Vietnam

Anthology and Guide to
A Television History

Vietnam

Anthology and Guide to A Television History

Edited by
Steven Cohen

ALFRED A. KNOPF   NEW YORK

THIS IS A BORZOI BOOK PUBLISHED BY ALFRED A. KNOPF, INC.

First Edition
98765

Cover art by Garry Trudeau
Text design by WGBH Design

ISBN: 0-394-33251-2

Manufactured in the United States of America

Credits and Permissions Acknowledgments

Introduction

Gerald V. Flannery "The Documentary as Essay". Southern Speech Communication Journal. Winter 1968 Vol XXXIV Number 2 pp 147–153.

Arthur Barron "Traditions of Documentary". Reprinted from the Journal of University Film Association, vol 21, no 3, 1969, by permission.

Andy Rooney "But Anyone Can Fool Around With Words". Reprinted with permission from TV Guide® Magazine. Copyright © 1971 by Triangle Publications, Inc. Radnor, Pennsylvania.

Burton Benjamin "In Defense of Talking Heads". TV Quarterly Winter 1973. Reprinted with the permission of the National Academy of Television Arts and Sciences. pp 42–44

Jerry Kuehl "History on Film". Journal of Social History © History Workshop Journal pp 127–135. Reprinted by permission.

Chapter 1   Roots of a War

Charles Depincé, "Protection of Indigenous Peoples," *La Quinzaine Coloniale,* September 25, 1900, translated by Judith Vecchione.

"The Worker's Life, January 4, 1924," *Ho Chi Minh: Selected Works,* Hanoi: Foreign Language Publishing House, 1960, vol. 1, pp. 62–65.

"Program of the Communist Party of Indochina, February 18, 1930," *Ho Chi Minh: Selected Works,* Hanoi: Foreign Language Publishing House, 1960, vol 2, pp. 145–148.

"Call for the Revolutionary League for the Independence of Vietnam," *Ho Chi Minh: Selected Works,* Hanoi: Foreign Language Publishing House, 1960, vol 2, pp. 151–154.

Viet-Nam Tan Bao, in Ngo Vinh Long, *Before the Revolution: The Vietnamese Peasants Under the French,* Copyright ©. 1973 by The Massachusetts Institute of Technology. pp. 132–133.

"Instructions of the Standing Bureau of the Central Committee of the Indochinese Communist Party, March 12, 1945," *Breaking Our Chains: Documents of the Vietnamese Revolution of August 1945,* Hanoi: Foreign Language Publishing House, 1960, pp 7–17.

Cover letter from Lord Halifax to Edward Stettinius, November 23, 1944 Aide memoire on the use of the French in Indochina British Embassy Washington, D.C. March 22, 1944 Department of State files.

Response to the British Embassy's aide memoire of November 22, 1944 by the United States Department of State. Department of State files.

Draft memorandum for the President April 20, 1945. Division of European Affairs, Department of State. United States Vietnam Relations, Book 8, pp 6–8.

"Declaration of Independence of the Democratic Republic of Vietnam, September 2, 1945," *Breaking Our Chains: Documents on the Vietnamese Revolution of August 1945,* Hanoi: Foreign Language Publishing House, 1960, pp. 94–97.

Chapter 2   The First Vietnam War: 1946–1954

"Agreement on the Independence of Vietnam, March 6, 1946," *The Pentagon Papers,* Boston: Beacon Press, © 1971, vol 1, pp 18–19.

"Appeal to the Entire People to Wage This Resistance War, December 20, 1946," *Ho Chi Minh: Selected Works,* Hanoi: Foreign Language Publishing House, 1961. vol. 3, pp 81–82.

"Message to the Vietnamese People, the French People, and the People of the Allied Nations," *Ho Chi Minh: Selected Works,* Hanoi: Foreign Language Publishing House, 1961, vol. 3, pp 83–86.

"Telegram from Dean Acheson to the U.S. Consulate in Hanoi May 20, 1949," and "Memorandum by the Department of State to the French Foreign Office, June 6, 1949," *Foreign Relations of the United States, 1949.* Washington: Government Printing Office, 1975, vol 7, pp 29–30 and 39–45.

"Final Declaration of the Geneva Conference on the Problem of Restoring Peace in Indo-China, July 21, 1954," *The Pentagon Papers,* Boston: Beacon Press, © 1971, vol 1, pp 571–573.

"Statement by the Under Secretary of State, Walter Bedell Smith, at the Concluding Plenary Session of the Geneva Conference, July 21, 1954," *The Pentagon Papers,* Boston: Beacon Press, © 1971, vol. 1, pp 570–571.

"Statement Regarding the Agreements of the Geneva Conference by Premier Ngo Dinh Diem, July 22, 1954," *The Reunification of Vietnam,* Saigon: Ministry of Information, 1958. p. 29.

Ho Chi Minh, "Long Live Peace, Unity, Independence and Democracy in Vietnam, July 30, 1954," *For A Lasting Peace, For a People's Democracy,* Bucharest: Communist Information Bureau, 1954. p. 3.

Chapter 3   America's Mandarin: 1954–1963

John Foster Dulles, "Opposition to the Spread of Communism 'By Any Means' " Speech to the Overseas Press Club, New York, March 29, 1954, in Department of State *Bulletin* (April 12, 1954), pp. 539–540.

Ngo Dinh Diem, "On Elections in Vietnam, July 16, 1955," Press and Information Service, Embassy of Vietnam, Washington, D.C., vol 1, no. 18 (July 22, 1955)

Dwight D. Eisenhower, "The Importance to the United States of the Security and Progress of Viet-Nam," Address by the President, Gettysburg College, Gettysburg, PA, April 4, 1959, Department of State *Bulletin*, April 27, 1959, pp. 579–583.

"Manifesto of the Eighteen, April 26, 1960," *The Pentagon Papers*, Boston: Beacon Press, © 1971, vol 1, pp. 316–317.

"Program of the National Liberation Front of South Vietnam," *North Vietnam Daily Report*, U.S. Foreign Broadcast Information Service, February 14, 1961.

John F. Kennedy, *Inaugural Address*, January 20, 1961. *Public Papers of the Presidents, Kennedy*, 1961.

"Ngo Dinh Diem, letter to President John F. Kennedy, December 7, 1961," Department of State *Bulletin* (January 1, 1962), pp 13–14.

"John F. Kennedy, letter to President Ngo Dinh Diem, December 14, 1961," Department of State *Bulletin* (January 1, 1962) p. 14.

Robin Moore, *The Green Berets* © 1965 Crown Publishers, Inc. Library of Congress Catalog Card 65-15849. Robin Moore. pp. 1–11.

"Cablegram from the Department of State to Ambassador Henry Cabot Lodge, August 24, 1963," *The Pentagon Papers*, Boston: Beacon Press, © 1971, vol. 2, p 734.

"Cablegram from Ambassador Henry Cabot Lodge to Secretary of State Dean Rusk and Assistant Secretary of State Roger Hilsman, August 25, 1963," *The Pentagon Papers*, Boston: Beacon Press, © 1971, vol. 2, p. 735.

Chapter 4 LBJ Goes to War: 1964–1965

Robert McNamara, "Memo for the President, December 21, 1963," *The Pentagon Papers*, Boston: Beacon Press, © 1971, vol. 3, pp 494–6.

From *Where I Stand* by Barry Goldwater. Copyright © 1964 Barry Goldwater. Used with the permission of McGraw-Hill Book Company. pp 28–29.

"Record of a meeting, December 20, 1964 between Ambassador Maxwell Taylor and a Group of Vietnamese Military Officers," *The Pentagon Papers*, Boston: Beacon Press, © 1971. vol. 2, pp 346–348.

Hans J. Morgenthau, "The Realities of Containment," Reprinted with permission of *The New Leader*, June 8, 1964. Copyright © American Labor Conference on International Affairs, Inc.

White Paper, February 1965, Department of State Publication #7839.

Richard M. Nixon, "Address To the Commonwealth Club of California, April 2, 1965."

Lyndon Baines Johnson, "Peace Without Conquest," Address at Johns Hopkins University, April 7, 1965, Department of State *Bulletin*, April 26, 1965, p. 607.

George Ball, "A Compromise Solution in South Vietnam," Memorandum for the President, July 1, 1965, *The Pentagon Papers*, Boston: Beacon Press, © 1971, vol. 2, pp 615–7.

From *South Vietnam*, Volume 1, *U.S.—Communist Confrontation in Southeast Asia 1961–65*, edited by Lester A. Sobel, © 1966, 1973, by Facts on File, Inc. Reprinted with permission of Facts on File, Inc. pp 5–16.

Tom Paxton, "Lyndon Johnson Told the Nation," Copyright © 1965, 1968 UNITED ARTISTS MUSIC CO., INC. All rights reserved. Used by permission.

Chapter 5 America Takes Charge: 1965–1967

"The White House Declaration of Honolulu," White House Press Release February 8, 1966

"Actions Recommended for Vietnam," Draft memorandum for President Lyndon B. Johnson from Secretary of Defense Robert S. McNamara, October 14, 1966, *The Pentagon Papers*, Boston: Beacon Press, © 1971 vol 4, pp 348–353.

"Memo from the Joint Chiefs of Staff to Secretary of Defense McNamara October 14, 1966," *The Pentagon Papers* as published by the *New York Times*, Chicago: Quadrangle Press, © 1971, p. 564–565.

From *The Village of Ben Suc*, by Jonathan Schell. Copyright © 1967 by Jonathan Schell. Reprinted by permission of Alfred A. Knopf, Inc. Originally appeared in *The New Yorker* in slightly different form. pp 3–11.

Letter from Lyndon B. Johnson to Ho Chi Minh, February 8, 1967," *President Ho Chi Minh Answers President L. B. Johnson*, Hanoi: Foreign Languages Publishing House, 1967, p. 27–29.

"Ho Chi Minh's Reply to Lyndon B. Johnson, February 15, 1967," *President Ho Chi Minh Answers President L. B. Johnson*, Hanoi: Foreign Languages Publishing House, 1967, p. 9–12.

William G. Westmoreland, "Address Before a Joint Session of Congress April 28, 1967," News Release from the Office of Assistant Secretary of Defense (Public Affairs)

John P. Roche, *Vietnam Settlement: Why 1973, Not 1969?*, pp. 152–156. © 1973 American Enterprise Institute.

"Memorandum for the President on Vietnam Policy from McGeorge Bundy," undated, *The Pentagon Papers*, Boston: Beacon Press, © 1971, vol. 4, pp 157–159.

Lyndon B. Johnson, "Address Before the National Legislative Conference, September 29, 1967," San Antonio Texas. Department of State Publication 8305, East Asian and Pacific Series 167.

Chapter 6   America's Enemy: 1954–1967

Pham Van Dong, "Note to the Two Co-Chairmen of the 1954 Geneva Conference on Indo-China, August 17, 1955," *Documents Related to the Implementation of the Geneva Agreements Concerning Viet Nam,* Democratic Republic of Vietnam, Hanoi: Ministry of Foreign Affairs, 1956. pp 45–50.

Le Duan, "The Path of Revolution in the South, November 1956," translated by Gareth Porter. From Gareth Porter, ed. *Vietnam: The Definitive Documentation of Human Decisions,* vol 2, pp. 24–26. © 1979 Earl M. Coleman Enterprises, Inc.

From *No Other Road to Take: Memoir of Mrs. Nguyen Thi Dinh,* translated by Mai V. Elliott © 1976, published and distributed by Cornell University Southeast Asia Program. pp 73–77.

"Resolution of the Ninth Conference of the Lao Dong Party Central Committee, December 1963," *Viet-Nam Documents and Research Notes,* July 1971 U.S. Embassy, Saigon. pp 4–10.

From Bernard B. Fall, *Viet-Cong: The Unseen Enemy in Viet-nam,* April 1965. Copyright NEW SOCIETY. Reprinted by permission.

Che Lan Vien, "Sparkling Fires in the South," in Douglas Pike, *Viet Cong,* Copyright © 1966 by The Massachusetts Institute of Technology. pp 437–439.

Huynh Tan Phat, "Letter to General Nguyen Khanh, January 28, 1965," English translation distributed by Nguyen Khanh.

Nguyen Huu Tho, "Reply to the Japanese Newspaper "Akahata," February 24, 1966," Hanoi: Vietnam Courier.

Chapter 7   Tet: 1968

"Do you think the U.S. and its allies are losing ground in Vietnam? . . ." Reprinted from *The Gallup Poll, 1935–1971,* by George Gallup. © 1972 by permission of Random House, Inc.

"Intelligence Memorandum: Bomb Damage Inflicted on North Vietnam Through April 1967, May 12, 1967," Directorate of Intelligence, Central Intelligence Agency. *Vietnam: The Definitive Documentation of Human Decisions,* edited by Gareth Porter © 1979 Earl M. Coleman Enterprises, Inc. Stanfordville, New York pp 466–468.

"Directive from Province Party Standing Committee to District and Local Party Organs on Forthcoming Offensive and Uprisings, November 1, 1967." *Vietnam Documents and Research Notes,* April 1968

"Circular from Central Office of South Vietnam (COSVN) Current Affairs Committee and Military Affairs Committee of South Vietnam Liberation Army (SVNLA) Headquarters Concerning a Preliminary Assessment of the Situation, January 31, 1968," translated by Patrick McGarvey. Reprinted from *Visions of Victory* by Patrick J. McGarvey with the permission of the publishers, Hoover Institution Press. Copyright © 1969 by the Board of Trustees of the Leland Stanford Junior University

Walt William Rostow, *The Diffusion of Power: an Essay in Recent History,* New York: Macmillan, Inc. Reprinted with permission of Macmillan Publishing Co., Inc. from *The Diffusion of Power* by W. W. Rostow. Copyright © 1972 by W. W. Rostow.

"Report of the Chairman, Joint Chiefs of Staff, General Earle G. Wheeler, on the Situation in Vietnam and MACV Force Requirements, February 27, 1968." *Vietnam: The Definitive Documentation of Human Decisions,* edited by Gareth Porter © 1979 Earl M. Coleman Enterprises, Stanfordville, NY. pp 501–504.

LBJ and the Credibility Gap, copyright 1967, Jules Feiffer. Reprinted with permission of Universal Press Syndicate. All rights reserved.

Graph by Sandra N. Kautz, "President Johnson and President Nixon—Their Use of Television and the Relationship to Gallup Poll Ratings," M.A. Thesis, University of Wisconsin 1973; based on Gallup Poll data.

Lyndon Baines Johnson, "The President's Address to the Nation Announcing Steps to Limit the War in Vietnam and Reporting His Decision Not to Seek Reelection, March 31, 1968," *Public Papers of the Presidents,* Washington: Government Printing Office, 1970, vol 1, pp 469–476.

Chapter 8   Vietnamizing the War: 1968–1973

William C. Westmoreland, "Combat Fundamentals for Advisors" *and* "Guidance for Commanders in Vietnam," from *Report on the War in Vietnam,* Saigon: United States Military Assistance Command, 1968.

"Vietnam: December 1969," A Staff Report Prepared for the Use of the Committee on Foreign Relations, United States Senate, February 2, 1970. 91st Congress, Second Session. Washington: US Government Printing Office. 1970.

"A Program for Peace In Viet-Nam," *Current Foreign Policy,* Department of State, Bureau of Public Affairs, Washington: Government Printing Office, 1971.

Eugene Linden, "Fragging and Other Withdrawal Symptoms," January 8, 1972, Copyright © 1972 by *Saturday Review.* Reprinted by permission.

Orville Schell, "Cage for the Innocents," January 1968, Copyright © 1967 by The Atlantic Monthly Company, Boston, Mass. Reprinted with permission.

"United States Assistance Programs in Vietnam," Statement of Ambassador William Colby before a Subcommittee of the Committee on Government Operations, House of Representatives, 92nd Congress, First Session, July 15–August 2, 1971.

Chapter 9   Cambodia and Laos

Chapter 10   Peace Is at Hand: 1968–1973

Chapter 11   Homefront USA

Benjamin Spock and William Sloane Coffin, "Overt Act #1, A Call to Resist Illegitimate Authority," August 1967.

"Revolution Towards a Free Society: Yippie!" by A. Yippie, August 25, 1968.

"Dear Brats" by Tom Anderson first appeared in the June 1969 issue of *American Opinion* (Belmont, Massachusetts 02178) and is reprinted by permission of the publisher.

Speech at a Citizen's Testimonial Dinner, by Spiro T. Agnew. From *The Impudent Snobs* by John R. Coyne, Jr. © 1972 New Rochelle, NY: Arlington House.

"Vietnam Veterans Against the War," Statement by John Kerry, April 22, 1971 before the Senate Committee on Foreign Relations. Congressional Record Vol. 117:57. Coverage edited and telecast by NBC Nightly News on April 23, 1971; telecast by ABC News on April 23, 1971.

Ron Ridenhour, "Letter to the Congress of the United States," March 29, 1969. *The My Lai Massacre and Its Cover-up: Beyond the Reach of Law?* The Peers Commission Report with a Supplement and Introductory Essay on the Limits of Law. Joseph Goldstein, Burke Marshall, Jack Schwartz. New York: The Free Press, 1976, pp 34–37

Bill Moyers, "Vietnam: What Is Left of Conscience?" February 13, 1971, *Saturday Review*. Reprinted with permission.

James Fallows "What Did You Do in the Class War, Daddy?" Reprinted with permission from *The Washington Monthly*. Copyright 1975 by The Washington Monthly Co., 1712 Ontario Road, N.W., Washington, D.C. 20009.

Chapter 12   The End of the Tunnel: 1973–1975

Richard M. Nixon, "Remarks of the President at a Reception for Returned Prisoners of War, May 24, 1973," Office of the White House Press Secretary.

Charles W. Wiley, "The United States Stake in Southeast Asia," *The New York Times,* February 19, 1975. © 1975 by The New York Times Company. Reprinted by permission.

"Commitment?" unsigned editorial from *The New York Times,* April 6, 1975. © 1975 by The New York Times Company. Reprinted by permission.

Gerald R. Ford, "Press Conference of the President of the United States, April 3, 1975." Office of the White House Press Secretary

Nguyen Van Thieu "Resignation speech, April 21, 1975," translated and edited by the Monitoring Service of the British Broadcasting Corporation.

Stephen T. Hosmer, Konrad Kellen, and Brian M. Jenkins *The Fall of South Vietnam: Statements by Vietnamese Military and Civilian Leaders,* a report prepared for Historian, Office of the Secretary of Defense, December 1978, Santa Monica, CA: Rand Corporation. pp 129–131.

"Notes and Comment," May 5, 1975. Reprinted by permission; © 1975 The New Yorker Magazine, Inc.

Chapter 13   Legacies

Jim Goodwin, "The Etiology of Combat-Related Post-Traumatic Stress Disorders," from *Post-Traumatic Stress Disorders of the Vietnam Veteran,* edited by Tom Williams, Cincinnati: Disabled American Veterans, 1980.

W. D. Ehrhart, "To Those Who Have Gone Home Tired," *The Awkward Silence,* Stafford, Va: Northwoods Press, 1980.

Paul Goldberger, "Vietnam Memorial: Questions of Architecture," October 7, 1982. © 1982 by The New York Times Company. Reprinted by permission.

Stanley Karnow, " 'Liberated' But Still Capitalist," November 1981, Copyright © 1981, by The Atlantic Monthly Company, Boston, Mass. Reprinted with permission.

Michael J. Arlen, "The Falklands, Vietnam, and Our Collective Memory," August 16, 1982, © 1982 Michael J. Arlen. Reprinted by permission, The New Yorker Magazine.

H. Bruce Franklin, "Teaching Vietnam Today: Who Won, and Why?" Appeared in *The Chronicle of Higher Education* (November 4, 1981). Reprinted with permission. Copyright 1981 by the Chronicle of Higher Education, Inc.

"Letters to the Editor" Appeared in *The Chronicle of Higher Education* (December 9, 1981). Reprinted with permission. Copyright 1981 by the Chronicle of Higher Education, Inc.

From Bill Moyers Journal: "Vietnam, Remembered" copyright © 1980 by Educational Broadcasting Corporation. Reprinted by permission.

Strobe Talbott, "El Salvador: It Is Not Viet Nam," February 22, 1982, Copyright 1982 Time Inc. All rights reserved. Reprinted by permission from TIME.

Transcribed from interviews by THE VIETNAM PROJECT with George Ball, Henry Kissinger, Dean Rusk, William Sloane Coffin, Gerald Ford, Daniel Ellsberg, James Fallows, William D. Ehrhart. Printed with permission.

Preface: "Vietnam" as Telehistory

Every history project has a history. This one dates from 1977 when Stanley Karnow, a journalist with years of experience in Asia during the Vietnam War, and I, a television producer who had never set foot in Vietnam, discovered a mutual interest in making a series about that country and conflict. We soon found an equally interested third party in Lawrence Lichty, professor of communications and student-extraordinary of the media coverage of the Vietnam War. Karnow, Lichty, and I were convinced that the United States stood in need of a full-scale television history that would deal with Vietnamese culture and traditions, the century of French colonial domination of Indochina, the eight-year war between the French and the Vietminh, and of course with the American involvement that has no official name, which we have come to call the Vietnam War.

At first it seemed that we three were alone in our conviction. The prevailing wisdom was that the American public had "had" it on Vietnam and "didn't want to know." The prevailing wisdom was wrong. Emerson's *Winners & Losers* had just been published; Herr's *Dispatches,* Shawcross's *Sideshow,* Lewy's *America in Vietnam,* and a flood of other books and articles would follow, along with *Heroes, The Deer Hunter, Apocalypse Now,* and "Friendly Fire" heading a list of movies and TV programs whose end is not in sight.

We were also beginning to hear more about "delayed stress syndrome," the dramatic and sometimes violent release of psychic energy in veterans who had been numbed by traumatic experiences in Vietnam. Men and women who thought they had put the war behind them found searing memories forcing their way into consciousness. The nation, too, had tried to forget Vietnam—with some initial success, but now the books and films, the news accounts of troubled veterans and suffering refugees, were breaking through the crust of public indifference. It was clearly time to "do" the Vietnam War.

That was easier said than done. In most countries, a television elite allocates resources to the programs it considers worthy, quite apart from their potential popularity. In the United States, commercial television commands huge resources but takes a populist line, letting the ratings control programming. Public television is less bound to ratings, but lacks the means fully to live up to its standards of excellence. The Vietnam Project early on got significant support within public television—notably from PBS's Lawrence Grossman and the management of Boston's WGBH-TV, but not from public television's traditional funders. Before we could make the series, we had to make the budget.

The project used its seed money from PBS and WGBH to create a research and development strategy for the series. The first major success was in persuading the National Endowment for the Humanities to make a modest grant that enabled the project to carry out basic research, recruit Southeast Asia scholars and other consultants, and write a proposal detailing its intentions for the series. In response to this proposal the NEH made what was to prove to be the largest single grant to the production of the series.

The major corporations and foundations that usually underwrite public television series did not rush to support this one. (With one exception: the Chubb Group of Insurance Companies became an underwriter in 1982.) The search extended to Europe, where eventually two partners were found. Antenne-2, the French second channel, agreed to provide program materials dealing with Vietnamese history, French colonialism, and the first Vietnam war; and a British program service, Associated TV (now Central Independent TV) joined as a full co-producer pledged to contribute four episodes to the thirteen-hour series. Three years had passed and the project was still not fully funded, but the gap had narrowed. The management of WGBH elected to assume the remaining financial risk. The Vietnam Project could start.

The four weeks of project seminars, held in September and October 1980, were unique in the history of television. The new Vietnam Project staff was exposed to a succession of distinguished Southeast Asia specialists discussing everything from the traces of Stone Age Vietnamese precursors (John Whitmore) to the image of the Vietnam War reflected in American movies (Peter McInerney and Larry Suid). From Canada (Alexander Woodside, Ton That Tien), England (Christopher Thorne, Jerry Kuehl), France (Philippe Devillers, Dominique Moisi), and as far away as Thailand (Jeffrey Race) they came to project headquarters at WGBH, Boston, to share their experiences and, it was devoutly hoped, impart a measure of their knowledge to the assembled, mind-boggled television types, who soon dubbed the seminars "Vietnam School."

The seminars brought the project producers face to face with many of the specialists they would be consulting in the months ahead. They also became a crucible in which the members of the project staff were formed into a team. Teamwork was essential to our planned mode of production. The four production units had to be prepared to share research, to film interview materials for other units on occasion, and even to tolerate critiques of one another's work in progress. Though Karnow, Lichty, and I were present to arbitrate—or dictate, as the occasion required—these critique sessions were always intense and sometimes abrasive. They were also useful correctives to the filmmakers' natural tendency to get too close to their work. The resulting films bear the stamp of the individual producers, and at the same time they reflect the project style and philosophy of presenting history for television.

That style is best described as "plain." No fancy intercut editing, no emotive music, no omniscient narrator. Plainness is in the interests of the philosophical objective, which is to manipulate the viewer as little as possible. The archival film is what it purports to be; sources are identified when necessary;

contradictory viewpoints are clearly articulated; conclusions and value judgments are expressed by the participants and interview subjects, not by the program makers.

But if the treatment is sober-sided, the history itself is complex, emotionally
charged, and still controversial. On any given issue, there are at least two, and
frequently three, or four, or more sides, held with stubborn passion. That is
true of American opinions on the rightness (or wrongness) of the U.S. military
and political commitment; it is probably even more true of Vietnamese attitudes. Barriers of politics and recent history as well as race, culture, and language, divide Americans and Vietnamese and helped shape the tragic course of
events from 1945 to 1975. For our series to deal adequately with those events,
it was in our view essential that Vietnamese viewpoints and experiences be included. Those of our recent allies were relatively easy to come by, since so
many of them had become refugees in America. Those of our erstwhile enemies
were more problematical.

Fortunately, the project had British and French partners, and the Vietnamese
have embassies in London and Paris, as well as a United Nations delegation in
New York. Through contacts made at all three points, we were eventually
granted permission, first to dispatch one producer on a survey trip to Hanoi,
then to send an American-British unit to film the length and (narrow) breadth
of Vietnam, and finally to send a French unit that filmed, among others, the
legendary General Vo Nguyen Giap and·visited the site of his greatest victory
over the French, Dienbienphu.

Despite the difficulties and delays attendant on filming in poor, underdeveloped countries and dealing with Communist bureaucracies, we were able to record well over a hundred interviews with Vietnamese who fought or supported
the fight against the Americans and the Saigon government. Their testimony is
essential to a complete understanding of the Vietnam War.

So of course is the testimony of Americans and allies, hawks and doves, civilians and soldiers, policy-makers and PFCs. Of Ambassador Bui Diem and
Ambassador Henry Cabot Lodge. Of Madame Nhu and General Ky. Of Walt
Rostow who still thinks the United States could and should have won the war
and George Ball who doesn't. All those and scores more gave generously of
their time and subjected themselves to our cameras and questions in the hope
that their witness would shed light on this troubled and troubling time.

Television viewers were eye-witnesses to part of this history, so it is appropriate to recount it in the form of a television series. But from the onset the
Vietnam Project has looked beyond that audience, hoping that the series will
bear closer scrutiny and have a longer life in classrooms across the country. Students too young to remember the world's first television war should have
the opportunity, not only to see the images that fascinated and horrified their
elders, but also to get behind the images to those large, difficult questions—of
tactics and strategy, of ends and means, of right and wrong, of life and death—
that were posed by this war, as indeed they are posed by every war.

I do not mean to suggest that this film series, however closely studied, can provide the answers. But if we have done our work well, the films will help viewers form the questions and invite them to draw their own conclusions.

Richard Ellison
Executive Producer

Acknowledgments

This anthology would not have been possible without help from a number of sources and to all of them we give our sincere thanks. First, the Fund for the Improvement of Postsecondary Education provided a grant which made the work possible and gave us the challenge of combining usefulness and excellence.

The producers, staff, and advisors for VIETNAM took time to share their knowledge, to review material, to suggest resources. Dick Ellison, Stanley Karnow, and Larry Lichty deserve special thanks for the many hours they spent making sure that our work reflected the goals of the series.

In creating this guide and in evaluating the early drafts, we had help from a number of people, starting with our educational advisory board: Betty Tenore, Bunker Hill Community College; John C. Donnell, Temple University; Paul Miles, U.S. Military Academy, West Point; Kevin Sullivan, Bergen County Community College; Joan Hoff-Wilson, University of Indiana; Anthony Lake, Amherst College. Joe Beckmann, Hilda Moscowitz, Jinny Goldstein, and Hazel Hertzberger all offered excellent suggestions, and RMC Research conducted an evaluation of our sample chapter that was a model of lucidness and useful advice.

The Suggestions for Further Reading included with each chapter provide the only current, selective reading list on the history of Vietnam for a college-level audience. Sharon Breakstone accomplished this with untold hours on the telephone, conferring with the series' advisors about the most recent and accessible scholarship in the field, reading suggested books, and annotating each listing to give readers an idea of the scope and approach of each entry.

There are many others who gave generously of their time, their concern, and their knowledge: from Nancy Gooden and Alan Melchior, who donated typing and research, to Seibert Adams and David Follmer at Knopf, whose belief in our project supported us through a number of difficult times. We can only hope that the final book reflects their contributions in some small measure.

Steven D. Cohen
Editor

Margaret Ann Roth
Director of Educational Projects
for THE VIETNAM PROJECT

December 28, 1982

How to Use This Guide

The Vietnam era is so recent that scholars and participants still argue passionately over the meaning and importance of events. "Vietnam: A Television History" and this companion guide provide materials which invite you to look closely at parts of this period, to search for meanings in the experience, and to participate in the struggle to arrive at conclusions. We also hope that, in the process, you will learn ways of thinking critically about current events as they are presented in newspapers, on television, and on radio.

This guide is not intended to be a definitive historical overview, or even a critique. It is a summary and a collection of documents which can help enlarge your perspective. The chapters of the guide follow the order of the television programs. They include introductory and concluding sections to help prepare for viewing and then for thinking about events and issues.

Each chapter has several sections to encourage study and discussion. The *Historical Summary* which begins each chapter gives a brief history of the period or topic covered in the companion television program. Where necessary, a three-part *Chronology* has been included to place events in Vietnam in the wider context of international and U.S. affairs. *Points to Emphasize* identifies ideas and events which you will want to note while viewing—aspects of which are expanded later in the chapter. The *Glossary of Names and Terms* serves as a permanent reference for people, places, and terms you will encounter in the television program. *Documents* have been selected to recapture debates about the war which are still relevant; with the *Critical Issues for Discussion* they help to examine some of the issues in detail. A *Follow Up* question selects a single theme which can be used for broader discussion.

Suggestions for Further Reading includes a number of excellent general histories of Vietnam—especially *Vietnam* by Stanley Karnow, which was written in conjunction with the television series and which supplements the viewing material. Other books are listed for each program to help you explore particular topics in depth.

The telecourse material was developed with a grant from the Fund for the Improvement of Postsecondary Education.

Suggestions for Further Reading

A word about these suggestions:

Given the controversial nature of the war, no single source can be expected to offer an objective history. Students will need to weigh each author's background, motives, and assumptions in evaluating the many versions of the truth about the war.

These suggestions, chosen in consultation with series advisors, were judged most appropriate for (or most accessible to) a college audience. Readability and availability were major criteria; although many of the books are now out of print, they can be found in most university libraries. Readers wishing to pursue a topic in more depth should consult a comprehensive bibliography such as *The Vietnam Conflict* by Milton Leitenberg and Richard Dean Burns (ABC-CLIO Santa Barbara, 1973).

General Histories

Books to Start With

Committee of Concerned Asian Scholars. *The Indochina Story*. New York: Pantheon, 1970.

Written by antiwar Asian scholars in the wake of the invasion of Cambodia, this popular handbook presents basic information about the war in all three countries of Indochina in easily usable form.

Gettleman, Marvin E. *Vietnam: History, Documents and Opinions on a Major World Crisis*. Rev. ed. New York: New American Library, 1970.

This popular anthology of primary materials and essays can serve either as an introduction to key issues in the history of the war or as a tool for further study. The revised edition includes information on the war in Laos and Cambodia.

Herring, George C. *America's Longest War: The United States and Vietnam, 1950–1975*. New York: Wiley, 1979.

Of the brief histories of the war now in print, Herring's readable, carefully researched overview is the best for understanding U.S. policy.

Kahin, George McTurnan, and John W. Lewis. *The United States in Vietnam*. Rev. ed. New York: Dial Press, 1969.

Drawing on their backgrounds in Asian history, Kahin and Lewis aimed to give Americans a Vietnamese context for challenging the assumptions underlying U.S. policy in Vietnam. Written in 1966, their book is still an excellent starting place for understanding the positions held by antiwar critics in later debates about the war.

Karnow, Stanley. *Vietnam: A History*. New York: Viking, 1983.

The first full history of the war going back to its origins. Chief correspondent for the television series, Karnow combines current scholarship with information from thirty years of reporting on the French and American wars in Indochina.

Other General Histories

Doyle, Edward, and Samuel Lipsman. *The Vietnam Experience*. Vol. 1, *Setting the Stage*. Boston: Boston Publishing, 1981.

Doyle, Edward, Samuel Lipsman, and Stephen Weiss. *The Vietnam Experience*. Vol. 2, *Passing the Torch*. Boston: Boston Publishing, 1981.

Duiker, William J. *The Communist Road to Power in Vietnam*. Boulder, Colo.: Westview, 1981.
Duiker's careful study begins with the founding of the Communist Party of Vietnam in 1930 and traces its development to the present.

Fall, Bernard B. *The Two Viet-Nams: A Political and Military Analysis*. Rev. ed. New York: Praeger, 1967.
This thorough study by a French-American scholar has been a classic for twenty years. Based on his research and travel in Vietnam, Fall gives a brief history and describes the complexity of Vietnam in the early sixties.

Harrison, James Pinckney. *The Endless War: Fifty Years of Struggle in Vietnam*. New York: Free Press, 1982.
An Asia scholar presents the Vietnamese view of the war—"to give some historical understanding of how the Communists took command of the Vietnamese Revolution and went on to defeat enemies so many times more powerful than they."

Kattenburg, Paul M. *The Vietnam Trauma in American Foreign Policy, 1945–75*. New Brunswick, N.J.: Transaction, 1982.
Kattenburg, a former U.S. Foreign Service Officer and early dissenter on aspects of Vietnam policy, places U.S. involvement in the context of its foreign policy generally. Especially interesting is Chapter 4, "Ten Fateful Decisions on Vietnam, 1961–75."

Lewy, Guenter. *America in Vietnam*. New York: Oxford Univ. Press, 1978.
Its use of classified Army, Air Force, and Marine Corps records makes this work helpful to those interested in American military operations in Vietnam. Much of the book is devoted to defending the U.S. against charges of immoral conduct in Vietnam and to justifying the war as legal and necessary.

Maclear, Michael. *The Ten-Thousand-Day War: Vietnam: 1945–1975*. New York: Avon, 1981.
Based on a Canadian-produced television history series with Peter Arnett, Maclear's book draws on interviews with participants to present vivid images of key moments in the American war.

Maitland, Terrence, and Stephen Weiss. *The Vietnam Experience*. Vol. 3, *Raising the Stakes*. Boston: Boston Publishing, 1982.
The first three volumes in a many-volume project intended to tell "how we became involved in Vietnam and what it was like once we were there." The text is often ambivalent and confusing in its treatment of the Vietnamese, but the excellent photos and illustrations provide a fascinating visual history of the war.

Nguyen Khac Vien. *The Long Resistance (1858–1975)*. Hanoi: Foreign Languages Publishing House, 1975.
Larger university libraries may have a copy of this readable history of the first and second Indochina Wars by North Vietnam's leading writer for Western audiences.

O'Ballance, Edgar. *The Wars in Vietnam, 1954–80*. Rev. ed. New York: Hippocrene, 1981.

Major O'Ballance gives a brief history of U.S. involvement from a military historian's point of view.

Porter, Gareth, ed. *Vietnam: A History in Documents*. Stanfordville, N.Y.: Earl M. Coleman, 1979; abridged edition, 1981.
Porter includes documents from the Pentagon papers as well as United States diplomatic and presidential papers, and internal documents from Vietnamese sources. His introduction is helpful in highlighting the broad historical themes which emerge from the documentary record.

Sheehan, Neil, Hedrick Smith, E. W. Kenworthy, and Fox Butterfield. *The Pentagon Papers as Published by the New York Times*. New York: New York Times, 1971.
The Pentagon papers, commissioned by Secretary of Defense Robert McNamara in 1967 for internal government use, cover the history of U.S. involvement in Indochina from 1945 to 1968. The sections vary in quality and reflect the bias of the Pentagon civilians who wrote them.

The Pentagon Papers (Senator Gravel Edition) Boston: Beacon, 1971.
The four-volume Senator Gravel Edition looks forbidding, but a fifth volume of critical essays (edited by Noam Chomsky and Howard Zinn) contains an excellent index. The one-volume New York Times edition is a good starting point.

Sobel, Lester A., ed. *South Vietnam*. 7 volumes. New York: Facts on File, 1966–1973.
A series of books published yearly that used press and government sources for narrative. Useful for reference work.

Woodside, Alexander Barton. *Community and Revolution in Modern Vietnam*. Boston: Houghton Mifflin, 1976.
Although Woodside deals only with the period 1925–1945, the themes he develops are of general interest. Woodside is widely respected for his ability to articulate conflicting interpretations of Vietnamese society, but his dense style makes him best read with Harrison and/or Duiker for orientation.

Contents

Chapter 3   America's Mandarin: 1954–1963   57

Chapter 4   LBJ Goes to War: 1964–1965   89

Chapter 5   America Takes Charge: 1965–1967   129

Introduction: History on Television

By Lawrence W. Lichty, Professor of Communication Arts, University of Maryland

The purpose of this short essay and the materials that follow are (1) to introduce you briefly to the form of non-fiction film called documentary and (2) to discuss briefly the elements that were used to make one documentary series, *Vietnam: A Television History*.

John Grierson, in a 1926 newspaper review, was apparently the first to write in English about film as documentary. He described the Robert Flaherty movie *Moana*, a poetic vision of life on a South Sea island, as "being a visual account of events in the daily life of a Polynesian youth and his family, which has documentary value." An important and pioneering factual filmmaker, Grierson defined documentary as "creative treatment of actuality."

Before 1900, documentary films were primarily short scenes of exotic places and things. (Some of these, including a view of Saigon and scenes of elephants in Cambodia, are in the first episode of the television series.) In the 1920s and 1930s the documentary took different forms in various countries: some were romantic travelogs, while others were propaganda designed to stir emotions and sway public opinion.

The American documentary movement developed from newsreels and from true stories dramatized on the radio. During the Depression, the U.S. government became a major producer, with its own motion picture service that made films of praise for Roosevelt's New Deal programs in conservation and economic development. Late in the 1930s, when Republicans gained control of Congress and the budget, this office was abolished. But, during World War II, propaganda films were again produced by the government, explaining America's role in the war. These, as well as instructional and combat history films, were made by people who had worked in the Hollywood film and newsreel industries before the war.

Based on their experiences and strongly influenced by an important documentary movement in Britain, producers and critics argued that the most important role for documentary films was to inform and persuade. Their point of view is captured by Richard Dyer MacCann's definition, which states that a documentary:

(a) is primarily concerned with the area of social studies;
(b) presents facts selected for relevance from thorough research;
(c) is edited by artists;

(d) in terms of a central idea;

(e) takes into account more than one viewpoint but does not necessarily shy away from offering a conclusion.

The distinction between films of fact and those of fiction is described by Erik Barnow in the conclusion to his history of the documentary:

> The documentarist has a passion for what he *finds* in images and sounds—which always seem to him more meaningful than anything he can *invent*. Unlike the fiction artist, he is dedicated to *not* inventing. It is in selecting and arranging his findings that he expresses himself; these choices are, in effect, comments.

The series *Vietnam: A Television History* is of the genre of documentary usually described as "compilation," in which films are made, at least in part, from existing, usually archival or historic film, videotape, and other earlier recordings. This kind of filmmaking can be very different from working with original material. But Jay Leyda, who has written a history of compilation documentaries, notes:

> No doubt, though, that "documentary" and "compilation" have one element in common: manipulation of actuality. This manipulation, no matter what its motive— art, propaganda, instruction, advertisement—usually tries to hide itself so that the spectator sees only "reality"—that is, the especially *arranged* reality that suits the film-maker's purpose.

More than sixty different archives were used for film and tape sources in making *Vietnam*. The largest quantity came from the files kept by the news departments of the three U.S. commercial networks. Other film came from the Army, Air Force, Navy, and Marines, and from other government agencies, presidential libraries, private organizations and personal collections. (Much of this material is available from the Library of Congress or the National Archives.)

Selection of television news material was based on the analysis of more than 10,000 network evening news reports about Vietnam from 1965 to 1977. A similar inventory was made of all of the network documentaries, public affairs discussions, live hearings, and other broadcasts related to Vietnam. Additionally, many archives outside the U.S. were consulted, particularly those in Britain, France, and Vietnam.

The programs in the *Vietnam* series average more than 50 percent archival film. The rest of the footage was shot especially for the series and includes interviews with observers of specific incidents and personalities, maps, and some still photographs.

The number of interviews in any episode is limited, both because this kind of filming is expensive and because too many "talking heads" can cause viewers to become confused or forget identifications. Using these interviews effectively is a challenge in terms of selection, handling of the subject, and editing (discussed more fully in Document 5). Usually, ten to fifteen times more material—archival and original footage—is collected than can be used in a finished documentary. And, even more people are interviewed, more film is viewed, and more sources consulted before the actual filming and editing of a particular program begins.

In *Vietnam,* a narrator weaves these elements together, to help shape the final program. Some filmmakers prefer not to use a narrator, but to have the camera as observer (cinema verité or direct cinema). Although cinema verité can be effective for contemporary topics, historical documentaries need a narrator to provide background and context. The way this narrator is used can give authority to speakers and scenes—or it can take importance away from them. The narrator, therefore, speaks for the producers of the film and has a role that one critic has described as "guarantor of truth." To this extent, as Andy Rooney argues in Document 3, documentary films are as much written as made.

It took almost six years to bring *Vietnam: A Television History* to the screen. An early statement of the purpose for which the project began, and for which it should be judged, was to

> provide the opportunity for serious viewers to examine the entire record, giving due weight to the Vietnamese and French as well as the American experience, and thus to form a basis for reaching their own conclusions about the nature of the conflict, what was won and lost, by whom, and why.

Points to Emphasize

Vietnam: A Television History presents more than twenty years of contemporary history in twelve one-hour episodes. In viewing them critically you will want to judge
- Factual accuracy. Does the producer provide adequate evidence and analysis? Does each film develop the social context of the time period and the subject matter?
- Interest and organization. Does the presentation help the viewer learn or experience what the filmmaker is trying to convey? Does each program present a balanced approach to alternative versions and interpretations of what happened and why?

Documents

Documents 1 and 2

Gerald Flannery, in Document 1, compares the newer documentary form with
the traditional prose essay, providing a context for understanding film documentaries and for evaluating compilations and other types of nonfiction films.
In Document 2, Arthur Barron, who made a number of reportage films for
CBS News, makes it clear that he would rather work with the personal or "human revelation" film. His description of the form and purpose of the other
filmmaking traditions, though used to support his preference for the personal
film, shows briefly and clearly that he understands and appreciates the function
of each genre.

1   The Documentary as Essay
Gerald V. Flannery

An examination of the form of the television documentary reveals that it is basically
a written essay given visual and dramatic force or emphasis. An essay of classic design is traditionally thought to involve four elements: argument, definition, narration, and exposition. The television documentary involves these same elements in
terms of its own techniques and methods: use of the camera, staging, lighting, narration, and sound effects.

                                   . . .

There is—or should be—a message in every documentary, be it educational, religious, technical, business, or reportorial. Robert F. Wagner, writing in *Audio-Visual
Review,* believes that the message should be there because the sponsors want it, audiences expect it and sometimes need it; and that when the documentary is well
done, "it grows naturally and inevitably out of the beliefs and feelings of someone
involved in the production—a writer, the director, the producer, the editor."[1] He
believes that the message will be there because at least one of those people was trying
to say something "with skill, some warmth, and a measure of conviction."

The purpose of the documentary, then, is what often serves to shape its production. Buchanan, in *Film-Making From Script to Screen,* gives this explanation of the
purpose:

> The documentary film brings you the everyday world, and surprises you with little
> known facts about the work of the man who lives around the corner. It aims to widen
> experience and vision by making you fully conscious of your relation to the community
> as a whole, at home and abroad.[2]

If the aim of the documentary is to influence or educate, to lead the viewer to

---

[1]Robert F. Wagner, "The Creative Educational Film," *Audio-Visual Review,* X (July–August, 1962),
   275–277.
[2]Buchanan, p. 89.

place himself somewhere in relation to the subject it is necessary that the producer/ creator of the project understand how to establish this relationship. In *The Television Manual,* William Hodapp writes:

> A significant decision to be made is whether to regard the documentary job as one of reporting or interpreting. A guide to follow is to ask yourself whether you can assume sufficient knowledge on the part of your audience or whether you must first sketch a brief background for orientation before you can come to the major part of your story. You must always be sure the viewer knows what you're talking about every step of the way.[3]

Robert Louis Shayon, television critic for the *Saturday Review,* criticized a network documentary in April, 1961, for avoiding the purposeful handling of its subject matter. The documentary was about Hong Kong, somewhat of a relaxed travelogue. Shayon criticized it for not editorializing, for having no special viewpoint. In earlier writings he surveyed documentaries and found them to fall in two categories: one that merely seeks to reflect a viewpoint; one that goes further and tries to arouse action.[4] His castigation of the Hong Kong documentary came because "it dealt merely with episodes in the outer eye."[5]

> For years in the entertainment business "documentary" has been a dirty word; the observation of reality, a deterrent to the enjoyment of illusion, has been considered dull. "Documentary" is still a dirty word, now that it has been discovered that the observation of reality can be dangerous.[6]

Marya Mannes, television reviewer for *The Reporter,* made that judgment in 1955 in the era of the early *See It Now* programs by Edward R. Murrow. Her comments were occasioned by the defection of several sponsors from Murrow's program and from the newly created series on NBC called *Project 20.* Advertisers were pleased to sponsor documentary travelogues of Europe and the Orient; but,

> . . . when Edward R. Murrow presented his visual essay on Joseph McCarthy, people began to feel the intense emotions which facts, used as an instrument of art, can stir. It set up a reaction in the industry of television which is gathering momentum daily.[7]

The documentary thus became the vehicle for the essayist to broaden his communication with the general public. In effect, the essayist is cooperating in the vivid portrayal of his essay, leaving the technique of its portrayal to the documentarian. The medium itself determines in what manner this emphasis will be given. This intricate relationship of purpose and technique is the reason documentary creation involves continuing editorial judgments, just as the original essay did.

Elements

The television documentary argues when it takes an editorial position or seeks to persuade the viewer to understand its subject; it defines by explaining its subject in

[3]Hodapp, p. 31.

[4]Robert Louis Shayon, "The Fuse in the Documentary," *Saturday Review,* XLIII (December 17, 1960), 29.

[5]Robert Louis Shayon, "Our Man in Hong Kong," *Saturday Review,* XLIV (April 8, 1961), 61.

[6]Marya Mannes, "Channels: The Hot Documentary," *The Reporter,* XIII (November 17, 1955), 37–39.

[7]Mannes, pp. 37–39.

terms the viewer can understand and by giving this explanation visual presence. This visual explanation is given emphasis by narration, which both argues and defines and provides for continuity of thought. The fourth element of exposition is composed of the other three. In television documentaries the exposition of the subject determines the technique used.

The techniques used are scholarly research; the camera, to obtain meaningful silent footage and descriptive sound footage; the expert, to relate, comment, or deliver judgments in his special area; the narrator, to provide the continuity and comment necessary in addition to that of the expert; the creation of a final script, fully marked for direction—a script that lists in television language all of the foregoing elements and includes advice on the selection of a wide range of special effects: staging, lighting, costuming, music, sound effects, and volume.

The documentary thus employs every communication technique known to television, radio, movies, and the theatre; yet it remains a technique in itself, separate from the elements it utilizes. The writing, narration, and creative exposition in the television documentary correspond to the media but remain analogous to the written essay.

To summarize:

1. The documentary should be viewed as a pictorial essay reflecting the creative treatment of reality.

2. The documentary should be about a specific subject of general interest, and its purpose should be clearly understood by the creator and the viewer.

3. The exposition of the subject should form the purpose of the documentary, be it education or editorial.

4. A decision should be made whether the documentary will report or interpret, examine or advocate.

5. The subject matter should be so narrowed as to allow reasonable exploration of one or several facets, yet not be so general as to merely billboard a variety of subjects.

6. Careful attention should be given to the form of the documentary in the utilization of its separate parts, these parts being: *(a)* documentation of the subject, using the best available research in terms of men, methods, and machines; *(b)* exposition, using narration, interviews, and careful camera work to depict the narration or the interview matters; *(c)* atmosphere or mood, using background sounds and sound effects to highlight or deepen the expository goals.

7. The documentary creator should understand his job as that of giving visualization and dramatic force to what is basically a classical essay.

The final judgment of the effectiveness of a television documentary rests with the audience. . . .

2   Traditions of Documentary
Arthur Barron
1969

. . . Our bag, I suppose, is educational films. Films whose chief purpose is not to entertain, not to make money, but rather to inform. And within that central purpose of information, it seems to me, there exist three great film traditions: the tradition of reportage, the tradition of instruction, and the tradition of human revelation. . . . For too long, our bag has been reportage and instruction. For too long we have neglected the great tradition of human revelation. For too long we have been pedagogues, not poets, reporters, not artists, communicators, not explorers. . . .

Films made in the tradition of reportage have these elements in common: They are *political;* they seek to inform people on matters of public policy and to motivate, to move people to collective action. They are *topical;* they deal with events in the news. They are *issue-oriented;* they focus not on individuals but on masses of people viewed in a large social context. They are *expert;* they presuppose a special knowledge, possessed by the film maker but not by the audience. They are *verbal;* they are scripted films, word-logic films. Turn off the picture and play only the sound track and you will be able to understand them perfectly. The image, as such, is illustrative of the verbal content; it does not exist in its own right. They are *pre-determined;* they are not emergent, they do not emerge in the process of being made, they are not discovered. Finally, these films *advocate;* they take a position "for" or "against" something. What they advocate usually is determined by who pays for them. Sometimes the advocacy is muted, cloaked in a subtle pretension of "balance" or "objectivity." Sometimes, the films are openly propagandistic.

Because they are what they are, films of reportage usually follow a standard authoritative and omniscient style. A narrator is usually present; the interview technique is much used; experts are appealed to and gladly declaim; the editing is logical and conventional; opposing viewpoints are often aired and cross-cut; there is a summation, some editorializing, a call to action of one sort or another. *CBS Reports* is the prototype model.

. . .

Films made in the tradition of instruction have these elements in common: They are *specialized;* they deal with narrow, delimited subject matter. They are *cognitive,* not *affective;* they address themselves to the intellect, not to the emotions. They are *pedagogic;* they teach mastery of factual information. They are *academic;* they do not attempt to move to action or to mobilize, but to add to knowledge for its own sake. They are *objective;* they do not take a position of advocacy in human affairs. Indeed, they are most often and necessarily irrelevant to social action. They are *subject-oriented;* they do not deal primarily with people, either as individuals or groups, with issues or events, but with the subject matter of a formal intellectual discipline. Finally, like films of reportage, films in the tradition of instruction are *expert, pre-determined,* and *verbal.*

Films in the instructional tradition also have a marked style. Here, a narrator is almost a necessity. Statistics, animation, charts, graphs, and other "visuals" are inevitable. There is a firm sense of structure: a logical beginning, middle, and end. Actors often are involved in very scripted and staged presentations. In short, all the paraphernalia of the classroom, the lecture, or the sales presentation are present. . . .

Finally, there are films in the tradition of human revelation. Such films have these elements in common: They are *experimental,* not *didactic;* the experience of the film itself as a process is central and paramount, not the informational content. Said another way, "the medium is the message." These films are people-oriented, even *individual-oriented.* Uppermost in the content of such films is the quality, meaning, and emotion of individual human beings in their total complexity. They are *universal* and *timeless;* they deal not with specialized events, narrow subject matter, time-bound subject matter, but with experience that is part of the total human situation.

Such films are as meaningful and relevant in Samoa as here in Pennsylvania, as relevant 100 years from now as today. They are *cinematic,* not verbal, not word-logic. Turn off the sound and you will still understand the picture. They are *emergent;* they are not prescripted, preplanned. They are discovered. If, for example, one decides, as I did for the film "Birth and Death," to make a film about a young couple having their first child and about a fifty-two-year-old man dying of cancer, and if these are real people (as they were), life itself, as it is lived, creates the story. The film emerges from life; it is discovered as it is made. Such a film is actually lived and it has the quality of life. Films of human revelation are *passionate,* not objective, not academic, not cognitive. They appeal directly and unashamedly to the emotions. Such films are *non-expert;* rather, let us say they are *democratic.* They presuppose no special knowledge possessed only by the film maker and not by the audience. The film maker shares a human experience with the audience—an experience immediately comprehensible to both, since both are part of the family of man.

The style of films in the tradition of human revelation tends to be, almost always, cinéma vérité. No narrator, no experts, no interviews, no charts and graphs, no setting the scene through explanations and devices, no analysis. Instead, life itself, captured as it happens—with a minimum of intrusion; life itself, unpredictable and uncontrollable; life itself, intimate, emotional, dramatic, human. The film maker is deeply involved, not on the outside with a tripod, but in the middle of it all, camera hand-held . . . involved.

. . .

There is another way to say all this: The purpose of reportage films is to report, to inform, motivate, and mobilize the public on issues of social concern. The purpose of instructional films is to increase academic knowledge. The purpose of films of human revelation is, . . . when you get down to it, the purpose of art, of *all* art, nothing more and nothing less than to make the joy of one man comprehensible to *all* men; the grief of one man comprehensible to *all* men. . . .

Documents 3 and 4

Clearly in opposition to Mr. Barron, in Documents 3 and 4 two of his former CBS colleagues argue strongly for the importance of the writer (especially of narration) and the interview in documentary films. As Mr. Rooney says, "nothing matches words for clarity and brevity."

3   But Anyone Can Fool Around with the Words
Andrew A. Rooney
October 2, 1971

The producers are producing, the directors are directing and the actors are acting, but the writers aren't writing anything.

Writing is hard; that's why there is so little of it that is any good in the theater, motion pictures or television. While everyone else is having meetings, going to lunch or talking about *cinema-vérité,* the writer is making a fool of himself putting it down on paper where everyone can see it.

Nothing anyone puts down on paper can match the misty vision of an idea that hasn't really been had, and the writer's work looks pale beside the dream. As a result, a lot of writers give up and start calling themselves "filmmakers," where no one is sure whether they're making fools of themselves or not.

The tendency to avoid writing irritates me most in the area of television nonfiction, where I have been working since there was one. The writer in the television news department has very little stature and no authority.

Most documentary films for television are more produced than written. The writing is something that is laid in afterward along with a little music and sound effects. If the word fits, use it. The pictures are seldom made to fit the writer's idea; the writing is used to fill a void or make up for any deficiencies in the film. The reports are made up largely of edited interviews intercut with small amounts of connective material supplied by the narrator or reporter.

The hard and expensive way to make an informational film for television is to know what it is you want to say and then set out to get large amounts of film that illustrate in detail what you are writing about. The great advantage of the interview is that it is cheap; and by putting the onus of what is being said on the subject, the trouble and danger of writing is eliminated.

Writing is dangerous for television because it puts the medium in a position of saying something and making a statement. A writer usually has more ideas but less of a sense of responsibility to stockholders and government agencies than a network executive. There are so many people ready to jump on television for any remark that is not down the middle of the road that networks avoid them. There is, unfortunately, no place for a little wild irresponsibility that might turn over a new idea, and writers are watched carefully.

Writing is troublesome and more expensive than producing because it is a creative process often accompanied by uncertainty, doubt and chaos. Producing, on the other hand, is orderly; and order is cheaper and neater than chaos.

In January [1971] I wrote a broadcast concerned with the health of the young for CBS News. The written part of the script consisted of an opening, a closing and six brief essays over film that divided the segments. I had been with CBS as a writer off and on for 20 years without ever having been actually fired for incompetence; but no fewer than five producers, executive producers or network executives checked the script and made suggestions for change. None of them had any comments to make to the lighting director, the cameraman or the people who chose the doctors to be interviewed.

My five editors were, with two or three possible exceptions, perfectly sound judges of material, but no writer's work can stand up to that kind of dissection.

. . .

The low status of writing in communications and the arts puzzles and angers me. The arty, wordless film is a mirror of our times . . . a bathroom mirror and someone has just taken a shower. It reflects the steamed-up inarticulateness of the young who behave as though they have so much to say, but don't ever quite say it so we can understand what the hell it is they mean.

People have a great preference for not knowing the truth, and the inexactness of communicating an idea without our most precise tool, the written word, makes it too easy for them to indulge themselves in an orgy of misinformation. Nothing matches words for clarity and brevity. They are the most efficient way of passing a thought from one mind to another. The writer extends the reader or the listener the courtesy of having thought about what it is he wants to say in advance. He is not blurting it out on a late-night television show, hoping to hit one or two good ones in his 15 minutes.

A film producer who puts the job of completing the idea on his audience may get the reputation for being some kind of genius without ever having had to finish a thought in his own mind. If an idea exists in a man's head, he ought to be able to say it with words. If he can't, there is a strong suspicion in my mind that no thought exists.

Because television writing has been held in such low esteem, many good writers shy away from it. Several years ago Luigi Barzini, author of "The Italians," was working on a project with Perry Wolff, CBS producer. Barzini showed some irritation with the slow progress of the work.

"All I want," Barzini said, "is my typewriter, my two hands and the words on the paper."

Although it is often my inclination to agree with him, if it is a writer's intention to communicate ideas and reveal the world to itself, it does not seem as though there is any reason not to use any extension of the power of the words on the paper that is available to him. Pictures and sounds are effective as a means of amplifying or punctuating words. They recall other words from the past and make it unnecessary for a writer to repeat them. . . .

The future for the written word in television or any of the visual arts is not bright. Most of the students interested in the field are known among themselves as "young filmmakers." What television needs right now is fewer young filmmakers and more old papermakers.

4 In Defense of Talking Heads
Burton Benjamin
1973

Let us now praise talking heads.

Let us now praise Walter Lippmann, Eric Hoffer, Dwight David Eisenhower, Lyndon Baines Johnson, Hugo Black, William O. Douglas, Dean Acheson, Richard Cardinal Cushing, Carl Sandburg, J. Robert Oppenheimer and Lauris Norstad.

All of them were talking heads on CBS News broadcasts. Each of them enriched television. And that is what this piece is all about—a defense of the head that talks on a television screen and has too often been maligned for doing so.

Let us begin by defining a talking head. The description may sound inelegant but it explains the phenomenon fairly accurately. A talking head is a closeup of a human head talking on television. Sometimes the subject is being interviewed. You hear the questions off camera. Sometimes he is making a statement. . . .

There are several kinds of talking-head broadcasts. There is the hour with six to twelve heads prominently participating. This format is often dismissed as "heavy with talking heads." If more than a dozen heads are used the complaint is that the film is "just a collection of talking heads." If the entire hour is one man talking . . . the purists will call it a "one-on-one" (the other "one" being the reporter); "illustrated radio;" or "just one goddamn talking head."

In praising talking heads (I believe they have given us some of our most memorable television) I know I am going against the tide. The filmmakers and the cinema verité devotees consider talking heads worse than out-of-focus. As a matter of fact they don't mind out-of-focus all that much. But the thought of a camera properly focusing on one head for an hour is intolerable. And some of the critics have taken this up and now use "talking heads" to disparage a broadcast. . . .

Now, admittedly, it depends how you use the heads and how you use the clips, but 1972 seemed to me an odd time to find fault with the technique. The year's most distinguished documentary in my view was Marcel Ophuls' four-and-a-half hour

"The Sorrow and the Pity." It consists exclusively of talking heads and news film clips.

When I screened Ophuls' film, I was deeply struck by the talent and passion that went into it. A not inconsiderable part of my own career is bound up with films of this genre. For nine years I produced *The Twentieth Century* for CBS News. Because the series dealt with history, and since I was not relying on reenactments, I went to the treasury a producer goes to when he requires historical footage—the film library. I believe we used our stock extremely well. I have always equated the use of historical film with what a writer would have to do today were he were preparing a biography of Woodrow Wilson. He would, of necessity, turn to the libraries and archives simply because Mr. Wilson would not be available to him. The spirit world has been of scant use to scholars in the recreation of history.

But assuming the subject were available, what would he do? He would certainly do what we have done: interview him. We have had the rare experience of putting some of the great figures in world history on America's home screens. We have turned the probing eye of a camera on them; pitted them against bright, tough-minded reporters. In short, we have made them Talking Heads. . . .

Ophuls put it well in a conversation in Paris with the writer, Jack Nessel:—

"Most modern non-fiction filmmakers detest the interview technique," Ophuls said. "It is almost the opposite of cinema verité. The great prejudice against it is usually that it is not visual, that it is talk and therefore not so graphic. But I think it's very visual to look at a man's face, to see the flicker in his eyes when he decides he doesn't quite want to hear the truth. Sometimes you can see it in the way he fidgets with a napkin or the paper, or the way he takes a photo out of his pocket. I think that this idea that you have to show people in action rather than people talking about themselves is an old-fashioned one, and it also has to do with the fact that most documentary filmmakers are frustrated fiction film directors. They haven't done film with actors and action and therefore they think they must get the film direction into the documentary."

The defense rests. Onward and upward with talking heads!

Document 5

Jerry Kuehl, an American working in Britain, was trained as a historian, and is now a filmmaker and teacher. Drawing examples from two important British series, *World at War* and *Destination America,* he describes the problems that arise when a filmmaker uses interviews—problems that apply to the production of all documentaries.

5   History on Film
Jerry Kuehl

In this note I want to talk about some of the constraints under which producers of television documentaries operate. I don't mean the kind of political pressures which every producer is subject to, whether working for British, French, Soviet or American television. I mean rather the structural constraints which shape historical documentaries (and I intend to concentrate on them to the exclusion of news and current affairs) everywhere in the world. These structural constraints are not often discussed in public—not because it is dangerous or risky to do so, but because they are so much a part of the professional lives of television producers that no-one really thinks consciously about them very much. Only when outsiders wonder why things are done the way they are is anyone liable to bring them out in the open.

Let us begin at the beginning. Historical documentaries are composed of a limited number of elements: film first of all. To a documentary producer, there are only two sorts: archive film and specially shot material. Archive film is film shot by someone else for some other purpose. Specially shot material is material shot by the producer for a specific film. It can be either filmed interviews—a 'talking head' as it's called, or film of something else. . . . In addition to film, there are 'stills'. Still photographs, maps, documents, charts, way-bills, bus tickets—anything written or drawn or photographed or painted—that can themselves be recorded on film. And finally, there is sound. Music, sound effects or voices. Again, these can be specially recorded or they can come from some pre-existing source: All films, however complex, are constructed from these elements, and these alone.

Though they may seem to offer a wealth of possibilities—image, speech, music—in fact, what films show is severely limited. For once an event is over, or once a person has died, nothing further of that life or that event can ever be recorded. And no events that take place in the absence of cameramen, or utterances that are made in the absence of recorders, can ever be preserved on film or tape at all. In other words, whoever sets out to make an historical documentary is limited to what is already to hand, and what he can have recorded on his own initiative. And what can he record? And what is recorded for him? Not as much as he would like. Official cameramen don't as a rule lavishly record disasters. Statesmen and politicians don't as a rule lovingly retail their own incompetencies. Private individuals don't as a rule expose their own humiliation and despair (although one kind of popular television is devoted to trying to get ordinary people to do just that).

Now, this reticence takes several forms. Public figures have a particular kind of reticence: for instance, in *The World at War,* Charles Bohlen was interviewed about American diplomacy in the years after the Second World War. He was an affable, indeed loquacious interviewee. But there was one matter which he flatly refused to discuss on film, although he had discussed it at some length in his published memoirs. He was asked to retell the story of how, when the Americans launched the Marshall Plan, they tried to frame the invitation in such a way as to oblige the Russians to reject it, whilst making the blame for the rejection appear to lie wholly with the Russians; and how, when the Soviets appeared to be about to accept, official Washington was thrown into consternation. Why did Bohlen refuse to repeat a published story in a television interview? I don't know, but I can guess. His memoirs were not widely read—except by specialists. Most copies were sold to libraries or to students of politics—hardly the sort of people to be surprised or shocked by the tale. But to tell the story to an audience of 8 million was something else again, especially since very few of those 8 million could be expected to be as worldly as the highly educated, politically conscious minority to which Bohlen addressed his written work. So that's one form of constraint. The refusals of public figures to share with a television audience statements that they have made for a restricted public.

There is a much broader area of refusal: where public figures refuse to repeat in public in *any* medium, things which they happily say in private. In other words, the stuff which makes dinner parties go around seldom appears on the screen, or in books, or even in the pages of *Foreign Affairs*. Only very rarely will a television interview with a public figure produce a story told in public by that person for the first time. I can think of one example from *The World at War;* where Lord Mountbatten gave an account of how Churchill told him at Potsdam that the war's end was imminent and that he, Lord Mountbatten, would be obliged to take political control of South East Asia, and asked him what he would do about it. Mountbatten replied he hadn't 'The faintest idea'. To my knowledge, this was the first and only time that Lord Mountbatten ever publicly admitted that he was at a loss to know what to do about *anything*. It's a trivial example—and with good reason. Public figures are circumspect in what they say in public, and that is one reason why they become and remain public figures. They are too wary to be trapped into scandalous revelations, particularly when they know that what they say is being recorded for posterity.

This kind of reticence is particularly striking in the case of military figures. Senior officers are notoriously gossipy, vain and rough-tongued. There's no question, for example, that General Eisenhower was one of the most foul-mouthed of all American commanders: yet his public utterances were models of decorum—if not of syntax. This should not surprise anyone. . . .

There is a final, forbidden area, involving matters which public figures will neither talk about in public nor allude to in private to producers. Sexual adventures, personal tragedies, secret ambitions, betrayals and alcoholism—and so on. (Everyone can doubtless provide their own favourite, libellous examples.)

Private persons don't often refuse to repeat a story told in their memoirs, because private persons don't often publish memoirs. But certainly there are subjects which interviewees will not usually discuss on camera, though they freely talk about them in private conversation. It may be from discretion, or the desire to avoid offending third parties, or embarrassment, or fear of damaging their own reputations in their neighbourhoods, or fear of reprisals—and of course it is not only public figures who suffer from mental illness, divided sexual loyalties, drug addiction.

. . .

Now this tendency to replace a candid, private version of events, with a softer public version, is worth pondering, because what it implies is that though they appear to be very intimate, the kind of interviews which go into historical documentaries really make a very formal and a very public kind of history. Only rarely are private persons prepared to speak with candour and, as it happens, the people mostly likely to speak truthfully are the very old and the young.

. . .

The second great set of constraints affects the *choice* of interviewees—and is quite unconnected with the question of the *content* of their interviews. How are people found, and who finds them? Consider first the constraints which are imposed by the nature of the budget. Major productions have major budgets. . . . They need budgets as large as these because they are popular entertainment, competing for the viewer's attention with situation comedies and variety shows. To compete successfully, they have to have what the industry calls 'production values': colour, music, stylish editing. They are much more like coffee table books than scholarly monographs. Such major series, because they mobilize and immobilize large resources, have to be planned long in advance, and they have to work to strict deadlines. . . .

Once the great machine starts, it can't really stop. This means that though budgets are lavish by the standards of university audio-visual departments, the production team must be extremely cost-conscious. If J. H. Plumb wishes to postpone the publication of his learned monograph until next year because he has discovered new documents, that's perfectly alright. But if Jack Plumb doesn't deliver his coffee-table manuscript to the publishers early enough to make the Christmas season, he throws an enormously complicated commercial machine out of kilter. And so it is with television documentaries—and all manner of consequences follow from this. If the best woman to interview is in California she may *not* be interviewed because the crew is in New York and it will [be costly] to fly them across the continent. She *could* be flown to New York, but she may be ill in bed and unable to come, or she simply may not want to. If the best scenes of Polish farm life take place just after the spring thaw, and the thaw is two weeks late this year, they won't be filmed, because the crew cannot possibly afford to spend the extra two weeks in Poland waiting for the thaw, even if they could have their visas extended, because they're needed in Seattle to film the man whose interview is the key to the programme, which is in the cutting room at this very moment, and so on. Such interlocking dependency runs backwards from the date of transmission, like a shockwave.

· · ·

Some changes—the most important—came about because of the speed with which [a] series has to be made in order to meet the scheduled transmission dates. Once it was clear that the [*Destination America*] series would have to be made in a year and a half, rather than two or two and a half years, the pace of production altered accordingly, and inevitably, the kind of films that were made. The researchers were sent off to look for ethnic individuals who would serve as Ideal Types for *Destination America* and found them difficult to locate. They might find someone from County Mayo, whose great great grandfather emigrated to escape the famine, who had worked as a labourer, and whose descendants became nuns, firechiefs, local politicians, but in Rhode Island, not in Boston—useless, because the programme was about the Irish in *Boston*.

Or they might find an elderly Jewish Socialist garment worker, whose life exemplified the experiences of a generation of Jews who grew up on New York's lower east side, but who himself lived in Paterson, New Jersey. Again, unusable in a story about Jews in *New York*.

There might be those who would object on principle to the idea of searching for an Ideal Type, and would regard the inability of our researchers to discover nine of them as confirmation of their own belief that individuals are irredeemably particular. I sympathize with that point of view, but am not convinced by it. It is possible, naturally, to people a film with highly individual individuals—philosemitic SS Officers, Americans who emigrated to Europe in 1900 to escape religious persecution in their native land—but to do so in a popular series would be, I think, simply perverse. The notions of 'typical' and 'characteristic' experiences do make sense, and it seems to me wholly proper that series for large audiences should seek out people who exemplify them, rather than search for idiosyncratic participants—but that is another issue.

· · ·

Schedules, budgets, and costs affect programmes in another way. Filming—including crew and lab services [is very expensive.] So the question the producer must always ask himself is: Is *this* . . . worth while? That is, is this man going to say in the *next* reel [of film] something he told us when we were chatting before we started filming, or is he going to continue to ramble as he has for the last three reels . . . ? And if the person isn't saying what we expect him to say, what can, or should, we do about it? We can't force him to change his story, or to say things he doesn't believe, but on the other hand he has been selected in the first place to represent one thing and not another.

· · ·

As the . . . roll of film goes through the camera, the producer asks himself other questions: Is the interviewee 'good television'? Public figures from the pre-television era never worried about whether they were 'good' media performers but it is something that television producers, because they are making films for popular audiences, must worry about on behalf of their interviewees. . . . Academic jargon is simply not comprehensible to most television viewers and that—rather than any crass anti-intellectualism—is why producers are so wary of putting Professors on the screen.

Interviewees may even be too professional themselves. That is, their behaviour is so polished that if they are used they may dominate the film, regardless of the substantive importance of their contribution.

Sam Levenson, a professional entertainer, was a valuable informant [in our production *Destination America*] but one who might have been used more in the programme on the New York Jews, had he not given such a striking *performance* on camera, and so threatened to overshadow less flamboyant interviewees.

Finally, there are the Tellers of Tales; people who say things which are true, but not necessarily about themselves. The best example is that of John Featherstone, a Wisconsin octogenarian whose accounts of frontier life are persuasive and detailed but, I believe, hopelessly muddled chronologically. I do not believe that his account of land clearing in the 1830s is an account of that period at all; it is rather, a description of life in the 1880s and 1890s. But since, in my view, conditions at the end of the century were, in the relevant respects, similar, we had little hesitation in using him to describe what he *claimed* to be describing—life in his grandfather's time.

Now, before academic historians cast the first stone, they should search their own consciences. Do they really behave so differently themselves? Do they *never* omit from their accounts people who awkwardly refuse to confirm what the historian *knows* to be the case? Do they never blur the edges of what they are doing in order to avoid having to make a return trip to the archives in Ulan Bator (or Wigan) simply to look up the reference they *know* they will find there anyhow? Do they never use printed rather than manuscript documents because they're less trouble to decipher in the time available?

I do not really mean to sound polemical when I raise this matter; but I think it is indisputable that professional historians have more in common with television craftsmen than they may like to think. Both work in an environment whose boundaries they so take for granted that they no more question them than football players question the rules of the game while they are playing a match—though they naturally dispute interpretations of the rules.

A television producer may make a programme proposal, and have it rejected by his superiors on the grounds that it's 'not television'—that is it's not a subject which will attract favourable attention from viewers, advertisers, critics, or national opinion leaders. The same thing happens to historians when they propose subjects for, e.g. dissertations or books, only to have their supervisor or editor reject them because they think examiners will not accept that it is a genuine contribution to historical knowledge, or the University press will not publish it. (And clearly, one of the purposes of this very journal is to extend the agreed limits of what subjects *are* suitable for historians to investigate, just as one of the purposes of alternative television is to widen the area of legitimate activity for television).

There is a final constraint on the producer of television programmes: the reactions of other members of the production team. 'Reactions' is perhaps the wrong word: it is their very *existence* which counts. Writing history is a solitary business; the same person does research, organizes material, writes the text. But film making is a cooperative, if not always a harmonious enterprise, and no producer can possibly do it all on his own. The other members of his team are all professionals, with ideas and skills of *their* own; they are not the mindless executors of the producers' will. . . .

The way television documentaries are made may well be determined, in some last analysis, by high politics. But in the world occupied by people who actually make films, the day to day considerations under which they operate are much more mundane. The kind of history they can do is largely shaped by the kind of cooperation they receive from the people they interview, and by the *technical* restraints under which *all* production teams operate in the last quarter of the twentieth century. What they produce is not *distorted* history; it is simply the kind of history that it is: Television History.

Suggestions for Further Reading

Barnow, Erik. *Documentary: A History of the Non-Fiction Film*. New York: Oxford University Press, 1974.
    A very readable, comprehensive history, covering many types of documentaries from many countries.
Bluem, A. William. *Documentary in American Television*. New York: Hastings House, 1965.
    A review of the early history of television documentary and its roots in motion picture film, with a description of various types of programs.
Leyda, Jay. *Films Beget Films: A Study of the Compilation Film*. New York: Hill and Wang, 1971.
    Types of documentaries produced from archival film, and their history.
MacCann, Richard Dyer. *The People's Films: A Political History of U.S. Government Motion Pictures*. New York: Hastings House, 1973.
    This book describes the development of documentaries produced by the federal government, particularly in the 1930s, and the political problems of the U.S. Film Service. There is more recent information on film production at U.S.I.A.

Vietnam

**Anthology and Guide to
A Television History**

Rebels with a Cause
Vo Nguyen Giap (on the left), the military strategist of the Vietminh, standing with
Ho Chi Minh, the leading Vietnamese political tactician. The photo was taken in
September 1945 shortly after Ho had read the Vietnamese Declaration of Independence
and had established the Democratic Republic of Vietnam. *Wide World Photo*.

Chapter 1
Roots of a War

Background

Historical Summary

Vietnam is a basically agricultural society whose people have struggled against foreign invaders for centuries. Its traditional enemy was China, which dominated Vietnam for more than a thousand years. In reaction, the Vietnamese long ago developed a warrior tradition and a strong sense of national identity.

In the 15th century, having gained their autonomy from China, the Vietnamese started to expand southward, eventually gaining control of the fertile Mekong Delta, until then a part of Cambodia. By 1800, they occupied virtually all the territory that is Vietnam today.

Throughout its history, however, Vietnam was torn by civil wars between rival claimants to power. In one of these internal conflicts, waged in the early 19th century, the head of a southern faction unified the country with the help of French mercenaries. His reliance on the French opened the way to their conquest of Vietnam which began in 1850 under the pretext of protecting Vietnamese Catholics—French missionary work having introduced Catholicism centuries earlier. By 1884, Vietnam had come under French colonial domination.

Having conquered Vietnam, France divided it into three distinct but interdependent regions. The southernmost area, Cochinchina, was ruled as an outright colony, while Annam in the center was ruled by a French-controlled emperor, and Tonkin in the north was a French protectorate. The French also conquered the neighboring states of Laos and Cambodia. They named the entire colonial region Indochina, which reflected its contrasting Indian and Chinese cultural influences.

The economic development of Indochina by the French was typically colonial. The French built cities, roads, bridges, and railways, opened coal and tin mines, and introduced rubber cultivation—all in order to improve the balance sheets of private French companies. In the process, they exploited the Vietnamese peasantry and disrupted traditional Vietnamese society.

But the French also brought education and fresh political ideas to Vietnam—and, paradoxically, their principles of liberty and equality inspired young Vietnamese who later became their nationalist adversaries. The most distinguished of these nationalists was Ho Chi Minh.

Born in 1890, Ho left Vietnam as a young man to travel the world, working

3

as a cook's assistant aboard freighters. He lived briefly in the United States and Britain before settling in Paris during World War I. There he labored to win independence for Vietnam, writing tracts and lobbying among French politicians and Vietnamese expatriates. He called himself Nguyen Ai Quoc, "Nguyen the Patriot."

Ho joined the French Communist party, moved to the Soviet Union and later to China, where he operated as a secret agent. He saw communism as the ideology through which the Vietnamese could be organized to overthrow their capitalist, colonialist oppressors—as the route to national independence for Vietnam.

In Vietnam itself, meanwhile, the Depression of the 1930s had dislocated the economy and impoverished the peasants. Their conditions were aggravated by droughts and floods, and they revolted against the French in some areas. But the French crushed them easily.

World War II brought cataclysmic change. In 1940, German armies overran France, and later that same year Germany's partner, Japan, compelled the French colonial administration in Indochina to cooperate in their expanding war. The French yielded without a fight.

The Japanese domination of Indochina discredited the French and inspired many Vietnamese nationalists, who welcomed the defeat of Europeans by Asians. But Ho feared the Japanese as much as he hated the French. In 1941, returning to Vietnam covertly for the first time in a generation, he organized the Vietminh, the League for Vietnamese Independence. It was then that he adopted the name Ho Chi Minh, which means "He Who Enlightens."

Though led by veteran Communists, the Vietminh sought to enlist Vietnamese of all classes. It formed guerrilla groups to harass both the French and the Japanese. Late in the war, the Vietminh received arms and training from a small American mission sent from China by the OSS, the Office of Strategic Services, precursor of the Central Intelligence Agency.

The Vietminh's nationalist appeals attracted many Vietnamese, especially in the north. A famine caused in part by Japanese pressures on the economy, in which an estimated two million died, turned many survivors toward the movement.

With Japan's defeat in 1945, Ho and his comrades moved quickly to assert their authority. They entered Hanoi, the former French colonial capital of Tonkin, and set up a provisional government, which they called the Democratic Republic of Vietnam. On September 2, 1945, Ho proclaimed Vietnam's independence, including in his speech the passage from the American Declaration of Independence that states: "All men are created equal . . ."

President Franklin D. Roosevelt had issued anticolonial statements during World War II, and Ho may have hoped for American support. But Roosevelt was dead and Truman unresponsive. The situation in Vietnam was confused and chaotic in the wake of the war, and Ho's hopes evaporated. Under an agreement reached by the wartime Allies, British forces arrived in Saigon to accept the Japanese surrender in the south, while Chinese Nationalist troops

Chronology

	3rd Cent. B.C.	221 B.C.	40–43 A.D.	965	1545	1626	1802	1841	1848
Vietnam	Kingdom of Au Lac with a Court and a regular army forms.	China invades. Long war follows.	Trung Sisters lead revolt against Chinese rule. Revolt fails.	Vietnam is totally liberated. Long period of independence follows.	Civil War begins. Vietnam split for nearly two centuries.	French priest, Alexandre de Rhodes, brings Catholicism.	Gia Long rules Vietnam.	Vietnam completely incorporates Cambodia.	
France							Napoleon becomes Consul for life in France.	Louis Philippe's bourgeois monarchy rules France.	Year of Revolution. Louis Philippe flees. 2nd Republic is set up.
World Wide		China unifies after 260 years of civil wars.	Claudius succeeds Caligula as Emperor of Rome. (41 A.D.)		European explorations of North and South America.	First Parliament of Charles I in England. (1625)	First practical steamboat is operated.		Karl Marx writes *Communist Manifesto.* Revolutions throughout Europe.

	1858	1859	1867	1884	1914	1919	1930	1936	1939
Vietnam	France invades Danang.	France occupies Saigon.	France annexes Cochinchina.	France imposes its rule throughout Vietnam.		Nguyen Ai Quoc petitions for Vietnamese independence at Versailles.	Indochinese Communist party is set up.	Unrest throughout Vietnam.	
France	Napoleon III rules the Second Empire. (1852–1870)			3rd French Republic now rules.	World War I begins in Europe.	Clemenceau represents France at Versailles.		Popular front government under Léon Blum.	World War II begins.
World Wide	Work begins on Suez Canal.		U.S. buys Alaska.			First commercial radio broadcast.	Economic depression worldwide.	Spanish Civil War begins.	

Chronology (cont.)

	1940	1941	1944	1945 Mar	Apr	May	Jun	Jul	Aug	Sep
Vietnam	Japanese troops in Vietnam. French arrive at an understanding with them.	Vietminh is founded. Fights Japanese and French.	Giap sets up the Liberation Army.	Japanese coup removes French from power in Vietnam. Bao Dai cooperates with Japanese.					Vietminh seize power from Japanese. Bao Dai abdicates.	Ho announces Declaration of Independence. British and Chinese forces accept Japanese surrender. British let French take control in the South.
France			Paris is liberated			War in Europe ends.				
World Wide		Japanese attack Pearl Harbor.	D-Day invasion of France.		President Roosevelt dies. Truman takes over. U.N. meets.			Potsdam Conference meets to discuss postwar plans.	Atom bombs dropped on Japan.	Japan surrenders.

performed the same function in the north. But on their arrival, the British at first allowed the Japanese to keep their arms, released French soldiers who had been imprisoned by the Japanese, and then helped the French and Japanese drive the Vietminh out of Saigon.

One of the earliest casualties of the fighting was a Lieutenant Colonel Peter Dewey, who was shot by Vietminh at a roadblock as he was preparing to leave the country. Dewey was the first American to die in Vietnam—the first of many.

Points to Emphasize

- the reasons for the French conquest of Indochina
- the factors which forced the Vietnamese rulers to capitulate to the French
- the economic role of Vietnam within the French Empire
- the explanations for the failures of most Vietnamese independence movements and anti-French struggles from 1880s to 1930s
- the impact of French colonial policies on the social and economic fabric of Vietnam
- the nature of the Vietnamese revolutionary movement in the 1930s and 1940s and of Ho Chi Minh's role in it
- the effects of the Japanese presence in Vietnam on the Vietnamese people and on their struggle for independence
- the reasons for the success of the August 1945 Revolution led by the Vietminh
- the circumstances which forced the United States to get involved in Southeast Asia during and after World War II
- the attitudes of the different Allied Powers toward the status of Indochina during and after World War II

Glossary of Names and Terms

Bao Dai last emperor of Vietnam. Served as emperor of Annam under the French, 1932–1945. Cooperated with the Japanese during World War II. Abdicated in 1945 in favor of Ho Chi Minh's government. Returned under the French as Chief of State in Vietnam, 1949–1955.

Jean Cedile French colonel who took command of French forces in Vietnam south of the 16th parallel in September 1945. In June 1946 signed the convention which set up an independent Cochinchina under a pro-French president.

Charles de Gaulle Army general and leader of the Free French during World War II. Head of the Provisional Government of the French Republic, 1945–1946. Later, first president of the Fifth French Republic, 1959–1969.

Peter Dewey American lieutenant colonel in the Office of Strategic Services (OSS) during World War II. Killed in Vietnam in the fall of 1945.

Douglas Gracey British general who accepted the surrender of Japanese forces in Vietnam south of the 16th parallel. Helped Colonel Cedile and the French return to power in the southern part of Vietnam on September 23, 1945. Served in Vietnam until January 1946.

Ho Chi Minh born Nguyen That Than in 1890. Became known as Nguyen Ai Quoc (Nguyen the Patriot) and later as Ho Chi Minh (He Who Enlightens). Vietnamese nationalist and a founder of the Indochinese Communist Party in 1930. Proclaimed Vietnamese independence from France on September 2, 1945. President of the Democratic Republic of Vietnam (known as North Vietnam) from that point until his death in 1969.

Jacques Philippe Leclerc French general, born Philippe, Vicomte de Haute-clocque, but adopted Leclerc in World War II. Commander of the Free French forces in North Africa, 1942–1943, and at the liberation of Paris, August 1944. Commander of French forces in Indochina, 1945.

Abbot Low Moffat American foreign service officer. Served as Chief of the State Department's Division of Southeast Asian Affairs in 1946.

Archimedes Patti American officer who served in the OSS during World War II. Organized the Deer Team to go into the mountains of northern Vietnam and work with the Vietminh of Ho Chi Minh.

Harry S. Truman Democratic senator from Missouri, 1935–1945. Elected vice president in 1944 for President Franklin D. Roosevelt's fourth term. Became the 33rd president after Roosevelt's death in April 1945. Re-elected as president in 1948.

Trung Sisters Vietnamese noblewomen who led a short-lived and ultimately unsuccessful rebellion against the Chinese in the first century A.D. Became symbols of the Vietnamese desire and demand for independence from all foreign rule.

Hoang Quoc Viet early member of the Indochinese Communist Party Central Committee. Active in the Vietnamese trade union movement throughout the wars in Vietnam.

Annam central region of Vietnam under the rule of the French, who outlawed the use of the word "Vietnam." The Vietnamese emperor, controlled by the French, maintained his court at Hue, the capital of Annam. Europeans used the term "Annamese" to refer to all of the inhabitants of Vietnam.

Cochinchina southernmost section of Vietnam under the rule of the French. The richest and most fertile section of the country.

Indochinese Communist Party founded in 1930 during the worldwide Depression. Became the spearhead of rebellion against French rule in Indochina.

La mission civilisatrice the French notion of their duty as colonialists to bring French culture to "less advanced peoples."

Mekong Delta fertile southern section of Vietnam located in Cochinchina. Vietnam's "rice bowl."

Office of Strategic Services (OSS) branch of the American armed forces which specialized in intelligence work during World War II. The Central Intelligence Agency, founded after the war, emerged from this organization.

Tonkin northernmost section of Vietnam under the French. The area of
Vietnam most affected by the famine of 1944–1945.

Vietnam Doc-Lap Dong Minh Hoi the anti-Japanese and anti-French Vietnamese liberation group organized by Ho Chi Minh in 1941, known as the Vietminh. Many communists were involved in this group but noncommunists
also participated. The most effective Vietnamese nationalist group.

Documents

Document 1

European imperialism changed the map of the world in the nineteenth century
as huge empires were carved out of African and Asian territory. These con-
quests were rationalized in various ways. In France, the Union Coloniale Fran-
caise, founded in 1894 and one of the leading proponents of empire, consistently
emphasized the duty "civilized" peoples owed those who were less advanced.

Many of these attitudes were expressed in the Union Coloniale's publication, *La Quinzaine Coloniale*. In its pages in September 1900, Charles Depincé,
the head of Union's Indochina department, expressed his reasons for advocating
a colonial policy that would care for the "indigenous populations in its charge."

1 Protection of Indigenous Peoples
Charles Depincé
September 25, 1900
Conquest—whether effected by peaceful means or by force of arms—has only one
justification: the improvement, as a result of the conquering nation's efforts, of the
material and moral standards of the conquered race. If the progress of industrializa-
tion and the new needs created by a more refined civilization compel certain nations
to move outside of the limited spaces in which nature has confined them and compel
them to create for themselves outlets beyond their own borders in the form of territorial expansion, and if to primitive and ignorant peoples a necessary consequence
of this expansion is that their land is expropriated and they lose their independence,
at least it must bring them as compensation the advantages which justify this dis-
possession. Conquest is no longer a matter of exercising superior force; it is the su-
perimposition on a primitive race of rudimentary civilization and elementary moral
standards by a more enlightened race that has higher moral standards and is further
advanced in civilization. If this conquering race only exploits, for purely material
profits, the territories it has taken and the people that inhabit them, it fails in its
social duty, it lies to itself and to humanity, and it loses its position as a superior
race because it has not carried out its obligations. On the other hand, it will fulfill
these duties and justify its conquest if, in taking by the hand, so to speak, the indigenous populations in its charge, it tries to raise them bit by bit to its own level by

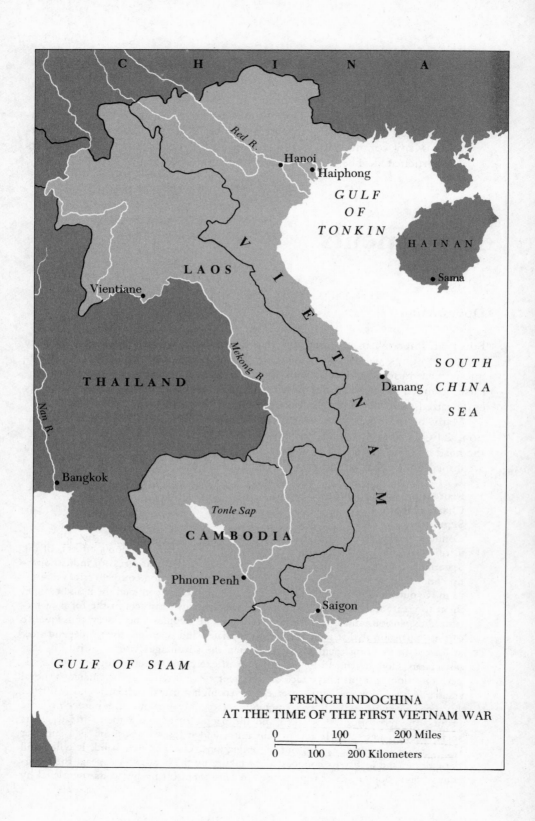

FRENCH INDOCHINA
AT THE TIME OF THE FIRST VIETNAM WAR

0   100   200 Miles

0   100   200 Kilometers

improving their welfare, teaching them morality, and developing their intelligence.

This is the colonizing nation's duty—and it is also in its best interests . . . because native populations are part of a country's wealth; and managing the life of a country, defending it against murderous influences, and improving its health at the same time manages, defends, and improves its economic resources and assures European enterprises the means, the only means, of exploiting the natural richness of the soil.

And it's in the interests of the colonizing race to improve the conditions under which its subjects live, not only for the material profit it will gain, but also because in exercising a rule that is no longer founded on violence and maintained by force, but is instead a protective system based on justice, marked by benevolence, and justified by mutual services rendered, the colonizing nation will secure its subjects' loyalties. A sentiment of sympathy and confidence will be established between them that will make the exercise of government easier, more stable, and less burdensome. . . .

Benevolence, respect for local customs and habits, prudence in the choice and application of the means by which this transformation of indigenous races will occur—these appear to be the principal characteristics of the policy to follow regarding these races. This policy will be as far removed from the ideas of those out-of-date people who still believe in repression as from those impatient people who dream of a premature exportation of the Declaration of the Rights of Man. The policy will have to triumph over many obstacles before it is adopted. It will have as adversaries both those colonists for whom exploitation of the natives remains the last word in colonization, and, at home, those more generous spirits whose thirst for equality can only be satisfied when every inhabitant of the world has the vote. Yet this is a policy which can satisfy both our self-interest and our conscience. In adopting it, we will be working both for ourselves and for humanity.

Documents 2 and 3

The Vietnamese peasants did not thrive under the rule of the French, who behaved as though the land and the people of Vietnam existed for the use and exploitation of the colonial power. Ho Chi Minh, living abroad in 1924, wrote critically about the conditions in which the Vietnamese peasants lived. Ho's comments (Document 2) were barbed, and he blamed capitalism and Christianity for the roles they played in the sufferings of his people.

Document 3 is the program for the Indochinese Communist party, founded in 1930. This statement, drafted by Ho Chi Minh, expressed his hatred for French imperialism and his belief in the Soviet Union as the nation that would lead the oppressed of the world into the glorious future. Note that he writes of the "Vietnamese revolution" as the force that will "make Indochina completely independent," reflecting a Vietnamese attitude toward neighboring states whose consequences are still unfolding today.

2   The Worker's Life
Ho Chi Minh
January 4, 1924
The Annamese in general are crushed by the blessings of French protection. The Annamese peasants especially are still more odiously crushed by his protection; as

Annamese they are oppressed, as peasants they are robbed, plundered, expropriated, and ruined. It is they who do all the hard labor, all the corvées. It is they who produce for the whole horde of parasites, loungers, civilizers, and others. And it is they who live in poverty while their executioners live in plenty, and die of starvation when their crops fail. This is due to the fact that they are robbed on all sides and in all ways by the Administration, by modern feudalism, and by the Church. In former times, under the Annamese regime, lands were classified into several categories according to their capacity for production. Taxes were based on this classification. Under the present colonial regime, all this has changed. When money is wanted, the French Administration simply has the categories modified. With a stroke of their magic pen, they have transformed poor land into fertile land, and the Annamese peasant is obliged to pay more in taxes on his fields than they can yield him. . . .

One can see that behind a mask of democracy, French imperialism has transplanted in Annam the whole cursed medieval regime, including the salt tax; and that the Annamese peasant is crucified on the bayonet of capitalist civilization and on the cross of prostituted Christianity.

3   Program of the Communist Party of Indochina
Ho Chi Minh
February 18, 1930

Workers, peasants, soldiers, youth, and pupils!
Oppressed and exploited compatriots!
Sisters and brothers! Comrades!

Imperialist contradictions were the cause of the 1914–1918 World War. After this horrible slaughter, the world was divided into two camps: one is the revolutionary camp including the oppressed colonies and the exploited working class throughout the world. The vanguard force of this camp is the Soviet Union. The other is the counter-revolutionary camp of international capitalism and imperialism whose general staff is the League of Nations.

During this World War, various nations suffered untold losses in property and human lives. The French imperialists were the hardest hit. Therefore, in order to restore the capitalist forces in France, the French imperialists have resorted to every underhand scheme to intensify their capitalist exploitation in Indochina. They set up new factories to exploit the workers with low wages. They plundered the peasants' land to establish plantations and drive them to utter poverty. They levied many heavy taxes. They imposed public loans upon our people. In short, they reduced us to wretchedness. They increased their military forces, firstly to strangle the Vietnamese revolution, secondly to prepare for a new imperialist war in the Pacific aimed at capturing new colonies; thirdly to suppress the Chinese revolution; fourthly to attack the Soviet Union because the latter helps the revolution of the oppressed nations and the exploited working class. World War Two will break out. When it breaks the French imperialists will certainly drive our people to a more horrible slaughter. If we give them a free hand to prepare for this war, suppress the Chinese revolution, and attack the Soviet Union, if we give them a free hand to stifle the Vietnamese revolution, it is tantamount to giving them a free hand to wipe our race off the earth and drown our nation in the Pacific.

However, the French imperialists' barbarous oppression and ruthless exploitation have awakened our compatriots, who have all realized that revolution is the only road to life; without it they will die out piecemeal. This is the reason why the

Vietnamese revolutionary movement has grown ever stronger with each passing day: the workers refuse to work, the peasants demand land, the pupils strike, the traders boycott. Everywhere the masses have risen to oppose the French imperialists.

The Vietnamese revolution has made the French imperialists tremble with fear. On the one hand, they utilize the feudalists and comprador bourgeois in our country to oppress and exploit our people. On the other, they terrorize, arrest, jail, deport, and kill a great number of Vietnamese revolutionaries. If the French imperialists think that they can suppress the Vietnamese revolution by means of terrorist acts, they are utterly mistaken. Firstly, it is because the Vietnamese revolution is not isolated but enjoys the assistance of the world proletarian class in general and of the French working class in particular. Secondly, while the French imperialists are frenziedly carrying out terrorist acts, the Vietnamese Communists, formerly working separately, have now united into a single party, the Communist Party of Indochina, to lead our entire people in their revolution.

Workers, peasants, soldiers, youth, pupils!

Oppressed and exploited compatriots!

The Communist Party of Indochina is founded. It is the party of the working class. It will help the proletarian class lead the revolution in order to struggle for all the oppressed and exploited people. From now on we must join the Party, help it and follow it in order to implement the following slogans:

1—To overthrow French imperialism, feudalism, and the reactionary Vietnamese capitalist class.

2—To make Indochina completely independent.

3—To establish a worker-peasant and soldier government.

4—To confiscate the banks and other enterprises belonging to the imperialists and put them under the control of the worker-peasant and soldier government.

5—To confiscate all of the plantations and property belonging to the imperialists and the Vietnamese reactionary capitalist class and distribute them to poor peasants.

6—To implement the eight hour working day.

7—To abolish public loans and poll tax. To waive unjust taxes hitting the poor people.

8—To bring back all freedoms to the masses.

9—To carry out universal education.

10—To implement equality between man and woman.

Document 4

During World War II, after the defeat of France in Europe in June 1940, the Japanese demanded and received concessions that enabled them to control and exploit Indochina while leaving the administration in French hands. In June 1941, as Document 4 indicates, the Vietnamese were preparing to fight back. Ho Chi Minh, returning to his country for the first time in thirty years, founded the Vietnam Doc-Lap Dong Minh Hoi, or Vietminh, whose aim was to liberate Vietnam from the double oppression of the Japanese and the French. Recalling past triumphs of the Vietnamese people, Ho Chi Minh and his new organization hoped to rally the population to fight for their freedom.

4   Call for the Revolutionary League for the Independence of Vietnam
Ho Chi Minh
June 1941

Elders! Prominent personalities! Intellectuals, peasants, workers, traders, and soldiers! Dear compatriots!

Since the French were defeated by the Germans, their forces have been completely disintegrated. However, with regard to our people, they continue to plunder
us pitilessly, suck all our blood, and carry out a barbarous policy of all-out terrorism
and massacre. Concerning their foreign policy, they bow their heads and kneel
down, shamelessly cutting our land for Siam; without a single word of protest, they
heartlessly offer our interests to Japan. As a result, our people suffer under a double
yoke: they serve not only as buffaloes and horses to the French invaders but also as
slaves to the Japanese plunderers. Alas! What sin have our people committed to be
doomed to such a wretched plight!

Now, the opportunity has come for our liberation. France itself is unable to
dominate our country. As to the Japanese, on the one hand they are bogged in
China, on the other, they are hamstrung by the British and American forces, and
certainly cannot use all their forces to contend with us. If our entire people are united
and single-minded, we are certainly able to smash the picked French and Japanese
armies.

Some hundreds of years ago, when our country was endangered by the Mon-
golian invasion, our elders under the Tran dynasty rose up indignantly and called on
their sons and daughters throughout the country to rise as one in order to kill the
enemy. Finally they saved their people from danger, and their good name will be
carried into posterity for all time. The elders and prominent personalities of our
country should follow the example set by our forefathers in the glorious task of national salvation.

Rich people, soldiers, workers, peasants, intellectuals, employees, traders, youth,
and women who warmly love your country! At the present time national liberation
is the most important problem. Let us unite together! As one in mind and strength
we shall overthrow the Japanese and French and their jackals in order to save people
from the situation between boiling water and burning heat.

Dear compatriots! National salvation is the common cause to the whole of our
people. Every Vietnamese must take part in it. He who has money will contribute
his money, he who has strength will contribute his strength, he who has talent will
contribute his talent. I pledge to use all my modest abilities to follow you, and am
ready for the last sacrifice.

Revolutionary fighters! The hour has struck! Raise aloft the insurrectionary banner and guide the people throughout the country to overthrow the Japanese and
French! The sacred call of the fatherland is resounding in your ears; the blood of our
heroic predecessors who sacrificed their lives is stirring in your hearts! The fighting
spirit of the people is displayed everywhere before you! Let us rise up quickly! Compatriots throughout the country, rise up quickly! Unite with each other, unify your
action to overthrow the Japanese and the French. Victory to Vietnam's Revolution!
Victory to the World's Revolution!

Document 5

As the tide of war turned in the Pacific and the Japanese were forced to retreat
from newly conquered territories, they bore down harder on lands still under

occupation. In addition to exporting Vietnamese rice to Japan, they forced many peasants to grow peanuts and jute instead of rice. These policies combined with a shortage of transport from the rice bowl of the Mekong Delta to produce a catastrophic famine in the northern part Vietnam in 1945, as described in Document 5. It is estimated that as many as two million Vietnamese died as a result of the famine.

5   The Starvation Crisis
In an article published in the April 28, 1945, issue of *Viet-Nam Tan Bao,* a Hanoi newspaper, an author had this to write:

Old men of 80 to 90 years of age that we have talked with all told us that they had never before seen a famine as terrible as this one. When we passed through areas that once had seen rice and potatoes growing in abundance and had been thriving with activity, now all we could see were dry paddy fields and people who were weak and tired.

Why was there this desolation?
    Because no sooner did the population grow the crops than the government took most of it away.
    Because the population had been so hungry that their strength had wasted away and they could not continue working.

When we entered market places we seldom saw foods like rice or potatoes. If there was any rice, the rice was full of husks, and if there were any potatoes, the potatoes looked not much bigger than the circumference of a chopstick. . . .
    When we entered the villages we saw the peasants miserably dressed. Many of them had only a piece of mat to cover their bodies. They wandered about aimlessly in the streets like skeletons with skin, without any strength left, without any thoughts, and totally resigned to the ghosts of starvation and disease. Their rice had all been taken away from them by the government. They did not have any potatoes or corn. They were forced to eat everything, whether poisonous or not, they did not care. They had eaten up all the vegetation around them. They ate even those plants that had been formerly reserved for animals. A family which still had a little bran to eat considered it a heavenly blessing. When a dog or a rat died, it was the occasion for the whole village to come around to prepare it and parcel it out among themselves. . . .

Document 6

By the beginning of 1945, the Axis plan for world conquest was in ruins, the Nazis faced immediate defeat, and the Japanese were in retreat. On the evening of March 9, the Japanese Army in Indochina staged a *coup de force,* quickly defeating the French garrisons and jailing the French political leaders. Their primary motive was to forestall the development of an active French underground resistance to their occupation. They proceeded to declare Vietnam independent, under Emperor Bao Dai.
    Document 6 summarizes the decisions of the Central Committee of the

Indochinese Communist Party made in the wake of the Japanese coup. These instructions guided all the activities of the Party and the Vietminh in the period
from March to August 1945 and had a decisive influence on the success of the
August Revolution.

**6   Instructions of the Central Committee of the Indochinese Communist Party
     March 12, 1945**
I. Analysis of the situation
    1. The Japanese *coup de force*.—At 8:25 p.m. on the March 9, 1945, the Japanese
opened fire upon the French and occupied the main towns and important strategic
points. The French put up but a weak resistance. They will lose in the end for three
reasons:
    a) Lack of fighting spirit.
    b) Lack of modern weapons.
    c) Lack of united action with the anti-Japanese forces of the Indochinese
       peoples.
    2. Character and objective of the *coup de force*.—The March 9, 1945 *coup de force*
was a *coup d'etat,* that is to say one group of rulers seized power from another. Its
objective was to deprive the French of all power, to occupy Indochina and to turn
it into an exclusive colony of Japanese imperialism.
    3. Causes of the *coup d'etat*.—Three causes have led to this *coup d'etat*:
    a) Two imperialist wolves could not share between them so rich a spoil as
       Indochina.
    b) Facing imminent attack by the Chinese and the Americans in Indochina,
       the Japanese were compelled to overthrow the French to remove the dan-
       ger of being stabbed in the back by the French on the landing of the Allied
       forces.
    c) Japan had at all costs to defend the land-link with its colonies in the In-
       donesian region since, following the occupation of the Philippines by the
       Americans, its sea-lines were completely cut off.
    4. Political crisis arising from the Japanese *coup d'etat*.—We can at this very mo-
ment see the characteristic signs of an acute political crisis:
    a) The two robbers are engaged in mortal combat
    b) French power is disintegrating
    c) Japanese power has not yet been consolidated
    d) The "neutral" strata of the population are in consternation
    e) The revolutionary masses are ready for action.

II. New conditions created by the new situation
    1. Conditions not yet ripe for an uprising.—The political crisis is acute but the
conditions are not yet ripe for an uprising because:
    a) French resistance was so weak and the Japanese *coup d'etat* was relatively
       easy; though the division between the French and Japanese ruling cliques
       has reached its climax, and the French ranks in Indochina are in extreme
       confusion and are disintegrating; extreme division, confusion and indeci-
       sion do not yet prevail among the Japanese ruling clique.
    b) The "neutral" strata of the population must necessarily go through a pe-
       riod of disillusionment with the disastrous results of the *coup d'etat* before
       they give way to the revolutionary forces and become determined to help
       the vanguard elements.

    c) Except in localities where the natural features are favourable and where we have fighting units, in the country as a whole the vanguard, still engaged in preparations for the uprising, is not yet ready to fight nor resolved to make every sacrifice.

    2. Circumstances favouring the rapid maturing of conditions for insurrection.— Three circumstances are creating conditions for the rapid maturing of the insurrection and launching of a vast revolutionary movement:

    a) The political crisis (the enemy's hands are tied, preventing them from dealing with the revolution)

    b) The terrible famine (deep hatred of the people for the aggressors)

    c) The war is entering the decisive phase (imminent Allied landing in Indochina to attack the Japanese).

III. Changes in the Party's tactics

    1. Enemy's ranks and allied forces after the Japanese *coup de force*.—The Japanese *coup de force* has brought about the following big changes.

    a) French imperialism having lost its ruling power in Indochina is no longer our immediate enemy, although we still have to be on our guard against the manoeuvres of the Gaullist group, who are trying to restore French rule in Indochina.

    b) After the *coup de force,* the Japanese fascists have become the main, immediate, and sole enemy of the Indochinese peoples.

    c) The French who are conducting a resistance to the Japanese are, for the moment, objectively allies of the Indochinese peoples.

    2. Main slogans change and whole tactics change. We must energetically renounce the old slogans and old forms of struggle and pass over to new forms of propaganda, organization and struggle. Particular attention must be paid to the following points:

    a) We must replace the slogan "Drive out the Japanese and French!" by "Drive out the Japanese fascists!" We must use the slogan "Establish the revolutionary power of the Indochinese peoples" in the struggle against Japanese power and the puppet government of the pro-Japanese traitors.

    b) We must switch the central point of our propaganda over to two themes:

      1. The Japanese bandits will not liberate our people; on the contrary, they will increase oppression and exploitation.

      2. The Japanese invaders cannot consolidate their power in Indochina and will certainly be annihilated.

      3. We must change to forms of propaganda, agitation, organization and struggle which are best suited to the pre-insurrectionary period, intensively mobilizing the masses for the revolutionary front and training them to march boldly forward to general insurrection.

    c) A powerful anti-Japanese movement for national salvation will be launched as a pre-requisite of the general insurrection. This movement could include actions ranging from non-cooperation, strikes in workshops and markets, and sabotage, to forms of a higher degree such as armed demonstrations and guerilla activity.

    d) We must be ready to switch over to general insurrection when the right conditions are obtained (e.g. on the Japanese capitulation, or when the Allied troops have established a firm position and are advancing firmly on our territory).

IV. Our attitude towards the French resistance and the setting up of an anti-Japanese front in Indochina

1. The French resistance has a relatively progressive character.—We entirely approve the French resistance although it has no other aims than disputing imperialist interests with the Japanese; because, objectively, it is directed against our principal enemy, the Japanese fascists. Thus it has a relatively progressive character.

2. Fundamental conditions for the formation of a United Democratic Front against the Japanese in Indochina.—The French resistants can stand by the side of the Indochinese revolutionary peoples in the United Democratic Front against the Japanese if they accept the four conditions laid down by our Party in 1943 and since amended as follows:

a) The foreigners who are fighting the Japanese in Indochina must recognize the complete and immediate independence of the Indochinese peoples.

b) The foreign anti-Japanese forces in Indochina and the Indochinese revolutionary forces must achieve united action in all fields including the military field. This united action must be based on the principle of equality and mutual assistance.

c) All Indochinese and foreign political prisoners must be released unconditionally.

d) The revolutionary governments in Indochina will ensure the protection of the lives and property of the foreigners who are fighting the Japanese fascists in Indochina and give them freedom of resistance and of trade.

. . .

3. Fight the Japanese first!—We shall not mechanically stick to all these four conditions in all circumstances and let slip opportunities to realize united action with the French who are fighting the Japanese in Indochina. Should this united action occur, we are ready to shake hands with the French who are truly and thoroughly resolved to resist the Japanese and are fighting them arms in hand. We call on them to supply us with arms and together with us, to fight the Japanese first! This does not mean that we surrender our claims to national independence. On the contrary, we see clearly that in the end, the slogan "national independence" will be realized by the strength of the armed masses of the population, and not by the promises of the French resistants.

4. United action with the rank and file.—But if the French resistants do not accept these four conditions and refuse to supply us with arms to fight the Japanese, our task is to strive to unite action with the rank and file of the French resistance army, to win over resolute anti-fascist elements of internationalist tendency, so that they can unite their actions with ours in the fight against the Japanese or, over the heads of selfish and irresolute higher army personnel, join our side bringing with them the weapons of the French imperialists and, together with us, set up the anti-Japanese Democratic Front of Indochina.

VI. To hold ourselves in readiness to unite action with the Allied troops

1. We cannot launch the general insurrection immediately upon the arrival of the Allied forces in Indochina to fight the Japanese. We should not only wait for the Allied forces to get a firm foothold, we must also wait until they are advancing. At the same time, we must wait until the Japanese send forces to the front to intercept the Allied forces, thus relatively exposing their rear, before we launch the general insurrection; only then will the situation be favourable to us.

↲ 2. Wherever the Allied forces land, we should mobilize the people to organize demonstrations to welcome them and at the same time arm the masses, set up militia forces to fight the enemy side by side with the Allied forces. In localities where our guerillas are active, they should enter into contact with the Allied forces and together with them fight the Japanese according to a common plan. But in any case, our guerillas must always keep the initiative in the operations.

Documents 7, 8, and 9

As the Allies began to take the offensive in the war in the Pacific, the prospect of victory led them to speculate about the face of Southeast Asia after the war had ended. The role of the French in the coming battles for Indochina, the areas of responsibility for each of the Allies, and the political ramifications of who fought where were all subject to high-level, top-secret consideration. Documents 7, 8, and 9 discuss the issues being raised among British and American military and political planners in the fall of 1944.

7 Cover Letter from Lord Halifax to Edward Stettinius
British Embassy
November 23, 1944

My dear Ed:

I send you herewith an Aide-Memoire concerning proposals for the use of the French in pre-operational activities in Indo-China.

This is a matter which Mountbatten and all of us have very much at heart. Until we have the all-clear from your side he cannot effectively carry out sabotage etc.

You will see that the matter is urgent and I would be grateful if you could let us have a very early reply.

HALIFAX

The Honourable
Edward R. Stettinius, Jr.,
Department of State,
Washington, D.C.

8 Aide Memoire on the Use of the French in Indochina
British Embassy
November 22, 1944

1. In August last His Majesty's Government invited the concurrence of the United States Government in the following proposals:

(1) The establishment of a French military mission with the South East Asia Command. This would facilitate the work of the Secret Operations Executive and of the Office of Strategic Services and would serve as the nucleus of the operational headquarters which may be required later. The function of the mission would be primarily to deal with matters concern-

ing French Indo-China and it would not participate in questions of general strategy. It would, therefore, be much on the same basis as the Dutch and Chinese missions attached to the South East Asia Command.

(2) The establishment in India of a "Corps Leger d'Intervention" composed at the start of 500 men and designed to operate exclusively in Indo China on Japanese lines of communication. The activities of this body would correspond to those of the American and British Secret Operational organizations and its establishment would be without prejudice to the wider question of from what sources French forces participating in the Far East should be equipped.

(3) French participation in the planning of political warfare in the Far East. This would be a matter for arrangement between the South East Asia Command and the French Military Mission.

2. The United States Chiefs of Staff, from a military point of view concurred with these proposals except that they believed that French participation in the planning of political warfare should be restricted to the area of the South East Asia Command. No further action could be taken by them in this matter as it was understood that the President had expressed the desire first to discuss the question of French Indo China orally with the Prime Minister.

3. The United States Chiefs of Staff took occasion to point out that in their view, French Indo China was part, not of South East Asia Command, but of the China Theatre and was an American sphere of strategic responsibility. They recognized that an oral understanding had been come to between Admiral Mountbatten and the Generalissimo by which both Commanders would be free to attack Thailand and French Indo China, and boundaries between the two Theatres would be decided at an appropriate time in the light of progress made by the two forces.

4. This agreement was recognized by the Generalissimo after Sextant as applying to pre-operational activities. It has however never been formally confirmed by the Combined Chiefs of Staff.

5. No further steps could be taken in obtaining the necessary approval by the Combined Chiefs of Staff to the proposals outlined in paragraph 1 of this aide memoire until the President and the Prime Minister had had an opportunity to discuss them. It was anticipated that this discussion would take place at the Quebec Conference, but in fact the subject was never raised. Consequently no further progress has been made in this matter which is becoming increasingly urgent.

6. Admiral Mountbatten is strongly of the opinion that useful and important work on irregular lines could immediately be done in French Indo China. The French Army and Civil Service are unquestionably anxious to take part in the liberation of the country from the Japanese and constitute virtually a well-organized and ready-made Maquis. The secret organizations operating from South East Asia Command have made contact with these elements and are now in regular communication with them. All that is necessary to exploit the situation is the presence in South East Asia Command of the necessary French personnel from whom alone the French in French Indo China will take the direction necessary to produce the action required.

7. Admiral Mountbatten has pointed out that French Indo China constitutes an area of vital importance to the operation of his Command since it lies on the Japanese land and air reinforcement route to Burma and Malaya. Irregular activities therefore on the lines envisaged in the proposals which are the subject of this aide memoire are for him a matter of urgency.

8. His Majesty's Government, therefore, earnestly hope that the United States Government will concur as to the desirability and urgency of pushing on with the irregular operations outlined above and will take such action as will make possible the issue of a directive by the Combined Chiefs of Staff

(a) confirming the oral understanding already existing between the Generalis-simo and Admiral Mountbatten, and

(b) approving the program set out in the opening paragraph of this aide memoire.

Such action would in no way prejudice the question of the ultimate settlement of the boundary between the China Theatre and the South East Asia Command, which, by the agreement between Admiral Mountbatten and the Generalissimo, is at present left open, nor the wider question of the participation of regular French armed forces in the Far Eastern War.

BRITISH EMBASSY,
WASHINGTON, D.C.
22nd November, 1944.

9 Response to the British Embassy's Aide Memoire
U.S. Department of State
TOP SECRET

The British Embassy's aide memoire of November 22, 1944 has been referred to the President. The State Department is authorized to make the following reply. In the aide memoire left by Lord Halifax with the Department of State on August 26, reference was made to a French request for British approval of:

(a) Sending a French military mission to be attached to S.E.A.C. headquarters;

(b) Sending to India a light intervention force for later use in Indo-China;

(c) Sending, later on, a French expeditionary force to participate in the liberation of Indo-China;

(d) Participation by the French in planning the war against Japan;

(e) Participation by the French in planning political warfare in the Far East.

In this aide memoire there was expressed on behalf of the British Government: disapproval as to proposal (d); approval of proposal (c), but only "in the later stages of the war and on the understanding that they are made up of good and experienced fighting men"; approval of proposal (e) "in areas in which the French are inter-ested", this to "be a matter for arrangement between the SEAC and the French Mil-itary Mission"; and approval of proposals (a) and (b). American concurrence on these last two was requested if possible in time to advise Monsieur Massigli before he should leave London on August 29.

As indicated in the Embassy's aide memoire of November 22, no formal reply was made to this request as it was expected that the entire matter would be discussed and a decision reached by the President and the Prime Minister at the Quebec con-ference. No such decision, however, was made.

This Government, meanwhile, has given serious consideration to the French re-quests referred to in the Embassy's aide memoire of August 25, and again in the Embassy's aide memoire of November 22. It concurs fully with the British Govern-ment that the French should not participate in planning the war against Japan; it feels that no plans should now be made for a French expeditionary force to participate in the liberation of Indo-China; and it has reached the conclusion that American ap-proval cannot be given at this time to the accrediting of a French Military Mission to the S.E.A.C.

In particular, it does not believe that pending final decisions on the future of Indo-China, such a Mission should participate in the planning of political warfare in the Far East where French interests center primarily in Indo-China.

Reports, which would appear reliable, have recently been received by this Government that a French Military Mission under General Blaizot has arrived in Kandy, that such Mission has been accorded by Admiral Mountbatten official recognition and approval and the same status as the Chinese and Dutch Missions accredited to the South East Asia Command, and that discussions are proceeding between officers of the South East Asia Command and the French Mission. Reports have also been received that two thousand French troops have arrived in India and the French are recruiting and training personnel in metropolitan France with the hope of increasing this group ultimately to about two divisions.

This Government is surprised by these reports, which would imply that the British Government has already given approval to the French Military Mission without the concurrent approval of this Government.

Finally, the British aide memoire of November 22 expresses the earnest hope that this Government will concur in taking such action as will make possible the issue of a directive by the Combined Chiefs of Staff confirming that the oral understanding said to exist between Admiral Mountbatten and Generalissimo Chiang Kai-shek concerning the boundaries between their two theaters should be applicable to pre-operational activities. It is felt that in view of the military considerations involved decision in regard to this question should be left to the appropriate military authorities.

Department of State,
   Washington

Document 10

Within the government of the United States, the question of American support for the French return to Indochina was hotly debated. Early in the war, President Roosevelt had seemed to want to see the end of French colonialism in Indochina. The French, of course, intended to hold on.

After Roosevelt's death, the Division of European Affairs of the State Department re-evaluated this policy. Document 10 outlines the reasons why the Europeanists thought that the United States should support France's return to Indochina.

10 Draft Memorandum for the President
U.S. Department of State
April 20, 1945
General Observations

1. The Japanese aggression against the French in Indo-China last month has brought about a marked increase in the number of proposals advanced by the French for the use of French forces and resources in the Pacific.

2. The consequences of these military developments make it clear that our last policy, which held that the disposition of Indo-China was a matter for post-war determination and that the United States should not become involved in military effort

for its liberation, is in urgent need of reexamination and clarification. This is particularly so in order that American military and naval authorities may have guidance to enable them to take appropriate action with respect to the French proposals referred to above.

3. The United States Government has publicly taken the position that it recognizes the sovereign jurisdiction of France over French possessions overseas when those possessions are resisting the enemy and had expressed the hope that it will see the reestablishment of the integrity of French territory. In spite of this general assurance, the negative policy so far pursued by this Government with respect to Indo-China has aroused French suspicions concerning our intentions with respect to the future of that territory. This has had and continues to have a harmful effect on American relations with the French Government and people.

4. On April 3, 1945, the Secretary of State with the approval of the President issued a statement of which the following excerpt is pertinent to the present problem:

> "As to territorial trusteeship, it appeared desirable that the Governments represented at Yalta, in consultation with the Chinese Government and the French Provisional Government, should endeavor to formulate proposals for submission to the San Francisco Conference for a trusteeship structure as a part of the general organization. This trusteeship structure, it was felt, should be defined to permit the placing under it of the territories taken from the enemy in this war, as might be agreed upon at a later date, *and also such other territories as might voluntarily be placed under trusteeship.*"

5. General de Gaulle and his Government have made it abundantly clear that they expect a proposed Indo-Chinese federation to function within the framework of the "French Union." There is consequently not the slightest possibility at the present time or in the foreseeable future that France will volunteer to place Indo-China under an international trusteeship, or will consent to any program of international accountability which is not applied to the colonial possessions of other powers. If an effort were made to exert pressure on the French Government, such action would have to be taken by the United States alone for France could rely upon the support of other colonial powers, notably Great Britain and the Netherlands. Such action would likewise run counter to the established American policy of aiding France to regain her strength in order that she may be better fitted to share responsibility in maintaining the peace of Europe and the world.

Recommendations

In the light of the above considerations, the following recommendations, which have been communicated to the War and Navy Departments, are submitted for your approval.

1. The Government of the United States should neither oppose the restoration of Indo-China to France, with or without a program of international accountability, nor take any action toward French overseas possessions which it is not prepared to take or suggest with regard to the colonial possessions of our other Allies.

2. The Government of the United States should continue to exert its influence with the French in the direction of having them effect a liberalization of their past policy of limited opportunities for native participation in government and administration, as well as a liberalization of restrictive French economic policies formerly pursued in Indo-China.

3. The French Provisional Government should be informed confidentially that, owing to the need of concentrating all our resources in the Pacific on operations al-

ready planned, large-scale military operations aimed directly at the liberation of Indo-China cannot be contemplated at this time.

4. French offers of military and naval assistance in the Pacific should be considered on their merits as bearing upon the objective of defeating Japan, as in the case of British and Dutch proposals. The fact that acceptance of a specific proposal might serve to strengthen French claims for the restoration of Indo-China to France should not be regarded as grounds for rejection. On the contrary, acceptance of French proposals for military assistance in the defeat of Japan should be regarded as desirable in principle, subject always to military requirements in the theater of operations.

5. While avoiding specific commitments with regard to the amount or character of any assistance which the United States may give to the French resistance forces in Indo-China, this Government should continue to afford all possible assistance provided it does not interfere with the requirements of other planned operations.

6. In addition to the aid which we are able to bring from the China theater of operations to the French forces resisting the Japanese in Indo-China, the United States should oppose no obstacle to the implementation of proposals looking toward the despatch of assistance to those forces from the southeast Asia theater of operations, provided such assistance does not constitute a diversion of resources which the Combined Chiefs of Staff consider are needed elsewhere.

Document 11

On September 2, 1945, before a crowd of over half a million people assembled in Ba Dinh Square in Hanoi, President Ho Chi Minh introduced the Provisional Government of the Democratic Republic of Vietnam and read the Vietnamese Declaration of Independence. Ho's declaration purposely echoed some of the ideas and even the phrases of those earlier declarations of independence and freedom written in the United States and in France. These reminders were then contrasted with his description of the horrible conditions in Vietnam under the rule of the Japanese and the French.

11 Declaration of Independence of the Democratic Republic of Vietnam
Ho Chi Minh
September 2, 1945

All men are created equal. They are endowed by their Creator with certain inalienable rights, among these are Life, Liberty and the pursuit of Happiness.

This immortal statement was made in the Declaration of Independence of the United States of America in 1776. In a broader sense, this means: All the peoples on the earth are equal from birth, all the peoples have a right to live, to be happy and free.

The Declaration of the French Revolution made in 1791 on the Rights of Man and the Citizen also states: « All men are born free and with equal rights, and must always remain free and have equal rights ».

Those are undeniable truths.

Nevertheless, for more than eighty years, the French imperialists, abusing the standard of Liberty, Equality and Fraternity, have violated our Fatherland and oppressed our fellow-citizens. They have acted contrary to the ideals of humanity and justice.

In the field of politics, they have deprived our people of every democratic liberty.

They have enforced inhuman laws; they have set up three distinct political regimes in the North, the Centre and the South of Viet Nam in order to wreck our national unity and prevent our people from being united.

They have built more prisons than schools. They have mercilessly slain our patriots; they have drowned our uprisings in rivers of blood.

They have fettered public opinion; they have practised obscurantism against our people.

To weaken our race they have forced us to use opium and alcohol.

In the field of economics, they have fleeced us to the backbone, impoverished our people and devastated our land.

They have robbed us of our ricefields, our mines, our forests and our raw materials. They have monopolized the issuing of bank-notes and the export trade.

They have invented numerous unjustifiable taxes, and reduced our people, especially our peasantry, to a state of extreme poverty.

They have hampered the prospering of our national bourgeoisie; they have mercilessly exploited our workers.

In the Autumn of 1940, when the Japanese fascists violated Indochina's territory to establish new bases in their fight against the Allies, the French imperialists went down on their bended knees and handed over our country to them.

Thus, from that date, our people were subjected to the double yoke of the French and the Japanese. Their sufferings and miseries increased. The result was that from the end of last year to the beginning of this year, from Quang Tri province to the North of Viet Nam, more than two millions of our fellow-citizens died from starvation. On the 9th of March, the French troops were disarmed by the Japanese. The French colonialists either fled or surrendered; showing that not only were they incapable of « protecting » us, but that, in the span of five years, they had twice sold our country to the Japanese.

On several occasions before the 9th of March, the Viet Minh League urged the French to ally themselves with it against the Japanese. Instead of agreeing to this proposal, the French colonialists so intensified their terrorist activities against the Viet Minh members that before fleeing they massacred a great number of our political prisoners detained at Yen Bay and Cao Bang.

Notwithstanding all this, our fellow citizens have always manifested towards the French a tolerant and humane attitude. Even after the Japanese putsch of March 1945, the Viet Minh League helped many Frenchmen to cross the frontier, rescued some of them from Japanese jails and protected French lives and property.

From the autumn of 1940, our country had in fact ceased to be a French colony and had become a Japanese possession.

After the Japanese had surrendered to the Allies, our whole people rose to regain our national sovereignty and to found the Democratic Republic of Viet Nam.

The truth is that we have wrested our independence from the Japanese and not from the French.

The French have fled, the Japanese have capitulated, emperor Bao Dai has abdicated. Our people have broken the chains which for nearly a century have fettered them and have won independence for the Fatherland. Our people at the same time have overthrown the monarchic regime that has reigned supreme for dozens of centuries. In its place has been established the present Democratic Republic.

For these reasons, we, members of the Provisional Government, representing the whole Vietnamese people, declare that from now on we break off all relations of a colonial character with France; we repeal all the international obligations that France has so far subscribed to on behalf of Viet Nam and we abolish all the special rights the French have unlawfully acquired in our Fatherland.

The whole Vietnamese people, animated by a common purpose, are determined to fight to the bitter end against any attempt by the French colonialists to reconquer their country.

We are convinced that the Allied nations which at Teheran and San Francisco have acknowledged the principles of self-determination and equality of nations, will not refuse to acknowledge the independence of Viet Nam.

A people who have courageously opposed French domination for more than eighty years, a people who have fought side by side with the Allies against the fascists during these last years, such a people must be free and independent.

For these reasons we, members of the Provisional Government of the Democratic Republic of Viet Nam, solemnly declare to the world that Viet Nam has the right to be a free and independent country—and in fact it is so already. The entire Vietnamese people are determined to mobilize all their physical and mental strength, to sacrifice their lives and property in order to safeguard their independence and liberty.

Hanoi, the Second of September 1945

HO CHI MINH, President

Tran Huy Lieu	Vo Nguyen Giap
Chu Van Tan	Pham Van Dong
Duong Duc Hien	Nguyen Van To
Nguyen Manh Ha	Cu Huy Can
Pham Ngoc Thach	Nguyen Van Xuan
Vu Trong Khanh	Dao Trong Kim
Vu Dinh Hoe	Le Van Hien

Critical Issues for Discussion

1. The French regarded Vietnam as the "pearl" of their empire. Why did they have this attitude? What was so worthwhile about Vietnam? Why did the French struggle to hold onto it?

2. The majority of the Vietnamese people were peasants. See Document 2.
How did Ho Chi Minh evaluate the living conditions of the peasantry? Who was responsible for their predicament? Why did Ho refer to his fellow countrymen as the "Annamese"? What institutions did Ho attack with the greatest venom? Why?

3. In 1930 and 1931 there was an unprecedented wave of revolts in Vietnam.
The Indochinese Communist Party was organized in 1930. Were these two facts coincidental? Why or why not? Was there any relationship between those two facts?
See Document 3. What points was this manifesto making? What did the In-

dochinese Communist Party hope to accomplish? How? Why? How effectively were their slogans chosen? Explain.

4. During the period between 1936 and 1939 there was great public opposition to colonial rule. What were the Vietnamese seeking? Was this an isolated reaction of theirs? How do you explain the fervor of the Vietnamese people for independence?

5. The Japanese were able to take over Indochina almost overnight. Why? What could the French and the Vietnamese have done to stop this occupation? What was the French attitude toward the Japanese takeover? How do you explain this point of view? Did it surprise you? Why or why not?

6. The founding of the Vietnam Doc-Lap Dong Minh Hoi (Vietminh) in June 1941 was a major event in the history of Southeast Asia. See Document 4. To whom were the Vietminh speaking? What were the major points raised by the Vietminh? What did they want? Were their plans effective? Who was the main target in this war of words? Why?

7. The Japanese occupation led to great trials and tribulations in Vietnam. The food shortage of 1944 and 1945 was particularly catastrophic. See Document 5. Who suffered the most from the famine? Why was it so devastating? How did the Japanese occupation government respond? What could have been done? What did the famine and starvation mean in terms of Vietnamese politics?

8. The Japanese coup in March 1945 changed the Vietnamese situation once again. See Document 6.
Why did the Japanese stage their coup at that time? Why not earlier in the war? What did they hope to gain? How did the Indochinese Communist Party react? How did the party analyze the event? What did the party decide to do? Why? What did they hope to accomplish? Was that a practical goal? Why or why not?

9. The Vietnamese situation was rarely discussed on its own merits. The international political scene consistently influenced the decisions of all the Allied powers. For a look at the British and American attitudes, compare Documents 7, 8, and 9.
Why were the British interested in this part of the world? What did they desire? What stance did they want their Allies to take on Vietnam? Why were these documents top secret? What might have happened if they had been released and published?

10. American policy makers saw Vietnam as a piece in a larger international puzzle. What would be a good title for that puzzle? Look at Document 10. What were the American concerns? Were they similar to the British hopes? What factors most influenced the American attitudes? Any surprises? Why? Why was the Division of European Affairs in the State Department writing about this issue? What was their focus? Would there have been any difference in emphasis if the Asian desk had written on the same subject?

11. A great deal can be learned from a nation's Declaration of Independence.
    Look at Document 11. Why was this declaration so similar to the American
Declaration of Independence? What did this document mean? What were its authors trying to accomplish? What were Ho Chi Minh's primary concerns? Who
was his audience for this speech? Explain.

12. Joseph Gallieni, a French hero during World War I who had served in Viet-
    nam earlier, once commented on the difficulties of ruling a captive popu-
lation. "A country is not conquered and pacified by crushing its people through
terror. After overcoming their initial fear, the masses grow increasingly rebel-
lious, their accumulated bitterness steadily rising in reaction to the brutal use of
force."
    Were Gallieni's comments applicable to what had happened in Vietnam?
Were his warnings heeded? On what basis had Gallieni made these observations? Could a country be conquered and pacified without using "brutal" force?
Of what use was Vietnam to the French? What purpose did any colonies serve?
Why were they worth fighting over?

Follow Up The French colonial societies argued, as Document 1 indicates,
that imperialism, if conscientiously and humanely undertaken, benefited those
who ruled and those who were governed. How did Depincé justify this argument? What benefits accrued to the "indigenous populations"? How could
oppression be avoided?
    A black leader in the United States, W.E.B. DuBois, viewed the prevailing
notion of governing and subject races rather differently. He predicted in 1900
that "the problem of the twentieth century is the problem of the colour line—
the relation of the darker to the lighter races of men in Asia and Africa, in
America and the islands of the sea."
    Was DuBois's prophecy true? Why have there been problems between races
in the twentieth century? What has been the nature of the relationships between
the races? Did this prediction have any relevance to what happened in Vietnam?
How might Depincé have answered DuBois? Would DuBois have been able to
counter Depincé's argument? How?

Suggestions for Further Reading

Introduction to the People of Vietnam
Chagnon, Jacqui, and Don Luce, eds. *Of Quiet Courage: Poems from Vietnam.*
    Washington: Indochina Mobile Education Project, 1974; distributed by
    Southeast Asia Resource Center East.
    The emphasis in this collection of poems, photos, and drawings is on the
    destructive impact of the war on Vietnamese life and on the people's
    strength to resist foreign domination. It is strongly antiwar without being
    rhetorical.

Hickey, Gerald Cannon. *Village in Vietnam*. New Haven: Yale Univ. Press, 1964.

An anthropological study of the religions, family life, economic system, legal administration, and social organization of a small rural village near Saigon.

Huynh Sanh Thong. *The Heritage of Vietnamese Poetry*. New Haven: Yale Univ. Press, 1979.

The poems in this annotated anthology date from the tenth century through the early part of the French colonial period.

Nguyen Du. *The Tale of Kieu*. Bilingual edition translated and annotated by Huynh Sanh Thong. New Haven: Yale Univ. Press, 1983.

The best-loved work in Vietnamese literature, this long narrative poem provides insight both into Vietnam's cultural roots and into how its people interpret the meaning of their long suffering.

Nguyen Khac Vien. *Tradition and Revolution in Vietnam*. Berkeley: Southeast Asia Resource Center, 1974.

In seven essays, Nguyen Khac Vien analyzes how Vietnam's revolution grew out of the history and culture of its people; in particular, how Confucianism paved the way for socialism.

Nguyen Khac Vien, gen. ed. *Vietnamese Studies #14: Literature and National Liberation in South Vietnam*. Hanoi.

Literary works from Vietnam are difficult to obtain but worth searching for in university libraries. Other worthwhile titles:

    Anthology of Vietnamese Literature. Hanoi: Foreign Languages Publishing House.

    Poems of South Vietnam, 1960–70. South Vietnam: Giai Phong Editions, National Front for Liberation Documents.

Nguyen Khac Vien, gen. ed. *Vietnamese Studies #21: Traditional Viet-Nam: Some Historical Stages*. Hanoi, 1969.

A brief collection of articles surveys Vietnam's development from the Stone Age through the eighteenth century.

Shaker, Peggy, and Holmes Brown. *Indochina Is People*. New York: United Church Press, 1973.

This introduction to Vietnamese history and culture was written as part of the antiwar effort to help Americans feel their common humanity with the peoples of Indochina. Simply written and attractively illustrated, it is still a good starting point.

Steinberg, David Joel, ed. *In Search of Southeast Asia*. New York: Praeger, 1971.

Alexander Woodside's section on Vietnam is a useful summary of social and cultural aspects of the eighteenth and nineteenth centuries.

Sully, François, ed. *We the Vietnamese: Voices from Vietnam*. New York: Praeger, 1971.

Sully's collection contains scenes from everyday life in North and South Vietnam and selections from Vietnamese leaders: Emperor Bao Dai, Ngo Dinh Diem, Ho Chi Minh, Thich Nhat Han, General Giap, Nguyen Van Thieu, and others.

Vietnam Under the French

Buttinger, Joseph. *The Smaller Dragon* and *Vietnam: A Dragon Embattled,* Vol.
1. Condensed in *Vietnam: A Political History.* New York: Praeger, 1967.

Together, Buttinger's books offer a widely-respected history of Vietnam
from its semilegendary beginnings to the fall of Ngo Dinh Diem. *The
Smaller Dragon* covers the period to 1900; *A Dragon Embattled,* Vol. 1, to the
end of World War II. Though wrong in some details, it remains the most
complete historical summary in English. The condensed edition omits the
scholarly notes of the more detailed original works.

Cady, John. *The Roots of French Imperialism in Indochina.* Ithaca: Cornell Univ.
Press, 1954.

This is a good general history of the period from a French point of view,
based on French sources.

Lamb, Helen. *Vietnam's Will to Live: Resistance to Foreign Aggression From Early
Times Through the Nineteenth Century.* New York: Monthly Review Press,
1972.

Focusing on the second half of the nineteenth century, Lamb shows Vietnam's earliest struggles against French domination forging its later resistance
movements.

Marr, David G. *Vietnamese Anticolonialism, 1885–1925.* Berkeley: Univ. of California Press, 1971.

Marr, David G. *Vietnamese Tradition on Trial, 1920–1945.* Berkeley: Univ. of
California Press, 1981.

Marr's books offer an intellectual history of the colonial period; aimed at a
scholarly audience, they are nonetheless rich in cultural detail and stories.
Vietnamese Anticolonialism shows how, during the time when Vietnam's very
identity was threatened by the French, its people created symbols of resistance which came to have deep meaning to later anticolonial leaders. *Vietnamese Tradition on Trial* studies the period of intense national debate just
prior to full-scale revolution when every part of Vietnamese tradition was
critically examined in a new light.

Ngo Vinh Long. *Before the Revolution: The Vietnamese Peasants Under the French.*
Cambridge: The M.I.T. Press, 1973.

Ngo Vinh Long. *Vietnamese Women in Society and Revolution.* Vol. 1, *The French
Colonial Period.* Cambridge: Vietnam Resource Center, 1974.

Each of these books begins with an historical analysis of the effects of French
colonial policies on peasant life, followed by brief stories which bring the
history painfully to life. They enable American readers to identify with people who otherwise seem far removed from their own experience. The last
three stories in *Vietnamese Women* take place during the war of resistance
against the French in the early 1950s.

Ho Chi Minh and the Vietminh

Chu Van Tan. *Reminiscences on the Army for National Salvation.* Tr. with an introduction by Mai Elliott. Ithaca: Cornell Data Paper series, 1974.

As an ethnic minority leader and key Vietminh tactician, General Chu Van Tan was crucial to early revolutionary success in Vietnam.

Fall, Bernard B., ed. *Ho Chi Minh on Revolution: Selected Writings, 1920–66.* New York: Praeger, 1967.

In contrast to the reserve of his prison diary, Ho here expresses his fervent commitment to ending the evils of colonialism.

Halberstam, David. *Ho.* New York: Random House, 1971.

Lacouture, Jean. *Ho Chi Minh: A Political Biography.* New York: Random House, 1968.

Because Lacouture's widely-respected biography of Ho assumes a background in European colonial history, American students may find it difficult. Halberstam's *Ho* is a more readable account but difficult to locate. Both are somewhat dated now.

Marr, David G., ed. *Reflections from Captivity: Phan Boi Chau's Prison Notes and Ho Chi Minh's Prison Diary.* Athens, Ohio: Ohio Univ. Press, 1978.

Fresh translations of Ho's poems from prison are paired with the journals of a Vietnamese patriot jailed by the French from 1914–17.

Patti, Archimedes L. A. *Why Vietnam? Prelude to America's Albatross.* Berkeley: Univ. of California Press, 1980.

A dramatic first-hand account of the early years of American involvement in Indochina. Colonel Patti, then head of a U.S. intelligence mission, met Ho Chi Minh in 1945, agreed to work with the Vietminh against the Japanese, and was present when the Vietnamese declared their independence.

Vo Nguyen Giap. *Unforgettable Months and Years.* Tr. with an introduction by Mai Elliot. Ithaca: Cornell Data Paper series, 1975.

North Vietnam's paramount military leader reminisces about Ho Chi Minh during the crucial period from August 1945 to December 1946, the start of the first Indochina War.

Hell in a Very Small Place
A French soldier watches as reinforcements and supplies land at Dienbienphu, near the
Laotian border. The Vietminh's ability to put artillery on top of the hills (shown in the
background) led to the French defeat in a decisive battle in the spring of 1954. *U.P.I.*

Chapter 2
The First Vietnam War

Background

Historical Summary

In August 1945, World War II ended with Japan's surrender to the Allied powers. But there would be no durable peace in Indochina, where a chain of complicated and confusing events triggered a fresh conflict—the first Vietnam war.

Ho Chi Minh, the Vietnamese Communist leader whose nationalist movement had sided with the Allies against the Japanese, had declared Vietnam's independence from French colonial rule on September 2. Almost immediately, however, a challenge confronted him.

Under an Allied plan, British troops entered the southern part of Vietnam to disarm the defeated Japanese, while Chinese Nationalist forces arrived in the north to perform the same function. The British released and rearmed interned French soldiers, who promptly clashed with Vietnamese nationalists. New French units landed to reassert France's authority in the south. Vietnamese resistance spread, and soon the area was engulfed in war.

In the spring of 1946, seeking to stop the conflict, Ho offered concessions to the French. He agreed to permit them to return to the north to displace the Chinese. He also agreed to affiliate an autonomous Vietnam with the French Union, a loose federation of states linked to France. Ho went to Paris in May 1946 to conclude the accord, but during his absence, the French commissioner in Saigon, Admiral Thierry d'Argenlieu, violated the agreement by separating the southern region, Cochinchina, from the rest of Vietnam.

Mounting tensions finally erupted in violence in November 1946 over a minor incident in the northern port of Haiphong. French warships shelled the city, causing thousands of casualties. The Vietnamese rejected French demands to capitulate, and the fighting intensified. Ho and his followers, unable to hold Hanoi, fled to the countryside, and a struggle began that was to last for eight more years.

Ho's military commander, Vo Nguyen Giap, organized guerrillas against the French. With their superior weapons, the French were able to control the cities and the country's main roads. But they were no match for the guerrillas in rural areas, where Ho had won the support of a large proportion of the peasant population. The French "pacification" effort, as they called it, made little headway.

In 1949, in an attempt to undermine Ho politically, the French set up a rival Vietnamese regime headed by Bao Dai, the former emperor. It was not a credible alternative. For one thing, Bao Dai spent most of his time in France, gambling and womanizing. Moreover, his claims to represent true nationalism were thin, since the French dictated nearly all his political actions. To many Vietnamese, therefore, he was merely a puppet.

Following the Communist takeover of China in 1949, the United States saw Indochina as an important arena in its crusade against global communism, and this perception grew after the outbreak of the Korean War. Thus the Truman administration supported the "Bao Dai solution" and began to furnish the French with military and economic assistance for their conflict in Indochina. By the end of the war in 1954, American aid had accounted for 80 percent of French expenditures in the struggle. The sum amounted to more than the United States had given France under the Marshall Plan.

The Communist victory in China changed the nature of the war as the Chinese, now at the Vietnamese border, provided Ho's forces with modern weapons. Giap staged daring offensives, but he was stopped by the French, commanded by General Jean de Lattre de Tassigny, who inspired his troops to fight vigorously. But De Lattre, sick with cancer, retired, and his successors lacked his ability. As the war continued, the French sank deeper into the quagmire of Vietnam.

General Henri Navarre, a new French commander, proclaimed that he had a winning plan. He committed a grave strategic error, however. Late in 1953—determined to prevent Ho's forces from invading adjacent Laos, which the French were committed to defend—he chose to block them at Dienbienphu, near the Laotian border. Contrary to French expectations, Giap equipped his men with artillery given to him by China, and they were able to trap the French garrison in the valley.

As the siege dragged on into early 1954, the French appealed to the United States to intervene with air support—even the possibility of deploying nuclear weapons was discussed. But President Eisenhower refused to become involved without the assent of Congress and the cooperation of Britain, both of which opposed intervention. On May 7, 1954, the French capitulated at Dienbienphu.

The next day, an international conference already in session in Geneva began to deliberate the Indochina issue, but made virtually no progress for weeks. Meanwhile, public opinion in France clamored for an end to the conflict. Joseph Laniel, the French premier, lost support over the question, and he was replaced by Pierre Mendès-France, who pledged to find a solution within thirty days or resign.

Mendès-France's determination to resolve the problem was echoed by China's foreign minister, Chou En-lai. Though the Chinese Communists had helped Ho, they feared that a prolonged war would bring the United States into Southeast Asia. Thus they exerted pressure on Ho's delegation to settle for a compromise.

The only accord signed at Geneva was a cease-fire. The Final Declaration of the Geneva Conference provisionally divided Vietnam at the 17th parallel pend-

Chronology

	1946	1947	1949	1950	1951	1953	1954
Vietnam	Negotiations and conferences on the status of Vietnam satisfy neither side. War breaks out by end of the year		Elysée Agreement is signed. Bao Dai becomes chief of state in French-controlled Vietnam	Mao and Stalin recognize Ho's government. U.S. recognizes Bao Dai's government; sends increased aid and a military assistance advisory group	Ho Chi Minh establishes Lao Dong party. General Giap's offensive fails	Navarre becomes commander of French forces in Vietnam	Dienbienphu falls to the Vietminh. Bao Dai appoints Ngo Dinh Diem as premier. Vietnam is temporarily divided at the 17th parallel
United States	Republicans gain in the fall elections	Truman Doctrine and Marshall Plan establish American foreign policy	Truman inaugurated for second term in office	Alger Hiss found guilty of perjury. Rise of Joseph McCarthy	Truman relieves MacArthur of command in Korea	Eisenhower becomes president	U.S. tests hydrogen bomb
World Wide	Cease fire in the Chinese civil war is signed and falls apart		NATO established. Mao takes control of China. U.S.S.R. tests nuclear weapon	Korean War begins		Stalin dies. Armistice in Korea	Geneva Conference brings peace for a time to Vietnam. Southeast Asia Treaty Organization (SEATO) set up under U.S. auspices

ing an election, scheduled for 1956, that would unify the country. A regime under Bao Dai, with Ngo Dinh Diem as his premier, would govern until then in the south, while Ho's government, the Democratic Republic of Vietnam, ruled in the north. The United States did not join in the Final Declaration but made its own unilateral statement supporting peace and self-determination in Southeast Asia.

So the first Vietnam war ended. But the elections would never take place, and though the future could not be forecast then, another war was in the making.

Points to Emphasize

- the reasons the French were interested in reestablishing colonialism in Indochina
- the attitudes of the United States toward Indochina during President Truman's first term
- the factors which convinced Ho Chi Minh to enter into agreements with the French in 1946
- the explanations for the failure of those agreements and conferences to preserve peace in Vietnam in 1946
- the aims of both sides when the fighting began
- the ways in which the rationale for fighting changed over time
- the political strategy behind France's "Bao Dai solution"
- the circumstances which led the United States to increase its aid to the French
- the pressures involved in the uneasy alliance between the United States and France
- the explanations for the French military defeat at Dienbienphu
- the reasoning behind the American decision not to join the Final Declaration of the Geneva Conference on Indochina
- the goals of each nation attending the Geneva Conference

Glossary of Names and Terms

Dean Acheson Assistant Secretary of State, 1941–1945. Undersecretary of State, 1945–1947. Secretary of State, 1949–1952. Helped establish NATO and U.S. containment policy.

Georges Louis Marie Thierry d'Argenlieu French naval officer who rose to the rank of Vice Admiral. Also a Roman Catholic priest in the Carmelite Order of monks. Served in de Gaulle's Free French Navy. Became High Commissioner of France for Indochina in August 1945.

Chiang Kai-shek aide to Sun Yat-sen in China who finally became head of the Nationalist government in China in 1928. Fought against Chinese Communists and the Japanese. Became President of China in 1948. Defeated by

Mao's army, he fled to Taiwan where he set up a new Nationalist government.

Chou En-lai a founder of the Chinese Communist Party. Became premier and foreign minister in 1949 after victory over Chiang Kai-Shek. Major figure at the Geneva Conference and in diplomacy until the 1970s.

Jean de Lattre de Tassigny French general known as the French MacArthur. A charismatic leader who defeated the Vietminh under General Giap in a series of battles in 1951. Became ill and died shortly after resigning his command.

John Foster Dulles counsel to the U.S. Delegation to the Paris Peace Conference, 1919. U.S. delegate to the United Nations, 1945–1949. Senator from New York, 1949–1951. Secretary of State under Eisenhower, 1953–1959. Staunch anti-Communist.

Dwight D. Eisenhower commander of the European theater of operations, June 1942. Commander of U.S. forces in North Africa, Nov. 1942. Supreme Commander of Allied Expeditionary Force, 1943. After war served as president of Columbia University and Supreme Commander of Allied Powers in Europe before serving as the 34th president of the United States, 1953–1961.

Mao Tse-tung Chinese communist leader who fought against Chiang Kai-shek. Founder of the People's Republic of China in 1949 and a major figure in world politics for a quarter of a century after that.

Pierre Mendès-France pilot with the Free French during World War II. French premier 1954–1955. Major figure at the Geneva Conference.

Henri Navarre French general in overall command of the French forces in Indochina at the time of the battle at Dienbienphu.

Jean Sainteny son-in-law of Albert Sarraut, a former Governor General of Indochina. Served in French Intelligence during World War II. Appointed commissioner of the Republic of France for Tonkin and northern Annam, 1945. Negotiated agreement with Ho Chi Minh in March 1946.

Bao Dai solution According to many French and American observers, the answer to the Indochina problem. They hoped that Bao Dai would provide an attractive Vietnamese alternative to the communist Ho Chi Minh. Bao Dai would rule his country with popular support, according to this plan, and remain friendly to the West.

Containment The use of diplomatic, political, and military means to keep communism from spreading all over the globe. The shorthand phrase for American foreign policy in the years after World War II.

Dienbienphu French outpost near the Laotian border which fell to the Vietminh in May 1954 after fifty-five days of fighting. Last battle of the first Vietnam war.

Elysée Agreements understandings reached between Bao Dai and the French in 1949 which provided for his return as chief of state. Vietnam's unity and independence were promised, but the French retained control of Vietnam's defense, diplomacy, and finances.

Geneva Conference international conference held in Geneva, Switzerland, between April and July 1954 in an attempt to restore peace to Korea and Indochina. Participating in the conference were France, Great Britain, the Soviet Union, the People's Republic of China, North Korea, South Korea, the Democratic Republic of Vietnam, the State of Vietnam, Laos, Cambodia, and the United States. An armistice and a plan for bringing peace to Indochina were agreed upon.

guerrilla a member of a small independent band of soldiers which harasses the enemy by surprise raids and attacks on communications and supply lines in an unconventional manner. From the Spanish, diminutive of "guerra" or a little war.

jaunissement literally "yellowing." The French term for using Vietnamese soldiers to take over the military role from French troops.

Korean War a conflict between Communist and non-Communist forces in Korea which lasted from June 25, 1950, until the armistice of July 27, 1953. North Korean forces attacked the South across the 38th parallel, precipitating the struggle. South Korea, backed by a United Nations force under the command of Gen. Douglas MacArthur and consisting mostly of Americans, fought back.

17th parallel latitude at which Vietnam was temporarily divided by the 1954 Geneva Conference.

Documents

Document 1

In early March 1946, faced with 200,000 Chinese troops in the North and French and British troops in the South, the Vietnamese government in Hanoi sought a compromise with the French to end the Chinese occupation of the northern part of their country. For their part, the French, who were not ready to wage war throughout the country, wanted a compromise with the Vietnamese to gain time. Therefore, President Ho Chi Minh of the Democratic Republic of Vietnam and Jean Sainteny, who represented the French government, signed the Agreement on the Independence of Vietnam on March 6, 1946.

This understanding was the high point of Franco-Vietnamese relations after World War II. Both sides agreed to let a referendum decide the stickiest issue of the day—the question of the reunification of Vietnam. Each side made concessions, and each promised to let the will of the people settle the problems which were still outstanding.

1 **Agreement on the Independence of Vietnam**
   March 1946
   1. The French Government recognizes the Vietnamese Republic as a Free State having its own Government, its own Parliament, its own Army and its own Finances, forming part of the Indochinese Federation and of the French Union. In that which concerns the reuniting of the three "Annamite Regions" [Cochinchina, Annam, Tonkin] the French Government pledges itself to ratify the decisions taken by the populations consulted by referendum.
   2. The Vietnamese Government declares itself ready to welcome amicably the French Army when, conforming to international agreements, it relieves the Chinese Troops. A Supplementary Accord, attached to the present Preliminary Agreement, will establish the means by which the relief operations will be carried out.
   3. The stipulations formulated above will immediately enter into force. Immediately after the exchange of signatures, each of the High Contracting Parties will take all measures necessary to stop hostilities in the field, to maintain the troops in their respective positions, and to create the favorable atmosphere necessary to the immediate opening of friendly and sincere negotiations. These negotiations will deal particularly with:
   a. diplomatic relations of Viet-nam with Foreign States
   b. the future law of Indochina
   c. French interests, economic and cultural, in Viet-nam.
   Hanoi, Saigon or Paris may be chosen as the seat of the conference.
                                                            Signed: Sainteny
   Signed: Ho-chi Minh
         and Vu Hong Khanh

Documents 2 and 3

The French violated the March 6 agreement almost immediately, and on December 19, 1946, they issued an ultimatum demanding that the Vietminh government dissolve its paramilitary and police forces and let the French army assume control of Hanoi, the capital of the Democratic Republic of Vietnam. Recognizing that he must now choose either to resist or to capitulate, Ho Chi Minh issued a plea to his fellow Vietnamese (Document 2) on December 20, 1946.

The next day, appealing to Frenchmen and all who believed in the United Nations charter, Ho Chi Minh reviewed the circumstances behind the conflict (Document 3). And he repeated the determination of the Vietnamese people to fight to the death for their independence.

2   Appeal to the Entire People to Wage This Resistance War
Ho Chi Minh
December 20, 1946

Compatriots all over the country!

As we desired peace we made concessions. But the more we made concessions, the further the French colonialists went because they are resolved to invade our country once again.

No! We would rather sacrifice all than lose our country. We are determined not to be enslaved.

Compatriots! Rise up!

Men and women, old and young, regardless of creeds, political parties or nationalities, all the Vietnamese must stand up to fight the French colonialists to save the the fatherland. Those who have rifles will use their rifles; those who have swords will use their swords; those who have no swords will use spades, hoes, or sticks. Everyone must endeavor to oppose the colonialists and save his country.

Army men, self-defense guards and militiamen!

The hour for national salvation has struck! We must sacrifice even our last drop of blood to safeguard our country.

Even if we have to endure hardship in the Resistance war, with the determination to make sacrifices, victory will surely be ours.

Long live an independent and unified Vietnam!

Long live the victorious Resistance!

3   Message to the Vietnamese, the French, and the Peoples of the Allied Nations
Ho Chi Minh
December 21, 1946

We, the Vietnamese Government and people, are determined to struggle for our independence and national unification, but we are also ready for friendly co-operation with the French people. We therefore signed a preliminary Agreement on March 6, 1946 and the Modus Vivendi on September 14, 1946.

But the French reactionary colonialists lack sincerity and regard those agreements as mere pieces of waste paper.

In the South they continue to arrest, massacre and provoke the Vietnamese patriots. They oppress honest Frenchmen who advocate sincerity, and have set up a puppet Government in order to divide our people.

In the southern part of Central Viet Nam they continue to terrorize our compatriots, attack the Vietnamese army and invade our territory.

In the North, they provoke clashes to occupy Bac Ninh, Bac Giang, Lang Son and many other localities. They blockade the port of Haiphong, thus making it impossible for the Chinese, Vietnamese, other foreigners and also the French residents to carry out their business. They try to strangle the Vietnamese people and wreck our national sovereignty. At present they use tanks, aircraft, cannons and warships to massacre our compatriots, and occupy the port of Haiphong as well as other provinces lying along the rivers.

That is not all. They have gone so far as to mobilize their naval, land and air forces and send us many ultimatums. They have massacred old people, women and children in Hanoi, the capital, itself.

On December 19, 1946, at 8 p.m. Hanoi was attacked.

The French colonialists' actions aimed at invading our country are glaring and undeniable.

The Vietnamese people are now facing two alternatives: either to stay with hands bound and heads bowed as slaves again, or to struggle to the end to win back freedom and independence.

No! the Vietnamese people cannot accept foreign domination being imposed on them again.

No! the Vietnamese people never want to be enslaved again. They would prefer to die than lose their independence and freedom.

French people!

We have affection for you and sincerely want to cooperate with you within the framework of the French Union because we have a common ideal which is freedom, equality and independence.

It is the reactionary French colonialists who have blemished France's honour and are seeking to divide us by provoking a war. As soon as France acknowledges our independence and unification and calls back home the bellicose French colonialists, friendly relations and co-operation between the peoples of Viet Nam and France will be restored immediately.

French soldiers!

There is no grudge or rancour between us. It is for the sake of their selfish interests that the reactionary colonialists provoke clashes. Profits will be theirs, death yours, and medals of victory will be conferred on the militarists. But for you and your families, there is only suffering and poverty. Think it over and think again. Can you be content with sacrificing your bones and blood and your lives for the reactionaries? In joining us you will be treated as friends.

Peoples of the Allied powers!

After the recent World War, peace was restored by the democratic countries. However, the French reactionaries trampled underfoot the Atlantic and San Francisco Charters. They are waging an aggressive war in Viet Nam. They must bear the whole responsibility. The Vietnamese people ask you to intervene.

Compatriots!

The Resistance war will be long and fraught with sufferings. Whatever sacrifices we have to make and however long the Resistance war will last, we are determined to fight to the end, until Viet Nam is completely independent and unified. We are 20 million against 100,000 colonialists. Our victory is firmly guaranteed.

On behalf of the Government of the Democratic Republic of Viet Nam, I give the following orders to the Armymen, self-defence guards, militiamen and compatriots in the three parts of Viet Nam:

1—If the French troops attack us, we must fiercely counter-attack them with all the weapons at our disposal. All Vietnamese people must stand up to safeguard their Fatherland.

2—We must protect the lives and property of foreign residents and treat the prisoners of war well.

3—Those who collaborate with the enemy will be punished. Those who help and defend their country will be rewarded.

Compatriots!

The Fatherland is in danger. All of us must rise up!

Long live independent and united Viet Nam!

Long live the successful Resistance War!

Documents 4 and 5

As the fighting in Vietnam continued, the United States monitored the situation closely. President Truman and Secretary of State Dean Acheson were discouraged by the lack of French military success and by the lack of a French political agreement with the nationalists. Document 4 reproduces a telegram from Acheson to the U.S. Consulate in Hanoi in 1949. Although he was convinced that, as a Communist, Ho Chi Minh had to be opposed, Acheson was not prepared to support a French government in Vietnam. He urged the acceptance of a "Bao Dai solution," in which the former Vietnamese emperor could be brought in as an appealing Vietnamese nationalist to oppose Ho. Acheson felt that without such a maneuver, Vietnam would definitely fall to the Communists.

Document 5 contains the same recommendations but phrased in the diplomatic language of the State Department. The United States tried to convince the French that the demands of the Vietnamese nationalists would have to be met if the French wanted to wean popular support away from Ho Chi Minh. Despite its acknowledged dislike for Ho and the Communists, the United States believed that Ho would win unless an authentic Vietnamese alternative was offered.

4   Telegram from Acheson to the U.S. Consulate in Hanoi
May 20, 1949

. . . In light Ho's known background, no other assumption possible but that he outright Commie so long as (1) he fails unequivocally repudiate Moscow connections and Commie doctrine and (2) remains personally singled out for praise by internatl Commie press and receives its support. Moreover, US not impressed by nationalist character red flag with yellow stars. Question whether Ho as much nationalist as Commie is irrelevant. All Stalinists in colonial areas are nationalists. With achievement natl aims (i.e., independence) their objective necessarily becomes subordination state to Commie purposes and ruthless extermination not only opposition groups but all elements suspected even slightest deviation. On basis examples eastern Eur it must be assumed such wld be goal Ho and men his stamp if included Baodai Govt. To include them in order achieve reconciliation opposing polit elements and "national unity" wld merely postpone settlement issue whether Vietnam to be independent nation or Commie satellite until circumstances probably even less favorable nationalists than now. It must of course be conceded theoretical possibility exists estab National Communist state on pattern Yugoslavia in any area beyond reach Soviet army. However, US attitude cld take acct such possibility only if every other possible avenue closed to preservation area from Kremlin control. Moreover, while Vietnam out of reach Soviet army it will doubtless be by no means out of reach Chi Commie hatchet men and armed forces.

Fol is for urinfo and such reference as you deem judicious:

Dept naturally considers only Fr can through concessions to nationalist movement lay basis for solution Indochina problem. As suggested Deptel 83 to Saigon, if nationalists find concessions Mar 8 agreements inadequate, much may depend upon willingness Fr put agreements in most favorable possible context by emphasizing expectations rapid evolution Vietnam beyond status envisaged those agreements. Provided Fr display realistic and generous attitude, most important part remainder immed program - viz, winning support nationalists away from Commie leadership - must devolve upon Baodai and Xuan group seconded by other South Asian govts who stand in most immed danger from Commie conquest Indochina and who by full polit and propaganda support Baodai solution might more that anyone else be able to deprive Ho of talking-points in event he continues demand armed resistance Baodai regardless circumstances (which appears certain in light vitriolic tone current Vietminh broadcasts on Baodai which give no recognition any Fr concessions to nationalist demands). Even with conditions for US support Baodai realized it futile expect US be able assist effectively this initial task beyond stressing requirements situation in talks South Asian govts and providing materials evidencing realities of Communism through USIS for distribution as you and Congen Saigon consider desirable in conjunction with Baodai efforts arouse compatriots to Commie menace. Experience Chi has shown no amt US mil and econ aid can save govt, even if recognized by all other powers and possessed full opportunity achieve natl aims, unless it can rally support people against Commies by affording representation all important natl groups, manifesting devotion to natl as opposed to personal or Party interests, and demonstrating real leadership.

Re Viet opinion reported Saigon's 145 that US abandonment Nationalist China presents unfavorable augury for non-Commie regime Vietnam, there no objection emphasizing to persons with this view that Nationalist China came to present pass through deficiency above qualities and lack will to fight, not because US "wrote it off".

Re Xuan query whether US wld propose Vietnam for membership UN shld Fr renege, you sld avoid discussion this matter, at most if pressed state circumstances at moment will of course determine US action. For urinfo only it unlikely US cld even vote for Vietnam membership UN if as it appears now Fr wld remain in control Vietnam for relations.

5 Memorandum by the Department of State to the French Foreign Office June 6, 1949

The Government of the United States is most appreciative of the action of the French Government in making available to it the text of the agreement concluded on March 8 between the President of France and the former Emperor of Annam defining the future status of the State of Vietnam. The agreement has been studied with the greatest interest by the Department of State.

As the French Government is aware, the United States Government has followed with some concern the course of events in French Indochina since the end of the war in the Pacific. This concern, it is needless to say, has been prompted by a realization that the forces which have contributed predominantly to the character of the Vietnamese nationalist movement are manifestations of the same forces which have worked profound changes in southern Asia generally and that the outcome of these forces can be of considerable consequence for the world in general.

When at the end of the war it became evident that in most of the dependent countries of southern Asia the indigenous peoples were determined to control their own destinies in the future, the United States Government ventured to hope that the western nations would appreciate the strength of this resolution and willingly grant the essential demands of the nationalist movements. It was believed that in so doing, the metropolitan powers would be yielding what in any case they could expect to hold only by military force at great cost. In such event it seemed probable that the costs to the Metropolitan Government would be unrecoverable and the value of the colony and its possible contribution to world stability would be reduced by the ensuant hostilities. On the other hand it was believed that by promptly offering the necessary political concessions to the nationalist demands the metropolitan power would be adopting the course most likely to result in a continued close and mutually fruitful relationship with the former colony, in the preservation of patterns of trade and economy long intermeshed, and in a readiness on the part of the colonial people to welcome the continued technical and administrative assistance of the metropolitan power. It appeared that only on such a basis would there be any real hope that the Western powers could retain their legitimate interests in the countries so closely associated with them over such long periods, and that among the new nations of southern Asia conditions of political stability and of freedom of political and economic development could be achieved enabling them to realize their potentialities and make their full contribution to the world.

Conversely, it seemed that an intention on the part of the metropolitan power to restrain an authority which the dependent people was determined to exercise itself could result only in turning the nationalist movement into destructive channels. In these circumstances it could be expected that widespread hostilities would result and that the consequent destruction of the facilities of production in the dependent area would cause economic setbacks seriously injurious to both peoples. Furthermore, it could be anticipated that the nationalist forces would turn increasingly to an uncompromising leadership which would react against cooperation with the West and against those free institutions which European civilization has evolved through long experience in self-government.

Events in southern Asia in the past four years have caused no revision of these views; and it is in the light of this estimate that the United States Government has examined the agreement of March 8 and offers its views.

Because of its conviction that concession by France to the Nationalist movement commensurate with the strength of that movement can alone provide the basis for a resolution of the Indochinese situation and the creation of a stable, representative Vietnamese Government, the United States Government welcomes the step taken by the President of France in arriving at an agreement with ex-Emperor Bao Dai whereby the territorial unity of Vietnam, comprising Tonkin, Annam, and Cochinchina, may be realized and the Vietnamese State enjoy far reaching powers of internal autonomy. It may be stated at once that in the opinion of the United States Government the Vietnamese people would be guilty of a mistake disastrous to their future should they reject this solution and give their support not to the Vietnamese Government formed under the March 8 agreement but to the so-called Democratic Republic of Vietnam. For those in command of this Republic are men trained in the methods and doctrine of international communism, and regardless of their present espousal of the nationalist cause, it cannot be ignored that they have never disavowed their Kremlin connections or repudiated the techniques and objectives of communism, which are the cause of so much suffering in the world today. It must be assumed, therefore, that should their government succeed in its aims with the support or through the acquiescence of the Vietnamese people, the pattern of a foreign totalitarianism will be clamped upon Vietnam under which all liberties, national and personal, will be lost. Such an outcome would not only be fatal to the welfare and hopes of the Vietnamese but would be most detrimental to the interests of all free peoples, particularly those of southern Asia who stand in most immediate danger of further Communist aggression.

However, the United States Government does not feel confident that the Vietnamese people in general will see the choice confronting them in these terms, especially in view of the isolating factors in their situation during most of the past decade. The Vietnamese nationalists who for the most part have been supporting the so-called Democratic Republic of Vietnam as the one agency which appeared to promise independence may not, it is feared, find the provisions of the March 8 agreement entirely appealing. In this connection, it should be pointed out that the United States Government is considering only this agreement since it is not familiar with the contents of any associated documents which may bear upon the matter and does not know whether the March 8 agreement is intended to define the status of Vietnam permanently or to provide a basis for the further early evolution of the Vietnamese State.

The United States Government is inclined to believe that one of the strongest motivating forces behind nationalist movements among dependent peoples is resentment of the imputation of inferiority implicit in a subordinate status. When a people has fought for the goal of independence with such tenacity as that displayed by the Vietnamese resistance forces, it appears unlikely that it will be content with a position of anything less than equality with other peoples. It is feared that the concessions granted by the French Government may be obscured in the eyes of the Vietnamese people by those terms of the agreement which are incompatible with Vietnamese national pride.

Should such feelings determine the reaction of the majority of Vietnamese to a Government formed under the March 8 agreement, then it must be supposed that the Communist-dominated "Democratic Republic of Vietnam" will continue to receive the support of these Vietnamese. Certainly as long as the Vietnamese are persuaded that the two-and-a-half-year-old war with France must be prosecuted to a conclusion if the goals for which they have fought are to be won, they will continue to regard the dominant Communist element of the Vietnamese League in the light of its effective leadership of the nationalist movement and not of its inevitable intention to subvert the nationalist cause in the end to the requirements of international Communism, with which they have little acquaintance as yet.

The United States Government would be lacking in frankness if it did not state that in its considered estimation the paramount question in Indochina now is whether the country is to be saved from communist control. Under the circumstances, all other issues must be considered as irrelevant. Much time has already been lost. The years since the end of the Pacific War have seen the Communist threat to Indochina intensified rather than otherwise. The southward progress of Chinese Communist armies toward the northern frontier of Indochina introduces a new element that transforms an already serious situation into an emergency.

As it has made clear in the past, the United States Government is of the opinion that it must prove difficult to save this situation, and to preserve Indochina from a foreign tyranny unless the French Government offers the Vietnamese the attainment of those nationalist goals which they would continue to fight for rather than forego and unless the Vietnamese can be convinced that they can, in fact, fully realize their patriotic aims through cooperation with the Government envisaged in the March 8 agreement. In its view, developments have reduced the choice in Indochina to simple alternatives: will Vietnam achieve independence through an agreement with France and with the assistance of France and maintain this independence fortified by collaboration with France, or will it achieve independence from France while at the same time falling victim to Communist totalitarianism?

The United States Government believes that the Vietnamese will willingly accept a partnership with France only if the equality of Vietnam is recognized and if, as a prior condition to the determination of the character of this relationship, the sovereignty of Vietnam is acknowledged. Observation of developments in southern Asia since the end of the war would seem to leave little doubt that a union between France and Vietnam would be far more likely of attainment and would prove more fruitful and enduring if attained were the Union conceived not as an instrument for the control of one member by the other but as an agency of cooperation in the fields of common interest, diplomatic, military, economic, and cultural, voluntarily espoused on both sides. . . .

A dispassionate appraisal leads the United States Government to believe, in short, that the preservation of Indochina's integrity depends, in the first place, upon the willingness of the metropolitan country to give assurances that Vietnam is to exercise control of its destinies; that its participation in the French Union will be upon terms freely accepted by representatives enjoying the confidence of the Vietnamese people when these shall have been assembled; that the powers of administration exercised by France in Vietnam will be transferred to the Vietnamese as soon as conditions permit the institution and functioning of the new regime; and that the deployment of French forces in Vietnam outside their bases to be accounted for in terms of the defense of Vietnam against the protagonists of a supranational totalitarianism who would surrender Vietnam to alien controls.

In the second place, much would appear to depend upon the readiness of the heads of the Vietnamese Government formed under the March 8 agreement to invite the participation in this Government of bonafide and truly nationalist leaders of Vietnam, including those who have heretofore supported the "Democratic Republic of Vietnam", to the end that this Government may provide dynamic leadership and obtain the confidence of the nationalist elements comprising the major part of the resistance forces.

Such an approach to the problem would best appear to lay the basis for the clear separation of nationalists from Communist elements in Vietnam; for those who persisted in resisting a Vietnamese Government through which all nationalist aims could be realized in favor of continued adherence to the "Democratic Republic of Vietnam" would in effect be acknowledging that their goals were not nationalist but Communist. The achievement of this distinction would appear to be the *sine qua non* of a solution of the Indochina problem.

Having determined its capacity to rally the nationalist majority of Vietnamese to its support, the Government formed under the March 8 agreement would - it would seem to the United States Government - have grounds for appealing for the support of all free nations. The United States Government would hope that this appeal would be generally heeded, especially by the other Governments of Southern Asia which, themselves having every reason to regard the further extension of Communist controls in the region with alarm, could fill a vitally important role by clarifying for the Vietnamese people the issues confronting them on the basis of their own experience and undoubted fidelity to the cause of self-determination by the Asian peoples.

The United States Government is, however, convinced that if the requisite concessions by the French Government to the nationalist demands are not forthcoming, the task of the Government envisaged in the March 8 agreement must prove most difficult of accomplishment and the countries adjacent to Indochina will likely be confronted by the prospect of the appearance of sizable Communist-controlled forces on their frontiers.

It goes without saying that the earnest hope of the United States Government is that the Government formed under the March 8 agreement will succeed in its crucial task. At the same time it would appear axiomatic that insofar as the probabilities of its success are related to the extent of international support it obtains, the decision of a third party in respect of the feasibility of its extending support or assistance must be governed by the extent to which the French Government has itself provided that Government with the political advantages upon which its appeal to the Vietnamese must be based. Clearly the success of this Government must rest in the first instance upon those means of accomplishing its purpose which only the French Government can provide.

In taking advantage of the relations of cordiality and mutual understanding it enjoys with the French Government by offering this frank appraisal, the United States Government has been prompted by the thought that it should not leave the direction of its thinking a matter of doubt and that an exchange of views might be advantageous considering all that is involved in the outcome of the situation in Indochina.

Documents 6 and 7

The Geneva Agreements on Vietnam included a bilateral armistice agreement between France and the Vietminh which was signed on July 20, 1954, and a multilateral "Final Declaration" (Document 6), which was issued on the following day. The Final Declaration was the much-discussed document referred to as the Geneva Accords of 1954.

The United States refused to join in the Final Declaration. Instead, Under Secretary of State Walter Bedell Smith, head of the American delegation to Geneva, made the "unilateral declaration" which is reprinted as Document 7. Smith did not say why the United States would not assent to the Final Declaration, but he did promise that the American government would not disturb the agreements and that it would oppose the "renewal" of aggression in Southeast Asia.

6   Final Declaration of the Geneva Conference
July 21, 1954

Final declaration, dated the 21st July, 1954, of the Geneva Conference on the problem of restoring peace in Indo-China, in which the representatives of Cambodia, the Democratic Republic of Viet-Nam, France, Laos, the People's Republic of China, the State of Viet-Nam, the Union of Soviet Socialist Republics, the United Kingdom, and the United States of America took part.

1. The Conference takes note of the agreements ending hostilities in Cambodia, Laos and Viet-Nam and organizing international control and the supervision of the execution of the provisions of these agreements.

2. The Conference expresses satisfaction at the ending of hostilities in Cambodia, Laos and Viet-Nam; the Conference expresses its conviction that the execution of the provisions set out in the present declaration and in the agreements on the cessation of hostilities will permit Cambodia, Laos, and Viet-Nam henceforth to play their part, in full independence and sovereignty, in the peaceful community of nations.

3. The Conference takes note of the declarations made by the Governments of Cambodia and of Laos of their intention to adopt measures permitting all citizens to take their place in the national community, in particular by participating in the next general elections, which, in conformity with the constitution of each of these countries, shall take place in the course of the year 1955, by secret ballot and in conditions of respect for fundamental freedoms.

4. The Conference takes note of the clauses in the agreement on the cessation of hostilities in Viet-Nam prohibiting the introduction into Viet-Nam of foreign troops and military personnel as well as of all kinds of arms and munitions. The Conference also takes note of the declarations made by the Governments of Cambodia and Laos of their resolution not to request foreign aid, whether in war material, in personnel or in instructors except for the purpose of the effective defence of their territory and, in the case of Laos, to the extent defined by the agreements on the cessation of hostilities in Laos.

5. The Conference takes note of the clauses in the agreement on the cessation of hostilities in Viet-Nam to the effect that no military base under the control of a foreign State may be established in the regrouping zones of the two parties, the latter having the obligation to see that the zones allotted to them shall not constitute part of any military alliance and shall not be utilized for the resumption of hostilities or in the service of an aggressive policy. The Conference also takes note of the declarations of the Governments of Cambodia and Laos to the effect that they will not join in any agreement with other States if this agreement includes the obligation to participate in a military alliance not in conformity with the principles of the Charter of the United Nations or, in the case of Laos, with the principles of the agreement on the cessation of hostilities in Laos or, so long as their security is not threatened, the obligation to establish bases on Cambodian or Laotian territory for the military forces of foreign Powers.

6. The Conference recognizes that the essential purpose of the agreement relating to Viet-Nam is to settle military questions with a view to ending hostilities and that the military demarcation line is provisional and should not in any way be interpreted as constituting a political or territorial boundary. The Conference expresses its conviction that the execution of the provisions set out in the present declaration and in the agreement on the cessation of hostilities creates the necessary basis for the achievement in the near future of a political settlement in Viet-Nam.

7. The Conference declares that, so far as Viet-Nam is concerned, the settlement of political problems, affected on the basis of respect for the principles of independence, unity and territorial integrity, shall permit the Viet-Namese people to enjoy the fundamental freedoms, guaranteed by democratic institutions established as a result of free general elections by secret ballot. In order to ensure that sufficient progress in the restoration of peace has been made, and that all the necessary conditions obtain for free expression of the national will, general elections shall be held in July 1956, under the supervision of an international commission composed of representatives of the Member States of the International Supervisory Commission, referred

to in the agreement on the cessation of hostilities. Consultations will be held on this subject between the competent representative authorities of the two zones from 20 July 1955 onwards.

8. The provisions of the agreements on the cessation of hostilities intended to ensure the protection of individuals and of property must be most strictly applied and must, in particular, allow everyone in Viet-Nam to decide freely in which zone he wishes to live.

9. The competent representative authorities of the Northern and Southern zones of Viet-Nam, as well as the authorities of Laos and Cambodia, must not permit any individual or collective reprisals against persons who have collaborated in any way with one of the parties during the war, or against members of such persons' families.

10. The Conference takes note of the declaration of the Government of the French Republic to the effect that it is ready to withdraw its troops from the territory of Cambodia, Laos, and Viet-Nam, at the requests of the Governments concerned and within periods which shall be fixed by agreement between the parties except in the cases where, by agreement between the two parties, a certain number of French troops shall remain at specified points and for a specified time.

11. The Conference takes note of the declaration of the French Government to the effect that for the settlement of all the problems connected with the re-establishment and consolidation of peace in Cambodia, Laos and Viet-Nam, the French Government will proceed from the principle of respect for the independence and sovereignty, unity, and territorial integrity of Cambodia, Laos and Viet-Nam.

12. In their relations with Cambodia, Laos and Viet-Nam, each member of the Geneva Conference undertakes to respect the sovereignty, the independence, the unity and the territorial integrity of the above-mentioned states, and to refrain from any interference in their internal affairs.

13. The members of the Conference agree to consult one another on any question which may be referred to them by the International Supervisory Commission, in order to study such measures as may prove necessary to ensure that the agreements on the cessation of hostilities in Cambodia, Laos and Viet-Nam are respected.

7 Statement by Walter Bedell Smith at the Geneva Conference July 21, 1954

As I stated on July 18, my Government is not prepared to join in a declaration by the Conference such as is submitted. However, the United States makes this unilateral declaration of its position in these matters:

Declaration

The Government of the United States being resolved to devote its efforts to the strengthening of peace in accordance with the principles and purposes of the United Nations takes note of the agreements concluded at Geneva on July 20 and 21, 1954 between (a) the Franco-Laotian Command and the Command of the Peoples Army of Viet-Nam; (b) the Royal Khmer Army Command and the Command of the Peoples Army of Viet-Nam; (c) Franco-Vietnamese Command and the Command of the Peoples Army of Viet-Nam and of paragraphs 1 to 12 inclusive of the declaration presented to the Geneva Conference on July 21, 1954 declares with regard to the aforesaid agreements and paragraphs that (i) it will refrain from the threat or the use of force to disturb them, in accordance with Article 2(4) of the Charter of the United Nations dealing with the obligation of members to refrain in their international relations from the threat or use of force; and (ii) it would view any renewal of the aggression in violation of the aforesaid agreements with grave concern and as seriously threatening international peace and security.

In connection with the statement in the declaration concerning free elections in Viet-Nam my Government wishes to make clear its position which it has expressed in a declaration made in Washington on June 29, 1954, as follows:

> In the case of nations now divided against their will, we shall continue to seek to achieve unity through free elections supervised by the United Nations to insure that they are conducted fairly.

With respect to the statement made by the representative of the State of Viet-Nam, the United States reiterates its traditional position that peoples are entitled to determine their own future and that it will not join in an arrangement which would hinder this. Nothing in its declaration just made is intended to or does indicate any departure from this traditional position.

We share the hope that the agreements will permit Cambodia, Laos and Viet-Nam to play their part, in full independence and sovereignty, in the peaceful community of nations, and will enable the peoples of that area to determine their own future.

Documents 8 and 9

Ho Chi Minh's Democratic Republic of Vietnam and the newly founded, Saigon-based Government of Vietnam reacted quite differently to the Geneva Accords. Premier Ngo Dinh Diem of the Bao Dai regime in Saigon announced (Document 8) that he regarded the agreement as tantamount to a "seizure by Soviet China—through its satellite the Vietminh—of over half of our national territory."

Ho Chi Minh, on the other hand, considered the accords "a great victory" and vowed that the Democratic Republic of Vietnam would carry out the terms of the agreements in good faith. His statement appears as Document 9.

8   Statement Regarding the Geneva Agreements
Ngo Dinh Diem
July 22, 1954

Dear Compatriots,

You know the facts: a cease-fire concluded at Geneva without the concurrence of the Vietnamese delegation has surrendered to the Communists all the north and more than four provinces of the central part of our country.

The national Government, constituted less than two weeks ago, in spite of its profound attachment to peace, has lodged the most solemn protest against that injustice. Our delegation at Geneva has not signed that agreement, for we cannot recognise the seizure by Soviet China—through its satellite the Vietminh—of over half of our national territory. We can neither concur in the enslavement of millions of compatriots faithful to the nationalist ideal, nor to the complete destitution of those who, thanks to our efforts, will have succeeded in joining the zone left to us.

Brutally placed before an accomplished fact, Vietnam cannot resort to violence, for that would be moving toward a catastrophe and destroying all hope [of] remaking one day a free Vietnam from the South to the North.

In spite of our grief, in spite of our indignation, let us keep our self-control and remain united in order to give our brother refugees help and comfort and begin at once the peaceful and difficult struggle which will eventually free our country from all foreign intervention, whatever it may be, and from all oppression.

9 **Long Live Peace, Unity, Independence, and Democracy in Vietnam**
Ho Chi Minh
July 30, 1954

The Geneva Conference has ended. We have won a big victory in the diplomatic field.

On behalf of the Government I cordially address myself to all compatriots, soldiers and cadres.

1. For the sake of the peace, unity, independence and democracy of our homeland, our people, the army, cadres and the Government, closely united, enduring hardship and overcoming numerous difficulties, resolutely fought during the past eight, nine years and won brilliant victories. On this occasion I convey, on behalf of the Government, my cordial congratulations to all compatriots, soldiers and cadres throughout the country, from the North to the South. I respectfully bow before the memory of the fighters and all patriots who heroically sacrificed their lives for the homeland, and convey sincere condolences to the sick and wounded servicemen.

Our great victories are also due to the fact that our fight for a just cause enjoys the support of the peoples in the friendly countries, the people of France and the peace-loving peoples of the world.

Negotiations were opened between our Government and the Government of France at the Geneva Conference thanks to these victories and to the efforts of the delegation of the USSR at the Berlin Conference. The efforts of our delegation and the aid from the delegations of the USSR and the People's Republic of China enabled us to achieve a big victory at the Geneva Conference. The Government of France has recognised the independence, sovereignty, unity and territorial integrity of our country and agreed to withdraw the French armed forces from our land, etc.

In the future too we must strive to consolidate peace, ensure unity and achieve independence and democracy throughout the country.

2. In order to achieve peace the first thing is the cessation of hostilities by the armed forces of both sides.

To ensure cessation of hostilities it is necessary to regroup the armed forces of the two sides in the two separate zones, that is, to readjust the areas occupied by the armed forces of each side.

The establishment of a military demarcation line is a temporary and transitional measure for carrying out the armistice, restoring peace and for making progress towards national unification by means of a general election. The demarcation line does not mean in any way a political or territorial boundary.

During the period of the armistice our armed forces shall be concentrated in Northern Viet Nam and the French Union armed forces in Southern Viet Nam. This means that there will be an exchange of zones: a number of localities occupied by the French will become liberated areas; on the other hand, French troops will be quartered temporarily, before their return to France, in a number of our liberated areas.

This is a necessary measure. But Northern, Central and Southern Viet Nam are integral parts of our territory, and our country will undoubtedly be unified and our compatriots throughout the country liberated.

Our compatriots in the South were the first to launch the patriotic war and displayed a high degree of consciousness. I am confident that they will place the interests of the whole country above local interests, and permanent interests above present ones, and, hand in hand with the rest of our people, do everything to consolidate peace, ensure unity and achieve independence and democracy throughout the country. The Viet Nam Working People's Party (Lao Dong), the Government and I personally have always followed the efforts of our compatriots in the South, and we are confident that they will achieve success.

3. The fight for the consolidation of peace, for effecting unity, for achieving independence and democracy is also a long and hard struggle. To ensure victory the entire people, all soldiers and cadres in the country, from North to South, must still more enhance their solidarity and be united in thought and action.

We are fully determined honestly to adhere to the terms we have signed with the French Government and at the same time urge the French Government honestly to observe the terms it has signed with us.

We shall do our utmost to consolidate peace and shall be vigilant in relation to encroachments by the enemies of peace. We shall do everything for the holding of a free, general election throughout the country in order to achieve national unity. We shall do our utmost to rehabilitate, build up, consolidate and develop our forces in all spheres so as to ensure the complete independence of the homeland.

We must strive to carry out social reforms in order to improve the conditions of our people and ensure genuine democracy.

We shall strengthen further our fraternal contact with the peoples of Laos and Cambodia.

We will reinforce still more the great friendship between Viet Nam and the Soviet Union, the People's Republic of China and other friendly countries. We shall strengthen our solidarity with the people of France, the peoples of Asia and the world for the sake of safeguarding peace.

4. I wholeheartedly call on the entire people, all soldiers and cadres, correctly to carry out the political line and policy of the Party and the Government, to work for the consolidation of peace and achieve unity, independence and democracy throughout the country.

I earnestly call on all who sincerely love their homeland, irrespective of social status, religious beliefs or political conviction, irrespective of the party they supported in the past, sincerely to cooperate with each other and work for the good of the nation and homeland, and to fight for the realisation of peace, unity, independence and democracy in our beloved Viet Nam.

Given nation-wide unity, given the monolithic solidarity of the entire people we will, undoubtedly, win victory.

Long live peace, unity, independence and democracy in Viet Nam!

Critical Issues for Discussion

1. The political vacuum produced by the Japanese surrender in August 1945 left many groups jockeying for control of Vietnam. Vietnamese, French,

Japanese, Chinese, British, and American military and political figures each kept a careful watch on what the other might be doing. What were the attitudes of each of these governments? What did they claim in public? On what did they base these claims? Evaluate the relative strength of each of these groups.

2. On September 30, 1945, French General Jean Leclerc announced: "I did not come back to Indochina to give Indochina back to the Indochinese." What did he come back for? Why did he say "give Indochina back"? Who had it before? To whom did he think it belonged? Why?

3. In March 1946, Ho Chi Minh's government arrived at a compromise agreement with a representative of the French Government (Document 1). What procedures did it establish? Why did Ho sign it? Why did the French agree to it? What do you think an average Vietnamese peasant might have felt about it? Explain.

4. Other conferences were held in 1946, but all of them failed either to reestablish the March Agreements or to move Vietnam further toward independence. At one of those discussions, Ho told the French that the Vietnamese were serious about gaining their independence. "If we have to fight, we will fight. You will kill ten of our men and we will kill one of yours, and in the end it will be you who will tire of it." What would he have said about General Leclerc's comments about Indochina? On what did Ho base his assessment of the relative commitment of both sides?

5. After fighting broke out in the fall of 1946, both sides prepared for the military showdown that began in December 1946. Documents 2 and 3 are part of Ho's effort to inspire his people to fight and to explain to the rest of the world why they were fighting.

How do you evaluate Ho's appeal? Would he have convinced his fellow Vietnamese? Frenchmen? Outsiders? Was bloodshed inevitable? At what point? Why?

6. The fighting in Vietnam took place during the Cold War, and U.S. decisions about Vietnam were always colored by that larger issue. According to Documents 4 and 5, what did the United States fear in Vietnam? How could that be avoided? What role should the French play? What policies did the Americans think would be most effective? What differences did the Americans see between "nationalists" and "Communists" in Vietnam? What differences did the Vietnamese see?

7. Throughout the late 1940s and early 1950s the French made various plans for a "Bao Dai solution," but each plan attempted to give the appearance, not the substance, of power to the Vietnamese emperor. Bao Dai himself once remarked: "What's the matter with the French—they're always giving us our independence. Can't they give it to us once and for all?" What was he getting at? What frustrated him? Why didn't the French give the power to Bao Dai? What were they trying to accomplish?

8. In 1949 and 1950, major events in the Cold War hardened the American attitude toward the Indochina War. What were these events? Why did they cause the United States government to take a harder line in Vietnam? What were the practical measures which the United States took to carry out its more stringent policy?

9. As the guerrilla war continued, the French General Pellet explained the increasing frustrations of his men. "The enemy is everywhere. No continuous front, no fixed lines of defense where our powerful and modern war means could be effectively used. Each cluster of bamboo, each hut perhaps, gives shelter to the enemy. How strained our soldiers' nerves are, for they face an elusive enemy in every place and at every moment."

How would General Pellet have responded to Ho's comment that the French would tire of the war? Why did these things happen to the French soldiers? Were they badly trained and led? Did this happen to the Vietnamese soldiers as well? Why or why not?

10. Reread Document 6, the Final Declaration of the Geneva Conference, to determine what was "declared" on July 21, 1954? What steps were to follow the conference? What was the precise status of Vietnam?

What did the American statement in Document 7 mean? Why do you think the United States refused to join in the Final Declaration? Why was America standing apart at Geneva?

11. Ho Chi Minh and Ngo Dinh Diem disagreed about the meaning and significance of the Geneva Agreements, as their statements in Documents 8 and 9 show. What pleased Ho? What was he looking forward to? What scared Diem? What did he desire in the future?

Follow Up The first Vietnam war lasted from 1946 until 1954, and the struggle was as much a political as a military one. Commandant A. M. Savani, the head of the Deuxième Bureau, the French intelligence command, noted before the end of that war that "pacification will be fully realized not when we will have occupied each inch of earth but when we will have conquered all the hearts and won all the minds."

What did he mean? How could that be accomplished? As 1954 ended, who was in a better position to conquer hearts and win minds—Ho Chi Minh or Ngo Dinh Diem? Why? Why had the French been unable to do so?

Suggestions for Further Reading

Devillers, Philippe, and Jean Lacouture. *End of a War: Indochina, 1954.* Rev. ed. New York: Praeger, 1969.

This excellent diplomatic history by two French scholars places the French war and the Geneva negotiations in the context of international relations at the time. Part III, "America Takes Over," explains how France's responsibilities were transferred to the United States in 1954 and 1955.

Eden, Anthony. *Full Circle*. London: Gassell, 1960.

Eden's is a reliable, readable, first-hand account of the Geneva negotiations.

Fall, Bernard B. *Hell in a Very Small Place: The Siege of Dien Bien Phu*. Philadelphia: Lippincott, 1967.

The classic account of this decisive battle, complete with maps and photos.

Vo Nguyen Giap. *People's War, People's Victory*. New York: Praeger, 1962.

On pages 154–188, the commander-in-chief of the Vietnam People's Army gives a brief account of the battle of Dienbienphu.

Hammer, Ellen. *The Struggle for Indochina, 1940–1955*. Rev. ed. Stanford: Stanford Univ. Press, 1966.

This early study of politics and diplomacy still offers a good overview.

Irving, R. E. M. *The First Indochina War: French and American Policy, 1945–54*. London: Croom Helm, 1975.

Irving examines the motives behind the French, American, and South Vietnamese policies of this period, focusing specifically on the influence of political parties in France.

Kattenburg, Paul M. *The Vietnam Trauma in American Foreign Policy, 1945–75*. New Brunswick, N.J.: Transaction, 1980.

In Chapter 2, "The Effects of Containment on U.S. Policies, 1945–59," Kattenburg explains how U.S. foreign policy came to be preoccupied with the perceived Soviet threat, and how that shaped its goals in Vietnam.

Oglesby, Carl, and Richard Shaull. *Containment and Change: Two Dissenting Views of American Foreign Policy*. Toronto: Macmillan, 1967.

In contrast to Kattenburg's more liberal view, Chapter 5, "The Vietnam Case," presents a radical view of containment as an ideological mask for Free World imperialism.

A Friend in Need
President Ngo Dinh Diem (second from right), dressed in his customary white suit, seen with his Finance Minister, Tan Huu Phuong, after receiving an American aid check for $11,720,000. U.S. Ambassador G. Frederick Reinhardt stands at the right in this 1955 photo while Justice William O. Douglas and Leland Barrows of the U.S. Aid Mission look on from the left. *Wide World Photo*.

Chapter 3
America's Mandarin: 1954–1963

Background

Historical Summary

The major figure in South Vietnam from 1954, when he became prime minister, to 1963, when he was assassinated, was Ngo Dinh Diem. After years abroad in the United States and Europe, Diem joined Emperor Bao Dai's government as prime minister just before a ceasefire agreement divided North and South Vietnam at the 17th parallel. The following year, Diem defeated Bao Dai in a referendum, proclaimed the Republic of Vietnam, and became its first president. Diem's strengths and weaknesses, his prejudices and policies, his unwillingness to compromise, and his desire for security helped shape the newly created state.

Diem took over a chaotic situation. The French had been defeated militarily in 1954 and were on their way out of Vietnam. They had provided structure and stability, and their departure left both a political and a bureaucratic vacuum. In the confusion surrounding and following the French departure, various factions jockeyed for power. Two indigenous religious sects, the Cao Dai and the Hoa Hao, controlled the loyalties of thousands of adherents. The leader of another armed faction, Bay Vien, ran both the underworld and the secret police in Saigon. In effect, there was civil war in Saigon. But Diem managed to subdue some of his enemies and buy off others as the United States gave him both money and arms.

The United States saw Diem as a staunch anticommunist, and that was enough to guarantee him political support. When Diem refused to go along with the electoral process for the reunification of Vietnam, as proposed by the Geneva Accords of 1954, the United States supported him. Diem used the large amounts of aid sent by President Dwight D. Eisenhower's administration to secure his government. He carefully controlled politics, permitting no significant opposition. But as long as Diem's enemies were presumed to be communists, the United States continued to support him. Thus, in a sense, Ngo Dinh Diem was America's mandarin—an official remote from the people and maintained in office by virtue of American support. The American press praised him as a miracle worker.

Diem's harsh rule, however, failed to eliminate all opponents of his regime. Indeed, his heavy-handed tactics created new enemies. Much of the opposition to Diem crystallized in 1960 with the formation of the National Liberation Front of South Vietnam (NLF), which was organized and supported by the Communist party and backed by Hanoi. An organization with wide-ranging appeal, the NLF got its impetus from the many former Vietminh supporters who agreed that armed struggle against Diem's rule was essential. By the time John F. Kennedy was inaugurated as president of the United States, South Vietnam was a nation in turmoil. Fighting had spread throughout much of the southern countryside.

Faced with numerous foreign policy problems in 1961, Kennedy hesitated to take any active role in the Vietnamese fighting. But he increased financial aid to Diem's government, and he sent the South Vietnamese leader more military advisors to help his army. Kennedy also sent a string of civilian experts to South Vietnam. They suggested that Diem make his government less autocratic, implement land reforms to win over the peasants, and allow opposing opinions to be expressed at the ballot box. Diem rejected this advice not only from the Americans, but also from former colleagues. He was convinced that liberalized policies would encourage dissent, and that dissent meant weakness.

Despite Diem's rejection of the advisors' suggestions, he was, the United States government concluded, the best man available for the job of stemming communist imperialism. After exchanging letters with Diem in December 1961, Kennedy further increased aid. The joint efforts of the United States and the Saigon governments included the use of American helicopters in battle and the Strategic Hamlet program that re-located peasants in fortress-like settlements. These efforts appeared successful in 1962 as NLF assaults decreased; however, optimism soon vanished. The NLF, generally known as the Vietcong, began employing new tactics of their own and by 1963 they were again on the offensive.

The situation in South Vietnam deteriorated further in May 1963 when Diem's government tried to prevent the Buddhists of Hue from celebrating the 2,587th birthday of the Buddha with traditional flags and parades. Protesting Buddhists were fired upon by government troops, and a major crisis was underway. Complaining that the Catholic Diem had always favored his co-religionists, the Buddhists expanded their protests and held hunger strikes as well as marches. Other dissidents in South Vietnam joined them. When a Buddhist monk, Thich Quang Duc, committed suicide by setting himself on fire to protest Diem's policies, the crisis came to world attention.

Diem's brother Ngo Dinh Nhu, who now was head of the secret police, made the situation even worse by raiding Buddhist pagodas throughout the country with his special forces. The new American ambassador, Henry Cabot Lodge, who arrived in Saigon one day after the raids, reported pessimistically to Washington about Diem's ability to rule. His negative reports were echoed by other American officials.

Chronology

	1954 Jan	May	Jun	Jul	Sep	Nov	1955 Jan	Mar	Apr
South Vietnam		Fall of Dienbienphu to Vietminh	Diem returns to South Vietnam	Geneva Conference Accords reached				Diem defeats Binh Xuyen	
United States	Nautilus, first atomic submarine	Brown vs Board of Education decision rules segregation illegal	Army-McCarthy hearings end				Congress passes Formosa Resolution		
World Wide				British surrender Suez Canal	South East Asia Treaty Organization (SEATO) established	French commit forces to Algeria			Bandung conference of Asian and African Peoples

	1955 May	Jul	Oct	1956 Feb	Apr	Jul	Sep	Oct	Nov	1957 Mar	May
South Vietnam		Diem refuses to plan for 1956 elections with North	Diem defeats Bao Dai in referendum. Republic of Vietnam established		Military Assistance Advisory Group (MAAG) set up by U.S.						Diem makes successful U.S. tour
United States	Geneva summit with Russia								Eisenhower re-elected	Eisenhower Doctrine for Middle East declared	
World Wide	Warsaw Pact signed			Khrushchev denounces Stalin				USSR intervenes in Polish and Hungarian uprisings	Suez Crisis	Ghana becomes independent of Great Britain	

Chronology *(cont.)*

	1957 Oct	1958 Feb	Oct	Dec	1959 Jan	May	Jun	Sep	1960 Apr
South Vietnam						Repressive Law 10/59 goes into effect			Manifesto of the 18 protests Diem's policies
United States	John F. Kennedy wins Pulitzer Prize for *Profiles in Courage*	Jets used on overseas flights					Vice President Nixon goes to Moscow	Khrushchev tours U.S.	
World Wide	Sputnik I launched	United Arab Republic established	Pope John XXIII elected	Fifth French Republic proclaimed	Castro comes to power in Cuba				

	1960 May	Jun	Nov	Dec	1961 Mar	Apr	May	Jun	Aug
South Vietnam			Coup attempt against Diem fails	National Liberation Front emerges			Vice President Johnson visits		
United States	U.S. U-2 spy plane shot down by USSR Paris summit fails		John F. Kennedy elected President		Peace Corps established	Bay of Pigs Invasion of Cuba fails		Vienna summit with USSR fails to ease relations	
World Wide		Civil war in Congo				USSR launches first man in space			Berlin Wall separates city

	1961 Sep	Oct	Dec	1962 Feb	Jun	Jul	Sep	Oct	Nov
South Vietnam		General Maxwell Taylor and W. W. Rostow visit	Diem and Kennedy exchange letters. U.S. aid increases	MAAG becomes Military Assistance Command, Vietnam (MACV)	Strategic Hamlet Program in full operation				
United States			State Department White Paper concludes North Vietnam is invading South	John Glenn orbits the earth	Students For a Democratic Society (SDS) started	Telstar communications satellite launched	James M. Meredith enrolls at University of Mississippi	Cuban Missile Crisis	
World Wide	UN Secretary General Dag Hammarskjold dies in plane crash					Algeria wins independence from France		India-China Border War	U Thant becomes Secretary General of United Nations

	1963 Jan	Apr	May	Jun	Aug	Sep	Nov
South Vietnam	South Vietnamese Army with U.S. advisors defeated at Ap Bac. 3 Americans killed.		Buddhist protests begin	Thich Quang Duc burns himself to death	Nhu's Special Forces raid Buddhist pagodas		Coup overthrows Diem / Diem and Nhu killed / General Minh takes over
United States		Birmingham sees civil rights demonstrations			Martin Luther King, Jr leads march on Washington	Network television news goes to half-hour format	President Kennedy assassinated
World Wide			Organization of African Unity formed		U.S. and USSR negotiate Nuclear Test Ban Treaty		

Word of America's wavering support soon circulated among top officers in South Vietnam's army. On November 1, 1963, General Duong Van Minh, known as Big Minh, led a cabal of officers in a *coup d'état*. Both Diem and his brother Nhu were killed. Three weeks later President Kennedy was also assassinated. New leaders now faced the problems posed by Vietnam.

Points to Emphasize

- the reasons why the United States was interested in South Vietnam and became involved in its political and social problems
- the early relationship between the American leaders and Ngo Dinh Diem
- the policies by which Diem sought to govern South Vietnam
- the reasons for the rise in opposition to Diem
- the explanation for the increased American help for Diem under the Kennedy administration
- the growing American dissatisfaction with Diem throughout 1963
- the events and attitudes among Vietnamese and Americans that led to the *coup d'état* against Diem in November 1963

Glossary of Names and Terms

John Foster Dulles American diplomat and political figure. Delegate to the United Nations, 1945–1949. Secretary of State under Eisenhower, 1953–1959.

Roger Hilsman Director of the State Department Bureau of Intelligence and Research, 1961–1963. Assistant Secretary of State for Far Eastern Affairs, 1963–1964.

Edward Lansdale Brigadier General, U.S. Air Force. Served with the C.I.A. in South Vietnam. Expert in guerrilla warfare.

Henry Cabot Lodge Republican Senator from Massachusetts. Vice Presidential nominee of his party, 1960. Ambassador to South Vietnam, 1963–1964 and 1965–1967.

Robert McNamara President, Ford Motor Company, before he became Secretary of Defense under Presidents Kennedy and Johnson, 1961–1968.

Ngo Dinh Diem Vietnamese nationalist. Prime Minister under Emperor Bao Dai, June 1954–October 1955. President of the Republic of Vietnam, 1955–1963. Catholic, bachelor, traditionalist. Assassinated in coup of November 1–2, 1963.

Ngo Dinh Nhu younger brother of Ngo Dinh Diem. Head of Secret Police. Served as brother's advisor, political counselor, and government policy maker.

Madame Nhu Tran Le Xuan, wife of Ngo Dinh Nhu. Outspoken defender of South Vietnamese policy and the Diem regime.

Frederick Nolting U.S. Foreign Service Officer. Ambassador to South Vietnam, 1961–1963.

Dean Rusk Assistant Secretary of State for Far Eastern Affairs under President Truman. President of the Rockefeller Foundation, 1952–1960. Secretary of State under Presidents Kennedy and Johnson, 1961–1969.

counterinsurgency American plan to fight against guerrilla warfare.

mandarin traditional Chinese term for a high ranking public official. Used in relation to Diem to indicate a ruler or official who is far removed from his base of support.

Strategic Hamlets program that attempted to move peasants off their farms and into fortified stockades to protect them from Vietcong influence and attacks and to allow the Diem government to control them more easily. Based on a successful British program in Malaya. Unpopular with the South Vietnamese people.

Vietcong Diem government's term for the National Liberation Front of South Vietnam. Shortened version of "Vietnamese Communist."

Documents

Document 1

John Foster Dulles had extensive experience in foreign affairs both as a diplomat and an international lawyer, and served as Dwight Eisenhower's Secretary of State from 1953 until 1959. As a delegate to the United Nations from 1945 to 1949, Dulles had participated in the debates on international affairs at the beginning of the Cold War.

A strong anticommunist, he saw the problems in South Vietnam as part of the global struggle between the communist world and the free world. The United States, he concluded, was the only nation that could restrain the communist advances.

1 Opposition to the Spread of Communism "By Any Means"
John Foster Dulles
March 1954
. . . If the Communist forces won uncontested control over Indochina or any substantial part thereof, they would surely resume the same pattern of aggression against other free peoples in the area.

The propagandists of Red China and Russia make it apparent that the purpose is to dominate all of Southeast Asia. . . .

The United States has shown in many ways its sympathy for the gallant struggle being waged in Indochina by French forces and those of the Associated States. Congress has enabled us to provide material aid to the established governments and their peoples. Also, our diplomacy has sought to deter Communist China from open aggression in that area.

President Eisenhower, in his address of April 16, 1953, explained that a Korean armistice would be a fraud if it merely released aggressive armies for attack else-where. I said last September that if Red China sent its own army into Indochina, that would result in grave consequences which might not be confined to Indochina.

Recent statements have been designed to impress upon potential aggressors that aggression might lead to action at places and by means of free-world choosing, so that aggression would cost more than it could gain.

The Chinese Communists have, in fact, avoided the direct use of their own Red armies in open aggression against Indochina. They have, however, largely stepped up their support of the aggression in that area. Indeed, they promote that aggression by all means short of open invasion.

Under all circumstances it seems desirable to clarify further the United States position.

Under the conditions of today, the imposition on Southeast Asia of the political system of Communist Russia and its Chinese Communist ally, by whatever means, must be a grave threat to the whole free community. The United States feels that that possibility should not be passively accepted but should be met by united action. This might involve serious risks. But these risks are far less than those that will face us a few years from now if we dare not be resolute today.

The free nations want peace. However, peace is not had merely by wanting it. Peace has to be worked for and planned for. Sometimes it is necessary to take risks to win peace just as it is necessary in war to take risks to win victory. The chances for peace are usually bettered by letting a potential aggressor know in advance where his aggression could lead him.

I hope that these statements which I make here tonight will serve the cause of peace. . . .

Document 2

Ngo Dinh Diem opposed the 1954 Geneva Accords and announced publicly in July 1955 that he would not abide by them. By then, the French, who had signed the military ceasefire and were supposed to make sure that Diem's government followed the decisions that had been reached in Geneva, no longer controlled events in South Vietnam. The United States, which was aiding Diem's young government and which had pledged not to interfere with the letter or the spirit of the Geneva Accords, supported Diem's decision not to hold elections in 1956 in conjunction with the North.

In this government press release, Diem explained why he would not take part in nationwide elections. His decision became a major rallying point for those who opposed his increasingly authoritarian rule.

2   On Elections in Vietnam
Ngo Dinh Diem
July 16, 1955

The National Government has emphasized time and time again the price it has paid for the defense of the unity of the country and of true democracy. We did not sign the Geneva Agreements. We are not bound in any way by these Agreements, signed against the will of the Vietnamese people. Our policy is a policy of peace, but nothing will lead us astray from our goal: the unity of our country—a unity in freedom and not in slavery.

Serving the cause of our nation more than ever, we will struggle for the reunification of our homeland. We do not reject the principle of free elections as peaceful and democratic means to achieve that unity. Although elections constitute one of the bases of true democracy, they will be meaningful only on the condition that they are absolutely free.

Faced now with a regime of oppression as practiced by the Vietminh, we remain skeptical concerning the possibility of fulfilling the conditions of free elections in the North. We shall not miss any opportunity which would permit the unification of our homeland in freedom, but it is out of the question for us to consider any proposal from the Vietminh if proof is not given that they put the superior interests of the national community above those of Communism, if they do not cease violating their obligations as they have done by preventing our countrymen of the North from going South or by recently attacking, together with the Communist Pathet Lao, the friendly state of Laos.

The mission falls to us, the Nationalists, to accomplish the reunification of our country in conditions that are most democratic and most effective to guarantee our independence. The free world is with us. Of this we are certain. I am confident that I am a faithful interpreter of our state of mind when I affirm solemnly our will to resist Communism.

To those who live above the 17th Parallel, I ask them to have confidence. With the agreement and the backing of the free world, the National Government will bring you independence in freedom.

Document 3

In this speech at Gettysburg, President Dwight D. Eisenhower explained why he considered Indochina of vital interest to the United States. Although Eisenhower made passing references to the importance of raw materials in South Vietnam elsewhere in the speech, its thrust was that South Vietnam was important in the rivalry between two competing world views. Freedom, he argued, demanded that the United States aid a small nation in its desire for independence.

3   The Importance to the United States of the Security and Progress of Vietnam
Dwight D. Eisenhower
April 4, 1959
Let us consider briefly the country of Viet-Nam and the importance to us of the security and progress of that country. It is located, as you know, in the southeastern corner of Asia, exactly halfway round the world from Gettysburg College.

Viet-Nam is a country divided into two parts, like Korea and Germany. The southern half, with its 12 million people, is free but poor. It is an underdeveloped country; its economy is weak, average individual income being less than $200 a year. The northern half has been turned over to communism. A line of demarcation running along the 17th parallel separates the two. To the north of this line stand several

Communist divisions. These facts pose to south Viet-Nam two great tasks: self-defense and economic growth.

Understandably the people of Viet-Nam want to make their country a thriving, self-sufficient member of the family of nations. This means economic expansion.

For Viet-Nam's economic growth, the acquisition of capital is vitally necessary. Now, the nation could create the capital needed for growth by stealing from the already meager rice bowls of its people and regimenting them into work battalions. This enslavement is the commune system, adopted by the new overlords of Red China. It would mean, of course, the loss of freedom within the country without any hostile outside action whatsoever.

Another way for Viet-Nam to get the necessary capital is through private investments from the outside and through governmental loans and, where necessary, grants from other and more fortunately situated nations.

In either of these ways the economic problem of Viet-Nam could be solved. But only the second way can preserve freedom.

And there is still the other of Viet-Nam's great problems—how to support the military forces it needs without crushing its economy.

Because of the proximity of large Communist military formations in the north, Free Viet-Nam must maintain substantial numbers of men under arms. Moreover, while the Government has shown real progress in cleaning out Communist guerrillas, those remaining continue to be a disruptive influence in the nation's life.

Unassisted, Viet-Nam cannot at this time produce and support the military formations essential to it or, equally important, the morale—the hope, the confidence, the pride—necessary to meet the dual threat of aggression from without and subversion within its borders.

Still another fact! Strategically south Viet-Nam's capture by the Communists would bring their power several hundred miles into a hitherto free region. The remaining countries in Southeast Asia would be menaced by a great flanking movement. The freedom of 12 million people would be lost immediately and that of 150 million others in adjacent lands would be seriously endangered. The loss of south Viet-Nam would set in motion a crumbling process that could, as it progressed, have grave consequences for us and for freedom.

Viet-Nam must have a reasonable degree of safety now—both for her people and for her property. Because of these facts, military as well as economic help is currently needed in Viet-Nam.

We reach the inescapable conclusion that our own national interests demand some help from us in sustaining in Viet-Nam the morale, the economic progress, and the military strength necessary to its continued existence in freedom.

Document 4

The following document, known as the "Manifesto of the Eighteen," was the work of prominent members of South Vietnamese society, including ten men who had served as cabinet ministers under Diem. Their opposition to Diem indicated that he had lost a great deal of support nationwide. These men felt that conditions in 1960 were worse than when Diem had first come to power.

4   Manifesto of the Eighteen
April 26, 1960
The President of the Republic of Viet-Nam
Saigon
Mr. President:

We the undersigned, representing a group of eminent citizens and personalities, intellectuals of all tendencies, and men of good will, recognize in the face of the gravity of the present political situation that we can no longer remain indifferent to the realities of life in our country.

Therefore, we officially address to you today an appeal with the aim of exposing to you the whole truth in the hope that the government will accord it all the attention necessary so as to urgently modify its policies, so as to remedy the present situation and lead the people out of danger.

Let us look toward the past, at the time when you were abroad. For eight or nine years, the Vietnamese people suffered many trials due to the war: They passed from French domination to Japanese occupation, from revolution to resistance, from the nationalist imposture behind which hid communism to a pseudo-independence covering up for colonialism; from terror to terror, from sacrifice to sacrifice—in short, from promise to promise, until finally hope ended in bitter disillusion.

Thus, when you were on the point of returning to the country, the people as a whole entertained the hope that it would find again under your guidance the peace that is necessary to give meaning to existence, to reconstruct the destroyed homes, put to the plow again the abandoned lands. The people hoped no longer to be compelled to pay homage to one regime in the morning and to another at night, not to be the prey of the cruelties and oppression of one faction; no longer to be treated as coolies; no longer to be at the mercy of the monopolies; no longer to have to endure the depredations of corrupt and despotic civil servants. In one word, the people hoped to live in security at last, under a regime which would give them a little bit of justice and liberty. The whole people thought that you would be the man of the situation and that you would implement its hopes.

That is the way it was when you returned. The Geneva Accords of 1954 put an end to combat and to the devastations of war. The French Expeditionary Corps was progressively withdrawn, and total independence of South Viet-Nam had become a reality. Furthermore, the country had benefited from moral encouragement and a substantial increase of foreign aid from the free world. With so many favorable political factors, in addition to the blessed geographic conditions of a fertile and rich soil yielding agricultural, forestry, and fishing surpluses, South Viet-Nam should have been able to begin a definitive victory in the historical competition with the North, so as to carry out the will of the people and to lead the country on the way to hope, liberty, and happiness. Today, six years later, having benefited from so many undeniable advantages, what has the government been able to do? Where has it led South Viet-Nam? What parts of the popular aspirations have been implemented?

Let us try to draw an objective balance of the situation, without flattery or false accusations, strictly following a constructive line which you yourself have so often indicated, in the hope that the government shall modify its policies so as to extricate itself from a situation that is extremely dangerous to the very existence of the nation.

Policies

In spite of the fact that the bastard regime created and protected by colonialism has been overthrown and that many of the feudal organizations of factions and parties which oppress the population were destroyed, the people do not know a better life or more freedom under the republican regime which you have created. A constitution has been established in form only; a National Assembly exists whose deliberations always fall into line with the government; antidemocratic elections—all those are methods and "comedies" copied from the dictatorial Communist regimes, which obviously cannot serve as terms of comparison with North Viet-Nam.

Continuous arrests fill the jails and prisons to the rafters, as at this precise moment; public opinion and the press are reduced to silence. The same applies to the popular will as translated in certain open elections, in which it is insulted and trampled (as was the case, for example, during the recent elections for the Second Legislature). All these have provoked the discouragement and resentment of the people.

Political parties and religious sects have been eliminated. "Groups" or "movements" have replaced them. But this substitution has only brought about new oppressions against the population without protecting it for that matter against Communist enterprises. Here is one example: the fiefs of religious sects, which hitherto were deadly for the Communists, now not only provide no security whatever but have become favored highways for Viet-Minh guerrillas, as is, by the way, the case of the rest of the country.

This is proof that the religious sects, though futile, nevertheless constitute effective anti-Communist elements. Their elimination has opened the way to the Viet-Cong and unintentionally has prepared the way for the enemy, whereas a more realistic and more flexible policy could have amalgamated them all with a view to reinforcing the anti-Communist front.

Today the people want freedom. You should, Mr. President, liberalize the regime, promote democracy, guarantee minimum civil rights, recognize the opposition so as to permit the citizens to express themselves without fear, thus removing grievances and resentments, opposition to which now constitutes for the people their sole reason for existence. When this occurs, the people of South Viet-Nam, in comparing their position with that of the North, will appreciate the value of true liberty and of authentic democracy. It is only at that time that the people will make all the necessary efforts and sacrifices to defend that liberty and democracy.

Administration

The size of the territory has shrunk, but the number of civil servants has increased, and still the work doesn't get done. This is because the government, like the Communists, lets the political parties control the population, separate the elite from the lower echelons, and sow distrust between those individuals who are "affiliated with the movement" and those who are "outside the group." Effective power, no longer in the hands of those who are usually responsible, is concentrated in fact in the hands of an irresponsible member of the "family," from whom emanates all orders; this slows down the administrative machinery, paralyzes all initiative, discourages good will. At the same time, not a month goes by without the press being full of stories about graft impossible to hide; this becomes an endless parade of illegal transactions involving millions of piastres.

The administrative machinery, already slowed down, is about to become completely paralyzed. It is in urgent need of reorganization. Competent people should be put back in the proper jobs; discipline must be re-established from the top to the bottom of the hierarchy; authority must go hand in hand with responsibility; efficiency, initiative, honesty, and the economy should be the criteria for promotion;

professional qualifications should be respected. Favoritism based on family or party connections should be banished; the selling of influence, corruption, and abuse of power must be punished.

Thus, everything still can be saved, human dignity can be re-established; faith in an honest and just government can be restored.

Army

The French Expeditionary Corps has left the country, and a republican army has been constituted, thanks to American aid, which has equipped it with modern matériel. Nevertheless, even in a group of the proud elite of the youth such as the Vietnamese Army—where the sense of honor should be cultivated, whose blood and arms should be devoted to the defense of the country, where there should be no place for clannishness and factions—the spirit of the "national revolutionary movement" or of the "personalist body" divides the men of one and the same unit, sows distrust between friends of the same rank, and uses as a criterion for promotion fidelity toward the party in blind submission to its leaders. This creates extremely dangerous situations, such as the recent incident of Tay-Ninh.

The purpose of the army, pillar of the defense of the country, is to stop foreign invasions and to eliminate rebel movements. It is at the service of the country only and should not lend itself to the exploitation of any faction or party. Its total reorganization is necessary. Clannishness and party obedience should be eliminated; its moral base strengthened; a noble tradition of national pride created; and fighting spirit, professional conscience, and bravery should become criteria for promotion. The troops should be encouraged to respect their officers, and the officers should be encouraged to love their men. Distrust, jealousy, rancor among colleagues of the same rank should be eliminated.

Then in case of danger, the nation will have at its disposal a valiant army animated by a single spirit and a single aspiration: to defend the most precious possession—our country, Viet-Nam.

Economic and Social Affairs

[A rich and fertile country enjoying food surpluses; a budget which does not have to face military expenditures; important war reparations; substantial profits from Treasury bonds; a colossal foreign-aid program; a developing market capable of receiving foreign capital investments—those are the many favorable conditions which could make Viet-Nam a productive and properous nation.] However, at the present time many people are out of work, have no roof over their heads, and no money. Rice is abundant but does not sell; shop windows are well-stocked but the goods do not move. Sources of revenue are in the hands of speculators who use the [government] party and group to mask monopolies operating for certain private interests. At the same time, thousands of persons are mobilized for exhausting work, compelled to leave their own jobs, homes, and families, to participate in the construction of magnificent but useless "agrovilles" which weary them and provoke their disaffection, thus aggravating popular resentment and creating an ideal terrain for enemy propaganda.

The economy is the very foundation of society, and public opinion ensures the survival of the regime. The government must destroy all the obstacles standing in the way of economic development; must abolish all forms of monopoly and speculation; must create a favorable environment for investments coming from foreign friends as well as from our own citizens; must encourage commercial enterprises, develop industry, and create jobs to reduce unemployment. At the same time, it should put an end to all forms of human exploitation in the work camps of the agrovilles.

Then only the economy will flourish again; the citizen will find again a peaceful life and will enjoy his condition; society will be reconstructed in an atmosphere of freedom and democracy.

Mr. President, this is perhaps the first time that you have heard such severe and disagreeable criticism—so contrary to your own desires. Nevertheless, sir, these words are strictly the truth, a truth that is bitter and hard, that you have never been able to know because, whether this is intended or not, a void has been created around you, and by the very fact of your high position, no one permits you to perceive the critical point at which truth shall burst forth in irresistible waves of hatred on the part of a people subjected for a long time to terrible suffering and a people who shall rise to break the bonds which hold it down. It shall sweep away the ignominy and all the injustices which surround and oppress it.

As we do not wish, in all sincerity, that our Fatherland should have to live through these perilous days, we—without taking into consideration the consequences which our attitude may bring upon us—are ringing today the alarm bell in view of the imminent danger which threatens the government.

Until now, we have kept silent and preferred to let the Executive act as it wished. But now time is of the essence; we feel that it is our duty—and in the case of a nation in turmoil even the most humble people have their share of responsibility—to speak the truth, to awaken public opinion, to alert the people, and to unify the opposition so as to point the way. We beseech the government to urgently modify its policies so as to remedy the situation, to defend the republican regime, and to safeguard the existence of the nation. We hold firm hope that the Vietnamese people shall know a brilliant future in which it will enjoy peace and prosperity in freedom and progress.

Yours respectfully,

1. TRAN VAN VAN, *Diploma of Higher Commercial Studies, former Minister of Economy and Planning*
2. PHAN KHAC SUU, *Agricultural Engineer, former Minister of Agriculture, former Minister of Labor*
3. TRAN VAN HUONG, *Professor of Secondary Education, former Prefect of Saigon-Cholon*
4. NGUYEN LUU VIEN, *M.D., former Professor at the Medical School, former High Commissioner of Refugees*
5. HUYNH KIM HUU, *M.D., former Minister of Public Health*
6. PHAN HUY QUAT, *M.D., former Minister of National Education, former Minister of Defense*
7. TRAN VAN LY, *former Governor of Central Viet-Nam*
8. NGUYEN TIEN HY, *M.D.*
9. TRAN VAN DO, *M.D., former Minister of Foreign Affairs, Chairman of Vietnamese Delegation to the 1954 Geneva Conference*
10. LE NGOC CHAN, *Attorney at Law, former Secretary of State for National Defense*
11. LE QUANG LUAT, *Attorney at Law, former Government Delegate for North Viet-Nam, former Minister of Information and Propaganda*

12. LUONG TRONG TUONG, *Public Works Engineer, former Secretary of State for National Economy*
13. NGUYEN TANG NGUYEN, *M.D., former Minister of Labor and Youth*
14. PHAM HUU CHUONG, *M.D., former Minister of Public Health and Social Action*
15. TRAN VAN TUYEN, *Attorney at Law, former Secretary of State for Information and Propaganda*
16. TA CHUONG PHUNG, *former Provincial Governor for Binh-Dinh*
17. TRAN LE CHAT, *Laureate of the Triannual Mandarin Competition of 1903*
18. HO VAN VUI, *Reverend, former Parish Priest of Saigon, at present Parish Priest of Tha-La, Province of Tay-Ninh*

Document 5

The "Manifesto of the Eighteen" indicated that many well-established citizens of South Vietnam were questioning the judgments and policies of President Ngo Dinh Diem. Those who wrote the manifesto were jailed. But eight months later an even more forceful and strident document voiced opposition to Diem's government.

This manifesto, the Program of the National Liberation Front of South Vietnam, expressed the view that Diem had overstayed his welcome; reform was no longer possible, and a reorganization of South Vietnamese government and society was a necessity. The National Liberation Front also felt that the removal of Diem would lead to the departure of the Americans from Vietnam.

5   Program of the National Liberation Front of South Vietnam
February 14, 1961

. . . The program of the NFLSV includes the following 10 points:

1—To overthrow the disguised colonial regime of the U.S. imperialists and the dictatorial Ngo Dinh Diem administration, lackey of the United States, and to form a national democratic coalition administration.

The present regime in South Vietnam is a disguised colonial regime of the U.S. imperialists. The South Vietnamese administration is a lackey which has been carrying out the U.S. imperialists' political lines. This regime and administration must be overthrown, and a broad national democratic coalition administration formed to include representatives of all strata of the people, nationalities, political parties, religious communities, and patriotic personages; to wrest back the people's economic, political, social, and cultural interests; to realize independence and democracy; to improve the people's living conditions; and to carry out a policy of peace and neutrality and advance toward peaceful reunification of the fatherland.

2—To bring into being a broad and progressive democracy.

a—To abolish the current constitution of the Ngo Dinh Diem dictatorial administration, lackey of the United States, and to elect a new National Assembly through universal suffrage.

b—To promulgate all democratic freedoms: freedom of expression, of the press, of assembly, of association, of movement; to guarantee freedom of belief with no discrimination toward any religion on the part of the state; and to grant freedom of action to the patriotic political parties and mass organizations, irrespective of political tendencies.

c—To grant general amnesty to all political detainees, dissolve all concentration camps under any form whatsoever, abolish the fascist law 10–59 and other antidemocratic laws; and to grant the right of repatriation to all those who had to flee abroad due to the U.S.-Diem regime.

d—To strictly ban all illegal arrests and imprisonments and tortures, and to punish unrepenting cruel murderers of the people.

3—To build an independent and sovereign economy, and improve the people's living conditions.

a—To abolish the economic monopoly of the United States and its henchmen; to build an independent and sovereign economy and finance, beneficial to the nation and people; and to confiscate and nationalize the property of the U.S. imperialists and the ruling clique, their stooges.

b—To help the industrialists and trades people rehabilitate and develop industry both large and small and to encourage industrial development; and to actively protect homemade products by abolishing production taxes, restricting or ending the import of those goods which can be produced in the country, and reducing taxes on import of raw materials and machinery.

c—To rehabilitate agriculture, and to modernize planting, fishing, and animal husbandry; to help peasants reclaim waste land and develop production; and to protect crops and insure the consumption of agricultural products.

d—To encourage and accelerate the economic interflow between the town and the countryside, between plains and mountainous areas; and to develop trade with foreign countries without distinction of political regimes and on the principle of equality and mutual benefit.

e—To apply an equitable and rational system to abolish arbitrary fines.

f—To promulgate labor regulations, that is: to prohibit dismissals, wage cuts, fines and ill-treatment of workers; to improve the life of workers and office employees; and to fix wages and guarantees for the health of teenage apprentices.

g—To organize social relief: jobs for unemployed; protection of orphans, elders, and the disabled; assistance to those who have become disabled or lost their relatives in the struggle against U.S. imperialism and its stooges; and relief to localities suffering crop failures, fire, and natural calamities.

h—To help northern compatriots who had been forced or enticed by the reactionaries to go south after the restoration of peace to return to their native places if they so desire, and to provide jobs to those who decide to remain in the south.

i—To strictly prohibit forcible house removals, arson, usurpation of land, and the herding of the people into concentration centers; and to insure the country folk and urban working people of the opportunity to earn their living in security.

4—To carry out land rent reduction in preparation for the settlement of the agrarian problem so as to insure land to the tillers.

a—To carry out land rent reduction; to guarantee the peasants' right to till their present plots of land and insure the right of ownership for those who have reclaimed waste land; and to protect the legitimate right of ownership by peasants of the plots of land distributed to them during the resistance war.

b—To abolish the "prosperity zones" and the policy of herding the people into "resettlement centers" and to grant the right of those forcibly herded into "prosperity zones" or "resettlement centers" (disguised concentration camps) (parentheses as received) to return home freely and earn their living on their own plots of land.

c—To confiscate the land usurped by the U.S. imperialists and their agents and distribute it to landless and land-poor peasants; and to redistribute communal land in an equitable and rational way.

d—Through negotiations, the state will purchase from landowners at equitable and rational prices all land held by them in excess of a given area, fixed in accordance with the concrete situation in each locality, and distribute it to landless and land-poor peasants. This land will be distributed free and will be free of any conditions.

5—To build a national and democratic education and culture.

a—To eliminate the enslaving and gangster-style American culture and education; and to build a rational, progressive culture and education serving the fatherland and the people.

b—To wipe out illiteracy; to build sufficient general education schools for the youth and children; to expand universities and professional schools; to use the Vietnamese language in teaching; to reduce school fees or exempt fees for poor pupils and students; and to reform the examination system.

c—To develop science and technology and the national literature and art; and to encourage and help intellectuals, cultural, and art workers to develop their abilities in service of national construction.

d—To develop medical service in order to look after the people's health; and to expand the gymnastic and sports movement.

6—To build an army to defend the motherland and the people.

a—To build a national army defending the fatherland and the people; and to cancel the system of U.S. military advisers.

b—To abolish the pressganging regime; to improve the material life of the armymen and insure their political rights; to prohibit the ill-treatment of soldiers; and to apply a policy of assistance to families of poor armymen.

c—To renumerate and give worthy jobs to those officers and soldiers who have rendered meritorious services in the struggle against the domination of the U.S. imperialists and their henchmen; and to observe leniency toward those who had before collaborated with the U.S.-Diem clique and committed crimes against the people, but have now repented and serve the people.

d—To abolish all the military bases of foreign countries in South Vietnam.

7—To guarantee the right of equality between nationalities and between men and women; to protect and legitimate rights of foreign residents and overseas Vietnamese.

a—To insure the right of autonomy of the national minorities; to set up, within the framework of the great family of the Vietnamese people, autonomous regions and areas inhabited by minority peoples; to insure equal rights among different nationalities, allowing all nationalities to have the right to use and develop their own spoken and written languages and to preserve or change their customs and habits; to abolish the U.S.-Diem clique's present policy of ill-treatment and forced assimilation of the minority nationalities; and to help the minority peoples to catch up with the common level of the people by developing the economy and culture in the areas inhabited by them, by training skilled personnel from people of minority origin.

b—To insure the right of equality between men and women, so women can enjoy the same rights as men in all fields: political, economic, cultural, and social.

c—To protect the legitimate rights of foreigners residing in Vietnam; and to defend and care for Vietnamese nationals abroad.

8—To carry out a foreign policy of peace and neutrality.

a—To cancel all unequal treaties signed with foreign countries by the U.S. henchmen which violate national sovereignty.

b—To establish diplomatic relations with all countries irrespective of political regime, in accordance with the principles of peaceful coexistence as put forth at the Bandung conference.

c—To unite closely with the peace-loving and neutral countries; and to expand friendly relations with Asian and African countries, first of all, with neighboring Cambodia and Laos.

d—To refrain from joining any bloc or military alliance or forming a military alliance with any country.

e—To receive economic aid from any country ready to assist Vietnam without conditions attached.

9—To establish normal relations between North and South Vietnam as a first step toward peaceful reunification of the country.

The urgent demand of our people throughout the country is to reunify the country by peaceful means. The NFLSV undertakes the gradual reunification of the country by peaceful means, on the principle of negotiations and discussions between the two zones of all forms and measures beneficial to the people and fatherland. Pending the national reunification, the governments of the two zones will negotiate and undertake not to spread propaganda to divide the peoples or favor war, nor to use military forces against each other; to carry out economic and cultural exchanges between the two zones; and to insure for people of both zones freedom of movement, of livelihood, and the right of mutual visits and correspondence.

10—To oppose aggressive war and actively defend world peace.

a—To oppose aggressive wars and all forms of enslavement by the imperialists; and to support the national liberation struggles of peoples in various countries.

b—To oppose war propaganda; and to demand general disarmament, prohibition of nuclear weapons, and demand the use of atomic energy for peaceful purposes.

c—To support the movements for peace, democracy, and social progress in the world; and to actively contribute to the safeguarding of peace in Southeast Asia and the world.

Document 6

John F. Kennedy's powerful inaugural address, delivered on January 20, 1961, inspired the nation. During his campaign, Kennedy had charged that the United States was falling behind in the global competition with the Communists, and now his aim was to make the United States first again. The new American leader asked his people to live up to the ideals of their country and meet the challenges of the world head on. By doing so, concluded Kennedy, the United States would not only demonstrate its preeminence, but would also create a better world for all humanity.

6 John F. Kennedy Inaugural Address, January 20, 1961

We observe today not a victory of party but a celebration of freedom—symbolizing an end as well as a beginning—signifying renewal as well as change. For I have sworn before you and Almighty God the same solemn oath our forebears prescribed nearly a century and three quarters ago.

The world is very different now. For man holds in his mortal hands the power to abolish all forms of human poverty and all forms of human life. And yet the same revolutionary beliefs for which our forebears fought are still at issue around the globe—the belief that the rights of man come not from the generosity of the state but from the hand of God.

We dare not forget today that we are the heirs of that first revolution. Let the word go forth from this time and place, to friend and foe alike, that the torch has been passed to a new generation of Americans—born in this century, tempered by war, disciplined by a hard and bitter peace, proud of our ancient heritage—and unwilling to witness or permit the slow undoing of those human rights to which this nation has always been committed, and to which we are committed today at home and around the world.

Let every nation know, whether it wishes us well or ill, that we shall pay any price, bear any burden, meet any hardship, support any friend, oppose any foe to assure the survival and the success of liberty.

This much we pledge—and more.

To those old allies whose cultural and spiritual origins we share, we pledge the loyalty of faithful friends. United, there is little we cannot do in a host of cooperative ventures. Divided, there is little we can do—for we dare not meet a powerful challenge at odds and split asunder.

To those new states whom we welcome to the ranks of the free, we pledge our word that one form of colonial control shall not have passed away merely to be replaced by a far more iron tyranny. We shall not always expect to find them supporting our view. But we shall always hope to find them strongly supporting their own freedom—and to remember that, in the past, those who foolishly sought power by riding the back of the tiger ended up inside.

To those peoples in the huts and villages of half the globe struggling to break the bonds of mass misery, we pledge our best efforts to help them help themselves, for whatever period is required—not because the communists may be doing it, not because we seek their votes, but because it is right. If a free society cannot help the many who are poor, it cannot save the few who are rich.

To our sister republics south of our border, we offer a special pledge—to convert our good words into good deeds—in a new alliance for progress—to assist free men and free governments in casting off the chains of poverty. But this peaceful revolution of hope cannot become the prey of hostile powers. Let all our neighbors know that we shall join with them to oppose aggression or subversion anywhere in the Americas. And let every other power know that this Hemisphere intends to remain the master of its own house.

To that world assembly of sovereign states, the United Nations, our last best hope in an age where the instruments of war have far outpaced the instruments of peace, we renew our pledge of support—to prevent it from becoming merely a forum for invective—to strengthen its shield of the new and the weak—and to enlarge the area in which its writ may run.

Finally, to those nations who would make themselves our adversary, we offer not a pledge but a request: that both sides begin anew the quest for peace, before the dark powers of destruction unleashed by science engulf all humanity in planned or accidental self-destruction.

We dare not tempt them with weakness. For only when our arms are sufficient beyond doubt can we be certain beyond doubt that they will never be employed.

But neither can two great and powerful groups of nations take comfort from our present course—both sides overburdened by the cost of modern weapons, both rightly alarmed by the steady spread of the deadly atom, yet both racing to alter that uncertain balance of terror that stays the hand of mankind's final war.

So let us begin anew—remembering on both sides that civility is not a sign of weakness, and sincerity is always subject to proof. Let us never negotiate out of fear. But let us never fear to negotiate.

Let both sides explore what problems unite us instead of belaboring those problems which divide us.

Let both sides, for the first time, formulate serious and precise proposals for the inspection and control of arms—and bring the absolute power to destroy other nations under the absolute control of all nations.

Let both sides seek to invoke the wonders of science instead of its terrors. Together let us explore the stars, conquer the deserts, eradicate disease, tap the ocean depths and encourage the arts and commerce.

Let both sides unite to heed in all corners of the earth the command of Isaiah—to "undo the heavy burdens . . . (and) let the oppressed go free."

And if a beach-head of cooperation may push back the jungle of suspicion, let both sides join in creating a new endeavor, not a new balance of power, but a new world of law, where the strong are just and the weak secure and the peace preserved.

All this will not be finished in the first one hundred days. Nor will it be finished in the first one thousand days, nor in the life of this Administration, nor even perhaps in our lifetime on this planet. But let us begin.

In your hands, my fellow citizens, more than mine, will rest the final success or failure of our course. Since this country was founded, each generation of Americans has been summoned to give testimony to its national loyalty. The graves of young Americans who answered the call to service surround the globe.

Now the trumpet summons us again—not as a call to bear arms, though arms we need—not as a call to battle, though embattled we are—but a call to bear the burden of a long twilight struggle, year in and year out, "rejoicing in hope, patient in tribulation"—a struggle against the common enemies of man: tyranny, poverty, disease and war itself.

Can we forge against these enemies a grand and global alliance, North and South, East and West, that can assure a more fruitful life for all mankind? Will you join in that historic effort?

In the long history of the world, only a few generations have been granted the role of defending freedom in its hour of maximum danger. I do not shrink from this responsibility—I welcome it. I do not believe that any of us would exchange places with any other people or any other generation. The energy, the faith, the devotion which we bring to this endeavor will light our country and all who serve it—and the glow from that fire can truly light the world.

And so, my fellow Americans: ask not what your country can do for you—ask what you can do for your country.

My fellow citizens of the world: ask not what America will do for you, but what together we can do for the freedom of man.

Finally, whether you are citizens of America or citizens of the world, ask of us here the same high standards of strength and sacrifice which we ask of you. With a good conscience our only sure reward, with history the final judge of our deeds, let us go forth to lead the land we love, asking His blessing and His help, but knowing that here on earth God's work must truly be our own.

Documents 7 and 8

The National Liberation Front of South Vietnam presented President Diem with a committed foe, capable of gaining support wherever Diem's policies created enemies. Although Saigon and many of the urban areas were relatively tranquil, Diem was quite unpopular with citizens living in the rural districts. There the National Liberation Front was especially active and was responsible for the assassination of many village government officials.

As NLF activity increased, Diem wrote to President Kennedy in December 1961 asking for more aid. Both leaders were worried about the growing insurgency in the countryside and determined to maintain an independent, noncommunist South Vietnam by force of arms if necessary.

This exchange of letters between Diem and Kennedy in the last days of 1961 helped set the stage for further American support of Diem's government.

7   Letter from President Diem to President Kennedy
December 7, 1961

Dear Mr. President:

Since its birth, more than six years ago, the Republic of Vietnam has enjoyed the close friendship and cooperation of the United States of America.

Like the United States, the Republic of Vietnam has always been devoted to the preservation of peace. My people know only too well the sorrows of war. We have honored the 1954 Geneva Agreements even though they resulted in the partition of our country and the enslavement of more than half of our people by Communist tyranny. We have never considered the reunification of our nation by force. On the contrary, we have publicly pledged that we will not violate the demarcation line and the demilitarized zone set by the Agreements. We have always been prepared and have on many occasions stated our willingness to reunify Vietnam on the basis of democratic and truly free elections.

The record of the Communist authorities in the northern part of our country is quite otherwise. They not only consented to the division of Vietnam, but were eager for it. They pledged themselves to observe the Geneva Agreements and during the seven years since have never ceased to violate them. They call for free elections but are ignorant of the very meaning of the words. They talk of "peaceful reunification" and wage war against us.

From the beginning, the Communists resorted to terror in their efforts to subvert our people, destroy our government and impose a Communist regime upon us. They have attacked defenseless teachers, closed schools, killed members of our antimalarial program, and looted hospitals. This is coldly calculated to destroy our government's humanitarian efforts to serve our people.

We have long sought to check the Communist attack from the North on our people by appeals to the International Control Commission. Over the years, we have repeatedly published to the world the evidence of the Communist plot to overthrow our government and seize control of all of Vietnam by illegal intrusions from outside our country. The evidence has mounted until now it is hardly necessary to rehearse it. Most recently, the kidnapping and brutal murder of our Chief Liaison Officer to the International Control Commission, Colonel Noang Thuy Nam, compelled us to speak out once more. In our October 24, 1961 letter to the ICC, we called attention again to the publicly stated determination of the Communist authorities in Hanoi to "liberate the South" by the overthrow of my government and the imposition of a Communist regime on our people. We cited the proof of massive infiltration of Communist agents and military elements into our country. We outlined the Communist strategy, which is simply the ruthless use of terror against the the whole population, women and children included.

In the course of the last few months, the Communist assault on my people has achieved high ferocity. In October they caused more than 1,800 incidents of violence and more than 2,000 casualties. They have struck occasionally in battalion strength, and they are continually augmenting their forces by infiltration from the North. The level of their attacks is already such that our forces are stretched to the utmost. We are forced to defend every village, every hamlet, indeed every home against a foe whose tactic is always to strike at the defenseless.

A disastrous flood was recently added to the misfortunes of the Vietnamese people. The greater part of three provinces was inundated, with a great loss of property. We are now engaged in a nationwide effort to reconstruct and rehabilitate this area. The Communists are, of course, making this task doubly difficult, for they have seized upon the disruption of normal administration and communications as an opportunity to sow more destruction in the stricken area.

In short, the Vietnamese nation now faces what is perhaps the gravest crisis in its long history. For more than 2,000 years my people have lived and built, fought and died in this land. We have not always been free. Indeed, much of our history and many of its proudest moments have arisen from conquest by foreign powers and our struggle against great odds to regain or defend our precious independence. But it is not only our freedom which is at stake today, it is our national identity. For, if we lose this war, our people will be swallowed by the Communist bloc, all our proud heritage will be blotted out by the "Socialist society" and Vietnam will leave the pages of history. We will lose our national soul.

Mr. President, my people and I are mindful of the great assistance which the United States has given us. Your help has not been lightly received, for the Vietnamese are proud people, and we are determined to do our part in the defense of the free world. It is clear to all of us that the defeat of the Vietcong demands the total mobilization of our government and our people, and you may be sure that we will devote all of our resources of money, minds and men to this great task.

But Vietnam is not a great power and the forces of international Communism now arrayed against us are more than we can meet with the resources at hand. We must have further assistance from the United States if we are to win the war now being waged against us.

We can certainly assure mankind that our action is purely defensive. Much as we regret the subjugation of more than half of our people in North Vietnam, we have no intention, and indeed no means, to free them by use of force.

I have said that Vietnam is at war. War means many things, but most of all it means the death of brave people for a cause they believe in. Vietnam has suffered many wars, and through the centuries we have always had patriots and heroes who were willing to shed their blood for Vietnam. We will keep faith with them.

When Communism has long ebbed away into the past, my people will still be here, a free united nation growing from the deep roots of our Vietnamese heritage. They will remember your help in our time of need. This struggle will then be a part of our common history. And your help, your friendship, and the strong bonds between our two peoples will be a part of Vietnam, then as now.

**8   Letter from President Kennedy to President Diem
December 14, 1961**
Dear Mr. President:

I have received your recent letter in which you described so cogently the dangerous condition caused by North Vietnam's efforts to take over your country. The situation in your embattled country is well known to me and to the American people. We have been deeply disturbed by the assault on your country. Our indignation has mounted as the deliberate savagery of the Communist program of assassination, kidnapping, and wanton violence became clear.

Your letter underlines what our own information has convincingly shown—that the campaign of force and terror now being waged against your people and your Government is supported and directed from the outside by the authorities at Hanoi. They have thus violated the provisions of the Geneva Accords designed to ensure peace in Vietnam and to which they bound themselves in 1954.

At that time, the United States, although not a party to the Accords, declared that it "would view any renewal of the aggression in violation of the Agreements with grave concern and as seriously threatening international peace and security." We continue to maintain that view.

In accordance with that declaration, and in response to your request, we are prepared to help the Republic of Vietnam to protect its people and to preserve its independence. We shall promptly increase our assistance to your defense effort as well as help relieve the destruction of the floods which you describe. I have already given the orders to get these programs underway.

The United States, like the Republic of Vietnam, remains devoted to the cause of peace and our primary purpose is to help your people maintain their independence. If the Communist authorities in North Vietnam will stop their campaign to destroy the Republic of Vietnam, the measures we are taking to assist your defense efforts will no longer be necessary. We shall seek to persuade the Communists to give up their attempts of force and subversion. In any case, we are confident that the Vietnamese people will preserve their independence and gain the peace and prosperity for which they have sought so hard and so long.

Document 9

One of President Kennedy's aims had been to establish a military force that was capable of flexible response. The Green Berets, part of the United States Special Forces units, became the models of well-trained, devoted, intelligent, freedom-fighting counterinsurgents who could beat back Communist-inspired wars around the world.

In a popular song and a film, as well as in a novel, the Green Berets enjoyed a great deal of adulation during the early days of the American experience in Vietnam. It was hoped that these men could provide a new way to win the support of the people of South Vietnam and, thereby, ensure the triumph of America's ally.

Robin Moore, a popular writer of the day, expressed the widespread interest in this new type of combatant in his novel, *The Green Berets*. Document 9 is excerpted from "Badge of Courage," the first chapter of Moore's book.

9   Badge of Courage
Robin Moore
The Green Berets is a book of truth. I planned and researched it originally to be an account presenting, through a series of actual incidents, an inside informed view of the almost unknown marvelous undercover work of our Special Forces in Vietnam and countries around the world. It was to be a factual book based on personal experience, first-hand knowledge and observation, naming persons and places. But it turned out that there were major obstacles and disadvantages in this straight reportorial method. And so, for the variety of reasons mentioned below, I decided I could present the truth better and more accurately in the form of fiction.

You will find in these pages many things that you will find hard to believe. Believe them. They happened this way. I changed details and names, but I did not change the basic truth. I could not tell the basic truth without changing the details and the names. Here's why.

Many of the stories incorporate a number of events which if reported merely in isolation would fail to give the full meaning and background of the war in Vietnam. Saigon's elite press corps, and such excellent feature writers as Jim Lucas of Scripps-Howard, Jack Langguth of *The New York Times,* and Dickey Chappell of *The Reader's Digest,* have reported the detailed incidents in the war. I felt that my job in this book was to give the broad overall picture of how Special Forces men operate, so each story basically is representative of a different facet of Special Forces action in wars like the one in Vietnam.

Also, as will be seen, Special Forces operations are, at times, highly unconventional. To report such occurrences factually, giving names, dates, and locations, could only embarrass U.S. planners in Vietnam and might even jeopardize the careers of invaluable officers. Time and again, I promised harried and heroic Special Forces men that their confidences were "off the record." To show the kind of men they are, to present an honest, comprehensive, and informed picture of their activities, one must get to know them as no writer could who was bound to report exactly what he saw and heard.

Moreover, I was in the unique—and enviable—position of having official aid and assistance without being bound by official restrictions. Even though I always made it clear I was in Vietnam in an unofficial capacity, under these auspices much was shown and told to me. I did not want to pull punches; at the same time I felt it wasn't right to abuse these special privileges and confidences by doing a straight reporting job.

The civic action portion of Special Forces operations can and should be reported factually. However, this book is more concerned with special missions, and I saw too many things that weren't for my eyes—or any eyes other than the participants' themselves—and assisted in too much imaginative circumvention of constricting ground rules merely to report what I saw under a thin disguise. The same blend of fact and "fiction" will be found in the locations in the book, many of which can be found on any map, while others are purely the author's invention.

So for these reasons *The Green Berets* is presented as a work of fiction.

Some means were sought to give the elite Special Forces man a distinctive type of insignia, and the green beret was adopted. The original crest on the beret was a silver Trojan horse worn on the left side above the ear. Now the flash denoting the wearer's group is worn directly above the left eye.

Conventional Army generals disliked the jaunty headgear and outlawed it. But the late President John F. Kennedy, recognizing the value of Special Forces, threw his full support behind the unit and restored the green beret in a message that exhorted the men to "wear the beret proudly, it will be a mark of distinction and a badge of courage in the difficult days ahead."

A green beret was returned to President Kennedy under the most tragic of circumstances two years later. Special Forces men formed the honor guard at the President's burial in Arlington National Cemetery. At the ceremony's end Sergeant Major Francis Ruddy sorrowfully took the beret from his head and placed it on his commander-in-chief's grave. It (that is, its replacement) is still there, along with the hats of the Army, Navy, and Air Force. Special Forces men insure that a fresh green beret will always lie above the President, who so loved and respected his tough, highly competent guerrilla fighters.

The basic unit of a Special Forces group is the 12-man A detachment or A team.

The A team is commanded by a captain, the CO. The XO (executive officer) is a 1st lieutenant (there are no 2nd lieutenants in Special Forces). There are ten intensively trained and experienced enlisted men on the A team, most of them senior sergeants. These are undoubtedly the most multiskilled enlisted men in the armed forces today.

The team sergeant is a master sergeant and—the officers will be the first to confirm—runs the detachment. One of the primary jobs of the sergeant specialists is to train their officers in the skills they have spent many years perfecting. Only after an officer graduates from the Special Warfare Center and forms his team does his training really begin.

The second-ranking enlisted man on an A team is usually the intelligence sergeant who keeps track of what the enemy is doing and recruits and trains agents—particularly tricky in Asia for an American.

There are two medical specialists on the A team, skilled in the exotic diseases to be found in the remote areas to which teams are sent. Much of their training is in war wounds. Two communications experts, who could probably make radios out of sea shells should the need arise, keep the A teams in touch with each other and with the B and C teams which are field headquarters for the operational A detachments.

Two demolition-engineer specialists can do everything from building bridges to blowing them up. Demolition men receive a richly deserved extra $50 a month in hazardous-duty pay. One light and one heavy-weapons specialist complete the team. These two men have to be good teachers since they must instruct native or indigenous troops in the use of the latest weapons. Many of the local people have never seen anything more modern than a crossbow before a Special Forces A detachment comes to their area.

Besides their specialties, the men on a Special Forces team have further capabilities.

Every man on an A team speaks a second language, some several tongues. On any given A team all the languages in use in the area are spoken, including those of the enemy. Every man is cross-trained in at least two other basic team skills. A medic, say, can not only efficiently patch up the wounded and care for the sick, but knows how to lay down a deadly accurate mortar barrage and blow up the enemy's rail lines and bridges.

In hand-to-hand combat the men of Special Forces have no superiors, blending judo, karate, wrestling, and boxing techniques into their own lethal brand of bare-handed, close-in fighting.

All Special Forces men are expert parachutists.

The Special Forces role is twofold. In a hot war situation the A detachment infiltrates enemy territory by parachuting in, or coming in by sea either in boats or with underwater apparatus, or across land routes. The job of the team is to build up, equip, train, and direct a guerrilla force of indigenous people. Special Forces men are carefully trained in all aspects of psychological warfare to both fan the flames of anti-Communist feeling among their civilian irregular troops and the citizens of the enemy country they are subverting, and keep the enemy government frightened and off-balance at all times.

In the type of counterinsurgency operations the United States has been backing in South Vietnam, the Special Forces teams train and equip the civilian irregular defense group (CIDG) troops, known as a strike force when organized in a Special Forces camp, as opposed to the conventional U.S. Army advisers in Vietnam who are assigned to the Army of the Republic of Vietnam (ARVN) regular troops. The strikers, as strike-force men are called, sign a contract to fight in a Special Forces–advised strike-force battalion for periods ranging from six months to two years. Basically, the A teams in Vietnam are training civilians to fight the Communist Viet Cong guerrillas as anti-guerrillas—much the same as killer submarines go after enemy subs. . . .

Documents 10 and 11

In the spring and summer of 1963, as Diem's war against the National Liberation Front faltered, major problems developed in another area. The Buddhists led the civilian population in protest against Diem's harsh policies. Diem, however, retained his determination to take a hard line against dissenters. At the time of Nhu's raids on the Buddhist pagodas on August 21, 1963, the United States, which had been carefully monitoring events in South Vietnam, was reassessing its support of Diem.

On Saturday, August 24, 1963, a group of White House advisers, including Roger Hilsman, sent a cable to Henry Cabot Lodge, who had just taken over as the new American ambassador to South Vietnam. Although subsequent communications somewhat modified the hard line taken against Diem, the August 24 cable and Lodge's reply represented a significant shift in the American attitude toward the Saigon regime, setting in motion a chain of events that led to Diem's overthrow.

The cable from Washington and the reply from Saigon were first made public when the Pentagon Papers appeared in June 1971.

10 Cablegram from the State Department to Ambassador Henry Cabot Lodge in Saigon
August 24, 1963
It is now clear that whether military proposed martial law or whether Nhu tricked them into it, Nhu took advantage of its imposition to smash pagodas with police

and Tung's Special Forces loyal to him, thus placing onus on military in eyes of world and Vietnamese people. Also clear that Nhu has maneuvered himself into commanding position.

U.S. Government cannot tolerate situation in which power lies in Nhu's hands. Diem must be given chance to rid himself of Nhu and his coterie and replace them with best military and political personalities available.

If, in spite of all of your efforts, Diem remains obdurate and refuses, then we must face the possibility that Diem himself cannot be preserved.

We now believe immediate action must be taken to prevent Nhu from consolidating his position further. Therefore, unless you in consultation with Harkins perceive overriding objections you are authorized to proceed along the following lines:

(1) First we must press on appropriate levels of GVN following line:

(a) USG cannot accept actions against Buddhists taken by Nhu and his collaborators under cover martial law.

(b) Prompt dramatic actions redress situation must be taken, including repeal of decree 10, release of arrested monks, nuns, etc.

(2) We must at same time also tell key military leaders that U.S. would find it impossible to continue support GVN militarily and economically unless above steps are taken immediately which we recognize requires removal of Nhus from the scene. We wish give Diem reasonable opportunity to remove Nhus, but if he remains obdurate, then we are prepared to accept the obvious implication that we can no longer support Diem. You may also tell appropriate military commanders we will give them direct support in any period of breakdown central government mechanism.

(3) We recognize the necessity of removing taint on military for pagoda raids and placing blame squarely on Nhu. You are authorized to have such statements made in Saigon as you consider desirable to achieve this objective. We are prepared to take same line here and to have Voice of America make statement along lines contained in next numbered telegram whenever you give the word, preferably as soon as possible.

Concurrently, with above, Ambassador and country team should urgently examine all possible alternative leadership and make detailed plans as to how we might bring about Diem's replacement if this should become necessary.

Assume you will consult with General Harkins re any precautions necessary protect American personnel during crisis period.

You will understand we cannot from Washington give you detailed instructions as to how this operation should proceed, but you will also know we will back you to the hilt on actions you take to achieve our objectives.

Needless to say we have held knowledge of this telegram to minimum essential people and assume you will take similar precautions to prevent premature leaks.

11 Cablegram from Ambassador Lodge to Secretary of State Dean Rusk and Assistant Secretary of State Roger Hilsman
August 25, 1963

Believe that chances of Diem's meeting our demands are virtually nil. At same time, by making them we give Nhu chance to forestall or block action by military. Risk, we believe, is not worth taking, with Nhu in control combat forces Saigon.

Therefore, propose we go straight to Generals with our demands, without informing Diem. Would tell them we prepared have Diem without Nhus but it is in effect up to them whether to keep him. Would also insist generals take steps to release Buddhist leaders and carry out June 16 agreement.

Request immediate modification instructions. However, do not propose move until we are satisfied with E and E plans. Harkins concurs. I present credentials President Diem tomorrow 11 A.M.

Critical Issues for Discussion

1. After Ngo Dinh Diem began to govern the area south of the 17th parallel, hundreds of thousands of refugees from the northern zone fled to the South. Why did they flee? Why did they think that living in the South would be better for them?

What might their arrival have meant to Diem? What conclusions could he have drawn from their support?

What did the rest of the South Vietnamese population think about the influx of people? Recalling northerners who had traveled south after the American Civil War, General Lawton Collins said that some South Vietnamese considered the refugees "carpetbaggers." What did he mean? Was that a useful analogy? Why or why not?

2. President Eisenhower worried about the United States "losing" Indochina. What did he mean by that? Why did he feel that that part of the world was an American concern?

John Foster Dulles went further in Document 1. Who worried him? Why did he think that Southeast Asia was important? What did he propose to do about it?

In Document 3 Eisenhower talked about South Vietnam. What did South Vietnam need to do? What choices did that government have to make? Would American aid mean progress for the South Vietnamese? What kind?

3. Countrywide elections were an important issue in Vietnam. See Document 2. What reasons did Diem give for refusing to take part in the elections which had been scheduled for 1956? Why did the United States support Diem's decision? What did this decision indicate about Diem's attitude toward democracy?

4. Madame Nhu once argued that "you open a window to let in light and air, not bullets. We want freedom, but we don't want to be exploited by it." Did she think that freedom was worthwhile? What did she mean by being "exploited" by it?

For a view of Diem's government, see Document 4. What were these men saying to Diem? Did they agree with Madame Nhu's fears about freedom? Which did they desire more—freedom or stability? Why? What were their goals for society? What did they consider progress to be?

For another view of Diem, see Document 5. What did the National Liberation Front hate? How would they have reacted to Madame Nhu's comments? What were their goals for society? What did they consider progress to be?

5. President Kennedy's inaugural address, reprinted as Document 6, had given
Americans a sense of the role they should play in the world. What was the
subject of Kennedy's speech? How did he see America's place in the world?
What did he think the United States should be doing? Why?

6. President Kennedy faced the same questions about Southeast Asia that Eisenhower had faced. See Documents 7 and 8. Why did Diem need more
help in 1961? How did he explain his troubles at home? Had his government
made any progress under his leadership? Why did he think that the United
States would be willing to help?

How did Kennedy explain the troubles in South Vietnam? Why did he agree
to give more aid? What problems did he face in his first year in office? Would
he have agreed with the analyses of the situation in Southeast Asia that Dulles
and Eisenhower had offered?

7. President Kennedy had high hopes for counterinsurgency efforts in Vietnam
like those of the Green Berets. Document 9 explores the appeal of this
group. What made the Green Berets special? What was their view of warfare?
Why were the Special Forces created?

8. By 1963 there was a great deal of controversy among Americans about
Diem's future in South Vietnam. What spurred this discussion? Had Diem's
programs failed? Had Diem changed? Had the Americans changed? What had
happened?

Some American journalists in South Vietnam quipped that U.S. policy
could best be expressed as "sink or swim with Ngo Dinh Diem." Vice President Johnson cut off a critic of Diem by saying "don't tell me about Diem. He's
all we've got out there." What did these comments indicate? Did Johnson and
the writers agree?

9. When did the U.S. government suspect that Diem was not going to survive
as an effective leader in South Vietnam? What could they do about it? What
alternate strategies did they envision?

Documents 10 and 11 come from the Pentagon Papers. What caused these
cables to be exchanged? What had the U.S. government decided about South
Vietnam? At this point, what steps would constitute progress? What was the
long-range goal?

10. In her explanation of the events which led to the deaths of her husband and
her brother-in-law, Diem, Madame Nhu argued that the United States was
"arrogant." She contended that the American government was "convinced it possessed the truth and was full of contempt." What did she mean? What truth did
the United States think that it possessed? Was the United States arrogant toward South Vietnam? How do you evaluate Madame Nhu's conclusions?

Follow up From 1954 to 1963, President Diem of South Vietnam received
a great deal of American aid but did not always follow American advice. Should
a condition of American foreign aid be that the recipient of this support be

friendly to American policy and mindful of American wishes? Should foreign aid promote progress? Who should decide what progress is—the donor or the recipient? Should foreign aid create vassals or subordinates? Clients or customers? Friends? Allies? What is its use?

Suggestions for Further Reading

General
Fall, Bernard B. *The Two Viet-Nams: A Political and Military Analysis*. Rev. ed. New York: Praeger, 1967.
> In Chapters 12–17, Fall's meticulous analysis of developments in the south after 1954 is highly critical of the Diem regime and of U.S. policy generally. Chapter 16, "National Liberation," is especially useful for its clear descriptions of the nature of the NLF and of American counterinsurgency efforts.

Kahin, George McTurnan and John W. Lewis. *The United States in Vietnam*. Rev. ed. New York: Dial Press, 1969.
> Drawing on their backgrounds in Asian history, Kahin and Lewis aimed to give Americans a Vietnamese context for challenging the assumptions underlying U.S. policy in Vietnam. Chapter 4 describes the reorganization of forces on either side of the 17th parallel; Chapter 5, the origins of the civil war in Diem's oppressive policies and the organization of the National Liberation Front; Chapter 6, U.S. military intervention under Kennedy.

Scigliano, Robert. *South Vietnam: Nation Under Stress*. Boston: Houghton Mifflin, 1963.
> Scigliano interviewed U.S. government officials for this political analysis of the years 1954–1962.

Related Novels
Greene, Graham. *The Quiet American*. New York: Penguin, 1962.
> Supposedly based on the career of Edward Lansdale in Vietnam, Greene's novel gives an accurate picture of the ambience of the late 1950s.

Lederer, William J. and Eugene Burdick. *The Ugly American*. New York: Norton, 1958.
> The story of an American ambassador to a small Asian country, who lived in urban comfort, ignorant of the native language and culture and insensitive to the people's needs. A best-seller of this era.

Accounts by U.S. Participants
Buttinger, Joseph. *Vietnam: The Unforgettable Tragedy*. New York: Horizon, 1977.
> Buttinger, once a vigorous supporter of Diem, here describes how his personal involvement led to a rejection of Diem's brutal course. With this book Buttinger's purposes changed from recording historical events to condemning U.S. involvement in Vietnam.

Halberstam, David. *The Making of a Quagmire*. New York: Random House, 1964.
> The *New York Times* correspondent to South Vietnam during the sixties,

David Halberstam, became frustrated by the ineffectiveness of U.S. policies there. *Quagmire* is his impressionistic description of events prior to Diem's overthrow.

Hilsman, Roger. *To Move a Nation.* Garden City, N.Y.: Doubleday, 1967.

Hilsman, who played an important part in counterinsurgency planning in South Vietnam (including the decision to drop Diem), describes John F. Kennedy's Vietnam decision-making in the context of the president's foreign policies generally.

Lansdale, Edward G. *In the Midst of Wars.* New York: Harper and Row, 1972.

The memoirs of the Major General behind the campaign for the "hearts and minds" of the Vietnamese people. Chapters 9–19 convey the arrogant idealism of the early years of the U.S. mission.

Shaplen, Robert. *The Lost Revolution: The Story of Twenty Years of Neglected Opportunities in Vietnam and of America's Failure to Foster Democracy There.* Rev. ed. New York: Harper and Row, 1966.

Based on his experience as a journalist and his contacts within South Vietnam, in Chapters 4–6 Shaplen gives a dramatic account of Diem's rise to power and eventual assassination.

Taylor, Maxwell. *Swords and Plowshares.* New York: Norton, 1972.

Taylor served on the Joint Chiefs of Staff under Eisenhower and Kennedy. His autobiography includes several chapters on the Vietnam War he saw as a general and as a diplomat. His assessments of people and policy are thoughtful and provocative.

(For readings on the origins of the National Liberation Front, see chapter 6.)

In Step
Secretary of Defense Robert McNamara seen with South Vietnamese head of state
General Nguyen Khanh, who had overthrown General Minh in January 1964.
McNamara made frequent trips to South Vietnam to meet with the many South
Vietnamese leaders and to get a first-hand picture of American progress in the war.
Francois Sully.

Chapter 4
LBJ Goes to War: 1964–1965

Background

Historical Summary

The situation in South Vietnam was precarious after the Diem regime was overthrown in November 1963. The country's administration was crumbling. Diem's successors, squabbling among themselves, were unable to govern effectively.

In the countryside, meanwhile, peasants were dismantling the strategic hamlets constructed to isolate them from the Vietcong. The Communists, taking advantage of the chaos, increased their attacks against the Saigon government forces with more sophisticated equipment sent by North Vietnam down the Ho Chi Minh Trail.

In the United States, President Kennedy had been assassinated in November 1963, and Vice President Lyndon Johnson had inherited not only the presidency but also America's commitment to support the anti-Communist government in South Vietnam.

Johnson was initially ambivalent toward the commitment. He wanted to steer the United States into a period of vast social reforms, programs he called the Great Society. But he also feared that, without U.S. support, South Vietnam would fall to the Communists. After some hesitation, he gradually deepened America's involvement in the war.

Almost immediately after moving into the White House, Lyndon Johnson had to confront the political challenge of the 1964 presidential election campaign. His Republican opponent was Senator Barry Goldwater of Arizona, a vigorous anti-Communist. But Johnson planned to defeat Goldwater by winning bipartisan backing in Congress, and thus removing the war from the campaign debate.

Johnson's aides drafted a congressional resolution designed to give the president the political approval he sought, and they seized on an incident in Vietnam to secure its passage.

Early in August 1964, two U.S. destroyers deployed in the Gulf of Tonkin off North Vietnam clashed with North Vietnamese patrol boats. American spokesmen claimed that the North Vietnamese attacks had been "unprovoked." The North Vietnamese claimed that the U.S. ships were linked to covert South Vietnamese commando operations against North Vietnam. They also denied that the second of two alleged attacks ever occurred.

Nevertheless, Johnson ordered retaliatory American air raids against North Vietnam for the first time. Simultaneously, both chambers of Congress overwhelmingly passed the Gulf of Tonkin Resolution, which gave the president full authority to commit U.S. forces to Southeast Asia as he saw fit. His attorney general, Nicholas Katzenbach, would later describe the resolution as "the functional equivalent of a declaration of war."

The situation continued to deteriorate in South Vietnam through the latter half of 1964, and once Johnson had won the election his aides pressed him to react strongly. Finally, in February 1965, a Vietcong assault against a U.S. military base in central Vietnam prompted Johnson to respond. He ordered American aircraft to bomb targets in North Vietnam that had been pinpointed by Pentagon strategists months earlier—a sustained air offensive afterward called Operation Rolling Thunder. And to defend the U.S. air fields in South Vietnam, two marine battalions were landed at the coastal town of Danang in March 1965. They were the first American ground combat troops to arrive.

The marines were originally supposed to engage only in defensive actions. But they were soon directed to conduct offensive operations that foreshadowed the massive "search and destroy" missions later carried out by the American forces.

Despite the bombing of the North, the Communists stepped up their infiltration of men and supplies into the South through the spring of 1965. Johnson and his aides, reasoning that South Vietnam could not survive without the introduction of large American units, decided in July 1965 to commit an additional 125,000 U.S. troops. By the end of the year, the U.S. force in Vietnam numbered nearly 200,000 men.

In appealing to the president for the additional troops, General Westmoreland, the U.S. commander in Vietnam, had warned that the Communists were planning to sweep down from the central highlands and cut the country in two. Westmoreland deployed the American forces in the Ia Drang Valley against three North Vietnamese regiments—and the big war had begun.

Points to Emphasize

- the meaning of the domino theory and the reasons for its acceptance by American policy makers
- the strengths and weaknesses of the new president in foreign and domestic affairs
- the incident in the Gulf of Tonkin and its repercussions
- the influence of the 1964 elections on American policy in South Vietnam
- the theory behind the American decision to make continual bombing runs over North Vietnam after February 1965
- the situation which led the United States to send ground troops to South Vietnam
- the debate among President Johnson and his advisors over the wisdom of expanding American military involvement
- the concept of limited war in the nuclear age

Chronology

	1964 Jan	Feb	Mar	Apr	May	Jun	Jul	Aug	Sep
South Vietnam	Nguyen Khanh's coup overthrows Big Minh					General William C. Westmoreland takes command of MACV Maxwell Taylor becomes new U.S. ambassador		Gulf of Tonkin incident U.S. bombs North Vietnam Khanh gives new constitution Musical chairs in Saigon government	Governmental instability in Saigon
United States		Cassius Clay (later Mohammed Ali) wins heavyweight crown				Three civil rights workers murdered in Mississippi	Civil Rights Act becomes law in U.S. Riots in Harlem and other ghettoes	Tonkin Gulf Resolution passed	Warren Commission Report accepted Free speech movement begins at Berkeley
World Wide	France recognizes People's Republic of China Unrest in Panama has anti-American flavor				Nehru dies in India Palestine Liberation Organization established	De Gaulle calls for an end to all foreign intervention in Vietnam			

Chronology *(cont.)*

	1964 Oct	Nov	Dec
South Vietnam			Buddhists and students demonstrate in Saigon
United States	Martin Luther King wins Nobel Peace Prize	Johnson defeats Goldwater	
World Wide	Brezhnev and Kosygin replace Khrushchev China explodes atomic bomb		

Glossary of Names and Terms

George Ball Counsel in Lend Lease Administration and the Foreign Economic Administration, 1942–1944. Undersecretary of State for Economic Affairs, 1961. Undersecretary of State, 1961–1966.

Barry Goldwater Republican Senator from Arizona, 1953–1965 and 1969–present. Republican nominee for President in 1964.

Wayne Morse Senator from Oregon, 1945–1969. Republican turned Independent and eventually Democrat. With Senator Ernest Gruening of Alaska opposed the Gulf of Tonkin Resolution.

Nguyen Cao Ky Air Vice-Marshal, South Vietnam. Prime Minister, South Vietnam, 1965–1967. Vice President of South Vietnam, 1967–1971.

Nguyen Khanh Major General, Army of the Republic of Vietnam (ARVN). Overthrew General Minh, January 30, 1964. Stormy period of rule marked by instability. Ousted within the year.

Maxwell Taylor Chief of Staff, U.S. Army, 1955–1959. Personal military representative to President Kennedy, 1961–1962. Chairman, Joint Chiefs of Staff, 1962–1964. Ambassador to South Vietnam, 1964–1965.

William Westmoreland Superintendent of West Point, 1960–1964. Commander, U.S. Military Assistance Command, Vietnam (MACV), 1964–1968. Chief of Staff, U.S. Army, 1968–1972.

domino theory idea that if South Vietnam fell to the Communists, all of the other states in that region of the world would also topple—like a line of dominoes. First used during Truman administration but widely identified with President Eisenhower and accepted by his successors.

Great Society the object of President Johnson's legislative program. He hoped to extend the measures begun by Democratic administrations since the time of Franklin Roosevelt to bring an end to poverty and ignorance and to facilitate civil rights for all.

Gulf of Tonkin Resolution resolution passed by Congress on August 7, 1964, which became Johnson's "blank check" to set policy in Vietnam. Repealed by Congress in 1970.

Pleiku town in South Vietnam where the United States built a base. After an attack by Viet Cong guerrillas on February 7, 1965, the United States responded by bombing North Vietnam. Sustained reprisals followed later that month. American ground combat troops were sent to Vietnam shortly thereafter.

Thirty-Four A series of covert operations in North Vietnamese waters which were planned by Americans although carried out by the South Vietnamese. Attempted to stop North Vietnamese infiltration into the South by sea and to harass North Vietnamese ports. Kept secret from the American public.

Documents

Document 1

President Johnson had been in office for one month when he received this analysis of the Vietnam situation in December 1963. Defense Secretary Robert McNamara had just returned from one of his frequent trips to South Vietnam and urged in this report that new policies be implemented in that country even though the United States publicly expressed hope for a more stable government under Big Minh. Privately, McNamara was unimpressed by Big Minh's administration and reported that the Strategic Hamlet program had failed to win over the peasants in the countryside. The Secretary of Defense feared that unless the United States took strong steps, South Vietnam would be lost to the free world.

1   **Memorandum for the President**
    Robert McNamara
    December 21, 1963
    Subject: Vietnam Situation
    In accordance with your request this morning, this is a summary of my conclusions after my visit to Vietnam on December 19–20.
       1. *Summary.* The situation is very disturbing. Current trends, unless reversed in the next 2–3 months, will lead to neutralization at best and more likely to a Communist-controlled state.
       2. *The new government* is the greatest source of concern. It is indecisive and drifting. Although Minh states that he, rather than the Committee of Generals, is making decisions, it is not clear that this is actually so. In any event, neither he nor the Committee are experienced in political administration and so far they show little talent for it. There is no clear concept on how to re-shape or conduct the Strategic Hamlet program; the Province Chiefs, most of whom are new and inexperienced, are receiving little or no direction; military operations, too, are not being effectively directed because the generals are so preoccupied with essentially political affairs. A specific example of the present situation is that General Dinh is spending little or no time commanding III Corps, which is in the vital zone around Saigon and needs full-time direction. I made these points as strongly as possible to Minh, Don, Kim, and Tho.
       3. *The Country Team* is the second major weakness. It lacks leadership, has been poorly informed, and is not working to a common plan. A recent example of confusion has been conflicting USOM and military recommendations both to the Government of Vietnam and to Washington on the size of the military budget. Above all, Lodge has virtually no official contact with Harkins. Lodge sends in reports with major military implications without showing them to Harkins, and does not show Harkins important incoming traffic. My impression is that Lodge simply does not know how to conduct a coordinated administration. This has of course been stressed

to him both by Dean Rusk and myself (and also by John McCone), and I do not think he is consciously rejecting our advice; he has just operated as a loner all his life and cannot readily change now.

Lodge's newly-designated deputy, Davis Nes, was with us and seems a highly competent team player. I have stated the situation frankly to him and he has said he would do all he could to constitute what would in effect be an executive committee operating below the level of the Ambassador.

As to the grave reporting weakness, both Defense and CIA must take major steps to improve this. John McCone and I have discussed it and are acting vigorously in our respective spheres.

4. *Viet Cong progress* has been great during the period since the coup, with my best guess being that the situation has in fact been deteriorating in the countryside since July to a far greater extent than we realize because of our undue dependence on distorted Vietnamese reporting. The Viet Cong now control very high proportions of the people in certain key provinces, particularly those directly south and west of Saigon. The Strategic Hamlet Program was seriously over-extended in these provinces, and the Viet Cong has been able to destroy many hamlets, while others have been abandoned or in some cases betrayed or pillaged by the government's own Self Defense Corps. In these key provinces, the Viet Cong have destroyed almost all major roads, and are collecting taxes at will.

As remedial measures, we must get the government to re-allocate its military forces so that its effective strength in these provinces is essentially doubled. We also need to have major increases in both military and USOM staffs, to sizes that will give us a reliable, independent U.S. appraisal of the status of operations. Thirdly, realistic pacification plans must be prepared, allocating adequate time to secure the remaining government-controlled areas and work out from there.

This gloomy picture prevails predominantly in the provinces around the capital and in the Delta. Action to accomplish each of these objectives was started while we were in Saigon. The situation in the northern and central areas is considerably better, and does not seem to have deteriorated substantially in recent months. General Harkins still hopes these areas may be made reasonably secure by the latter half of next year.

In the gloomy southern picture, an exception to the trend of Viet Cong success may be provided by the possible adherence to the government of the Cao Dai and Hoa Hao sects, which total three million people and control key areas along the Cambodian border. The Hoa Hao have already made some sort of agreement, and the Cao Dai are expected to do so at the end of this month. However, it is not clear that their influence will be more than neutralized by these agreements, or that they will in fact really pitch in on the government's side.

5. *Infiltration* of men and equipment from North Vietnam continues using (a) land corridors through Laos and Cambodia; (b) the Mekong River waterways from Cambodia; (c) some possible entry from the sea and the tip of the Delta. The best guess is that 1000–1500 Viet Cong cadres entered South Vietnam from Laos in the first nine months of 1963. The Mekong route (and also the possible sea entry) is apparently used for heavier weapons and ammunition and raw materials which have been turning up in increasing numbers in the south and of which we have captured a few shipments.

To counter this infiltration, we reviewed in Saigon various plans providing for cross-border operations into Laos. On the scale proposed, I am quite clear that these would not be politically acceptable or even militarily effective. Our first need would be immediate U-2 mapping of the whole Laos and Cambodian border, and this we are preparing on an urgent basis.

One other step we can take is to expand the existing limited but remarkably effective operations on the Laos side, the so-called Operation HARDNOSE, so that it at least provides reasonable intelligence on movements all the way along the Laos corridor; plans to expand this will be prepared and presented for approval in about two weeks.

As to the waterways, the military plans presented in Saigon were unsatisfactory, and a special naval team is being sent at once from Honolulu to determine what more can be done. The whole waterway system is so vast, however, that effective policing may be impossible.

In general, the infiltration problem, while serious and annoying, is a lower priority than the key problems discussed earlier. However, we should do what we can to reduce it.

6. *Plans for Covert Action into North Vietnam* were prepared as we had requested and were an excellent job. They present a wide variety of sabotage and psychological operations against North Vietnam from which I believe we should aim to select those that provide maximum pressure with minimum risk. In accordance with your direction at the meeting, General Krulak of the JCS is chairing a group that will lay out a program in the next ten days for your consideration.

7. *Possible neutralization* of Vietnam is strongly opposed by Minh, and our attitude is somewhat suspect because of editorials by the *New York Times* and mention by Walter Lippmann and others. We reassured them as strongly as possible on this—and in somewhat more general terms on the neutralization of Cambodia. I recommend that you convey to Minh a Presidential message for the New Year that would repeat our position in the strongest possible terms and would also be a vehicle to stress the necessity of strong central direction by the government and specifically by Minh himself.

8. *U.S. resources and personnel* cannot usefully be substantially increased. I have directed a modest artillery supplement, and also the provision of uniforms for the Self Defense Corps, which is the most exposed force and suffers from low morale. Of greater potential significance, I have directed the Military Departments to review urgently the quality of the people we are sending to Vietnam. It seems to have fallen off considerably from the high standards applied in the original selections in 1962, and the JCS fully agree with me that we must have our best men there.

Conclusion. My appraisal may be overly pessimistic. Lodge, Harkins, and Minh would probably agree with me on specific points, but feel that January should see significant improvement. We should watch the situation very carefully, running scared, hoping for the best, but preparing for more forceful moves if the situation does not show early signs of improvement.

Document 2

Senator Barry Goldwater, the Republican nominee for president, set forth his proposals for U.S. policy in Vietnam in a section of his 1964 book, *Where I Stand*. Goldwater felt that the Democrats were not using American power effectively and stated that his aim as president would be, simply, victory—a goal which, he concluded, could only be achieved through strength.

Goldwater was often attacked for being an extremist, but he made no apologies for the positions he took. In accepting the presidential nomination in 1964 he argued "extremism in the defense of liberty is no vice. Moderation in the pursuit of justice is no virtue." And, convinced that most Americans would soon agree with him, Goldwater's campaign slogan was "In your heart, you know he's right."

2 Victory in Asia
Barry Goldwater

The basic requirement for an effective U.S. policy in Southeast Asia is the decision—and the will to back it up—that *victory* is our goal.

American fighting men are being killed in Vietnam by the Communists. We are not out there in great numbers; but to our boys on the firing line—and to their loved ones back home—they are in a war. If we have learned anything from the tragic lesson of Korea, if we can draw any guidance from the life of one of history's great military figures, Douglas MacArthur, it might well be this—that in war there is no substitute for victory.

No responsible world leader suggests that we should withdraw our support from Vietnam. To do so would unhinge a vast and vital area, thereby committing to Communist domination its resources and its people. This we cannot do. Therefore, we need the dedication and the courage to face some hard and unpleasant facts. We are at war in Vietnam and we must have the will to win that war.

With that key decision made, we can by every diplomatic and military means at our disposal begin to give our armed forces engaged there the kind of support they deserve. They have not been getting it. There is no more shameful episode in this Administration's record of fumbling and futility than the plain fact that we have required American boys to fight this war with obsolete, cast-off World War II equipment.

It is more than a question of morale: it is a question of life-or-death for our American fighting men. This, I repeat, is no minor skirmish. It is a major battlefield of the free-world struggle against the Communist threat to engulf all of free Asia. And our allies, in Europe as well as in Asia, ought to be supporting our efforts.

This nation must back up its resolve with whatever manpower, equipment, and weaponry it may take, first to stem the Communist advance in Laos and Vietnam, and then to help these countries, along with their neighbors in Thailand, to create conditions of stability and freedom in Southeast Asia. The security of all Asia hinges on this crucial battle.

The Communists have violated neutral territory to maintain supply routes to the Viet Cong guerrillas. Sound military tactics call for the interdiction of these supply lines, a basic military move as old as history. We must not again—as we did in Korea—tolerate a so-called "privileged sanctuary" from which Communism feeds its military aggression in Vietnam. America cannot again afford the tragedy of sending our boys into a war we will not permit them to win.

Peace in Asia depends on our strength, and on our purpose to use that strength to achieve peace. Nowhere in the world today is there a clearer road to *peace through strength* than in Vietnam.

Document 3

In 1964 the government of South Vietnam changed seven times. Frequently, the same individuals remained in the cabinet, but in different roles. Nevertheless, the changes were disturbing to anyone trying to work with the South Vietnamese government, and the American ambassador was particularly upset. After several young Vietnamese officers became involved in yet another political reshuffling in December of that year, Ambassador Taylor called them together and spoke bluntly.

3   Record of Meeting Between Ambassador Taylor and a Group of Vietnamese Military Officers
December 20, 1964

. . . AMBASSADOR TAYLOR: Do all of you understand English? (Vietnamese officers indicated they did, although the understanding of General Thi was known to be weak.) I told you all clearly at General Westmoreland's dinner we Americans were tired of coups. Apparently I wasted my words. Maybe this is because something is wrong with my French because you evidently didn't understand. I made it clear that all the military plans which I know you would like to carry out are dependent on governmental stability. Now you have made a real mess. We cannot carry you forever if you do things like this. Who speaks for this group? Do you have a spokesman?

GENERAL KY: I am not the spokesman for the group but I do speak English. I will explain why the Armed Forces took this action last night.

We understand English very well. We are aware of our responsibilities, we are aware of the sacrifices of our people over twenty years. We know you want stability, but you cannot have stability until you have unity . . . But still there are rumors of coups and doubts among groups. We think these rumors come from the HNC, not as an organization but from some of its members. Both military and civilian leaders regard the presence of these people in the HNC as divisive of the Armed Forces due to their influence.

Recently the Prime Minister showed us a letter he had received from the Chairman of the HNC. This letter told the Prime Minister to beware of the military, and said that maybe the military would want to come back to power. Also the HNC illegally sought to block the retirement of the generals that the Armed Forces Council unanimously recommended be retired in order to improve unity in the Armed Forces.

GENERAL THIEU: The HNC cannot be bosses because of the Constitution. Its members must prove that they want to fight.

GENERAL KY: It looks as though the HNC does not want unity. It does not want to fight the Communists.

It has been rumored that our action of last night was an intrigue of Khanh against Minh, who must be retired. Why do we seek to retire these generals? Because they had their chance and did badly . . .

Yesterday we met, twenty of us, from 1430 to 2030. We reached agreement that we must take some action. We decided to arrest the bad members of the HNC, bad politicians, bad student leaders, and the leaders of the Committee of National Salvation, which is a Communist organization. We must put the trouble-making organizations out of action and ask the Prime Minister and the Chief of State to stay in office.

After we explain to the people why we did this at a press conference, we would like to return to our fighting units. We have no political ambitions. We seek strong, unified, and stable Armed Forces to support the struggle and a stable government. Chief of State Suu agrees with us. General Khanh saw Huong who also agreed.

We did what we thought was good for this country; we tried to have a civilian government clean house. If we have achieved it, fine. We are now ready to go back to our units.

AMBASSADOR TAYLOR: I respect the sincerity of you gentlemen. Now I would like to talk to you about the consequences of what you have done. But first, would any of the other officers wish to speak?

ADMIRAL CANG: It seems that we are being treated as though we were guilty. What we did was good and we did it only for the good of the country.

AMBASSADOR TAYLOR: Now let me tell you how I feel about it, what I think the consequences are: first of all, this is a military coup that has destroyed the government-making process that, to the admiration of the whole world, was set up last fall largely through the statesman-like acts of the Armed Forces.

You cannot go back to your units, General Ky. You military are now back in power. You are up to your necks in politics.

Your statement makes it clear that you have constituted yourselves again substantially as a Military Revolutionary Committee. The dissolution of the HNC was totally illegal. Your decree recognized the Chief of State and the Huong Government but this recognition is something that you could withdraw. This will be interpreted as a return of the military to power . . .

AMBASSADOR TAYLOR: Who commands the Armed Forces? General Khanh?

GENERAL KY: Yes, sir . . .

GENERAL THIEU: In spite of what you say, it should be noted that the Vietnamese Commander-in-Chief is in a special situation. He therefore needs advisors. We do not want to force General Khanh; we advise him. We will do what he orders . . .

AMBASSADOR TAYLOR: Would your officers be willing to come into a government if called upon to do so by Huong? I have been impressed by the high quality of many Vietnamese officers. I am sure that many of the most able men in this country are in uniform. Last fall when the HNC and Huong Government was being formed, I suggested to General Khanh there should be some military participation, but my suggestions were not accepted. It would therefore be natural for some of them now to be called upon to serve in the government. Would you be willing to do so? . . .

GENERAL KY: Nonetheless, I would object to the idea of the military going back into the government right away. People will say it is a military coup.

AMBASSADOR TAYLOR and AMBASSADOR JOHNSON: (Together) People will say it anyway . . .

AMBASSADOR TAYLOR: You have destroyed the Charter. The Chief of State will still have to prepare for elections. Nobody believes that the Chief of State has either the power or the ability to do this without the HNC or some other advisory body. If I were the Prime Minister, I would simply overlook the destruction of the HNC. But we are preserving the HNC itself. You need a legislative branch and you need this particular step in the formation of a government with National Assembly . . .

AMBASSADOR TAYLOR: It should be noted that Prime Minister Huong has not accepted the dissolution of the HNC . . .

GENERAL THIEU: What kind of concession does Huong want from us?

Ambassador Taylor again noted the need for the HNC function.

GENERAL KY: Perhaps it is better if we now let General Khanh and Prime Minister Huong talk.

GENERAL THIEU: After all, we did not arrest all the members of the HNC. Of nine members we detained only five. These people are not under arrest. They are simply under controlled residence . . .

AMBASSADOR TAYLOR: Our problem now, gentlemen, is to organize our work for the rest of the day. For one thing, the government will have to issue a communique.

GENERAL THIEU: We will still have a press conference this afternoon but only to say why we acted as we did.

AMBASSADOR TAYLOR: I have real troubles on the U.S. side. I don't know whether we will continue to support you after this. Why don't you tell your friends before you act? I regret the need for my blunt talk today but we have lots at stake . . .

AMBASSADOR TAYLOR: And was it really all that necessary to carry out the arrests that very night? Couldn't this have been put off a day or two? . . .

In taking a friendly leave, Ambassador Taylor said: You people have broken a lot of dishes and now we have to see how we can straighten out this mess.

Document 4

Hans Morgenthau, an academic commentator on the events in South Vietnam, questioned a fundamental principle upon which American policy was built—the idea that the average inhabitant of South Vietnam was willing to fight against the National Liberation Front on the side of the South Vietnamese government. Morgenthau was not convinced that the North Vietnamese had started the war or that, in the wake of the Sino-Soviet split, there was a monolithic Communist plan to take over the world.

Morgenthau argued that the fighting in Vietnam was a civil war and that the United States should not be involved.

4   The Realities of Containment
Hans J. Morgenthau
June 8, 1964

It is difficult, hazardous and painful to try to discover beneath the layers of official pronouncements the hard rational core of the alternatives open to us in Southeast Asia. There can be no doubt that much of what is being said officially about what we shall do in that part of the world is aimed at deterring the enemy, hardening our friends, disarming the domestic opposition and preventing a catastrophe from occurring before Nov. 1964. What we shall do in the end will not depend so much upon what we now say we are going to do as upon what we think we can do without undue risks and with a chance for success.

Our presence in Vietnam and our general commitment to the preservation of the status quo in Southeast Asia has a dual purpose: the containment of Communism and the containment of China. While 10 years ago these two purposes indeed coincided, they do not necessarily do so today when the Communist world is rent by polycentrism and the Soviet-Chinese split. In order to understand the rational choices open to us it is therefore necessary to distinguish these two purposes.

Ten years ago, anti-Communism was the prevailing mood of South Vietnam. Almost a million refugees had come from the north to escape Communism, and it will remain the historic merit of the late President Ngo Dinh Diem that he personified and organized resistance to it. Of that anti-Communist mood, little is left today. When 10 years ago we committed ourselves to the support and defense of the anti-Communist regime of South Vietnam, our policies and the aspirations of the people of South Vietnam coincided. They do not coincide now.

The great mass of the South Vietnamese people are today either indifferent or hostile to our policies. They have one aim: to be done with what they regard as senseless slaughter and destruction. Thus our main immediate problem is apparently not to win the war against the Viet Cong but to prevent the ascendancy of an anti-war government in Saigon. What we are saying and doing must, then, have as its main purpose to prevent the collapse of the morale of General Nguyen Khanh's government and of its military forces.

We are not fully informed—to put it mildly—of the degree to which that morale has already deteriorated. The government of Saigon is lucky when its troops just desert rather than join the Viet Cong. Some time ago, 600 Viet Cong were surrounded by 2,000 government troops. When the Communists attacked, the commander of the government forces "lost control" of his troops—that is, his troops ran away. It is not surprising, therefore, that the Viet Cong are primarily supplied with U.S. weapons, abandoned or surrendered by government troops.

It is futile, of course, to expect that our latest remedy—the quantitative expansion of such an army, already enjoying approximately a 10–1 superiority over the Viet Cong—can have any effect upon the political and military situation except to increase Viet Cong chances of acquiring additional recruits and weapons. As the Saigon *Post* put it on May 20, 1964: "It is plain common sense that it takes much more than money to win a war. What we need are men to do the job, men with the will to undergo sacrifices in order to win." It is tiresome but necessary to say again what has been said so many times before: The problem is political and not military, and it is impossible to win the war in Vietnam without the political support of at least a very substantial segment of the population.

Popular support can be strengthened from the outside where it exists; but it cannot be created from the outside. When we found the anti-Communist mood in South Vietnam 10 years ago, we could support it, and we were successful in doing so. When Diem lost popular support and was kept in power long after he had become a political liability, the known evils of a discredited anti-Communism seemed to many Vietnamese to be at least as bad as the unknown evils of Communism. Short of the miraculous appearance of an anti-Communist national leader with charismatic powers, there appears to be no chance of restoring those ties between government and people which, once severed, are severed forever.

The French found that out in Indochina and Algeria. A few weeks ago, I asked the opinion of a French general who commanded French forces in Indochina. He told me that when he was offered that command, his predecessor warned him not to take it because he could not win and it would ruin his health. A year later, his health was ruined and victory was not in sight, and he gave the same warning to his presumptive successor, with the same negative result. Once they are emotionally committed, men and nations do not appear to be susceptible to rational argument.

Adverse experience must teach them what reason cannot, and the best reason can do is to shorten the time which experience needs to teach its lessons.

If the war in South Vietnam cannot be won without the political support of the population, it cannot be won either by expanding it northward. The proposal to extend the war to North Vietnam rests upon two assumptions; that there exists a direct causal nexus between the war in South Vietnam and the policies of the North Vietnamese government, and that the war in South Vietnam can be won by rupturing this causal nexus. Neither assumption has any basis in fact.

The war in South Vietnam is a civil war, aided and abetted by the North Vietnamese government but neither created nor sustained by it. To call it "foreign aggression" is to misrepresent the facts and thereby confuse the issue with which our policy must come to terms. The distances and terrain in Vietnam make it impossible for anything more than token support to reach the guerrillas in the Mekong Delta from the north.

Yet even if the government of North Vietnam had the power to end the civil war in the south by withdrawing its support, it would certainly require more than some token raids to bring North Vietnam to its knees. And is it conceivable that China, in view of its national interests confirmed by 2,000 years of history and recent experiences in Korea and Laos, would remain idle if this should come to pass?

. . .

It is probably idle, but nevertheless illuminating, to speculate on how a Richelieu or Bismarck, given responsibility for our foreign policy, would approach the problem of Southeast Asia. They would not have allowed themselves to get committed in a civil war which cannot be won short of a political miracle. Nor would they have allowed themselves to get involved elsewhere in piecemeal military commitments at the periphery of China. Instead, they would have sought to appear to the governments of Southeast Asia, Communist or non-Communist, as the protector from Chinese domination by committing the total power of the United States to that end. And they would have put the vaunted new amenability of Soviet foreign policy to the test by marshalling its support for the Communist governments of the area against Chinese domination.

The unreality of these propositions is the measure of the irrationality of our policies in Southeast Asia. Only humiliation or catastrophe awaits us there as long as we persist in our simple-minded combination of indiscriminate ideological opposition to all Communist governments with peripheral military containment of a potentially great power. For such opposition, driving the Communist governments of Asia into the arms of China, defeats containment, and the end of containment is in the long run not likely to be achieved with the limited military means chosen.

Document 5

In February 1965, a State Department White Paper asserted that the North Vietnamese "inspired, directed, supplied, and controlled" the Vietcong, and that therefore the conflict in South Vietnam was not a civil war as some had claimed. The report equated the "North Vietnamese invasion of South Vietnam" with the North Korean invasion of South Korea, when American intervention had been sanctioned by the United Nations.

Also in February 1965 Operation Rolling Thunder, the bombing of North

Logevall pp 358 elsewhere

Vietnam, began. American policy makers claimed that bombing the North would make Ho Chi Minh stop supporting the Vietcong and would thus hasten the end of the war.

5 State Department White Paper
February 1965

South Viet-Nam is fighting for its life against a brutal campaign of terror and armed attack inspired, directed, supplied, and controlled by the Communist regime in Hanoi. This flagrant aggression has been going on for years, but recently the pace has quickened and the threat has now become acute.

The war in Viet-Nam is a new kind of war, a fact as yet poorly understood in most parts of the world. Much of the confusion that prevails in the thinking of many people, and even many governments, stems from this basic misunderstanding. For in Viet-Nam a totally new brand of aggression has been loosed against an independent people who want to make their own way in peace and freedom.

Viet-Nam is *not* another Greece, where indigenous guerrilla forces used friendly neighboring territory as a sanctuary.

Viet-Nam is *not* another Malaya, where Communist guerrillas were, for the most part, physically distinguishable from the peaceful majority they sought to control.

Viet-Nam is *not* another Philippines, where Communist guerrillas were physically separated from the source of their moral and physical support.

Above all, the war in Viet-Nam is *not* a spontaneous and local rebellion against the established government.

There are elements in the Communist program of conquest directed against South Viet-Nam common to each of the previous areas of aggression and subversion. But there is one fundamental difference. In Viet-Nam a Communist government has set out deliberately to conquer a sovereign people in a neighboring state. And to achieve its end, it has used every resource of its own government to carry out its carefully planned program of concealed aggression. North Viet-Nam's commitment to seize control of the South is no less total than was the commitment of the regime in North Korea in 1950. But knowing the consequences of the latter's undisguised attack, the planners in Hanoi have tried desperately to conceal their hand. They have failed and their aggression is as real as that of an invading army.

This report is a summary of the massive evidence of North Vietnamese aggression obtained by the government of South Viet-Nam. This evidence has been jointly analyzed by South Vietnamese and American experts.

The evidence shows that the hard core of the Communist forces attacking South Viet-Nam were trained in the North and ordered into the South by Hanoi. It shows that the key leadership of the Viet-Cong (VC), the officers and much of the cadre, many of the technicians, political organizers, and propagandists have come from the North and operate under Hanoi's direction. It shows that the training of essential military personnel and their infiltration into the South is directed by the Military High Command in Hanoi.

The evidence shows that many of the weapons and much of the ammunition and other supplies used by the Viet-Cong have been sent into South Viet-Nam from Hanoi. In recent months new types of weapons have been introduced in the VC army, for which all ammunition must come from outside sources. Communist China and other Communist states have been the prime suppliers of these weapons and ammunition, and they have been channeled primarily through North Viet-Nam.

The directing force behind the effort to conquer South Viet-Nam is the Communist Party in the North, the Lao Dong (Workers) Party. As in every Communist state, the party is an integral part of the regime itself. North Vietnamese officials have expressed their firm determination to absorb South Viet-Nam into the Communist world. . . .

Document 6

In the spring of 1965, former Vice President Richard M. Nixon made a speech on the Vietnam War. In this speech, Nixon agreed with the aim of President Johnson's policy—an independent, non-Communist South Vietnam. Like Johnson, Nixon believed in the domino theory and that the United States had to stop Communist expansion. Although not simply advocating victory as Goldwater had, Nixon faulted the president for not going far enough. Nixon urged that a long-range diplomatic plan be formulated to insure the independence and security of Asia.

6   Address by Richard M. Nixon to the Commonwealth Club of California
April 2, 1965

Today the most difficult decision facing President Johnson is South Vietnam, the most difficult decision he will make during his Presidency, I believe, at home or abroad. And it is the most important decision for the United States and the free world.

There are times when the loyal opposition should support an administration. Lyndon B. Johnson needs this support not only because of the validity of his policy but because there is a deep division in his own party.

Our greatest danger to the future of our policy on Vietnam is because the Democratic party is divided. Forty-five Democratic Senators have indicated opposition.

The interests of America, the free world and of South Vietnam are being served by the present policy.

Some claim the United States has no legal right in South Vietnam and that we are involved in a civil war. Some say the war will not be won because the Vietnamese are not willing to do what is necessary.

Others believe that, even if the war could be won, the risks are too great. Many suggest another way out—negotiation—neutralization.

Lyndon Johnson should answer each of these objections now. He might well have done this before now. Not enough people know why we should support the South Vietnamese.

First, who is responsible for the war? If it were not for support of the guerrillas by North Vietnam there would be no war; no war, at least, which would require our support. If it were not for Chinese support for North Vietnam there would be no war requiring American support.

This is a confrontation—not fundamentally between Vietnam and the Vietcong or between the United States and the Vietcong—but between the United States and Communist China.

This must not be glossed over because if we gloss it over we underestimate the risks and do not understand the stakes.

Those who question our presence ignore certain facts. In 1954 a convention was signed in Geneva guaranteeing South Vietnam its independence. The North Vietnamese are there as lawbreakers. We are there as law enforcers, by invitation of the South Vietnamese Government.

What are the risks, the stakes? First, the fate of 15,000,000 Vietnamese. Two hundred thousand Vietnamese casualties in the fight against Communism over the years, prove they have the desire and will to keep their country free and independent.

In Vietnam today there is determination of the people to save their freedom—provided they have the conviction they will win.

These are fundamental reasons the stronger course of action will be more effective than may seem today.

Fifteen million people are worth saving but many argue that this is not enough to risk major confrontation and Chinese Communist intervention.

If South Vietnam fails, through U.S. withdrawal, political settlement, or neutralization (which is surrender on the installment plan), there is no doubt that Cambodia (already on the brink) will go; that Laos, practically gone now because of our gullibility, will go; that Thailand (which wants to be on our side but has held her independence by being on the winning side) will go; that Burma, an economic basket case; and that Indonesia will go.

Indonesia will follow Sukarno and Sukarno once said that because of the American failure in Asia, the Communists were the wave of the future and he would be on the winning side.

Indonesia has half the world's tin; half the world's rubber. It is only 14 miles from the Philippines where guerrillas and Huk activity have begun again—guerrilla activity easily supported by Indonesian Communists.

In three or four years, then, we would have the necessity of saving the Philippines. Could we avoid a major war to save the Philippines?

Japan is the biggest prize in Asia, a miracle of economic recovery, the only possible economic counterpart to China. Strong neutralist forces are now growing in Japan. If Southeast Asia goes Communist, Japan will eventually be pulled irresistibly into the Red orbit.

If the United States gives up on Vietnam, Asia will give up on the United States and the Pacific will become a Red sea. These are the stakes. And this is the reason the Johnson administration has decided to win in Vietnam—no more, no less.

The possibilities of winning? How could it be possible that, where 300,000 Frenchmen on the ground failed, 25,000 Americans can expect success? But when the French were in Vietnam they were fighting to stay in—while the United States is fighting to get out.

The Vietnamese had very little interest in fighting to preserve French colonialism. The Vietnamese have a very great interest in fighting against Communist colonialism. That's why they fight with a will today.

Risks must always be weighed. There is a risk of Russian intervention. This risk is small due to the logistic problems involved, and because the Soviets are not particularly interested in seeing the Chinese Communists succeed in their foreign policy objectives for Asia.

A greater risk is Chinese Communist intervention. Some say this is inevitable, that the Chinese Communists would come in to save North Vietnam from defeat. That is subject to serious question.

Comparing the situation now with Korea in 1950, there are major differences. Now Russia and Communist China are opponents. Then they were allies.

China without Russia is a fourth-rate military power. And that is the situation

China must confront if it decides to intervene. That is probably the reason Communist China is talking big but acting little without risking a confrontation with the United States, at this point, over Vietnam.

Adding it all, we must assume that Communist China might intervene. What should our decision be, weighing that risk and that possibility? It must be the same, because it is a choice not between that risk and no risk—but that risk and a greater risk.

In the event that Vietnam falls, and in the event that the balance of Southeast Asia falls, in four to five years, the United States would be confronted inevitably with a war to save the Philippines or in some other area in Asia and we would be confronting a China stronger than she is now. China today is diplomatically and militarily weaker than she will ever be in the future.

Today China has a minimal nuclear capability but that capability increases daily. It is a risk we must weigh. Do we stop Chinese Communist aggression in Vietnam now or wait until the odds and the risks are much greater?

The United States must make a decision as to what our goals are to be. Our goals are presently limited to winning the war, without unconditional surrender, without destroying North Vietnam, without destroying Communist China. It is a limited objective but one which must be achieved.

What are the alternatives? Many well-intentioned people have suggested, Why not negotiate? Negotiation is a good word. All wars are ended by negotiation. But to negotiate now would mean that the United States could negotiate only surrender, coalition government, a division of South Vietnam, or neutralization, which is surrender on the installment plan.

Negotiating with the Communists now would be like negotiating with Hitler when he had France practically occupied.

We must negotiate independence and freedom for Vietnam. We cannot do that now. Once we have gained the military advantage, once North Vietnam and Communist China are convinced they cannot take over South Vietnam, then we can negotiate the freedom and independence of South Vietnam. Until then, we cannot.

Neutralization? Neutralism, where Communists are concerned, means only three things: we get in, we get out; they stay in, and they take over. That is why we can't agree to a neutralization of South Vietnam. The choice we have is to get out completely or to stay in until we achieve freedom and independence for Vietnam.

The future is our main problem. The world has been given the impression that this is our war; that we are there unilaterally for our own selfish purposes. We are there for our purposes, true, but we are there because the freedom of all Asia, not just Vietnam, is involved.

Several suggestions can be made for future policy. Once the war is won in Vietnam, we must recognize that it will only be the winning of a single battle as far as the Communists are concerned.

It took Mao twenty years to conquer China. This is Mao Tse-tung's theory of a long war. He lost many battles, but he won the long war. If Vietnam is lost to Communist China, the long war will be stepped up in Indonesia or somewhere else.

There must be a counterforce, an alternative to Mao's long war. Let me make several suggestions. There is no question as to Communist China's purpose and plan. They have one. And they are determined. But free Asia does not have a plan. It does not have a purpose. It is necessary to mobilize free Asia's economic and military resources so there will be the lasting alternative of peace under freedom as against the long war of Communism.

President Johnson started down this road when he suggested an Asian economic plan. Let's go further; we need a conference of free Asian nations, including South Vietnam, Cambodia, Laos, Thailand, Malaysia, Burma, Indonesia, Taiwan, the Philippines, Japan, South Korea, and possibly Australia and New Zealand.

Such a conference would have three major objectives: One, economic development—a Marshall plan for Asia; a Marshall plan involving industrial development, free trade areas, and all other aspects which mean economic development for the whole area.

The difficulty is in stopping there and that is all that is suggested by the administration. Economic strength alone is not enough to stop Communism, for in South Vietnam, economic conditions are much better than in the North.

Second, in Europe, the Marshall plan could not have succeeded economically unless it had the NATO military shield. There needs to be a military alliance of free Asian nations to stop any Communist aggression against freedom.

The third step is to meet the problem of indirect aggression. There should be something like the Caracas resolution of 1954 that in event of a revolution with Communist support from abroad (as in Vietnam), all nations involved would band together to resist conquest by indirect aggression.

Now that we've stepped up military activity in Vietnam, we need to step up our diplomatic offensive in all of Asia.

We need a charter for freedom for the Pacific—an alternative to the seeming inevitability, at least to many in Asia, of Chinese Communist domination.

Often overlooked today is the fact that the economic power of the nations cited is twice as great as that of Communist China today—if it can be mobilized, if it can be united, if the United States can support it.

There is no question but that this could be the great step forward which would stop Chinese Communist aggression and the inevitable takeover of the heartland and peripheral areas of Asia as well.

I spoke of the stakes—Southeast Asia, Japan, the Pacific—but they're much greater than that. A great debate is going on in the Communist world and what happens in Vietnam will determine its course. The debate is between the hardliners in Peiping and the so-called softliners in Moscow. The softliners (oversimplified), because of a risk of confrontation with the United States, are not supporting revolutions to the same extent that they did. The hardliners say, "We must step up our tactics and support of revolution all over the world."

In the event the hardliners succeed in Vietnam, that will be the green light for aggression in Africa, Latin America—all over the world. If they are stopped in Vietnam, that will be a lesson just as Korea was a lesson on the use of overt aggression.

It will be a lesson to the Communists attempting to take over a nation through indirect aggression that the United States and the free world have an answer to it.

So what is involved here is not just Asia, but a battle for the whole world and because that is so, risks must be taken—risks which, I believe, in the long run will bring peace and freedom. But the alternatives could be war and loss of freedom.

In 1938, immediately after Munich, Winston Churchill said: "The belief that you can gain security by throwing a small state to the wolves is a fatal delusion." He was right about Czechoslovakia in 1938. And today, with regard to Vietnam, the belief that we can gain security by throwing a small state to the wolves is a fatal delusion. In this year when we honor Churchill the man, we will do well to heed Churchill's principles.

Document 7

In his speech at Johns Hopkins University on April 7, 1965, President Johnson described his determination to safeguard the existence of South Vietnam. The address was noteworthy because in it Johnson offered incentives which he hoped would bring North Vietnam to the bargaining table.

Negotiation became the theme of most of the president's speeches for the rest of his term in office. To protect the independence of South Vietnam, Johnson was trying to fight a limited war, without using the full arsenal of the United States, and without destroying North Vietnam. But, Johnson warned the world, as long as the North Vietnamese sought military confrontation, there would be war.

7   Peace Without Conquest
Lyndon Baines Johnson
April 7, 1965

. . . Tonight Americans and Asians are dying for a world where each people may choose its own path to change.

This is the principle for which our ancestors fought in the valleys of Pennsylvania. It is the principle for which our sons fight tonight in the jungles of Viet-Nam.

Viet-Nam is far away from this quiet campus. We have no territory there, nor do we seek any. The war is dirty and brutal and difficult. And some 400 young men, born into an America that is bursting with opportunity and promise, have ended their lives on Viet-Nam's steaming soil.

Why must we take this painful road?

Why must this Nation hazard its ease, and its interest, and its power for the sake of a people so far away?

We fight because we must fight if we are to live in a world where every country can shape its own destiny. And only in such a world will our own freedom be finally secure.

This kind of world will never be built by bombs or bullets. Yet the infirmities of man are such that force must often precede reason, and the waste of war, the works of peace.

We wish that this were not so. But we must deal with the world as it is, if it is ever to be as we wish.

The Nature of the Conflict

The world as it is in Asia is not a serene or peaceful place.

The first reality is that North Viet-Nam has attacked the independent nation of South Viet-Nam. Its object is total conquest.

Of course, some of the people of South Viet-Nam are participating in attack on their own government. But trained men and supplies, orders and arms, flow in a constant stream from north to south.

This support is the heartbeat of the war.

And it is a war of unparalleled brutality. Simple farmers are the targets of assassination and kidnapping. Women and children are strangled in the night because their men are loyal to their government. And helpless villages are ravaged by sneak attacks. Large-scale raids are conducted on towns, and terror strikes in the heart of cities.

The confused nature of this conflict cannot mask the fact that it is the new face of an old enemy.

Over this war—and all Asia—is another reality: the deepening shadow of Communist China. The rulers in Hanoi are urged on by Peking. This is a regime which has destroyed freedom in Tibet, which has attacked India, and has been condemned by the United Nations for aggression in Korea. It is a nation which is helping the forces of violence in almost every continent. The contest in Viet-Nam is part of a wider pattern of aggressive purposes.

Why Are We in Viet-Nam?

Why are these realities our concern? Why are we in South Viet-Nam?

We are there because we have a promise to keep. Since 1954 every American President has offered support to the people of South Viet-Nam. We have helped to build, and we have helped to defend. Thus, over many years, we have made a national pledge to help South Viet-Nam defend its independence.

And I intend to keep that promise.

To dishonor that pledge, to abandon this small and brave nation to its enemies, and to the terror that must follow, would be an unforgivable wrong.

We are also there to strengthen world order. Around the globe, from Berlin to Thailand, are people whose well-being rests, in part, on the belief that they can count on us if they are attacked. To leave Viet-Nam to its fate would shake the confidence of all these people in the value of an American commitment and in the value of America's word. The result would be increased unrest and instability, and even wider war.

We are also there because there are great stakes in the balance. Let no one think for a moment that retreat from Viet-Nam would bring an end to conflict. The battle would be renewed in one country and then another. The central lesson of our time is that the appetite of aggression is never satisfied. To withdraw from one battlefield means only to prepare for the next. We must say in southeast Asia—as we did in Europe—in the words of the Bible: "Hitherto shalt thou come, but no further."

There are those who say that all our effort there will be futile—that China's power is such that it is bound to dominate all southeast Asia. But there is no end to that argument until all of the nations of Asia are swallowed up.

There are those who wonder why we have a responsibility there. Well, we have it there for the same reason that we have a responsibility for the defense of Europe. World War II was fought in both Europe and Asia, and when it ended we found ourselves with continued responsibility for the defense of freedom.

Our Objective in Viet-Nam

Our objective is the independence of South Viet-Nam, and its freedom from attack. We want nothing for ourselves—only that the people of South Viet-Nam be allowed to guide their own country in their own way.

We will do everything necessary to reach that objective. And we will do only what is absolutely necessary.

In recent months attacks on South Viet-Nam were stepped up. Thus, it became necessary for us to increase our response and to make attacks by air. This is not a change of purpose. It is a change in what we believe that purpose requires.

We do this in order to slow down aggression.

We do this to increase the confidence of the brave people of South Viet-Nam who have bravely borne this brutal battle for so many years with so many casualties.

And we do this to convince the leaders of North Viet-Nam—and all who seek to share their conquest—of a very simple fact:

We will not be defeated.

We will not grow tired.

We will not withdraw, either openly or under the cloak of a meaningless agreement.

We know that air attacks alone will not accomplish all of these purposes. But it is our best and prayerful judgment that they are a necessary part of the surest road to peace.

We hope that peace will come swiftly. But that is in the hands of others besides ourselves. And we must be prepared for a long continued conflict. It will require patience as well as bravery, the will to endure as well as the will to resist.

I wish it were possible to convince others with words of what we now find it necessary to say with guns and planes: Armed hostility is futile. Our resources are equal to any challenge. Because we fight for values and we fight for principles, rather than territory or colonies, our patience and our determination are unending.

Once this is clear, then it should also be clear that the only path for reasonable men is the path of peaceful settlement.

Such peace demands an independent South Viet-Nam—securely guaranteed and able to shape its own relationships to all others—free from outside interference—tied to no alliance—a military base for no other country.

These are the essentials of any final settlement.

We will never be second in the search for such a peaceful settlement in Viet-Nam.

There may be many ways to this kind of peace: in discussion or negotiation with the governments concerned; in large groups or in small ones; in the reaffirmation of old agreements or their strengthening with new ones.

We have stated this position over and over again, fifty times and more, to friend and foe alike. And we remain ready, with this purpose, for unconditional discussions.

And until that bright and necessary day of peace we will try to keep conflict from spreading. We have no desire to see thousands die in battle—Asians or Americans. We have no desire to devastate that which the people of North Viet-Nam have built with toil and sacrifice. We will use our power with restraint and with all the wisdom that we can command.

But we will use it.

This war, like most wars, is filled with terrible irony. For what do the people of North Viet-Nam want? They want what their neighbors also desire: food for their hunger; health for their bodies; a chance to learn; progress for their country; and an end to the bondage of material misery. And they would find all these things far more readily in peaceful association with others than in the endless course of battle.

A Cooperative Effort for Development

These countries of southeast Asia are homes for millions of impoverished people. Each day these people rise at dawn and struggle through until the night to wrestle existence from the soil. They are often wracked by disease, plagued by hunger, and death comes at the early age of 40.

Stability and peace do not come easily in such a land. Neither independence nor human dignity will ever be won, though, by arms alone. It also requires the work of peace. The American people have helped generously in times past in these works. Now there must be a much more massive effort to improve the life of man in that conflict-torn corner of our world.

The first step is for the countries of southeast Asia to associate themselves in a greatly expanded cooperative effort for development. We would hope that North Viet-Nam would take its place in the common effort just as soon as peaceful cooperation is possible. . . .

The task is nothing less than to enrich the hopes and the existence of more than a hundred million people. And there is much to be done.

The vast Mekong River can provide food and water and power on a scale to dwarf even our own TVA.

The wonders of modern medicine can be spread through villages where thousands die every year from lack of care.

Schools can be established to train people in the skills that are needed to manage the process of development.

And these objectives, and more, are within the reach of a cooperative and determined effort.

I also intend to expand and speed up a program to make available our farm surpluses to assist in feeding and clothing the needy in Asia. We should not allow people to go hungry and wear rags while our own warehouses overflow with an abundance of wheat and corn, rice and cotton. . . .

For centuries nations have struggled among each other. But we dream of a world where disputes are settled by law and reason. And we will try to make it so.

For most of history men have hated and killed one another in battle. But we dream of an end to war. And we will try to make it so.

For all existence most men have lived in poverty, threatened by hunger. But we dream of a world where all are fed and charged with hope. And we will help to make it so.

The ordinary men and women of North Viet-Nam and South Viet-Nam—of China and India—of Russia and America—are brave people. They are filled with the same proportions of hate and fear, of love and hope. Most of them want the same things for themselves and their familes. Most of them do not want their sons to ever die in battle, or to see their homes, or the homes of others, destroyed.

Well, this can be their world yet. Man now has the knowledge—always before denied—to make this planet serve the real needs of the people who live on it.

I know this will not be easy. I know how difficult it is for reason to guide passion, and love to master hate. The complexities of this world do not bow easily to pure and consistent answers.

But the simple truths are there just the same. We must all try to follow them as best we can.

Conclusion

We often say how impressive power is. But I do not find it impressive at all. The guns and the bombs, the rockets and the warships, are all symbols of human failure. They are necessary symbols. They protect what we cherish. But they are witness to human folly.

A dam built across a great river is impressive.

In the countryside where I was born, and where I live, I have seen the night illuminated, and the kitchens warmed, and the homes heated, where once the cheerless night and the ceaseless cold held sway. And all this happened because electricity came to our area along the humming wires of the REA. Electrification of the countryside—yes, that, too, is impressive.

A rich harvest in a hungry land is impressive.

The sight of healthy children in a classroom is impressive.

These—not mighty arms—are the achievements which the American Nation believes to be impressive.

And, if we are steadfast, the time may come when all other nations will also find it so.

Every night before I turn out the lights to sleep I ask myself this question: Have I done everything that I can do to unite this country? Have I done everything I can to help unite the world, to try to bring peace and hope to all the peoples of the world? Have I done enough?

Ask yourselves that question in your homes—and in this hall tonight. Have we, each of us, all done all we could? Have we done enough?

We may well be living in the time foretold many years ago when it was said: "I call heaven and earth to record this day against you, that I have set before you life and death, blessing and cursing: therefore choose life, that both thou and thy seed may live."

This generation of the world must choose: destroy or build, kill or aid, hate or understand.

We can do all these things on a scale never dreamed of before.

Well, we will choose life. In so doing we will prevail over the enemies within man, and over the natural enemies of all mankind. . . .

Document 8

This memo to President Johnson was written in July 1965 when he decided to increase the number of American ground troops in Vietnam and to draft more young men in the future. George Ball, an Undersecretary of State, disagreed with this policy and suggested a compromise solution.

Ball's memo presented a pragmatic argument against becoming involved in a land war in Asia. The devil's advocate within the President's inner circle, Ball did not ask for an immediate withdrawal from Vietnam, but hoped instead to influence Johnson not to jump "onto the tiger's back." Ball feared that the bigger the American commitment became, the harder it would be to extricate this country.

8 A Compromise Solution in South Vietnam
George Ball
July 1965

(1) *A Losing War:* The South Vietnamese are losing the war to the Viet Cong. No one can assure you that we can beat the Viet Cong or even force them to the conference table on our terms, no matter how many hundred thousand *white, foreign* (U.S.) troops we deploy.

No one has demonstrated that a white ground force of whatever size can win a guerrilla war—which is at the same time a civil war between Asians—in jungle terrain in the midst of a population that refuses cooperation to the white forces (and the South Vietnamese) and thus provides a great intelligence advantage to the other side. Three recent incidents vividly illustrate this point: (a) the sneak attack on the Da Nang Air Base which involved penetration of a defense parameter guarded by 9,000 Marines. This raid was possible only because of the cooperation of the local inhabitants; (b) the B-52 raid that failed to hit the Viet Cong who had obviously been tipped off; (c) the search and destroy mission of the 173rd Air Borne Brigade which spent three days looking for the Viet Cong, suffered 23 casualties, and never made contact with the enemy who had obviously gotten advance word of their assignment.

(2) The Question to Decide: Should we limit our liabilities in South Vietnam and try to find a way out with minimal long-term costs?

The alternative—no matter what we may wish it to be—is almost certainly a protracted war involving an open-ended commitment of U.S. forces, mounting U.S. casualties, no assurance of a satisfactory solution, and a serious danger of escalation at the end of the road.

(3) Need for a Decision Now: So long as our forces are restricted to advising and assisting the South Vietnamese, the struggle will remain a civil war between Asian peoples. Once we deploy substantial numbers of troops in combat it will become a war between the U.S. and a large part of the population of South Vietnam, organized and directed from North Vietnam and backed by the resources of both Moscow and Peiping.

The decision you face now, therefore, is crucial. Once large numbers of U.S. troops are committed to direct combat, they will begin to take heavy casualties in a war they are ill-equipped to fight in a non-cooperative if not downright hostile countryside.

Once we suffer large casualties, we will have started a well-nigh irreversible process. Our involvement will be so great that we cannot—without national humiliation—stop short of achieving our complete objectives. *Of the two possibilities I think humiliation would be more likely than the achievement of our objectives—even after we have paid terrible costs.*

(4) Compromise Solution: Should we commit U.S. manpower and prestige to a terrain so unfavorable as to give a very large advantage to the enemy—or should we seek a compromise settlement which achieves less than our stated objectives and thus cut our losses while we still have the freedom of maneuver to do so.

(5) Costs of a Compromise Solution: The answer involves a judgment as to the cost to the U.S. of such a compromise settlement in terms of our relations with the countries in the area of South Vietnam, the credibility of our commitments, and our prestige around the world. In my judgment, if we act before we commit substantial U.S. troops to combat in South Vietnam we can, by accepting some short-term costs, avoid what may well be a long-term catastrophe. I believe we tended grossly to exaggerate the costs involved in a compromise settlement. An appreciation of probable costs is contained in the attached memorandum.

(6) With these considerations in mind, I strongly urge the following program:

    (a) Military Program

        (1) Complete all deployments already announced—15 battalions—but decide not to go beyond a total of 72,000 men represented by this figure.

        (2) Restrict the combat role of the American forces to the June 19 announcement, making it clear to General Westmoreland that this announcement is to be strictly construed.

(3) Continue bombing in the North but avoid the Hanoi–Haiphong area and any targets nearer to the Chinese border than those already struck.

(b) Political Program

    (1) In any political approaches so far, we have been the prisoners of whatever South Vietnamese government that was momentarily in power. If we are ever to move toward a settlement, it will probably be because the South Vietnamese government pulls the rug out from under us and makes its own deal *or* because we go forward quietly without advance prearrangement with Saigon.

    (2) So far we have not given the other side a reason to believe there is *any* flexibility in our negotiating approach. And the other side has been unwilling to accept what *in their terms* is complete capitulation.

    (3) Now is the time to start some serious diplomatic feelers looking towards a solution based on some application of a self-determination principle.

    (4) I would recommend approaching Hanoi rather than any of the other probable parties, the NLF, _____ or Peiping. Hanoi is the only one that has given any signs of interest in discussion. Peiping has been rigidly opposed. Moscow has recommended that we negotiate with Hanoi. The NLF has been silent.

    (5) There are several channels to the North Vietnamese, but I think the best one is through their representative in Paris, Mai van Bo. Initial feelers of Bo should be directed toward a discussion both of the four points we have put forward and the four points put forward by Hanoi as a basis for negotiation. We can accept all but one of Hanoi's four points, and hopefully we should be able to agree on some ground rules for serious negotiations—including no preconditions.

    (6) If the initial feelers lead to further secret, exploratory talks, we can inject the concept of self-determination that would permit the Viet Cong some hope of achieving some of their political objectives through local elections or some other device.

    (7) The contact on our side should be handled through a nongovernmental cutout (possibly a reliable newspaper man who can be repudiated).

    (8) If progress can be made at this level a basis can be laid for a multinational conference. At some point, obviously, the government of South Vietnam will have to be brought on board, but I would postpone this step until after a substantial feeling out of Hanoi.

(7) Before moving to any formal conference we should be prepared to agree once the conference is started:

(a) The U.S. will stand down its bombing of the North

(b) The South Vietnamese will initiate no offensive operations in the South, and

(c) The DRV will stop terrorism and other aggressive action against the South.

(8) The negotiations at the conference should aim at incorporating our understanding with Hanoi in the form of a multinational agreement guaranteed by
the U.S., the Soviet Union and possibly other parties, and providing for an
international mechanism to supervise its execution. . . .

Document 9

The escalation of the Vietnam War forced the United States to look at South
Vietnam with an eye toward its tactical advantages and disadvantages in a military situation. The topography, climate, vegetation, methods and problems of
transportation and communication, population mixture, and economic pressures were all weighed in terms of the war.

This document contains part of an article written by the geographer of the
U.S. Department of State, for a Department of State Bulletin which was published in the fall of 1965—after the massive buildup of American forces had
begun.

9   **Geographic Aspects of the Struggle**
    G. Etzel Pearcy
    September 20, 1965
All physical relations between the United States and South Vietnam involve distances of global proportions. In a westerly direction 176° of longitude separate
Washington from Saigon; in an easterly direction, 184°. Thus the capitals of the two
countries are within about 250 miles of being halfway around the world from each
other.

A direct, or great circle, route from Seattle to Saigon measures 7,400 miles. Were
the flight to go via Honolulu, 1,625 miles would be added to the distance. By ship,
the distance from San Diego to Saigon via the shortest sea route, skirting the coast
of Japan, would run around 8,400 miles. Modern jet aircraft seem to shrink these
overwhelming distances, but even the latest and fastest of naval vessels would require from a week to 10 days for the trip. In any event, the transpacific supply lines
to South Vietnam are staggering in dimensions. Sustained operations through staging points for any significant volume of men and materiel present logistic problems
too complex to evaluate simply by route distances or ton-miles.

The approach to South Vietnam is via its east coast. On the Asian continent
much of the quadrant containing this area is generally hostile or nonaligned with the
West, forcing U.S. staging operations to take place primarily in the western part of
the Pacific defense zone. 2 outlying areas presently controlled by the U.S. have reasonably strategic locations along supply routes: Guam, an unincorporated territory,
and Okinawa in the U.S.-administered part of the Ryukyus. Even here mileages remain high: Guam to Saigon, 2,600 miles; Okinawa to Saigon, 1,825 miles.

South Vietnam, with its marginal position on the continent, can be readily approached. But its relatively small size and attenuated shape pose serious problems for
its defense. Although a little larger than Florida in area, the country in the north
narrows to no more than 33 miles in one place. Even Saigon, an "east coast" city,
lies only 35 miles from the Cambodian boundary to the west. The widest part of the

country, in the central portion, measures less than 130 miles. In contrast, South Vietnam's eastern coast curves in a long arc for almost 800 miles, nearly equal to California's arcuate west coast.

Geopoliticians cite compact shape as a decided asset for defense purposes and refer to France, with its hexagonal form, as approaching the ideal. South Vietnam represents the opposite extreme: a narrow ledge of land clinging to the great interior mountain system of Asia and presenting a classic example of exposed territory. So lengthy are the country's boundaries in relation to its size that those who would infiltrate have a rich choice of spots from which to select for entry.

Diversity of Topography

About 60% of South Vietnam consists of relatively high mountains and plateau lands. Maximum elevation is 8,500 feet, about 1,500 feet lower than in North Vietnam. Lowlands with little or no relief make up most of the remaining 40% of the country and are located chiefly in the Mekong Delta area.

Thus it can be seen that well over half of the countryside presents obstacles to penetration and movement but offers protection to offensive forces engaged in guerrilla-type warfare. And even in the lowlands, swamps and heavy vegetative growth afford the invaders a certain immunity against government security forces.

The Indochina Peninsula is dominated by a series of mountain spurs thrusting south from the great mountain systems of Central Asia, particularly the Yunnan Plateau of South China. Almost all of Laos, as well as most of both North and South Vietnam, is encompassed by these outliers, which reach to within 50 miles of Saigon. A cordillera running from north-northwest to south-southeast, known as the Chaine Annamitique, forms a physical barrier separating South Vietnam from Laos in the northern part of the country and from Cambodia in the central part. The eastern slopes of the chain rise abruptly from the narrow coastal zone. In places high altitudes are as much as 40 miles from the sea, but in others the eastward extensions of these mountain spurs crowd to the shoreline itself and separate the coastal region into a number of small, partially enclosed plains.

In the past the impingement of mountain spurs on the lowland fringe north of Saigon has inhibited development, and at present it limits the scope of operations against guerrilla strongholds in the higher lands to the west.

With very few exceptions the southernmost 1/3 of the country lies at an altitude of less than 500 feet. The great Mekong River flows through this flat landscape, its 4 major distributaries emptying into the South China Sea over a wide delta. Where the river enters South Vietnam from Cambodia, 125 miles from the east coast and 55 miles from the Gulf of Siam, the elevation of the land is scarcely 15 feet above sea level. An elaborate system of waterways includes canals as well as minor distributaries. Reliance on water transportation is very high, severely handicapping strategic operations. Heavily vegetated areas in this low-lying region often provide strongholds for well-armed guerrillas, and the central government finds it exceedingly difficult to penetrate this tortuous water route with its services, its authority, and its security program.

The delta lands of the Mekong seldom flood seriously. In western Cambodia the Tonle Sap, an inland lake fluctuating in area from 1,000 to 3,900 square miles, serves as a reservoir to stabilize the flow of the lower Mekong. When the water rises, the surplus backs up into this lake and prevents heavy flooding. In turn, during low water the process is reversed and from the Tonle Sap the extra accumulation of water drains back into the river.

Notwithstanding this fortunate regulation by nature, there are seasons of relatively high water which further isolate the delta. But the South is spared the ravaging floods quite common to the Tonkin Delta in North Vietnam, except upon rare occasions when the Mekong picks up an unusually heavy load on its 2,600-mile course from Tibet.

Climate & Vegetation

The thermometer in South Vietnam never skyrockets; the highest temperature ever recorded at Saigon has only been 104° F. Nevertheless, a temperature which never goes much below 80° F. definitely has a debilitating effect on human energy, particularly when it is accompanied by high humidity. Sustained periods in the steaming lowlands of the Mekong Delta place a severe strain on anyone accustomed to the climate of higher latitudes. At higher elevations temperatures are more agreeable, but here other handicaps, such as pounding rainfall and dense vegetation, may well offset the advantage of a cool breeze.

The controlling factor in Vietnam's climate is its position deep in the tropics. Another basic climatic control is Vietnam's location on the southeastern margin of the great Eurasian land mass. Pressure differences between continent and ocean result in major air-mass movements which pour seaward during the winter and landward during the summer. This dynamically effective wind system, which reverses itself twice yearly, gives rise to a monsoon influence—a "when the rains come" type of climate.

For Southeast Asia in general the rainy season thus occurs in summer, but along the coast in the northern part of South Vietnam (Hue-Danang area) the wettest period lasts from September to January. This exception is caused by the northeast monsoon winds, which are normally dry but are onshore in this particular location and so contain moisture. In short, the monsoon does not appreciably alter temperature values but brings a notoriously wet season each summer and fall.

Heavy rainfall handicaps security measures in several ways. Mobility is reduced, equipment becomes difficult to maneuver, and better protection is offered the aggressor. Air action may be limited by the poor visibility resulting from high humidity and low cloud cover during the rainy season.

The quantity of rain falling in South Vietnam is impressive. At Saigon the annual precipitation amounts to 78 inches, of which 67 inches fall during the 6-month period from May to October. June and September average over 13 inches each, registering frequent downpours of torrential proportions. On the exposed east coast north of Saigon, steep slopes lift the moist, humid air as it blows landward and upward, unloading even greater amounts of water. Hué, onetime capital of the old Annamese Empire, annually receives 115 inches.

In their extreme form the unequal atmospheric pressures give rise to typhoons which pound the east coast of the Indochina Peninsula. These devastating storms occur from July into November; in October and especially in November they are concentrated on the Vietnamese coast south of the 17th Parallel.

Over ⅚ of South Vietnam has a cover of natural vegetation—rain forests, monsoon forests, and some savanna lands. When the original forest is cut away or burned, a secondary forest cover takes over in many places, poorer in timber but with heavier undergrowth. These tangles of vegetation are a marked disadvantage for forces seeking out an enemy which moves quickly on foot, with a good knowledge of the terrain. For example, roadways cleared through heavy vegetative growth must be maintained or they soon revert to the jungle. In contrast, dense foliage offers excellent concealment from both air and land observation. From such terrain guerrillas may operate with relative safety and on a time schedule of their own making.

Transportation

Transportation facilities in South Vietnam are too limited to provide unity and cohesion within the country. Physical factors handicap the development of communications to many remote and marginal areas; in numerous instances towns and villages have had little or no contact with the Central government.

The obstacles of inaccessibility also handicap those fighting against the guerrilla aggressors from the North. Inadequate lines of communication allow guerrillas to infiltrate large areas and remain under cover while at the same time they prevent effective offensive action to rout them. American military operations, ordinarily geared to efficient transportation systems, contrast markedly with those of the Viet Cong along the infiltration routes, where guerrillas slip in with their less-than-complex supplies and equipment.

Economic development on the Indochina Peninsula has been largely limited to the Mekong Delta region in the south, the Tonkin Basin in the north, and the lowlands fringing the coast between them. When Vietnam was partitioned in 1954, the southern part inherited only one of the larger lowland areas and about ⅗ of the string of coastal lowlands. Modern transportation facilities within the country do not generally extend beyond these areas.

Within South Vietnam there are only about 870 miles of operable railway lines, comprising for the most part the coastal line from Saigon to Dongha, 40 miles north of Hué and within 12 miles of the demarcation line from North Vietnam. From this longitudinal railroad, a few short spurs branch off, the most important of which reaches Dalat, high on the plateau of the same name. The slim traffic artery completely bypasses the extensive "back country" of South Vietnam with its thousands of hamlets and villages.

Highways in South Vietnam form a rather sketchy network but have much greater coverage than the railway lines. When Indochina was a part of France's colonial empire, the French established a road pattern in some ways resembling that of metropolitan France. The more important routes carry numbers, identifying them with major axes of travel between key points. For example, National Route 14 leads from Danang (Tourane) on the coast, 50 miles south of Hué, to the northern part of the Mekong lowlands and gives access to Saigon. The over-all route system, however, has been truncated, for it was developed to cover French Indochina. Now an appreciable proportion of the net lies in Cambodia, Laos, and North Vietnam.

Route 9 extends nearly straight westward from Dongha near the coast, through Laobao on the Laos boundary, to Savannakhet on the Mekong border between Laos and Thailand. This particular route, paralleling the demarcation line on the south for about 10 or 15 miles, is at least partially responsible for deflecting the infiltration route of the Viet Cong to the west into Laotian territory. Although the demarcation line itself crosses relatively empty countryside and would entice infiltrators, Route 9 provides some access for security measures.

The northern approach to South Vietnam for the Viet Cong is not limited to any given itinerary but corresponds to a band of rough landscape where improvised paths and trails can carry the traffic. This zone does not correlate in any way with the established road pattern for that part of the Indochina Peninsula. It serves as the principal access route from north to south; into it and from it finger a labyrinth of trails for assembly and deployment of the Viet Cong forces.

Water transportation plays a heavy role in the heart of the Mekong Delta. Some 3,000 miles of waterways crisscross these lowlands, giving access to areas where roads are difficult to construct and maintain. Unfortunately the lack of approach by land hampers security precautions, and the Viet Cong have installed themselves in certain of these low-lying and often saturated areas. Elsewhere in South Vietnam navigable waters are limited or altogether lacking.

In North Vietnam watercourses provide excellent transportation facilities in the delta of the Red River of Tonkin. Hanoi and the port city of Haiphong are both in the midst of true delta country, whereas Saigon lies somewhat off center of the Mekong Delta.

Air transportation in South Vietnam has superficially alleviated some of the problems involving appreciable distance and inadequate means of movement on the surface. Saigon is well known as one of the leading international air terminals in Southeast Asia, but in addition there are local flights from here to the larger cities in South Vietnam. The fact that the Viet Cong have been unable to overrun urban areas permits commercial air transportation to continue even during heated warfare.

The People of Vietnam

The Vietnamese people range from highly cultured and sophisticated individuals who dwell in the larger cities to tribal folk who eke a living out of the countryside by the most primitive of methods. Well-to-do Vietnamese in Saigon live in European-style homes, dress and entertain as do Westerners, and send their children abroad to school. Peasants may live in villages amounting to nothing more than collections of straw huts.

Throughout most urban centers French culture is at once apparent. The French language continues to be used by many of the better educated Vietnamese. Most administrative and educational practices of the former French colonial regime also continue in use. French methods persist in most of the routine necessary to the country's political and economic existence.

Any ethnological map of South Vietnam must be considered as a segment of a larger one encompassing the entire Indochina Peninsula and its environs. Ceaseless migrations during past millennia have brought numerous racial types and social patterns to the area. Predominant influences stem not only from what is now the Indo-Pakistan subcontinent and China proper, but from deep within the interior of the Asian Continent. Most of the present-day inhabitants of South Vietnam, however, may be directly related to the people of the old Annamite Kingdom in the eastern part of the Indochina Peninsula. Known racially as well as nationally as Vietnamese, they comprise about 85% of South Vietnam's some 16 million population.

As a powerful majority the Vietnamese south of the 17th Parallel dominate the country and represent a new national group. Height of the men averages around 5 feet 1 or 2 inches, and their weight around 120 pounds. The most common physical type is characterized by straight black hair, broad face, high cheekbones, dark eyes with an epicanthic fold of the eyelid, and light- or medium-brown skin.

Minority Groups

Several minority groups, while not great in total numbers, complicate the racial picture. The Chinese, forming the largest minority, have not fared especially well politically. Their skill and energy brought them economic success as entrepreneurs, but with the rise of nationalism a prejudiced policy of discrimination gave many the feeling of persecution. Under the French they were allowed to retain Chinese citizenship and could appeal to their motherland in the case of denied rights (before the Communist conquest of mainland China). But the Vietnamese government required that all Chinese become citizens of the new state in response to the special need for loyalty in the face of aggression from the North by a power friendly to their former homeland.

The second most significant minority are the *montagnards*. (The word in French means "dwellers in the mountains.") Estimates of their number range from 500,000 to 700,000. These highlanders live in relative isolation from the rest of the country, speak their own languages, and maintain distinctive cultural traditions. The remote and sparsely settled habitat of the *montagnards* is a region that is definitely vulnerable to guerrilla infiltration. Some steps have been taken by the Central government to lessen this danger. The Viet Cong have gone so far as to assure these primitive peoples in Communist propaganda that they may have their own autonomy "when the Communists conquer South Vietnam."

Another minority, the Khmers, are actually Cambodians living in South Vietnam. Numbering from 350,000 to 400,000, they are largely concentrated southwest of Saigon. Like the *montagnards,* they have not assimilated well with the Vietnamese. On the other hand, they have generally not proved to be a primary security problem.

The Chams, numbering only about 35,000, represent the least significant of the minorities. A fragmented remainder of a once great people, they are poor economically. Scattered through less desirable sections of the south-central part of the country, they live in humble little villages quite apart from the general flow of Vietnamese life.

Europeans, especially French, do not enjoy the privileges they once did under colonial rule. Nevertheless there are still some close associations between Europeans and Vietnamese which prove mutually beneficial.

The last extended period of peace and stability for the inhabitants of what is now South Vietnam dates back to the pre-World War II years, and even that was marred by a serious economic depression. Any person under 40, then, could not be expected to have experienced any type of life other than a troubled one. Political instability has been the general rule. What progress has been made has been achieved in the face of serious handicaps.

Economic Pressures

In the 1954 split of territory between North and South Vietnam, the latter came out a poor 2d in natural resources. In mineral resources the division was especially uneven; North Vietnam has copious quantities of coal, zinc, phosphates, tin, and graphite, while South Vietnam's share, pending further investigation at least, is quite meager. Further, the French promoted greater industrial development in the North than in the South.

Partially offsetting these advantages of the North, however, is the fact that there is a considerably greater population pressure on the fertile lowlands around Hanoi and Haiphong than on those tributary to Saigon. As a result, in normal years South Vietnam exports rice, while North Vietnam traditionally has to import rice.

The economic pattern of South Vietnam is hardly a complex one. Agriculture provides the basic sustenance, ranging from rubber and rice as the prime products entering trade down to a number of provision crops for local consumption, including corn, cassava, and beans. Other products, commercial in nature, are tea, coffee, tobacco, sugar cane, and coconuts. By Western standards industrial processes are largely the community type, wherein simple manufactured goods are produced for domestic consumption.

The U.S., by its aid program, has done much in recent years to stimulate economic activity in South Vietnam, somewhat countering the war-induced decline in production and welfare. Projects include the improving of agricultural techniques, pest and insect control, an agricultural credit system, better transportation and communication facilities, and land reclamation.

Problems in Perspective

From a geographic point of view there can be no doubt that the U.S. faces disadvantages in Vietnam that far outweigh the advantages. While factors of relief, climate, and vegetation which handicap the defenders are not necessarily in themselves assets to the guerrillas, the guerrillas, of course, take advantage of the landscape as it is. They turn heavy foliage into camouflage, use light arms on terrain too rough for most conventional weapons, and seek strategic advantages during the monsoon season, when aircraft cannot be fully effective.

Tactics of the Viet Cong are likewise tailored to the cultural environment, including the abstract struggle for the minds and sympathies of the inhabitants. A recent estimate identifies well over a million villagers as dominated by Communists, with other millions subjected to some degree of Viet Cong control or pressure. Methods of obtaining cooperation from these rural inhabitants vary—from terrorism to the promise of concession. By holding small, scattered areas, the Viet Cong can erode government control more than they could if they gained larger but fewer blocks of territory. Hit-and-run tactics can be extended in more widespread fashion for greater psychological effect. Also, control of areas as close as possible to Saigon tends to give the impression that a rice-roots rebellion is closing in on the capital.

Document 10

America's deeper military involvement in Vietnam was not unquestioningly accepted by all segments of the population. Tom Paxton was one of the politically conscious folksingers who opposed the step in his music of the early 1960s. The Paxton song reprinted here never made the Top 40, but the substance of his commentary was representative of the criticisms voiced by early figures in the antiwar movement.

This protest song complains that a military solution to the Vietnamese situation was impossible because the Vietnamese themselves opposed American intervention. It further attacks President Johnson for having promised moderation in the 1964 campaign and then escalating the war.

10 Lyndon Johnson Told the Nation
   Tom Paxton
   I got a letter from L.B.J.,
   It said, "This is your lucky day.
   It's time to put your khaki trousers on.
   Though it may seem very queer,

We've got no jobs to give you here,
So we are sending you to Viet Nam."
And Lyndon Johnson told the nation,
"Have no fear of escalation,
I am trying ev'ryone to please.
Though it isn't really war,
We're sending fifty thousand more
To help save Viet Nam from Viet Namese."

I jumped off the old troop ship,
I sank in mud up to my hips,
And cussed until the captain called me down,
"Never mind how hard it's raining,
Think of all the ground we're gaining,
Just don't take one step outside of town."

Every night the local gentry
Slip out past the sleeping sentry
They go out to join the old V.C.
In their nightly little dramas,
They put on their black pajamas
And come lobbing mortar shells at me.

We go 'round in helicopters
Like a bunch of big grasshoppers
Searching for the Viet Cong in vain.
They left a note that they had gone,
They had to get back to Saigon,
Their government positions to maintain.

Well, here I sit in this rice paddy,
Wondering about Big Daddy,
And I know that Lyndon loves me so;
Yet how sadly I remember
Way back yonder in November
When he said I'd never have to go.

The word came from the very top
That soon the shooting war would stop
The pockets of resistance were so thin.
There just remained some trouble spots
Like Vietnam, Detroit & Watts
Gene McCarthy and Ho Chi Minh.

They sent me to some swampy hole
We went out on a night patrol
Just who was who was very hard to tell.
With Martha Raye and 13 Mayors,
Half of Congress, 6 ball players
And Ronald Reagan yelling, "Give 'em hell!"

Critical Issues for Discussion

1. Within his first month in office, President Johnson learned that the situation in South Vietnam had greatly deteriorated as noted in Document 1. What were the problems in South Vietnam? Why hadn't the situation been resolved? What could be done to improve things? What did people think would happen if the United States did nothing?

2. Senator Barry Goldwater felt that Johnson's policy was a weak one and he made this clear in his speeches and in his writing, as Document 2 shows. What were Goldwater's specific complaints about the Democratic policy in Asia? What would he have done? How would Johnson have answered this criticism?

3. In March 1964, Johnson told Senator William Fulbright that in Vietnam "the only thing I know to do is more of the same and do it more efficiently and effectively." What did he mean? Did he have other alternatives? If so, what were they? Why did he reject them?

4. Secretary of State Rusk cabled Ambassador Lodge about the situation in Vietnam in May 1964, to say that "somehow we must change the pace at which these people move and I suspect that this can only be done with a pervasive intrusion of Americans into their affairs" (in Gibbons, "Vietnam Decision-Making Paper"). Who were "these people?" What had to be done? Why did Rusk feel that intrusion was necessary? What kind of intrusion did he have in mind?

After another in a series of governmental reorganizations in South Vietnam in 1964, Ambassador Maxwell Taylor called in the young military men who had shaken up the government for a meeting described in Document 3. What was the tone of Taylor's remarks? How do you think the Vietnamese reacted? What did this episode reveal about relations between the Americans and the South Vietnamese?

5. The question of who was responsible for the war in Vietnam remained an important issue. According to Document 5, how did the State Department view the origins of the war? With what wars was Vietnam compared? Why? Why was it called a "new" kind of war? Who was responsible for the war?

Compare Documents 4 and 6 with the State Department White Paper. Who would have agreed with the White Paper? What were the basic differences between Nixon and Morgenthau? What were their assumptions? With whom would Johnson have agreed? To what kinds of policies did these analyses lead? Nixon called the proposal for neutralizing Vietnam "surrender on the installment plan." What did he mean by that? What would Morgenthau have said?

6. President Johnson escalated the war but talked about negotiations at the same time. Was such a stance reasonable as stated in Document 7? What points did he make? How did he present himself and his views? What did he expect the North Vietnamese to do?

7. George Ball was very wary of increasing American military involvement in
Vietnam. In Document 8, for example, he argued that "once on the tiger's
back, we cannot be sure of picking the place to dismount." What did he mean
by that? Who was the tiger? What alternatives did Ball offer? What was his view
of the origin of the war? Was his solution really a compromise?

8. The terrain of South Vietnam and other geopolitical features of the country
were studied with great seriousness as American forces began to arrive in
the country. How did the topography of the country affect the military tactics?
How did other attributes of South Vietnam change the ways in which the war
would have to be fought? What might a geographer have emphasized in a description of South Vietnam in 1955? How would it have differed from Document 9?

9. The American military had many problems during the Vietnam war as it
attempted to find an efficient and practical way to win. What did "winning"
mean?

Maxwell Taylor later remarked (in Charlton and Moncrieff, *Many Reasons
Why*) that "the fear which we always had, even at the outset, was: 'We don't
want to take this war over, we want to do just those things the Vietnamese
can't do for themselves.' Now this turned out to be very difficult when our
military forces arrived. . . . And there was every tendency to push the little
brown men to one side: 'Let us go do it.' And we erred many times in allowing
that to go too far." Why did Taylor feel that the Americans made a mistake by
trying to do too much in Vietnam? What was the role of the American military
in 1965? How had it changed from 1964? Had the United States gone "too far"
at this point?

At the other extreme, General Earle Wheeler once complained that "no one
ever won a battle sitting on his ass" (in Gelb and Betts, *The Irony of Vietnam*).
What did he want the United States to do? Would he have agreed with Taylor?

10. The first teach-ins about the Vietnam War began in the spring of 1965 and
with them came the first protest songs (see Document 10). What points was
Paxton making? Is the song convincing?

Follow Up Shortly after the first American ground troops were sent to
Vietnam in March 1965, Brigadier General Fred Karsh chafed about the rules of
combat. "When I put a kid out there in a foxhole, I'm responsible for him. And
if I'm responsible for him I've go to do everything I can to support and protect
him. If that involves more patrolling, then we'll just have to do it" (in Mc-
Culloch, "Vietnam: Jan. 1964–Jan. 1968"). What was his preferred policy?
Would he have agreed with Taylor or Wheeler? Why? Would he have been
happy with the introduction of search and destroy missions? Why?

Suggestions for Further Reading

LBJ and His Advisors
Berman, Larry. *Planning a Tragedy: The Americanization of the War in Vietnam.*
New York: Norton, 1982.
> This brief book, based on classified papers in the LBJ Library, looks in
> depth at how the decision to commit ground troops was made in June and
> July 1965.

Halberstam, David. *The Best and the Brightest.* New York: Random House,
1969.
> Rambling and undocumented, it nevertheless offers vivid sketches of the
> policymakers in the Kennedy-Johnson years and insight into their percep-
> tions of Vietnam.

Johnson, Lyndon Baines. *The Vantage Point: Perspectives of the Presidency, 1963–
1969.* New York: Holt, Rinehart and Winston, 1971.
> Johnson's version of the period is detailed and sometimes defensive but con-
> tains information not available elsewhere.

Kearns, Doris. *Lyndon Johnson and the American Dream.* New York: Harper and
Row, 1976.
> Kearns' biography contains valuable insights into Johnson's personality,
> leadership style, and Vietnam policy.

Stavins, Ralph, Richard J. Barnet, and Marcus G. Raskin. *Washington Plans an
Aggressive War: A Documented Account of the United States Adventure in Indochina.* New York: Random House, 1971.
> Written while controversy over the war was raging, the combination of
> sound documentation and easy readability continues to make this a good
> book to read first. In Part I, Chapters 4 and 5 by Stavins chronicle the plan-
> ning process from November 1963 to July 1965. Part II, "The Men Who
> Made the War" by Barnet, is a political-psychological analysis of how the
> bureaucratic process narrowed the options which Kennedy and Johnson con-
> sidered viable.

Analysis of Policy
These books consider American policy-making generally, not only in the Johnson years.

Barnet, Richard J. *Roots of War: The Men and Institutions Behind U.S. Foreign
Policy.* New York: Atheneum, 1972.
> Barnet offers a radical critique, indicting the "national security managers"
> behind the war who defined the national interest to serve a narrow elite.

Ellsberg, Daniel. *Papers on the War.* New York: Simon and Schuster, 1972.
> Ellsberg draws on the Pentagon Papers to review decision making from
> Truman's administration to Nixon's. He believes that presidents were aware
> of the risks of intervention but chose to continue in the same pattern of
> stalemate at increasing levels of violence.

Gallucci, Robert L. *Neither Peace Nor Honor: The Politics of American Military Policy in South Vietnam.* Baltimore: Johns Hopkins University Press, 1975.

Arguing that military leaders didn't know what they were getting into in Vietnam, Gallucci finds the decision-making process within the military flawed by professionalism and a closed bureaucratic system.

Gelb, Leslie H., and Richard K. Betts. *The Irony of Vietnam: The System Worked.* Washington: Brookings Institute, 1979.

This analysis of recurrent patterns in presidential decision making "attempts to explain why American leaders felt it was necessary to prevent defeat in Vietnam, to fight the war by gradual escalation, and to persevere despite pessimism about the final outcome." The authors conclude that, in spite of policy failures, the system succeeded in steering a compromise course toward the core goal of containing communism.

Joseph, Paul. *Cracks in the Empire: State Politics in the Vietnam War.* Boston: South End Press, 1981.

Joseph, a sociologist, analyzes the patterns of differences among U.S. foreign policy makers. His study is helpful in understanding the range of positions from which government leaders were speaking.

Thies, Wallace J. *When Governments Collide: Coercion and Diplomacy in the Vietnam Conflict, 1964–1968.* Berkeley: Univ. of California Press, 1980.

Using the Johnson administration's bomb-and-negotiate policy as his example, Thies inquires into the role force and the threat of force should have in international relations. His complex analysis of U.S. processes makes this the most difficult of the books in this section, but worth the effort.

Gulf of Tonkin Incident

Austin, Anthony. *The President's War: The Story of the Tonkin Gulf Resolution and How the Nation was Trapped in Vietnam.* Philadelphia: Lippincott, 1971.

A dramatic and readable presentation of evidence that, Austin says, shows that "managers of the national security establishment . . . deliberately misled Congress and the American people . . . to obtain authorization for a war they had secretly decided on months before."

Windchy, Eugene. *Tonkin Gulf.* Garden City, N.Y.: Doubleday, 1971.

Windchy's thorough reconstruction of events surrounding the incident reveals a pattern of systematic deception of the American people and a consequent erosion of congressional authority over foreign policy.

Young Robin Hood
Pfc. Bernard A. Roe, Durango, Colo., chats with a trio of Vietnamese boys, one of whom wears a Robin Hood-style hat. Roe is a member of C Co., 1st Bn. (Abn), 327th Inf. of the 1st Brigade, 101st Airborne Division. This photograph and its title represent the American effort to "win the hearts and minds" of the Vietnamese. *USA Photo by Spec. 4 Ben Croxton.*

Chapter 5
America Takes Charge:
1965–1967

Background

Historical Summary

General William C. Westmoreland had conceived a strategy for Vietnam even before President Johnson granted his request for additional U.S. combat troops in the summer of 1965. He would use part of the force to protect American bases and other installations along the coast and in the area around Saigon, deploy units in the central highlands in order to prevent the Communists from cutting across the country, and bomb North Vietnam to cut off supplies to the South.

The strategy was founded on the theory that, where limited numbers of men in an advisory capacity had failed, the sheer weight of American industry and technology could grind down the enemy. As General William Depuy explained, it called for "more bombs, more shells, more napalm . . . til the other side cracks and gives up." American troops—"the flower of our youth", Lyndon Johnson called them—began to arrive in Vietnam by the thousands. They came prepared to fight, but many found that they were not prepared for the tropical climate, the strangeness of the people and their language, or the complexities of a war in which allies and enemy looked alike and might be discovered at any turn. Troops were deployed in mountains, plains and deltas, fighting highly trained North Vietnamese regulars and lightly armed South Vietnamese guerrillas.

The American military performed logistical miracles. Engineers constructed air fields and harbors, and thousands of tons of equipment poured into Vietnam to field the American forces. They were also helped by the most sophisticated devices, among them electronic sensors intended to detect guerrillas by smell. The Post Exchange system provided the luxuries that are necessities for U.S. soldiers away from home—beer and cigarettes, radios, stereo sets, and tape recorders. So enormous was the flow of American money into Vietnam that Wall Street brokerage firms opened offices in Saigon to sell GIs stocks and bonds.

For many U.S. combat troops, the war consisted of patrolling through dense jungles and across flooded rice fields where they were chronically plagued by an ingenious assortment of enemy mines and booby traps. Nor could they easily distinguish friend from foe among the peasants; thus they tended to suspect all villagers as Vietcong sympathizers.

In addition to reliance on American ground fire, Westmoreland's plan called for bombing raids on supply lines in North Vietnam to discourage the Hanoi regime from infiltrating men and supplies into the South, to bring the enemy to the negotiating table, and to strengthen the South Vietnamese government's ability to conduct pacification programs. But supplies continued to reach the South by sea and along the Ho Chi Minh trail. And the enemy continued to use South Vietnamese villages as cover for their operations.

Though Westmoreland and his generals paid lip service to the need to "win the hearts and minds" of the peasant population, they now saw the war as essentially a military operation. Their measure of success became the "body count," which determined progress by the number of North Vietnamese and Vietcong corpses found after battle. American soldiers were used for massive maneuvers called "search and destroy" missions. In January 1967, Operation Cedar Falls was launched: a major attempt to move civilian populations from their villages to refugee camps, to search out the enemy, and to destroy anything remaining that might be used as a base of operation. Villages were burned and plowed under, tunnels blown up, crops poisoned, and vegetation erased with chemical defoliants.

Not long after American commitment began to intensify, the United States had been troubled by the recurrence of internal political disorder within the South Vietnamese establishment. The convulsions erupted soon after the Honolulu conference, at which President Johnson acclaimed Premier Nguyen Cao Ky's leadership of the Saigon government. Factions mobilized against each other until it seemed for a period as if South Vietnam faced a civil war within a civil war. In the United States, as American casualties mounted, disapproval of the war grew and took the form of antiwar demonstrations. Perhaps more important, senior figures within the Johnson administration began to voice doubts. Foremost among them was Secretary of Defense Robert McNamara, who argued that the bombing of North Vietnam was ineffective. Westmoreland's plans had failed to take into account the readiness of the North Vietnamese and the Vietcong to sacrifice themselves to attain their objective. So, instead of wearing down the Communists, the strategy was eroding the will of the United States and its South Vietnamese allies.

By the end of 1967, the war was draining off experienced officers and men who, at the end of their one-year tour of duty, were increasingly replaced by draftees and officers on their first assignments. There were nearly half a million American troops in Vietnam and the Joint Chiefs of Staff were asking the President for more.

The U.S. soldiers who had gone into battle in Vietnam in the middle of 1965 were filled with optimism. But as the war dragged on, they were overtaken by frustration at the lack of results. Philip Caputo, a marine lieutenant, summed up their feelings after the war: "When we marched into the rice paddies on that damp March afternoon, we carried, along with our packs and rifles, the implicit convictions that the Vietcong would be quickly beaten. We kept the packs and rifles; the convictions, we lost."

March 1965

Chronology

	1965 Mar	Dec	1966 Jan	Feb	Mar	Apr	May	Jun	Jul	Aug	Sep
Vietnam	First American combat troops at Danang	U.S. combat strength reaches almost 200,000	37-day bombing pause ends on January 31.		Demonstrations against Ky in Hue and Danang	B-52s attack North Vietnam for first time		U.S. bombs outskirts of Hanoi and Haiphong			
United States	Prime Minister Ky and President Johnson meet in Hawaii										
World Wide											De Gaulle urges U.S. to withdraw and then negotiate

Chronology (cont.)

	1966 Oct	Nov	Dec	1967 Jan	Feb	Mar	Apr	May	Jun
Vietnam				Operation Cedar Falls—major U.S. search and destroy mission		Ellsworth Bunker becomes U.S. ambassador to Saigon		Operation Junction City—another major search and destroy mission	Ky withdraws from presidential election campaign
United States	McNamara discouraged by slow U.S. progress		Harrison Salisbury reports that U.S. had hit civilian targets in Hanoi				Antiwar protests in New York and San Francisco		"Haight-Ashbury Summer" begins
World Wide	Johnson meets with Asian leaders in Manila			Treaty between U.S., U.S.S.R., and Britain bans nuclear weapons in outer space					6-Day War between Israel and Arab states

	1967 Jul	Aug
Vietnam		
United States	Race riots in many U.S. cities	
World Wide		

Points to Emphasize

- the justifications for the large increase in American troops in Vietnam between 1965 and 1968
- the explanations for the American military tactics in use during this period
- the role of technological innovations in the Vietnam War
- the reactions of the Vietnamese civilians to the American soldiers
- the reactions of the American soldiers to the Vietnamese civilians
- the rationale behind the pacification programs of both sides
- the reasons why the United States talked about negotiating while continuing to fight
- the definition of progress in the war
- the reasons why victory seemed sure but far away

Glossary of Names and Terms

J. William Fulbright Democratic Representative from Arkansas, 1943–1945. Democratic Senator from Arkansas, 1945–1975. Chairman of the Senate Foreign Relations Committee, 1959–1974. Helped guide the Gulf of Tonkin Resolution through the Senate but later became a leading opponent of the escalation of the war.

Robert Komer early advocate of the importance of the pacification program who took charge of that program in 1966 and worked as General Westmoreland's assistant in charge of CORDS in 1967.

Don Luce American civilian who worked in Vietnam beginning in 1958, originally as an agriculturalist in the International Voluntary Services. Directed IVS, 1961–1967. Returned to Vietnam and later worked with the World Council of Churches.

Nguyen Chanh Thi military figure in South Vietnam who rose to the rank of general. One of the "Young Turks" with Ky and Thieu in 1965. Fired as 1st Corps Commander by Ky in March 1966.

Truong Dinh Dzu Buddhist layman and lawyer who opposed Thieu and Ky in the September 1967 presidential election. Despite his relative anonymity, collected 17 percent of the vote. Proposed the recognition of and negotiations with the National Liberation Front. Jailed soon after the election.

body count American tally of enemy killed during the war.

Cedar Falls and *Junction City* two major American search and destroy operations in Vietnam in 1967.

Civil Operations and Revolutionary Development Support (CORDS) the program charged with the pacification of the South Vietnamese people.

doves Americans who opposed the U.S. military intervention in Vietnam.

hawks Americans who supported the war effort or wanted to use more force in Vietnam.

Honolulu Conference meeting between President Johnson and Premier Nguyen
  Cao Ky in February 1966 which resulted in Ky's promise to reform the
  South Vietnamese government and Johnson's assurance of continued Amer-
  ican aid to South Vietnam.

Iron Triangle Vietcong stronghold just north of Saigon which was the setting
  for Operation Cedar Falls in January 1967.

Military Units for the U.S. Army
  squad ten infantrymen under a staff sergeant.
  platoon four infantry squads under a lieutenant (40 men).
  company headquarters section and four platoons under a captain (160 +).
  battalion headquarters section and four or more companies under a lieuten-
    ant colonel (640 +).
  brigade headquarters section and three or more battalions under a colonel
    (1920 +).
  division headquarters section and three brigades with artillery combat sup-
    port and combat service support units under a major general (5,760 +).

San Antonio formula President Johnson's late 1967 proposal that the United
  States would stop bombing North Vietnam "with the understanding" that
  "productive discussions" would ensue. Johnson added that he expected that
  the North would not take advantage of any bombing halt to infiltrate more
  men or material into the South.

Documents

Document 1

In February 1966, President Johnson met with Nguyen Cao Ky, the premier of
South Vietnam, in Honolulu. Johnson was pleased that Ky had managed to
maintain his power for nearly a year and used this meeting to publicly acknowledge Ky's achievement.

Their meeting resulted in a joint statement, the White House Declaration of
Honolulu, which set forth the goals of the Republic of Vietnam, those of the
United States, and the commitment common to both. However, the meeting
was less successful for Ky than for Johnson. Ky's association with Johnson in
Hawaii and his change in policy when he returned to Vietnam caused some
Vietnamese to see him as a Diem-style puppet. Buddhists returned to the streets
to protest aspects of Ky's policy, and serious civil disturbances erupted inside
South Vietnam. President Johnson on the other hand, thought the Honolulu
summit successful and viewed its declaration as binding.

1   The White House Declaration,
Honolulu
February 8, 1966
Part I
> The Republic of Viet-Nam and the United States of America jointly declare:
>> their determination in defense against aggression,
>> their dedication to the hopes of all the people of South Viet-Nam,
>> and their commitment to the search for just and stable peace.
> In pursuit of these objectives the leaders of their governments have agreed upon this declaration, which sets forth:
>> the purposes of the Government of Viet-Nam,
>> the purposes of the Government of the United States,
>> and the common commitment of both Governments.

Part II: The Purposes of the Government of Viet-Nam

Here in the mid-Pacific, halfway between Asia and North America, we take the opportunity to state again the aims of our government.

We are a government—indeed a generation—of revolutionary transformation. Our people are caught up in a mortal struggle.

This struggle has four sides.

1. We must defeat the Viet-Cong and those illegally fighting with them on our soil. We are the victims of an aggression directed and supported from Hanoi. That aggression—that so-called "War of National Liberation"—is part of the communist plan for the conquest of all of Southeast Asia. The defeat of that aggression is vital for the future of our people of South Viet-Nam.

2. We are dedicated to the eradication of social injustice among our people. We must bring about a true social revolution and construct a modern society in which every man can know that he has a future; that he has respect and dignity; that he has the opportunity for himself and for his children to live in an environment where all is not disappointment, despair and dejection; that the opportunities exist for the full expression of his talents and his hopes.

3. We must establish and maintain a stable, viable economy and build a better material life for our people. In spite of the war, which creates many unusual and unpredictable economic situations, we are determined to continue with a policy of austerity; to make the best possible use of the assistance granted us from abroad; and to help our people achieve regular economic growth and improved material welfare.

4. We must build true democracy for our land and for our people. In this effort we shall continue to imbue the people with a sense of national unity, a stronger commitment to civic responsibility. We shall encourage a widened and more active participation in and contribution to the building of a free, independent, strong and peaceful Viet-Nam. In particular, we pledge again:

—to formulate a democratic constitution in the months ahead, including an electoral law;

—to take that constitution to our people for discussion and modification;

—to seek its ratification by secret ballot;

—to create, on the basis of elections rooted in that constitution, an elected government.

These things shall be accomplished mainly with the blood, intelligence, and dedication of the Vietnamese people themselves. But in this interdependent world we shall need the help of others:—to win the war of independence; to build while we fight; to reconstruct and develop our nation when terror ceases.

To those future citizens of a free, democratic South Viet-Nam now fighting with the Viet-Cong, we take this occasion to say come and join in this national revolutionary adventure:

—come safely to join us through the Open Arms Program.

—stop killing your brothers, sisters, their elders and their children.

—come and work through constitutional democracy to build together that life of dignity, freedom and peace those in the North would deny the people of Viet-Nam.

Thus, we are fighting this war. It is a military war, a war for the hearts of our people. We cannot win one without winning the other. But the war for the hearts of the people is more than a military tactic. It is a moral principle. For this we shall strive as we fight to bring about a true social revolution.

Part III: The Purposes of the Government of the United States

1. The United States of America is joined with the people and Government of Viet-Nam to prevent aggression. This is the purpose of the determined effort of the American armed forces now engaged in Viet-Nam. The United States seeks no bases. It seeks no colonial presence. It seeks to impose no alliance or alignment. It seeks only to prevent aggression, and its pledge to that purpose is firm. It aims simply to help a people and government who are determined to help themselves.

2. The United States is pledged to the principles of the self-determination of peoples, and of government by the consent of the governed. It therefore gives its full support to the purpose of free elections proclaimed by the Government of South Viet-Nam and to the principle of open arms and amnesty for all who turn from terror toward peace and rural construction. The United States will give its full support to measures of social revolution including land reform based upon the principle of building upward from the hopes and purposes of all the people of Viet-Nam.

3. Just as the United States is pledged to play its full part in the world-wide attack upon hunger, ignorance, and disease, so in Viet-Nam it will give special support to the work of the people of that country to build even while they fight. We have helped and we will help them—to stabilize the economy—to increase the production of food—to spread the light of education—to stamp out disease.

4. The purpose of the United States remains a purpose of peace. The United States Government and the Government of Viet-Nam will continue in the future, as they have in the past, to press the quest for a peaceful settlement in every forum. The world knows the harsh and negative response these efforts have thus far received. But the world should know, too, that the United States Government and the Government of Viet-Nam remain determined that no path to peace shall be unexplored. Within the framework of their international commitments, the United States and Viet-Nam aim to create with others a stable peace in Southeast Asia which will permit the governments and peoples of the region to devote themselves to lifting the condition of man. With the understanding and support of the Government of Viet-Nam the peace offensive of the United States Government and the Government of South Viet-Nam will continue until peace is secured.

Part IV: The Common Commitment

The President of the United States and the Chief of State and Prime Minister of the Republic of Viet-Nam are thus pledged again:

to defense against aggression,
to the work of social revolution,
to the goal of free self-government,
to the attack on hunger, ignorance, and disease,
and to the unending quest for peace.

Documents 2 and 3

Secretary of Defense Robert McNamara's frequent trips to Vietnam and his obvious commitment to the ideas behind America's involvement there had led some reporters to call the struggle "Mr. McNamara's War." McNamara advocated the escalation of the Vietnam War until the fall of 1966, when he became uncertain that an ever-increasing number of troops or bombing sorties would win the war. At that time, McNamara recommended a new five-point program (Document 2) which would build on America's successes in Vietnam without further expanding the war. He now felt that the focus of American efforts should be the pacification of the South Vietnamese people rather than further military escalation.

The Joint Chiefs of Staff, under the chairmanship of General Earle G. Wheeler, disagreed with McNamara's recommendations to limit Operation Rolling Thunder. They argued, in Document 3, that bombing was a major part of the American strategy and that limiting it would adversely affect the American war effort and give the wrong message to America's friends and foes.

2 Actions Recommended for Vietnam
Robert S. McNamara
October 14, 1966
1. Evaluation of the situation.

In the report of my last trip to Vietnam almost a year ago, I stated that the odds were about even that, even with the then-recommended deployments, we would be faced in early 1967 with a military stand-off at a much higher level of conflict and with "pacification" still stalled. I am a little less pessimistic now in one respect. We have done somewhat better militarily than I anticipated. We have by and large blunted the communist military initiative—any military victory in South Vietnam the Viet Cong may have had in mind 18 months ago has been thwarted by our emergency deployments and actions. And our program of bombing the North has exacted a price.

My concern continues, however, in other respects. This is because I see no reasonable way to bring the war to an end soon. Enemy morale has not broken—he apparently has adjusted to our stopping his drive for military victory and has adopted a strategy of keeping us busy and waiting us out (a strategy of attriting our national will). He knows that we have not been, and he believes we probably will not be, able to translate our military successes into the "end products"—broken enemy morale and political achievements by the GVN.

The one thing demonstrably going for us in Vietnam over the past year has been the large number of enemy killed-in-action resulting from the big military operations. Allowing for possible exaggeration in reports, the enemy must be taking losses—deaths in and after battle—at the rate of more than 60,000 a year. The infiltration routes would seem to be one-way trails to death for the North Vietnamese. Yet there is no sign of an impending break in enemy morale and it appears that he can more than replace his losses by infiltration from North Vietnam and recruitment in South Vietnam.

Pacification is a bad disappointment. We have good grounds to be pleased by the recent elections, by Ky's 16 months in power, and by the faint signs of development of national political institutions and of a legitimate civil government. But none of this has translated itself into political achievements at Province level or below. Pacification has if anything gone backward. As compared with two, or four, years ago, enemy full-time regional forces and part-time guerrilla forces are larger; attacks, terrorism and sabotage have increased in scope and intensity; more railroads are closed and highways cut; the rice crop expected to come to market is smaller; we control little, if any, more of the population; the VC political infrastructure thrives in most of the country, continuing to give the enemy his enormous intelligence advantage; full security exists nowhere (not even behind the U.S. Marines' lines and in Saigon); in the countryside, the enemy almost completely controls the night.

Nor has the ROLLING THUNDER program of bombing the North either significantly affected infiltration or cracked the morale of Hanoi. There is agreement in the intelligence community on these facts.

In essence, we find ourselves—from the point of view of the important war (for the complicity of the people)—no better, and if anything worse off. This important war must be fought and won by the Vietnamese themselves. We have known this from the beginning. But the discouraging truth is that, as was the case in 1961 and 1963 and 1965, we have not found the formula, the catalyst, for training and inspiring them into effective action.

2. Recommended actions. In such an unpromising state of affairs, what should we do? We must continue to press the enemy militarily; we must make demonstrable progress in pacification; at the same time, we must add a new ingredient forced on us by the facts. Specifically, we must improve our position by getting ourselves into a military posture that we credibly would maintain indefinitely—a posture that makes trying to "wait us out" less attractive. I recommend a five-pronged course of action to achieve those ends.

a. Stabilize U.S. force-levels in Vietnam. It is my judgment that, barring a dramatic change in the war, we should limit the increase in U.S. forces in SVN in 1967 to 70,000 men and we should level off at the total of 470,000 which such an increase would provide.* It is my view that this is enough to punish the enemy at the large-unit operations level and to keep the enemy's main forces from interrupting pacification. I believe also that even many more than 470,00 would not kill the enemy off in such numbers as to break their morale so long as they think they can wait us out. . . .

b. Install a barrier. A portion of the 470,000 troops—perhaps 10,000 to 20,000—should be devoted to the construction and maintenance of an infiltration barrier. Such a barrier would lie near the 17th parallel—would run from the sea, across the neck of South Vietnam (choking off the new infiltration routes through the DMZ) and across the the trails in Laos. This interdiction system (at an approxi-

---

*Admiral Sharp has recommended a 12/31/67 strength of 570,000. However, I believe both he and General Westmoreland recognize that the danger of inflation will probably force an end 1967 deployment limit of about 470,000.

mate cost of $1 billion) would comprise to the east a ground barrier of fences, wire, sensors, artillery, aircraft and mobile troops; and to the west—mainly in Laos—an interdiction zone covered by air-laid mines and bombing attacks pinpointed by air-laid acoustic sensors.

The barrier may not be fully effective at first, but I believe that it can be effective in time and that even the threat of its becoming effective can substantially change to our advantage the character of the war. It would hinder enemy efforts, would permit more efficient use of the limited number of friendly troops, and would be persuasive evidence both that our sole aim is to protect the South from the North and that we intend to see the job through.

c. Stabilize the ROLLING THUNDER program against the North. Attack sorties in North Vietnam have risen from about 4,000 per month at the end of last year to 6,000 per month in the first quarter of this year and 12,000 per month at present. Most of our 50 percent increase of deployed attack-capable aircraft has been absorbed in the attacks on North Vietnam. In North Vietnam, almost 84,000 attack sorties have been flown (about 25 percent against fixed targets), 45 percent during the past seven months.

Despite these efforts, it now appears that the North Vietnamese-Laotian road network will remain adequate to meet the requirements of the Communist forces in South Vietnam—this is so even if its capacity could be reduced by one-third and if combat activities were to be doubled. North Vietnam's serious need for trucks, spare parts and petroleum probably can, despite air attacks, be met by imports. The petroleum requirement for trucks involved in the infiltration movement, for example, has not been enough to present significant supply problems, and the effects of the attacks on the petroleum distribution system, while they have not yet been fully assessed, are not expected to cripple the flow of essential supplies. Furthermore, it is clear that, to bomb the North sufficiently to make a radical impact upon Hanoi's political, economic and social structure, would require an effort which we could make but which would not be stomached either by our own people or by world opinion; and it would involve a serious risk of drawing us into open war with China.

The North Vietnamese are paying a price. They have been forced to assign some 300,000 personnel to the lines of communication in order to maintain the critical flow of personnel and material to the South. Now that the lines of communication have been manned, however, it is doubtful that either a large increase or decrease in our interdiction sorties would substantially change the cost to the enemy of maintaining the roads, railroads, and waterways or affect whether they are operational. It follows that the marginal sorties—probably the marginal 1,000 or even 5,000 sorties—per month against the lines of communication no longer have a significant impact on the war.

When this marginal inutility of added sorties against North Vietnam and Laos is compared with the crew and aircraft losses implicit in the activity (four men and aircraft and $20 million per 1,000 sorties), I recommend, as a minimum, against increasing the level of bombing of North Vietnam and against increasing the intensity of operations by changing the areas or kinds of targets struck.

Under these conditions, the bombing program would continue the pressure and would remain available as a bargaining counter to get talks started (or to trade off in talks). But, as in the case of a stabilized level of U.S. ground forces, the stabilization of ROLLING THUNDER would remove the prospect of ever escalating bombing as a factor complicating our political posture and distracting from the main job of pacification in South Vietnam.

At the proper time, I believe we should consider terminating bombing in all of North Vietnam, or at least in the Northeast zones, for an indefinite period in connection with covert moves toward peace.

d. Pursue a vigorous pacification program. As mentioned above, the pacification (Revolutionary Development) program has been and is thoroughly stalled. The large-unit operations war, which we know best how to fight and where we have had our successes, is largely irrelevant to pacification as long as we do not lose it. By and large, the people in rural areas believe that the GVN when it comes will not stay but that the VC will; that cooperation with the GVN will be punished by the VC; that the GVN is really indifferent to the people's welfare; that the low-level GVN are tools of the local rich; and that the GVN is ridden with corruption.

Success in pacification depends on the interrelated functions of providing physical security, destroying the VC apparatus, motivating the people to cooperate and establishing responsive local government. An obviously necessary but not sufficient requirement for success of the Revolutionary Development cadre and police is vigorously conducted and adequately prolonged clearing operations by military troops, who will "stay" in the area, who behave themselves decently and who show some respect for the people.

This elemental requirement of pacification has been missing. . . .

The U.S. cannot do this pacification security job for the Vietnamese. All we can do is "Massage the heart." For one reason, it is known that we do not intend to stay; if our efforts worked at all, it would merely postpone the eventual confrontation of the VC and GVN infrastructures. The GVN must do the job; and I am convinced that drastic reform is needed if the GVN is going to be able to do it.

The first essential reform is in the attitude of GVN officials. They are generally apathetic, and there is corruption high and low. Often appointments, promotions, and draft deferments must be bought; and kickbacks on salaries are common. Cadre at the bottom can be no better than the system above them.

The second needed reform is in the attitude and conduct of the ARVN. The image of the government cannot improve unless and until the ARVN improves markedly. They do not understand the importance (or respectability) of pacification nor the importance to pacification of proper, disciplined conduct. Promotions, assignments and awards are often not made on merit, but rather on the basis of having a diploma, friends or relatives, or because of bribery. The ARVN is weak in dedication, direction and discipline. . . .

e. Press for Negotiations. I am not optimistic that Hanoi or the VC will respond to peace overtures now (explaining my recommendations above that we get into a level-off posture for the long pull). The ends sought by the two sides appear to be irreconcilable and the relative power balance is not in their view unfavorable to them. But three things can be done, I believe, to increase the prospects:

(1) Take steps to increase the credibility of our peace gestures in the minds of the enemy. There is considerable evidence both in private statements by the Communists and in the reports of competent Western officials who have talked with them that charges of U.S. bad faith are not solely propagandistic, but reflect deeply held beliefs. Analyses of Communists' statements and actions indicate that they firmly believe that American leadership really does not want the fighting to stop, and that we are intent on winning a military victory in Vietnam and on maintaining our presence there through a puppet regime supported by U.S. military bases.

As a way of projective U.S. bona fides, I believe that we should consider two possibilities with respect to our bombing program against the North, to be undertaken, if at all, at a time very carefully selected with a view to maximizing the chances of influencing the enemy and world opinion and to minimizing the chances that failure would strengthen the hand of the "hawks" at home: First, without fanfare, conditions, or avowal, whether the stand-down was permanent or temporary, stop bombing all of North Vietnam. It is generally thought that Hanoi will not agree to negotiations until they can claim that the bombing has stopped unconditionally. We should see what develops, retaining freedom to resume the bombing if nothing useful was forthcoming.

Alternatively, we could shift the weight-of-effort away from "Zones 6A and 6B"—zones including Hanoi and Haiphong and areas north of those two cities to the Chinese border. This alternative has some attraction in that it provides the North Vietnamese a "face saver" if only problems of "face" are holding up Hanoi peace gestures; it would narrow the bombing down directly to the objectionable infiltration (supporting the logic of a stop-infiltration/full-pause deal); and it would reduce the international heat on the U.S. . . .

To the same end of improving our credibility, we should seek ways—through words and deeds—to make believable our intention to withdraw our forces once the North Vietnamese aggression against the South stops. In particular, we should avoid any implication that we will stay in South Vietnam with bases or to guarantee any particular outcome to a solely South Vietnamese struggle.

(2) Try to split the VC off from Hanoi. The intelligence estimate is that evidence is overwhelming that the North Vietnamese dominate and control the National Front and the Viet Cong. Nevertheless, I think we should continue and enlarge efforts to contact the VC/NLF and to probe ways to split members or sections off the VC/NLF organization.

(3) Press contacts with North Vietnam, the Soviet Union and other parties who might contribute toward a settlement.

(4) Develop a realistic plan providing a role for the VC in negotiations, postwar life, and government of the nation. An amnesty offer and proposals for national reconciliation would be steps in the right direction and should be parts of the plan. It is important that this plan be one which will appear reasonable, if not at first to Hanoi and the VC, at least to world opinion.

3. The prognosis.

The prognosis is bad that the war can be brought to a satisfactory conclusion within the next two years. The large-unit operations probably will not do it; negotiations probably will not do it. *While we should continue to pursue both of these routes in trying for a solution in the short run, we should recognize that success from them is a mere possibility, not a probability.*

The solution lies in girding, openly, for a longer war and in taking actions immediately which will in 12 to 18 months give clear evidence that the continuing costs and risks to the American people are acceptably limited, that the formula for success has been found, and that the end of the war is merely a matter of time. All of my recommendations will contribute to this strategy, but the one most difficult to implement is perhaps the most important one—enlivening the pacification program. The odds are less than even for this task, if only because we have failed consistently since 1961 to make a dent in the problem. But, because the 1967 trend of pacification will, I believe, be the main talisman of ultimate U.S. success or failure in Vietnam, extraordinary imagination and effort should go into changing the stripes of that problem. . . .

3   Memo from the Joint Chiefs of Staff to Secretary of Defense McNamara
October 14, 1966
The Joint Chiefs of Staff do not concur in your recommendation that there should be no increase in level of bombing effort and no modification in areas and targets subject to air attack. They believe our air campaign against NVN to be an integral and indispensable part of over all war effort. To be effective, the air campaign should be conducted with only those minimum constraints necessary to avoid indiscriminate killing of population. . . .

The Joint Chiefs of Staff do not concur with your proposal that, as a carrot to induce negotiations, we should suspend or reduce our bombing campaign against NVN. Our experiences with pauses in bombing and resumption have not been happy ones. Additionally, the Joint Chiefs of Staff believe that the likelihood of the war being settled by negotiation is small, and that, far from inducing negotiations, another bombing pause will be regarded by North Vietnamese leaders, and our Allies, as renewed evidence of lack of U.S. determination to press the war to a successful conclusion. The bombing campaign is one of the two trump cards in the hands of the President (the other being the presence of U.S. troops in SVN). It should not be given up without an end to the NVN aggression in SVN. . . .

The Joint Chiefs of Staff believe that the war has reached a stage at which decisions taken over the next sixty days can determine the outcome of the war and, consequently, can affect the overall security interests of the United States for years to come. Therefore, they wish to provide to you and to the President their unequivocal views on two salient aspects of the war situation: the search for peace and military pressures on NVN.

A. The frequent, broadly-based public offers made by the President to settle the war by peaceful means on a generous basis, which would take from NVN nothing it now has, have been admirable. Certainly, no one—American or foreigner—except those who are determined not to be convinced, can doubt the sincerity, the generosity, the altruism of U.S. actions and objectives. In the opinion of the Joint Chiefs of Staff the time has come when further overt actions and offers on our part are not only nonproductive, they are counter-productive. A logical case can be made that the American people, our Allies, and our enemies alike are increasingly uncertain as to our resolution to pursue the war to a successful conclusion. The Joint Chiefs of Staff advocate the following:

(1) A statement by the President during the Manila Conference of his unswerving determination to carry on the war until NVN aggression against SVN shall cease;

(2) Continued covert exploration of all avenues leading to a peaceful settlement of the war; and

(3) Continued alertness to detect and react appropriately to withdrawal of North Vietnamese troops from SVN and cessation of support to the VC. . . .

Document 4

These first few pages from Jonathan Schell's history, *The Village of Ben Suc,* look at how the inhabitants of a village thirty miles from Saigon were affected by the opposing sides in the war. From this a reader can understand a great deal about the success of the National Liberation Front and the difficulties the United States and South Vietnamese governments faced in trying to pacify the population of South Vietnam. The entrenched position of the NLF among the 3,500 people of Ben Suc made it and much of the nearby countryside unexpectedly hard to win over and prompted the major search and destroy mission Operation Cedar Falls in 1967.

4   The Village of Ben Suc
Jonathan Schell

Up to a few months ago, Ben Suc was a prosperous village of some thirty-five hundred people. It had a recorded history going back to the late eighteenth century, when the Nguyen Dynasty, which ruled the southern part of Vietnam, fortified it and used it as a base in its campaign to subjugate the natives of the middle region of the country. In recent years, most of the inhabitants of Ben Suc, which lay inside a small loop of the slowly meandering Saigon River, in Binh Duong Province, about thirty miles from the city of Saigon, were engaged in tilling the exceptionally fertile paddies bordering the river and in tending the extensive orchards of mangoes, jackfruit, and an unusual strain of large grapefruit that is a famous product of the Saigon River region. The village also supported a small group of merchants, most of them of Chinese descent, who ran shops in the marketplace, including a pharmacy that sold a few modern medicines to supplement traditional folk cures of herbs and roots; a bicycle shop that also sold second-hand motor scooters; a hairdresser's; and a few small restaurants, which sold mainly noodles. These merchants were far wealthier than the other villagers; some of them even owned second-hand cars for their businesses. The village had no electricity and little machinery of any kind. Most families kept pigs, chickens, ducks, one or two cows for milk, and a team of water buffaloes for labor, and harvested enough rice and vegetables to sell some in the market every year. Since Ben Suc was a rich village, the market was held daily, and it attracted farmers from neighboring villages as well as the Ben Suc farmers. Among the people of Ben Suc, Buddhists were more numerous than Confucianists, but in practice the two religions tended to resemble each other more than they differed, both conforming more to locally developed village customs practiced by everyone than to the requirements of the two doctrines. The Confucianists prayed to Confucius as a Buddha-like god, the Buddhists regarded their ancestors as highly as any Confucianist did, and everyone celebrated roughly the same main holidays.

. . .

Troops of the Army of the Republic of Vietnam (usually written "ARVN" and pronounced "Arvin" by the Americans) maintained an outpost in Ben Suc from 1955 until late 1964, when it was routed in an attack by the National Liberation Front (or N.L.F., or Vietcong, or V.C.), which kidnapped and later executed the government-appointed village chief and set up a full governing apparatus of its own. The Front demanded—and got—not just the passive support of the Ben Suc villagers but their active participation both in the governing of their own village and in the war effort. In the first months, the Front called several village-wide meetings. These began with impassioned speeches by leaders of the Front, who usually opened with a report of victories over the Americans and the "puppet troops" of the government, emphasizing in particular the downing of helicopters or planes and the disabling of tanks. Two months after the "liberation" of the village, the Front repelled an attack by ARVN troops, who abandoned three American M-113 armored personnel-carriers on a road leading into the village when they fled. The disabled hulks of these carriers served the speakers at the village meetings as tangible proof of their claimed superiority over the Americans, despite all the formidable and sophisticated weaponry of the intruders. Occasionally, a badly burned victim of an American napalm attack or an ex-prisoner of the government who had been tortured by ARVN troops was brought to Ben Suc to offer testimony and show his wounds to the villagers, giving the speakers an opportunity to condemn American and South Vietnamese-government atrocities. They painted a monstrous picture of the giant Americans, accusing them not only of bombing villages but also of practicing cannibalism and slitting the bellies of pregnant women. The speeches usually came to a close with a stirring call for support in the struggle and for what was sometimes called "the full coöperation and solidarity among the people to beat the American aggressors and the puppet troops." The speeches were often followed by singing and dancing, particularly on important National Liberation Front holidays, such as the founding day of the Front, December 20th, and Ho Chi Minh's birthday, May 19th. At one meeting, the dancers represented the defeat of a nearby "strategic hamlet." Usually, some of the women from Ben Suc itself danced, after being instructed by dancers from the Front. During the first year of Front government, a group of village teen-agers formed a small band, including a guitar, a trumpet, and various traditional Vietnamese instruments, and played for the meetings, but toward the end of 1965 they were replaced by a professional itinerant band. In all its meetings to boost morale and rally the villagers, the Front attempted to create an atmosphere combining impassioned seriousness with an optimistic, energetic, improvised gaiety that drew the villagers into participation. At every opportunity, it attempted to make the villagers aware of their own collective power and of the critical necessity of their support in winning the war.

The Front organized the entire village into a variety of "associations" for the support of the war effort. The largest were the Youth Liberation Association, the Farmers' Liberation Association, and the Women's Liberation Association. Each of these three associations met twice a month, and in times of emergency they met more often. At the meetings, leaders again reported news of recent victories and also delivered instructions from higher authorities for the coming month. The Youth Liberation Association exacted dues of one piastre (about three-quarters of a cent) a month. The usual duties of its members were to carry supplies and rice for the troops, build blockades to make the roads impassable to jeeps and slow for armored personnel-carriers, and dig tunnels, usually as bomb shelters for the village but sometimes as hideouts or hospitals for the Front's troops. Every once in a while, the members were called to the scene of a battle to remove the dead and wounded. The Farmers' Liberation Association asked for dues of two piastres a month. The farmers also had to pay the Front a tax of up to ten per cent of their harvest. Taxes were assessed on a graduated scale, with the richest farmers paying the most and the poorest paying nothing, or even receiving a welfare allotment. In its propaganda, the Front emphasized the fact that rich peasants, who had the most to lose from the Front's policy of favoring the poor as a "priority class," would not be allowed to slip out of their obligations to the war effort or to play a merely passive role in it. Soldiers were recruited from both the Youth Association and the Farmers' Association, with members of the priority class most often entrusted with positions as officers and leaders. In one case, the Front supported a young orphan on welfare until he became established as a farmer, and then made him a soldier and promoted him to the rank of squad commander within a few months. Generally speaking, rich families and families with relatives in ARVN were mistrusted and kept under close watch. The duties of members of the Women's Liberation Association were not fixed. They supported the war effort through a number of miscellaneous jobs, among them making clothes. A few young women served as nurses, helping roving Front doctors at a large underground hospital in the jungle, only a few miles from the village. On the non-military side, the Women's Association took a strong stand on the need to break the bonds imposed on women by the "dark feudal society" and to raise women to an equal position with men. There was no Front organization for old people—formerly the most influential group in village life. As an ex-member of the Farmers' Association has put it, the Front's policy toward old people was to "recruit them if they were smart" and otherwise leave them alone with their old ways. The activities of the three large associations were coordinated by the Village Committee, a group of three men in close contact with higher officials of the Front. The three men on the Village Committee were the village chief, who dealt with military and political matters; the village secretary, who dealt with taxes and supplies; and the education officer, who was responsible for the schools and the propaganda meetings. The Front was particularly diligent in establishing schools where the children, along with reading and their multiplication tables, learned anti-American slogans. In short, to the villagers of Ben Suc the National Liberation Front was not a band of roving guerrillas but the full government of their village. . . .

In late 1965, the Front permitted a team of ARVN troops to come into Ben Suc and attempt their own version of the Front's village meetings. This kind of ARVN meeting, which the Americans call a Hamlet Festival, is, like so many of the techniques employed by the South Vietnamese government and the United States Army, a conscious imitation of the Front's programs. (In a full-scale Hamlet Festival, troops will surround a village and order everyone into the center. Then, while intelligence men set up a temporary headquarters to interrogate the males caught in the roundup, searching for draft dodgers as well as for the enemy, a special team of entertainers will put on a program of propaganda songs and popular love songs for the women and children. Sometimes a medical team will give shots, hand out pills, and offer medical advice. Lunch is usually served from a mess tent. In the most abbreviated version of the Hamlet Festival, only a medical team will go into a village.) The fact that the Front allowed an ARVN medical team to enter the village in 1965 was quite consistent with the Front's continuing policy of deriving whatever benefit it can from government programs and facilities. One American official has noted, "If they don't try to blow up a certain power station, it usually means they're drawing power off it for themselves." . . .

Documents 5 and 6

Although the American military role in South Vietnam grew swiftly after 1965, President Johnson wanted to retain the option to negotiate; he called an extended bombing halt and launched a well-publicized "peace offensive" in January 1966. Even though this attempt was unsuccessful, Johnson tried again with another bombing pause in honor of the Tet holidays in February 1967.

During this truce, President Johnson wrote to Ho Chi Minh, outlining his proposals for the initiation of negotiations (Document 5). Ho Chi Minh's response, Document 6, was not conciliatory. Each leader had a different sense of how to begin a discussion, and that first step was the hardest one to take.

5   **Letter from Lyndon B. Johnson
to Ho Chi Minh
February 8, 1967**

Dear Mr. President,

I am writing to you in the hope that the conflict in Vietnam can be brought to an end. The conflict has already taken a heavy toll—in lives lost, in wounds inflicted, in property destroyed, and in simple human misery. If we fail to find a just and peaceful solution, history will judge us harshly.

Therefore, I believe that we both have a heavy obligation to seek earnestly the path to peace. It is in response to that obligation that I am writing directly to you. We have tried over the past several years, in a variety of ways and through a number of channels, to convey to you and your colleagues our desire to achieve a peaceful settlement. For whatever reasons, these efforts have not achieved any results.

It may be that our thoughts and yours, our attitudes and yours, have been distorted or misinterpreted as they passed through these various channels. Certainly that is always a danger in indirect communication.

There is one good way to overcome this problem and to move forward in the search for a peaceful settlement. That is for us to arrange for direct talks between trusted representatives in a secure setting and away from the glare of publicity. Such talks should not be used as a propaganda exercise but should be a serious effort to find a workable and mutually acceptable solution.

In the past two weeks. I have noted public statements by representatives of your government suggesting that you would be prepared to enter into direct bilateral talks with representatives of the U.S. Government, provided that we ceased "unconditionally" and permanently our bombing operations against your country and all military actions against it. In the last days, serious and responsible parties have assured us indirectly that this is in fact your proposal.

Let me frankly state that I see two great difficulties with this proposal. In view of your public position, such action on our part would inevitably produce worldwide speculation that discussions were under way and would impair the privacy and secrecy of those discussions. Secondly, there would inevitably be grave concern on our part whether your government would make use of such action by us to improve its military position.

With these problems in mind, I am prepared to move even further toward an ending of the hostilities than your government has proposed in either public statements or through private diplomatic channels. I am prepared to order a cessation of bombing against your country and the stopping of further augmentation of U.S. forces in South Vietnam as soon as I am assured that infiltration into South Vietnam by land and by sea has stopped. These acts of restraint on both sides would, I believe, make it possible for us to conduct serious and private discussions leading toward an early peace.

I make this proposal to you now with a specific sense of urgency arising from the imminent New Year holidays in Vietnam. If you are able to accept this proposal I see no reason why it could not take effect at the end of the New Year, or Tết, holidays. The proposal I have made would be greatly strengthened if your military authorities and those of the government of South Vietnam could promptly negotiate an extension of the Tết truce.

As to the site of the bilateral discussions I propose, there are several possibilities. We could, for example, have our representatives meet in Moscow where contacts

have already occurred. They could meet in some other country si
may have other arrangements or sites in mind, and I would
suggestions.

The important thing is to end a conflict that has brought bi
peoples, and above all to the people of South Vietnam. If you
about the actions I propose, it would be most important that I re
as possible.

Sincerely,
Lyndon B. Johnson

6 Ho Chi Minh's Reply to Lyndon B. Johnson February 15, 1967

Your Excellency,

On February 10, 1967, I received your message. This is my reply.

Vietnam is thousands of miles away from the United States. The Vietnamese
people have never done any harm to the United States. But contrary to the pledges
made by its representative at the 1954 Geneva Conference, the U.S. Government
has ceaselessly intervened in Vietnam, it has unleashed and intensified the war of
aggression in South Vietnam with a view to prolonging the partition of Vietnam
and turning South Vietnam into a neo-colony and a military base of the United
States. For over two years now, the U.S. Government has, with its air and naval
forces, carried the war to the Democratic Republic of Vietnam, an independent and
sovereign country.

The U.S. Government has committed war crimes, crimes against peace and
against mankind. In South Vietnam, half a million U.S. and satellite troops have
resorted to the most inhuman weapons and the most barbarous methods of warfare,
such as napalm, toxic chemicals and gases, to massacre our compatriots, destroy
crops, and raze villages to the ground. In North Vietnam, thousands of U.S. aircraft
have dropped hundreds of thousands of tons of bombs, destroying towns, villages,
factories, roads, bridges, dykes, dams, and even churches, pagodas, hospitals,
schools. In your message, you apparently deplored the sufferings and destructions in
Vietnam. May I ask you: Who has perpetrated these monstrous crimes? It is the U.S.
and satellite troops. The U.S. Government is entirely responsible for the extremely
serious situation in Vietnam.

The U.S. war of aggression against the Vietnamese people constitutes a challenge
to the countries of the socialist camp, a threat to the national independence movement, and a serious danger to peace in Asia and the world.

The Vietnamese people deeply love independence, freedom and peace. But in the
face of the U.S. aggression, they have risen up, united as one man, fearless of sacrifices and hardships; they are determined to carry on their Resistance until they have
won genuine independence and freedom and true peace. Our just cause enjoys
strong sympathy and support from the peoples of the whole world including broad
sections of the American people.

The U.S. Government has unleashed the war of aggression in Vietnam. It must
cease this aggression. That is the only way to the restoration of peace. The U.S.
Government must stop definitively and unconditionally its bombing raids and all
other acts of war against the Democratic Republic of Vietnam, withdraw from
South Vietnam all U.S. and satellite troops, recognize the South Vietnam National

Front for Liberation, and let the Vietnamese people settle themselves their own affairs. Such is the basic content of the four-point stand of the Government of the Democratic Republic of Vietnam, which embodies the essential principles and provisions of the 1954 Geneva Agreements on Vietnam. It is the basis of a correct political solution to the Vietnam problem.

In your message, you suggested direct talks between the Democratic Republic of Vietnam and the United States. If the U.S. Government really wants these talks, it must first of all stop unconditionally its bombing raids and all other acts of war against the Democratic Republic of Vietnam. It is only after the unconditional cessation of the U.S. bombing raids and all other acts of war against the Democratic Republic of Vietnam that the Democratic Republic of Vietnam and the United States could enter into talks and discuss questions concerning the two sides.

The Vietnamese people will never submit to force; they will never accept talks under the threat of bombs.

Our cause is absolutely just. It is to be hoped that the U.S. Government will act in accordance with reason.

Sincerely,
Ho Chi Minh

Document 7

The Commander of the United States Military Assistance Command, Vietnam, General William C. Westmoreland, frequently commented on the status of the war and he was consistently optimistic.

In Document 7, an address delivered before a Joint Session of Congress on April 28, 1967, Westmoreland reported that the American and South Vietnamese troops were more than equal to the challenge posed by North Vietnam and the Vietcong.

7 Address to Congress
William Westmoreland
April 28, 1967

. . . The Republic of Vietnam is fighting to build a strong nation while aggression—organized, directed and supported from without—attempts to engulf it. This is an unprecedented challenge for a small nation such as the Republic of Vietnam. But it is a challenge which will confront any nation that is marked as a target for the communist stratagem called "war of national liberation." I can assure you here and now that militarily this stratagem will not succeed in Vietnam.

In three years of close study and daily observation, I have seen no evidence that this is an internal insurrection. And I have seen much evidence to the contrary—documented by the enemy himself—that it simply is aggression from the North.

Since 1954, when the Geneva Accords were signed, the North Vietnamese have been sending leaders, political organizers, technicians and experts on terrorism and sabotage into the South. Clandestinely directed from the North, they and their Hanoi-trained southern counterparts have controlled the entire course of the attack against the Republic of South Vietnam.

More than two years ago, North Vietnamese divisions began to arrive, and the control no longer was as clandestine. Since then, the buildup of enemy forces has been formidable. During the last 22 months, the number of enemy combat battalions in the South has increased significantly, and nearly half of them are North Vietnamese. In the same period, overall enemy strength has nearly doubled in spite of large battle losses.

Enemy commanders are skilled professionals and provide good leadership. In general, their troops are thoroughly indoctrinated, well trained, aggressive and under tight control.

The enemy's logistic system is primitive in many ways. Forced to transport most of his supplies down through Southeastern Laos, he uses combinations of trucks, bicycles, men and animals. But he does this with surprising effectiveness. In South Vietnam, the system is well organized. Many of the caches we have found and destroyed have been stocked with enough supplies and equipment to support months of future operations.

The enemy emphasizes what he calls strategic mobility although his tactics are based on foot mobility, relatively modest firepower, and often primitive means of communications. However, his operational planning is meticulous. He gathers intelligence, makes careful plans, assigns specific tasks in detail and then rehearses the plan of attack until he believes it cannot fail. The enemy impresses local villagers into his service, demanding that they provide food, shelter and laborers to carry supplies and equipment for combat units, and to evacuate the dead and wounded from the battlefield.

When all is ready he moves his large military formations covertly from concealed bases into the operational area. His intent is to launch a surprise attack designed to achieve quick victory by the sudden application of overwhelming power. This tactic has failed because of our firepower and spoiling attacks.

For months now we have been successful in destroying a number of main force units. We will continue to seek out the enemy, catch him off guard, and punish him at every opportunity.

But success against his main forces alone is not enough to insure a swift and decisive end to the conflict.

This enemy also uses terror—murder, mutilation, abduction and the deliberate shelling of innocent men, women and children—to exercise control through fear. This tactic, which he employs daily, is much harder to counter than his best conventional moves.

During the week ending 22 April Viet Cong terrorists killed 126 innocent civilians, wounded 86 and abducted 100 others. The victims included 27 Revolutionary Development workers, 11 village or hamlet officials or candidates, six policemen, and 13 refugees or defectors from VC control.

Last Sunday, terrorists, near Saigon, assassinated a 39-year old village chief. The same day in the delta, they kidnapped 26 civilians assisting in arranging for local elections. The next day the Viet Cong attacked a group of Revolutionary Development workers, killing one and wounding 12 with grenades and machine-gun fire in one area, and in another they opened fire on a small civilian bus and killed three and wounded four of its passengers. These are cases of calculated enemy attack on civilians to extend by fear that which they cannot gain by persuasion.

One hears little of this brutality here at home. What we do hear about is our own aerial bombing against North Vietnam, and I would like to address this for a moment.

For years the enemy has been blowing bridges, interrupting traffic, cutting roads, sabotaging power stations, blocking canals and attacking airfields in the

South, and he continues to do so. Bombing in the North has been centered on precisely these same kinds of targets and for the same military purposes—to reduce the supply, interdict the movement and impair the effectiveness of enemy military forces.

Within his capabilities the enemy in Vietnam is waging total war all day—every day—everywhere. He believes in force, and his intensification of violence is limited only by his resources and not by any moral inhibitions.

To our forces, a cease fire means just that. Our observance of past truces has been open and subject to public scrutiny. The enemy permits no such observation. He traditionally has exploited cease fire periods when the bombing has been suspended to increase his resupply and infiltration activity.

This is the enemy—this has been the challenge. The only strategy which can defeat such an organization is one of unrelenting military, political and psychological pressure on his whole structure—at all levels.

From his capabilities and his recent activities, I believe the enemy's probable course in the months ahead can be forecast.

In order to carry out his battlefield doctrine I foresee that he will continue his buildup across the Demilitarized Zone and through Laos, and he will attack us when he believes he has a chance for a dramatic blow. He will not return exclusively to guerrilla warfare, although he certainly will continue to intensify his guerrilla activities.

I expect the enemy to continue to increase his mortar, artillery, rocket and recoilless rifle attacks on our installations. At the same time he will step up his attacks on hamlet, village and district organizations to intimidate the people, and to thwart the democratic processes now underway in South Vietnam.

Given the nature of the enemy, it seems to me that the strategy we are following at this time is the proper one, and that it is producing results. While he obviously is far from quitting, there are signs that his morale and his military structure are beginning to deteriorate. Their rate of decline will be in proportion to the pressure directed against him.

Faced with this prospect, it is gratifying to note that our forces and those of the other free world allies have grown in strength and profited from experience. In this connection it is well to remember that Korea, Australia, New Zealand, Thailand and the Philippines all have military forces fighting and working with the Vietnamese and Americans in Vietnam. It also is worthy of note that 30 other nations are providing non-combat support, and that all of these free world forces are doing well, whether in combat or in support of nation-building. Their exploits deserve recognition, not only for their direct contributions to the overall effort, but for their symbolic reminder that the whole of free Asia opposes communist expansion.

As the focal point of this struggle in Asia the Republic of Vietnam Armed Forces merit special mention.

In 1954 South Vietnam had literally no armed forces in being. There was no tradition of leadership, nor was there an educational system to provide leaders. The requirement to build an army, navy and air force in the face of enemy attack and political subversion seems, in retrospect, an almost impossible task. Yet, in their determination to resist the communists, the Vietnamese have managed to do it.

What I see now in Vietnam is a military force that performs with growing professional skill. During the last six months, Vietnamese troops have scored repeated successes against some of the best Viet Cong and North Vietnamese Army Units.

Perhaps more important in this total effort is the support given by the Vietnamese military to the government's nation-building or Revolutionary Development program. Nearly half of the Vietnamese Army now is engaged in or training for this vital program which will improve the lot of the people. This is a difficult role for a military force. Vietnamese are not only defending villages and hamlets, but with spirit and energy they have turned to the task of nation building as well.

In 1952 there were some who doubted that the Republic of Korea would ever have a first rate fighting force. I wish those doubters could see the Korean units in Vietnam today. They rank with the best fighters and the most effective civic action workers in Vietnam. And so today when I hear doubts about the Vietnamese armed forces, I am reminded of that example.

As you know we are fighting a war with no front lines since the enemy hides among the people, in the jungles and mountains, and uses covertly border areas of neutral countries. Therefore one cannot measure the progress of battle by lines on a map. We therefore have to use other means to chart progress. Several indices clearly point to steady and encouraging success:

Two years ago the Republic of Vietnam had fewer than 30 combat ready battalions. Today it has 154.

Then there were three jet-capable runways in South Vietnam. Today there are 14.

In April 1965 there were 15 airfields that could take C-130 transport aircraft. Now there are 89.

Then there was one deep water port for sea-going ships. Now there are seven.

In 1965 ships had to wait weeks to unload. Now we turn them around in as little as one week.

Then there was no long-haul highway transport. Last month alone 161,000 tons of supplies were moved over the highways. During the last year the mileage of essential highways open for our use has risen from about 52% to 80%.

During 1965 the Republic of Vietnam Armed Forces and its allies killed 36,000 of the enemy and lost approximately 12,000 in return. During recent months this three to one ratio in favor of the allies has risen significantly and in some weeks has been as high as ten or twelve to one.

In 1965, 11,000 Viet Cong rallied to the side of the government. In 1966 there were 20,000. In the first three months of 1967 there have been nearly 11,000 ralliers, a figure that equals all of 1965 and more than half of all of 1966.

In 1964 and the first part of 1965 the ratio of weapons captured was two to one in favor of the enemy. The ratio for 1966 and the first three months of this year is two and one-half to one in favor of the Republic of Vietnam and its allies.

Our President and the representatives of the people of the United States, the Congress, have seen to it that our troops in the field have been well supplied and equipped. And when a field commander does not have to look over his shoulder to see whether he is being supported, he can concentrate on the battlefield with much greater assurance of success. I speak for my troops, when I say—we are thankful for this unprecedented material support.

As I have said before, in evaluating the enemy strategy it is evident to me that he believes our Achilles' heel is our resolve. Your continued strong support is vital to the success of our mission.

Our soldiers, sailors, airmen, marines and coastguardsmen in Vietnam are the finest ever fielded by our nation. And in this assessment I include Americans of all races, creeds and colors. Your servicemen in Vietnam are intelligent, skilled, dedicated and courageous. In these qualities no unit, no service, no ethnic group and no national origin can claim priority.

These men understand the conflict and their complex roles as fighters and builders. They believe in what they are doing. They are determined to provide the shield of security behind which the Republic of Vietnam can develop and prosper for its own sake and for the future and freedom of all Southeast Asia.

Backed at home by resolve, confidence, patience, determination and continued support, we will prevail in Vietnam over communist aggression.

Documents 8 and 9

Despite General Westmoreland's public satisfaction with the progress of the fighting in South Vietnam, American strategy was continually questioned by presidential advisers and others. The military's great reliance on the aerial bombardment of Vietnam struck some as a grave error.

Documents 8 and 9 are memoranda for President Johnson submitted in May 1967. The authors, John Roche and McGeorge Bundy, remained staunch supporters of the American program in South Vietnam but felt that the methods needed to be rethought. Bombing North Vietnam and continuing to increase the American presence in South Vietnam, these men concluded, would not result in the victory the president referred to as the "coonskins on the wall."

8 Memo for the President
John P. Roche
May 1, 1967

I don't know whether it makes me a hawk, a dove, or a penguin, but for a year or more I have had very serious doubts about our Vietnamese strategy.

I don't think we have taken a "hard" enough line on what is really required to achieve our objectives.

—I have no objection to bombing North or South so long as we realize that air power, in anything short of a nuclear context, is merely *mobile artillery*.

—What has distressed me is the notion (expressed time and again by the Air Force boys) that air power would provide a *strategic* route to victory;

—And the parallel assumption that by bombing the North we could get a cut-rate solution in the South and escape from the problems of building a South Vietnamese army.

I raised the question of the rebuilding of ARVN in several memos to you last fall. Regrettably, I could write the same memos today. There are about 650,000 South Vietnamese under arms (in various categories), but we have still not done the job we did in Korea. Or even started to do it.

And the lead-time remains the same—stretched into the future—and the same argument seems to be employed against reforming ARVN—namely, that it will require too much lead-time.

As you know by now (I hope), I am not intellectually or temperamentally inclined to play "Rover Boy with the Joint Chiefs." But I do know that if I were a professional military man, I would be making demands upon you that would be contrary to the political strategy you have laid down for Vietnam.

Essentially the very concept of "limited war" runs against the grain of a dedicated military professional.

—And I don't *blame* him for this in the slightest. He is not trained, or paid, to think about political considerations.

(In this connection, I had a very interesting talk with General Clay in Bad Godesberg. I asked him why we had not insisted on land access to Berlin in 1945. He said that F.D.R. had not so instructed Ike, and that anyone who blamed Ike for the decision (me among others) was a "dumb son of a bitch." Ike, he said, was paid to make military decisions—and made one. Those of us who didn't like the decision, should blame F.D.R. and Truman. I am not in the habit of admitting that I am a "dumb son of a bitch," but in fact Clay was absolutely right.)

The simple military answer to the war in Vietnam is "destroy the enemy," and they could do a very good job of it if you turned them loose, doubled or tripled our commitment, authorized nuclear weapons, etc., etc.

In essence, they are like doctors who have a cure for pneumonia but not for a common cold—they therefore have a vested interest in the patient *getting* pneumonia.

To all of this you can correctly say "So what?" So let me try to set out what seems to me the outline of an effective strategy.

1. Our problems in the South, while sponsored and buttressed from the North, cannot be solved *in* the North unless we are prepared to abandon the strategy of limited war.

2. Specifically, we must win the war on the ground *in* the South. Ky and others have advocated an "Inchon landing" around Dong Hoi. Perhaps they should meditate on Anzio rather than Inchon—the analogy, in my judgment, is far more exact. Even by MACV's figures (which I profoundly mistrust), only a small percentage of the PAVN is in the panhandle.

3. At the risk of sounding banal, the war *in* the South can be won either by one to two million United States troops or by 500-750,000 United States troops and a *well-trained ARVN*.

4. The key to "pacification" is *not* "winning the hearts and minds of the peasantry." All they want is peace and quiet. The key to pacification is the capacity to pacify, i.e., to beat the hell out of the guerrillas and thereby convince the peasants that the VC is a loser. Like others in the world, peasants love a winner, and are much too smart to pick a winner by reading one of Zorthian's seven billion leaflets.

5. The decision to win the war in the South does not necessarily involve cessation of bombing. But I would suggest that a utility study of bombing should accompany it. When I was in Saigon, I asked a high ranking Air Force officer who was two sheets to the wind why they had flown 350 sorties the day before. He said: "We have to fly 1.2 sorties per plane per day—weather permitting. Last week we were down to 1.16, but yesterday brought it up. The goddamned Navy was up to 2.25 last week."

There may be something to this, but more fundamentally the problem is that the Air Force does not *want* to do the job that needs doing. For example, in South Vietnam the most useful *mobile artillery* are helicopters and prop aircraft (the A-1 for example). Every time an Air Force General sees a prop-plane, he has an aesthetic shudder: he wants jets—*beautiful jets*. Jets are beautiful, but they are lousy mobile artillery in terms of close ground support.

6. Finally, the constant pressure to *do something* must be resisted. Sometimes the only thing on the shelf worth buying is *time*. Assuming as I do that nothing in the limited war range will force Hanoi to negotiate (and that total war is out of the question), we have a force in Vietnam that can buy time and hopefully do something with it, namely, make ARVN into an army.

9   Memo on Vietnam Policy
McGeorge Bundy

Since the Communist turndown of our latest offers in February, there has been an intensification of bombing in the North, and press reports suggest that there will be further pressure for more attacks on targets heretofore immune. There is also obvious pressure from the military for further reinforcements in the South, although General Westmoreland has been a model of discipline in his public pronouncements. One may guess, therefore, that the President will soon be confronted with requests for 100,000–200,000 more troops and for authority to close the harbor in Haiphong. Such recommendations are inevitable, in the framework of strictly military analysis. It is the thesis of this paper that in the main they should be rejected and that as a matter of high national policy there should be a publicly stated ceiling to the level of American participation in Vietnam, as long as there is no further marked escalation on the enemy side.

There are two major reasons for this recommendation: the situation in Vietnam and the situation in the United States. As to Vietnam, it seems very doubtful that further intensifications of bombing in the North or major increases in U.S. troops in the South are really a good way of bringing the war to a satisfactory conclusion. As to the United States, it seems clear that uncertainty about the future size of the war is now having destructive effects on the national will.

On the ineffectiveness of the bombing as a means to end the war, I think the evidence is plain—though I would defer to expert estimators. Ho Chi Minh and his colleagues simply are not going to change their policy on the basis of losses from the air in North Vietnam. No intelligence estimate that I have seen in the last two years has ever claimed that the bombing would have this effect. The President never claimed that it would. The notion that this was its purpose has been limited to one school of thought and has never been the official Government position, whatever critics may assert.

I am very far indeed from suggesting that it would make sense now to stop the bombing of the North altogether. The argument for that course seems to me wholly unpersuasive at the present. To stop the bombing today would be to give the Communists something for nothing, and in a very short time all the doves in this country and around the world would be asking for some further unilateral concessions. (Doves and hawks are alike in their insatiable appetites; we can't really keep the hawks happy by small increases in effort—they come right back for more.)

The real justification for the bombing, from the start, has been double—its value for Southern morale at a moment of great danger, and its relation to Northern infiltration. The first reason has disappeared but the second remains entirely legitimate. Technical bombing of communications and of troop concentrations—and of airfields as necessary—seems to me sensible and practical. It is strategic bombing that seems both unproductive and unwise. It is true, of course, that all careful bombing does some damage to the enemy. But the net effect of this damage upon the military capability of a primitive country is almost sure to be slight. (The lights have not stayed off in Haiphong, and even if they had, electric lights are in no sense essential to the Communist war effort.) And against this distinctly marginal impact we have to weigh the fact that strategic bombing does tend to divide the U.S., to distract us all from the real struggle in the South, and to accentuate the unease and distemper which surround the war in Vietnam, both at home and abroad. It is true that careful polls show majority support for the bombing, but I believe this support rests upon an erroneous belief in its effectiveness as a means to end the war. Moreover, I think those against extension of the bombing are more passionate on balance than those who favor it. Finally, there is certainly a point at which such bombing does increase the risk of conflict with China or the Soviet Union, and I am sure there is no majority for that. In particular, I think it clear that the case against going after Haiphong Harbor is so strong that a majority would back the Government in rejecting that course.

So I think that with careful explanation there would be more approval than disapproval of an announced policy restricting the bombing closely to activities that support the war in the South. General Westmoreland's speech to the Congress made this tie-in, but attacks on power plants really do not fit the picture very well. We are attacking them, I fear, mainly because we have "run out" of other targets. Is it a very good reason? Can anyone demonstrate that such targets have been very rewarding? . . .

There is one further argument against major escalation in 1967 and 1968 which is worth stating separately, because on the surface it seems cynically political. It is that Hanoi is going to do everything it possibly can to keep its position intact until after our 1968 elections. Given their history, they are *bound* to hold out for a possible U.S. shift in 1969—that's what they did against the French, and they got most of what they wanted when Mendes took power. Having held on so long this time, and having nothing much left to lose—compared to the chance of victory—they are bound to keep on fighting. Since only atomic bombs could really knock them out (an invasion of North Vietnam would not do it in two years, and is of course ruled out on other grounds), they have it in their power to "prove" that military escalation does not bring peace—at least over the next two years. They will surely do just that. However much they may be hurting, they are not going to do us any favors before November 1968. (And since this was drafted, they have been publicly advised by Walter Lippmann to wait for the Republicans—as if they needed the advice and as if it was his place to give it!)

It follows that escalation will not bring visible victory over Hanoi before the election. Therefore the election will have to be fought by the Administration on other grounds. I think those other grounds are clear and important, and that they will be obscured if our policy is thought to be one of increasing—and ineffective—military pressure.

If we assume that the war will still be going on in November 1968, and that Hanoi will not give us the pleasure of consenting to negotiations sometime before then what we must plan to offer as a defense of Administration policy is not victory over Hanoi, but growing success—and self-reliance—in the South. This we can do, with luck, and on this side of the parallel the Vietnamese authorities should be prepared to help us out (though of course the VC will do their damnedest against us). Large parts of Westy's speech (if not quite all of it) were wholly consistent with this line of argument.

. . . if we can avoid escalation-that-does-not-seem-to-work, we can focus attention on the great and central achievement of these last two years, on the defeat we have prevented. The fact that South Vietnam has not been lost and is not going to be lost is a fact of truly massive importance in the history of Asia, the Pacific, and the U.S. An articulate minority of "Eastern intellectuals" (like Bill Fulbright) may not believe in what they call the domino theory, but most Americans (along with nearly all Asians) know better. Under this Administration the United States has already saved the hope of freedom for hundreds of millions—in this sense, the largest part of the job is done. This critically important achievement is obscured by seeming to act as if we have to do much more lest we fail.

Document 10

In this speech, delivered in San Antonio, Texas, in September 1967, President Johnson reviewed, once again, the reasons for American intervention in Vietnam. He praised the results of the recent elections in South Vietnam and saw that country as started on the road to a fully functioning democracy. However, Johnson's most important point in this speech was that the United States was always willing to negotiate. His San Antonio formula—stopping the bombing in return for "productive discussions" during which the North Vietnamese "would not take advantage" of the situation—was seen by some observers as a new and potentially helpful step in finding a negotiated end to the war.

10 San Antonio Address
Lyndon Johnson
September 29, 1967

. . . Why should three Presidents and the elected representatives of our people have chosen to defend this Asian nation more than 10,000 miles from American shores?

We cherish freedom—yes. We cherish self-determination for all people—yes. We abhor the political murder of any state by another, and the bodily murder of any people by gangsters of whatever ideology. And for 27 years—since the days of lend-lease—we have sought to strengthen free people against domination by aggressive foreign powers.

But the key to all that we have done is really our own security. At times of crisis—before asking Americans to fight and die to resist aggression in a foreign land—every American President has finally had to answer this question:

Is the aggression a threat—not only to the immediate victim—but to the United States of America and to the peace and security of the entire world of which we in America are a very vital part?

That is the question which Dwight Eisenhower and John Kennedy and Lyndon Johnson had to answer in facing the issue in Vietnam.

That is the question that the Senate of the United States answered by a vote of 82 to 1 when it ratified and approved the SEATO treaty in 1955, and to which the Members of the United States Congress responded in a resolution that it passed in 1964 by a vote of 504 to 2, ". . . the United States is, therefore, prepared, as the President determines, to take all necessary steps, including the use of armed force, to assist any member or protocol state of the Southeast Asia Collective Defense Treaty requesting assistance in defense of its freedom."

Those who tell us now that we should abandon our commitment—that securing South Vietnam from armed domination is not worth the price we are paying—must also answer this question. And the test they must meet is this: What would be the consequences of letting armed aggression against South Vietnam succeed? What would follow in the time ahead? What kind of world are they prepared to live in 5 months or 5 years from tonight?

. . .

I cannot tell you tonight as your President—with certainty—that a Communist conquest of South Vietnam would be followed by a Communist conquest of Southeast Asia. But I do know there are North Vietnamese troops in Laos. I do know that there are North Vietnamese trained guerrillas tonight in northeast Thailand. I do know that there are Communist-supported guerrilla forces operating in Burma. And a Communist coup was barely averted in Indonesia, the fifth largest nation in the world.

So your American President cannot tell you—with certainty—that a Southeast Asia dominated by Communist power would bring a third world war much closer to terrible reality. One could hope that this would not be so.

But all that we have learned in this tragic century strongly suggests to me that it would be so. As President of the United States, I am not prepared to gamble on the chance that it is not so. I am not prepared to risk the security—indeed, the survival—of this American Nation on mere hope and wishful thinking. I am convinced that by seeing this struggle through now, we are greatly reducing the chances of a much larger war—perhaps a nuclear war. I would rather stand in Vietnam, in our time, and by meeting this danger now, and facing up to it, thereby reduce the danger for our children and for our grandchildren.

I want to turn now to the struggle in Vietnam itself.

There are questions about this difficult war that must trouble every really thoughtful person. I am going to put some of these questions. And I am going to give you the very best answers that I can give you.

First, are the Vietnamese—with our help, and that of their other allies—really making any progress? Is there a forward movement? The reports I see make it clear that there is. Certainly there is a positive movement toward constitutional government. Thus far the Vietnamese have met the political schedule that they laid down in January 1966.

The people wanted an elected, responsive government. They wanted it strongly enough to brave a vicious campaign of Communist terror and assassination to vote for it. It has been said that they killed more civilians in 4 weeks trying to keep them from voting before the election than our American bombers have killed in the big cities of North Vietnam in bombing military targets.

On November 1, subject to the action, of course, of the Constituent Assembly, an elected government will be inaugurated and an elected Senate and Legislature will be installed. Their responsibility is clear: To answer the desires of the South Vietnamese people for self-determination and for peace, for an attack on corruption, for economic development, and for social justice.

There is progress in the war itself, steady progress considering the war that we are fighting; rather dramatic progress considering the situation that actually prevailed when we sent our troops there in 1965; when we intervened to prevent the dismemberment of the country by the Vietcong and the North Vietnamese.

The campaigns of the last year drove the enemy from many of their major interior bases. The military victory almost within Hanoi's grasp in 1965 has now been denied them. The grip of the Vietcong on the people is being broken.

Since our commitment of major forces in July 1965 the proportion of the population living under Communist control has been reduced to well under 20 percent. Tonight the secure proportion of the population has grown from about 45 percent to 65 percent—and in the contested areas, the tide continues to run with us.

But the struggle remains hard. The South Vietnamese have suffered severely, as have we—particularly in the First Corps area in the north, where the enemy has mounted his heaviest attacks, and where his lines of communication to North Vietnam are shortest. Our casualties in the war have reached about 13,500 killed in action, and about 85,000 wounded. Of those 85,000 wounded, we thank God that 79,000 of the 85,000 have been returned, or will return to duty shortly. Thanks to our great American medical science and the helicopter.

I know there are other questions on your minds, and on the minds of many sincere, troubled Americans: "Why not negotiate now?" so many ask me. The answer is that we and our South Vietnamese allies are wholly prepared to negotiate tonight.

I am ready to talk with Ho Chi Minh, and other chiefs of state concerned, tomorrow.

I am ready to have Secretary Rusk meet with their foreign minister tomorrow.

I am ready to send a trusted representative of America to any spot on this earth to talk in public or private with a spokesman of Hanoi.

We have twice sought to have the issue of Vietnam dealt with by the United Nations—and twice Hanoi has refused.

Our desire to negotiate peace—through the United Nations or out—has been made very, very clear to Hanoi—directly and many times through third parties.

As we have told Hanoi time and time and time again, the heart of the matter is really this: The United States is willing to stop all aerial and naval bombardment of North Vietnam when this will lead promptly to productive discussions. We, of course, assume that while discussions proceed, North Vietnam would not take advantage of the bombing cessation or limitation.

But Hanoi has not accepted any of these proposals.

So it is by Hanoi's choice—and not ours, and not the rest of the world's—that the war continues.

Why, in the face of military and political progress in the South, and the burden of our bombing in the North, do they insist and persist with the war?

From many sources the answer is the same. They still hope that the people of the United States will not see this struggle through to the very end. As one Western diplomat reported to me only this week—he had just been in Hanoi—"They believe their staying power is greater than ours and that they can't lose." A visitor from a Communist capital had this to say: "They expect the war to be long, and that the Americans in the end will be defeated by a breakdown in morale, fatigue, and psychological factors." The Premier of North Vietnam said as far back as 1962: "Americans do not like long, inconclusive war. . . . Thus we are sure to win in the end."

Are the North Vietnamese right about us?

I think not. No. I think they are wrong. I think it is the common failing of totalitarian regimes that they cannot really understand the nature of our democracy:

—They mistake dissent for disloyalty.

—They mistake restlessness for a rejection of policy.

—They mistake a few committees for a country.

—They misjudge individual speeches for public policy.

They are no better suited to judge the strength and perseverance of America than the Nazi and the Stalinist propagandists were able to judge it. It is a tragedy that they must discover these qualities in the American people, and discover them through a bloody war.

And, soon or late, they will discover them.

In the meantime, it shall be our policy to continue to seek negotiations—confident that reason will some day prevail; that Hanoi will realize that it just can never win; that it will turn away from fighting and start building for its own people.

Since World War II, this Nation has met and has mastered many challenges—challenges in Greece and Turkey, in Berlin, in Korea, in Cuba.

We met them because brave men were willing to risk their lives for their nation's security. And braver men have never lived than those who carry our colors in Vietnam at this very hour.

The price of these efforts, of course, has been heavy. But the price of not having made them at all, not having seen them through, in my judgment would have been vastly greater.

Our goal has been the same—in Europe, in Asia, in our own hemisphere. It has been—and it is now—peace.

And peace cannot be secured by wishes; peace cannot be preserved by noble words and pure intentions. "Enduring peace," Franklin D. Roosevelt said, "cannot be bought at the cost of other people's freedom."

The late President Kennedy put it precisely in November 1961, when he said: "We are neither warmongers nor appeasers, neither hard nor soft. We are Americans determined to defend the frontiers of freedom by an honorable peace if peace is possible but by arms if arms are used against us."

The true peace-keepers in the world tonight are not those who urge us to retire from the field in Vietnam—who tell us to try to find the quickest, cheapest exit from that tormented land, no matter what the consequences to us may be.

The true peace-keepers are those men who stand out there on the DMZ at this very hour, taking the worst that the enemy can give. The true peace-keepers are the soldiers who are breaking the terrorist's grip around the villages of Vietnam—the civilians who are bringing medical care and food and education to people who have already suffered a generation of war.

And so I report to you that we are going to continue to press forward. Two things we must do. Two things we shall do.

First, we must not mislead the enemy. Let him not think that debate and dissent will produce wavering and withdrawal. For I can assure you they won't. Let him not think that protests will produce surrender. Because they won't. Let him not think that he will wait us out. For he won't.

Second, we will provide all that our brave men require to do the job that must be done. And that job is going to be done.

These gallant men have our prayers—have our thanks—have our heart-felt praise—and our deepest gratitude.

Let the world know that the keepers of peace will endure through every trial—and that with the full backing of their countrymen, they are going to prevail.

Critical Issues for Discussion

1. As the war in South Vietnam grew bigger and bigger, President Johnson continually reminded his fellow citizens how and why the United States was fighting there. Compare Documents 1 and 10. According to those sources, how had the war in Vietnam begun? What were the reasons given for the American intervention? What did the United States hope to accomplish? What role did the South Vietnamese play?

2. Escalation by itself did not solve all of the problems which the war raised. Compare and contrast Documents 2 and 3. What was McNamara's message? Why was his five-point program needed? How had he evaluated the American role in Vietnam up to that point? Where had the Americans succeeded? Where had they failed?

What did the Joint Chiefs of Staff think about McNamara's recommendations? What were their reasons for this attitude? How did they think the war could be won?

Bombing remained an issue of contention in 1967 as well. Read Documents 8 and 9 and compare them to Documents 2 and 3. Was there any agreement here? Complete? Partial? None at all? Who was most qualified to make strategic judgments in Vietnam? Was it a purely military undertaking? A political one? Evaluate all four policy-makers' pleas. Who seemed most convincing to you? Why?

3. Operation Cedar Falls was a major American search and destroy mission. It occurred near Saigon in an area which had been the subject of intense political maneuvering by both Viet Cong units and United States and South Vietnamese pacification groups, as described in Document 4.

What did Schell report about the success and failures of the pacification policies of both sides? Compare the procedures used by the National Liberation Front to those used by the United States Army and the Army of the Republic of Vietnam.

4. Pacification of Vietnamese villages was a challenge to Americans. They were, simultaneously, hiding spots for the enemy and the places which had to be won over to support the Saigon government. How did the Americans want to handle this double-edged sword? Villages sometimes were, as one G.I. put it, "cleaned out." What did that mean? Another American claimed that pacification often turned into destruction. "It was as if we were trying to build a house with a bulldozer and a wrecking crane." Why were such harsh measures taken? What alternatives existed? What was the basic problem?

General Wheeler defended the search and destroy strategy in this way. "We must continue to seek out the enemy in South Vietnam—in particular, destroy his base areas where the enemy can rest, retrain, recuperate, resupply, and pull up his socks for the next military operation." Was that the same as "cleaning out" an area? What would Wheeler have said about the use of bulldozers and Rome plows? What else could have been done?

5. President Johnson's attempts to pursue negotiation while building up the war effort were not successful. The war continued and grew while the peace talks remained elusive. Read Documents 5 and 6. Was Johnson's letter a good first step toward peace talks? What did he offer? How did Ho Chi Minh respond? How do you evaluate that answer to Johnson's letter? What were the long-range goals of each leader? How would you rewrite Johnson's letter? How would you rewrite the response?

Reread Document 10. Have Johnson's offers changed? Do they respond to any of Ho Chi Minh's demands? Why didn't these offers bring real peace talks? What were the obstacles to sitting down and talking about peace?

6. General Westmoreland's address to the Joint Session of Congress (Document 7) was an optimistic assessment of the war in Vietnam. What problems faced the American troops in Vietnam? How were these problems being overcome? How did Westmoreland measure success? Were you convinced? What steps would Westmoreland have recommended to ensure success against the enemy?

7. At the end of 1966, Robert Komer, then a special assistant to the President, reported back to Mr. Johnson that all was going much better in South Vietnam. When some reporters questioned Komer about his optimism, he explained: "Gentlemen, gentlemen. I think you misunderstood what my mission for the president was. I was sent to South Vietnam to report on the *progress* there."

How had Komer understood his mission? How had he responded? Had he done well? What did reports such as his indicate? What did statements such as his indicate?

8. One observer of the American escalation in Vietnam described the American policy as one of continuous pummelling of North Vietnam. Each blow, however, was "like a sledgehammer on a floating cork. Somehow the cork refused to stay down."

Was this image a helpful one? Why a "floating" cork? Why did it refuse to stay down? Could it have been forced to stay down? How?

Follow Up One analyst of the Vietnam War claimed that the American effort in Vietnam brought him a feeling of *déjà vu*. He argued that the United States went into Vietnam "dreaming different dreams than the French but walking in the same footsteps." What did this statement mean? Were the Americans "walking in the same footsteps"? Compare and contrast the American effort in the years 1965 to 1967 with the French effort between 1946 and 1954. How would you evaluate each of them?

Suggestions for Further Reading

Soldiers' Accounts
Caputo, Philip. *A Rumor of War*. New York: Ballantine, 1977.
> Caputo, a Second Lieutenant in the Marine Corps, arrived in Vietnam in 1965 exhilarated by the adventure of stopping communism. At the end of the year he counted "our idealism lost, our morals corrupted, and purpose forgotten."

Downs, Frederick. *The Killing Zone: My Life in the Vietnam War*. New York: Norton, 1978.
> Downs is preoccupied with proving himself as a young platoon leader in grim search-and-destroy missions.

Herr, Michael. *Dispatches*. New York: Knopf, 1968.
> A journalist's impressions of the grunts' experience, *Dispatches* is chilling, often surreal in the horrors it portrays.

Indochina Curriculum Group. *Front Lines: Soldiers' Writings from Vietnam*. Cambridge, Mass.: Indochina Curriculum Group, 1975.

Compiled for high school use, this collection of first-hand accounts is worth reading by adults as well. Included are Black and white, American and Vietnamese, pro- and antiwar, GIs and officers—all raising questions about the war in some way.

Kovic, Ron. *Born on the Fourth of July*. New York: McGraw-Hill, 1976.

Paralyzed from the chest down during his year in Vietnam, Kovic describes his struggle to readjust to American life as a wounded vet and his participation in the veterans' rights and antiwar movements.

Moore, Robin. *The Green Berets*. New York: Crown, 1965.

This popular fictionalized version of "the marvelous undercover work of our Special Forces in Vietnam" gave Americans a romantic view of the U.S. mission early in the war.

O'Brien, Tim. *If I Die in a Combat Zone, Box Me Up and Ship Me Home*. New York: Dell, 1969.

O'Brien, a reluctant recruit, continued to debate the war while serving and being wounded in Vietnam. His battalion was in charge of the My Lai area in 1969 while investigations of the massacre were going on.

Rottmann, Larry, Jan Barry, and Basil T. Paquet, eds. *Winning Hearts and Minds: War Poems by Vietnam Veterans*. New York: McGraw-Hill, 1972; distributed by Southeast Asia Resource Center.

Some of these poems are passionately antiwar, others vividly descriptive of the veterans' experience of the war.

Webb, James. *Fields of Fire*. New York: Prentice-Hall, 1978.

A fictional version of the GI experience, *Fields of Fire* dramatizes many of its common elements, including the preoccupation with surviving one year and the corrupting influence of having absolute power of life and death in an ambiguous situation.

The Air War

Littauer, Raphael, and Norman Uphoff, eds. *The Air War in Indochina*. Boston: Beacon, 1972.

This collection of articles, based on government statistics, gathers everything known about the tonnage of bombs dropped, the cost of the bombing, the loss of planes and pilots, and the damage done to all of Indochina.

Schell, Jonathan. *The Military Half: An Account of Destruction in Quang Ngai and Quang Tin*. New York: Knopf, 1968.

Flying with American pilots who located targets for bombing in South Vietnam, Schell observed the missions as well as how villagers were removed to refugee camps and how the progress of the war was reported and evaluated.

Impact on the Vietnamese

Chung, Ly Qui, ed. *Between Two Fires: The Unheard Voices of Vietnam*. New York: Praeger, 1970.

The winners in a short story contest sponsored by a Third Force (moderate Vietnamese) newspaper give personal expression to the effects of the war. Included are "Refugee Hamlet," "When the Americans Came" and "The Old Man in the Free Fire Zone."

FitzGerald, Frances. *Fire in the Lake: The Vietnamese and the Americans in Vietnam*. Boston: Little, Brown, 1972.

FitzGerald portrays the vast cultural gap between the Americans and the Vietnamese. In Part II, "The Americans and the Saigon Government," she follows its destructive consequences in the years after Diem's assassination.

Griffiths, Philip Jones. *Vietnam Inc.* New York: Collier, 1971.

Griffiths' photographs contrast the dignity and beauty of traditional Vietnamese life with the grotesqueness of U.S. militarism, technology, and Coca-Cola culture.

Luce, Don, and John Sommer. *Viet Nam: The Unheard Voices*. Ithaca: Cornell Univ. Press, 1969.

Two young International Voluntary Services workers, living with Vietnamese in the countryside, report on the human effects of programs such as pacification, defoliation, and the creation of refugees. Although sympathetic to the American mission, they find it working against the real needs of the Vietnamese people.

Schell, Jonathan. *The Village of Ben Suc.* New York: Knopf, 1967.

Ben Suc, a prosperous South Vietnamese village, was governed by the NLF from 1964 to 1967, when the U.S. Army "Operation Cedar Falls" evacuated or killed everyone and obliterated what was left with bulldozers and bombers. Schell's eyewitness description, contrasted with the Americans' enthusiasm for their "model project," painfully demonstrates the counterproductivity of this U.S. strategy.

Weisberg, Barry, ed. *Ecocide in Indochina*. San Francisco: Canfield, 1970.

Articles on the effects of chemical warfare, carpet bombing, and other technological strategies to make the countryside uninhabitable make the meaning of "ecocide" devastatingly clear.

The Long and Winding Road
The Ho Chi Minh Trail was a series of footpaths which North Vietnamese troops took to the South. The trails, some of which traveled through the neighboring countries of Laos and Cambodia, were, as seen here, often quite narrow and primitive, but were modernized as the war went on. *Wide World Photo*.

Chapter 6
America's Enemy:
1954–1967

Background

Historical Summary

In the summer of 1954, an international conference in Geneva oversaw the end of the war that had been raging in Indochina for nine years. The French and the Vietminh, the main belligerents in the war, signed a cease-fire agreement that partitioned Vietnam pending a permanent political settlement. No other agreements were signed. Under the Geneva Accords, however, it was understood that nationwide elections would be held within two years to reunify Vietnam. In the meantime, the French forces would leave the North while the Vietminh troops would depart from the South. Families of the Vietminh soldiers were permitted to remain in the South, along with Vietminh political cadres designated to prepare for the elections.

The division of Vietnam at the 17th parallel imposed severe hardships on the Democratic Republic of Vietnam, the Vietminh regime in the north. The southern part of the country had traditionally supplied rice to the north, and now these shipments were cut off, causing serious food shortages. In an attempt to spur agricultural production, the government in Hanoi launched a program to distribute land to poor peasants.

The agrarian reform was also designed by the Communists to destroy the political power of rural landlords. Officials set up "people's courts" at which the landlords were tried. Many landlords were the victims of local vendettas or quotas set by officials. Between 3,000 and 15,000 were executed, and thousands more were sent to labor camps. Ho Chi Minh, the president of the country, later apologized personally for the excesses, which he feared might create disunity at a time when North Vietnam desperately needed to rebuild from the ruins of war.

Ngo Dinh Diem, the president of the regime in the South, refused to participate in the nationwide elections. He launched a campaign aimed at uprooting the Vietminh cadres who had remained behind, and his repression nearly wiped out the residual movement. He gave the Vietminh a pejorative name—the Vietcong, which meant Communist Vietnamese, and the name stuck.

By 1957, using weapons they had hidden during the French war, Vietcong

165

groups began to resist Diem's troops. They relied on guerrilla tactics and terrorism, primarily directed against South Vietnamese officials. For the most part, though, they focused on constructing a political organization. The Vietcong was helped inadvertently by Diem's ineptitude. Among other things, he alienated peasants by requiring them to pay for land that they had been given by the Vietminh earlier. Peasants were antagonized as well by the corruption and brutality of his officials, many of whom had served the French.

Preoccupied with economic problems in the North, Ho Chi Minh had initially sought to discourage the Vietcong from resorting to violence. But, after considerable debate, the Communist leaders in Hanoi determined that their southern wing would be liquidated unless it turned to armed struggle.

Adopting a tactic he had used against the French by forming the Vietminh, Ho authorized the creation of a front organization in the South, contrived to attract various opponents of the Diem government. Proclaimed in December 1960, it was called the National Liberation Front. Nguyen Huu Tho, its figurehead leader, was a non-Communist, French-educated lawyer, but the Communists exercised the real power in the movement.

Diem had at first refused to recognize the existence of an insurrection, because the admission would cast doubts on his ability to rule. But as the Vietcong insurgency spread in 1961, he appealed to the United States for help. He also embarked on several projects aimed at isolating peasants from the rebels. The most ambitious of these was the strategic hamlet program, undertaken with the help of the United States. Thousands of peasants were shunted into fortified villages. Removed from their own land and ancestral grave sites, numbers of peasants reacted by sympathizing with the Vietcong, which by late 1963 could count on 25,000 active guerrillas and another 60,000 irregulars.

Diem was overthrown by his own dissident generals in November 1963. And the Hanoi leadership, seeing an opportunity to take advantage of the confusion that followed, accelerated the movement of men and supplies into the south. By the end of 1964, with Diem's successor government in Saigon crumbling and its army in disarray, more than 10,000 northern troops and southern regroupees had filtered into the South.

In an effort to block the infiltration, the United States began a sustained bombing campaign of the North in March 1965, calling it Operation Rolling Thunder. But the air strikes failed to stop the movement. Helped by the Soviet Union and China, the North Vietnamese also set up an impressive air defense system that took a high toll of American aircraft. In addition, the Communist regime in Hanoi was able to mobilize the population for defense and safety. Factories and schools were dispersed, and people dug a vast network of shelters and tunnels. American officials soon realized, too, that the primitive North Vietnamese economy offered few bombing targets.

In March 1965, U.S. marines landed in the South Vietnamese coastal city of Danang to guard the air base there. They were the forerunners of a massive American expedition of combat troops—and, from the viewpoint of Ho Chi Minh and his comrades, yet another foreign invasion of Vietnam. Despite heavy casualties, there is no evidence that their determination to eject the foreigners ever wavered during the months of warfare leading up to the Tet offensive of January 1968.

Points to Emphasize

- the attitude of the old Vietminh political cadres to Diem's government
- the problems which faced Ho Chi Minh's Democratic Republic of Vietnam in its early years
- the reasons for the outbreak of hostilities between Diem and his opponents
- the methods used by the Vietcong for winning over the Vietnamese people
- the ways in which the fighting in South Vietnam changed in response to the American involvement in Vietnam
- the effects of Operation Rolling Thunder on the government and people of North Vietnam
- the differences between American and North Vietnamese methods of waging war

Glossary of Names and Terms

Le Duan leading political figure throughout the war years. Vietcong organizer in South Vietnam in the 1950s. Secretary, Lao Dong party Central Committee for the Southern Region, 1956. Secretary General, Lao Dong party, 1959. First Secretary, Lao Dong party, 1960.

Nguyen Huu Tho French-educated Saigon lawyer. Imprisoned by President Diem, 1954. Headed National Liberation Front of South Vietnam, 1961.

Pham Van Dong led Vietminh delegation to Geneva Conference, 1954. Premier of North Vietnam, 1955. Minister for Foreign Affairs, 1954–1961.

Vo Nguyen Giap Commander-in-chief of the Army of the Vietminh, 1946. Also held positions as Deputy Prime Minister and Defense Minister. Author of *People's War   People's Army*.

Democratic Republic of Vietnam (D.R.V.) official name of Ho Chi Minh's government, known as North Vietnam from 1954 to 1975.

Government of Vietnam (G.V.N.) the government below the 17th parallel, officially called the Republic of Vietnam and known as South Vietnam from 1954 to 1975.

Ho Chi Minh Trail a series of paths leading from North Vietnam to South Vietnam. Major route for soldiers and supplies throughout the war. Expanded as the war continued. Some branches of the trail went through Laos and Cambodia.

Lao Dong party short form of Dang Lao Dong Vietnam, the Workers' Party of Vietnam. The official party of Ho's government.

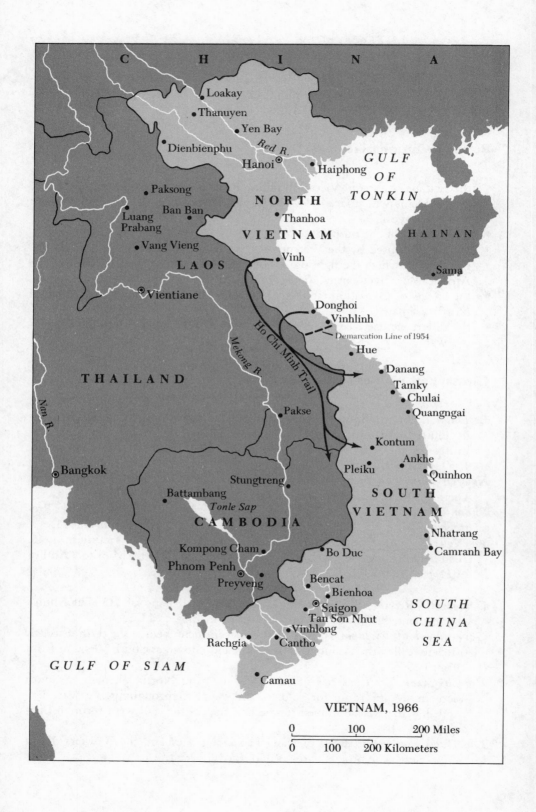

VIETNAM, 1966

0   100   200 Miles

0   100   200 Kilometers

napalm a jellylike gasoline substance used in incendiary bombs, flame-throwers, and other weapons.

Operation Rolling Thunder the American policy of sustained bombing of North Vietnam. Originally planned to last a few months, the policy was in effect from 1965 to 1968 with only a few short pauses.

shadow government in South Vietnam, the *de facto* government in rural areas set up by the Vietcong. This Vietcong administration often taxed families and recruited soldiers just like the Saigon government. Also known as the government of the night.

Documents

Document 1

Participants in the Vietnam war often cited the Geneva Accords of 1954 in defending their own actions or criticizing their opponents. The accords projected national elections to be held in 1956, but President Diem—who had publicly condemned the accords from the beginning—refused to go ahead on the grounds that there could be no free elections while the Communists ruled in Hanoi. Diem was condemned for this refusal by many, but the United States and its allies supported his decision.

This document is a note from Pham Van Dong, then Prime Minister of the Democratic Republic of Vietnam, to the Co-chairmen of the 1954 Geneva Conference on Indochina. Dong, writing in August 1955, protested Diem's arbitrary decision and asked that the Co-chairmen force the French and the South Vietnamese governments to live up to the letter and the spirit of the July 1954 agreements. Dong included the French government in his note because of the important role played by that government in Vietnamese affairs for over a century.

1 Note to the Two Co-chairmen of the 1954 Geneva Conference on Indochina
Pham Van Dong
August 17, 1955
Messrs. Co-Chairmen,
    I have the honour to address the present note to you, Messrs. Co-Chairmen of the Geneva Conference, to inform you of the grave situation now menacing the political settlement in Viet-nam in conformity with the Geneva Agreements—that is the holding of the consultative conference between the competent representative authorities in North and South Viet-nam to discuss the organization of free general elections which will bring about the reunification of Viet-nam—and to expound to you our position in face of this grave situation.

After 8 to 9 years of atrocious war, the Geneva Conference has re-established peace in Indo-China on the basis of respect for the principles of the independence, sovereignty, unity and territorial integrity of Viet-nam, Cambodia and Laos.

. . .

Thanks to the efforts of the interested parties and to the collaboration of the International Commission for Supervision and Control, the first 300 days of the execution of the Armistice Agreement have brought good results, the regroupment and transfer of military forces have been completed.

That is a notable success in the implementation of the Geneva Agreements, thereby creating *"the necessary basis for the achievement in the near future of a political settlement in Viet-nam"*.

In view of the political settlement in Viet-nam, the Government of the Democratic Republic of Viet-nam declared on June 6, 1955, its *"readiness to hold a consultative conference with the competent representative authorities in South Viet-nam to discuss the question of preparing for the general elections in order to achieve the reunification of Viet-nam"*.

Following the June 6, 1955 declaration of the Government of the Democratic Republic of Viet-nam, the Sai-gon Radio broadcast on July 16 a statement on the position of the Government in South Viet-nam in connection with the question of general elections in view of unifying the national territory; according to this statement, the authorities in South Viet-nam have repudiated the Geneva Agreements and did not touch upon the question of conducting a consultative conference to discuss the free general elections to achieve Viet-nam's reunification as provided for by the Geneva Agreements.

On July 19, 1955, the President and Prime Minister of the Democratic Republic of Viet-nam addressed to the Government of South Viet-nam a note in which he clearly said:

"The Government of the Democratic Republic of Viet-nam proposes that you appoint your representatives and that they and ours hold the consultative conference from July 20, 1955 onwards, as provided for by the Geneva Agreements, at a place agreeable to both sides, on the Vietnamese territory, in order to discuss the problem of reunification of our country by means of free general elections all over Viet-nam".

The position and attitude of the Government of the Democratic Republic of Viet-nam fully conform to the interests and intimate aspirations of the entire Vietnamese people, and have their warm response and enthusiastic support.

On August 9, 1955, the authorities in South Viet-nam, without officially replying to the July 19 note of the Government of the Democratic Republic of Viet-nam, made public, again through the Sai-gon Radio, another statement the contents of which did not in the least differ from that of the July 16 declaration, inasmuch as it continued to repudiate the Geneva Agreements and refused all consultations to discuss the holding of free general elections with a view to achieving the reunification of Viet-nam by peaceful means.

The Government of the Democratic Republic of Viet-nam deems that the implementation of the Geneva Agreements and the political settlement in Viet-nam are being seriously menaced owing to the attitude of the authorities in South Viet-nam.

The consultative conference between the competent representative authorities of the Northern and Southern zones in accordance with the Geneva Agreements, would have started by July 20, 1955, but so far it has not yet been convened; that is a grave situation for the consolidation of peace and the achievement of Viet-nam's unity and also a factor which aggravates tension in Indo-China and South East Asia.

The Government of the Democratic Republic of Viet-nam therefore addresses this note to the Co-Chairmen of the Geneva Conference to expound its position and ask for the intervention of the Co-Chairmen:

1. The Government of the Democratic Republic of Viet-nam has executed and continues to execute strictly and scrupulously the Geneva Agreements. The Government of the Democratic Republic of Viet-nam is resolved to exhort the interested parties to execute the Geneva Agreements strictly and scrupulously. . . .

2. The Government of the Democratic Republic of Viet-nam holds that the French Government and the Government in South Viet-nam should assure their obligation in the execution of the Geneva Agreements, in the cessation of hostilities as well as in the political settlement. . . .

Document 2

The 1956 deadline for elections to unite all of Vietnam passed without any negotiation between the two governments on that topic. Although the failure to hold elections was a blow to Ho Chi Minh, who was expected to win any nationwide election, the D.R.V. concentrated on consolidating its position in the North. The unification of all Vietnam was not the D.R.V's immediate goal in response to Diem's cancellation of the elections.

In this document, Le Duan, then Secretary of the Lao Dong party's Central Committee for the Southern Region, outlined the main tasks for the whole nation. Although Le Duan wanted to see Vietnam united, he did not advocate military aid for the southern political cadres. His anger at the role played by the United States in South Vietnam was an early expression of an emotion which soon intensified among North Vietnamese.

2   The Path of the Revolution in the South
Le Duan
November 1956
During two years of struggle for peace, unification, independence and democracy, the people of the South have shown clearly their earnest feelings of patriotism and the firm will of Vietnamese.

Meanwhile, the past two years have also made the people of South Vietnam see clearly the poisonous scheme of the Aggressive American imperialists, and the traitorous, country-selling crimes of Ngo Dinh Diem.

On July 20, 1954, was the day the ceasefire agreement was signed at the Geneva Conference, requiring a free national general election to unify Vietnam, but has not been carried out. The reason is the Aggressive American imperialists and dictatorial feudalist Ngo Dinh Diem have sought by every means to sabotage and not carry out the agreement with hope of maintaining long-term division of our country, and turning the South into a colony and military base of the imperialists in order to provoke war and hoping to rob us of our rivers and mountains.

The Vietnamese people, who defeated the French imperialists and American intervention after nine years of heroic resistance, forcing the imperialists at the Geneva Conference to recognize the national independence and territorial integrity of our country, definitely will not allow the imperialists and feudalists to provoke war, or to prolong the division of our country, and the cruel imperialist-feudal regime in the Southern part of our beloved country.

Three Main Tasks of the Whole Nation at Present

In order to cope with that situation created by the U.S.-Diem, and in order to complete the work of national liberation, to liberate the Southern people from the imperialist-feudalist yoke, the Party Central has put forward three main tasks to make a general line for the whole revolution work at present for the entire country.

Those tasks are:

1) Firmly consolidate the North.
2) Strongly push the Southern revolutionary movement.
3) Win the sympathy and support of the people who love peace, democracy and national independence in the world.

Why must we firmly consolidate the North?

Because the North is one half of the country which has been completely liberated from the yoke of imperialism and feudalism, has an independent and democratic government of the people. Independent, democratic North Vietnam is the result of the victory of the revolution due to the fact that the entire people from North to South struggled heroically through 9 years against French imperialism and U.S. intervention. The North at present must be the firm and strong base to serve as rear area for the revolutionary movement to liberate the South. That is why we must firmly consolidate the North.

Why must we push the Southern revolutionary movement?

Because the South at present is still under the yoke of imperialist and feudalist rule. The U.S.-Diem imperialists and feudalists are using a policy of fascist dictatorship by imperialist and class rule in order to occupy the South, are sabotaging peace, and national unification and are oppressing and exploiting our people, scheming to provoke war, hoping to invade the entire country. In order to resist the U.S.-Diem regime, the Southern people have only one way to save the country and themselves, and that is the Revolutionary path. There is no other path but Revolution.

That is why we must push the revolutionary movement of the South in order to resist the U.S.-Diem regime.

Why must we win the sympathy and support of the people who love peace, democracy, and national independence in the world?

Because our work in maintaining peace, achieving unity and completing our independence and democracy is at present a part of the movement of progressive people throughout the world which is struggling to achieve peace, democracy and independence for all mankind. Because the work of peaceful unification of the country is in keeping with the legal principles recognized by the Geneva Conference, and therefore, all actions opposing peaceful unification of our country are illegal, and are denounced by the world's people. We are strengthened further by that, while the enemy will be isolated and weakened, and we will have further favorable conditions to defeat the enemy and finish the complete liberation of our whole nation.

Those are the three tasks of the whole revolutionary line of the entire people nation-wide at present. Those three tasks cannot be separated; they are closely linked with each other. Only by fulfilling those tasks, can our people's national liberation revolution succeed.

The entire Party Committee in the South as well as the entire Southern people must clearly realize that general revolutionary line for the whole country.

In order to fulfill its task, the Party Committee of the South must firmly grasp the Revolutionary Path of the South in order to preserve and push the revolutionary movement forward.

Document 3

Mrs. Nguyen Thi Dinh, known as Ba Dinh, was a leader of the Vietnamese
resistance against the French in the First Vietnam War. Mrs. Dinh took charge
of the women's movement in Ben Tre province in the Mekong Delta. She was
part of the political cadre which remained in the South after the 1954 Geneva
Conference, and she was instrumental in organizing the first opposition to President Diem in Ben Tre province.

Mrs. Dinh quickly rose in the ranks of the opposition. At the end of 1960,
she became one of the founders of the National Liberation Front in Ben Tre
province. In 1961 she was chosen to be Chairman of the South Vietnam Liberation Women's Association, a member of the Presidium of the South Vietnam
National Liberation Front, and Deputy Commander of the South Vietnam Liberation Armed Forces. In this excerpt from her memoir, *No Other Road To
Take,* Mrs. Dinh describes the jubilation in Ben Tre province after open resistance to the Diem government began in 1960.

3   No Other Road to Take
Mrs. Nguyen Thi Dinh

The people of Ben Tre province who had endured untold miseries during the past
six years could now laugh, sing and live. A new spirit was burning all over the
countryside. The political forces held animated discussions about the struggle. Car-
penters and blacksmiths raced to produce knives and machetes to kill the enemy.
The workshops improved the sky-horse rifles, making them more lethal, and produced a batch of new weapons called "mút nhét" (primed rifles). At this time, the
armed forces of the province were over one company in strength and each district
had from one to two squads. Each village had from one to three rifles, but the majority of these were French muskets. Young girls stayed up many nights to sew
"Main Force" green uniforms for the troops. An information office was set up in
each hamlet in Giong Trom, Mo Cay and Chau Thanh districts. On each side of the
road, slogans were drawn on tree trunks and caught everyone's eyes. On some days
people from the province town came by the hundreds to visit the liberated areas.

After the gigantic foray of a 15,000 strong political force into Ben Tre province
town, the Ben Tre Province Committee of the National Front for the Liberation of
South Vietnam was officially presented to the people. The creation of the Front was
of vital significance for its aim was to consolidate the people's right to be masters of
the countryside. While the high point of the concerted uprising was rising like a tidal
wave sweeping everything in its path, the people became more insistent in their demand that the revolution set up an official organization to represent the strength,
unity and fighting force of the people, which would continue to lead the people to
advance forward toward new successes in the resistance to save the country and oppose the American imperialist invaders and their henchmen—Ngo Dinh Diem and
the gang of traitors. This was why the "National Front for the Liberation of South
Vietnam"—the sole organization leading the resistance by the entire population of
the South—was timely created and presented to the people on December 20th, 1960.

Aware of this spirit, we made urgent preparations in order to present the Ben
Tre Province Liberation Front Committee to the people on December 26th, 1960,

that is to say six days after the birth of the National Front for the Liberation of South Vietnam. We decided to make it a big occasion by convoking a conference which would be attended by representatives of every population strata in order to set up the Province Liberation Front Committee, and organizing a ceremony for about 10,000 people representing the countryside, the urban areas, all the religious groups and the families of soldiers. We selected My Chanh, located less than five kilometers from Ba Tri district town, as the site for the presentation ceremony. The population here was large and the village was located in a favorable strategic terrain and had a big market, the Ben Bao market.

At dusk on the 26th, the rally began. We had electric lights and microphones which had been sent by workers in the province town as their contribution to the rally. Seeing the flag being hoisted which brightened up a whole section of the sky, we all felt very moved. So much blood shed by the comrades and people had dyed this glorious and eternal flag.

The Liberation Front Committee comprised 15 people who represented every social strata, religious group and political party. The committee solemnly appeared in front of the people and each member gave a speech. Mr. Ngôi, the representative of the Cao Dai Thien Tien sect, Mr. Ho Hao Nghia, representing university and high school students, Mr. Ngôi, representing the national bourgeoisie, Mrs. Muoi Quoi, representing the women, brother Ba, representing the peasants—they all condemned the crimes of the enemy and expressed their gratitude toward and their confidence in the revolution, and pledged to unite and fight to the end to overthrow the Americans and Diem.

I had the honor of representing the People's Revolutionary Party and the Front, and on their behalf I made promises and pledges, and called on the people to propel the fight strongly forward. When I stepped down from the podium, many women embraced me and inquired after me with great concern. An old lady grasped my hand and wept:

—I'm Bich's aunt. Heavens, if he were still alive today he would be so happy seeing this scene.

Heavens! We embraced each other in happiness and sorrow. I was very moved and told her:

—Besides Bich, both my parents have been killed. I don't have anyone left, but there are so many other mothers and fathers who love me even more than their own children.

Talking about Bich in this place where he was born, I thought that this ceremony, by evoking an old memory, had taken on an added significance for me. I felt greatly cheered and asked my husband's aunt:

—If the enemy comes tomorrow and asks what you're doing here tonight, what will you say?

She replied without hesitating:

—What do you think I'll say? I'll say that the Front was born, that liberation troops and people attended in great numbers, in the tens of thousands. I wasn't afraid of them before, so why should I be afraid of them now that our forces are as strong as this?

I looked at the large popular force and felt overjoyed. The armed units had expanded rapidly. Ben Tre province now had close to a battalion of adequately armed troops. This was a real battalion, not a "fake" one. As for the strong and large "long haired" force, I did not even know how many battalions of them there were. From now on, on the road of resisting the Americans and their lackeys, our people would stand firm on the two powerful legs of military and political strength to fight and achieve victory. There was no other road to take.

In the face of this enormous and imposing force of the people, I felt very small, but I was full of self-confidence, like a small tree standing in a vast and ancient forest. In struggling against the enemy, I had come to fully realize that we had to have the strength of the whole forest in order to be able to stay the force of the strong winds and storms. As I thought about the protection and support of the people, about the enormous efforts that the revolution had expanded in educating and nurturing me, about the countless comrades and beloved people—some of whom I had mentioned but whose names I could never exhaustively enumerate—I felt more intimately bound, more so than ever before, to the road I had taken and had pledged to follow until my last days. This was the road for which I would sacrifice everything for the future of the revolution and for the interests of the masses. For me there was no other road to take.

After the ceremony broke up, I walked among the troops, carrying my knapsack. A few shots echoed from an enemy post nearby. A fighter joked:

—Hey, they're firing to salute the birth of the Front!

Another one immediately brushed his remark aside:

—Saluting like that isn't adequate. One of these days we'll have to go to the post and force them to kneel down to greet the Front and to surrender!

Everyone burst out laughing. We made our way leisurely on the large road, talking noisily as we walked under the sky of liberation full of stars and cooled by a strong breeze. And from all four directions of the island I could hear the rifle shots of the guerrillas encircling and destroying the posts, as though urging everyone to quickly rush forward and eliminate the Americans and Diem to liberate the South, so that the people of the whole country could soon be reunited under the spring sky of our native land full of the sweet fragrance of the milk fruit.

Document 4

As time went on, North Vietnam's involvement in anti-Diem activities in the South increased. In the first years after Dienbienphu, the Lao Dong party actively cautioned against any armed response to Diem; then in 1960 Hanoi sponsored the National Liberation Front. For some time after this major step, however, North Vietnam's support for the guerrilla movement in South Vietnam remained cautious and moderate.

This policy began to change after Diem was assassinated during a military coup in November 1963. The following document from the Ninth Conference of the Lao Dong Party Central Committee gives a new assessment of South Vietnam's capabilities.

4   **Resolution of the Ninth Conference of the Lao Dong Party Central Committee**
December 1963
Assessment of the Balance of Power, the Capability for Development and Prospects of the South Vietnamese People's Revolutionary Movements

In order to assess and compare our force with the enemy's force, we have to *consider them in the frame of a "special" war being currently waged by the U.S. imperialists in SVN.*

After the 2nd World War, the U.S. imperialists became imperialist ringleaders, the main force of the international reactionaries and aggressors. In addition, the U.S. imperialists were also international gendarmes. At first, the Americans relied on their temporary superiority in nuclear weapons and set forth their "on-the-brink-of-the war" policy together with a military strategy of an offensive nature called "massive retaliation" in the hope of making their dream of world domination come true. However, the balance of force was changed rapidly but not in favor of the imperialists. On the one hand, our side has achieved superiority in nuclear weapons and become a decisive factor in the development of mankind. The people's national liberation movement has risen strongly, bringing about not only the establishment of countries which have full national sovereignty, but also the establishment of socialist countries such as China, Viet-Nam, Korea and Cuba. On the other hand, the contradictions among imperialist countries have increased more and more. The more the imperialists, especially the U.S. imperialists, make preparations for another world war, the more preventive measures against that world war are taken by our side. If the imperialists madly launch a new world war, they will be smashed by the world people. In this situation, the U.S. imperialists had to admit their failure in their old military strategy and set forth a new strategy which consists of both offensive and defensive measures. This is a strategy of "flexible response" in three types of war: World war, limited war and special war. . . .

The "special" war is chosen to regain the initiative in areas where they are on the defensive. They also conduct this type of war to face the violent revolutionary movements of the peoples in the countries of Africa, Asia, and Latin America. In these areas, both the national liberation movement and the workers' and peasants' revolutionary movement are making great progress. This situation not only disintegrated the imperialists' colonial system but also shanked the newly formed bourgeois regimes and posed a serious danger to the entire capitalist system of the world. This danger forced the imperialists to compromise with the bourgeois reactionaries of countries in Africa, Asia, and Latin America to maintain colonialism under new forms and with new methods. In addition, as the revolutionary movement in countries of Africa, Asia, and Latin America was increased, the bourgeois elements in these countries cooperated with the imperialists to counter the revolutionary movement of the workers-peasants. Neocolonialism was born from this situation. The special war is a type of war of aggression conceived to fit neocolonialism. In the economic field in nationalist countries, the imperialists relied on the bourgeois government to exploit the people of these countries. When they initiated their war of aggression and counterrevolutionary war, they primarily use the troops of the bourgeois reactionary government while they retain the command, supply weapons and money and only introduce their own troops to directly participate in the war at a definite level.

The U.S. imperialists not only used the special war to repress the national liberation movement and the masses' revolutionary movement. In definite conditions, they may also resort to limited war. However, they cannot conduct this type of war wherever and whenever they like. Though possessing a great military strength, they had to scatter their forces over many areas, and as a result, their reaction capability was limited. For this reason their force commitment is contingent upon the attainable objective and the balance of power in each area.

Southeast Asia is a place where the imperialists have many interests. After being defeated in China, Korea and together with the French, being defeated in Indochina, the U.S. imperialists cooperated with the British and French imperialists to establish a Southeast Asia aggressive bloc. South Viet-Nam is an important link in the Southeast Asia strategy of the Americans. It is also a place where the revolutionary movement was most seething and where the U.S. troops and lackey troops were increased to a great extent. The U.S. imperialists waged the special war in SVN and established the Southeast Asia aggressive bloc in order to achieve the following three objectives:

—Repress the national liberation movement and carry out the neocolonialist policy.

—Build up military bases and prepare to attack our side.

—Keep socialism from spreading throughout Southeast Asia.

If the U.S. imperialists are after the third objective, it is because all national liberation movements tend unavoidably to develop into socialist revolutions, especially in Southeast Asia in general and in South Viet-Nam in particular. In these areas, the national democratic revolutions are being conducted by the strong Marxist-Leninist parties.

. . .

As for us, we become more confident in the victory of our armed forces. Our technical and tactical skills are improved and our fighting spirit is heightened. The people in South Viet-Nam have stood up against the imperialists for almost 20 years, so they have a high political enlightenment. At the present time, the more they fight, the bigger victories they win, the revolutionary movement has created favorable conditions for building up the armed forces. If we properly guide the political and military struggle and the force building program, our military force will grow up rapidly. To create a basic change in the balance of forces between the enemy and us is within our grasp. In the days ahead, our force will be increasingly developed, whereas the enemy will certainly encounter a great deal of difficulty and he will be demoralized. His weaknesses are obvious and have increased after his defeat at Ap Bac, especially after the overthrow of Diem's regime. A strong development of the Revolution will cause many more troubles for the enemy and bring about a quicker disorganization of his armed forces and government. *The Revolution in SVN will inevitably evolve into a General Offensive and Uprising to achieve the complete victory.*

If the U.S. imperialists send more troops to Viet-Nam to save the situation after suffering a series of failures, *the Revolution in Viet-Nam will meet more difficulties, the struggle will be stronger and harder but it will certainly succeed in attaining the final victory.* With 800,000 well trained troops, the French imperialists could not defeat the 12 million courageous Algerians and finally had to give independence and freedom to them. For the same reason, the U.S. imperialists cannot win over 14 million Vietnamese people in the South who have taken arms to fight the imperialists for almost 20 years, and who, with all the compatriots throughout the country, have defeated the hundreds of thousands of troops of the French expeditionary force. Now the South Vietnamese people show themselves capable of beating the enemy in any situation. They certainly have the determination, talents, strength and patience to crush any U.S. imperialists' schemes and plans, and finally to force them to withdraw from Viet-Nam as the French imperialists did.

There is the possibility that the South Viet-Nam Revolution must go through a transitional period which entails complex forms and methods of struggling before it attains the final victory. The reunification of the country must be carried out step by step. In the present national democratic revolutionary phase in South Viet-Nam, *we must strive to attain victory step by step and gradually push back the enemy before reaching the General Offensive and Uprising to win complete victory.* However, we may pass through a transitional period before we attain complete victory. In any case, we must encourage the entire Party, people, and army to attain the maximum victory, and we should not have a hesitating attitude or to pause at the transitional period. If we are highly determined to win and prepared to face any situation, the final victory will certainly be in the hands of our people.

Document 5

Bernard B. Fall was a scholar who had studied the history of Vietnam and the roots of its post–World War II problems. Fall understood the American reasoning behind intervention in Southeast Asia but also saw misperceptions and weaknesses in that policy. In this article, published in 1965, Fall presented an informed view of the Vietcong. Acknowledging that the term was an imprecise and confusing one, Fall believed that an understanding of the background and motivation of the Vietcong was critical to a clear understanding of the Vietnam War. Fall was killed in Vietnam in 1967 while reporting on the war.

5   Vietcong—The Unseen Enemy in Vietnam
Bernard B. Fall
April 22, 1965
Much has been said and written lately about the war in Viet-Nam, the bombs and the aircraft that are being used, and the large political issues that are involved. But relatively little is being said by either side about the furtive enemy who actually holds much of South Viet-Nam's terrain and effectively administers perhaps as much as 50 per cent of the country's rural population.

To the South Viet-Nam government in Saigon, the enemy is simply the Viet-Cong, or VC, which stands for "Vietnamese Communist." To the United States and its closest allies, the VC is an Orwellian unperson. It simply does not exist, except as an emanation of North Viet-Nam's People's Army and its political masters in Hanoi. The State Department devoted in recent weeks a whole White Book to prove that, by contrast with such guerrilla wars as Greece, Malaya, or the Philippines, "the war in Viet-Nam is *not* a spontaneous and local rebellion against the established government . . . In Viet-Nam a Communist government has set out deliberately to conquer a sovereign people in a neighboring state."

If that view were entirely correct, then the whole Viet-Nam insurrection would be little else but an invasion from the outside, like Germany's aggression against Poland; and any measures taken against North Viet-Nam would fall within the inherent right of a nation to self-defense against attack.

The insurrectionists in South Viet-Nam must, for obvious reasons, convince the world of the opposite—namely, that they represent a genuine uprising against a series of unpopular regimes and are willing to offer the South Vietnamese people a valid alternative both to the current Saigon regimes and to domination by Hanoi. For the time being, neither the United States (and Saigon) nor the guerrillas (and their backers in Hanoi) seem to have made their case to the point where it carries full conviction. That may be mainly so because the actual truth lies somewhere in between the two views.

First of all, it must be understood that armed opposition to the Ngo Dinh Diem regime inside South Viet-Nam, in one form or another, had never ceased between

Viet-Nam's partition in 1954 and the demise of the Diem regime in November, 1963. Apart from the Communists, there existed in South Viet-Nam a variety of political-religious sects, such as the Hoa-Hao and the Cao-Dai; and at least one well-organized semipiratical band, the Binh-Xuyên, which never fully surrendered to the South Viet-Nam government.

. . .

As President Eisenhower was to remark in his memoirs later, every responsible observer estimated that the North Viet-Nam leader Ho Chi Minh would win even an uncoerced pan-Vietnamese election by 80 per cent of the popular vote. With elections only two years away, there was no reason for the Communists to risk precious cadre personnel on short-term adventures.

This is exactly what the later leader of the "National Liberation Front of South Viet-Nam" (NLF), a Saigon barrister named Nguyen Huu Tho, meant when he explained to the Australian Communist writer Wilfred Burchett: "There were mixed feelings about the two years' delay over reunification but the general sentiment was that this was a small price to pay for the return to peace and a normal life, free of foreign rule."

Nguyen Huu Tho had first been involved in politics when he led, in March, 1950, a student demonstration in Saigon against the presence of three American warships on a courtesy call to the French. He paid for this with three years' detention in the northern mountain town of Lai-Chau. In August, 1954, he set up what in Communist parlance is called a "legal-struggle" organization in the form of a "Committee of Defense of Peace and the Geneva Agreements," whose aim was to keep up the pressure on the South Viet-Nam government of Diem, as well as on the still-present French, to make sure that the Geneva Agreements would be observed.

But Diem had already made up his mind not to observe the agreements (which South Viet-Nam had not signed), and his repression against all oppositionists also covered Nguyen Huu Tho's peace committee and the local branches it had set up in various provincial towns.

On November 11, 1954, security police closed in on the peace committees and arrested its members. These included Nguyen Huu Tho, who now found himself jailed in the Central Viet-Nam detention house at Tuy-Hoa. He escaped only in 1961, after his appointment as president of the NLF.

"We had no idea at that time," Tho told Burchett in 1964, "but . . . we had created the embryo for the National Liberation Front, set up more than six years later."

When the South Viet-Nam government, with the open encouragement of most Western powers, defied the July, 1956, deadline for elections, it was obvious that a struggle to the death would ensue with Hanoi, unless Hanoi could be made to see that it was to its advantage to coexist with a southern rival too strong for overthrow through subversion. That could have happened if the Diem regime had chosen a set of policies which would have provided it with maximum popular support and left the Communists reduced to the role of an ineffectual harasser. The regime did exactly the opposite.

By a presidential decree of June, 1956, Diem abolished elected village councils and mayors. This imposed directly on the Viet-Nam peasantry the dictatorial regime which he already wielded at the center. In March, 1957, the regime openly violated the last restraints placed upon it by the Geneva Agreements with regard to reprisals exercised against "former resistance members"—that is, ex-guerrillas of the Viet-Minh who had fought against the French, and many of whom were not Commu-

nists. Such highly respected, non-Communist French observers as *Le Monde's* Jean
Lacouture and Philippe Devillers (author of the French classic *Histoire du Viet-Nam
de 1940 à 1952*) aver that, faced with physical extermination along with the sect
units, some of the former Viet-Minh guerrillas simply banded together for survival.
In Devillers's words, "the overriding needs of the world-wide strategy of the socialist camp meant little or nothing to guerrilla fighters being hunted down in Nam-Bô
[South Viet-Nam] . . . Hanoi preferred diplomatic notes, but it was to find that its
hand had been forced."

In my view, the actual situation probably lay somewhere in between: Hanoi, to
be sure, was distressed about what was happening to its faithful followers in the
South. But other Communist regimes had abandoned failing guerrilla movements
before: in Greece, Azerbaijan, Indonesia, Malaya, and elsewhere. In the case of Viet-
Nam, however, Hanoi may well have made the judgment that:

(a) The South Viet-Nam government was in the process of alienating its own
people to such an extent that even a modestly encouraged and supported guerrilla
movement could well succeed in overthrowing it;

(b) Saigon's American advisers were so blinded by Diem's "successes," and so
oblivious to the real weaknesses of the situation, that a rebellion might succeed before the cumbersome American apparatus could shift into high gear.

As events were to show, the plan almost worked. How well it did, even without
outside aid, is best shown by the progressive shift in village official killings between
1957–58 and 1959–1960. The new guerrillas began to take over control of the only
thing worth holding in a revolutionary warfare situation: people, and rural people at
that. With a method showing long-standing professionalism, the guerrillas first established "resistance base areas" in certain Mekong Delta provinces such as Chau-
Doc and My-Tho. They then proceeded to seal off Saigon from the rice-rich and
densely populated delta area.

But terrorism was not the whole program. There were sound propaganda, like
the "Three Withs" program ("a good cadre lives with, eats with, works with the
population"); some modest reforms; and even a measure of physical improvement.

In a remarkable book *(Mission in Torment)* John Mecklin, whose credentials are
that he was America's chief information officer in Viet-Nam during the critical
1962–64 period, writes about a village called Binh Yen Dong, only twenty miles
from Saigon. The village had "gone Viet-Cong" without apparent coercion and a
study was made of how the process had worked. As it turned out, the NLF had
forced a local landlord to allow the farmers to take a short cut through his property
to the village well, which until then they had been forced to reach via a detour.

Organizationally, the movement rose apace. In March, 1960, the "Nam-Bô Resistance Veterans Organization" met in hiding and issued a proclamation in which
it announced that it had taken up "arms in self-defense." At the third congress of
North Viet-Nam's Communist Lao-Dong (Workers') Party, held in Hanoi on September 5, 1960, Lê Duan, the party secretary and a former leader of the Viet-Minh
in the South, issued a report which for the first time took cognizance of the "southern people's revolutionary struggle" and advocated the creation there of a "broad
national united front against the U.S.-Diem clique." And on December 20, 1960, on
the day after the fourteenth anniversary of Ho Chi Minh's uprising against France,
a provisional Central Committee of southern resistance leaders created the National
Liberation Front. The guerrilla movement had matured into a full-fledged revolutionary apparatus.

The newborn NLF led a very shadowy life for almost two years, although its military arm, the "People's Self-Defense Forces," began to roam far and wide throughout South Viet-Nam. By May, 1960, the situation had deteriorated enough for the Saigon government to report to the International Control Commission (I.C.C.) set up by the Geneva Agreements that the "southern liberation forces" constituted a "grave menace for peace."

Statistics now began to pile up inexorably: 452 village chiefs were lost by South Viet-Nam in 1957–58. By January, 1960, they were being lost at the rate of fifteen a week. On May 25, 1961, President Kennedy told Congress that minor officials were being killed in Viet-Nam at the rate of 4,000 a year: eleven a day. In 1964, over 1,500 small officials were lost, and over 400 during the first four months of 1965.

The guerrillas' strength was estimated at 3,000 in 1959. By mid-1961 they were 15,000: half of them fully armed. There were 35,000 hard-core elite troops by January this year [1965], in addition to 60,000–80,000 "local force" guerrillas. By this month the Pentagon revised the figures to 45,000 and 100,000, respectively, grouped in five or six regimental-size units and about 60 battalions and over 150 companies.

In terms of administration, the killed or fleeing officials of the Diem administration were replaced by Administrative Committees, soon capped by District and Provincial Committees of the NLF. By February, 1962, the movement was ready to present itself to the world in the course of a clandestine congress attended by over 100 delegates. Whether by coincidence or design, the congress was convened just a few days after the United States had set up its Military Advisory Command in Saigon—just as the NLF had originally proclaimed its existence one month after Diem had almost been overthrown, in November, 1960, by his own best paratroops.

. . .

The program of the Front is by now well known and need hardly be repeated here. Much has been made in some quarters of the fact that the program in itself is quite moderate, which is true. Its ten points make hardly any doctrinaire references to the United States and none whatever in favor of communism. Its points dealing with foreign policy restate the Geneva Agreements' position on South Viet-Nam's nonengagement in military alliances, and reunification is left to later negotiations rather than to an iron clad two year provision as provided for in 1954. It must, however, be remembered that this program represents at best a set of "electoral promises." After all, North Viet-Nam had a constitution until 1960, which embodied phrases from the American Declaration of Independence. It was changed for a strikingly doctrinaire document once North Viet-Nam had been made secure for its regime. . . .

In the American official view, there can be no doubt but that the NLF is nothing but a suboffice of the Reunification Commission operating under the Council of Ministers of the Hanoi government. The state Department White Book shows elaborate charts which demonstrate ties with northern military and political agencies.

But to many people, that can only be part of the story. There is, for example, the high-ranking spokesman of the Front who told Le Monde's Georges Chaffard that the NLF had got along without the North for "a long time" and would "prefer to settle our affairs among 'southerners'." And he added something which many a resistance fighter (as I was in France in the Second World War) will fully understand: "We have not fought all these years simply to end up by installing one set of dictators in place of the old."

It is this aspect of resistance war that seems to be too often glibly overlooked in the case of the NLF. One does not fight for eight long years, under the crushing weight of American armor, napalm, jet bombers and, finally, vomiting gases, for the sheer joy of handing over whatever one fights for to some bureaucrat in Hanoi, merely on the say-so of a faraway party apparatus. The NLF *and* South Viet-Nam have both had to pay a heavy price for NLF victories. Officially, the US Army Chief of Staff, General Harold K. Johnson, claims that 75,000 Viet-Cong had been killed between 1961 and February, 1965. By April, the "kill" figure had risen to 89,000. The French Press Agency, on the basis of earlier Saigon reports, stated that casualties between 1957 and 1961 amounted to 29,000 on the government side and 66,000 on the Viet-Cong side. This is not too far off the NLF's own claim that over 160,000 South Vietnamese (on its side, presumably) have thus far been killed in this war.

There has been increasing evidence of differences in view as well as in tone between Hanoi and the NLF, just as there have been between Hanoi and Peking or Moscow. Thus, an important policy statement issued by the Front on March 22, found itself seriously toned down by Hanoi. In recent weeks there have been reports from Paris that Peking, fearing that Hanoi might weaken under the impact of American pressure, has attempted to "leap-frog" it by dealing directly with the Front through the NLF delegation in Peking and through emissaries in Laos and Cambodia.

There are some doubts among many observers as to whether the apparent intransigence of Hanoi does not in reality hide its relative inability to "deliver" the NLF bound hand and foot at a problematical conference table. Having sold out the guerrilla movement twice before, in 1954 and 1956, it may find the task difficult, if not altogether impossible. Yet it is on this assumption—that is, that the whole southern guerrilla movement would rapidly wither away if only it were abandoned by Hanoi—that the whole present policy of bombing North Viet-Nam into negotiating the NLF out of existence is based. The next few weeks may show whether this expectation is not somewhat too simple to be entirely true.

Document 6

The United States was the main enemy for the North Vietnamese and the Vietcong. In the days of Diem, during the revolving door governments that followed him, and later, when Thieu and Ky brought relative stability to South Vietnam, the Communists taunted the southern rulers as "puppets." As the war spread and the American military buildup increased, the Americanization of the conflict bred more hatred.

In this brief document a soldier of the National Liberation Front voiced a crude anti-American propaganda line. Unlike the preceding North Vietnamese documents in this chapter, this work was designed to move the Vietnamese masses rather than persuade the political cadres. It served, therefore, to dehumanize the Americans and to fire up the Vietnamese to keep fighting.

6   Sparkling Fires in the South
Che Lan Vien
Through a paradox of history and the evil plots of the U.S.-Diem clique the peaceful Hien Luong River, the river of my childhood, which flows along the 17th parallel,

has for eight years played the role of a sword, splitting the country asunder. My parents, who live south of this river that I know so well, who live in a house only a stone's throw from the river, have for years given me no sign that they are alive and well. But let us not blame the river.

The "clever" Americans are using the river and the barbed wire running along it to accomplish more than physical separations. They want to split the human heart as well, to make wives fearful of showing love for their husbands, to drive parents to repudiate their children, and to force friends to avoid each other, to make fellow countrymen bitter antagonists. . . .

Awaiting those [in the South] are strategic hamlets, prisons, napalm bombs, chemical defoliants, poisoned food, American planes and guillotines, American paratroops, arson, rape, and police dogs. The nationalists [that is, the GVN] are showered with such American treasures as liquor, clothes, automobiles, and even an American "God" when needed. . . . An American gun is pushed into his hands and he is separated from his fellow men whom he hunts for his American master. This separation is incomparably more terrifying than any barbed wire along a peaceful river.

Even more terrifying is American lust. This is apparent everywhere. You have probably heard about the U.S.-Diem troops indulging in cannibalism, disemboweling a man, and eating his liver raw. Talking to newsmen when he paid a visit to a joint security post north of the demilitarized zone, a young Diemist officer calmly said that cannibalism was hardly a novelty to him and that, although he had never tasted human flesh, all cadets at the officers' school had eaten human liver more than once. This must be the officers' school with American-type training, where young men eat human liver in a sophisticated manner during an evening dancing party or a fishing trip. Training is dispensed in a cruder manner at lower levels. Back from his tour of sentry duty a new recruit asked for his meal. He was shown a huge pot of soup, and he fainted when he saw human skulls in it. Not only did no one help to revive him but fists rained upon him and he was threatened with being shot on the grounds that Viet Cong blood must be running in his veins, making him faint at the first whiff of Viet Cong flesh. Then these commanding officers—who bear likeness to the image of Christ and pray "Thou shalt not kill, thou shalt love thy neighbor as thyself "—forced the recruit down on his back and made him swallow the flesh of his own kind. Now whether this young soldier soon forced human soup into others, committed suicide, or turned his rifle against the U.S.-Diemists, I cannot tell. Suffice it to say this is how to turn men into fiends, lesson one.

A man named Ty was captured at Ben Tre by the U.S.-Diemists, eviscerated, his liver taken out, and then turned loose. Blood streaming all over, he ran aimlessly, shrieking with pain, stumbled a few meters, and dropped dead amid the enemy's merry laughter. They raped a pregnant woman and then beat her stomach until she aborted to their great jubilation. A seven-year-old boy suspected of serving as a Viet Cong sentry was caught and tied to a tree and burned alive. His mother, forced to watch, screamed helplessly and then fainted, much to the amusement of the U.S.-Diemists. This—the fact that they are trying to make man unfit for society—is what hurts me most about my country's partition. . . .

Why do the Americans scheme so? They want the sun to rise and set according to their whims. Do they not plan to turn heroes into slaves? To turn the people into prisoners and Vietnam into an American land? . . .

A certain hamlet was the target for bombing by 50 U.S.-piloted planes for six hours; one hundred tons of bombs were dropped on one thousand persons. Each received one hundred kilograms of explosives, but they did not have even one kilogram of rice. The Americans may lack humanity and intelligence, but they do not lack bombs. . . .

This is why men smile on their way to the firing squad, why a patriot sacrificed himself trying to prevent the enemy from tearing up a national flag and died eviscerated and with his skull crushed, why a young man whose stomach was slashed open by the enemy took out his bowels and with his own hands held them up to the enemy.

Documents 7 and 8

The common theme of these documents, produced within the National Liberation Front, is the destructive influence which the United States had on South Vietnam. These authors, writing as southerners seeking to end the warfare among Vietnamese, urge their countrymen to expel the Americans. Only then, they argued, could peace reign in Vietnam.

In Document 7 Huynh Tan Phat, the vice president of the Central Committee of the National Liberation Front of South Vietnam, writes to General Nguyen Khanh, who had had a stormy year as the major political leader in South Vietnam from January 1964 to January 1965. Phat hoped that Khanh had tired of the American presence in South Vietnam and that he could be convinced to send them home.

Nguyen Huu Tho, the moderate leader of the National Liberation Front, became more extreme over time. In Document 8, a 1966 interview, Tho told a Japanese newspaperman that the United States was at the root of the troubles in Southeast Asia.

7   Letter to General Nguyen Khanh
Huynh Tan Phat
January 28, 1965

Dear General Khanh,

Replying to a number of your ideas, I previously had occasion to write you a long letter in which I clearly set forth our point of view, and also informed you that we were prepared to offer you our friendly cooperation and join with all who manifested these same desires and aspirations.

I heartily approve of your determined declaration against American intervention and I congratulate you for having made it. You stated quite clearly, in fact, that "the USA must let South Vietnam settle the problem of South Vietnam!" In your recent press-conference, your attitude was equally clear: "For national sovereignty and against foreign intervention in South Vietnam's domestic affairs."

You have now committed yourself, as well as your friends, to pursuing the struggle for peace and independence from American intervention. You are, so to speak, the first in the South Vietnamese administration to choose a new, more advanced orientation, one that is more independent of the United States of America. The road you have taken will be a difficult one and the pitfalls will be many. But with your ardent patriotism, your indomitable spirit in the face of imperialist, colonialist oppression, your determination to oppose any kind of intervention by outsiders, you will undoubtedly receive the support of the people. And as you pursue this goal, you may rest assured that you also have our support, as we stated in our last letter.

We are convinced, given our common determination to serve our people and our country, valiantly to combat for national sovereignty and independence, and against foreign intervention, that whatever our differences of political opinion, we can join together and coordinate our efforts to accomplish our supreme mission, which is, to save our homeland.

Signed: Huynh-Tan-Phat, Vice-President
Central Committee, FNL/SVN.

8   Reply to the Japanese Newspaper "Akahata"
Nguyen Huu Tho
February 24, 1966

QUESTION: Would you please describe the main features of the South Vietnamese people's heroic struggle against the U.S. imperialists and their henchmen over the last five years under the skilful and correct leadership of the NLF?

ANSWER: After defeating, together with the entire Vietnamese people, the U.S.-backed French colonialists, and winning glorious victory in the first War of Resistance (1945–1954) the South Vietnamese people have, over the last eleven years, had to cope with the utterly atrocious intervention and aggression of the U.S. imperialists, the extremely ferocious and dangerous ringleader of imperialism. Making untold sacrifices and overcoming indescribable hardships, the South Vietnamese people's patriotic movement has constantly developed and led to the founding of the South Viet-Nam National Front for Liberation five years ago, on December 20, 1960. With the coming into being of the NLF the South Vietnamese people's valiant struggle switched on to a new stage, that of big and repeated victories in all fields. The main features of this new stage are:

1. By upholding the banner of patriotism and justice with the aim of driving out the U.S. aggressors, overthrowing the puppet administration, achieving independence, democracy, peace and neutrality in South Viet-Nam and the reunification of the country, the NLF, reflecting the most legitimate aspirations of the South Vietnamese people and meeting the most urgent demands of patriots from all strata in South Viet-Nam, has therefore succeeded in forming the broadest and strongest ever solidarity bloc of the entire people to oppose the U.S. aggressors and save the country. This first great achievement of the NLF is precisely the most basic step which has paved the way for later successes of the South Vietnamese people's patriotic struggle. It is also the root cause which has led to the defeat of all colonialist maneuvers and aggressive military plans of the U.S. imperialists at their inception.

2. Though at the beginning the odds against the South Vietnamese people were overwhelming in the balance of forces between them on one side, and the aggressors and traitors on the other, the NLF has resolutely led the people's self-defense struggle and developed it into a real people's war which has become more and more effective day after day against the U.S. aggressive war. This was possible thanks to the Front's deep confidence in the tremendous strength of the masses which have risen up against oppression, its spirit of thorough-going revolution without the least illusion about the enemy's extremely stubborn and wicked nature.

From the jungle to the countryside and even in the towns temporarily controlled by the enemy, the people's war has developed vigorously and widely, thus making a closely combined action possible between various areas, drawing millions of people to the frontline to wage a political and armed struggle, attack and harass the enemy everywhere and repeatedly foil their aggressive plans.

In only five years, led and inspired by the NLF the South Vietnamese people, starting from scratch have succeeded in founding a powerful political army and powerful armed forces. The political army composed of millions of people of different ages, with the great contingent of women as its core, is better and better organized and has constantly taken the initiative in attacking the enemy, and has shaken and disintegrated to its foundations the enemy administration in the rural and urban areas, destroyed by big chunks the "strategic hamlets" system—backbone of the enemy's aggressive plans.

The armed forces have also developed quickly in all fields—politics, tactics, technique, organization and command.

Organized into three armed forces—guerilla, regional forces and regular army—along the line of people's war defined by the NLF, the Liberation Armed Forces, together with the rest of the people, have during five years' fighting recorded brilliant achievements: wiped out or disintegrated a force of over 550,000 American and puppet troops, captured nearly 70,000 guns of different kinds, shot down or destroyed nearly 2,500 aircraft, destroyed nearly 6,000 of the 8,000 "strategic hamlets" set up by the enemy. The tremendously quick tempo of growth in both effectiveness and quality of the Liberation Armed Forces have gone beyond all calculations of the U.S. aggressive ringleaders and upset all their war plans.

3. As a result of the repeated victories recorded by the South Viet-Nam armed forces and people, the South Viet-Nam NLF now controls over four-fifths of the South Viet-Nam territory inhabited by more than 10 million people. . . .

For the South Vietnamese people, the prospect of a South Viet-Nam completely liberated, really independent and democratic is no longer a dream and a matter of conviction, but has become a living truth: a new and really democratic society of the people is taking shape in the liberated area. Revolutionary administrative organs have been set up down to liberated hamlet and village levels in the form of people's self-governing committees. These not only care for, mobilize and organize the people to carry out the resistance war and see to the security of the liberated areas but also do their best to improve the people's life in all fields. Two million hectares of rice fields have been allotted by the Front to the peasants, thus increasing many times the fighting power of the main army of the revolution. Developing production has been able to meet in a more and more adequate fashion the needs of the people and the resistance war. Cultural and educational work has also been developed widely and incessantly along a national, scientific and popular line. Though faced with many difficulties created by the enemy, the protection of the people's health continues to record great achievements thanks to the closely combined use of popular traditional medicine and modern medicine.

As a result of the ever greater successes of the South Viet-Nam army and people, the liberated areas have consolidated and developed continually, thereby creating a situation in which the areas still under the enemy's temporary control are subject to an encirclement and pressure. At the same time, thanks to its ever greater attraction, they have contributed to promoting the people's struggle in the enemy-controlled areas.

Frightened by the growth and influence of the liberated areas, the U.S. aggressors and their henchmen have stopped at no barbarous and cruel scheme to sabotage these tremendous achievements of the people and to misrepresent and slander the liberated areas. However, all these schemes and tricks have met with failure.

Inspired by the results gained at the cost of their own blood, the South Vietnamese people are resolved to fight to the end to safeguard and develop these gains and to march forward and sweep off the enemy from the whole country.

4. The U.S. imperialists are the sworn enemy of the South Vietnamese people and the cruel enemy number one of the peoples throughout the world. They are committing aggression in South Viet-Nam while using it as a testing ground of methods of repression and aggression to be applied in other countries. The South Vietnamese people are determined to foil this dark design.

The South Vietnamese people's just cause of national liberation is closely linked with the struggle of the world's peoples for independence, democracy, peace and social progress, and constitutes at the same time an active contribution to that common cause. That is precisely why an international front of solidarity with the South Vietnamese people against U.S. aggression has been formed in practice and has been growing in size and strength with every passing day.

The peoples and governments of all socialist countries and many Asian and African countries, and peoples of many other countries including the American people have been giving the South Vietnamese people an extremely great and effective assistance, not only political and moral but also material.

The international movement of solidarity with, and support for, the South Vietnamese people has also developed in the form of continual drives of stirring struggle on a world scale with the participation of thousands of millions of people, inspiring and encouraging us, energetically denouncing and condemning the U.S. imperialists and urging them to end their aggressive war in South Viet-Nam.

It may be said that never has a national liberation movement been so strongly supported by the world, and never have the U.S. imperialists been so isolated and decried by world public opinion.

5. The U.S. imperialists' neo-colonialist policy and "special war" have received deadly blows from the South Vietnamese people in their most fundamental aspects.

To carry out their aggressive war in South Viet-Nam, the U.S. imperialists have been relying on the puppet army and administration set up by them. But now the former is disintegrating at an increasing tempo on the battlefield, and the latter has also decayed to such a point that it has become only a moribund administration, hated by the South Vietnamese people and spurned by world public opinion. The fact that the U.S. imperialists had to resort to war as a means to realize their neo-colonialism spelled out a most basic step toward the collapse of U.S. policy of aggression in the present world situation. Now, they have been compelled to send combat troops for direct aggression in South Viet-Nam and engage deeper and deeper in the intensification and expansion of the war. This is another new step towards bankruptcy bearing a great significance for the world's peoples. Today, in spite of all kinds of double talk about "peace" and "negotiation," they have appeared under their true colors as the most cruel and bloodthirsty aggressive colonialist devil. . . .

Critical Issues for Discussion

1. The failure of the Diem government to plan for and hold elections in Vietnam in 1956 was a serious issue in Vietnamese politics. In Document 1, Pham Van Dong, Hanoi's foreign minister, protests Diem's policy.

How did Pham Van Dong describe the government of North Vietnam? Is his argument convincing? Turn back to Chapter 3, "America's Mandarin." In Document 2 Diem explained his reasons for not holding elections. Which argument do you find more compelling? Why?

2. As Document 2 shows, the Vietminh had been forced to retreat from their dream of a unified Vietnam in 1954.

Was unity still important to Le Duan? What did he hope to see in the future? How would these goals be reached? What was the tone of his argument? What relationship did he see between the two Vietnams?

3. The birth of the National Liberation Front in December 1960 in Hanoi gave expression to the spirit of revolt in South Vietnam as indicated in Document 3. What were the "liberated areas" liberated from? Who were Mrs. Dinh's enemies? Who were her allies? What were her goals? How would they be achieved?

4. Soldiers in the Vietnam War coined many phrases to express the essence of a situation. Americans, for instance, often referred to areas held by the National Liberation Front as "Indian country." What images did that bring to mind? What did it mean in the Vietnam situation? What had happened to the Indians in the United States? How did that happen? Did the fate of the Indians in the United States have any relevance for Vietnam?

5. The North Vietnamese decision to escalate the war in December 1963 was a major change in strategy. See Document 4.

To understand why the Lao Dong party decided to make this change, consider the following questions. How did they assess the situation in South Vietnam in 1963? What was their image of American policy in Southeast Asia? What results did they expect their new strategy to achieve?

6. One South Vietnamese farmer said to an American reporter in 1959 that "we are always for the government—no matter which government is in control. But in our hearts we like the government that takes the least from the people, and gives them abundance and happiness. We do not yet have that government."

How could the South Vietnamese government give the people "abundance and happiness?" How could the Vietcong shadow government? Which side do you think would convince the farmer? Why?

7. The question of the identity of the enemy in Vietnam consistently plagued American observers.

How did Bernard Fall describe the Vietcong in Document 5? Who were they? How could they be distinguished from other groups in Vietnam? What were their goals? How did they hope to achieve these goals?

8. The picture of the United States in the minds of the North Vietnamese and many of the South Vietnamese was not an attractive one.

What was the image of the Americans presented in Documents 6 and 8? How did the authors explain the reasons for American behavior in Vietnam? What did they desire? How could Americans answer these charges? Why did

Americans believe they were in Vietnam? How did they view their situation? Did all Vietnamese agree with the perceptions presented in these documents?

Follow Up One of Mao Tse-tung's most famous analogies occurred in his explanation of guerrilla warfare. "There are those who cannot imagine how guerrillas could survive for long in the rear of the enemy. But they do not understand the relationship between the people and the army. The people are like water and the army is like the fish. How can it be difficult for the fish to survive where there is water?"

What did Mao mean? Was this applicable to the Vietnam experience? What was the relationship between the people of the countryside and the Vietcong? Did Diem see the relationship in this way, too? What did he try to do to counteract it? Why did that fail?

Suggestions for Further Reading

General

Bergman, Arlene Eisen. *Women of Vietnam*. San Francisco: Peoples Press, 1974.
 Writing out of her political sympathy for the Vietnamese and the women's movement, Arlene Eisen Bergman describes how women overcame their traditional oppression to develop a culture of resistance. The final chapters evaluate the gains women have made in Vietnam through the revolution.

Harrison, James Pinckney. *The Endless War: Fifty Years of Struggle in Vietnam*. New York: Free Press, 1982.
 Chapter 6, "Nationalism and Ideology," and Chapter 7, "Organization and Practice," offer a general discussion of the strengths of the Vietnamese Communists, North and South.

Nguyen Khac Vien, Gen. ed. *Vietnamese Studies*. Hanoi.
 Each of these small books, written by the government of North Vietnam for Western readers, covers one topic in Vietnamese culture, economics, and history. They are available in many university libraries. The Southeast Asia Resource Center may have copies of some back issues for sale.

Popkin, Samuel. *The Rational Peasant: The Political Economy of Rural Society in Vietnam*. Berkeley: Univ. of California Press, 1979.

Scott, James. *The Moral Economy of the Peasant: Rebellion and Subsistence in Southeast Asia*. New Haven: Yale Univ. Press, 1976.
 Both Scott and Popkin focus on the peasant nature of the Vietnamese revolution, developing theories of the processes by which rural societies recreate themselves when their norms are violated.

Vo Nguyen Giap. *The Military Art of People's War*. Ed. Russell Stetler. New York: Monthly Review Press, 1970.

Vo Nguyen Giap. *Banner of People's War: The Party's Military Line*. New York: Monthly Review Press, 1970.

Either of these books is a good introduction to the concept of people's war as it has developed in Vietnam.

Wolf, Eric. *Peasant Wars of the Twentieth Century*. New York: Harper and Row, 1979.

Comparing Vietnam to Mexico, Russia, China, Algeria, and Cuba, in Chapter 4, Wolf sees in each case a peasant society building on earlier forms within its tradition toward its idea of a just organization of society.

The National Liberation Front

Burchett, Wilfred G. *Vietnam: Inside Story of the Guerrilla War*. New York: International, 1965.

Burchett, an Australian war correspondent who enthusiastically identified with the Vietnamese revolution, spent eight months with the NLF in 1963–1964. He gives a firsthand account of his stay, including interviews that provide background on the origins of the NLF.

Hunt, David. "Villagers at War: The National Liberation Front in My Tho, 1965–1967," *Radical America* 8 (nos. 1 & 2, January–April, 1974).

Hunt, David, "Village Culture and the Vietnamese Revolution," *Past and Present* 94 (1982).

Hunt used Rand Corporation interviews with defectors from the NLF to study political aspects of NLF resistance. In "Villagers at War" he gives a sympathetic picture of Front organizers responding to the needs of their people but demoralized by the U.S. escalation. The second study examines the impact of guerrilla war and revolution on religious practice, family relations, and other aspects of private life.

Nguyen Thi Dinh. *No Other Road to Take*. Tr. Mai Elliot. Ithaca: Cornell Univ. Press, 1976.

The history of the revolution comes to life in these memoirs of a woman who joined the struggle against the French in her teens, became a leader of the NLF, and eventually was promoted to the Party's Central Committee in Hanoi.

Pike, Douglas. *Viet Cong: The Organization and Techniques of the National Liberation Front*. Cambridge: M.I.T. Press, 1966.

A U.S. foreign service officer in Vietnam, Pike based his influential study on Rand Corporation interviews with defectors from the NLF. He concluded that the NLF's strength was in their superior organization rather than the appeal of their cause.

Race, Jeffrey. *War Comes to Long An: Revolutionary Conflict in a Vietnamese Province*. Berkeley: Univ. of California Press, 1972.

In 1967–1968, Race (a political scientist originally sent to Vietnam as a military advisor) interviewed hundreds of Vietnamese in a single province to determine how the revolutionary movement was able to win control there. Chapter 4, "Lessons from Long An," presents his conclusions; Chapter 5 analyzes how the American war effort ignored those conclusions.

Sansom, Robert. *The Economics of Insurgency in the Mekong Delta of Vietnam*. Cambridge: M.I.T. Press, 1970.

Sansom interviewed villagers in Mai Tho Province about their experience of land policies under the French, Vietminh, NLF, and Diem. He found that Diem's land reform worsened the lot of the peasants.

Trullinger, James Walker. *Village at War*. New York: Longman, 1980.
Trullinger studied a village near an American base which was classified as "safe" by the Saigon government; he found that more than half the villagers supported the NLF, who continued working there in secret.

The Democratic Republic of Vietnam

Burchett, Wilfred G. *Vietnam North*. New York: International, 1966.
Daily life under the bombs in 1966, stressing the Vietnamese people's ingenuity and their determination to resist.

Chaliand, Gérard. *The Peasants of North Vietnam*. Baltimore: Penguin, 1969.
Chaliand briefly describes his 1967 visit to rural communities, then lets the peasants speak for themselves. They tell of their suffering from the bombing and their efforts to build socialism in their own villages.

Porter, Gareth. "The Myth of the Bloodbath: North Vietnam's Land Reform Reconsidered." *Bulletin of Concerned Asian Scholars* 5 (1973): 2–15.
Using Vietnamese sources, Porter's study of the 1953–1956 Communist land reform documents its difficulties and excesses but challenges U.S. versions of systematic violence.

Riboud, Marc, and Philippe Devillers. *North Vietnam*. New York: Holt, Rinehart & Winston, 1970.
The 120 pages of captioned black and white photos in this book are divided into eight sections: Bombing, Countryside, Factories, Soldiers, School, Religion, Leadership, Hanoi.

Van Dyke, Jon M. *North Vietnam's Struggle for Survival*. Palo Alto: Pacific, 1972.
This scholarly analysis of the effects of the U.S. bombing uses Vietnamese sources to show "why the most sophisticated and sustained bombing campaign in history failed to force the North Vietnamese to sue for peace." Descriptions of programs of evacuation, labor reorganization, etc., are especially interesting.

The Shot Seen Round The World
This photo, showing South Vietnamese National Police Chief, Brigadier General
Nguyen Ngoc Loan, killing an enemy soldier with a single pistol shot to the head,
vividly demonstrated the horrors of the war. The summary execution was witnessed
nationwide on television and reported in the newspapers. *Wide World Photo*.

Chapter 7
Tet: 1968

Background

Historical Summary

By the end of 1967, U.S. combat troops had been fighting and dying in Vietnam for more than two years, and the American public was beginning to express growing doubts about the war. President Lyndon Johnson and his commander in Vietnam, General William Westmoreland, sought to lessen these doubts by declaring that the United States was making progress in the conflict.

But at the end of January 1968, events in Vietnam tested the president's credibility as well as his conduct of the war, and forced him to reverse his strategy. These events came to be known as the Tet Offensive.

Tet is the lunar new year, the time when the Vietnamese traditionally celebrate their most important holiday. Months earlier, the North Vietnamese and Vietcong had planned to take advantage of the holiday to launch surprise attacks on South Vietnam's cities, which they had never before assaulted. Their purpose was to break the deadlock in the long war of attrition that had seemed to favor neither side. They hoped to spark uprisings in the urban areas that would compel Nguyen Van Thieu, the South Vietnamese president, to accept a coalition government in Saigon.

North Vietnamese and Vietcong troops were able to penetrate deep into South Vietnam's major cities and provincial capitals, hitting army installations, police headquarters, and radio stations. They even broke into the compound of the U.S. embassy in Saigon. The extent and boldness of their actions startled senior American officers, who had expected the main confrontation to take place at Khesanh, in the northern part of South Vietnam, where the enemy had laid siege to a U.S. outpost.

From a strictly military viewpoint, the Communists failed to attain their objective. On the contrary, the Vietcong forces suffered heavy losses, leaving the burden of the war in the future largely on North Vietnamese units.

The most significant impact of the offensive occurred in the United States, where key members of the Johnson administration, along with the rest of the nation, saw reports on television that seemed to contradict the official optimism.

In Washington many of President Johnson's advisers were disillusioned. Foremost among them was Clark Clifford, the new secretary of defense and an

193

Chronology

	1967 Sep	Oct	Nov	Dec	1968 Jan	Feb	Mar	Apr	May
Vietnam	Thieu-Ky ticket receives 35% of the vote and wins				North Vietnam surrounds Khesanh. Tet Offensive begins	ARVN recaptures Hue	LBJ announces bombing halt. My Lai massacre takes place	U.S. Marines survive in Khesanh. North Vietnam agrees to talks	Peace talks begin in Paris
United States	LBJ announces San Antonio formula for peace	Antiwar demonstrators march on the Pentagon				Senate questions McNamara about Gulf of Tonkin	Eugene McCarthy gets 42% of New Hampshire primary vote. Robert Kennedy seeks Democratic nomination. LBJ announces he will not run for re-election	Martin Luther King assassinated. Unrest at Columbia University	
World Wide		Ché Guevara killed leading rebels in Bolivia			Students riot in Warsaw. North Korea seizes USN Pueblo				Students riot in Paris

	1968 Jun	Jul	Aug	Sep	Oct	Nov	Dec
Vietnam	U.S. troops leave Khe-sanh.	Abrams replaces Westmoreland as Commander of MACV			LBJ announces total halt of North Vietnam bombing		
United States	Robert Kennedy assassinated		Violence in Chicago during Democratic Convention		Black Power demonstrations at Mexico City Olympics	Nixon wins presidency, defeating Vice President Humphrey	
World Wide			Russian troops crack down on Czechoslovakia				

old friend of the president. He felt that a continued war of attrition would drain the United States, and he argued for an alternative approach. Clifford was supported by a group of elder statesmen, most of whom were retired prominent officials. Their disenchantment with the war was heightened when, on March 10, the *New York Times* published a report revealing that Westmoreland had requested 206,000 more men for Vietnam. They, too, now shared Clifford's pessimism about winning the war.

Meanwhile, antiwar sentiment seemed to be spreading through the country. In the Democratic primary election in New Hampshire, an avowed peace candidate, Senator Eugene McCarthy, won an unexpectedly large proportion of the votes, nearly defeating the incumbent president.

On March 31, 1968, President Johnson delivered a televised address in which he announced that he would curtail the bombing of North Vietnam and seek to negotiate peace with the Communists. At the end of his speech, Johnson disclosed that he would not run in the November elections.

He may have planned earlier to retire from politics. But his unexpected announcement created the impression that he had been a casualty of the Tet Offensive. To a large extent, certainly, his dream of building a Great Society in America had been a casualty of the Vietnam War.

Points to Emphasize

- the effects of television coverage on the public's perception of the Vietnam War
- the credibility problem of the Johnson administration
- the shock value of the Tet Offensive and the strategic and tactical goals of the North Vietnamese
- the question of increasing the size of American forces in Vietnam
- the disenchantment with the Johnson war policy among both hawks and doves
- President Johnson's options: whether to escalate or disengage
- the impact of the New Hampshire primary on American electoral politics in 1968
- the factors which led to President Johnson's March 31, 1968 speech

Glossary of Names and Terms

McGeorge Bundy dean of the Faculty of Arts and Sciences, Harvard University, 1953–1961. Special Assistant to the President for National Security, 1961–1966. President, Ford Foundation, 1966–1979.

Clark Clifford Washington lawyer. Special Counsel to the President, 1946–1950. Head of President Kennedy's transition team, 1960–1961. Secretary of Defense, 1968–1969.

Robert Kennedy younger brother of John Kennedy and his campaign manager in 1960. Attorney General of the United States, 1961–1964. U.S. senator from New York, 1965–1968. Candidate for the Democratic nomination for President, 1968. Assassinated June 5, 1968, after winning the California primary.

Eugene McCarthy U.S. representative and senator from Minnesota, 1958–1970. Candidate for the Democratic nomination for President, 1968.

Harry McPherson Deputy Under Secretary for International Affairs, Department of the Army, 1963–1964. Assistant Secretary of State, Educational and Cultural Affairs, 1964–1965. Special Assistant and Counsel to President Johnson, 1965–1966. Special Counsel to President Johnson, 1966–1969.

Mike Mansfield U.S. representative and senator from Montana, 1952–1976. Assistant Majority Leader, 1957–1961. Majority Leader, 1961–1976. Member of the Senate Committee on Foreign Relations.

Walt Whitman Rostow professor of economic history, Massachusetts Institute of Technology, 1950–1960. Deputy Special Assistant to the President for National Security Affairs, 1961. Counselor and Chairman, Policy Planning Council of State Department, 1961–1966. Special Assistant to the President, 1966–1969.

Earle Wheeler Deputy Commander-in-chief, U.S. European Command, 1962. Chief of Staff, U.S. Army, 1962–1964. Chairman, Joint Chiefs of Staff, 1964–1970.

credibility gap public disbelief in the government version of events. One of the major problems of the Johnson administration with regard to Vietnam.

disengagement the pulling back of U.S. troops to end the Americanization of the war. The goal of Secretary of Defense Clark Clifford after the Tet Offensive.

Hue former imperial capital of Vietnam. Communist troops captured it during the Tet Offensive and held it for more than three weeks.

Khesanh isolated U.S. Marine base near the Laotian border which was under siege by the Communists in the winter of 1967–1968. Khesanh never fell but was evacuated by the Americans later in 1968, then rebuilt into a base in 1971.

Tet the lunar new year celebrations in Vietnam.

Ton Son Nhut Airbase American-built airport outside of Saigon. Headquarters for General Westmoreland.

Wise Old Men government officials and military men, both active and retired, who served as unofficial advisors to President Johnson, including: Dean Acheson, George Ball, McGeorge and William Bundy, Abe Fortas, Cyrus Vance, Henry Cabot Lodge, Dean Rusk, Clark Clifford, Richard Helms, Walt Rostow, Arthur Goldberg, and Generals Bradley, Ridgway, and Taylor.

Documents

Document 1

The scope and intensity of the Tet Offensive were a surprise to American and South Vietnamese officials. Although some intelligence operatives had warned that an attack might be coming, holiday leaves had been granted to South Vietnamese forces. Because the Tet holiday was traditionally a time of heavy travel in Vietnam with families returning to their ancestors' burial places, the North Vietnamese and the Vietcong were able to prepare their multipronged assaults and move troops into position without being observed.

Document 1 is an excerpt from *Village in Vietnam* by Gerald C. Hickey, whose study of the cultural life of the Vietnamese points out the importance of the Tet holiday in the Vietnamese tradition and shows why the attackers were sure of finding a distracted population which could be easily surprised.

1   Village in Vietnam
Gerald C. Hickey

. . . As the lunar new year comes to a close and the harvest is gathered, the people of Khanh Hau give themselves over to a holiday mood, indulging in numerous village and family celebrations. Thuong Dien, the village feast marking the end of the harvest, is followed closely by Tet, as the lunar New Year celebration is commonly called. It is the time for everyone, even the urban dweller, to return to his natal village or to the village where his family tombs are located. There he re-establishes bonds with kinfolk, and for one week he becomes a villager again, participating in the simple pleasures of peasant life.

The first Tet ritual, held during the twelfth lunar month, is the fixing of family tombs, and it may be observed in one of two ways. First the family gathers at the house of the truong toc, and they may carry the necessary joss votive papers, and the prescribed offerings of cake, chicken, tea, rice alcohol, and paper money to the graves. After requesting the Spirit of the Soil for permission to disturb the earth, the truong toc offers the food to the ancestors, and adult members kowtow before the graves and place burning joss on them. They then weed the plot, pile earth on the graves, and whitewash the stone tombs—tasks which they perform scrupulously, for the state of the graves reflects on the family. When their labor is finished they settle down to a picnic of the food offerings.

It also is permissible to return to the house of the truong toc after refurbishing the tombs and make the food offerings at the main altar there. This is followed by a feast to which guests usually are invited. Most villagers prefer having the food offering and meal at the tombs, and only a few prosperous families consistently have feasts at their homes. Several villagers go about fixing the graves of those who no longer have kin in the village. Most of these burial places have been reduced to barely visible weathered mounds, and a few chunks of dried soil may mark them for the coming year. Joss also is placed on them to prevent the deceased from becoming errant spirits.

On the twenty-third day of the twelfth lunar month the family celebrates the departure of Ong Tao, the Spirit of the Hearth, who is represented in the kitchen by three stones on which cooking is done, and honored with a small altar in an auspicious corner. Ong Tao observes the daily activities of the family, and on this day he returns to the celestial realm where he reports to the Emperor of Jade all he has observed during the year. He consequently can influence the family's destiny, and it is not uncommon for parents to place their children under his protection. Daily offerings are placed on his altar, and for the Tet ritual, red paper containing a sketch, which depicts the departure of Ong Tao on a large carp, a celestial horse, or a phoenix, is burned on the altar. The family then partakes of a feast which should include two traditional Tet dishes—glutinous rice cakes and the excessively sweet soybean soup. A bowl of the rice usually is placed on Ong Tao's altar, but during his absence no joss is burned on it.

On the thirtieth day of the twelfth lunar month, each family gathers at its house to prepare for the arrival of the souls of the ancestors and the return of Ong Tao. A few families retain the traditional practice of placing before the house a symbolic tree made from bamboo branches on which votive paper, a rectangular talisman of straw, a small sack of rice, and a container of water are tied. Joss burns continuously on the altar of the ancestors. Around nine o'clock in the evening the usual calm of the village is shattered by bursts of exploding firecrackers intended to chase evil spirits, and anyone entering the house must wash his feet.

While awaiting midnight, the hour for receiving the ancestors and Ong Tao, women prepare the soybean soup while the men continue to set off firecrackers, careful to guard a good supply for midnight so the entrance of ancestors and Ong Tao will not be marred by the presence of evil spirits. At midnight all adult members of the family, dressed in traditional clothes, gather before the ancestral altar where the eldest male makes an offering of food and burns red votive paper. Each member than takes a stick of burning joss and kowtows before the altar. This ritual is followed by a meal in which special Tet dishes are served. Prayers are recited at the altar through the night as a vigil for the first day of the new lunar year.

Mon Mot is the first day of Tet, and with it comes a certain anxiety that bad luck will enter the house and plague the family during the entire year. The primary function of the symbolic tree is to bar the entrance to the Celestial Dog, a bearer of ill fortune. Since firecrackers have the same effect, the tree is not absolutely necessary (which probably explains why many villagers do not bother to prepare one). Many villagers purchase leafless branches of an apricot or pear tree that they hope will burst with exquisite blossoms on the first day of Tet, portending good fortune for the family. On this day there is a great deal of visiting, so some members of the family remain at home to receive guests and serve them tea, rice alcohol, and candied fruits and vegetables. Guests with favorable names such as Tho (longevity), Loc (abundance), and Kim (gold) are particularly welcome in the belief that they bring the good fortune their names import. On the other hand, those with unfavorable names such as Meo (cat), Cho (dog), or Lon (vagina) are not encouraged to visit. Around six o'clock in the evening, offerings are made at the altar of the ancestors, and the family sits down to another meal of Tet dishes.

On the third day of Tet some villagers observe a ritual honoring two military heroes of antiquity—Hanh Binh and Hanh Truong. Chicken boiled in a special way is served at a large feast during which the host invites the two heroes to participate, requesting that they in return protect the house during the coming year. After the meal the feet of the chicken are attached to one of the rafters. If the claws draw inward after a while, it is considered a good sign, but if they open out they release bad luck. The important ritual of the fourth day of Tet is the departure of the ancestors. This resembles the other rituals honoring the ancestors, and it also is an appropriate time for exploding firecrackers. The fifth day is inauspicious for traveling, having feasts, and engaging in a number of other activities, so it tends to be uneventful as is the sixth day. On the seventh and last day of Tet, the symbolic tree is removed, and the various talismans are kept in the house during the year. The family has a final meal to mark the end of the new year celebration. . . .

Document 2

Proponents of the use of air power in Vietnam believed that bombing had been effective in World War II and could bring victory in Southeast Asia. They advanced a number of arguments in favor of heavy bombing of North Vietnam. It would, they said, avoid the necessity of a large U.S. land force. It would bolster the morale of the South Vietnamese. It would destroy the industrial strength of North Vietnam, discourage the populace, and force Hanoi to move toward peace. And it would check the infiltration of soldiers and supplies from North to South Vietnam, without which, the argument ran, the southern insurgency would wither away. Under President Johnson, the argument carried the day. Although some bombing advocates complained that they never were allowed to unleash the full force of U.S. airpower, critics of the strategy argued that no amount of bombing alone could win that kind of war. In 1967, the Central Intelligence Agency issued the results of a study of Operation Rolling Thunder, the sustained bombing of the North, that supported the critics.

2   Bomb Damage Inflicted on North Vietnam Through April 1967
   CIA Intelligence Memorandum
   May 12, 1967
   Summary

Through the end of April 1967 the US air campaign against North Vietnam—Rolling Thunder—had significantly eroded the capacities of North Vietnam's limited industrial and military base. These losses, however, have not meaningfully degraded North Vietnam's material ability to continue the war in South Vietnam.

Total damage through April 1967 was over $233 million, of which 70 percent was accounted for by damage to economic targets. The greatest amount of damage was inflicted on the so-called logistics target system—transport equipment and lines of communication.

By the end of April 1967 the US air campaign had attacked 173 fixed targets, over 70 percent of the targets on the JCS list. This campaign included extensive attacks on almost every major target system in the country. The physical results have varied widely.

All of the 13 targeted petroleum storage facilities have been attacked, with an estimated loss of 85 percent of storage capacity. Attacks on 13 of the 20 targeted

electric power facilities have neutralized 70 percent of North Vietnam's power-gen-
erating capacity. The major losses in the military establishment include the neutralization of 18 ammunition depots, with a loss capacity of 70 percent. Over three
fourths of the 65 JCS-targeted barracks have been attacked, with a loss of about one
fourth of national capacity. Attacks on 22 of the 29 targeted supply depots reduced
capacity by 17 percent. Through the end of April 1967, five of North Vietnam's airfields had been attacked, with a loss of about 20 percent of national capacity.

North Vietnam's ability to recuperate from the air attacks has been of a high order. The major exception has been the electric power industry. One small plant—
Co Dinh—is beyond repair. Most of the other plants would require 3–4 months to
be restored to partial operations, although two plants—Haiphong East and Uong
Bi—would require one year. For complete restoration, all of the plants would require at least a year. Restoration of these plants would require foreign technical assistance and equipment.

The recuperability problem is not significant for the other target systems. The
destroyed petroleum storage system has been replaced by an effective system of dispersed storage and distribution. The damaged military target systems—particularly
barracks and storage depots—have simply been abandoned, and supplies and troops
dispersed throughout the country. The inventories of transport and military equipment have been replaced by large infusions of military and economic aid from the
USSR and Communist China. Damage to bridges and lines of communications is
frequently repaired within a matter of days, if not hours, or the effects are countered
by an elaborate system of multiple bypasses or pre-positioned spans.

Documents 3 and 4

The North Vietnamese and the Vietcong had planned the January 1968 Tet Offensive months earlier. Document 3, written at the beginning of November
1967, shows North Vietnam's goals for the offensive, the plan for beginning
the general uprising, and the strategy for success. These instructions were sent
to the local cadres, for each to implement its share of the plan.

Document 4 was issued by the Command Post of the Liberation Army in
the South. In it the Central Office of South Vietnam (COSVN) assessed the
first hours of the Tet Offensive on January 31, 1968, detailing the objectives
that had been met and the scope and difficulty of the work yet to be done.

3 Directive on Forthcoming Offensive and Uprisings
Provincial Party Standing Committee
November 1, 1967

1. Following is information on the new situation. Our troops are continuously
attacking the enemy everywhere, especially in district seats and province capitals.
We have started a partial uprising in the city. Several province capitals and district
seats have changed hands three or four times. The enemy troops in several districts
and provinces have been confused and disorganized.

In the rural, delta and mountain areas, an uprising movement to gain full control
of the rural areas has started. The rural people, together with town people, are rising
up to fight the U.S., overthrow the puppet government and seize power. In the face
of this situation, the enemy has shifted to the defensive and has been thrown into
utmost confusion. A new era, a real revolutionary period, an offensive and uprising

period has begun. The victorious day of the people and the trying hours are coming. This is the encouraging factor of the situation. This is what the entire Party, entire army and entire population have been expecting. The people often say: "It is wise to carry through to the end, no matter what the cost in lives and money may be." Now it is time to apply this motto to complete our work as soon as possible and without delay. . . .

Upon receipt of this letter, you are required to formulate a plan to prepare the minds of the Party, Group, agencies and the people by convening a Party Branch meeting (one night) to:

—Report the new situation in towns and rural areas. The time is now more favorable [for an offensive] than ever before. This is to notify you that an offensive and uprising will take place in the very near future and we will mount stronger attacks on towns and cities, in coordination with the widespread [uprising] movement in the rural areas. The enemy will be thrown into utmost confusion. No matter how violently the enemy may react, he cannot avoid collapse. This is not only a golden opportunity to liberate hamlets and villages but also an opportunity to liberate district seats, province capitals and South Viet-Nam as a whole.

Our victory is close at hand. The conditions are ripe. Our Party has carefully judged the situation. We must act and act fast. This is an opportunity to fulfill the aspirations of the entire people, of cadre, of each comrade and of our families. We have long suffered hardships, death and pain. We are looking for an opportunity to avenge evil done to our families, to pay our debt to the Fatherland, to display our loyalty to the country, affection for the people and love for our families. We cannot afford to miss this rare opportunity. All Party members and cadre must be willing to sacrifice their lives for the survival of the Fatherland.

This opportunity is like an attack on an enemy post in which we have reached the last fence and the enemy puts up a fierce resistance. We only need to make a swift assault to secure the target and gain total victory.

If we are hesitant and fearful of hardships and misery, we will suffer heavy losses, fail to accomplish the mission and feel guilty for failing our nation, our people, our families and our comrades who have already sacrificed themselves. It is time for us to take the initiative in penetrating into enemy bases in provinces, districts and villages, attacking him five or ten times more violently to score brilliant achievements.

Make all comrades realize that the purpose of the revolutionary activities conducted for many years is mainly to support this phase, in this decisive hour. Even though we make sacrifices, we will gain glorious victory, not only for the people, but also for our Fatherland and families. If we adopt a hesitant attitude, we will not only belittle the value of human beings but also lower the prestige of revolutionary party members. This means we will lose self-respect and we will not be worthy of enjoying the rights of man.

As Party members, we should not think and act in an inferior manner. For this reason all comrades must get together and speak their minds in order to become better acquainted and to transform the whole Party Branch into a determined-to-die unit. All comrades must write a heart-felt letter expressing their decision to the Central Party Committee, to Chairman Ho as well as to the Province Party Committee.

. . .

3. *How will the uprising be conducted?*
There are two fundamental steps:
First, annihilate the enemy's political power. It is fundamental that we capture all

tyrants from the village and hamlet administrative machinery and a number of spies. If we are not successful in this area the uprising will not be able to take place.

Second, organize our political power, specifically our [own] district, village and hamlet administrative machinery.

To conduct an uprising, you must have a roster of all the tyrants and spies and be familiar with the way they live and where they live. Then use suicide cells to annihilate them by any means. The following tasks should also be achieved on the same night:

Conduct meetings and give information on the current situation (about 10 to 15 minutes). *Make use of the populace immediately* in sabotage and support activities and in raid operations against the spies. The masses should be encouraged to go on strike. Dig trenches and make spikes all night long, and contribute to the transformation of the terrain. All people in each family, regardless of their ages, should be encouraged to take part [in the uprising]. This is the best way of motivating the populace and of elevating their pride. We must alter the terrain features at night to secure positions to oppress and attack the enemy in the morning. The cadre, together with the population, will be required to swear that they will stay close to their rice fields, defend their villages and do their utmost to wrest back control of the entire area, including district seats and towns. A number of old men, women and children should be made available the following morning and ordered to report to enemy district seats or posts to inform them [the GVN officials] that their [the demonstrators'] village has been occupied by the revolutionary army and that the personnel of the [village] administrative committee as well as their [own] husbands and children have been captured. This demonstration will be aimed at preventing the enemy from battering their village. Young men and healthy farmers will be retained for use in defense work construction, altering terrain, guard duty and combat. This is done to restrict escapees and limit our casualties. Place emphasis on encouraging enemy soldiers' dependents to struggle for the return of their husbands and children. Make appeals to enemy personnel from the Popular, Regional and Special Forces to surrender. Once the task is achieved, make use of a number of agents under legal cover to organize insurrection committees in white [GVN-controlled] hamlets and villages. At the same time, transfer the determined-to-die cells to the next hamlet or village to push the revolutionary movement forward quickly, observing the same principles applied recently in Tuy Phuoc and other areas of the province. Women and children must be recruited immediately to serve in the self-defense corps and guerrilla force.

A number of loyal farmers, youths and women will be selected for indoctrination. Upon termination of the course, and after the students have been acquainted with the regulations, an official selection of members for organizations and recruitment of personnel for hamlets will take place. This will facilitate the organization of people's cells, such as those for the youths, farmers, and women.

Instructions on carrying out such policies as that for land will be disseminated in the future. If all Party Branches, hamlets, and villages display a strong determination and unanimously carry out the aforesaid tasks, we will surely create various levels of supremacy and will continue to heighten our supremacy. . . .

4 A Preliminary Assessment of the Situation
COSVN and SVNLA
January 31, 1968

On the evening of January 31, [1968], the COSVN Current Affairs Committee and the Military Affairs Committee of SVNLA Headquarters held a meeting to assess the situation and decide on specific recommendations on matters related to leadership and guidance to be disseminated to, and implemented by [addresses].

1. We have launched simultaneous and timely attacks on almost all towns and cities, district seats, sectors and [enemy] military bases as planned. Generally speaking, the attacks were fruitful at the outset. In areas where the offensive and uprising were closely coordinated, or where the three-pronged attacks in mountainous and lowland areas were comparatively coordinated, the attacks were more successful. Within a short period of time we succeeded in paralyzing the puppet government administration from central to local echelons, and confusing the U.S. command channels. We succeeded in wearing down and destroying an important enemy force, many headquarters of the puppet troops, and a large quantity of war facilities. Timely and accurate fire was directed at main objectives. The attack was extremely fierce. The COSVN Current Affairs Committee and the Military Affairs Committee of the SVNLA Headquarters considered this achievement a very great one. This first achievement has an extremely momentous significance. [It gains revolutionary pride for the masses and places us in a position to advance and score greater achievements in both the military and the political field.] It enables us to make greater efforts to continue attacking and to be resolute in our determination to win final victory. We have struck the enemy accurately and successfully. The Current Affairs Committee and the Military Affairs Committee of the SVNLA Headquarters warmly cite and commend all cadre, party and group members of all echelons, both inside and outside the army, and all cadres and troops within the armed forces.

However, we still have the following shortcomings and weaknesses: We failed to seize a number of primary objectives and to completely destroy mobile and defensive units of the enemy. We also failed to hold the occupied areas. In the political field, we failed to motivate the people to stage uprisings and break the enemy's oppressive control. In cities as well as in rural areas and areas temporarily occupied by the enemy, the troop-proselytizing activities of the masses were not conducted on a broad front, and propaganda work was not carried out soon enough or continuously enough. Signal liaison and reporting in some areas, especially the signal liaison and command in charge of the immediate objectives of the SVNLA Headquarters and regions, were extremely slow and not closely coordinated, and so forth.

2. The enemy: Although he had taken precautionary measures, he was surprised strategically and suffered heavy losses in strength and equipment. The puppet's command agencies, installations, and central government administration were paralyzed. His troops were driven into disorder. The U.S. troops were put on the defensive. They became confused and demoralized. However, since we did not succeed in completely destroying many of his mobile and defensive units at the very start, or closely coordinate the offensive with uprisings and troop proselytizing, the enemy continued to resist and his units were not completely broken up. If in the coming days we fail to quickly motivate a large and powerful force of the masses to stand up against the enemy in time, and if we fail to concentrate our armed forces to attack him continuously, he will certainly recover his strength and counterattack us more strongly. Not only will this limit the impact of our victories, it will create new difficulties for us.

3. In accordance with the Resolution of the Politburo and the development of the situation during the past two days, the COSVN Current Affairs Committee and the Military Affairs Committee of the Liberation Army Headquarters would like to call the attention of the Region [Party] Committees, Military Region [Party] Committee and Party Committee agencies to the following basic problems:

a. It is imperative to be fully aware of the fact that the general offensive and general uprising, which are directed against an enemy with an army of more than 1,200,000 stubborn, reactionary, and well-equipped soldiers, is a prolonged strategic offensive that includes many military campaigns and local uprisings to break off all enemy counterattacks and that it is an extremely fierce struggle.

Only when we succeed in destroying the entire puppet army and government, neutralizing the actual political and military support of the Americans, and wiping out a large portion of the U.S. and satellite forces, thus depriving them of all war facilities and crushing their attempted invasion, can we drive them to total defeat and achieve final victory. At present, the victories that we gained at the outset show that we are now powerful and the enemy is on the decline. Our fierce attacks are bringing him closer to the threat of bitter defeat. Consequently, we are fully able to successfully achieve our plan. However, while preparing and implementing this plan, we have been guilty of many errors and shortcomings, as mentioned above. We cannot yet, therefore, achieve total victory in a short period.

Document 5

American reporters and cameramen were on hand within hours of the attack on the American Embassy in Saigon on the last day of January 1968, and by means of communications satellites, reports were televised in the United States the same day. Document 5 is a transcript of a fifteen-minute CBS News Special Report "Saigon Under Fire," hosted by Mike Wallace. An estimated 7,450,000 homes were tuned in to the report, which was telecast from 11:15 to 11:30 P.M., following "The Jonathan Winters Show."

Similar programs appeared simultaneously on ABC and NBC, and in the days that followed, the Tet Offensive became a major subject of television news programming.

5   **Saigon Under Fire**
    CBS News Special Report
    January 31, 1968
    WALLACE: Good evening. I'm Mike Wallace.

With a bold series of raids during the last three days the enemy in Vietnam has demolished the myth that Allied military strength controls that country. The Communists hit the very heart of Saigon, the capital of South Vietnam, and at least ten cities which correspond to state capitals here in the United States. And then, as if to demonstrate that no place in that war-torn nation is secure they struck at least nine American military strongholds and unnumbered field positions. Tonight the magnitude of those raids became apparent in the U.S. Command's report on casualties. The Communists paid a heavy toll for their strikes, almost 5,000 dead, including 660 in Saigon alone, and almost 2,000 captured. But Allied casualties also are high: 232

Americans killed, 929 wounded; 300 South Vietnamese killed, 747 wounded, and that toll is expected to climb.

The enemy's well-coordinated attacks occurred throughout South Vietnam, but the most dramatic demonstration of his boldness and capability came at the very symbol of America's presence in Vietnam, the brand new U.S. Embassy building there. CBS NEWS Correspondent Robert Schakne reports.

SCHAKNE: The American Embassy is under siege; only the besiegers are Americans. Inside, in part of the building, are the Vietcong terror squads that charged in during the night. Military Police got back into the compound of the $2½ million Embassy complex at dawn. Before that a platoon of Vietcong were in control. The Communist raiders never got into the main chancery building; a handful of Marines had it blocked and kept them out. But the raiders were everywhere else. By daylight (voice drowned out by gunfire) No one, unless identified, was allowed in the street. An Australian Military Policeman was standing guard, firing warning shots to keep the street clear.

Outside the building knots of Military Policemen held positions. There were bursts of wild shooting in the streets, perhaps snipers in other buildings and there had been casualties. The bodies of two Military Policemen who died as they tried to assault the compound lay near their jeep across the boulevard. But even after the Military Police fought their way back inside, there was more fighting to do. The raiders were still about the compound. They may have been a suicide cadre. In the end none of them were to surrender.

This is where the Vietcong raiders broke in. They sneaked up and blasted a hole in the reinforced concrete fence surrounding the compound. They were inside before anyone knew it. They had the big Embassy wall to protect them. But none of the raiders lived to tell of their exploit. By 8:00 o'clock, five hours after they first broke in, almost all of them were dead. Nineteen bodies were counted. All in civilian clothes, they had been armed with American M-16 rifles and also rocket-launchers and rockets. They had explosives, their purpose apparently to destroy the Embassy. In that purpose they did not succeed.

The fighting went on for a total of six hours before the last known Vietcong raider was killed. They were rooted out of bushes, from outlying buildings, and then the last one, the 19th, from the small residence of the Embassy's Mission Coordinator, George Jacobson, who had been hiding out all alone, all morning.

What could you see from your window? Were the—were the VC in the buildings?

JACOBSON: No, I did not see any VC in the building except that I knew that there was at least one VC in my house. I knew that he was on the bottom floor of my house.

SCHAKNE: You had quite an escape at the very end. How did that happen?

JACOBSON: Well, they [U.S. troops] put riot gas into the bottom floors of my house, which of course would drive whoever was down below up top where I was. They had thrown me a pistol about ten minutes before this occurred, and with all of the luck that I've had all of my life, I got him before he got me.

SCHAKNE: With the pistol. And he had what?

JACOBSON: An M-16.

SCHAKNE: And you got him.

Then the job of sweeping through the Embassy building and compound, trying to make sure no Vietcong were still hiding. The job of finding unexploded rockets,

grenades and satchel charges. And the casualties. The two American Military Policemen who had been guarding the side gate apparently killed at the very beginning
when the raiders blasted their way through the wall. All told, five Americans were
killed during the day; at least four others were wounded. All the known attackers
are dead too.

Saigon had been on the alert for Vietcong terror attacks during the night, but for
some reason the Embassy guard was not increased. Just two Military Policemen at
one gate, a handful of Marines inside. There wasn't anyone to stop the Vietcong
when they came. General William Westmoreland came by soon after. His version
was that all this represented a Vietcong defeat.

WESTMORELAND: In some way the enemy's well-laid plans went afoul. Some su-
perficial damage was done to the building. All of the enemy that entered the compound as far as I can determine were killed. Nineteen bodies have been found on the
premises—enemy bodies. Nineteen enemy bodies have been found on the premises.

SCHAKNE: General, how would you assess yesterday's activities and today's? What
is the enemy doing? Are these major attacks?

(Sound of explosions)

WESTMORELAND: That's POD setting off a couple of M-79 duds, I believe.

SCHAKNE: General, how would you assess the enemy's purposes yesterday and
today?

WESTMORELAND: The enemy very deceitfully has taken advantage of the Tet truce
in order to create maximum consternation within South Vietnam, particularly in the
populated areas. In my opinion this is diversionary to his main effort, which he had
planned to take place in Quang Tri Province, from Laos, toward Khesanh and across
the Demilitarized Zone. This attack has not yet materialized; his schedule has probably been thrown off balance because of our very effective air strikes.

Now yesterday the enemy exposed himself by virtue of this strategy and he suffered great casualties. When I left my office late yesterday, approximately 8:00
o'clock, we—we had accounted for almost 700 enemy killed in action. Now we had
suffered some casualties ourselves, but they were small by comparison. My guess is,
based on my conversations with my field commanders, that there were probably—
there were probably far more than 700 that were killed. Now by virtue of this audacious action by the enemy, he has exposed himself, he has become more vulnerable. As soon as President Thieu, with our agreement, called off the truce, U.S. and
American troops went on the offensive and pursued the enemy aggressively.

SCHAKNE: When they built this Embassy it was first to be a secure building. This
Embassy was designed as a bomb-proof, attack-proof building, but it turned out,
when the VC hit us, it wasn't attack-proof enough. Robert Schakne, CBS NEWS,
Saigon.

WALLACE: Washington regards the enemy raids as the first step in a strategy
aimed at strengthening their hand for any peace talks which may develop, and captured Communist documents lend weight to the theory.

CBS NEWS White House Correspondent Dan Rather reports.

RATHER: We knew this was coming—a well-coordinated series of enemy raids
against South Vietnamese cities. Our intelligence even pinpointed the exact day it
would happen. What we did not know was where. This is the official story, as given
out by White House news secretary George Christian, who went on to say there was
no way to completely insulate yourself against this kind of thing if the enemy is willing to sacrifice large numbers of men.

But if we knew it was coming, even to the exact day, Christian was asked, why wasn't extra protection placed around such an obvious place as the Saigon Embassy? The White House spokesman paused, then said, "I just don't know." At the Pentagon a high-ranking source said, "There simply were more of them and they were better than we expected."

Washington is startled but not panicked by the latest series of events. President Johnson privately is warning Congressmen that intelligence reports indicate the whole month of February will be rough in Southeast Asia. Mr. Johnson is emphasizing that the enemy's winter offensive is only beginning. Dan Rather, CBS NEWS, Washington.

WALLACE: The drama of the battle for Saigon captured most attention, but the South Vietnamese capital was only one of the Communist targets. In a moment we'll return with battle film from another city.

(ANNOUNCEMENT)

WALLACE: The U.S. Command's battle communique indicates that the Allies repulsed most of the enemy's attacks, but this success was not universal. In an assault today the Communists captured half of the Central Highlands city of Kontum and the Vietcong flag flies in the center of the northern city of Hue. The enemy claims also to control Quang Tri city, also in I Corps in the north, a claim as yet unconfirmed by the Allies.

But one place where American and South Vietnamese troops turned back the enemy was at Nhatrang, a coastal city about 190 miles northeast of Saigon. In peacetime a pleasant resort city, now Nhatrang is the headquarters for the Fifth Special Forces, the Green Berets; and the Green Berets were in the thick of the fighting. The Communist attack there had begun around midnight, and it developed into a street fight which, as you see here, carried over into the daylight hours. The enemy's apparent goal in this fight, down the street, was a provincial prison where many important Vietcong were held. During this battle many innocent civilians, friendly to the Allies, were trapped in their homes between the lines of fire between VC and the Green Berets. It was only after twelve hours of battle that the area was secure enough to call those civilians out to safety.

The Communist raids had a stunning impact, all of them, around the world, and the question is, what is it that the enemy is after in these attacks. Certainly he does not believe that these suicide assaults by terrorist squads are going to radically change the course of the war in Vietnam; but there can be no doubt that these attacks are calculated to impress indelibly on public opinion in North and South Vietnam and in the United States the resourcefulness and the determination of the Vietcong and his ability to strike almost at will any place in South Vietnam if he is willing to pay the price.

The story of the past three days, with heavy emphasis, of course, on American and South Vietnamese casualties will be trumpeted throughout Vietnam and around the world by Hanoi. Whether all of this is a prelude to an expression that Hanoi is willing now to go to the negotiation table remains to be seen, but there is little doubt that there will be more such stories from Khesanh and elsewhere in South Vietnam in the bitter month of February that lies ahead.

Mike Wallace, CBS NEWS, New York.

ANNOUNCER: This has been a CBS NEWS SPECIAL REPORT: "Saigon Under Fire."

Document 6

Walt Whitman Rostow served as Special Assistant to the President at the time of the Tet Offensive. Rostow staunchly supported government policy in Vietnam and, indeed, thought the Johnson administration should use even more military force in Vietnam. He believed that the United States was winning the war of attrition and was already improving its position in the wake of the Tet Offensive.

In this document, Rostow expresses his optimism that the Tet Offensive will help lead to an Allied victory as well as a shortening of the war.

6   The Diffusion of Power
Walt W. Rostow

Monday, February 5, 1968—9:00 A.M.

Mr. President:

Responding to a question from Elspeth [my wife] last night, I explained events in Vietnam as follows.

The war had been proceeding in 1967 on an attritional basis with our side gradually improving its position, the Communists gradually running down: like this

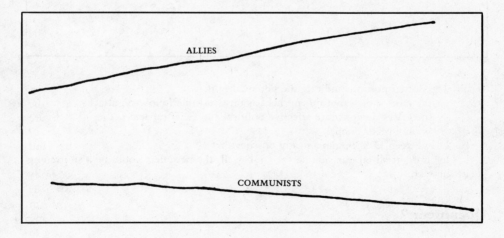

Behind these curves were pools of military forces and fire power which represented the working capital available to the two sides.

As the documents forecast, the Communists decided to take a large part of their capital and put it into:

an attack on the cities;

a frontier attack at Khe Sanh and elsewhere.

In the one case their objective was the believed vulnerability of GVN and the believed latent popular support for the Viet Cong.

In the other case, the believed vulnerability of the U.S. public opinion to discouragement about the war.

So the curves actually moved like this:

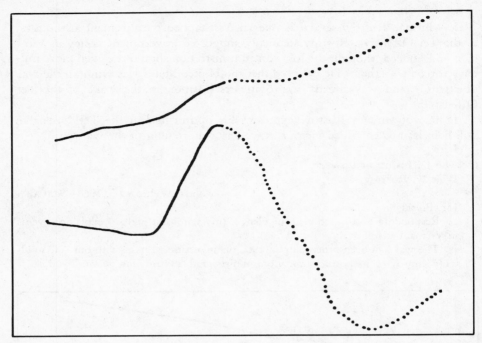

The dotted portions indicate the potentiality if:
    the cities are cleared up and held against possible follow-on attacks;
    the GVN demonstrate effective political and relief capacity;
    we hold Khe Sanh;
    we keep U.S. opinion steady on course.
    In short, if all on our side do their job well, the net effect could be a shortening
of the war.

Document 7

Lyndon Johnson sent General Earle G. Wheeler, Chairman of the Joint Chiefs
of Staff, to Vietnam in February 1968. The president wanted Wheeler's evaluation of the military situation in Vietnam and his recommendations for steps the
United States should take to insure the security of an independent, non-Communist South Vietnam.

    Document 7 contains portions of General Wheeler's report analyzing the sit-
uation in the wake of the Tet offensive, which he calls "a very near thing." The
report ends with a request for reinforcements totalling 206,000 men. That request was to be denied.

7   Report on the Situation in Vietnam and MACV Force Requirements
General Earle G. Wheeler
February 27, 1968

1. The Chairman, JCS and party visited SVN on 23, 24 and 25 February. This report summarizes the impressions and facts developed through conversations and briefings at MACV and with senior commanders throughout the country.

2. *Summary*

—The current situation in Vietnam is still developing and fraught with opportunities as well as dangers.

—There is no question in the mind of MACV that the enemy went all out for a general offensive and general uprising and apparently believed that he would succeed in bringing the war to an early successful conclusion.

—The enemy failed to achieve his initial objective but is continuing his effort. Although many of his units were badly hurt, the judgment is that he has the will and the capability to continue.

—Enemy losses have been heavy; he has failed to achieve his prime objectives of mass uprisings and capture of a large number of the capital cities and towns. Morale in enemy units which were badly mauled or where the men were oversold the idea of a decisive victory at TET probably has suffered severely. However, with replacements, his indoctrination system would seem capable of maintaining morale at a generally adequate level. His determination appears to be unshaken.

—The enemy is operating with relative freedom in the countryside, probably recruiting heavily and no doubt infiltrating NVA units and personnel. His recovery is likely to be rapid; his supplies are adequate; and he is trying to maintain the momentum of his winter-spring offensive.

—The structure of the GVN held up but its effectiveness has suffered.

—The RVNAF held up against the initial assault with gratifying, and in a way, suprising strength and fortitude.

However, ARVN is now in a defensive posture around towns and cities and there is concern about how well they will bear up under sustained pressure.

—The initial attack nearly succeeded in a dozen places, and defeat in those places was only averted by the timely reaction of US forces. In short, it was a very near thing.

—There is no doubt that the RD Program has suffered a severe set back.

—RVNAF was not badly hurt physically—they should recover strength and equipment rather quickly (equipment in 2–3 months—strength in 3–6 months). Their problems are more psychological than physical.

—US forces have lost none of their pre-TET capability.

—For these reasons, General Westmoreland has asked for a 3 division-15 tactical fighter squadron force. This force would provide him with a theater reserve and an offensive capability which he does not now have. . . .

Documents 8 and 9

Lyndon Johnson had won a landslide victory over Senator Barry Goldwater in the 1964 presidential election. Johnson had unified the old Democratic coalition from the days of the New Deal and managed to sweep in an overwhelmingly

Democratic Congress on his coattails. One of Johnson's slogans during the campaign had been "All The Way With L.B.J." By 1967, however, many former Johnson supporters had decided not to go any further.

The Vietnam War was the major cause of weakening support for the president. As Johnson tried to sell his policy to the American people, more and more listeners began to doubt the administration's claims. Jules Feiffer, one of the president's most effective and unrelenting critics, pictured this erosion of belief in the cartoon which appears as Document 8.

The Document 9 graph traces the popularity of President Johnson throughout his term in office and shows that public support for his presidency consistently declined, reaching a low of 25 percent approval shortly before his speech on March 31, 1968.

8   LBJ and the Credibility Gap
Jules Feiffer

9 President Johnson's Use of Television and His Rating in the Gallup Poll
Sandra N. Kautz

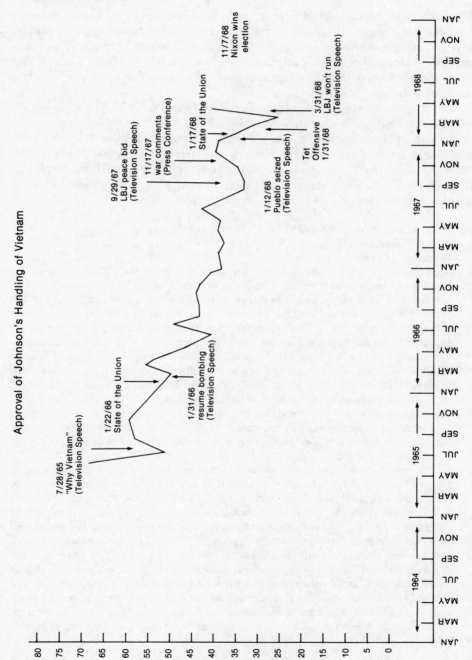

Document 10

If President Johnson suffered from a credibility gap, public opinion polls over two decades consistently reported that CBS News anchorman Walter Cronkite was among the most widely trusted Americans. Cronkite's reporting was perceived as calm and accurate, and the public believed what "Uncle Walter" told them. When Walter Cronkite reported from Vietnam after the Tet Offensive, Americans listened.

On Tuesday, February 27, 1968, Cronkite broadcast a half-hour report on Vietnam entitled "Who, What, When, Where, Why." His personal observations at the end of this fact-finding tour of Vietnam, printed here as Document 10, cast doubt on the widsom of continuing the present policy in Vietnam. Bill Moyers, a former Presidential Press Secretary, later reported that President Johnson took Cronkite's statement of concern over government policy in Vietnam as a signal that he had lost the support of his country.

10 Who, What, When, Where, Why: Report from Vietnam
Walter Cronkite
February 27, 1968

CRONKITE: Tonight, back in more familiar surroundings in New York, we'd like to sum up our findings in Vietnam, an analysis that must be speculative, personal, subjective. Who won and who lost in the great Tet offensive against the cities? I'm not sure. The Viet Cong did not win by a knockout, but neither did we. The referees of history may make it a draw. Another standoff may be coming in the big battles expected south of the Demilitarized Zone. Khesanh could well fall, with a terrible loss in American lives, prestige and morale, and this is a tragedy of our stubbornness there; but the bastion no longer is a key to the rest of the northern regions, and it is doubtful that the American forces can be defeated across the breadth of the DMZ with any substantial loss of ground. Another standoff. On the political front, past performance gives no confidence that the Vietnamese government can cope with its problems, now compounded by the attack on the cities. It may not fall, it may hold on, but it probably won't show the dynamic qualities demanded of this young nation. Another standoff.

We have been too often disappointed by the optimism of the American leaders, both in Vietnam and Washington, to have faith any longer in the silver linings they find in the darkest clouds. They may be right, that Hanoi's winter-spring offensive has been forced by the Communist realization that they could not win the longer war of attrition, and that the Communists hope that any success in the offensive will improve their position for eventual negotiations. It would improve their position, and it would also require our realization, that we should have had all along, that any negotiations must be that—negotiations, not the dictation of peace terms. For it seems now more certain than ever that the bloody experience of Vietnam is to end in a stalemate. This summer's almost certain standoff will either end in real give-and-take negotiations or terrible escalation; and for every means we have to escalate, the enemy can match us, and that applies to invasion of the North, the use of nuclear weapons, or the mere commitment of one hundred, or two hundred, or three hundred thousand more American troops to the battle. And with each escalation, the world comes closer to the brink of cosmic disaster.

To say that we are closer to victory today is to believe, in the face of the evidence, the optimists who have been wrong in the past. To suggest we are on the edge of defeat is to yield to unreasonable pessimism. To say that we are mired in stalemate seems the only realistic, yet unsatisfactory, conclusion. On the off chance that military and political analysts are right, in the next few months we must test the enemy's intentions, in case this is indeed his last big gasp before negotiations. But it is increasingly clear to this reporter that the only rational way out then will be to negotiate, not as victors, but as an honorable people who lived up to their pledge to defend democracy, and did the best they could.

This is Walter Cronkite. Good night.

Document 11

The speech which Lyndon Johnson made to a nationwide television and radio audience on March 31, 1968, went through numerous drafts, revisions, and alterations in the few days before he delivered it. In the weeks between the Tet Offensive and the end of March, Johnson had vacillated as he tried to decide what kind of policy to adopt.

The question of a bombing halt was one which took the president a long time to resolve. The arguments of Dean Rusk, that the poor weather which would soon occur in Vietnam would make bombing problematic at best, played a major role in convincing him to use the cut-back in bombing North Vietnam as a bargaining chip. That Hanoi would accept this offer had not been expected.

The president's decision not to seek re-election, on the other hand, was a well-kept secret and caught even many close advisors by surprise.

11 The President's Address to the Nation
Lyndon Baines Johnson
March 31, 1968

Good evening, my fellow Americans:

Tonight I want to speak to you of peace in Vietnam and Southeast Asia.

No other question so preoccupies our people. No other dream so absorbs the 250 million human beings who live in that part of the world. No other goal motivates American policy in Southeast Asia.

For years, representatives of our Government and others have traveled the world—seeking to find a basis for peace talks.

Since last September, they have carried the offer that I made public at San Antonio.

That offer was this:

That the United States would stop its bombardment of North Vietnam when that would lead promptly to productive discussions—and that we would assume that North Vietnam would not take military advantage of our restraint.

Hanoi denounced this offer, both privately and publicly. Even while the search for peace was going on, North Vietnam rushed their preparations for a savage assault on the people, the government, and the allies of South Vietnam.

Their attack—during the Tet holidays—failed to achieve its principal objectives.

It did not collapse the elected government of South Vietnam or shatter its army—as the Communists had hoped.

It did not produce a "general uprising" among the people of the cities as they had predicted.

The Communists were unable to maintain control of any of the more than 30 cities that they attacked. And they took very heavy casualties.

But they did compel the South Vietnamese and their allies to move certain forces from the countryside into the cities.

They caused widespread disruption and suffering. Their attacks, and the battles that followed, made refugees of half a million human beings.

The Communists may renew their attack any day.

They are, it appears, trying to make 1968 the year of decision in South Vietnam—the year that brings, if not final victory or defeat, at least a turning point in the struggle.

This much is clear:

If they do mount another round of heavy attacks, they will not succeed in destroying the fighting power of South Vietnam and its allies.

But tragically, this is also clear: Many men—on both sides of the struggle—will be lost. A nation that has already suffered 20 years of warfare will suffer once again. Armies on both sides will take new casualties. And the war will go on.

There is no need for this to be so.

There is no need to delay the talks that could bring an end to this long and this bloody war.

Tonight, I renew the offer I made last August—to stop the bombardment of North Vietnam. We ask that talks begin promptly, that they be serious talks on the substance of peace. We assume that during those talks Hanoi will not take advantage of our restraint.

We are prepared to move immediately toward peace through negotiations.

So, tonight, in the hope that this action will lead to early talks, I am taking the first step to deescalate the conflict. We are reducing—substantially reducing—the present level of hostilities.

And we are doing so unilaterally, and at once.

Tonight, I have ordered our aircraft and our naval vessels to make no attacks on North Vietnam, except in the area north of the demilitarized zone where the continuing enemy buildup directly threatens allied forward positions and where the movement of their troops and supplies are clearly related to that threat.

The area in which we are stopping our attacks includes almost 90 percent of North Vietnam's population, and most of its territory. Thus there will be no attacks around the principal populated areas, or in the food-producing areas of North Vietnam.

Even this very limited bombing of the North could come to an early end—if our restraint is matched by restraint in Hanoi. But I cannot in good conscience stop all bombing so long as to do so would immediately and directly endanger the lives of our men and our allies. Whether a complete bombing halt becomes possible in the future will be determined by events.

Our purpose in this action is to bring about a reduction in the level of violence that now exists.

It is to save the lives of brave men—and to save the lives of innocent women and children. It is to permit the contending forces to move closer to a political settlement. . . .

At Johns Hopkins University, about 3 years ago, I announced that the United States would take part in the great work of developing Southeast Asia, including the Mekong Valley, for all of the people of that region. Our determination to help build a better land—a better land for men on both sides of the present conflict—has not diminished in the least. Indeed, the ravages of war, I think, have made it more urgent than ever.

So, I repeat on behalf of the United States again tonight what I said at Johns Hopkins—that North Vietnam could take its place in this common effort just as soon as peace comes.

Over time, a wider framework of peace and security in Southeast Asia may become possible. The new cooperation of the nations of the area could be a foundation-stone. Certainly friendship with the nations of such a Southeast Asia is what the United States seeks—and that is all that the United States seeks.

One day, my fellow citizens, there will be peace in Southeast Asia.

It will come because the people of Southeast Asia want it—those whose armies are at war tonight, and those who, though threatened, have thus far been spared.

Peace will come because Asians were willing to work for it—and to sacrifice for it—and to die by the thousands for it.

But let it never be forgotten: Peace will come also because America sent her sons to help secure it.

It has not been easy—far from it. During the past 4½ years, it has been my fate and my responsibility to be Commander in Chief. I have lived—daily and nightly—with the cost of this war. I know the pain that it has inflicted. I know, perhaps better than anyone, the misgivings that it has aroused.

Throughout this entire, long period, I have been sustained by a single principle: that what we are doing now, in Vietnam, is vital not only to the security of Southeast Asia, but it is vital to the security of every American.

Surely we have treaties which we must respect. Surely we have commitments that we are going to keep. Resolutions of the Congress testify to the need to resist aggression in the world and in Southeast Asia.

But the heart of our involvement in South Vietnam—under three different Presidents, three separate administrations—has always been America's own security.

And the larger purpose of our involvement has always been to help the nations of Southeast Asia become independent and stand alone, self-sustaining, as members of a great world community—at peace with themselves, and at peace with all others.

With such an Asia, our country—and the world—will be far more secure than it is tonight.

I believe that a peaceful Asia is far nearer to reality because of what America has done in Vietnam. I believe that the men who endure the dangers of battle—fighting there for us tonight—are helping the entire world avoid far greater conflicts, far wider wars, far more destruction, than this one.

The peace that will bring them home someday will come. Tonight I have offered the first in what I hope will be a series of mutual moves toward peace.

I pray that it will not be rejected by the leaders of North Vietnam. I pray that they will accept it as a means by which the sacrifices of their own people may be ended. And I ask your help and your support, my fellow citizens, for this effort to reach across the battlefield toward an early peace.

Finally, my fellow Americans, let me say this:

Of those to whom much is given, much is asked. I cannot say and no man could say that no more will be asked of us.

Yet, I believe that now, no less than when the decade began, this generation of Americans is willing to "pay any price, bear any burden, meet any hardship, support any friend, oppose any foe to assure the survival and the success of liberty."

Since those words were spoken by John F. Kennedy, the people of America have kept that compact with mankind's noblest cause.

And we shall continue to keep it.

Yet, I believe that we must always be mindful of this one thing, whatever the trials and the tests ahead. The ultimate strength of our country and our cause will lie not in powerful weapons or infinite resources or boundless wealth, but will lie in the unity of our people.

This I believe very deeply.

Throughout my entire public career I have followed the personal philosophy that I am a free man, an American, a public servant, and a member of my party, in that order always and only.

For 37 years in the service of our Nation, first as a Congressman, as a Senator, and as Vice President, and now as your President, I have put the unity of the people first. I have put it ahead of any divisive partisanship.

And in these times as in times before, it is true that a house divided against itself by the spirit of faction, of party, of region, of religion, of race, is a house that cannot stand.

There is division in the American house now. There is divisiveness among us all tonight. And holding the trust that is mine, as President of all the people, I cannot disregard the peril to the progress of the American people and the hope and the prospect of peace for all peoples.

So, I would ask all Americans, whatever their personal interests or concern, to guard against divisiveness and all its ugly consequences.

Fifty-two months and 10 days ago, in a moment of tragedy and trauma, the duties of this office fell upon me. I asked then for your help and God's, that we might continue America on its course, binding up our wounds, healing our history, moving forward in new unity, to clear the American agenda and to keep the American commitment for all of our people.

United we have kept that commitment. United we have enlarged that commitment.

Through all time to come, I think America will be a stronger nation, a more just society, and a land of greater opportunity and fulfillment because of what we have all done together in these years of unparalleled achievement.

Our reward will come in the life of freedom, peace, and hope that our children will enjoy through ages ahead.

What we won when all of our people united must not now be lost in suspicion, distrust, selfishness, and politics among any of our people.

Believing this as I do, I have concluded that I should not permit the Presidency to become involved in the partisan divisions that are developing in this political year.

With America's sons in the fields far away, with America's future under challenge right here at home, with our hopes and the world's hopes for peace in the balance every day, I do not believe that I should devote an hour or a day of my time to any personal partisan causes or to any duties other than the awesome duties of this office—the Presidency of your country.

Accordingly, I shall not seek, and I will not accept, the nomination of my party for another term as your President.

But let men everywhere know, however, that a strong, a confident, and a vigilant America stands ready tonight to seek an honorable peace—and stands ready tonight to defend an honored cause—whatever the price, whatever the burden, whatever the sacrifice that duty may require.

Thank you for listening.

Good night and God bless all of you.

NOTE: The President spoke at 9 p.m. in his office at the White House. The address was broadcast nationally.

Critical Issues for Discussion

1. In November 1967, just before Tet, and in February 1968, just after it, the Gallup Poll asked Americans the same question: "Do you think the U.S. and its allies are losing ground in Vietnam, standing still, or making progress?" The results of those two surveys looked like this.

	Nov. 1967	Feb. 1968
Losing	8%	23%
Standing Still	33%	38%
Making Progress	50%	33%
No Opinion	9%	6%

What do these figures indicate? What effect did Tet have on American public opinion? What could President Johnson do to regain support?

2. The American military presence in Vietnam was immense. American soldiers and machines far outstripped the firepower of their foes. As outlined in Document 2, many tacticians saw the strategic bombing of the North as the shortcut to victory.

What conclusions had CIA analysts drawn? Why hadn't bombing worked? Would it ever work? What would happen if the bombing campaign was called off?

3. The Tet Offensive, as Documents 3 and 4 reveal, resulted from a decision in North Vietnam which was relayed to its cadres throughout the country. How was the coming offensive explained to the local cadres? What was the tone of the directive? What points did it make? Would such a directive have worked in the American army? The South Vietnamese army? Why or why not?

What are the differences between Documents 3 and 4? Why was this second one written? What is its message?

4. Different observers read the results and the meaning of the Tet Offensive in different ways. In Document 6, Walt Rostow, one of President Johnson's Special Assistants, saw the bright side of the fighting. Why was he optimistic? What did he think had to be done to insure American success in Vietnam? What did he mean by the "attritional basis" on which the war was proceeding? How did he think it would end?

5. General Westmoreland was quoted in *Tet* by Don Oberdorfer as saying that "this has been a limited war with limited objectives, fought with limited means and programmed for the utilization of limited resources. This was a feasible position on the assumption that the enemy was to fight a protracted war. We are now in a new ball game where we have to face a determined, highly disciplined enemy, fully mobilized to achieve a quick victory."

How had Westmoreland envisioned the war before Tet? What did he mean by a "limited war?" Why did he think that the war was no longer a limited one? What new strategy might he desire?

Look at Document 7. Did Westmoreland agree with Wheeler? What did Wheeler want? How did he summarize the meaning of the Tet Offensive? What lessons had Tet taught him?

President Johnson summed up his new strategy by saying that the United States would "do no more to win but refused to lose." What did that attitude imply? How could that be translated into military terms? How would Wheeler and Westmoreland have reacted to that strategy?

6. Clark Clifford's change of opinion on American strategy in Vietnam was a key influence on President Johnson's March 31, 1968 speech. Read Document 11 and describe how much the decisions announced in the President's speech owe to Clifford's work in the month preceding it.

7. Harry McPherson, President Johnson's Special Counsel, worked in the White House and had access to classified information on Vietnam. But during the Tet Offensive, he received his impressions about the fighting from television rather than from available government sources. Wondering about this later, McPherson concluded: "I assume the reason this is so, the reason I put aside my own interior access to confidential information and was more persuaded by what I saw on the tube and in the newspapers, was that like everyone else who had been deeply involved in explaining the policies of the war and trying to understand them and render some judgment, I was fed up with the 'light at the end of the tunnel' stuff. I was fed up with the optimism that seemed to flow without stopping from Saigon."

What had happened to McPherson? Was this an example of a credibility gap? How might a government avoid creating a credibility gap?

Follow Up Documents 5, 8, 9, and 10 deal directly with the relationship between the government, the media, and the public's perceptions of its administration. Did the televised reports on Vietnam differ from the government's statements? How? What did they imply? In the context of the events of 1967 and 1968, what impact did these reports have on the average citizen?

How do you evaluate the accuracy of the reporting of the Tet Offensive? Should newspapers, radio, and television be allowed to report the news about a war from an independent perspective? Should the government control the news in wartime in the interests of the nation? Should any line be drawn? Where? When? How? By whom? Why?

Suggestions for Further Reading

The Tet Offensive in Saigon and Washington

Braestrup, Peter. *Big Story: How the American Press and Television Reported and Interpreted the Crisis of Tet 1968 in Vietnam and Washington.* 2nd ed. New Haven: Yale University Press, 1983.

A condensation of the first edition. Braestrup's study analyzes in great detail the reporting of Tet by American TV and newspapers and the role it played in determining policy.

Oberdorfer, Don. *Tet.* New York: Avon, 1971.

This highly readable narrative by a journalist on the scene at the time looks at Tet as a "classic case study in the interaction of war, politics, the press and public opinion." Weighing Tet's impact in Vietnam and the United States, Oberdorfer judges that there were no winners.

Rostow, W. W. *The Diffusion of Power.* New York: Macmillan, 1972.

Rostow was a personal advisor to President Kennedy and Special Assistant for National Security Affairs under Johnson. In Chapters 37–40 he builds his case that, although the military effort was indecisive, the political effort to strengthen South Vietnamese nationalism could have succeeded if Americans hadn't lost their will to continue.

Schandler, Herbert Y. *The Unmaking of a President: Lyndon Johnson and Vietnam.* Princeton: Princeton University Press, 1977.

Based on extensive interviews with top administration officials, this scholarly book by a former Defense Department officer is the definitive study of the Washington debates after Tet.

Westmoreland, William C. *A Soldier Reports.* Garden City, N. Y.: Doubleday, 1976.

General Westmoreland was Vietnam field commander from 1964 to 1968 and Army Chief of Staff until 1972. In Chapters 17, 18 and 23 of his autobiography Westmoreland assesses the Tet/Khesanh battles as decisive U.S. victories which Washington officials failed to exploit because of public opinion against the war.

Zinn, Howard. *Vietnam: The Logic of Withdrawal.* Boston: Beacon Press, 1967.

This brief critique of U.S. policy culminates in a speech which President Johnson could have given in 1967, stating his reasons for withdrawing completely from Vietnam.

My Lai and the Question of War Crimes

Browning, Frank, and Dorothy Forman, eds. *The Wasted Nations.* Report of the International Commission of Enquiry into United States Crimes in Indochina. New York: Harper & Row, 1972.

Testimony against the United States is presented by U.S. soldiers, Indochinese victims of the war, medical doctors, scientists, and journalists, with a concluding section discussing its legal implications.

Hammer, Richard. *One Morning in the War: The Tragedy at Son My*. New York: Coward-McCann, 1970.

Hammer gives a brief, clear account and concludes that "Son My is inevitable, given the American policy of total war . . . when all people are considered the enemy."

Hersh, Seymour M. *My Lai 4: A Report on the Massacre and Its Aftermath*. New York: Random House, 1970.

Hersh, Seymour M. *Cover-up*. New York: Vintage, 1972.

My Lai 4 tells the basic story of the massacre from the point of view of the soldiers involved. *Cover-up* adds further information and details the attempts at every level to keep the story quiet.

Lifton, Robert Jay. *Home From the War: Vietnam Veterans: Neither Victims nor Executioners*. New York: Simon and Schuster, 1973.

A psychiatrist who spent two years in "rap groups" with veterans, Lifton portrays the guilt experienced by veterans who participated in criminal acts. His chapter on My Lai examines the step-by-step sequence by which the soldiers at My Lai became immersed in an "atrocity-producing situation."

Taylor, Telford. *Nuremberg and Vietnam: An American Tragedy*. Chicago: Quadrangle, 1970.

America's chief counsel for the prosecution at the Nazi war crimes trials at Nuremberg here considers the parallels between that war and Vietnam. Taylor carefully evaluates the conduct of all parties to the war in light of international law.

Trooboff, Peter B., ed. *Law and Responsibility in Warfare: The Vietnam Experience*. Chapel Hill: Univ. of North Carolina Press, 1975.

Articles by Falk, Baxter, Taylor and others offer differing viewpoints about the United States' legal responsibility.

The Battle of Khesanh

Nalty, Bernard. *Air Power at Khe Sanh*. Washington: Government Printing Office, 1970.

Nalty argues that air power played a more important part in the Khesanh victory than acknowledged in the Marine Corps history.

Pisor, Robert. *The End of the Line: The Siege of Khe Sanh*. New York: Norton, 1982.

This readable account by a war correspondent credits General Giap with diverting U.S. attention and resources to Khesanh while his own troops moved south for the Tet offensive.

U.S. Marine Corps. *The Battle for Khe Sanh*. Washington: History and Museums Division, Headquarters, U.S. Marine Corps, 1969.

The only controversy in this official history is over what part of the U.S. forces was responsible for the victory.

On the Street
Prostitution became a big business in wartime Saigon. *U.P.I.*

Chapter 8
Vietnamizing the War:
1968–1973

Background

Historical Summary

The massive American presence in South Vietnam had more than a military impact on the country. It also had a decisive—and often brutal—effect on South Vietnam's social fabric.

By the late 1960s, the United States had poured more than $100 billion into South Vietnam. The vast sum spawned new opportunities, new wealth, and a new commercial class. The money, combined with the introduction of 500,000 American soldiers into the country, corrupted the society. Prostitution, drugs, and a huge black market in consumer goods flourished, disrupting the traditional Vietnamese way of life.

The Communists took advantage of this dislocation. They promoted themselves as Vietnam's true nationalists, contending that the South Vietnamese government and army were "puppets" of the Americans.

The U.S. forces serving in Vietnam meanwhile found themselves in a complicated and sometimes incomprehensible situation. They were supposed to be fighting to save the South Vietnamese people from the North Vietnamese and Vietcong. But they could not distinguish between friend and foe. Many Americans began to regard all Vietnamese with suspicion.

The American bombing campaign, directed against both North and South Vietnam, was often conducted indiscriminately. More bombs were dropped in Vietnam than during all of World War II, creating some three million refugees, most of whom crowded into the already swollen cities.

The U.S. effort focused as well on pacification, known as the "other war." Its projects included land reform, education, agricultural help, and similar programs aimed at winning the support of the peasants. A parallel effort, the Phoenix Program, was initiated in 1968 to uproot the Vietcong political structure in the countryside.

The Phoenix Program, conducted by South Vietnamese officials and CIA advisers, aroused considerable controversy. It relied on a network of informants and secret agents, and its critics claimed that it promoted assassinations and torture of innocent suspects. William Colby, the former C.I.A. director who then managed the operation, has defended the effort, asserting that most of the

20,000 Vietcong who died during this period were killed in battles and skirmishes.

Heavily backed by the United States, the Saigon regime headed by President Nguyen Van Thieu was stable by early 1969. It was recognized by most Western nations, and its army numbered more than a million men. Some 400 South Vietnamese soldiers lost their lives every week, and another 2000 deserted. Very few defected to the enemy, however.

By 1969, U.S. casualties were mounting. During that year, 9000 Americans died, and President Nixon unveiled his policy of "Vietnamization." Its objective was to withdraw U.S. forces from Vietnam and turn the conduct of the war over to the South Vietnamese—giving them the money and equipment to wage the conflict.

The policy appeared to work. American casualties dropped as the U.S. troops were withdrawn. By 1971, there were fewer than 200,000 American soldiers in Vietnam, and combat deaths had declined to 10 per week. But morale in the U.S. forces was also deteriorating.

As they saw the United States pulling out, more and more Americans sent to Vietnam saw little purpose to the war. Many were preoccupied with survival rather than with victory. Drugs, venereal disease, and antiwar sentiment spread. Racial tensions within the U.S. Army intensified.

A symptom of the demoralization was "fragging." In 1970, more than 200 incidents were reported of American soldiers attempting to kill their officers with fragmentation grenades.

A test of "Vietnamization" came in March 1972, when regular North Vietnamese units equipped with tanks and artillery staged a frontal offensive across the 17th parallel into South Vietnam. The South Vietnamese army was routed in the northernmost provinces of the country, and the North Vietnamese occupied cities in the area.

President Nixon, then planning a summit meeting in Moscow, reacted by mining Haiphong Harbor and bombing the region around Hanoi. American aircraft also flew tactical missions, striking at the North Vietnamese units invading the South. The North Vietnamese offensive was blunted—thus suggesting that an American presence could be vital to South Vietnam's security.

The setback did not stop the North Vietnamese, however. They were then negotiating secretly with the United States for a cease-fire, and they intended to improve their position in the South before an agreement was reached. North Vietnamese troops continued to infiltrate the South.

The peace negotiations were finally concluded in early 1973, and an agreement was signed in Paris. The last American combat troops left Vietnam—just as Chinese, Japanese, and French forces had before them.

Points to Emphasize

- the image of the South Vietnamese in American eyes
- the image of the Americans in South Vietnamese eyes

Chronology

	1969 Jan	Feb	Mar	Apr	May	Jun	Jul	Aug	Sep
Vietnam			U.S. begins bombing of North Vietnamese bases in Cambodia			Provisional Revolutionary Government (P.R.G.) is formed by N.L.F. / Nixon and Thieu meet on Midway Island			Ho Chi Minh dies
United States	Lodge replaces Harriman at Paris Peace Talks			Unrest at Harvard and other campuses		First U.S. troop withdrawal is announced		Woodstock Music Festival	Second U.S. troop withdrawal announced
World Wide				De Gaulle resigns from office in France					

Chronology (cont.)

	1969 Oct	Nov	Dec	1970 Jan	Feb	Mar	Apr	May	Jun
Vietnam						ARVN troops first attack Vietnamese bases in Cambodia	U.S. forces join ARVN in Cambodian incursion	U.S. bombs North Vietnam for first time since 1968	U.S. troops leave Cambodia
United States	Vietnam moratorium. Nation-wide peace demonstrations	Another moratorium attracts record numbers. U.S. Army begins to investigate My Lai massacre	Harris Poll shows 46% in favor of the aims of the November moratorium					4 demonstrators killed at Kent State. 200 colleges close in protest. Demonstrations in Washington	Cooper-Church Amendment limits U.S. role in Cambodia. Senate repeals Gulf of Tonkin Resolution.
World Wide						Sihanouk deposed in Cambodia. Lon Nol takes over.			

	1970 Jul	Aug	Sep	Oct	Nov	Dec	1971 Jan	Feb	Mar
Vietnam								ARVN troops invade Laos with U.S. air support	ARVN forced out of Laos
United States	White House sets up "plumbers" to end information leakage								
World Wide			Allende elected President of Chile		De Gaulle dies		Idi Amin takes over in Uganda		

	1971 Apr	May	Jun	Jul	Aug	Sep	Oct	Nov	Dec
Vietnam					Big Minh withdraws from election		Thieu reelected with 80% of the vote		U.S. bombs North Vietnam as protective reaction strikes
United States	500,000 protest in Washington / U.S. table tennis team visits China	Disorderly May Day demonstrations in Washington	*New York Times* begins publication of the Pentagon Papers						
World Wide									

	1972 Jan	Feb	Mar	Apr	May	Jun	Jul	Aug	Sep
Vietnam			First major North Vietnamese ground offensive since 1968	Easter Offensive continues / U.S. bombs North Vietnam	ARVN retreats from Quang Tri / U.S. mines North Vietnamese ports. Bombing continues			Last U.S. ground troops leave	
United States	Nixon announces secret talks in Paris			Antiwar demonstrations protest bombings		Break-in at the Democratic National Committee headquarters at the Watergate Hotel			
World Wide		Nixon visits China			Nixon visits Russia				

Chronology (cont.)

	1972 Oct	Nov	Dec
Vietnam	Preliminary peace agreement	Thieu rejects the treaty	U.S. bombs Hanoi and Haiphong Bombing halt over the North announced on December 30.
United States	Kissinger says peace is at hand	Nixon reelected	
World Wide			

- the concept of Vietnamization and how it changed the strategy of the war
- the effect of Vietnamization on American soldiers
- the principle of pacification and how the United States planned to help President Thieu's government "win the hearts and minds" of the South Vietnamese population
- the controversy surrounding the Phoenix Program
- the significance of the North Vietnamese Easter Offensive of 1972
- the variety of problems which the war caused for Vietnamese civilians and for American and South Vietnamese soldiers

Glossary of Names and Terms

Creighton Abrams Deputy Commander, U.S. Military Assistance Command, Vietnam (MACV), 1967–1968. Commander, MACV, 1968–1972. U.S. Army Chief of Staff, 1972–1974.

Bui Diem South Vietnam's last ambassador to the United States.

Ellsworth Bunker American businessman and diplomat. Served in the Dominican Republic. Ambassador to South Vietnam, 1967–1973.

William Colby First Secretary, American Embassy, Saigon, 1959–1962. Chief of Far East Division, Central Intelligence Agency (CIA), 1962–1967. Director, CORDS, 1968–1971. Later, director of the CIA, 1973–1976.

Henry Kissinger professor of government at Harvard, appointed National Security Advisor by President Nixon. Served as Secretary of State under Nixon and Ford. Winner of the Nobel Peace Prize in 1973.

Nguyen Van Thieu Division Commander, ARVN. With Nguyen Cao Ky, a leading force in many South Vietnamese governments from 1963 to 1967. Elected president of South Vietnam in 1967. Reelected in 1971.

Army of the Republic of Vietnam (ARVN) the South Vietnamese army. Individual South Vietnamese soldiers were referred to by Americans as "Arvins."

Demilitarized Zone (DMZ) The area surrounding the 17th parallel, which was the temporary dividing line between the northern and southern zones of Vietnam set up in the Geneva Conference of 1954.

Easter Offensive The attack of North Vietnamese ground forces at the end of March 1972. First indication of renewed North Vietnamese commitment to conventional warfare since the offensives of 1968.

pacification a multifaceted and far-reaching policy which included land reform, the building of schools, and the resettling of refugees to gain support for the Thieu government among the South Vietnamese. The Phoenix Program was part of this policy.

Phoenix Program a program which sought to identify opponents of the South Vietnamese government and then to "turn" or "neutralize" them. Designed and directed by Americans to ensure the loyalty of the countryside to the South Vietnamese government.

Provisional Revolutionary Government (PRG) a shadow government for South Vietnam established in 1969 by the National Liberation Front and a few smaller groups.

Quang Tri province northernmost province of South Vietnam. The scene of heavy fighting during the Easter Offensive of 1972.

Third Force South Vietnamese groups who were opposed to the government of Thieu and Ky and were independent of the National Liberation Front. Pushed for peace negotiations rather than a continuation of the war.

Vietnamization the American policy of turning the war over to South Vietnamese soldiers while continuing to give American financial, military, and strategic support. Defined by the Department of State as "a military-economic program of South Vietnamese development which will permit rapid but phased withdrawals of the U.S. forces without radically upsetting the power balance in Southeast Asia."

Documents

Document 1

While General William C. Westmoreland completed his last year as commander of MACV in 1968, he put together notes for the military personnel who would follow him in South Vietnam. In the excerpts from his report reprinted here as Document 1, Westmoreland discusses unconventional enemy tactics, guidelines for troop behavior in the strained political atmosphere, and guidelines for commanders managing troops under the peculiar stresses of the war in Vietnam.

1 **Combat Fundamentals for Advisors and Guidance for Commanders in Vietnam**
   William C. Westmoreland
   1968
   Combat Fundamentals for Advisors
       The goal of the United States Government in Vietnam is to assist the Government of the Republic of Vietnam in its fight for freedom. Together we will win the struggle against the Viet Cong.
       In the prosecution of the war, American advisors are called upon to appraise the situation and to give sound advice. This advice must be based on an objective analysis grounded on fundamental military knowledge. Attached are combat precepts as they apply to the war in Vietnam, which are commended for your study and use. The effectiveness of your advisory efforts will be in direct proportion to the application of combat fundamentals, knowledge, past experience, and common sense.

A favorite tactic of the VC is the ambush. By use of the ambush, the VC seek to offset their overall inferiority in manpower and weaponry through surprise and concentration of force at one location. Recognizing this typical guerrilla maneuver, anti-ambush thinking and planning should become second nature to every U.S. Advisor in Vietnam.

The combat Fundamentals for Advisors which follow in this publication are applicable in general to all military operations—but they should be constantly applied to uncover, thwart, or destroy VC ambushes. For example, a standard VC tactic is to attack a hamlet or small post as "bait," then ambush on the route which government reinforcements must take to relieve or reinforce the hamlet or small post. Since every relief column is a potential target it must take the proper security measures en route and not rush headlong down the road. Where possible, the relief column should move by two or more routes and avoid the most obvious and direct route.

One of the main problems in anti-guerrilla war is to bring the enemy to combat. When he ambushes, he volunteers to fight. Thus, the destruction of the ambush must become a main objective of RVNAF forces—as important—in some cases more important to the overall effect than the relief column itself.

Anticipate ambushes—note potential ambush sites as a result of past experience and map reconnaissance—make detailed fire support plans—use reconnaissance by fire (artillery and small arms) against likely ambush areas—use air cover—adopt ultra-secure formations—take unorthodox approaches and routes—use multiple routes—be close-mouthed and deny VC advance information—be secure in planning troop movements—screen actual movements with ground patrols operating to front and flanks of the main body to discover ambush sites before the main body arrives. Be suspicious—be practical—be professional. Apply the fundamentals and avoid the—AMBUSH.

. . .

Nine Rules

For personnel of U.S. Military Assistance Command, Vietnam

The Vietnamese have paid a heavy price in suffering for their long fight against the Communists. We military men are in Vietnam now because their government has asked us to help its soldiers and people in winning their struggle. The Viet Cong will attempt to turn the Vietnamese people against you. You can defeat them at every turn by the strength, understanding, and generosity you display with the people. Here are nine simple rules:

1. Remember we are guests here: We make no demands and seek no special treatment.
2. Join with the people! Understand their life, use phrases from their language, and honor their customs and laws.
3. Treat women with politeness and respect.
4. Make personal friends among the soldiers and common people.
5. Always give the Vietnamese the right of way.
6. Be alert to security and ready to react with your military skill.
7. Don't attract attention by loud, rude or unusual behavior.
8. Avoid separating yourself from the people by a display of wealth or privilege.
9. Above all else, you are members of the U.S. Military Forces on a difficult mission, responsible for all your official and personal actions. Reflect honor upon yourself and the United States of America.

. . .

Guidance for Commanders in Vietnam

1. Make the welfare of your men your primary concern with special attention to mess, mail, and medical care.

2. Give priority emphasis to matters of intelligence, counterintelligence, and timely and accurate reporting.

3. Gear your command for sustained operations: keep constant pressure on the enemy.

4. React rapidly with all force available to opportunities to destroy the enemy; disrupt enemy bases, capturing or destroying his supply caches.

5. Open up methodically and use roads, waterways, and the railroad; be alert and prepared to ambush the ambusher.

6. Harass enemy lines of communication by raids and ambushes.

7. Use your firepower with care and discrimination, particularly in populated areas.

8. Capitalize on psywar opportunities.

9. Assist in "revolutionary development" with emphasis on priority areas and on civic action wherever feasible.

10. Encourage and help Vietnamese military and paramilitary units; involve them in your operations at every opportunity.

11. Be smarter and more skillful than the enemy; stimulate professionalism, alertness, and tactical ingenuity; seize every opportunity to enhance training of men and units.

12. Keep your officers and men well informed, aware of the nine rules for personnel of MACV, and mindful of the techniques of Communist insurgency and the role of Free World forces in Vietnam.

13. Maintain an alert "open door" policy on complaints and a sensitivity to detection and correction of malpractices.

14. Recognize bravery and outstanding work.

15. Inspect frequently units two echelons below your level to insure compliance with the foregoing.

Documents 2, 3, 4, and 5

Vietnamization was the gradual replacement of American soldiers by Vietnamese military forces, with continued American technological and strategic support. Announced in late 1969, Vietnamization formed the basis of President Nixon's attempt to gain "peace with honor," and was his main strategy until the signing of the peace agreement in January 1973.

The Senate Foreign Relations Committee had studied the prospects for Vietnamization in December 1969. In Document 2, excerpted from the committee staff report, many opinions about the potential strengths and weaknesses of this strategy were offered. The committee's uncertainty about what to believe was clearly revealed in the conclusions of the report.

Kevin Buckley's short article on the front-line "grunts" in Vietnam (Document 3) appeared in *Newsweek* on January 11, 1971. Buckley had spent Christmas with American soldiers in the field and reported their feelings about being in South Vietnam.

Document 4 describes the theory and practice of Vietnamization as the

Nixon administration saw it. The article is part of a Department of State publication, and it praised the accomplishments of the policy.

Document 5 appeared in the winter of 1972 in the *Saturday Review*. Eugene Linden reported the perceptions of American soldiers in the war at that time—how they saw Vietnamization, what their attitudes were toward drug use, and how they reacted to their officers.

2   Vietnam: December 1969
U.S. Senate Staff Report
I. Itinerary

We arrived in Vietnam on December 7 and left on December 18. We spent six days in Saigon, in the course of which we talked to Ambassador Bunker, General Abrams, Ambassador William Colby, who is General Abrams' deputy for Civil Operations and Revolutionary Development Support (CORDS), AID Director Donald MacDonald, other senior mission officers and the more junior officers in CORDS and in the political and economic sections of the Embassy.

We had a number of conversations in Saigon with American and foreign correspondents and also met with various foreign diplomats. In addition, we talked to many Vietnamese in the Government—including a number of cabinet officers—and in the National Assembly, as well as former government officials and private citizens. Among others, we talked to members of the Government bloc in the Assembly, politicians who support the Thieu administration, opposition leaders, army officers, former officials of various previous governments, lawyers, journalists and academicians. Some appointments were made by the Embassy but most were arranged by us through private channels. Many of our conversations were in French. . . .

II. Introduction

We concentrated our attention on three principal subjects: The progress of pacification; the prospects for Vietnamization; and the Saigon political scene, as it is intimately related to both pacification and Vietnamization. We attempt, in this report, to refrain from making judgments. To employ the analogy of the half-filled water glass, our objective is not to characterize the glass as half empty or as half full but rather to describe the water level.

Before turning to our observations, we believe that it is necessary to point to several considerations, perhaps not obvious to those who have not visited Vietnam:

A. From the first to the last hour of our stay, we were struck by the fact that no conclusion seems to stand up from one conversation or experience to the next. To illustrate: One evening a reporter, generally regarded as one of the most knowledgeable journalists in Vietnam, was talking about the disposition of North Vietnamese troops in the western highlands of I Corps. He said that they were forced to camp along river beds as they needed large quantities of running water to clean and cook their rice. The following day we talked with an American Army officer who is reputed to know as much about Vietnam as any American. When we advanced the reporter's theory, he assured us that anyone who knew anything about the country realized that at intervals the North Vietnamese cooked enough rice to last several days and then carried the rice with them as they traveled, and that they preferred to avoid the river beds in order to obtain the protection of the cover found at higher elevations.

B. It follows that a visitor to Vietnam can easily find evidence to support any case he wishes to make. Almost any number of Americans and Vietnamese can be found to substantiate, or refute, any thesis. In fact, disagreement exists even within official institutions, despite the constraints of institutional discipline. Within the American mission, below the very senior level, there are distinct differences of opinion and disagreements on the facts and their interpretation. The same is true in the military.

C. Briefings add to the difficulties of comprehension, in a situation where contradiction is the rule rather than the exception. Visitors receive briefings literally every step of the way in Vietnam—in Saigon, at Corps headquarters, in every province capital, by officials in district towns and even at the village and hamlet level. Every American and every South Vietnamese military unit seems to have a briefing board with acetate overlays, a stainless steel pointer and a set script—no matter how small the unit or how remote its location. At most briefings facts and figures are presented in such profusion and with such rapidity that it is impossible to correlate or analyze the information. In a few cases, we were able to secure the scripts of briefings and these proved to be of some value, although our impression, on carefully rereading these scripts, was that what had been omitted was often as significant as what had been included. In sum, whether inadvertently or deliberately, briefings do not objectively present the pros and cons but rather emphasize progress and accomplishment. Being briefed in Vietnam is somewhat like being told to buy product X without being told what is wrong with it or why to buy product Y.

D. Finally, there is another serious problem of communication and that is the almost hopeless task of trying to find out what the Vietnamese really think as distinct from what they say to Americans or in the presence of Americans. In fact, it is usually difficult even to know what they say. It would have been impossible for us to have meaningful conversations in English with many Vietnamese politicians in Saigon. Yet many American journalists, military officers and civilian officials do not speak French much less Vietnamese.

Vietnamese is, of course, essential in rural Vietnam. There are thousands of American military officers and civilians who have had between 28 days and a year of Vietnamese language training. But only a handful, at most, seem to have true fluency in the language and an appreciation of the manner that necessarily goes with using it effectively. For example, we visited one village in company with an American colonel who had spent a year in language training and a major who is one of the few U.S. military officers in Vietnam who is truly bilingual. The colonel asked us what we would like him to ask the villagers. We suggested that he simply talk to them about conditions there. He chatted with a group for ten minutes. We then asked him what questions he had posed. He said that he had asked them how many Vietcong had been killed or captured recently, how many terrorist incidents there had been, and so forth. After telling us what numerical replies had been received, he summed up by saying that the general attitude of the villagers was that everything was fine and that they were "relaxed" about the situation, a statement that was difficult to accept in light of the fact that his remarks were punctuated by intermittent mortar fire.

The bilingual major then talked with the villagers, laughing with them, and using his hands and facial expressions to make them smile. We asked him what questions he had asked. He said that he had asked only one and that was: "Is this village happy or sad?" The answers by the thirty or so villagers to this one question conveyed to us a rather different impression of the attitude of the villagers. The major summed up their replies by saying that they seemed to be on edge, to have little hope for the future and to have no faith in either the Communists or the Government. One villager said, in effect, that while they were being protected by the Americans, it was the presence of Americans that made protection necessary. . . .

VII. Conclusions

The assumptions regarding the present situation in Vietnam and the expected future course of developments in that country, on which U.S. policy is apparently based, seem to rest on far more ambiguous, confusing, and contradictory evidence than pronouncements from Washington and Saigon indicate. The success of present American policy appears to depend on three factors:

1. The progressive Vietnamization of the military effort,
2. The stability and cohesiveness of the Thieu government,
3. The expectation that the enemy can and will do nothing to inhibit the Vietnamization or disrupt the Thieu government's stability.

There is, of course, an intimate relationship among these three factors. Indeed, it may be said that all must succeed—or, perhaps more accurately, that none may fail—if present U.S. objectives in Vietnam are to be realized.

Vietnamization is perhaps the most important factor because the possibility of a continuing, progressive American withdrawal obviously depends upon its success. So does pacification, for the key to its success is security. Thus if Vietnamization fails, the United States cannot withdraw and still claim to have achieved its stated objectives.

The stability and cohesiveness of the Thieu government is of fundamental importance because there must be an agency through which the process of Vietnamization can be effected. Furthermore, given the importance which has been attached to the constitutional legitimacy of the Thieu government, its overthrow would probably plunge South Vietnam into a state of political anarchy and at the same time severely strain public patience in the United States.

As for the enemy's intentions and capabilities, the policy of Vietnamization is based on the assumption that the enemy is either willing to permit, or unable to prevent, the phased withdrawal of American combat forces and the progressive assumption of the combat burden by the Vietnamese. Were the North Vietnamese to launch a massive attack at any point in the course of this withdrawal, the United States would be faced with the agonizing prospect of either halting—or even reversing—the process of withdrawal, on the one hand, or being forced, on the other hand, to effect an accelerated, complete withdrawal which would be interpreted at home, and probably abroad, as a military and political defeat.

We believe that the evidence presented in this report leads to the inference that the prospects for a successful outcome of any one of the aforementioned three factors, much less all three, must be regarded as, at best, uncertain. Dilemmas thus seem to lie ahead in Vietnam, as they have throughout our involvement in this war that appears to be not only far from won but far from over.

3   You Can Have Your Own Little Castle
Kevin Buckley
January 11, 1971

It was cool, almost cold, on Christmas night and the grunts at Firebase Dragonhead sat in clusters around their bunkers. The scenes that they presented were diverse enough to support any opinion about the standards and behavior of the American

GI in South Vietnam. At one bunker, soldiers with hillbilly twangs were singing "The Green, Green Grass of Home," and to them the song title undoubtedly retained its conventional meaning. But at another bunker, the title would have produced waves of knowing giggles. The GI's there were listening to hard rock on a tape cassette. And as Iron Butterfly sang "In the Time of Our Lives," the grunts passed around a glowing pipe of "dew," the GI slang for marijuana.

Someone changed the tape to Jimi Hendrix's version of "Machine Gun" and one grunt, with a slight grin on his stubbly face, muttered, "Wow . . . wow . . . wow. That really spun my mind." A second soldier reached into the bunker and produced a sleeve which had been cut off a fatigue shirt. "You put this wide part over your nose and mouth," he began to explain. "Then someone blows the dew in from the cuff end and it can't escape. You're in a world of dew." Suddenly a siren sounded; this was the signal for a "mad minute"—one minute of small arms firing around the entire perimeter of the base in case enemy troops had infiltrated the area during the Chirstmas cease-fire. The soldier who had muttered "wow . . . wow . . . wow" slapped his M-16 rifle on full automatic and fired into the echoing underbrush. When silence returned, the aroma of cordite mingled with the fragrance of the powerful Vietnamese dew.

Outside the barbed wire surrounding the base, Claymore mines faced the area from which enemy soldiers might launch an attack. But on Christmas night at Dragonhead that was about as likely as the arrival of the Three Wise Men. Enemy activity in this area has been so slight that the grunts have trouble recalling when they took their last casualty. In fact, for many of the GI's the real threat that night came from within the base—from the "lifers," the career men, and especially the career NCO's, whose attitudes so often are diametrically opposed to those of the young draftees. As the Iron Butterfly tape moved on to "Filled With Fear" and "Lonely Boy" and the dew pipe was being passed, someone stood on lookout, whispering from time to time: "Watch it, a lifer."

Agreement: But the lifers never appeared, and the talk turned to the war. Everyone—pot smoker and non-pot smoker alike—agreed when one stoned soldier remarked: "You know what this war is like? It sucks. That's just about all you can say. It sucks. There's nothing good about us being here. There it is. All we want to do is get out of here alive. Morale is bad, man."

That, in fact, seemed to be the unifying theme at Dragonhead. The day after Christmas, I visited a company from the base which was on patrol, and while conditions were different—no one was stoned—the message was the same. "They ought to send over some of those people who are for the war," growled Sp/4 Steven Almond, 22. "Send some of those brave politicians and hard hats and let them see if they like it so much. I'll change places with any one of them." Others picked up the chant. "A lot of our buddies got killed here but they died for nothing," muttered one GI. "Our morale, man, it's so low you can't see it," said another.

Good Soldiers: Yet, around a jungle clearing where the soldiers rested there were indications of higher morale than the GI's might let on. For fifteen days, the men had been struggling through tangled, prickly vines that tear ferociously at clothes and skin alike—"wait a minute" vines, the grunts call them. Two soldiers had playfully written "Merry Xmas" on a tree trunk with shaving cream. And an officer, hardly older than the grunts in his company, insisted: "Sure they bitch and a lot of them smoke grass and they don't like it here. But these men are good soldiers."

After talking with these soldiers and with many others, I decided that flat statements about low grunt morale are not accurate. As much as they complain, they also boast about their work. And like soldiers in all wars, they recall exploits, tell war stories, chide and congratulate each other. They are proud of themselves and proud of each other. "We do everything together," said one. "It's like being brothers for a year." And they are proud to be grunts. "Those REMF's don't even know what Vietnam is all about," sneered one grunt, using the derisive acronym [Rear Echelon Mother F------] for men at support bases. An officer described one manifestation of the grunts' pride: "In the field they're always complaining they can't get new fatigues or have a shower. But if they ever have to go to the rear, all that changes. Then all they want is to look as funky as they can and terrorize the people in clean, pressed fatigues who work in air-conditioned offices."

Rhapsody: And the field itself—the "boonies"—has compensations now that the war is winding down and combat perils are less frequent. One grunt at Dragonhead, very stoned, went off into a rhapsodical speech. "Being a grunt ain't all bad," he mused. "Sometimes I really kind of like the bush. At the end of the day you drop your pack. You hack away a little piece of jungle and make a little space for yourself. You hang your hammock, you heat up some C-rations and maybe mix some together so they taste a little different. You put on your cassette for a little sound, really low. Maybe you smoke a little dew, just to relax. Man, that's not bad. Out in the bush you can have your own little castle."

4   A Program for Peace in Vietnam
Department of State
1971
Introduction

It is clear that a majority of Americans now favor the withdrawal of U.S. combat forces from Viet-Nam and an end to the Viet-Nam war.

Since June 1969, when President Nixon made his first announcement of U.S. troop withdrawals, the key issues have been the manner of the withdrawal and the way the war is ended.

A sudden departure of U.S. forces, however, could lead to: a North Vietnamese takeover of the South and imposition of a dictatorship; possibly the liquidation of thousands of those associated with the long anti-Communist struggle; and a dangerous weakening of the non-Communist effort in Asia to remain neutral and independent. In that belief, this administration has followed a two-fold program for limiting and ending U.S. participation in the Viet-Nam conflict.

The program is designed to:

1) seek a negotiated solution in Paris consistent with the legitimate interests of all parties; or,

2) in the event that a negotiated settlement is not achieved, provide a viable alternative course of action by preparing South Viet-Nam to carry the full burden of its defense after U.S. forces are withdrawn. This is the program known as "Vietnamization"—a military-economic program of South Vietnamese development which will permit rapid but phased withdrawals of U.S. forces without radically upsetting the power balance in Southeast Asia.

. . .

Vietnamization

While we continue to press for a reasonable settlement through negotiations, the U.S. Government is pursuing the alternative policy of Vietnamization, designed to reduce and eventually eliminate American participation in the war in a way which leaves the South Vietnamese a reasonable chance to survive as a free people. The rate of withdrawal of U.S. troops is determined on the basis of three criteria announced by the President at the beginning of the program: 1) the level of enemy military activity, 2) progress in the Paris talks, and 3) the ability of the South Vietnamese to assume an increasing share of the burden of their own defense. Two years ago:

—The authorized American troop strength in Viet-Nam in 1969 was 549,500. More than 316,200 have now been withdrawn. By December 1, 1971, the authorized troop strength will be 184,000. The current pace of U.S. withdrawal is ahead of schedule.

—Approximately three hundred Americans were being lost every week. This year that figure runs less than 50.

—The ratio of South Vietnamese forces to U.S. forces in Viet-Nam changed from 2 to 1 in 1969 to 4 to 1 in early 1971.

Thus the President could announce on April 7, 1971, "The American involvement in Viet-Nam is coming to an end. The day the South Vietnamese can take over their own defense is in sight. Our goal is a total American withdrawal from Viet-Nam. We can and we will reach that goal . . ."

The Vietnamization program, which the Communists have consistently denounced, is in general succeeding. In some areas it is, inevitably, a mixed picture; in others, the picture is one of uniform progress.

5   **Fragging and Other Withdrawal Symptoms**
     Eugene Linden
     January 8, 1972

Fragging is a macabre ritual of Vietnam in which American enlisted men attempt to murder their superiors. The word comes from the nickname for hand grenades, a weapon popular with enlisted men because the evidence is destroyed with the consummation of the crime. Fragging has ballooned into intra-Army guerrilla warfare, and in parts of Vietnam it stirs more fear among officers and NCOs than does the war with "Charlie." To predict who will be the assassin is impossible; it could be anyone, almost as though the act of murder chooses its executor at random. The victim, too, can be any officer or NCO in contact with enlisted men. Officers who survive fragging attempts often have no idea who their attackers were and live in fear that "they" will try to kill them again. Fraggings occur amid the detritus of a demoralized army: a world of heroin, racial tension, mutiny, and fear. They express the agony of the slow, internal collapse of our Army in Vietnam. Ultimately, the roots of these murder attempts lie outside the military and even the war. They lie in the clash of forces that have brought our Army in Vietnam to its present state.

Capt. Barry Steinberg, an Army judge who has presided over trials involving fraggings, has described the ritual as "the troops' way of controlling officers," adding that it is "deadly effective." Captain Steinberg argues that once an officer is intimidated by even the threat of fragging he is useless to the military because he can no longer carry out orders essential to the functioning of the Army. Through intimidation by threats—verbal and written—and scare stories, fragging is influential to the point that virtually all officers and NCOs have to take into account the possibility of fragging before giving an order to the men under them.

Fraggings have occurred in every war in this century. The available statistics are too spotty and inconsistent to make any direct comparison; however, they do show a spectacular increase in the number of violent attacks by enlisted men on their superiors. In World War I, which involved over 4,700,000 American military, fewer than 370 cases of violence directed at superiors were brought to courts-martial. This low ratio was fairly constant through World War II and the Korean police action. It did not change significantly until Vietnam. Since January 1970 alone, a period during which roughly 700,000 Americans were in Vietnam, there have been 363 cases involving assault with explosive devices (fraggings using hand grenades, mines, and the like) and another 118 cases termed "possible assault with explosive devices." Forty-five men died in those attacks, and these figures are exclusive of fraggings by such other weapons as rifle or knife. Officers in the Judge Advocate General Corps have estimated that only about 10 per cent of fraggings end up in court.

In World War I, World War II, and Korea, the typical fragging took place in the field and for the most part during skirmishes and firefights. An inexperienced or overly zealous lieutenant would be shot by his own men while the platoon or squad was preoccupied with the enemy. The victim would be listed as Killed in Action. The killing generally followed a cold reckoning by the men in the unit that the lieutenant was a danger to them. Albeit ruthless, this type of murder at least can be understood as the result of life or death assessment. Indeed, this type of fragging has occurred in Vietnam, and during 1967 and 1968 in the Mekong Delta region "bounty hunting" enjoyed a brief vogue: A pooled amount of money would be paid to the soldier who killed a marked NCO or officer. However, at present in Vietnam many fraggings take place in rear areas where the dangers are minimal, and many murder attempts occur without any visible provocation or motive at all. "Rear-echelon fraggings are a complete mystery to me," Jeff Jennings, a JAG lawyer at Camp Eagle, told me. "All it takes is a 'How are you, Joe?' and bang, somebody will shoot you."

The prevalence of fraggings, the passionless and often seemingly unprovoked nature of many fraggings, the grisly game of psychological warfare that GIs use to threaten and prepare a victim, and finally the climate of intimidation that effectively cripples numbers of NCOs and officers far greater in proportion than those actually involved in fragging incidents, all differentiate Vietnam from other wars the United States has fought this century. What was in World War I, World War II, and Korea an idiosyncratic yet understandable horror of war has become an obtrusive characteristic of our involvement in Southeast Asia.

Dr. Robert Landeen, an Army psychiatrist, believes that virtually all officers who are fragged are partially at fault. Although persuasive, this argument fails to explain why murder should be the primary resort of dissatisfied troops, nor does it offer any perspective on the changed conditions with which the officer has to contend.

The infantry or rear-echelon officer must be acutely sensitive to both the frustrations of his men and the demands of his superiors. He is expected to make sense of the war when his predecessors and leaders, both military and civilian, have all failed. Chances are he will fail as well, and then he is left with the task of surviving his tour without being court-martialed or fragged. One second lieutenant refused to obey an order from a superior to storm a hill during an operation in the Mekong Delta region. His first sergeant later told him that when his men heard him refuse that order they removed a $350 bounty earlier placed on his head when they thought he was "hard-line."

The overall futility and senselessness of the war make hollow all the individual acts that constitute it. The Army is installed in Vietnam; there is no front on which to advance, no cause to fight for that can be convincingly argued, and not even any real sense of withdrawal as we withdraw. The result of this stagnation is visible everywhere in the despair written on the GI's face, but it is suffered most keenly in the rear units. In the field a soldier's actions redound upon him in terms of survival. With a good combat officer the unnecessary formalities are relaxed, and some soldiers actually prefer the countryside, with its booby traps, firefights, and risk of death, to life in the rear, with its secure, lobotomized monotony.

Although the dangers of being in the rear echelon are minimal, the environment is still one of stress. The enlisted men are the pawns of an authoritarian system designed to deploy soldiers in combat efficiently; yet, the dangers that justify its discipline are absent. The system creates its own stress to match the demands of war; yet, without the particular type of war that fulfills the system, only the stress remains. Thus, in the rear, the enlisted men become acutely aware of the authoritarianism of the system and the privileges and luxuries enjoyed by officers; yet, they see little immediate justification for the discrepancies in status because both officers and enlisted men are doing essentially nothing. This resentment sometimes erupts into skirmishes that resemble class war. The officers' club near the 2/11 Artillery at Camp Eagle north of Hué was recently attacked by between twenty and thirty enlisted men. In a well-organized assault employing combat techniques, the enlisted men first stoned the building and then hit the confused officers with gas and smoke grenades as they streamed outside to see what the disturbance was. At this point, the EMs' plan had called for the use of an M-79 grenade launcher. Fortunately, this phase was abandoned. The next day the shaken officers called a meeting of the company to discuss grievances.

Indeed, through rigidity, pettiness, or hypocrisy, many officers exacerbate frustrations, but occasionally some of them make mistakes in handling situations they should not be expected to handle. Contending with heroin use in a mutinous unit with strained race relations is overwhelming to an officer trained only to order and deploy his men. The rear-echelon officer stands over a caldron where the soldier's every atavistic impulse is boiled to the surface by the heat of enforced proximity. He is expected to lubricate the wheels of the war machine, but much of the time all he has to work with is vitriol. . . .

Heroin is just one contender with a CO for the command of his troops. It is one device the GI uses to live through a tour in Vietnam without being there. The drug—or evidence of it—is everywhere. If you look down through the slats of a base bus station anywhere in Vietnam, you will see dozens of the little glass vials that once contained the 96 to 99 per cent pure heroin. Each $2 vial would sell for as much as $150 when cut to the 6 per cent dosage used in the U.S.A. Dr. Landeen, who was with the 101st Airborne for eight months in 1970, found that in several companies as many as 40 per cent of the men used heroin. Peer group pressure only partially explains the rapid spread of the use of heroin. Bill Karabaic, a drug counselor with the 101st Airborne, told me that for many GIs fighting a war in Vietnam is so confusing and unassimilable that when they are there they feel as though they are in a dream, that they are not really themselves. Because life there is not real, it becomes acceptable to snort skag and to frag the sarge. That's what your buddies are doing. When the dream stops and you return safely to the States, you will stop—or so goes the dream. "Vietnam is a bad place to be," said Karabaic, "and most people want to get through as quickly and painlessly as possible. Heroin makes the time fly."

Documents 6, 7, and 8

Pacification was the attempt to "win the hearts and minds" of the Vietnamese people and to sort out foes from friends. Document 6 describes the results of an American round-up of Vietnamese peasants.

As part of Vietnamization, pacification included land reform, education, and the Phoenix Program—the use of secret agents and spies to root out the Vietcong in the countryside. Suspects were offered a chance to side with the Thieu government or they were punished—sometimes in cruel and unusual ways, according to the program's critics.

In the summer of 1971, the Committee on Government Operations of the House of Representatives studied the Phoenix Program. As Documents 7 and 8 show, witnesses before the committee did not always agree.

6 Cage for the Innocents
Orville Schell
January 1968

Scores of GI's in combat fatigues who had been sprawled out on the benches in the Danang Air Base passenger shed started getting up and moving outside. Once outside they gathered in small knots on the rain-soaked aprons, watching. Some half-heartedly fumbled with cameras. Overhead, jets screamed off the runways into the fluffy early-morning clouds to their targets. A large army truck had just pulled up a short distance from the shed and disgorged about sixty barefoot Vietnamese dressed in ragged shorts and faded dirty shirts. Each had a gray sandbag pulled down over his head. They clung to each other in a disjointed human chain as they were herded by shotgun-toting GI's into an awaiting C-130 transport plane. Moving over closer to this faceless procession, I noticed that several captives had long hair flowing out from under their gray sacks. At the end of the groping line two people were limping and were being helped along by anonymous friends. A Japanese correspondent tried to take a picture and was waved off. He was told that it was against regulations. No one was quite sure what regulation it was against, so he took it anyway.

I walked over to the officer in charge and asked who these people were and where they were being taken.

"These here are hard-core V.C.," he drawled. "You can tell just by lookin' at 'em."

An assistant corrected him and said that he thought that they were CD's (Civil Defendants). I asked what that meant.

"We don't deal in the meanings of all these names," he said, "but we know they're Charlie—maybe saboteurs, collaborators, and like that."

Meanwhile the Vietnamese were slowly being loaded through the rear door of the tadpole-shaped C-130. Since they could not see, they were moving very cautiously, feeling their way slowly up on the hanging tail gate. A GI who was jabbing them along with the barrel of his shotgun said playfully, "If one of these slopes takes off his bag, I'll blow his fuckin' head off."

The officer in charge, who was not accompanying the flight, handed over the manifest of passengers to the pilot. "Well, Chief," he said, "here are the Mexicans. They're all yours."

Inside the aircraft the "sacked" Vietnamese sat utterly silent on the cabin floor. Four GI guards sat on the fold-down seats on both sides of the aircraft. In the dim light of the interior the Vietnamese looked like some sort of strange hooded religious order. Except for one or two pathetic parcels wrapped in brown paper, these people carried no personal possessions. As the engines started, they shrank back against one another in terror. Sensing this fear, one of the GI's poked the Vietnamese nearest to him in the foot with his rifle barrel. The man lunged back away from his unseen tormentor. Another guard commenced breaking his shotgun and cocking his pistol. The noise sent a wave of cringing down the line of huddling figures.

Finally the plane was cleared and started down the runway on its takeoff. As it got airborne the hydraulic system to retract the landing gear went on making a high-pitched scream. The Vietnamese clutched each other in fear.

One of the guards hooted above the noise of the engines, "Hang on, sweet-hearts!" Then he leaned over to me and said, "Hope none of 'em barfs."

I asked if they would be allowed to remove their sacks if they became sick.

"Hell, no!" he replied. "They're so dirty they don't give a shit, and neither do we because we're getting rid of 'em."

As we gained altitude, the Vietnamese began shaking their heads and hitting their ears. They apparently did not understand how to pop their ears. Several became quite frantic. One of the guards looked toward them and then at me in a feigned amazement that anyone could be so stupid.

In a half hour we landed at Chulai Air Base in Quangtin Province. The Vietnamese were herded off the plane and led into a small barbed-wire enclosure, about twenty-five feet by twenty-five feet, out under the blazing hot sun. Here they squatted on the sandy ground and waited. Within a half hour a large pickup truck arrived. The Vietnamese were then divided into two groups and thirty were jammed into the back of the truck. The fact that the vehicle was really too small to transport the whole group in two trips seemed to disturb no one. None of the captors spoke Vietnamese, and obviously none of the captives spoke English. When a guard's command was not immediately understood and obeyed, he would start swearing and shoving the Vietnamese as though they were some dumb stubborn animals refusing to leave the barn.

After some hesitation the driver agreed to let me accompany him to camp, and we set off across the Chulai Air Base, headquarters for Task Force Oregon. The giant runways stretched endlessly away, finally disappearing into mirages in the heat. Sandbag bunkers, gun emplacements, barracks, and hundreds of miles of barbed-wire fence were all that broke the monotony of the dry, sandy dunes upon which the base is built.

The truck finally pulled up in front of a large sign emblazoned with two crossed pirate pistols which read CHULAI POWC (Prisoner of War Camp). As the Vietnamese were being unloaded, I was ushered into the camp headquarters and introduced to the temporary commanding officer, a morose-looking sergeant from Cincinnati who had eyes like Robert Mitchum's. I explained that I was a journalist and that I had accompanied the newly arrived Vietnamese from Danang. I said that I was interested in finding out just who these people were, what they had done, and where they were being taken. The sergeant said that until he had had a chance to look at their papers he could not be certain. Five minutes later he returned and announced that the Vietnamese who had just flown down from Danang were what is known as IC's (Innocent Civilians). He said that this meant that they had been interrogated and found to be innocent of aiding or cooperating with the enemy. He proudly informed me, "These people will be returned to their villages just as soon as we get a chance to ship them out. And if their villages have been destroyed or lie in V.C. areas, well, then we'll turn them over to the Vietnamese refugee authorities and let them take care of them."

The Chulai camp lies on a sand dune bluff overlooking the blue ocean and a beautiful beach, where GI's can be seen riding on air mattresses in the surf and cooking barbecues. All day, low-flying jets, transports, gun ships (helicopters), and small Cessna spotters circle noisily overhead. The prisoners' compound itself consists of four barbed-wire enclosures known as "cages." In each cage the prisoners have built a small thatched roof structure faced on three sides by rattan matting to protect themselves from the sun and rain. Besides the prisoners, a latrine, and the sandy ground, there is nothing else inside the cages. At night the prisoners are given army cots on which to sleep. In the daytime these are stacked neatly outside the cages near the cooking area, into which the prisoners are brought three times a day in two shifts to cook their own meals over an open fire. The army provides dried meat, onion soup, tomato juice, and Texas long grain rice. The reasoning behind this bizarre bill of fare is unclear. The fact that it was not Vietnamese left the sergeant undisturbed.

"Since these people like American chow," he said, "there is no sweat. We treat these people like human beings, not animals."

The camp medic hastened to add, "You know, some of these folks really cry when they have to leave here. [This was said to me on numerous occasions during the next two days.] We give them four squares a day and all the pills they can eat. And we try and show them the American way of life so that when they go back to their villages . . ."

He trailed off, not knowing exactly how to finish his sentence. Outside the office the new arrivals were squatting in the sand up against a barbed-wire fence. They had removed their sandbag hoods. There were six women and several extremely young looking males. They sat listlessly looking up at the bare-chested Americans towering over them. No one talked. Their faces showed no trace of any kind of feeling.

Inside, the briefing continued: There were 141 people imprisoned at the camp. Chulai POWC is the collection point for Vietnamese "detained" in the area of operations of Task Force Oregon. In some areas and on some military operations only people with weapons are picked up and brought in. In other areas where there are known or suspected hostile forces, everyone is picked up and brought in. This includes the aged, women, and children. There are no systematic rules for determining who will be a "detainee." The decision is left up to the field commander's judgment. I asked several people to explain the difference between a "refugee" and a "detainee." Most of those asked assumed that the words were somehow self-explanatory. But none of them could systematically articulate the difference.

Like so many other terms in the Vietnam War lexicon, these words are adopted out of administrative necessity, although they may have very little relation to reality. In Vietnam the situation is very different from any previous war situation in which there have been "detainees" and "refugees": every Vietnamese in the field is potentially hostile. Yet the army needs categories to handle and process these people efficiently even if the categories do not accurately describe the people involved. Every Vietnamese encountered by U.S. forces must fit into one of the previously determined categories. The words "refugee" and "detainee" are really words without meaning. They bring with them old meanings which are irrelevant as designation for the people they are describing. For instance, both "detainees" and "refugees" are "generated" by U.S. and ARVN forces as they move through the countryside on operations destroying villages. These people are not fleeing Communism. They are forced to leave by an invading army. Their designation usually depends on a hasty battlefield decision. It is this decision which makes a person a "refugee" or "detainee." Often a suspect is questioned briefly in the field by a team of ARVN interrogators. But under combat conditions this intelligence-gathering can become extremely indiscriminate and brutal. The emphasis is on getting quick information which may save American lives as the operation moves on. Torture and intimidation are common. After this field interrogation, any villager who is still suspect is bound, blind-folded, and taken back to Chulai to be questioned at greater length and then finally classified. Until this time he is treated just like a prisoner, since there is no way to ascertain whether a "detainee" is hostile or friendly. He is guilty until proven innocent; then if found innocent he suddenly becomes a "refugee." As one colonel in J2 (intelligence) at the Saigon Pentagon put it, "Our job concerns us with the intelligence we can get so that we can take a hill or save a life—this is our interest. But we do respect the dignity of others and treat them in a humane Christian manner. But you mustn't forget that there is a war going on out here."

At Chulai, 52 out of the 127 prisoners (not including the 59 new arrivals) were designated as IC's. Throughout all of Vietnam 65 percent of all detainees finally prove to be IC's. In other words, two out of three suspects brought in from the field are innocent. There are only two other possible designations besides IC; PW (Prisoner of War) and CD (Civil Defendant). North Vietnamese regulars, Viet Cong, or any other person who has committed an act against a "friendly force" is designated as a PW. But an average of only 7 percent of all detainees prove to be PW's. These prisoners are turned over to the Vietnamese Army-run PW camps, of which there are now six with a capacity of over 10,000. One camp which is under construction on Phuquoc Island on the Cambodian border will have a capacity of 20,000 when finished. These camps are technically built according to Geneva Convention specifications, and the inmates are theoretically under the jurisdiction of the Treatment of Prisoners of War section of that convention. But because it is extremely difficult to gain access to these camps on anything more than a short formal tour, it is impossible to be certain of what conditions in them are really like.

The third possible designation for a detainee is CD. This is the vaguest and most poorly defined of the three categories. Officially, someone who is suspected of being a "spy, saboteur, or terrorist" comes under this category. But actually it is a convenient designation for anyone about whom the interrogation teams cannot make up their minds. These unfortunates fall into a limbo category. Since they have not committed a belligerent act against a friendly army they cannot be classified as PW's and therefore do not fall under the protection of the Geneva Convention. They are treated as criminal or political prisoners and thrown into local provincial jails, which are under the jurisdiction of the national police. Treatment is rough, and conditions are indescribably squalid. Such prisons are prime targets for raiding Viet Cong units. For instance, on August 29 the Viet Cong hit the capital city of Quangngai Province and sprang the local jail, freeing 1200 prisoners, many of whom were CD's. A national average of 28 percent of all detainees are finally designated as CD. During the time I was at the Chulai camp 30 out of 141 fell into this category.

In a situation where every Vietnamese is potentially hostile, the United States, as figures suggest, is forced to the desperate tactic of picking up vast numbers of questionable cases. A large number of civilians are simply shot in the field by scared trigger-happy GI's who have learned that it is risky business to trust any Vietnamese, especially any Vietnamese near or in a combat area. Of course, any dead Vietnamese is conveniently considered V.C., thereby raising the unit's enemy KIA (Killed in Action) body count, the summa of progress in Vietnam. As one enlisted man in Ducpho District, Quangngai Province, said, "Anything dead that's not white is V.C."

For instance, on an operation a unit may take sniper fire from the direction of a village. This is sufficient justification for calling in an air strike and wiping out part or all of the village. (The casualness with which Americans put air strikes on "suspected enemy positions" is disturbing.) The Vietnamese have learned to build bunkers under their huts for just such an eventuality. But when the ground forces finally do move into what is left of the village, anyone who is caught hiding in a bunker is automatically treated with great suspicion. He or she is usually detained.

In the month of June 10,000 Vietnamese were detained. In July the figure rose to 15,000. Only 2.5 percent of the July detainees were finally designated as PW's. This is a very small return and a very large catch. In the last six months in I Corps, where combat had been most intense, this mass detention of tens of thousands of people and the attendant disruption of rural life have created a critical but largely ignored social problem. These people are taken forcibly from their farms (which are usually burned), separated from their families, and taken to collection centers like Chulai to await interrogation and designation. Frequently they are moved again because of overcrowded facilities. It often takes weeks before a detainee is finally declared innocent and released. Then he is usually released into one of the badly overcrowded refugee camps. A military police spokesman in Saigon from the Plans and Policy branch, when asked what effect he thought this mass detention was having on "winning the hearts and minds of the people," merely said, "Bringing in so many people is just a problem which is necessarily inherent in this type of war. But it has not yet been presented as a problem area."

For the detainee it *is* a "problem area." At Chulai, no one had told any of the prisoners or detainees with whom I talked why they had been picked up. I talked to several Innocent Civilians who had no idea why they were being held, and had not even been told that in fact they had already been designated as IC's and were only waiting to be transported to refugee centers. The Americans seemed totally oblivious of this piteous information gap. It was blandly assumed that somehow these small unintelligible yellow-skinned people were different, that they could live anywhere, eat anything, and not be disturbed by common American emotions and concerns for one's family, oneself, and the future. None of the Americans I met spoke Vietnamese. They were totally dependent on the seven ARVN interpreters who had been assigned to them for communication with their captives. The only real communication took place during the interrogations. At this time the Americans asked all the questions, never the other way around.

Behind the "cages" at the Chulai camp, four small open interrogation huts have been constructed out of plywood. The head of Interrogation assigned one of them to me for interviewing some of the inmates. Then, accompanied by an interpreter and a Press Information Officer, we walked down to the cages to select some subjects.

Most of the prisoners were lying on the sand in the shade of the thatched roof shelter when we arrived. As we entered the cages they all stood up. One old man jumped to his feet and saluted in a pathetic attempt to please. He wore the black pajama-like garb which is the traditional peasant mode of dressing. Like all the other inmates, he had a large white cardboard tag fastened to his shirt which identified him not by name but by number. The prisoners stood uneasily as we walked between them checking their tags.

Two IC's were finally chosen and let out of the compound.

Nguyen Mê, the first of the group of prisoners whom I interviewed, is forty-six years old and comes from Phuondong village in Quangtin Province. He has been told that he has been designated an Innocent Civilian, but he does not know what that means. He is a slight man, under five feet tall. He wore a dirty pair of black cotton shorts and a black cotton shirt, which was fastened in the front by the large safety pin which secured his white numbered identity card. His feet were bare, archless, and splayed out from years of working in the fields. His skin had been burned a dark brown by the sun. During the whole interview he sat very upright. He smiled only once, when the PIO major offered him a Life-Saver (which at first he did not know what to do with). The rest of the time he listened intently and spoke simply and directly. He betrayed no hostility or any sense of having been wronged. His whole tone was so matter-of-fact that if it had not been for the brief moments when a mixture of pain and bewilderment would cross his face, one might have assumed that he was narrating the story of another person.

Q. How long has it been since you were detained?

A. I don't know. I can't exactly remember how many days. Each day is the same, so they are hard to count.

Q. How were you captured?

A. I was captured in the morning time when everyone was still in the village. We began to hear some shooting and then bombs started to fall [probably mortars]. So we all ran into the shelters under our houses.

Q. Did everyone in your village have a shelter?

A. Yes, every house has one. We dug them two years ago when the bombing and artillery fire first started coming. We really need our shelters.

Q. What happened after you went into your shelters?

A. We couldn't see much or hear much. It was difficult to tell what was happening outside. I was with my wife and children. After a while we heard someone yelling into our house with a voice that we did not understand saying something about Chieu Hoi [the official name for defectors from the Viet Cong]. They fired some shots. I was very scared, but I came out anyway. I thought that it must be the Americans because we had seen helicopters flying over our village earlier. When I came out they pointed guns at me and grabbed me. I was afraid because I could not understand them and didn't know what would happen to me. The Americans are very kind, but these Americans were very rough and hit me. They pushed me back into my house and gestured for me to call my family out of the shelter. I had no choice but to call them.

Q. What did they do after you were all out?

A. They ran off to get a Vietnamese soldier who asked us where the V.C. were and where the V.C. kept their rice. I told them that the V.C. came through our village every four days or so to get rice. But the soldiers were in a big hurry. They tied our hands and put sacks over our heads and led us away someplace. I couldn't see where we were going.

Q. Where was your family?

A. We got separated. We were led away someplace where there were lots of other people. I couldn't see and didn't dare call out to them. They never came to the camp. Now I don't know where they are.

Q. Was your rice already planted when you were picked up?

A. Yes, but now I don't know who will harvest it.

Q. What happened to everything that you owned, like your house, buffalo, et cetera?

A. I am not sure. We were not allowed to bring anything with us at all. Our hands were tied. How could we?

Q. Do you have an extra change of clothes with you?

A. No. I haven't been able to wash my clothes since I have been here.

Q. Did the soldiers destroy many houses?

A. They were burning many when they caught me. Do you know if they burned my house down? [Inmates constantly assumed that since I was American I must have some sort of authority and could help them.]

Q. How many houses had been destroyed before the day you were captured?

A. Six.

Q. How many houses were there in the village?

A. Twenty-seven.

Q. Why were the six houses destroyed?

A. They were near the mountain and the airplanes bombed them.

Q. Were many people killed?

A. Yes, quite a few because they didn't have time to get into their shelters.

Q. Where are they going to take you from here?

A. I don't know. Someone said to the Hoiduc refugee center. But I don't know if my family is there. I want to see them very badly. But that is up to the higher people.

Nguyen Luc, who is seventy-seven years old, came from Phuctien village, in Tienphuc District, Quangtin Province. He had also been designated an Innocent Civilian and was waiting to be shipped out. He was probably the oldest inmate in the Chulai camp. Although his hair was not completely gray, he was hunched over from years of bending down working in the rice paddies. He walked extremely slowly and finally had to be helped up the steps of the interrogation hut. I reached down to give him a hand. His wiry body could not have weighed more than eighty pounds. A major from the Press Information Office thrust out a glad hand in welcome. But Nguyen did not know the significance of shaking hands. Instead he placed both hands together in front of him in a prayer-like motion, which is the traditional form of Vietnamese greeting. The major gave a nervous laugh and then tried to clasp him around the back like a public relations man squiring a big client into his office. But Luc had already begun to sit down. His eyes were riveted to the ground the whole time. He wore an oversize pair of sawed-off army fatigues, and sat quietly on a small wood stool. He seemed neither nervous nor scared, just weary. I had the feeling that even if I had wished to, I could have done nothing which would have elicited any emotional response from him.

Q. How long have you been here?

A. Six days.

Q. How were you captured?

A. I was captured in the morning while out in the rice fields working. The Americans and the ARVN's came and ordered me to go with them.

Q. Did they allow you to return home and talk to your family or bring any possessions?

A. No, they were in a big hurry. They pointed guns at me and I just went.

Q. Had your fields been planted?

A. Yes.

Q. What will happen to them now?

A. I don't know who will harvest the rice. I would like to go back because now there are very few people in the village. They all live underground. All our houses have been bombed and destroyed. The bombs have made big holes in our rice fields.

Q. When did the bombing start?

A. [He paused.] It started three years ago—but then not as much as now.

Q. Did the people fear the V.C. or the bombing more in your village?

A. We don't like the Viet Cong because they take our rice and sometimes make us work.

Q. But which do you fear the most?

A. We fear the bombing because we don't know when it will come and we can't see it. [At this point Luc began fidgeting with his pants. I asked why, but he did not respond.]

Q. Who are the Americans?

A. [Pause.] The Americans are like the French. The French were very cruel.

Q. Are the Americans cruel?

A. The French beat the people.

Q. Do the Americans beat the people?

A. [Luc glanced over at the agitated but silent PIO officer.] Sometimes the Americans give candy. [Again he started tugging at his baggy fatigue shorts, which I noticed were missing most of the buttons on the fly.]

Q. Why are you fidgeting? Are you hurt?

A. [A long pause during which time Luc stared at his feet.] I want some underwear. I am embarrassed because my pants will not fasten.

Q. Have you asked the Americans for some new clothes? You know that they give clothes to inmates, don't you?

A. Yes.

Q. Have you asked them? [The PIO major interrupted here to assure me that all prisoners received all the clothing and medical attention that they needed.]

A. Yes, once.

Q. What happened?

A. I asked the Americans, but they did not understand me. They just laughed at me, and one struck me. He slapped me on my face. I was very scared. I didn't dare ask again.

Q. Why don't you ask now? I have explained that I am not in the army.

A. The atmosphere is good. [The PIO major acted shocked and assured me that this "oversight" would be corrected. After the interview he hurried to the office to launch his protest.]

Q. Do you know why your village was bombed?

A. The people said that it was because of the Communists.

Q. What is a Communist? Who are they?

A. [Long pause.] They are . . . I don't know.

Q. Have you ever heard of Nguyen Cao Ky or Nguyen Van Thieu?

A. No, I do not know them.

Q. Have you ever heard of Ho Chi Minh?

A. Yes, he sent troops from the North. He is well known.

Q. Why were you detained?

A. I don't know why. They just brought me in.

Q. But has anyone explained to you the reason for detaining you?

A. No. They do not speak Vietnamese. We cannot understand one another.

Q. What did they tell you in the interrogation?

A. They asked me questions. They asked me if I was a Viet Cong and if I knew where the Viet Cong were hiding. They just asked me questions.

Q. Do you know that you have been designated an Innocent Civilian?

A. What is that? [The PIO major moved forward on his chair ready to give an explanation.]

Q. Where are you going when you leave here?

A. I don't know what they are going to do with us. Will I be able to go back to my village? I am very worried because no one is there to look after our ancestral tombs.

Q. Do you have a family?

A. Yes, a wife, two sons, and some grandchildren.

Q. Where are they now?

A. I don't know. I am very sad because I don't know what has happened to them. Maybe they are worrying about me also.

Q. Perhaps they are in refugee camps. Do you know anything about the resettlement program?

A. No.

Q. Have the Americans ever dropped leaflets on your village explaining the refugee program and warning you to leave your village because it will be bombed?

A. Yes, sometimes they drop leaflets. But I can't read. Many people can't read. Now there are no schools in the countryside. They are all destroyed.

Q. Do you know what is going to happen to you?

A. No, I don't know. I need someone to help me. I am very scared here all alone.

7   United States Assistance Programs in Vietnam: Statement by William Colby

. . . Ambassador COLBY: On July 15, the members of the subcommittee devoted considerable attention to the Phoenix program. I have thus prepared the following statement in an attempt to put this program in perspective. It supplements the rather detailed and extensive testimony I provided on the same subject to the Senate Foreign Relations Committee in February, 1970.

The Phoenix program of the Government of South Vietnam is designed to protect the Vietnamese people from terrorism and political, paramilitary, economic and subversive pressure from the Communist clandestine organization in South Vietnam. The Vietcong infrastructure, or VCI, is the leadership apparatus of the Communist attempt to conquer the Vietnamese people and government. The VCI supports the military operations of the Vietcong and North Vietnamese Army units by providing intelligence, recruits or conscripts and logistics support. It also directs and implements a systematic campaign of terrorism against government officials, locally elected leaders and the general population. The result of this terrorism is as follows:

VC TERRORISM

	Incidents	Killed	Wounded	Abducted
1969	10,526	6,097	15,074	6,097
1970	11,680	5,951	12,588	6,872
1971 (May)	4,526	2,470	4,701	3,257

The Phoenix program is an integral part of the Vietnamese Government's war effort to bring security to its people since the VCI is a key element of the Communist war effort.

The Phoenix program includes an intelligence program to identify the members of the VCI, an operational program to apprehend them, a legal program to restrain them and a detention program to confine them.

. . .

Conclusion

The Phoenix program is an essential element of Vietnam's defense against VCI subversion and terrorism. While some unjustifiable abuses have occurred over the years, as they have in many countries, the Vietnamese and U.S. Governments have worked to stop them, and to produce instead professional and intelligent operations which will meet the VCI attack with stern justice, with equal stress on both words. Considerable evidence has appeared from enemy documents and from former and even current members of the enemy side that, despite some weaknesses, the program has reduced the power of the VCI and its hopes for conquest over the people of South Vietnam. Phoenix is an essential part of the GVN's defense as the VCI is to the Communist attack. U.S. support is fully warranted.

Mr. MOORHEAD: Thank you very much, Mr. Ambassador, for your statement. I am sure your suggestions will be studied closely by the subcommittee because CORDS is a new type of foreign operation.

Mr. Ambassador, did you see the article today in the Washington Post which is headed "Vietnam, a Fragile Security," and then in a smaller heading, "Population Still Up for Grabs"?

It seems to me that we face a situation which I have experienced before in Vietnam, where the official report is always positive. Intelligent people like you are always more optimistic, whether it is on the military side or the civilian side, than the information we get from independent observers like newspaper reporters.

On page 12 of your testimony, you talk about the traffic on the roads, the bustling marketplaces. This article gives a much less optimistic picture.

I looked also at your supplementary statement about the number of persons killed through VC terrorism. If my arithmetic is correct, if they keep on in 1971 at the rate that they have for the first 5 months, we have approximately the same number killed in 1971 as were killed in 1970. That is a statistic which indicates to me that progress toward pacification is at a slower rate than your general testimony would indicate.

Would you care to comment on this?

Ambassador COLBY: I was very interested in the headline there, Mr. Chairman, referring to a fragile situation. About a year ago, a journalist who had been there a while threw up to me the question whether the security situation there was still fragile. We had made quite a point over the previous year or so that the situation was quite fragile. I had to think back and say that I didn't think it was fragile anymore in that sense.

What you have there, I believe, quite frankly, is a situation we have had in our own staff to a considerable degree. The fellow who has been there a little while looks back on the situation a couple of years ago and has a great sense of how different the situation is from what it was a couple of years ago in terms of the security situation and the ability of the people to circulate, the markets work and so forth.

So he is inclined to tell his successor that the situation is good compared to what it was when he came. The new man looks around and realizes you can still get killed by a mine on the road, by a grenade in that very marketplace. Not many of those occur, but some do. He begins to think it is pretty bad.

I think the thrust of that article, Mr. Chairman, was that the security situation is really quite a bit better than it was, and is quite substantially in hand, but that the political problem is yet to be faced. I think that is what the writer of that article was essentially saying, that the political problem of the relationship of the people to the Government has not really been solved to that degree.

I would be inclined to agree that certainly the political identification of the people with the Government has not proceeded as fast as the security situation has, but this is a sequential development. This is the design of the plan. First you produce a reasonable climate of security in which the people dare to participate and maintain security, and then you develop the programs which invite the people's participation in a political sense and involve them in that sense. I think this has been done at the village level to a considerable degree, although it has not in every village, I hasten to say.

The process is building a new political base of this Government from the bottom up. This is just beginning at the local level and it is being gradually moved up the scale from the village to the province to the national level.

I think the sequence of elections at the village hamlet level in 1969 and 1970, and then in the Province councils in 1970, and later in 1970 for the Senate and this year for the National Lower House and the Presidency, shows this sequential development from the bottom up.

This is political development which is quite a different kind of political base than the former governments used to have where power went down to the people. I am well aware that spokesmen such as myself, and probably including myself, have stated a more positive view of the situation than some of our independent observers have. I do believe, though, that a full evaluation of the situation in Vietnam today shows that the momentum of the strengthening of the Government in security terms, in political terms, and in development terms, is continuing, and will continue in the near future.

Mr. MOORHEAD: Thank you, Mr. Ambassador. I still point out that the rate of VC killings seems to be at practically the same rate as last year.

Mr. Ambassador, a question with respect to the Phoenix program. That is the same thing as the Phung Hoang program?

Ambassador COLBY: It is, Mr. Chairman.

Mr. MOORHEAD: You mentioned that there have been some abuses. Have any of your subordinates reported to you instances of torture being used under the Phoenix program?

Ambassador COLBY: We have had reports of a few through our channels. We have also had allegations to the National Assembly and in the Vietnamese press of this kind of thing. We have looked into these. On occasion we have found abuses, as I say, unjustifiable abuses, and in collaboration with the Vietnamese authorities we have moved to stop that sort of nonsense.

Mr. MOORHEAD: It bothers me, Mr. Ambassador, that the pacification program by its very nature, includes the killing, torture, imprisonment, moving of people, destruction of villages, and the conscious creation of refugees. They may create new hatreds among the people in opposition to the Saigon government.

Have any studies been made on this point? There are certain aspects of the pacification program which make me wonder if we are making friends or enemies. If we are making enemies by this program, our assistance is not only wasteful from a dollar point of view, but in direct contravention of our goals and objectives in Vietnam.

Ambassador COLBY: I think, Mr. Chairman, that your characterization of the nature of the program is not quite the same as I would give it. I think the program is one of an expanding defense of the people against the rockets and raids such as were described in the New York Times this morning and some of this sort of thing. I think the purpose is to provide protection to the people and to give the people a voice in their own future and their own Government.

Thus, I believe that there have been a few cases of abuses, as I have mentioned, most people have been killed as the enemy attacked some of these places, either by the local forces or the self-defense forces, and in the course of active operations against the enemy units out in the jungle.

There have been very few movements of people from areas where they could not be defended.

This is in accordance with the Government's overall policy that security will be brought to the people and not the people brought to security, whenever it is possible. I think the trend of the program over the past several years, in terms of the millions of people it has protected more than overcomes the occasional unjustified abuse. . . .

8   Military Intelligence and the Phoenix Program: Statement by K. Barton Osborn

Mr. OSBORN: Thank you, Mr. Chairman.

My name is K. Barton Osborn. I am a resident of Washington, D.C.

I would like to describe my role as it was peripheral to the Phoenix program and give you an idea of the context in which I was associated with both military intelligence and the Central Intelligence Agency program.

I was in Vietnam from September 1967 until December 1968. At that time I was in the Army on active duty. I had been trained for 6 months at Fort Holabird, Md., in a covert classified program of illegal agent handling, which taught us to find, recruit, train, and manage and later terminate agents for military intelligence.

Mr. REID: Could you explain what you mean by "terminate"?

Mr. OSBORN: Terminate, that is to release agents from their duties as they performed them for the agent handler once they no longer were of use for the agent.

Mr. REID: Do you imply by that with extreme prejudice?

Mr. OSBORN: There are two ways: one is with prejudice and one is without prejudice.

With prejudice means simply—without prejudice first of all, is to tell the man or woman he has done a good job; give them a payoff or whatever and let them go; also to establish a future contact arrangement.

With prejudice is subcategorized into two areas. With prejudice may mean simply that the agent did a bad job; in some way was judged not loyal or whatever, and was not to be hired again and was to be put on a list of undesirable personalities which they call "black list."

With extreme prejudice is to murder the individual right out because he or she constitutes a knowledgeable person who may be compromising to present or future operations. That is a termination process. There is a whole cycle called "The intelligence cycle," from the point of needing an agent and going to find one through recruiting the person, training them, managing them, sending them out, receiving them back, having them perform missions and then debriefing them and then eventual termination.

Mr. REID: Were you aware of or did you participate in anything that reflected extreme prejudice?

Mr. OSBORN: Yes, I was. . . .

The Phoenix description was that it was designed to neutralize the core of the VC, interdiction politically, logistically and so forth. I found myself in possession of this information and in need of funds for my agents, because Military Intelligence, although I had been assigned by them to recruit agents, found themselves short on what Mr. Uhl described as the intelligence contingency funding and in fact, had no money to pay the agents once they had been recruited.

I had recruited these people on promises of money to come, but when it came time to pay I didn't have money so I took what incentive gifts—cigarettes and liquor, that were available and had them sold by interpreters on the black market in order to get money for my agents' payment.

The Phoenix coordinator offered me not only the opportunity to utilize the political information I was getting, but also additional money which I may have needed for my agents. From that point on I had no real financial struggle and found myself not only able to pay my agents, but utilize CIA facilities, such as Air America for transportation housing, covert housing in the city areas where I needed it; such things as safe houses which are areas to meet your agent covertly and debrief; money to rent hotel rooms in order to meet them covertly; agent payments, both overt money payments and incentive gifts such as an occasional motorcycle to a principal agent and so forth.

From the time of my association with the Phoenix program I no longer had any logistical problems. This is how the information was dealt with; I gave it to them in reciprocity for the money and information I received. . . .

I at one point was reporting regularly people in that area of Da Nang Air Base who may have constituted a threat to the air base's security. I remember at one time I reported an individual who lived in a local village who was reported to me by the local cell as being a logistical officer for the local farmers organization, which is the Vietcong structure at the village level, and the counterintelligence team from that unit went out and picked the individual up and detained him as a suspected VC.

I went back the next day to check out the utilization of my report and whether or not it had been accurately followed through on and so forth. They told me they had the individual detained there and I asked how they were going to deal with him; and they said they were preparing to interrogate him; would I like to attend the interrogation, and I said I would, because I had never seen one. They said it would be an airborne interrogation and I didn't quite conceive that. I went ahead with the marine officer who was a first lieutenant, head of the CI team.

We took two Marine enlisted men and two Vietnamese males in their 30's or so and we went out to the air wing and we got on a helicopter and flew northwest of Da Nang over some uninhabited area there of flat terrain.

Mr. REID: What unit was that?

Mr. OSBORN: Counterintelligence team of the 1st Marine Division.

Mr. REID: Of the 1st Marine Division?

Mr. OSBORN: That is right. They had a facility there on the 3d Marine Amphibious Force's air wing at Da Nang Air Base.

But we flew over some flat terrain, perhaps 20 miles out of Da Nang, and the two Vietnamese were bound with their hands behind their backs and the two Marine enlisted men kept them off in a sling seat inside the helicopter. The interrogation began not on the individual whom I had reported, but on the extra person, and I didn't know who he was at first and found out that he was a previous detainee who had already been interrogated who had been beaten and who had internal injuries and who was not able to respond to questions. They had brought him along for the purposes of interrogation.

I found out the purpose was this: They antagonized the individual and told him they needed certain information regarding VC activities and he couldn't give it. He hadn't given the information they wanted from him and they demanded it of him and he couldn't respond or wouldn't respond. They antagonized him several times by taking him with his elbows behind his back, hands tied, running him up to the door of the helicopter and saying: If you don't tell us what we need to know we are going to throw you out of the helicopter. They did this two or three times and he refused to say anything. He couldn't respond. He wouldn't respond. Therefore, on the fourth trip to the door they did throw him out from the helicopter to the ground. That had the effect directly of antagonizing the person I had reported, suspected Vietcong logistics officer, into telling them whatever information they wanted to know, regardless of its content, value or truth; he would tell them what they wanted to know simply because his primary objective at that point would be not to follow the first Vietnamese out the door, but rather to return safely to the ground.

Mr. REID: That was a purposeful, deliberate pushing out the door?

Mr. OSBORN: There was no question at all. This was the reason they took this first individual up and the reason that they antagonized him and went through the form of threatening him and throwing him out three times.

Mr. REID: Who gave the order that he should be pushed out?

Mr. OSBORN: The 1st Marine Division lieutenant.

Mr. REID: There was a lieutenant on board?

Mr. OSBORN: That is right. He was the counterintelligence team chief.

Mr. REID: Do you recall his name?

Mr. MOORHEAD: Because of the rules, we had better not mention names of individuals in such cases in public session.

Mr. OSBORN: In all due respect, I do recall his name, but I am not willing to go into that. You can see that that is irrelevant. In fact, the form of the thing is what we are talking about.

So that we returned to the ground and they proceeded with the interrogation of their own. This happened, not once as an aberration, but twice that I attended. The same airborne procedure; the same dummy on the first hand who was antagonized and then thrown from the helicopter; the second person who was then interrogated and gave whatever information they demanded of him.

They certainly did not know how to elicit information from this person without brutality, for there was no real interrogation session short of the brutalization.

I saw other interrogations, to describe them briefly: The use of the insertion of the 6-inch dowel into the canal of one of my detainee's ears and the tapping through the brain until he died. The starving to death of a Vietnamese woman who was suspected of being a part of the local political education cadre in one of the local villages. They simply starved her to death in a cage there they kept in one of the hooches at that very counterintelligence team headquarters.

There were other methods of operation which they used for interrogation, such as the use of electronic gear such as sealed telephones attached to the genitals of both the men and women's vagina and the men's testicles, and wind the mechanism and create an electrical charge and shock them into submission. I had a lot of conversations about the use of that kind of equipment, although I never saw it used.

Mr. MOORHEAD: Were these methods that you described conducted by American personnel or——

Mr. OSBORN: Americans only. These were unilateral operations not in coordination or with the knowledge of the South Vietnamese Government.

Mr. REID: And officers were present as well as enlisted men?

Mr. OSBORN: Each time. These were my experiences with reporting names of Vietnamese from my agents to American agencies and the resulting interrogations. . . .

Document 9

Tim O'Brien's novel portrays soliders with uncertainties about their roles in Vietnam. In this excerpt, one soldier wonders about the hopes and dreams of a Vietnamese girl he saw during the war.

9   Going After Cacciato
Tim O'Brien

After the war, perhaps, he might return to Quang Ngai. Years and years afterward. Return to track down the girl with gold hoops through her ears. Bring along an interpreter. And then, with the war ended, history decided, he would explain to her why he had let himself go to war. Not because of strong convictions, but because he didn't know. He didn't know who was right, or what was right; he didn't know if it was a war of self-determination or self-destruction, outright aggression or national liberation; he didn't know which speeches to believe, which books, which politicians; he didn't know if nations would topple like dominoes or stand separate like trees; he didn't know who really started the war, or why, or when, or with what motives; he didn't know if it mattered; he saw sense in both sides of the debate, but he did not know where truth lay; he didn't know if Communist tyranny would prove worse in the long run than the tyrannies of Ky or Thieu or Khanh—he simply didn't know. And who did? Who really did? He couldn't make up his mind. Oh, he had read the newspapers and magazines. He wasn't stupid. He wasn't uninformed. He just didn't know if the war was right or wrong. And who did? Who really *knew*? So he went to the war for reasons beyond knowledge. Because he believed in law, and law told him to go. Because it was a democracy, after all, and because LBJ and the others had rightful claim to their offices. He went to the war because it was expected. Because not to go was to risk censure, and to bring embarrassment on his father and his town. Because, not knowing, he saw no reason to distrust those with more experience. Because he loved his country and, more than that, because he trusted it. Yes, he did. Oh, he would rather have fought with his father in France, knowing certain things certainly, but he couldn't choose his war, nobody could. Was this so banal? Was this so unprofound and stupid? He would look the little girl with gold earrings straight in the eye. He would tell her these things. He would ask her to see the matter his way. What would *she* have done? What would *anyone* have done, not knowing? And then he would ask the girl questions. What did she want? How did she see the war? What were her aims—peace, any peace, peace with dignity? Did she refuse to run for the same reasons he refused—obligation, family, the land, friends, home? And now? Now, war ended, what did she want? Peace and quiet? Peace and pride? Peace with mashed potatoes and Swiss steak and vegetables, a full-tabled peace, indoor plumbing, a peace with Oldsmobiles and Hondas and skyscrapers climbing from the fields, a peace of order and harmony and murals on public buildings? Were her dreams the dreams of ordinary men and women? Quality-of-life dreams? Material dreams? Did she want a long life? Did she want medicine when she was sick, food on the table and reserves in the pantry? Religious dreams? What? What did she *aim* for? If a wish were to be granted by the war's winning army—any wish—what would she choose? Yes! If LBJ and Ho were to rub their magic lanterns at war's end, saying, "Here is what it was good for, here is the fruit," what would Quang Ngai demand? Justice? What sort? Reparations? What kind? Answers? What were the questions: What did Quang Ngai want to know?

Critical Issues for Discussion

1. One young American correspondent in Vietnam during the war noted that "we also knew that for years now there had been no country here but the war." What exactly did he mean? Was the same message conveyed in this program?

Michael Herr also reported in *Dispatches* that the American soldiers' ideas about the best way to win the war were sometimes remarkable. "What you do is, you load all the Friendlies onto ships and take them out to the South China Sea. Then you bomb the country flat. Then you sink the ships." This was a common joke during the Vietnam War. What did that joke demonstrate? Why did the Americans have that attitude?

American soldiers spoke about their colleagues in similar ways. A sign in one U.S. military camp said: "If you kill for money you're a mercenary. If you kill for pleasure you're a sadist. If you kill for both you're a Green Beret." What had happened to the popularity of that new breed of warriors?

2. The American commanders in Vietnam tried to manage the war in a businesslike fashion. When General Westmoreland left in 1968, he submitted rules and guidelines for his officers and men, reprinted as Document 1. How do you evaluate Westmoreland's suggestions? Were they helpful for wartime? Was there anything missing? Anything unexpected?

Westmoreland had worked hard in Vietnam, and according to Charlton and Moncrieff in *Many Reasons Why,* he saw the American role as "a concerted effort to put some backbone into the Vietnamese, stabilize their government, improve the economy, open roads, and increase and improve the proficiency of the Vietnamese armed forces." Were those goals realized? How? Would the successful completion of Westmoreland's objectives have won the war? Explain.

3. The life of the American soldier in Vietnam was the subject of countless articles and surveys such as the one which appears as Document 3. What did these troops say about the war and their role in it? Were they good soldiers? What is a good soldier? How is a good soldier molded?

4. Vietnamization was controversial. While some saw it as a legitimate and successful way to achieve peace with honor in Vietnam, others complained that it was morally reprehensible and left the basic issues of American involvement in the war unexamined. Compare Documents 2, 4, and 5.

How do you evaluate Vietnamization? What was its ultimate goal? Why was that goal chosen? Did Vietnamization succeed?

5. The Vietnamese peasants were often caught between American troops and the Vietcong. Why did the American soldiers capture the prisoners described in Document 6? What had these people done? How were they treated? Why? How did the soldiers and the peasants interact? Why did their relationship take this form?

What was the difference between a "refugee" and a "detainee"? How were these categories of people "generated"? What was the significance of this type of official army language?

6. The Phoenix Program had impassioned devotees and furious foes. When congressional hearings were held on the program, this aspect of pacification put American policy in Vietnam clearly before the public eye. Compare and contrast Documents 7 and 8.

Colby and Osborn did not have the same point of view toward the Phoenix program. How do you decide whom to believe? What could Congress do with such conflicting information? Since the Phoenix Program continued in spite of the testimony presented at this hearing, what probably convinced the Congress to carry on with it? Whose comments were the most convincing to you? Why?

7. Combat affected the attitudes that soldiers had toward each other and those around them. Many American infantrymen became frustrated with the villagers in the countryside. One soldier explained: "When, for example, we would patrol an area of villages for a number of weeks and continue to lose men to booby traps, and the people in the villages who pretended not to know anything about these booby traps walked the same trails that we did day after day without stepping on them, it became obvious that these people were well informed by the VC where the booby traps were" (Santoli, *Everything We Had*).

Why did incidents like this happen? What were the feelings of the South Vietnamese toward the Americans? What did the villagers want?

8. One black soldier remarked that racism in the Army was rampant—except at the front lines. "Out in the bush everybody was the same. You can't find no racism in the bush. We slept together, ate together, fought together. What else can you ask for?" (Santoli, *Everything We Had*.)

How do you explain this account of life in Vietnam? What was happening back at the bases? Why was there such a difference?

Follow Up Some critiques of the war were most effectively presented far away from the official setting of congressional investigations. Novels and poems about the Vietnam War, some by the soldiers themselves, captured the ideas, thoughts, and concerns of the participants in the conflict.

How did the soldier in Document 9 explain his presence in Vietnam? What did he worry about? How does this compare to the experiences presented in the television program? Was the Vietnam War different from previous ones for its participants or are all wars alike?

Suggestions for Further Reading

Vietnamization—Saigon

Buttinger, Joseph. *Vietnam: The Unforgettable Tragedy*. New York: Horizon, 1977.

In Part III, "The Turn of the Tide," Buttinger attributes the failure of Vietnamization in large part to widespread corruption within the South Vietnamese government and military.

Tran Van Don. *Our Endless War: Inside South Vietnam*. San Rafael, Cal.: Praesidio, 1978.

The memoirs of a top South Vietnamese official chronicle the corruption and intrigue which paralyzed the government.

FitzGerald, Frances. *Fire in the Lake: The Vietnamese and the Americans in Vietnam*. Boston: Little, Brown, 1972.

FitzGerald exposes the cultural gulf between the Americans and their "allies" and the surreal relations between the two governments. Chapter 16 describes the chaos and destruction of the Vietnamization period, which she judges to have been unnecessary except for Nixon's fear of appearing to lose.

Nguyen Khac Vien., gen. ed. *Vietnamese Studies #42, U.S. Neocolonialism in South Vietnam: The "Vietnamization" of the War*. Hanoi. Xunhasaba (Dist.), 1975.

Vietnamese writers show American money, consumer goods, films, drugs and propaganda destroying traditional values among those forced into cities by the war.

Vietnamization—Washington

Herring, George C. *America's Longest War: The United States and Vietnam, 1950–1975*. New York: Wiley, 1979.

Chapter 7, "A War for Peace: Nixon, Kissinger, and Vietnam, 1969–1973," is a good overview of the period as seen from Washington. Herring is sympathetic to Nixon's intentions but critical of the extreme measures he used under pressure from his opponents.

Nixon, Richard M. *RN: The Memoirs of Richard Nixon.* New York: Grosset and Dunlap, 1978.

Nixon's autobiography offers quotes from his private papers and some unconscious revelations about his own character.

Demoralization and Resistance Among U.S. Troops

Boyle, Richard. *Flower of the Dragon: The Breakdown of the U.S. Army in Vietnam.* San Francisco: Ramparts, 1972.

A dramatic eyewitness account, with photographs, including the "fragging" of an officer, the mutiny of a cavalry division, and a peace demonstration in Saigon with GIs and Vietnamese army deserters.

Cincinnatus (pseudonym of Cecil B. Currey). *Self-Destruction: The Disintegration and Decay of the United States Army During the Vietnam Era.* New York: Norton, 1980.

This very critical description was written by an Army insider on active duty.

Gabriel, Richard P., and Paul Savage. *Crisis in Command: Mismanagement in the Army.* New York: Hill and Wang, 1979.

Political science jargon makes this less readable than other books in the section, but it is important for the controversy that it has sparked in military circles.

Helmer, John. *Bringing the War Home: The American Soldier in Vietnam and After.* New York: Free Press, 1974.

Helmer's scholarly study examined the impact of the war on working-class men and found that, contrary to stereotype, they were more likely than middle-class men to rebel because the war hurt them more, physically and economically.

Jury, Mark. *The Vietnam Photo Book.* New York: Grossman, 1971.

Jury uses his own photos and interviews to show GI experiences of this period, including peace signs, Black power, antiwar grafitti, brothels, and drugs.

Starr, Paul. *The Discarded Army: Veterans After Vietnam.* New York: Charterhouse, 1973.

Chapter 5 of this report from Ralph Nader's Center for Study of Responsive Law examines the use of heroin by GIs and the limits of the armed services' ability to control it.

Taylor, Clyde, ed. *Vietnam and Black America: An Anthology of Protest and Resistance.* Garden City, N.Y.: Anchor, 1973.

Includes statements by Martin Luther King, Jr. and other Black leaders, poetry, diaries of Black soldiers, and radical analyses linking American Black liberation struggles with revolutionary movements in Vietnam and the rest of the Third World.

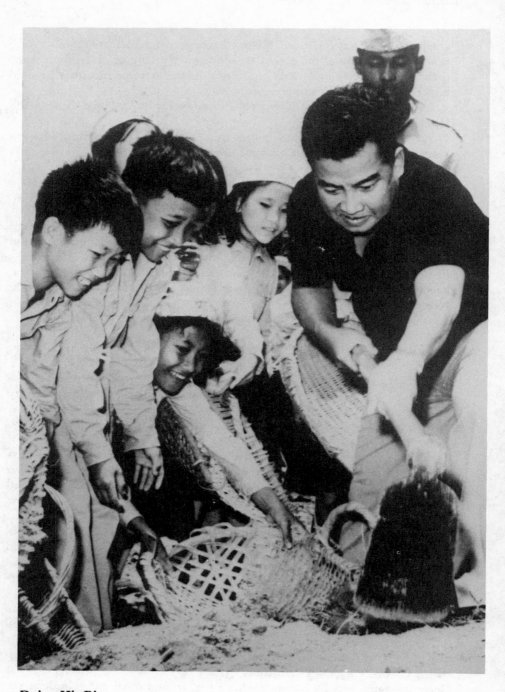

Doing His Bit
Prince Norodom Sihanouk of Cambodia was often photographed pitching in to help build a better Cambodia. Here he helps rural youth in a community project. *U.P.I.*

Chapter 9
Cambodia and Laos

Background

Historical Summary

The Geneva Conference of 1954 had guaranteed the neutrality of the remaining two countries of France's Indochinese Empire, Laos and Cambodia. But neither country could keep the war in neighboring Vietnam from spilling across its borders. Neither country could prevent American administrations from seeing them as pieces in an international game of dominoes.

Laos

In Laos, the government included members of the pro-Communist Pathet Lao, supported by the North Vietnamese who used Laotian trails to move supplies to South Vietnam. To counter this breach of neutrality the Kennedy administration sent special forces to equip and train the largest of the hill tribes, the Muong (or Meo) as guerrilla forces to fight against the Pathet Lao.

An international conference was held in 1962 to stop the fighting, but, as war in Vietnam escalated, the fragile Laotian coalition fell apart. In March 1964, five months before the first bombing raid on North Vietnam, the U.S. launched a secret bombing campaign in Laos against the Ho Chi Minh Trail—the increasingly important Communist supply route from North to South Vietnam. For eight years, Laos was the most bombed country in the world, with millions of peasants driven from their homes.

Pathet Lao forces, equipped with heavier weapons by the North Vietnamese, began to fight in battalion-sized units. The Muong tribes, backed by hundreds of millions of dollars in U.S. training and materiel—and eventually reinforced by 8,000 Thai mercenaries—fought back. But, while North Vietnamese forces grew, the Muong tribes were decimated. In early 1973, cease-fire agreements were reached in Laos as well as Vietnam. Two years later, the Pathet Lao took over the government.

Cambodia

For ten years after the 1954 Geneva Agreements, Cambodia remained at peace. The country was ruled by Norodom Sihanouk, son of the last king of Cambodia, whose base of support was a prosperous land-owning peasantry.

263

By 1963, however, the South Vietnamese were regularly pursuing Vietcong into Cambodia, and Sihanouk became concerned that the war would spread inside his country. Sihanouk looked everywhere for support against this impending disaster—to China's Mao Tse-tung, to France's President Charles de Gaulle, to leaders of nonaligned nations like Indonesia's President Sukarno. And, in 1965, Sihanouk broke off relations with the United States.

Sihanouk's problems, however, began to grow out of control: his army officers resented the lack of American military aid; Cambodian Communists, the Khmer Rouge, became more active and began recruiting peasants; and the Vietnamese Communists continued to build up sanctuaries along the border.

In 1969, newly elected President Richard M. Nixon launched secret B-52 bombing raids over Cambodia against the North Vietnamese and Vietcong sanctuaries, driving those forces deeper into the Cambodian countryside. The increased Vietnamese Communist presence caused great concern among Cambodians. And, in March 1970, while Sihanouk was abroad, he was ousted in a coup led by his former prime minister, Lon Nol, who promptly received secret American military aid. Sihanouk set up residence in China when Lon Nol assumed control, and announced support for the Khmer Rouge, his former opponents.

In the countryside, violence escalated: Lon Nol's government forces fought the Khmer Rouge, Sihanouk's non-Communist supporters, and the Vietnamese. But the Cambodian troops' main target was not the Vietnamese Communists; they slaughtered thousands of Vietnamese villagers and merchants whose families had lived in Cambodia for generations.

Taking advantage of Lon Nol's hostility towards the Vietnamese, 20,000 American and 40,000 South Vietnamese troops moved into Cambodia to wipe out Vietnamese Communist sanctuaries. The attack, announced as a means to save American lives in Vietnam, plunged Cambodia into full scale war, driving the North Vietnamese into the interior and helping the Khmer Rouge to organize and expand their support among the people. The incursion into Cambodia lasted sixty days.

In October 1970, Lon Nol ended the centuries-old Cambodian monarchy and created the Khmer Republic. Earlier American optimism that his government could defeat the Communists had crumbled, even though his army, with U.S. aid, had grown four-fold, to 100,000 men. Corruption was rampant, and the economy was a shambles.

On January 22, 1971, Vietnamese Communists hit the capital of Phnom Penh for the first time. American military aid and personnel were stepped up sharply. But no Americans were dying in Cambodia as they still were in Vietnam, and, for the moment, Congress went along with the expense of supporting the Cambodian military.

During six months of 1973, more than a quarter of a million tons of bombs were dropped on Cambodia, in raids coordinated by the U.S. embassy in Phnom Penh. It was war, waged without congressional approval, and not uncovered until July of 1973. Congress then forced a bombing halt on August 15, 1973.

Chronology

	1963	1965	1966–1967	1968	1969	1970 Mar	Apr	May	Jun	Sep
Cambodia	Prince Sihanouk renounces U.S. aid	Cambodia breaks relations with U.S.	Vietnamese Communists set up bases. U.S. Army occasionally crosses border in "hot pursuit" of enemy		Secret bombing of Cambodia begins (March 17)	Sihanouk deposed. Lon Nol takes over. ARVN troops first attack Vietnamese bases in Cambodia.	American "incursion" begins	Sihanouk announces the formation of a government in exile, from Peking.	American ground troops leave	First U.S. ambassador since 1965 arrives
Vietnam	Coup overthrows President Ngo Dinh Diem	Operation Rolling Thunder. U.S. troops in ground combat.	B-52s attack North Vietnam for the first time	Tet Offensive. Peace Talks begin in Paris.				U.S. bombs North Vietnam for the first time since 1968		
United States and World Wide		Kosygin visits North Vietnam			*N.Y. Times* reports on bombing of Cambodia. (May 9) Nixon Administration begins wiretapping of suspected information leaks. (May 10) First U.S. troop withdrawal announced. (June)				Cooper-Church Amendment prohibits U.S. ground forces from re-entering Cambodia. U.S. Senate repeals Gulf of Tonkin Resolution.	

Chronology (cont.)

	1971 Jan	Oct	1972 Aug	Oct	1973 Jan	May	Aug	1974	1975 Apr
Cambodia	MEDTC set up by U.S.	Lon Nol cancels democratic government due to "emergency"				U.S. Congress votes to block money for Cambodia bombing	Mistake results in bombing of Neak Luong. U.S. bombing ends		Lon Nol flees to Hawaii. U.S. Embassy staff leaves Phnom Penh. Khmer Rouge takes over.
Vietnam			Last U.S. ground troops leave		Peace Agreement signed in Paris			Communists make military gains.	Saigon surrenders.
United States and World Wide				Kissinger says peace is at hand				Nixon resigns. Ford takes over as president.	

	1975 Dec
Cambodia	
Vietnam	
United States and World Wide	King of Laos abdicates. People's Democratic Republic set up.

With the end of American bombing, the tiny Cambodian army was on its own. In the countryside, the Khmer Rouge grew from 3,000 to 60,000 members, some attracted by the figurehead leadership of Norodom Sihanouk, some motivated by fear or hatred of the Americans. The Khmer Rouge now prepared to launch their biggest offensive. In early 1975, Communist forces surrounded the capitol whose population was swollen by more than two million refugees from regions devastated by American bombing and Khmer Rouge brutality. U.S. air lifts of rice, fuel, and ammunition into Phnom Penh were under constant attack and convoys along the Mekong River life-line were completely cut off.

On April 12, 1975, the few remaining Americans were evacuated from Phnom Penh. Within a week the capitol was taken by the Khmer Rouge and its population driven into the countryside. The war had ended. Starvation and wholesale slaughter lay ahead for the once-prosperous and peaceful Cambodians.

Points to Emphasize

- the effects of the presence of foreign troops and supplies in Southeast Asia in the early 1960s
- the consequences of the neutralist solution sought by Prince Norodom Sihanouk of Cambodia
- the reasons behind the secret bombing of Laos and Cambodia by the United States
- the results of the ouster of Prince Sihanouk and the assumption of power by Lon Nol
- the American-South Vietnamese incursion into Cambodia and its effects on Cambodian life
- the reasons for the growth of the Khmer Rouge and the resultant civil war in Cambodia
- the results of the increased American aerial bombardment of Cambodia and of the congressional cutoff of funds for bombing in August 1973
- the explanations for the victory of the Khmer Rouge and the resulting genocide in Cambodia

Glossary of Names and Terms

John Gunther Dean Assistant Economic Commissioner, American Embassy, Saigon, 1953–1956. Political Officer, American Embassy, Laos, 1956–1958. Regional Director, Civilian Operations Revolutionary Development Staff (CORDS) in Central Vietnam, 1970–1972. Deputy Chief of Mission, American Embassy, Laos, 1972–1974. Ambassador to Cambodia, 1974–1975.

Khieu Samphan Received doctorate in economics from the University of Paris. Elected to the Cambodian National Assembly in 1966. Cabinet Minister,

1966–1967. Joined underground, 1967. Minister of Defense and Commander in Chief, Chairman of the State Presidium and Head of State of Democratic Kampuchea, 1976–1978.

Jonathan "Fred" Ladd Colonel in the Special Forces in Cambodia. Political-Military Counselor, U.S. Embassy, Phnom Penh, 1970–1972.

Lon Nol Minister of Defense under Sihanouk. Appointed Prime Minister by Sihanouk in August 1969. Led coup to overthrow the Prince, March 1970. Prime Minister, Commander in Chief, and Head of State of the Khmer Republic, March 1970–April 1, 1975, when he fled to Hawaii.

Pol Pot also known as Saloth Sar. Joined the *maquis*, 1963. Secretary General, Central Committee of the Communist Party of Kampuchea, 1963–1978. Prime Minister of Democratic Kampuchea, 1976–1978.

Lloyd "Mike" Rives *Chargé d'affaires,* U.S. Embassy, Phnom Penh, 1969–1970. Ranking American official in Cambodia at that time.

Norodom Sihanouk Prince of Cambodia, crowned king, 1941. Abdicated 1955 to become Prime Minister until 1960. Chief of State, 1960–1970. Deposed, March 1970. Head of government in exile, Royal Government of National Union of Kampuchea, 1970–1975. Nominal head of state, 1975–1976. Retired, 1976.

Emory Coblentz Swank Counselor of Embassy, Deputy Chief of Mission, American Embassy, Laos, 1964–1967. Minister, American Embassy, Moscow, 1967–1969. Deputy Assistant Secretary of State for European Affairs, 1969–1970. Ambassador to Cambodia, 1970–1973.

Central Office for South Vietnam (COSVN) purportedly the headquarters from which the North Vietnamese and the Vietcong were conducting the war in South Vietnam.

Force Armée Nationale Khmer (FANK) the Cambodian Army.

genocide the deliberate extermination of a race of people.

Kampuchea the new name for Cambodia adopted by the Khmer Rouge after their triumph in 1975.

Khmer Rouge literally, the Red Khmer. Shorthand for Cambodian Communists.

Lam Son 719 code name for the invasion of Laos by the Army of the Republic of Vietnam in February 1971.

maquis resistance fighters. Used by the Khmer Rouge to describe themselves in the days during which they fought Sihanouk and Lon Nol. Term also used by French resistance fighters against the Nazi occupation during World War II.

Military Equipment Delivery Team, Cambodia (MEDTC) set up by the United States in January 1971 to give military assistance to Cambodia.

Pathet Lao literally, the nation of Laos. Shorthand for the Laotian Communists.

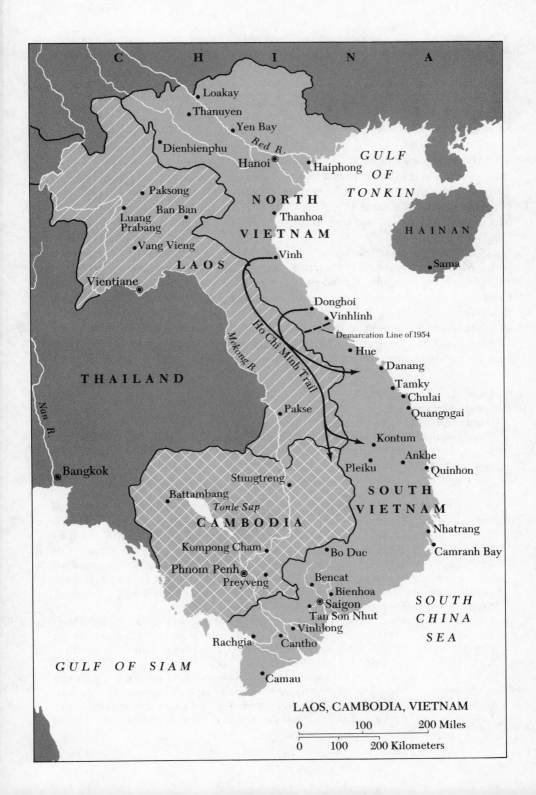

C H I N A

Loakay

Thanuyen

Yen Bay

Red R.

Dienbienphu

Hanoi

Haiphong

GULF
OF
TONKIN

Paksong

NORTH

Ban Ban

Luang
Prabang

Thanhoa

VIETNAM

HAINAN

Vang Vieng

LAOS

Vinh

Sama

Vientiane

Donghoi

Vinhlinh

Mekong R.

Demarcation Line of 1954

Ho Chi Minh Trail

Hue

THAILAND

Danang

Tamky

Chulai

Quangngai

Nan R.

Pakse

Kontum

Ankhe

Bangkok

Pleiku

Quinhon

Stungtreng

SOUTH

Battambang

VIETNAM

Tonle Sap

CAMBODIA

Nhatrang

Kompong Cham

Bo Duc

Camranh Bay

Phnom Penh

Preyveng

Bencat

Bienhoa

Saigon

SOUTH

Tan Son Nhut

CHINA

Rachgia

Vinhlong

SEA

Cantho

GULF OF SIAM

Camau

LAOS, CAMBODIA, VIETNAM

0   100   200 Miles

0   100   200 Kilometers

Documents

Documents 1 and 2

The United States had been active in Laos since the Eisenhower administration and, as in Vietnam, the American commitment had grown during the Kennedy years. Unlike the war in Vietnam, however, the struggle in Laos was not discussed publicly. Not until 1972, ten years after the Geneva Agreements of 1962 had purportedly ended the civil war there, did the American populace find out what was going on.

Document 1, an article written by Senator Stuart Symington, a Democrat from Missouri, indicates the secrecy with which the struggle in Laos was waged. Symington, who served on the Armed Services and Foreign Relations Committees, was upset by the extension of executive power demonstrated by this policy. Document 2, an article which appeared in the *Washington Monthly* in September 1972, looks at the fighting in Laos from the point of view of the Laotian peasants. The author, John Everingham, shared Symington's unhappiness with American policy in Laos but from a more personal perspective.

1   Laos: The Furtive War
Stuart Symington
August 29, 1972

The United States has been involved for more than a decade in an undeclared and largely unnoticed war in northern Laos. From the beginning, and as of today, this war has been characterized by a degree of secrecy never before true of a major American involvement abroad in which many American lives have been lost and billions of American tax dollars spent.

A perversion of the processes of government has been going on, a perversion inimical to our democratic system and to the nation's future.

Who is responsible? The Constitution has been bypassed by a small group of men in various departments of the Executive Branch who, under the direction of four Presidents, initiated and carried out policies without any real Congressional knowledge and thus any true Congressional authorization. Needless to say, these policies were also carried out without the knowledge and approval of the American people, on whose consent our government is supposed to rest.

The war in northern Laos, in which the United States has been a principal party, has been pursued without a declaration of war by the Congress. Moreover, in the past few years, the U.S. government has financed Thai troops fighting in northern Laos despite a clear legislative prohibition against such activity.

It has been possible for successive administrations to ignore the normal processes of government because, until recently, the Executive Branch has succeeded in concealing from the people and the Congress the true facts of our involvement in this little country. As long as Congress and the people did not know what the United

States was doing, as long as there was no public debate on the issues involved, Executive Branch policy-makers were free to do as they pleased without having to explain or justify their actions. John Foster Dulles, Secretary of State under President Eisenhower and an arch proponent of the Domino Theory, considered Laos a key domino that then stood between China and North Vietnam on the Communist side and Thailand, Cambodia, and South Vietnam on the free world side.

By an exchange of diplomatic notes in July 1955, the U.S. and the Royal Government of Laos called for economic cooperation and the defense of the Kingdom of Laos. During the late Fifties, U.S. aid to Laos was running $40-million a year, and 80 per cent of that went to the support of the Royal Laotian Army.

To guide the Lao Army, the State Department organized an incognito American military mission with headquarters in Vientiane. This group was attached to the U.S. Operations Mission, or more popularly, the PEO. Its members were called technicians and wore civilian clothes. At its head was an equally disguised American general. When the general assumed command of this force his name was erased from the list of active American army officers.

Thus for many years this war was a well-kept secret. When John F. Kennedy became President in 1961, there were 700 American military personnel in Laos as well as 500 Soviet operatives whose mission was to provide logistic support to local Communist forces. These forces included at least 10,000 North Vietnamese.

Soon thereafter, the military position of Royal Lao government forces began to deteriorate, whereupon President Kennedy and the Soviet and Chinese leaders entered into negotiations that led to a conference in Geneva. The Geneva Convention recessed when President Kennedy and Chairman Khrushchev met in Vienna and produced a joint statement on Laos in which both parties assured the neutrality and independence of Laos and "recognized the importance of an effective cease fire." In July, what became known as the Geneva agreements of 1962 were signed.

The Geneva Agreements prohibited Laos from joining any military alliances, including SEATO, banned the introduction of foreign military personnel and civilians performing quasi-military functions (with the exception of a small French training mission), and forbade the establishment of any foreign military installation in Laos.

After these agreements were signed, the United States and the Soviet Union withdrew their military personnel. The North Vietnamese, however, failed to withdraw most of their forces and advisers.

In the fall of 1962, because of the continuous presence of the North Vietnamese in Laos, the United States agreed to provide Souvanna Phouma, the Prime Minister and leader of the Neutralist faction in the tripartite government, with limited amounts of military equipment as permitted by the Geneva Agreements.

In 1962 the United States began, through the CIA, to support a force of Lao irregulars on the theory that it would be possible to deny officially that the Geneva Agreements were being violated. The decision to use the CIA as the instrument for waging what became a full-scale war was, in my view, a clear perversion of that agency's intended role.

With the outbreak of serious hostilities in 1963, the United States secretly began to train Lao pilots and ground crews in Thailand. In June 1964, American tactical fighter bombers began, again secretly, to strike targets in northern Laos far from the Ho Chi Minh Trail area in the south.

When these strikes were reported by the press, the Executive Branch clung to the story, even after it was no longer true, that the United States was flying reconnaissance missions at the request of the Lao government and that our planes were authorized to fire back if they were fired upon.

The United States also began to provide greater amounts of war material and other assistance and to transport Lao supplies and military personnel, using the airplanes and the services of Air America and Continental Air.

In 1965, as the war in South Vietnam intensified, American aircraft began to attack North Vietnamese supply routes in the southern panhandle region of Laos. These attacks were not officially acknowledged until 1970.

In 1966, about fifty U.S. Air Force officers and enlisted men, nominally assigned to the air attaché's office, were stationed at Lao air force bases as advisers to the local command.

In 1967, about the same number of U.S. Army personnel were assigned to the Lao regional headquarters for similar duty, and about twenty U.S. Air Force pilots stationed in Laos and others stationed in Thailand began to fly as forward air controllers directing tactical aircraft to their targets.

American air attacks on North Vietnam intensified in 1967 and 1968. Following the bombing halt in North Vietnam in 1968, a large part of the U.S. air effort there was redirected at Laos. During this period, the United States installed several navigational aid facilities in Laos, some manned by American Air Force personnel, and U.S. air strikes in Laos increased. By 1969, more than 100 sorties a day were being flown in northern Laos in addition to those being flown over the Ho Chi Minh Trail area in southern Laos, which was considered to be an adjunct of the battlefield in South Vietnam.

Since the Executive Branch, during the Kennedy, Johnson, and Nixon administrations, obviously intended not to give the Congress all the facts, it was necessary for the Legislative Branch to seek the information on its own. It determined to find out what the United States is doing now in northern Laos and which of its activities are still surrounded by secrecy. It did so by holding hearings and through staff reports of the United States Security Agreements and Commitments Abroad Subcommittee of the Committee on Foreign Relations.

As a result of these hearings and reports originally secret but subsequently made public after they had been sanitized by the Executive Branch, the American people now know that the United States, through Defense Department-funded military assistance, is training, arming, and feeding the Royal Lao Army and Air Force; that the United States, through the CIA, is training, advising, paying for, supporting, and organizing a 30,000-man Lao irregular force; and that the United States is also paying for, training, advising, and supporting a force of Thai troops in Laos, at a cost last year in the neighborhood of $100-million.

· · ·

This war in northern Laos, furtive and secret, will perhaps teach us all a lesson about the dangers of creeping involvements, hidden from the Congress and the public, that make a mockery of our governmental processes. It is a lesson we cannot afford to be taught again.

2   Let Them Eat Bombs
John Everingham
March, 1968

It was a three-day walk to Long Pot village from the nearest motor road. When I first arrived, I saw clusters of thatch and bamboo houses gripping the sides of a man-scraped ridge. The cries of small children scampering on the rust-colored clay mingled with the grunts and squeals of fat pigs rooting in the underbrush. It was a peaceful scene.

I was shown to the home of the district chief. He was a short, vigorous man in his late fifties, with a high forehead and the melancholy dignity of a senior statesman. Gair Su Yang wore loose black pants of traditional Meo cut and a U.S. military fatigue jacket; he wore no shoes.

According to Gair Su Yang, the first helicopter landed in Long Pot in 1960. The pilots were American, but a Meo officer climbed out to talk with him. The officer spoke of an alliance between the Americans and a Meo colonel of the Royal Lao Army named Vang Pao. He said that American officials had made a pact with Vang Pao, promising to build for the Meo their own army and independent state in the mountains. They guaranteed that the tribesmen would not fall under the control of either faction of lowland Lao then girding for civil war. The officer painted a picture of future prosperity for the Meo. All they had to do was become anti-communist, helping the Americans to fight the Pathet Lao revolutionaries controlling sections of Laos' northern provinces.

One of the problems that the people of Long Pot had in accepting the deal was that they were not sure who Vang Pao was. But there was a more basic problem— though Gair Su Yang did not inform me of it until sometime later: "If we joined the alliance, the Pathet Lao would have become our enemy and would have threatened our village. . . . I told him that Long Pot would not join Vang Pao and the Americans." According to Gair Su Yang, the officer then became angry and threatened that Vang Pao and the Americans considered those not friends to be enemies, and "enemy villages would be attacked and captured by Vang Pao's men."

"We couldn't do anything," Gair Su Yang later contended, pointing out that only fear of a helicopter-load of soldiers descending upon Long Pot forced him to accept involvement in the war venture.

By the end of 1960, every man in Long Pot village had received an M-1 rifle or carbine. Many had been flown to Long Cheng for three to four months' training by U.S. soldiers. (These were probably U.S. Special Forces, whom it was common to see in small up-country towns of Laos until 1968–69. Thereafter CIA "civilians" were used to train Vang Pao's army.) Long Pot's men were then given rank in irregular battalion 209.

Long Pot had been militarized in defense of "Meoland" nearly eight years when I first visited. It had not, however, gone to war. The M-1s were used for shooting squirrels and birds. Men, women, and children slashed, burned, and planted to reap harvests of rice, corn, and, of course, the opium poppy. Opium was the main cash crop, which from 1960 onwards had been bought by Meo soldiers and transported both by pony caravan and American-piloted Air America helicopters from Long Cheng.

. . .

December, 1971

It was mid-December, Meo Lunar New Year, when I last saw Gair Su Yang in Long Pot. He apologized that the festivities would not be as gay as in past years. Many families could not even offer a pig for sacrifice and feasting. In his 60 years he could not remember such poverty in the village. Nevertheless, unmarried girls adorned themselves with richly colored tunics and trousers, and with finely crafted silver rings around their necks. Atop a grassy hillock they tossed ceremonial cloth balls with boys from distant villages, part of the mass courtship game of swapping partners, compliments, and songs.

Gair Su Yang was more apprehensive than ever. The rains were over and the tracks dry. It was the time of the year for Pathet Lao guerrillas to attack the Vang Pao army outposts. Helicopters had recently landed 30 irregulars and 30 Royal Lao army soldiers in Long Pot. They had erected fortifications 400 yards outside the village limits. "Now," said Gair Su Yang, "the Pathet Lao won't be able to just walk into the village and take it. They'll have to clear out the soldiers first. And then the planes will bomb us." Rice denial, he said, was only one means, and not the most effective, that the Americans had to push his people to fight the Pathet Lao. The thought of bombs raining on a man's family would keep him fighting when nothing else would. For any village, Gair Su Yang said, falling behind Pathet Lao lines would mean devastation from the sky.

"To keep away the bombs we must keep away the Pathet Lao. And that's what the Americans want." But, said Gair Su Yang, if the Pathet Lao were to come to his village the people would not fight. "The villagers at Phou Miang fought to keep the Pathet Lao away. They lost; the planes leveled their village anyway. We won't fight. We will slip out the back way and go to the refugee camps."

February, 1972

I made my way by motorboat and sampan into Pak Sah village 17 miles southeast of the royal capital, Luang Prabang. Like Long Pot, Pak Sah was perched on the brink of the free-fire zone blanketing Pathet Lao territory; I had come to get photographs of its predicament. Five minutes' walk outside Pak Sah I found myself face to face with two Pathet Lao soldiers. Arrested and then marched to the east, I spent the next 29 days in "liberated territory." For the first four days I was held at gunpoint, kept in jail, and branded a "professional bomb dropper." Eventually I was sent to a small, jungle camp 20 miles west of the Plain of Jars and held for two weeks while my story and credentials were checked. The camp was near Muong Soui, the destination of the boy soldiers I had watched helicoptered out of Long Pot in 1970.

"Every village north of here has been bombed," Gair Su Yang had told me, and it seemed true. During my 29 days with the Pathet Lao I saw not a single village standing in the open. All human activity had gone underground or into the security of the forest. Though a large portion of the province had chosen to leave for the U.S.-run refugee camps, many had opted to remain. I saw nine different communities making a living in the shelter of the deep jungle. People from one village, Par Kheng, were living in caves.

When I was still thought to be a pilot, angry villagers yelled at me that American and Royal Lao air force bombers had been dropping explosives on them since 1967. Every day, T-28 bombers dumped aluminum canisters filled with anti-personnel bomblets into the protective canopy of vegetation. The six-foot containers would open as they fell and spew out more than 100 grenade-sized ball-bearing filled bomblets which spread over a sizeable area. Any person outside when the bomblet went off had little chance of escaping alive. The T-28s would saturate as much forest as possible with their six-canister loads and return to home base for more. Once an attack by three T-28s found the camp at which I was being held. Soldiers, civilians, and I jammed our bodies into one of the ever-present tunnel shelters and escaped with our lives.

I was finally sent back on the same route along which I had been marched into the "liberated zone." The Pathet Lao government was satisfied that I probably was a photo-journalist. I entered Luang Prabang with a personal appreciation of the terror in Gair Su Yang's voice as he tried to describe the zone of destruction he feared would envelop Long Pot.

May, 1972

"Nobody lives there," said the Royal Lao soldiers as I looked eastward from Route 13 towards Long Pot District. They found it queer that I should even stop and ask about Long Pot. . . .

I took my chances, striking off on one of the approaches I knew best. With the exception of nearly stepping on a mine on my return journey (fortunately it had been half-unearthed by the spring rains), I made the trip without trouble. What I found, however, more than matched the worst predictions and reports of Long Pot's fate. I wandered alone over the scorched hilltop where Gair Su Yang's home had stood. Ash and a few charred poles, a few pieces of metal plate and utensils were all that was left.

A single house somehow remained erect on the most prominent hill. It stood like a tombstone in memory of Long Pot's death, though with most of its walls blown away. It hardly promised to remain long.

The village's ruins had been deserted more than four months, but in the one remaining house I found Gair Su Yang's wife and his second son, Chao Cho. They had returned to the village with about 10 others to search for lost cattle and buffalo. Any animals they found would be taken south to the refugee camps, their new homes. Chao Cho told of the bombing of Long Pot. The Pathet Lao offensive had swept south, by-passing the village to get at the military garrison from Long Cheng. The Pathet Lao had the 30 Long Cheng irregulars and 30 Royal Lao regulars on the run within an hour. Caught behind Pathet Lao lines and fearful of the bombing that was sure to come, Long Pot's families fled to the forest.

Old Var Lur, the village's most respected medium, whom I had often photographed during his incantations, had returned from the forest late one day to feed the pigs and chickens. His wife and a Hill Lao man were with him. While they were in the village a T-28 spotted them, attacked, and dropped cluster bombs (CBUs). All three were killed trying to get inside Var Lur's house. The village was finished off with napalm, fragmentation bombs, and more CBUs the following few days, Chao Cho said.

Chao Cho and his friends said that most of the bombs were dropped by the propeller-driven T-28s, but, they said, jets bombed on some days, and the big crater in the middle of one cluster of Long Pot's houses was from a bomb released by a jet.

In Ban Nam Phak, a Hill Lao village and the biggest settlement in the district, 14 people had been killed by CBUs, according to Chao Cho. That had been the first village bombed, apparently before the inhabitants had had time to evacuate. After that, Chao Cho, said, the whole of Ban Nam Phak fled into the forest and joined the Pathet Lao. The village itself had subsequently been razed clean.

According to Chao Cho, the people of Long Pot never saw the Pathet Lao, who had passed the village and continued south in pursuit of the fleeing soldiers from Long Cheng. Nobody had heard of any Pathet Lao being killed by the bombing.

In five days I traveled to 10 of 11 villages in the district. All had been destroyed. A few people at Long Pot village assured me that the 11th had also been razed. Tong Ouie, whose headman had been so enraged at the kidnap-drafting of his men, was in cinders. At Ban Tam Geo, charred two-by-fours stood at attention before a dozen large craters.

People from two of the 11 villages had fled north into Pathet Lao territory.

Those from the nine others, including Gair Su Yang and his people, had fled south to the refugee centers. They would only come back to live in Long Pot, said Chao Cho, if the war finished and there were no more planes dropping bombs. Until then, they would live in refugee camps with the rest of the Meo people, who, according to the official American explanation, "are denied their homes by the presence of the Pathet Lao."

Document 3

Until the 1970s, when press criticism of the Central Intelligence Agency became common, the majority of articles on the CIA praised its accomplishments. This article, by I. F. Stone, was an early exception. Written in December 1963 soon after the assassinations of President Diem in South Vietnam and President Kennedy in the United States, Stone's concern with the role of the CIA "as a proper agency of government" was one which many other observers later echoed.

When this article was written, the American commitment to South Vietnam was still advisory, and Cambodia had just refused to accept economic and military aid from the United States. Cambodia's decision angered many Americans who believed that neutrality was impossible in the modern world. They wanted Prince Sihanouk to take sides in the struggles between the free world and Communism and saw all disagreements between and within nations in the context of that global competition.

3   A Crisis and a Turning Point Approaches in Vietnam
I. F. Stone
December 23, 1963
The war in Vietnam is being lost. Only a few weeks ago, Secretary McNamara and General Taylor reported on their return from Saigon that "the major part" of our military role there could be "completed by the end of 1965." Now Hanson W. Baldwin, our most respected military expert, writes *(New York Times,* Dec. 7) that "unless public support in the U.S. and among its allies can be maintained *during years of frustration,* there is no possibility of victory." The italics are ours. President Johnson at his first meeting with the press that same day announced that Secretary McNamara is going back to Vietnam on another tour of inspection. It begins to look as if the Secretary of Defense has become a commuter between Washington and Saigon.

A Shift in U. S. Policy
It is clear that we are heading for a new crisis in South Vietnam; rebel attacks are mounting in size and frequency; the loss of arms to them is growing. At the same time Cambodia has formally asked Britain and the Soviet Union as co-chairmen of the 1954 Geneva Conference on Indochina to reconvene it. In August of last year, when Cambodia asked the Geneva conferees to reassemble and guarantee its neutrality, President Kennedy shied away from the idea. But this time the attitude of the American government seems to have changed. When the Foreign Minister of Cambodia was here to attend the President's funeral, he spoke with Under Secretary of State Harriman and was assured that we would not place obstacles in the way of

reconvening the conference for this purpose. The first Geneva conference met, it will be recalled, to end the Korean War, and then went on to end the first Indochinese War as well. The new session could become a vehicle for the peaceful ending of the war in South Vietnam too. We are approaching a turning point, either to risk widening the conflict by intervening with our own combat troops, or settling the war at the conference table.

Prince Sihanouk of Cambodia indicated these wider possibilities when he called for an independent South Vietnam linked in a neutral confederation with Cambodia. "The reunification of Vietnam is the end to be attained but it is for the moment premature if not impossible, as responsible leaders of North Vietnam have admitted to me," said Prince Sihanouk (Agence France-Press, *Le Monde*, Dec. 4), adding that he thought "the Communist camp would content itself with a South Vietnam completely neutral as is Cambodia." An article in the *Peking Review* (Nov. 22) confirms this view. China would like new trade ties with the West to replace the broken trade ties with the Soviet Union. Peace in South Vietnam would remove a major obstacle to such relations. In South Vietnam itself the National Liberation Front has made clear in a clandestine interview (*Le Monde*, Aug. 24) that it did not wish to "exchange one dictatorship for another." A democratic South Vietnam, an honorable and face-saving peace are possible.

Unfortunately the U.S. public has been conditioned to such oversimplified and fallacious views on Asian foreign policy as to make negotiation difficult. The Cambodian Foreign Minister had a friendly talk with the new President, but if Mr. Johnson were a combination of Machiavelli and King Solomon he would still have trouble with this one. Three ideas widely held in this country are obstacles to a sensible settlement. One is that problems arising in the areas bordering China can be settled without taking its views into account. We had to negotiate with China to end the Korean war and we will have to sit down at Geneva with China again to end the Vietnamese war. The second is that neutralism is a menace second only to Communism, though the only one of the three Indochinese states which is stable today, free from guerrilla war and any internal Communist threat is neutralist Cambodia.

The third obstacle to peace is public acceptance of the CIA as a proper agency of government. The first thing to be said of the CIA is that in Southeast Asia, at least, it has proven itself politically incompetent. Its favorite Indochinese proteges, Diem in South Vietnam and Phoumi Nosavan in Laos, have been utterly discredited; the latter only opened the door to Communism, the former had to be "removed" when his failure and instability became too notorious. The one Indochinese ruler the CIA has always regarded with disfavor is the only one who has succeeded. Cambodia under Sihanouk's leadership, Majority Leader Mansfield told the Senate the other day (Nov. 20), "has developed within its borders a remarkable degree of progress and political cohesion and stability and a level of human freedom and political participation in the life of the nation which exceeds most if not all of the other nations of southeast Asia." Yet as the *Washington Post* said in a recent editorial (Nov. 14), the CIA "has for a long time tended to consider the non-aligned Sihanouk as a pernicious fellow."

Does The Right Hand Know?

The second thing to be said of the CIA is that the very existence of a secret agency which boasts of "cloak and dagger" activities in countries with which we are at peace creates suspicions which poison our foreign relations. Both President Johnson and Secretary Harriman denied to the Cambodian Foreign Minister that the CIA had been engaged in plots against its government. But no one can be sure that the right hand of our government really knows what this left hand is doing.

Cambodia's first charges of a CIA plot were made in 1959 when it expelled Victor Matsui, an official of the U.S. Embassy for activities incompatible with diplomacy; Cambodia claimed that rebel groups had been given radio transmitters with which they kept in touch with the U.S. Embassy. The next incident was the capture of an anti-Sihanouk emissary with 270 kilograms of pure gold for the rebels; he confessed that he had been in contact with CIA agents not only in Cambodia but in Washington. Later an elaborate "gift" was presented at the Royal Palace and turned out to be an ingenious bomb intended to kill the King and Queen; three members of the Court lost their lives when it exploded. It had come by ship from Vietnam and its intricacy led the Cambodians to suspect skilled CIA hands at work. Then they learned that the secret rebel radio was operating from a house in Saigon under the very nose of U.S. and Vietnamese authorities, and felt this could not happen without their connivance. Another assassination attempt came last spring, when the President of Communist China visited Cambodia. Conspirators were caught in an attempt to mine the road over which he would pass with Prince Sihanouk on his way from the airport. The latest incident was the confession of a rebel infiltrator from South Vietnam that anti-Sihanouk forces worked out of strategic hamlets near the Cambodian border in close liaison with both Vietnamese and U.S. military authorities. These are the incidents which led Prince Sihanouk to break off American aid, fearing that aid agencies were a means by which hostile American agents penetrated his country.

Again I ask—in the wake of our own President's assassination—how long are we going to maintain what other nations consider an assassination agency of our own?

Document 4

William Beecher reported in the *New York Times* on May 9, 1969, that American bombers had attacked North Vietnamese and Vietcong supply bases in Cambodia. Far from causing a nationwide furor, the report made little impression on the public. It did, however, make an impact on President Nixon.

The bombing of Cambodia was top-secret. Because the Nixon administration had taken careful steps to make sure that the public was not informed of this escalation of the war, Beecher's article infuriated the president. As a result, people whom the president and his advisors considered likely to have leaked the story to the press later found that their phones were tapped. The unauthorized use of listening devices to discover the source of William Beecher's information marked the beginning of the unlawful activities of the Nixon administration—the road that would lead to the Watergate burglary.

4 Raids in Cambodia by U.S. Unprotested
William Beecher
May 9, 1969
Washington, May 8—American B-52 bombers in recent weeks have raided several Vietcong and North Vietnamese supply dumps and base camps in Cambodia for the

first time, according to Nixon Administration sources, but Cambodia has not made any protest.

In fact, Cambodian authorities have increasingly been cooperating with American and South Vietnamese military men at the border, often giving them information on Vietcong and North Vietnamese movements into South Vietnam.

Information from knowledgeable sources indicates that three principal factors underlie the air strikes just inside the Cambodian border, west and northwest of Saigon:

Rising concern by military men that most of the rockets and other heavy weapons and ammunition being used by North Vietnamese and Vietcong forces in the southern half of South Vietnam now come by sea to Cambodia and never have to run any sort of bombing gantlet before they enter South Vietnam.

A desire by high Washington officials to signal Hanoi that the Nixon Administration, while pressing for peace in Paris, is willing to take some military risks avoided by the previous Administration.

Apparent increasing worry on the part of Prince Norodom Sihanouk, Cambodia's Chief of State, that the North Vietnamese and Vietcong now effectively control several of Cambodia's northern provinces and that he lacks sufficient power to disrupt or dislodge them.

No Desire to Extend War

Officials say that there is no Administration interest at this time in extending the ground war into Cambodia, or Laos either.

Discussing the on-again, off-again statements of Prince Sihanouk on the re-establishment of relations with the United States, one official said: "Although the Prince has made various statements in recent speeches questioning the sincerity of our recognition of his frontiers, he has made none of these protestations to us. It may be that he's simply demonstrating to his people that any new deal he makes will be on his own terms."

The Prince has made United States recognition of Cambodia's "present frontiers" a condition for the re-establishment of relations.

Some American ground commanders have long urged that battalion-size forces occasionally be allowed to sweep into sanctuaries in Laos and Cambodia to follow up air strikes. This plea has been rejected by President Nixon as it was by President Johnson.

But sources here say that to assure that accurate information can be obtained to provide "lucrative" targets for the bombers, small teams of men are permitted to slip across both the Cambodian and Laotian borders to locate enemy concentrations of men and matériel.

Coincided With Other Raids

The sources report, for instance, that to try to reduce losses in B-52 raids the enemy has dug in and dispersed supply caches in such a way that it is unlikely that all supplies in any one area would be hit by the linear pattern of bombs dropped by a B-52. Each plane, which normally carries about 30 tons of bombs, lays out a pattern that is 1,000 feet wide and 4 miles long.

The raids into Cambodia, the sources say, coincided with heavy B-52 raids on the Vietnamese side of the border 50 to 75 miles northwest of Saigon.

Over the last two weeks more than 5,000 tons of bombs have been dropped by B-52's in this area, according to one estimate.

There are reported to be three enemy divisions operating back and forth across the border in this area: the First and Seventh North Vietnamese Divisions and the Ninth Vietcong Division. Another division, the Fifth Vietcong, is now operating south and southeast of Saigon.

The decision to demonstrate to Hanoi that the Nixon Administration is different and "tougher" than the previous Administration was reached in January, well-placed sources say, as part of a strategy for ending the war.

Hints by Sihanouk Noted

Limited, selective bombing strikes into Cambodia, the sources say, were considered feasible because Prince Sihanouk had dropped hints that he would not oppose such actions and because they seemed to offer relatively little risk of either expanding the war or disrupting the Paris peace talks.

In the past, American and South Vietnamese forces had occasionally fired across the border and even called in fighters or helicopter gunships to counter fire they received from enemy units there. But there had been no bombing of supply stockpiles or base camps in Cambodia, military men say.

Over the last several weeks the military sources say, Cambodian Army officers in border posts have held secret meetings with Americans and South Vietnamese to "coordinate" some actions against enemy forces. . . .

Documents 5 and 6

On April 30, 1970, President Nixon told the nation that he had ordered an "incursion" into Cambodia. The president's speech, reprinted as Document 5, justified the widening of the war as a way to protect American soldiers still in Vietnam and as a major step toward ending the fighting. The address was significant because Nixon revealed both his vision of America's role in the world and his reasons for taking a step that would be criticized.

The resulting protests went beyond any that had occurred before. When four students at Kent State University in Ohio were killed by National Guardsmen on campus, unrest at home redoubled.

Although the president's popularity was rocked by these events, and although he was vehemently criticized by many opponents in the days after his speech, his supporters rallied around him. In its weekly publication, the Republican National Committee ran a letter from an entertainer who was in Vietnam at the time of the Cambodian invasion (Document 6). Johny Grant, of Los Angeles Station KTLA, argued that the Cambodian incursion raised the morale of the American soldiers directly involved in the struggle, and that critics of the president's policy were endangering the lives of American fighting men. Grant's note was printed under the title "A Significant Letter from Vietnam."

5 Address by the President on the Situation in Southeast Asia
Richard M. Nixon
April 30, 1970
Ten days ago, in my report to the Nation on Vietnam, I announced a decision to withdraw an additional one hundred and fifty thousand American troops over the

next year. I said then I was making that decision despite our concern over increased enemy activity in Laos, in Cambodia, and in South Vietnam.

At that time, I warned that if I concluded that increased enemy activity in any of these areas endangered the lives of Americans remaining in Vietnam, I would not hesitate to take strong and effective measures to deal with that situation.

Despite that warning, North Vietnam has increased its military aggression in all three areas—particularly in Cambodia.

After full consultation with the National Security Council, Ambassador Bunker, General Abrams and my other advisers, I have concluded that the actions of the enemy in the last ten days clearly endanger the lives of Americans who are in Vietnam now and would constitute an unacceptable risk to those who will be there after our withdrawal of 150,000.

To protect our men who are in Vietnam and to guarantee the continued success of our withdrawal and Vietnamization programs, I have concluded the time has come for action.

Tonight, I shall describe the actions of the enemy, the actions I have ordered to deal with that situation, and the reasons for my decision.

Cambodia, a small country of seven million people has been a neutral nation since the Geneva Agreement of 1954—an agreement signed by the Government of North Vietnam.

American policy since then has been to scrupulously respect the neutrality of the Cambodian people. We have maintained a skeleton diplomatic mission of fewer than fifteen in Cambodia's capital since last August. For the previous four years—from 1965–1969, we did not have any diplomatic mission whatever. For the past five years, we have provided no military assistance and no economic assistance whatever to Cambodia.

North Vietnam, however, has not respected that neutrality.

For the past five years—as indicated on this map—North Vietnam has occupied military sanctuaries all along the Cambodian frontier with South Vietnam. Some of these extend up to 20 miles into Cambodia. They are used for hit-and-run attacks on American and South Vietnamese forces in South Vietnam.

These Communist occupied territories contain major base camps, training sites, logistics facilities, weapons and ammunition factories, air strips and prisoner of war compounds.

For five years, neither the United States nor South Vietnam moved against those enemy sanctuaries because we did not wish to violate the territory of a neutral nation. Even after the Vietnamese Communists began to expand these sanctuaries four weeks ago, we counselled patience to our South Vietnamese allies and imposed restraints on our commanders.

In contrast to our policy, the enemy in the past two weeks has stepped up his guerrilla actions and he is concentrating his main forces in the sanctuaries where they are building up to launch massive attacks on our forces and those of South Vietnam.

North Vietnam in the last two weeks has stripped away all pretense of respecting the sovereignty or neutrality of Cambodia. Thousands of their soldiers are invading the country from the sanctuaries; they are encircling the Capital of Phnom Penh. Cambodia has sent out a call to the United States and a number of other nations for assistance.

If this effort succeeds, Cambodia would become a vast enemy staging area and springboard for attacks on South Vietnam along 600 miles of frontier—and a refuge where enemy troops could return from combat without fear of retaliation.

North Vietnamese men and supplies could then be poured into that country, jeopardizing not only the lives of our own men but the people of South Vietnam as well.

Confronted with this situation, we have three options.

First, we can do nothing. The ultimate result of that course of action is clear. Unless we indulge in wishful thinking, the Americans remaining in Vietnam after our next withdrawal would be gravely threatened.

Our second option is to provide massive military assistance to Cambodia. Unfortunately, while we deeply sympathize with the plight of seven million Cambodians whose country is being invaded, massive amounts of military assistance could not be rapidly and effectively utilized by the small Cambodian Army against the immediate threat. With other nations, we shall do our best to provide the small arms and other equipment which the Cambodian Army needs and can use now for its defense. The aid we will provide will be limited to the purpose of enabling Cambodia to defend its neutrality—not for the purpose of making it an active belligerent on one side or the other.

Our third choice is to go to the heart of the trouble. That means cleaning out major North Vietnamese and Viet Cong occupied sanctuaries which serve as bases for attacks on both Cambodia and American and South Vietnamese forces in South Vietnam. Some of these are as close to Saigon as Baltimore is to Washington.

This is my decision:

In cooperation with the armed forces of South Vietnam, attacks are being launched this week to clean out major enemy sanctuaries on the Cambodian-Vietnam border.

A major responsibility for the ground operations is being assumed by South Vietnamese forces. For example, the attacks in several areas including the Parrot's Beak are exclusively South Vietnamese ground operations under South Vietnamese command with the United States providing air and logistical support.

There is one area, however, where I have concluded that a combined American and South Vietnamese operation is necessary. Tonight, American and South Vietnamese units will attack the headquarters for the entire Communist military operation in South Vietnam. This key control center has been occupied by the North Vietnamese and Viet Cong for years in blatant violation of Cambodia's neutrality.

This is not an invasion of Cambodia. The areas in which these attacks will be launched are completely occupied and controlled by North Vietnamese forces. Our purpose is not to occupy the areas. Once enemy forces are driven out of these sanctuaries and their military supplies destroyed, we will withdraw.

These actions are in no way directed at the security interests of any nation. Any government that chooses to use these actions as a pretext for harming relations with the United States will be doing so on its own responsibility and at its own initiative and we will draw the appropriate conclusions.

A majority of the American people are for the withdrawal of our forces from Vietnam. The action I have taken tonight is indispensable for the continuing success of that withdrawal program.

A majority of the American people want to end this war rather than have it drag on interminably. The action I take tonight will serve that purpose.

A majority of the American people want to keep the casualties of our brave men in Vietnam at an absolute minimum. The action I take tonight is essential if we are to accomplish that goal.

We take this action not for the purpose of expanding the war into Cambodia but for the purpose of ending the war in Vietnam and winning the just peace we all desire. We have made and will continue to make every possible effort to end this war through negotiation at the conference table rather than through more fighting on the battlefield.

Let us look at the record. We have stopped the bombing of North Vietnam. We have cut air operations by over twenty percent. We have announced the withdrawal of over 250,000 of our troops. We have offered to withdraw all of our men if they withdraw theirs. We have offered to negotiate all issues with only one condition—that the future of South Vietnam be determined not by North Vietnam, not by the United States, but by the people of South Vietnam themselves.

Their answer has been intransigence at the conference table, belligerence in Hanoi, massive military aggression in Laos and Cambodia and stepped-up attacks in South Vietnam, designed to increase American casualties.

This attitude has become intolerable. We will not react to this threat to American lives merely by plaintive diplomatic protests. If we did, the credibility of the United States would be destroyed in every area of the world where only the power of the United States deters aggression.

Tonight, I again warn the North Vietnamese that if they continue to escalate the fighting when the United States is withdrawing its forces I shall meet my responsibility as Commander-in-Chief of our Armed Forces to take the action I consider necessary to defend the security of our American men.

This action puts the leaders of North Vietnam on notice that we will be patient in working for peace, we will be conciliatory at the conference table, but, we will not be humiliated. We will not be defeated. We will not allow American men by the thousands to be killed by an enemy from privileged sanctuaries.

The time came long ago to end this war through peaceful negotiations. We stand ready for those negotiations. We have made major efforts, many of which must remain secret. All the offers and approaches made previously remain on the conference table whenever Hanoi is ready to negotiate seriously.

But if the enemy response to our most conciliatory offers for peaceful negotiation continues to be to increase its attacks and humiliate and defeat us we shall react accordingly.

We live in an age of anarchy both abroad and at home. We see mindless attacks on all the great institutions which have been created by free civilizations in the last five hundred years. Here in the United States, great universities are being systematically destroyed. Small nations all over the world find themselves under attack from within and from without.

If when the chips are down the U.S. acts like a pitiful helpless giant, the forces of totalitarianism and anarchy will threaten free nations and free institutions throughout the world.

It is not our power but our will and character that is being tested tonight. The question all Americans must ask and answer tonight is this: Does the richest and strongest nation in the history of the world have the character to meet a direct challenge by a group which rejects every effort to win a just peace, ignores our warning, tramples on solemn agreements, violates the neutrality of an unarmed people, and uses our prisoners as hostages?

If we failed to meet this challenge all other nations will be on notice that despite its overwhelming power the United States, when a real crisis comes, will be found wanting.

My fellow Americans: During my campaign for the Presidency, I pledged to bring Americans home from Vietnam. They are coming home.

I promised to end the war. I shall keep that promise.

I promised to win a just peace. I shall keep that promise.

We shall avoid a wider war. But we are also determined to put an end to this war.

In this room, Woodrow Wilson made the great decisions which led to victory in World War I. Franklin Roosevelt made the decisions which led to our victory in World War II. Dwight D. Eisenhower made decisions which ended the war in Korea and avoided war in the Middle East. John F. Kennedy, in his finest hour, made the great decision which removed Soviet nuclear missiles from Cuba and the Western Hemisphere.

The decision I have announced tonight is not of the same magnitude. Between those decisions and this decision, however, there is a difference that is very fundamental. In those decisions, the American people were not assailed by counsels of doubt and defeat from some of the most widely known opinion leaders of the nation.

A Republican Senator has said that this action means my party has lost all chance of winning the November elections. Others are saying today that this move against the enemy sanctuaries will make me a one-term President.

No one is more aware than I am of the political consequences of the action I have taken. It is tempting to take the easy political path: (1) To blame this war on previous Administrations and to bring all of our men home immediately regardless of the consequences; even though that would mean defeat for the United States; (2) To desert 18 million South Vietnamese people, who have put their trust in us and to expose them to the same slaughter and savagery which the leaders of North Vietnam inflicted on hundreds of thousands of North Vietnamese who chose freedom when the Communists took over North Vietnam; (3) To get peace at any price now even though I know that a peace of humiliation for the United States will lead to a bigger war or surrender later.

But I have rejected all political considerations in making this decision.

Whether my party gains in November is nothing compared to the lives of 400 thousand brave Americans fighting for our country and for the cause of peace and freedom in Vietnam. Whether I may be a one-term President is insignificant compared to whether by our failure to act in this crisis the United States proves itself to be unworthy to lead the forces of freedom in this critical period. I would rather be a one-term President than to be a two-term President at the cost of seeing America become a second rate power and see this nation accept the first defeat in its proud 190-year history.

I realize that in this war there are honest and deep differences about whether we should have ever become involved in Vietnam. There are differences as to how the war should be conducted. But the decision I announce tonight transcends those differences.

For the lives of American men are involved. The opportunity for 150,000 American men to come home over the next twelve months is involved. The future of 18 million in South Vietnam and seven million people in Cambodia is involved. The possibility of winning a just peace in Vietnam and in the Pacific is at stake.

It is customary in a speech from the White House to ask support for the President of the United States. Tonight, what I ask for is more important. I ask for support of our brave men fighting tonight half-way around the world—not for territory—not for glory—but so that their younger brothers and their sons and your sons will be able to live in peace and freedom.

6   A Significant Letter from Vietnam
Johny Grant
May 7, 1970
A short note from a touring gypsy in Vietnam.

In view of the bitter attacks on the President in recent days by the public and the press, I thought you might pass on a few words of support and encouragement.

The young men who are fighting the war and stand to lose the most—their lives—are solidly behind the President's decision to go into the Vietcong sanctuary in Cambodia. Morale here was good but went to an all time high when the announcement was made.

They feel they now have an even chance at fighting Charlie at his own game.

They also feel that in the end lives will be saved and a quicker victory will be achieved on the battlefield or at the peace talks. They honestly feel they can win this thing and now have the support to do it.

They are greatly disappointed in the reaction of the back home press, public and some of the politicians. As one young GI put it, "Fullbright must be worth 3 Divisions to the enemy." It's really hard for a young soldier to understand this kind of reaction to a White House announcement of more support for him and his buddies. These are outstanding young men and they deserve all the help and encouragement we can give them.

This letter was prompted by a young GI at the 3rd Field Hospital this morning when he said, "For God's sake let the President know somebody's behind him—us."

As I have toured the area the past few days *many* others have expressed the same feelings. I have not found one man against the Cambodian move.

I promised the troops I would pass their support on to the President and figured this would be the fastest way.

Will be back in the states on the 16th or 17th and will do all I can to help the situation.

Regards to all.

Sincerely
Johny Grant

PS The men really love and respect General Abrams. They would walk to Cambodia if he asked them to.

Document 7

American policies in Southeast Asia during the sixties and seventies were quite controversial, and the fact that some of these policies were kept secret from the American public later caused a great deal of acrimonious debate. Congress, which had not questioned administration policies during the early days of the Vietnam War, after the war had ended demanded to know the facts.

One area of congressional investigation was the extension of the Vietnam War into Cambodia. Although Congress had never formally declared war in

Vietnam, the Gulf of Tonkin Resolution had been viewed as roughly equivalent to such a declaration. No such permission had been given regarding Cambodia or Laos, and the Department of Defense Report of September 10, 1973 (Document 7) indicates the extent to which Americans had not been told the truth about operations in Southeast Asia. The report shows how accounts of these operations were falsified. For example, the secrecy surrounding Operation MENU demonstrated the high regard in which the government held that program and its fear that public exposure would enflame the controversy over the Vietnam War.

7 Report on Selected Air and Ground Operations in Cambodia and Laos
Department of Defense
September 10, 1973
Menu Operations
General:
   On March 18, 1969, B-52s were used for the first time against Viet Cong and North Vietnamese Army elements located in Cambodian sanctuaries adjacent to the South Vietnamese border. The name MENU was given this operation, and it continued through May 26, 1970. The purpose of MENU was to protect American lives during the preparation for and actual withdrawal of U.S. military personnel from Southeast Asia by pre-empting imminent enemy offensive actions from the Cambodian sanctuaries into South Vietnam and against U.S. servicemen and women.
   Due to the unusual and sensitive diplomatic situation between the Cambodian government and the governments of the United States and South Vietnam, information on MENU was held very closely. Knowledge of the operation was limited to those personnel essential to its successful administration and execution. The special security or "back" channel communication system for insuring optimum security in highly sensitive matters was used for TOP SECRET sensitive aspects of MENU. Less highly classified channels were used to handle the routine mission requests and authorizations.
   The following is a summary of MENU methodology adopted and utilized by field units and in the military chain of command:
   A B-52 strike on a target in South Vietnam would be requested through normal communication and command channels.
   Through the special security communication and command channel, a strike on the MENU (Cambodian) target nearest a requested target in South Vietnam would be requested.
   Upon approval, the mission would be flown in such a way that the MENU aircraft on its final run would pass over or near the target in South Vietnam and release its bombs on the enemy in the MENU sanctuary target area.
   On return of the aircraft to its base, routine reports on the mission would be filed in normal communication channels which did not reveal the MENU aspect of the mission.
   Separate reports were provided by "back" channel on the MENU aspect.

   All MENU sorties occurred at night and were directed by ground control radar sites. These radar sites were used to direct aircraft throughout the Southeast Asia conflict, and their operation permitted extremely accurate strikes against the enemy. The name for this ground-directed bombing operation was COMBAT SKYSPOT.

In MENU operations, the radar site crews received instructions that resulted in the aircraft releasing their bombs on the MENU targets rather than on the targets in South Vietnam.

In their pre-take off mission preparation, all the B-52 crews were briefed on the South Vietnamese targets. Only the pilots and navigators of the aircraft to be directed to MENU targets were briefed to react to all directions for bomb release from the ground control radar sites. This special guidance to MENU pilots and navigators was necessary since the entire crew was briefed routinely, as they normally had been throughout the war, to make every effort not to bomb in Cambodia. The pilots and navigators, while not controlling the exact release point of their bombs, had indications from on-board radar and navigation instruments of their position. Other crew members had no indication that their aircraft was directed on other than the target in South Vietnam which had been covered in their routine briefing since the MENU target was in close proximity to and in alignment with the routine target. . . .

MENU mission reports were carried in both the routine and special security communications channels depending on their degree of security sensitivity. Reports on the sensitive aspects, which were sent through the special security channel, were available only to those in the command and control chain who had a "need-to-know". Reports based on the routine requests and containing routine data were forwarded via routine channels, so that for administrative and logistical purposes, MENU sortie information blended into other less highly classified information in the data base. MENU sorties thus properly were included in overall Southeast Asia statistical totals but not identified with Cambodia in any but the special security channels. When the routine data base was subsequently utilized in providing Congress a country-by-country breakout of sorties—first in classified and then in unclassified form—the MENU sorties were reflected in South Vietnam as they were routinely carried in that data base, rather than in Cambodia as they were carried in the closely held MENU records.

This error was subsequently discovered, corrected and apologized for.

. . .

Statistics:

During the MENU operation, six enemy base sanctuary areas along the South Vietnam/Cambodian border were struck. These base areas were named: BREAKFAST, DINNER, DESSERT, SNACK, SUPPER and LUNCH.

As the combat action developed during the ground operations in Cambodia in early May and June 1970, the requirement for special security procedures was lifted. The last MENU strike to use special procedures in South Vietnam was on May 26, 1970. The sorties and total tonnage of munitions dropped from March 18, 1969 to May 26, 1970, during MENU were as follows:

Base Area	Sorties	Tons
350 (DESSERT)	706	20,157
351 (SNACK)	885	25,336
352 (DINNER)	817	23,391
353 (BREAKFAST)	228	6,529
609 (LUNCH)	992	26,630
704 (SUPPER)	247	6,780
TOTALS	3,875	108,823

Documents 8, 9, and 10

Many Americans lost interest in Southeast Asia after the American troops and prisoners of war returned. But the United States government continued to support President Thieu of South Vietnam and President Lon Nol of Cambodia with economic and military aid. The wars in Vietnam and Cambodia were not yet over.

Indeed, in Cambodia the fighting between Lon Nol's government and the Khmer Rouge was particularly heated. After Congress cut off the use of American bombers in the summer of 1973, Cambodia's army had to fight alone. And by the spring of 1975, Lon Nol was in dire straits. As the Khmer Rouge gained territory and seemed poised on the brink of victory, President Gerald Ford tried to convince Congress to give Lon Nol's government more aid. The debate which followed his request juxtaposed the moral question of whether to help an ally in distress against the practical questions of whether what the United States had already done and could still do actually constituted help.

The three documents that follow all address this question. Russell Baker, the nationally syndicated humorist whose columns were a staple in the *New York Times,* used a far from humorous tone to write about Cambodia. Anthony Lake, who had been a member of the National Security Council staff and had resigned in protest at the time of the Cambodian incursion, questioned whether American aid could help that war-torn land. The *Wall Street Journal* acknowledged the possibility of Cambodia's fall even with U.S. aid, but took the position that the United States had to offer some help to its ally because America's credibility was at stake.

8   Cambodia: It's All in How One Looks at It
Russell Baker
March 12, 1975

New York, N.Y.—While President Ford and Henry Kissinger were whooping it up for more war in Cambodia the other day, Sydney Schanberg was writing for the New York Times from Pnompenh. If we juxtapose excerpts from Schanberg, Ford and Kissinger, we begin to understand how American policy relates to Cambodian reality.

Thus, Schanberg:

Cambodia before the war was a country so rich in her food produce that even the very poor were never hungry. Everyone had a piece of land and there were always bananas and other fruit growing wild and a river or stream nearby where fish could be easily caught.

"I wish to convey to the House of Representatives my deep concern over the present critical situation in Cambodia. An independent Cambodia cannot survive unless the Congress acts very soon to provide supplemental military and economic assistance."—President Ford.

Now it is a country of landless nomads with empty stomachs—human flotsam living amid damp and filth in the flimsiest of shanties, thatch shacks and sidewalk lean-tos. The countryside is charred wasteland that either belongs to the Cambodian insurgents or is insecure, so the population huddles in the cities and towns, doing marginal work that never pays enough to feed a family adequately. Growing numbers of children and adults are taking to begging.

"Unless such assistance is provided (by the Congress) the Cambodian army will run out of ammunition in less than a month."—President Ford.

In a World Vision clinic, Ah Srey, a 2 month old girl, grossly dehydrated from starvation, has just been brought in by her grandmother. Ten days before, they were caught in the maelstrom of a battle a few miles from Pnompenh. In the panic, the family became separated and the grandmother found herself alone with the child. For 10 days they had been surviving on handouts and scraps of garbage. The child had been malnourished before. Now she is a skeletal horror, little more than bulging eyes and a protruding rib cage. Every few seconds she produces a wail that racks her body. In three hours she is dead.

"If a supplemental is not voted within the next few weeks, it is certain that Cambodia must fall because it will run out of ammunition."—Kissinger.

Waves of mothers carrying gravely ill children—swollen children, children with sticklike concentration camp bodies, children with parchment skin hanging in flaccid folds, coughing children, weeping children, silent children too weak to respond anymore—press forward every day against the doors of the relief agency clinics, desperate to get in. But there are not enough doctors or nurses or medicine or food for them all, so for every 500 who come, only 200 or so can be treated.

"Therefore, the decision before us is whether the United States will withhold ammunition from a country which has been associated with us and which, clearly, wishes to defend itself."—Kissinger.

On the table next to Ah Srey is an older child—19 months—who is dying right now. His name is Nuth Saroeun. From his mouth comes a steady whimper and rattle. His father was killed by a rocket three months ago. His 25 year old mother, also suffering from malnutrition (she has beriberi and her feet are going numb), stands at his side sobbing. A doctor tries to force a tube down the child's throat to get out the mucus that is blocking his breathing. Suddenly the child utters a tiny cry that sounds like "mak" ("mother") and then his head slumps and he is gone.

"Our national security and the integrity of our alliances depend upon our reputation as a reliable partner. Countries around the world who depend on us for support—as well as our foes—will judge our performance."—President Ford.

At least every other person in this country of seven million is a refugee from war.

9 **At Stake in Cambodia**
   Anthony Lake
   March 9, 1975

The news from Indochina has a familiar ring these days. Rockets are falling on a city, innocent people are dying and a government propped up by American money is calling for more. Even more familiar are the arguments being used by President Ford and his administration to urge additional aid for Cambodia, arguments that echo years of similar pleas about Vietnam.

The fact that we have heard them before does not mean that the old arguments are necessarily wrong. But the passage of time and the continuing bloodshed do indicate that we may have been arguing the wrong issues all along.

If we are to turn an all too familiar and bitter debate into a practical discussion of what is to be done about the mess in Cambodia, we should resolve the questions on Indochina that no longer can be evaded.

Anyone who feels nostalgic about the rhetoric of the past must appreciate many recent pleas by the administration.

"Dominoes," for example, are back in fashion. The allegiance to the theory of falling dominoes is not as enthusiastic as in 1963, when President Kennedy exclaimed, "I believe it. I believe it." Now, Secretary of Defense James Schlesinger argues that "the domino theory . . . has been overly discredited."

The theory has changed, of course. In the 1950s and early 1960s, the prediction was that the dominoes might fall, one by one, as communism advanced across Asia.

Under Presidents Kennedy and Johnson, the concept was broadened. The Communists would promote "wars of liberation" around the world, if they were not licked in Vietnam. In May, 1965, the assistant secretary of state for Far Eastern affairs warned that "Africa and Latin America are already feeling the threat of such thrusts."

Now, with false alarms about Africa and Latin America no longer ringing, and with detente the cornerstone of our foreign policy, the dominoes are not physical but psychological; not countries that might fall to external subversion, they have become attitudes towards the United States that might change, with severe diplomatic consequences.

Secretary of State Dean Rusk sounded this warning in October, 1967. Our "credibility," he said, was at stake in Vietnam. "If any who would be our adversary should suppose that our treaties are a bluff, or will be abandoned if the going gets tough, the result could be catastrophe for all mankind."

President Nixon, similarly, feared the worldwide consequences of America's acting like a "pitiful, helpless giant."

The assistant secretary of state for East Asian affairs recently played on the same general theme: "Cambodia cannot be viewed as an isolated spot of small import to the U.S. Rather, it must be viewed in the larger context of Indochina which, in turn, affects Southeast Asia and Asia as a whole, which again affect the rest of the world. It is not to exaggerate to say that the eyes of the world are on the U.S. response to the needs of embattled countries."

But where are the voices and arms of our allies, if their eyes are riveted to our response? They are generally silent, because they, at least, understand the danger of drawing an analogy between a NATO country and a Cambodia. Indeed, they must prefer that the United States wake up from the Indochina nightmare whose commitment so debilitates it.

Related to the dominoes argument is another old acquaintance, the "commitment" refrain. It is unnecessary to recall how often we heard of our "commitment" to succeeding regimes in Saigon. Now we are told we have a commitment to Lon Nol, and the Congress will violate it only at our peril.

Yet surely the blame for this state of affairs should not be placed on Capitol Hill. The administration made whatever promises there were, despite constant congressional opposition since the war was extended to Cambodia by the "incursion" of 1970.

Section 655(g) of the Foreign Assistance Act, which states that aid to Cambodia "shall not be construed as a commitment by the United States to Cambodia for its defense," was passed by the Congress in 1971 and reaffirmed since. It was also signed by the President.

To "dominoes" and "commitment," add a third familiar phrase: "foreign aggression." American troops won't necessarily be sent to meet it any more, but according to President Ford's statement on Cambodia, "the policy of this country is to help those nations with military hardware . . . where the government and the people of a country want to protect their country from foreign aggression."

At best, the view that the struggle in Vietnam is not a civil war has always been arguable. To claim that Prince Sihanouk and his Communist but indisputably Cambodian allies in the field are "foreign" to Cambodia is simply inaccurate. Sixty-two governments recognize them as the legitimate rulers of Cambodia.

Yes, they do receive foreign aid as they attack the people who attacked and threw out Sihanouk in the first place. If that makes this a situation of "aggression," and "foreign" at that, what are we to say of our aid to the other side?

Cambodia must be recognized as a civil, not an international war as Vietnam should have been so long ago.

The Burden of Proof

Finally, there is the Cambodian "bloodbath" which so many in Washington now fear, should Phnom Penh fall. "Defeat in South Vietnam would be to deliver a friendly nation to terror and repression," warned President Johnson in April, 1965. Now one can all too clearly envisage the bloodshed that would accompany a final spasm of fighting around Phnom Penh.

But to warn of a new "bloodbath" is no justification for extending the current bloodbath. Rather, we should begin to consider the questions which must now— perhaps already too late—be addressed.

All of the arguments just mentioned warn of the penalties of failure, the consequences of allowing a defeat in Indochina. Yet the first question to be addressed is at least as important: What are the future penalties of a continuing effort to avoid defeat?

Throughout the sad history of American sacrifice in Vietnam, our Presidents justified our anguish not by predictions of success, but through fear of failure. And we never saw a careful analysis of what it would cost—in American lives, in American dollars, and in the sufferings of those we said we were trying to save.

The hope offered for so many years on Vietnam, and now on Cambodia, was that a "compromise settlement" could be achieved if we were tough enough to force one. But even with the so-called cease-fire of 1973, the fighting continues in Vietnam, and this flickering light at the end of the tunnel seems as far distant as ever.

We never should have waded into Cambodia in 1970, or into Vietnam before that. Now that we are over our heads, we are like a swimmer who strikes on *away* from shore, with only water to the horizon, because he wants to avoid looking weak to his friends and to the bullies back on the beach.

Especially with the situation in Cambodia now so desperate, the burden of proof must be on the administration to show us where it wants to take us: how more aid will lead to peace and how much it will cost us and the Cambodian people in the process.

Playing on vague, future fears will not do. For those concerns must be overpowered by our fears of continuing a conflict that has claimed the lives of 10 per cent of the Cambodian people in the last five years and made millions homeless.

The second and third questions make an assumption that the reader may not share: that whatever the United States does, short of armed intervention, the Lon Nol regime will fall, and sooner rather than later. This is an assumption supported by news reports and widely shared by analysts both in and out of the U.S. government.

Cutting Our Losses

The second question: How, in these circumstances, can we limit damage to and within the United States?

One way would be to stop falling into the same traps we so willingly entered in Vietnam, and cease overstating the stakes in our performance.

The more we *say* that the whole world is watching and judging us, the more it watches and judges. In claiming that Cambodia is a test of our will, we may make it one. It would be better to make it a test of our intelligence.

On Feb. 25, Secretary of State Henry Kissinger intoned the warning that ". . . if the collapse of Southeast Asia is caused by an American decision to withhold aid under conditions in which such a decision can have only one outcome, the conclusion will be inevitable that it was the United States which has the responsibility."

What of the responsibility of the corrupt and incompetent Cambodian regime that made such bad use of $1.75 billion of U.S. aid the past five years?

Kissinger has carefully tried to avoid parallels between American actions on Cambodia and our approach to Israel. Couldn't the same distinction be made in favor of our other allies? It would be in our interest to do so.

Another way to limit the damage of Cambodia would be to heed the administration's own fears, expressed by President Nixon on Nov. 3, 1969, that after disaster in Indochina, "inevitable and divisive recrimination would scar our spirit as a people."

What is it but "divisive recrimination" when the administration goes to such great lengths to blame the Congress for what most officials at State, Defense and the White House must know is an inevitable loss in Cambodia? There is a widespread suspicion in Washington that leaders of the administration privately concede defeat both in Cambodia and in the Congress, but plan to use the guilt they will lay on the Capitol doorsteps to force continuing appropriations for Vietnam. If this is the strategy, it presents a curious spectacle of self-defeat: an American government damaging us abroad and at home over Cambodia to avoid precisely those dangers over Vietnam.

A further measure of damage-limitation would involve adopting a diplomatic and rhetorical position which eschewed bitter attacks on Lon Nol's enemies. They are indeed supported by Hanoi, Peking and Moscow. But, to the extent we know much about them, they include many Khmer nationalists, Communist and non-Communist. Once they gain power, we must hope for as much nationalism on their part as possible. Why play up our enmity to them? It can only help push them further into the arms of their Communist supporters.

We are not, after all, really facing the "loss of Cambodia." It is not ours.

The third question concerns the damage done in Cambodia: How can we help keep future bloodshed there at a minimum?

As Sen. Hubert Humphrey recently put it, "It seems to me that events in Cambodia have gone far beyond the point where we should be concerned about trying to support continued military actions on the part of the Phnom Penh forces and should turn our attention instead to the alleviation of the terrible suffering and bloodshed occurring on both sides in this civil war. How does it make any sense to ask for $222 million worth of ammunition which can't be delivered when children are starving and the Cambodian people are desperate for peace?"

The dilemma is painful. If no more aid is forthcoming, Phnom Penh will collapse before too long and more children will starve in the meantime. If more aid is sent, the bloodshed will continue a while longer.

There is no good answer. Some find appealing the President's call for time for negotiations aimed at a compromise settlement. But that boat left port at least a year ago, as shown by the record of failed efforts just released by the State Department. Why should the Khmer Rouge agree to share power when they can expect to seize it?

As Kissinger aptly puts it, "negotiations cannot be a substitute for a situation on the ground . . . They will reflect a situation on the ground." And even with the new aid, the position of the Phnom Penh regime is hardly likely to return to 1973—when successful negotiations, we were told, were not possible.

What, then, is to be done?

The administration would like to buy some more time with further aid. If Lon Nol still loses in the near future, we would have gone down swinging. But all we would have accomplished is the provision of an indecent interval of further killing.

If, extraordinarily, our aid denied the Khmer Rouge victory through the coming rainy season, we would only have entered a new tunnel at the end of this tunnel, with still more bloodshed.

In either case, the administration's tired old arguments would have produced a terrible new suffering.

Perhaps the least bad choice would be to provide a little more aid, including food, to allow the government in Phnom Penh to negotiate—not an impossible compromise—but an immediate, peaceful turning over of power. This would stop the final, useless killing.

Free passage out of the country for those who wished to leave might be achieved. If it is not, and the aid is simply cut off, only those Cambodians who can commandeer the last flights out of Phnom Penh, assuming the airport is open, would be able to go. American officials would leave by plane or, if necessary, by the helicopters now standing by. And the departing generals and diplomats would leave chaos behind them.

The presence of an international group in Phnom Penh that could oversee the departure of refugees could also be sought. It might be given responsibilities for managing food and medicine distribution as well.

This approach would require absolutely limiting the further U.S. aid to no more than enough for one or two more months, so the handwriting on the wall is completely clear. And it should be accompanied by calls on the administration and the leaders in Phnom Penh to make such a diplomatic effort.

Kissinger is right when he argues that the time is not ripe for negotiations—but only if the administration and the generals still seek victory or substantive compromise. The time is now for negotiation to save lives, as the final act apparently unfolds.

As it does, a last question emerges. Cambodia was invaded in 1970 for the sake of American strategy in Vietnam. Shouldn't that strategy now be examined in the light of Cambodia? For the same basic choices seem to face us in Vietnam as well, even if the timetable and scale are different.

10 Senatorial Imperialism
Wall Street Journal editorial
March 12, 1975

So Mike Mansfield and Hugh Scott have decided that Lon Nol is not the right man to head the government of Cambodia, and that the State Department and presumably the CIA should use, in the Republican leader's words, "as much pressure as necessary" to secure his removal. These demands that Cambodia change its government are intended, we presume, to requite the sins of "American Imperialism."

Now, on a personal level, the Senators' suggestion makes a good deal of sense. Lon Nol and his associates would be well advised to resign while there is still air service between Phnom Penh and the Riviera, leaving to the faceless insurgents such problems as feeding the refugees. Yesterday there were in fact reports of an apparently indigenous shake-up in the Cambodian government, but even if Lon Nol himself leaves, so far it seems that the government will still prefer to hang on so long as it sees any chance of avoiding a North Vietnamized future for its tiny country. A foolish course, perhaps, but scarcely a dishonorable one.

In these unhappy circumstances, it seems to us the sensible course for the U.S. is to make clear it will not fight Cambodia's battle for it, but to supply it with enough arms to offset the external support being given the insurgents. The U.S. should be prepared to accept Cambodia's fall as not crucial to U.S. security, but it is not up to the U.S. to second-guess Cambodia's decision to fight on rather than surrender.

Least of all is it up to the U.S. to decide when Cambodia should change rulers. Our last adventure in helping to overthrow an ally, the 1963 coup against Ngo Dinh Diem, was the worst single mistake of postwar foreign policy. It was this act more than anything else that bogged the U.S. down in Vietnam.

Why is it that calls like those Senators Mansfield and Scott are now issuing always focus on our allies? Would the Senators favor a U.S. policy of trying to secure a new government in the Soviet Union, or North Vietnam? Would Senator Scott have favored using "as much pressure as necessary" to secure the removal of Salvador Allende as president of Chile? Or—to take two states where the present governments were established or maintained with heavy American assistance—how about trying for new rulers in Saudi Arabia and Iran? No doubt the Senate would be aghast at such suggestions, but to friendly governments it applies a different standard.

Today's cries to remove Lon Nol echo cries in late 1968 to remove Nguyen Van Thieu. Back then the essential point was neatly summed up by a university professor named Henry Kissinger: "If Thieu meets the same fate as Diem, the word will go out to the nations of the world that it may be dangerous to be America's enemy, but to be America's friend is fatal."

Documents 11 and 12

The victory of the Khmer Rouge in Cambodia in April 1975 did not end the fighting or the dying. The extremists who took over the country turned Phnom Penh into a deserted city as they set out to rebuild life in Cambodia according to their own model of rural cooperatives. The Khmer Rouge were not magnanimous in victory, and the genocide which followed their triumph was indescribable.

Anthony Lewis argues that the United States government must bear a great deal of the responsibility for the carnage in Cambodia. The incursion into Cambodia by American troops in the spring of 1970 followed by the massive aid for the Lon Nol government and the devastation caused by American bombs had, according to Lewis, destabilized a peaceful state and had led directly to a situation where "Khmer were fighting and killing Khmer."

The *Wall Street Journal* shared Lewis' pain and dismay at the events in Cambodia. The newspaper, however, rejected his argument that the United States had to bear responsibility for the "Cambodian horror." The editorial argued that the guilty party could be found in Cambodia.

11 But the Patient Died
Anthony Lewis
April 29, 1976

On April 30, 1970, six years ago tomorrow, President Nixon ordered United States forces into Cambodia. It is a day that will live in the shame of Americans who know the good in their country and suffer when evil is done in its name.

Mr. Nixon and his national security adviser, Henry Kissinger, gave assurance that the Cambodian operation would be limited in purpose and means and time. It was none of those things. It began five years of wanton, cruel, useless destruction: the destruction of a civilization. If there is a reckoning, in this life or another, some Americans will bear a heavy burden for what they did to Cambodia.

This is a time of remembrance generally for the tragedy of American intervention in Indochina. It all came to an end just one year ago: April 30, 1975, when the American-supported Government in Saigon surrendered. How much farther away it seems. How quickly we blot the unpleasant from memory. . . .

But Cambodia was worse. Very little of what goes wrong in the world deserves to be called evil; most is mere mistake. But Congressman Paul McCloskey, Republican of California, was right when he saw Cambodia in early 1975 and said that what American policy-makers had done there was "greater evil than we have done to any country in the world."

In Vietnam, the American intervention could be ascribed to ignorance. And the original mistake was hard to undo. Once in, U.S. officials found it hard to get out while preserving intact the image of strength that they regarded as vital to world order.

But there were no such excuses in Cambodia. In 1970 no rational American official could believe that more would mean less war in Indochina. None could plead ignorance or inadvertence.

Indeed, the very way the invasion was announced suggested that its wellspring was not reason but obsession. "We will not be humiliated," Mr. Nixon said: We would not act like "a pitiful, helpless giant." Mr. Kissinger said his own assistants who opposed the invasion were insufficiently "manly" and showed "the cowardice of the Eastern Establishment."

The President and his men said their aim was only to clean out sanctuaries of the *Vietnamese* Communists. They promised that the U.S. would not get involved in Cambodia's emerging civil war, would not supply military advisers to the Lon Nol regime just installed in Phnom Penh by a coup, would not fly any air missions in Cambodia except against the Vietnamese. The promises were quickly broken.

In the next three years and three months American planes dropped 400,000 tons of bombs on Cambodia. The U.S. sent $2 billion in aid to Lon Nol—and kept the civil war going for five terrible years.

A country that had once been a demi-paradise, where the poorest never went hungry, became a charred wasteland of starving refugees. A tenth of Cambodia's population, 600,000 people, were killed. Half the population was made homeless.

The evil of 1970 was mercilessly repeated. When the Vietnam "peace" was signed in 1973, Mr. Nixon shifted the B-52's to Cambodia, using them there without a shred of authority in any law or resolution or treaty—very likely the most flagrant Presidential violation of the Constitution in our history. When the end became inevitable, in 1974, Mr. Kissinger still refused to work for a settlement that would mitigate the damage. His policy was to fight to the last Cambodian.

In 1970 many foresaw that the sending of American forces into Cambodia would enlarge the war, but few could imagine the extent of the human and political disaster. The end result has been not only to decimate Cambodia but to give it one of the most xenophobic governments on earth, hating outsiders and reportedly imposing terrible cruelties on its own people.

One wonders about the American officials responsible. Apart from external accountability, does any one of these men ever think of Cambodia, look into himself and despair?

12 The Cambodian Horror
Wall Street Journal editorial
April 16, 1976

Time magazine's account of genocide in Cambodia is reminiscent of the horrors of Stalinist Russia and Nazi Germany; in Cambodia the horrors have taken the form of mass forced marches and forced labor, political purges and assassinations and massacres of entire villages, with people sometimes buried alive by bulldozers or clubbed to death to save ammunition.

The magazine estimates that upwards of 600,000 Cambodians, roughly one-tenth of the population, have died from mistreatment at the hands of the Communist Khmer Rouge. Even that estimate may be low. The French newspaper Le Monde, which has a center-left political orientation, recently published two detailed articles on Cambodia, translated by the Library of Congress and introduced into the Congressional Record by Senator Robert Griffin. Le Monde puts the casualties from the organized slaughter at close to 800,000.

The enormity of this kind of atrocity, conducted by a party in power against the people, is mind numbing. A generous person might hold that simple shock explains the relatively weak outcry from the usual wellsprings of moral outrage around the world. But while that may have some validity, we would guess that it is much too generous. There are undoubtedly other reasons, both puzzling and complex.

One answer could be that the crimes of the Khmer Rouge, even though they dwarf some other state crimes of our time—tortures in Brazil and Chile, for example—have attracted less attention because they are inflicted in the name of revolution. In our world, the wellsprings of moral outrage and the wellsprings of revolution are often the same.

The pain and discomfort experienced by revolutionary moralists in even discussing Cambodia are reflected in some recent remarks we heard from an Eastern college professor. In his view, the Khmer Rouge is murdering people in 1976 because the U.S. bombed Cambodia in 1970. That may well be the record extension to date of the politics of guilt.

But going more deeply, such a tortuous reasoning reflects the notion, not at all uncommon, that there is some inherent nobility in those of our world who would create a new man and thereby reform mankind. And that concept of nobility seems to remain untarnished even when the would-be reformers commit despicable acts in pursuit of their utopian dreams. Fervent moralism is no stranger to naked power.

It seems to be only after the fact, when those dreams collapse, that their admirers have second thoughts. Stalin, Hitler and Mussolini were men of such dreams, ruthless in their drives to create a new order and a new man. And while they were committing their wholesale cruelties, they did not lack for admirers.

The Khmer Rouge have had, as an immediate example, Hanoi. Scholar Robert F. Turner in his recent book "Vietnamese Communism: Its Origins and Development" (Hoover Institution), notes that when the Viet Minh first moved into Hanoi in 1954, they at first followed a policy of "moderation."

But he observes that later they conducted a reign of terror, executing perhaps 100,000 and were probably responsible for upwards of 500,000 deaths. The use of terror as a weapon continued throughout that long struggle to put all of Vietnam under Hanoi's control.

It remains an open question whether South Vietnam will escape a new genocide. Currently, there is the same moderation first employed in Hanoi. But there also are spreading controls over personal affairs, "re-education" classes, people's courts and public tribunals, the organization of families into manageable cells, and threats to ferret out enemies who owe a "blood debt to the people." Just last week, the official Saigon press announced the roundup of 110 "reactionaries" who failed to register with the government and are charged with "spreading false news designed to stir up confusion among the population."

We suspect that world opinion, if employed, could have some influence even on the revolutionaries of Hanoi. The best way that opinion could be registered would be through a world-wide outcry against the atrocities being committed in Cambodia.

But here again—not for the first time in the world's history—world opinion seems to be stupefied in the face of truly colossal crimes. When there is no censure from self-professed authorities on morality, is there any wonder that those hardened men who would slaughter thousands to fulfill their dreams so often think they are right?

Critical Issues for Discussion

1. Prince Sihanouk's neutrality was not popular with Americans in the mid-1960s. See Document 3. Why did the United States attack Sihanouk's policies? How do those policies look in retrospect? Why?

   According to Stone, what role did the Central Intelligence Agency play in Cambodian affairs? The mission of the CIA was debated in the 1970s in the United States. What do you think it should be? Justify your answer.

2. Prince Sihanouk once said that "the best way to make Communists is to put the American army into a place where there were no Communists before." What was the reasoning behind his statement? Is this a sufficient explanation for the growth of the Khmer Rouge in Cambodia? What other factors were involved? How do you evaluate Sihanouk's attitude toward the United States?

3. William Beecher's news report in the *New York Times*, reprinted as Document 4, appeared to be just another news story, but it had serious repercussions. Should the president have the right to wiretap the phones of people who

are suspected of "leaking" stories? What kinds of suspicions would justify such an act? Can anything be done about "leaks"? Should a leader be able to put a "plumber" on the job? What exactly is "national security"? What lines would you draw?

See Document 7. What did the Department of Defense report reveal? What was the attitude of the author toward the American bombing of Cambodia? What conclusions might Beecher have drawn from these revelations? What is your reaction?

4. In his speech, which appears as Document 5, President Nixon reviewed the risks and possible rewards of his decision to allow American troops to enter Cambodia. The President was willing to widen the war in order to gain military advantages. How do you evaluate his decision? What were his assumptions about American foreign policy? What were his beliefs about American patriotism? What did he mean when he warned that without taking this step the United States would turn into a "pitiful, helpless giant"?

Why did the Republican National Committee reprint the letter which appears as Document 6? What points did the author make? Was it an effective letter? To whom was it appealing? What do you think about the slogan "My Country Right or Wrong?"

5. William Shawcross's book on Cambodia was called *Sideshow*. What did that title connote? Was the Cambodian battle a sideshow to the war in Vietnam? If so, what did that say about American policy in Vietnam? Was Laos a sideshow, too? An opening act? How would you characterize it?

6. The Vietnamization of the war and the gradual withdrawal of American troops were very popular policies in the United States. Did they end the war or merely force the struggle to take a different form? Were the bombings of Laos and Cambodia ways to wind up the conflict or to wage war by other means? What were the effects of the bombings on the people and the governments of Southeast Asia?

See Documents 1 and 2. What messages were these authors trying to convey? What were the problems which allowed such actions to be taken by the American government? What solutions were needed? Were the bombings justified? Why or why not?

7. The bitter anguish about which Anthony Lewis wrote in Document 11 affected many Americans. Was the United States government the root cause of the great problems in Cambodia? If not, who or what was? What could have been done to prevent the bloodbath in Cambodia? Should any country have done anything to stop the gruesome slaughter? Could anything have been done? Whose business was it? Is there any way to prevent future genocides from happening?

Whom did the *Wall Street Journal* hold responsible for the Cambodian mass murder? See Document 12. How do you evaluate these arguments? What was the *Journal's* message to its readers?

Follow Up See Documents 8, 9, 10, which were written while Congress was debating whether or not to aid Lon Nol's government in 1975. What did each of these authors think? How would an opponent answer their charges?

Should the United States have continued to help Lon Nol? Why or why not? On what grounds should such a decision be made? Practical? Political? Military? Moral? A combination of these factors? Which ones? Why?

Was Lon Nol an ally who was stabbed in the back by Congress or was he a corrupt leader who reaped what he had sown? Or does the truth lie somewhere in between?

Suggestions for Further Reading

Laos
Adams, Nina, and Alfred McCoy, eds. *Laos: War and Revolution*. New York: Harper and Row, 1970.
> Documents and analyses provide the best overview of the land and people of Laos and the history of U.S. policy there.

Branfman, Fred, ed. *Voices from the Plain of Jars: Life Under an Air War*. New York: Harper and Row, 1972.
> Drawings and testimony by refugees tell of life during five and a half years of daily bombing. Branfman provides an introductory section on Laos' history.

Burchett, Wilfred. *Mekong Upstream: A Visit to Laos and Cambodia*. Berlin: Seven Seas, 1959.
> Much of Burchett's book is a chatty travelogue. In Laos he gives an enthusiastic account of the achievements of the Pathet Lao.

Fall, Bernard. *Anatomy of a Crisis: The Laotian Crisis of 1960–61*. Ed. Robert M. Smith. Garden City, N.Y.: Doubleday, 1969.
> Fall gives a feeling for Laos and one of the very few inside views (in his case, an unsympathetic one) of the Pathet Lao.

Haney, Walt. *The Pentagon Papers and the United States Involvement in Laos*. Vol. 5 of *The Pentagon Papers* (Senator Gravel Edition). Boston: Beacon, 1971.
> Haney gives a critical overview of "the forgotten war" from 1950 to 1970, supplementing the Pentagon Papers with other documents to give a fuller picture of the effects of U.S. policy.

Thee, Marek. *Notes of a Witness: Laos and the Second Indochinese War*. New York: Random House, 1973.
> A former Polish delegate to the International Commission for Supervision and Control in Laos gives an eyewitness account of the period 1961–1962 and early United States intervention in Laos.

Cambodia
Given that Kampuchea/Cambodia was closed to Westerners from 1975 to 1979, American scholars are just beginning to catch up with recent events there.

We suggest that you watch for forthcoming books including work from: Anthony Barnett (Schocken), Elizabeth Becker (Simon and Schuster), David P. Chandler (Yale University Press), Karl Jackson (Westview), William Shawcross (Simon and Schuster), and Michael Vickerey (South End Press).

Carney, Timothy Michael, trans. *Regrets of the Khmer Soul*. Ithaca: Cornell Data Papers, 1976.
The best thing by a Cambodian about the liberated zones in the early part of the war.

Etcheson, Craig. *Utopian Pandemonium: The Rise and Demise of Democratic Kampuchea*. Boulder, Colo.: Westview, 1982.
History of the Pol Pot regime based on secondary sources.

Kiernan, Ben, ed. *Peasants and Politics*. White Plains, N.Y.: M. E. Sharpe, 1982.
The articles, many historical, give a background to what happened in the 1970s. Included are translations of Khmer materials.

Kissinger, Henry. *White House Years*. Boston: Little, Brown, 1979.
President Nixon's Secretary of State and chief architect of his Indochina policies offers a controversial view of the last years of the war. The revised edition directly disagrees with Shawcross's accusations against Kissinger's Cambodia policy.

McCoy, Alfred W. *The Politics of Heroin in Southeast Asia*. New York: Harper and Row, 1972.
McCoy traces the roots of the drug epidemic among GIs to Laos, where the heroin was grown, and Saigon, where corrupt government officials organized and protected the illicit drug traffic. At several points he finds the U.S. government secretly involved in this complex network.

Pouchaud, Francois. *Cambodia: Year Zero*. Trans. Nancy Amphoux. New York: Holt, Rinehart & Winston, 1978.
Based on interviews with refugees, Pouchaud chronicles the horror of the Pol Pot years.

Shawcross, William. *Sideshow: Kissinger, Nixon and the Destruction of Cambodia*. Rev. ed. New York: Simon and Schuster, 1980.
"Cambodia was not a mistake; it was a crime," concludes Shawcross's highly critical assessment of the Nixon's administration's uses of power in Cambodia. The revised edition includes a first-hand description of Cambodia in 1980.

Sihanouk, Norodom. *War and Hope: The Case for Cambodia*. New York: Pantheon, 1980.
The former monarch of Cambodia makes a plea for what he believes is his people's best hope: a multi-nation conference on Cambodia to restore its neutrality.

Peace Is Finally at Hand
Henry Kissinger (background left), National Security Adviser to President Nixon, and North Vietnamese Politburo Member Le Duc Tho (seated foreground) initial the peace agreement in Paris on January 24, 1973. The men shared the Nobel Peace Prize for bringing an end to one stage of the conflict in Southeast Asia. *Wide World Photo*.

Chapter 10
Peace Is at Hand: 1968–1973
Background

Historical Summary

Hubert Humphrey and Richard Nixon approached the last days of the 1968 presidential campaign with the Paris peace negotiations still deadlocked. Humphrey was seen by many Democrats as representing Johnson's Vietnam policies—even though, in late October, Humphrey tried to disassociate himself by promising to stop the bombing if elected. Nixon, proclaiming a strong anti-Communist policy while promising peace, defeated Humphrey by a narrow margin.

Nixon took office and began to outline his approach to the war: withdraw American combat forces from Vietnam but intensify the training and firepower of the South Vietnamese army so that it could take over. Nixon called the plan "Vietnamization." Crucial to the program was the continued role of the U.S. air force in Vietnam to bulwark the South Vietnamese government against the North Vietnamese and the Vietcong.

Nothing in Nixon's strategy implied a desire on his part to see Vietnam fall to the Communists. On the contrary, he believed that, with American help, the South Vietnamese could hold back their enemies. This policy of bolstering the military might of "friendly" third-world countries assumed worldwide proportions in Nixon's mind. He labeled it the "Nixon Doctrine," and later described his actions in Cambodia as the doctrine "in its purest form."

The Nixon approach worked. As U.S. troops withdrew from Vietnam, American casualties declined and so did domestic political opposition. Meanwhile, Nixon's chief foreign affairs adviser, Henry Kissinger, undertook a series of secret diplomatic missions designed to persuade the North Vietnamese to agree to a settlement.

Nixon and Kissinger sought to fit Vietnam into a larger international context. In their view, an end to the war would be part of what they called a "structure of peace." Thus they established a link with the People's Republic of China and negotiated with the Soviet Union—both of which were furnishing the Vietnamese Communists with vital assistance. These diplomatic moves were intended to isolate the Hanoi regime from its Communist partners.

In March 1972, evidently hoping to improve their position on the battlefield in order to improve their bargaining posture, the North Vietnamese launched a major offensive. Big units crossed the 17th parallel frontally, using tanks and heavy artillery for the first time.

Though he was then preparing for a summit meeting in Moscow, Nixon reacted vigorously. He ordered the mining of the Haiphong harbor and stepped up the bombing of the area near Hanoi. B-52s and other aircraft gave massive, close support to the beleaguered South Vietnamese forces in Quang Tri province. This U.S. intervention succeeded in blocking the Communist offensive.

The diplomatic breakthrough came in October 1972. The North Vietnamese retreated from their demand that President Nguyen Van Thieu's regime in South Vietnam abdicate prior to an accord. The United States conceded that North Vietnamese troops could remain in the south.

Thieu stubbornly resisted the agreement, seeing the presence of North Vietnamese forces in the South as a threat to his security. It seemed, for a moment, that the settlement might collapse. Trying to salvage it, Kissinger went before the television cameras to assert that "peace is at hand." His forecast was premature. The signing of the pact, originally scheduled for October 31, had to be postponed.

Negotiations resumed following Nixon's defeat of Senator George McGovern in the November elections. Facing the Communists again, Kissinger submitted sixty-nine changes to the draft accord on behalf of the Saigon government. The North Vietnamese negotiator, Le Duc Tho, stiffened. The talks collapsed in December.

By now the Nixon administration was racing against the return of Congress in January, for the president feared that the legislature would prevent him from continuing to furnish U.S. aid to the Saigon regime. Nixon, determined to compel the North Vietnamese to return to the conference table, directed that the Hanoi-Haiphong area be heavily bombed for a period of eleven days during the Christmas season. His decision triggered worldwide criticism.

But the Communists did return to the conference table in Paris, where a cease-fire agreement was signed on January 11. Nixon secretly pledged to help Thieu if the Communists violated the accord. He also sent the Communists a secret promise of aid if they respected the accord.

Hostilities officially ended in Vietnam on January 27, and the war had apparently come to a conclusion. A month later, the last of the American prisoners held in Hanoi returned home to an emotional welcome. The Communists filmed their departure under the title "Goodbye Uninvited Guests."

Points to Emphasize

- Richard Nixon's strategy for ending the war in Vietnam
- the simultaneous policies of negotiating an end to the war while continuing to withdraw American soldiers from the battlefield
- the strategy behind Nixon's policies toward China and the Soviet Union
- the results of the North Vietnamese Easter Offensive and President Nixon's response

Chronology

	1969 Jan	Feb	Mar	Apr	May	Jun	Jul	Aug	Sep
Vietnam			U.S. begins bombing of North Vietnamese bases in Cambodia			Provisional Revolutionary Government (PRG) formed by NLF; Nixon and Thieu meet on Midway Island			Ho Chi Minh dies
United States		Lodge replaces Harriman at Paris peace talks		Unrest at Harvard and other campuses		First U.S. troop withdrawal announced		Woodstock music festival	Second U.S. troop withdrawal announced
World Wide									

	1969 Oct	Nov	Dec	1970 Jan	Feb	Mar	Apr	May	June
Vietnam						ARVN troops first attack North Vietnamese bases in Cambodia	U.S. forces join ARVN in Cambodia incursion	U.S. bombs North Vietnam for first time since 1968	U.S. troops leave Cambodia
United States	Vietnam moratorium. Nationwide peace demonstrations	Another moratorium attracts record numbers; U.S. Army begins investigation of My Lai massacre	Harris Poll shows 46% in favor of aims of November moratorium					4 demonstrators killed at Kent State. 200 colleges close in protest; Demonstrations in Washington	Cooper-Church Amendment limits U.S. role in Cambodia. Senate repeals Gulf of Tonkin Resolution
World Wide						Sihanouk deposed in Cambodia. Lon Nol takes over			

Chronology (cont.)

	1970 Jul	Aug	Sep	Oct	Nov	Dec	1971 Jan	Feb	Mar
Vietnam								ARVN troops invade Laos with U.S. air support	ARVN forced out of Laos
United States		White House sets up "plumbers" to end information leaks							
World Wide			Allende elected president of Chile		De Gaulle dies in France		Idi Amin takes over in Uganda		

	1971 Apr	May	Jun	Jul	Aug	Sep	Oct	Nov	Dec
Vietnam					Big Minh withdraws from election		Thieu re-elected with 80% of the vote		U.S. bombs North Vietnam as protective reaction strikes
United States	500,000 protest in Washington U.S. table tennis team visits China	Disorderly May Day demonstrations in Washington	N.Y. Times begins publication of the Pentagon Papers						
World Wide									

	1972 Jan	Feb	Mar	Apr	May	Jun	Jul	Aug	Sep
Vietnam			First major North Vietnamese ground offensive since 1968	Easter Offensive continues; U.S. bombs North Vietnam	ARVN retreats from Quang Tri; U.S. mines North Vietnamese ports; Bombing continues			Last U.S. ground troops leave	
United States	Nixon announces secret talks in Paris			Anti-war demonstrations protest bombings		Break-in at Democratic National Committee Headquarters in Watergate Hotel			
World Wide		Nixon visits China			Nixon visits Russia				

	1972 Oct	Nov	Dec
Vietnam	Preliminary peace agreement	Thieu rejects peace agreement	U.S. bombs Hanoi and Haiphong; Bombing halt over the North announced on December 30
United States	Kissinger says peace is at hand	Nixon re-elected president	
World Wide			

- the important concessions made by both sides in the negotiations in the fall of 1972
- the disagreements between the United States and South Vietnam over the draft treaty
- the rationale behind the Christmas bombing of North Vietnam
- why a treaty was finally accepted in January 1973

Glossary of Names and Terms

Alexander Haig Battalion and Brigade Commander, 1st Infantry Division, Vietnam, 1966–1967. Regimental Commander, Deputy Commandant, U.S. Military Academy, 1967–1969. Military Assistant to the Assistant to the President for National Security Affairs, 1969–1970. Deputy Assistant to the President for National Security Affairs, 1970–1973.

Morton Halperin staff member of the Department of Defense under Robert McNamara. Worked in the International Security Affairs Unit of the Pentagon. Staff member of the National Security Council under Kissinger.

Hoang Duc Nha Commissioner General for Information for South Vietnam. Relative and chief aide of President Thieu.

Melvin Laird U.S. Congressman from Wisconsin, 1953–1969. Secretary of Defense, 1969–1972. Domestic Advisor to the President, 1973–1974.

Le Duc Tho member of the Politburo of the Democratic Republic of Vietnam. North Vietnam's principal negotiator with Henry Kissinger in secret talks.

Thomas Moorer Commander in Chief of Pacific Fleet, 1964–1965. Chief of Naval Operations, 1967–1970. Chairman, Joint Chiefs of Staff, 1970–1974.

John Negroponte Foreign Service officer, Department of State, 1960. Vice Consul, Hong Kong, 1961–1963. Second Secretary, Saigon, 1964–1968. Member, U.S. Delegation to the Paris Peace Talks, 1968–1969. Member, National Security Council Staff, 1970–1973.

Nguyen Co Thach Vice Foreign Minister of the Democratic Republic of Vietnam (North Vietnam).

William Sullivan Deputy Assistant Secretary of State for Far Eastern and Pacific Affairs under Nixon. Worked as Head of the Interdepartmental Vietnam Task Force. Had served as Ambassador to Laos under Johnson.

Tuu Ky Secretary to Ho Chi Minh until the latter's death in 1969.

Easter Offensive the North Vietnamese invasion of South Vietnam which began at the end of March 1972.

MIAs American soldiers missing in action.

Operation Enhance Plus a program which supplied South Vietnam with a great deal of military equipment in the period up to the signing of the peace agreement. It followed Operation Enhance.

Pentagon Papers the massive, top-secret history of the United States' role in Indochina commissioned by Secretary of Defense McNamara in 1967.

Leaked to the public by Daniel Ellsberg and published in June 1971 by the *New York Times* and other newspapers.
POWs Prisoners of War.
Provisional Revolutionary Government (P.R.G.) the new designation of the National Liberation Front after June 1969.

Documents

Document 1

During the 1968 presidential campaign, both major candidates were acutely aware that a significant portion of the electorate had turned against the war. Hubert Humphrey had the disadvantage of his years of support of President Johnson's policies. Richard Nixon, on the other hand, was in an excellent position to convince Americans that to achieve peace in Vietnam there had to be a change of administration in Washington.

In his presentation to the Platform Committee at the Republican National Convention in 1968, Nixon stated that the war in Vietnam had to end and that the strategies for fighting and for negotiating might have to change. In order not to jeopardize the meetings going on in Paris, he did not reveal exactly how he planned to end the war, but with hindsight, hints of his Vietnamization policy can be found in this speech.

1 Presentation to the Platform Committee at the Republican National Convention
Richard M. Nixon
August 1, 1968
With regard to the war in Vietnam, the Republican party faces the question of how a complex, emotionally-charged and highly sensitive issue can be handled during an election year in a responsible way.

The manner in which we conduct ourselves on this issue can bear heavily on the chances for peace.

The Republican party must address this issue in its platform. What I intend to do, and what I believe the party should do, is to separate those questions that *can* responsibly be discussed from those that cannot. The present Administration's emissaries in Paris must be able to speak with the full force and authority of the United States. Nothing should be offered in the political arena that might undercut their hand.

But there is much that can and should be discussed.

The war must be ended.

It must be ended honorably, consistent with America's limited aims and with the long term requirements of peace in Asia.

We must seek a negotiated settlement. This will require patience.

Until it *is* ended—and in order to hasten a negotiated end—it must be waged more effectively. But rather than further escalation on the military front, what it requires now is a dramatic escalation of our efforts on the economic, political, diplomatic and psychological fronts. It requires a new strategy, which recognizes that this is a new and different kind of war. And it requires a fuller enlistment of our Vietnamese allies in their own defense.

I have long been critical of the Administration's conduct of the war. Specifically:

● Our massive military superiority has been wasted, our options frittered away, by applying power so gradually as to be ineffective. The swift, overwhelming blow that would have been decisive two or three years ago is no longer possible today. Instead, we find that we have been locked into a massive, grinding war of attrition.

● The Administration has done far too little, too late, to train and equip the South Vietnamese, both for fighting their own war now and for the task of defending their own country after the war is settled.

● The Administration has either not recognized that this is a new and more complex kind of war, or has not seen its significance. The result is that the old-style, conventional military aspects have been overemphasized, and its other dimensions—psychological, political, economic, even diplomatic—have gotten too little attention.

● The Administration has failed in candor at home and in leadership abroad. By not taking the American people into *its* confidence, the Administration has lost *their* confidence. Its diplomacy has failed to enlist other nations to use their influence toward achieving a peaceful settlement.

These are failures of the past. In terms of what the United States should do *now*, we start with the fact of the Paris talks. These impose limits on what a Presidential candidate can responsibly say—not because of what the American people might think, but because of how Hanoi's negotiators might interpret it.

A Presidential candidate is in a different position than is a private citizen, an editor or even a Senator. He may soon bear the responsibility for conducting the negotiations. Anything he might offer as a candidate would become unavailable for bargaining when he became President. Anything he might say, any differences he might express, would be taken by Hanoi as indicating the possible new direction of the next administration.

Our negotiators in Paris represent not only the present administration, but the United States. In the spirit of country above party, as long as they have a chance of success—and as long as the Administration remains committed to an honorable settlement—they should be free from partisan interference, and they should have our full support. The pursuit of peace is too important for politics-as-usual.

If the talks fail, or if they drag on indefinitely, new approaches both to the conduct of the war and to the search for peace will be needed.

There is no Republican way or Democratic way to end a war, but there *is* a difference between an administration that inherits the errors of the past, and an administration that can make a fresh beginning free from the legacy of those errors.

There is a difference between an administration burdened by accumulated distrust, and a new administration that can tell the truth to the American people and be believed.

However cruel its military aspects, this new kind of war is not primarily a military struggle in the conventional sense. It is primarily a political struggle, with the enemy conducting military operations to achieve political and psychological objectives. It is a war for people, not for territory. The real measure of progress is not the body-count of enemy killed, but the number of South Vietnamese won to the building and defense of their own country.

This new kind of war requires greater emphasis on small-unit action, on routing out the Viet Cong infrastructure, on police and patrol activities, on intelligence-gathering, on the strengthening of local forces. This kind of war can actually be waged *more* effectively with *fewer* men and at *less* cost.

The fact is that our men have not been out-fought; the Administration has been out-*thought*.

At the same time, we need far greater and more urgent attention to training the South Vietnamese themselves, and equipping them with the best of modern weapons. As they are phased in, American troops can—and should—be phased out. This phasing-out will save American lives and cut American costs. Further, it is essential if South Vietnam is to develop both the military strength and the strength of spirit to survive now and in the future.

It is a cruel irony that the American effort to safeguard the *independence* of South Vietnam has produced an ever-increasing dependency in our ally. If South Vietnam's future is to be secure, this process must now be reversed.

The context in which the final negotiations will occur cannot be predicted, but the far-reaching implications of the war in Vietnam plainly indicate that the conference table must be wide enough, and the issues placed upon it broad enough, to accommodate as many as possible of the powers and interests involved. In particular, there should be the most candid and searching conversations with the Soviet Union.

Vietnam does not exist in isolation. Around the world, we should mobilize our diplomatic forces for peace—through our embassies, through the United Nations and elsewhere. We need such effort not only to speed an end to the war in Vietnam, but also to lay the groundwork for the organization of a lasting and larger peace. Certainly one of the lessons from the agony of Vietnam is that we need a new diplomacy to prevent future Vietnams.

If the war is still going on next January, it can best be ended by a new Administration that has given no hostages to the mistakes of the past; an Administration neither defending old errors nor bound by the old record. A new Republican Administration will be pledged to conduct a thorough reappraisal of every aspect of the prosecution of the war and the search for peace. It will accept nothing on faith, reputation or statistics. In waging the war and making the peace, it will come with a fresh eye and act with a free hand. And it will do what the present Administration has so signally failed to do: it will arm the American people with the truth.

Document 2

David Halberstam, a *New York Times* reporter whose criticism of American methods in Vietnam and of Diem's policies had earned him the sharp rebukes of both governments, became increasingly convinced that American involvement in Vietnam was a mistake. In this January 1969 *Harper's* article, Halberstam expressed his hope that Richard Nixon would end the American presence in Vietnam. Halberstam argued that the newly elected Republican president had a golden opportunity to do so, and he warned that a president who did not stop the war would face domestic turmoil.

2   President Nixon and Vietnam
David Halberstam
January 1969

"It would take us 500,000 men—and even that would not be enough."
—*General Philippe Leclerc to Paul Mus, Indochina, 1945.*

There was a time, almost seven years ago in Saigon, when a steady stream of high American diplomats and generals would arrive at Tan Son Nhut airport and the television cameras would push forward to catch the words of these new arrivals because they were officials and their words were weighty. They were good men, all of them, or almost all, and they would talk about imminent victory, and then we whose words were not so weighty would listen, at first surprised, then cynical, and eventually amused at this procession. Finally Neil Sheehan, then with UPI and only twenty-five years old, would laugh and say, "Another foolish Westerner come to lose his reputation to Ho Chi Minh."

The story is particularly apropos right now because Lyndon Johnson, who once talked of Ho Chi Minh in terms of coonskins, is leaving office to return to Johnson City and to teach history and political science, and is being replaced by a man who has a chance, one chance and a very good one, of ending the war. Mr. Nixon will enter the White House enjoying the benefit of the doubt both from those who voted for him and those who did not. He knows the nation is tired of the war, and if he has as keen a political sense as his friends think, he must know by now that the war is unwinnable. He will be able to handle, should he seek peace, the one faction of Congress which partially supports the war, the Republicans. Most important, he is freed from past decisions and past mistakes; indeed, he can do what no one in official Washington has been able to do in the past—he can actually say that the war was a mistake and a miscalculation. The country will believe him.

He will have that chance. Perhaps one chance, and it will come and go very quickly, for Vietnam is not just a quagmire, it is a tar-baby as well. It will not be easy for President Nixon. The North Vietnamese will not be particularly generous or flexible; they have come a long way and fought a long time for this, and one senses they are perfectly willing and content to go a longer way and wait a longer time for the settlement they demand. Even a dovish President would probably be surprised by the stiffness of their terms. Yet President Nixon, because *he* can be flexible, can settle at terms that Lyndon Johnson never could. We had committed 500,000 men and $30 billion a year and about two-thirds of Lyndon Johnson's ego to Vietnam—the last was the most difficult to extricate. Nixon's chance will come perhaps in the first four months, and if he fails, then his speeches will have to justify the war, and the failure to end the war, and soon it will no longer be Johnson's war, it will be Nixon's. He will find himself justifying it more and more, and slowly but surely, without even realizing it, he will be pulled by the powerful currents around him into the same course as Johnson. For though Johnson and his staff will be leaving Washington, and Rusk will be leaving State, the institutional pull at both State and Defense to justify the war and to continue present policy will be surprisingly strong. There will, yes, be a notch or two more of flexibility but both of these giant, powerful institutions will be far from admitting that the last five years, all those speeches, all those meetings were one terrible mistake. Since Hanoi will seem, to American eyes, to be intransigent and since the generals will promise the usual imminent victory in return for a few more troops, the temptations for Nixon to hold out will be very great. He will be dependent upon the generals, he will have to accept their interpretation, and we will be back to where we were before, only worse. For if after this election, after all the protest, there is no move to end the war, then the entire rhythm of protest will be speeded up. People who were writing letters in the past will go into the streets, and the last year of the Johnson Administration will seem in retrospect a time of tranquility.

The real problem is mere human vanity; it is hard to explain this to people, the young radicals looking for deep Marxian explanation. This whole sad, tragic business is not economic. It has been powerful men with vast egos, acting out the mistakes of the past as though it were mandatory to do so. Each time they came to a crossroads and were faced with a choice of plunging us further into something that was at best dubious, or admitting to a mistake, they plunged us further and deeper into it, putting their own feeling of infallibility above decency and common sense.

Now Mr. Nixon ascends to the Presidency largely because of the war, and there is no longer a chance for a middle ground. He will not lack for strategists willing to explain the war, the need for toughness, the need to show an allegedly crumbling Hanoi a sense of purpose—just a few more bombs, a few more targets, a few more men, the end is around the corner. One remembered, in August 1967 Robert Komer, the chief of pacification, a poor man's Rostow, going around to the dinner parties telling people that he had told the President not to worry about the war, for it would not be an election issue.

The fact is that for twenty-two years the generals and their propagandists have been wrong, terribly wrong, about Indochina, and they are wrong now. The enemy has total political superiority, his system works, and he can keep coming, and he feels he was cheated at Geneva in 1954.

This war is hurting the Vietnamese more than it is helping them, it is weakening the U.S. throughout the world and tearing it apart at home. One can rationalize forever how it happened—all the chickens coming home to roost during the Johnson Administration, Johnson ill-served by all the Kennedy advisers, Johnson's own fatal misunderstanding of power—but all that is past. First it was McNamara's War. Then Rusk's War. Then Johnson's War. One hopes it will not become Nixon's War.

Documents 3, 4, and 5

Airpower was essential to American strategy and logistics in Vietnam. Troops were flown to Vietnam in transports and deployed in helicopters. Reconnaissance, supply, defoliation, close tactical support and long-range strategic bombing depended on the availability of vast numbers of sophisticated aircraft, many based outside Vietnam on carriers, in Thailand, and as far away as Guam.

As ground troops began leaving Vietnam in 1970, the U.S. military effort became increasingly dependent on air power. Bombing was at the heart of Nixon's attempt to convince the North Vietnamese to negotiate an end to the war. In Document 3, Robert Seamans, Jr., the Secretary of the Air Force during Nixon's first term, argued that bombing was "absolutely essential" to the

American purpose in Vietnam. Senator Gaylord Nelson of Wisconsin, however, was horrified by the results of the bombing campaign and told his Senate
colleagues why in the speech reproduced as Document 4. Yet another point of
view on airpower—that of an American pilot who flew missions over Vietnam—is presented in Document 5.

3   The Absolutely Essential Bombing
Robert C. Seamans, Jr.
January 28, 1972

Washington—Short of the negotiated settlement which we seek, if we are to continue phasing down U.S. involvement in the war in a safe way, U.S. air activity in
Southeast Asia—though diminishing—is absolutely essential.

Air operations make it more difficult for enemy forces to concentrate their units
for an attack and limit the scale of combat by interfering with North Vietnamese
delivery of munitions and other supplies that would endanger American lives.

We are withdrawing our ground forces at an increasing rate, and this is generally
understood. We have also substantially reduced our air effort in Southeast Asia, a
fact that is not often appreciated.

Air effort can be measured in terms of the numbers of aircraft in the theater, sorties flown or the weight of munitions delivered. On each of these counts, reductions
in the U.S. effort in the last three years are greater than 50 per cent.

The Air Force of the Republic of South Vietnam has become more effective and
has taken over a greater share of the air support task. They are currently providing
virtually all of the air support for their own ground forces. We are still providing
support for the ground forces of Cambodia and Laos, and in addition, the South
Vietnamese are now flying about as many sorties as the United States in support of
Cambodia forces.

The reduction in our air operations has also been aided by the use of new developments that have increased our effectiveness, particularly in the interdiction of munitions and supplies in transit from North Vietnam to the other countries of
Southeast Asia. Supplies of guns, rockets, ammunition, equipment and food are
transported by the North Vietnamese mostly at night along the Ho Chi Minh Trail,
a series of tortuous mountain and jungle roads.

Sensors on the ground alert our air crew that the trucks are in motion, and our
aircraft use new types of infrared and television devices to locate the moving traffic
and direct the ordnance. During the last year (November, 1970 to November, 1971)
our aircraft attacked their trucks on over 35,000 occasions, nearly 25,000 of these
attacks resulted in hits and, as a result, over ten thousand trucks were destroyed. We
estimate that only 15 per cent of the supplies entering the trails reached South Vietnam or Cambodia.

The operation of the Ho Chi Minh Trail employs 40,000 to 50,000 North Vietnamese who maintain the roads, drive and repair the trucks, man the communications and operate the anti-aircraft guns and missiles. During the rainy season when
the roads are impassable the supplies and trucks are massed in North Vietnam in
preparation for passage through the mountain passes and into Laos. The attacks in
North Vietnam late in December were against these logistic centers, as well as the
airfields used by MIG aircraft, air defense radars and surface-to-air missile sites. The
total number of U.S. attack sorties flown in Southeast Asia during the December

week when the five-day, limited-duration strike of North Vietnam took place, was 20 per cent less than the corresponding week a year earlier.

In conducting air strikes, U.S. air elements must adhere to stringent restrictions. These operating restrictions vary somewhat from region to region within Southeast Asia, but all have as an important objective the minimizing of civilian casualties. This is true not only in friendly territories, but also in North Vietnam. That is why the North Vietnamese often integrate military activities into their villages recognizing the increased safety this affords.

As we draw down our forces in Southeast Asia, air power provides protection and support for our remaining forces and those of our allies. Air power also helps stem the flow of enemy supplies into friendly countries giving them more time to develop their own defense capability.

Our objective is simple: to disengage our own forces as rapidly and as safely as possible, to obtain the release of our prisoners of war and to permit all the people of Southeast Asia to determine their own destiny.

4   The Tragedy of Vietnam
Gaylord Nelson
February 25, 1972

Suppose we took gigantic bulldozers and scraped the land bare of trees and bushes at the rate of 1,000 acres a day or 44 million square feet a day until we had flattened an area the size of Rhode Island, 750,000 acres.

Suppose we flew huge planes over the land and sprayed 100 million pounds of poisonous herbicides on the forests until we had destroyed an area of prime forests the size of Massachusetts or 5½ million acres.

We've Done This to South Vietnam

Suppose we flew B-52 bombers over the land, dropping 500 pound bombs until we had dropped almost 3 pounds per person for every man, woman and child on earth—8 billion pounds—and created 23 million craters on the land measuring 26 feet deep and 40 feet in diameter.

Suppose the major objective of the bombing is not enemy troops but rather a vague and unsuccessful policy of harassment and territorial denial called pattern or carpet bombing.

Suppose the land destruction involves 80% of the timber forests and 10% of all the cultivated land in the nation.

We would consider such results a monumental catastrophe. That is what we have done to our ally, South Vietnam.

While under heavy pressure the military finally stopped the chemical defoliation war and has substituted another massive war against the land itself by a program of pattern or carpet bombing and massive land clearing with a huge machine called a Rome Plow.

The huge areas destroyed, pockmarked, scorched, and bulldozed resemble the moon and are no more productive.

This is the documented story from on the spot studies and pictures done by two distinguished scientists, Prof. B. W. Pfeiffer and Prof. Arthur H. Westing. These are the same scientists who made the defoliation studies that alerted Congress and the country to the grave implications of our chemical warfare program in Vietnam, which has now been terminated.

The story of devastation revealed by their movies, slides, and statistics is beyond the human mind to fully comprehend. We have senselessly blown up, bulldozed over, poisoned and permanently damaged an area so vast that it literally boggles the mind.

Horror Defies Adequate Description

Quite frankly, I am unable adequately to describe the horror of what we have done there.

There is nothing in the history of warfare to compare with it. A "scorched earth" policy has been a tactic of warfare throughout history but never has a land been so massively altered and mutilated that vast areas can never be used again or even inhabited by man or animal.

This is impersonal, automated and mechanistic warfare brought to its logical conclusion—utter, permanent, total destruction.

The tragedy of it all is that no one knows or understands what is happening there, or why, or to what end. We have simply unleashed a gigantic machine which goes about its impersonal business, destroying whatever is there without plan or purpose. The finger of responsibility points everywhere but nowhere in particular. Who designed this policy of war against the land, and why? Nobody seems to know and nobody rationally can defend it.

Strategists, Victims Are Worlds Apart

Those grand strategists who draw the lines on the maps and order the B-52 strikes never see the face of that innocent peasant whose land has been turned into a pockmarked moon surface in 30 seconds of violence without killing a single enemy soldier because none were there.

If they could see and understand the result, they would not draw the lines or send the bombers.

If Congress knew and understood, we would not appropriate the money.

If the president of the United States knew and understood, he would stop it in 30 minutes.

If the people of America knew and understood, they would remove from office those responsible for it if they could ever find out who is responsible. But they will never know, because nobody knows.

By any conceivable standard of measurement, the cost-benefit ratio of our program of defoliation, carpet bombing with B-52's, and bulldozing is so negative that it simply spells bankruptcy. It did not protect our soldiers or defeat the enemy, and it has done far greater damage to our ally than to the enemy.

These programs should be halted immediately before further permanent damage is done to the landscape.

The cold, hard and cruel irony of it all is that South Vietnam would have been better off losing to Hanoi than winning with us. Now she faces the worst of all possible worlds with much of her land destroyed and her chances of independent survival after we leave in grave doubt at best.

This has been a hard speech to give and harder to write because I did not know what to say and how to say it—and I still do not know. But I do know that when the members of Congress finally understand what we are doing there, neither they nor the people of this nation will sleep well that night.

For many reasons I did not want to make this speech but someone has to say it, somewhere, sometime.

Mr. President, I ask unanimous consent that the following statistics, which were provided by Arthur H. Westing and which will appear in a forthcoming publication, be printed in the Congressional Record at this point.

There being no objection the statistics were ordered to be printed in the Record as follows:

MUNITIONS EXPENDITURES (in millions of dollars)

Year	South Vietnam	North Vietnam	South Laos	North Laos	Cambodia	Total Indochina
1965	594	65	60	10	0	630
1966	1,778	255	135	20	0	2,188
1967	3,634	415	200	30	0	4,278
1968	5,185	330	310	40	0	5,866
1969	4,674	0	490	420	0	5,583
1970	3,333	0	655	240	115	4,344
Total	19,099	1,065	1,850	760	115	22,889

ECOLOGICAL IMPACT

Country	Number of craters (in millions)	Area with "shrapnel" (in million acres)	Area cratered (in thousand acres)	Earth displaced (in million cu. yards)
South Vietnam	19.1	23.9	309.9	2,500
Military region I	(6.1)	(7.6)	(98.4)	(794)
Military region II	(3.8)	(4.8)	(62.0)	(500)
Military region III	(8.3)	(10.3)	(134.2)	(1,083)
Military region IV	(.9)	(1.2)	(15.3)	(124)
North Vietnam	1.1	1.3	17.3	139
Laos	2.6	3.3	42.4	342
Southern Laos	(1.8)	(2.3)	(30.0)	(242)
Northern Laos	(.8)	(1.0)	(12.3)	(99)
Cambodia	.1	.1	1.9	15

IMPACT OF U.S. MUNITIONS (in pounds)

Expenditure	South Vietnam	North Vietnam	Laos	Cambodia	Total Indochina
Per acre	446	26	45	3	125
Per person	1,091	58	992	18	513

ALL INDOCHINA (in millions of pounds)

Year	Air Munitions	Surface Munitions	Total Munitions
1965	630	—	630
1966	1,024	1,164	2,188
1967	1,866	2,413	4,279
1968	2,863	3,003	5,866
1969	2,744	2,808	5,582
1970	1,955	2,389	4,344
Total	11,112	11,777	22,889

B-52 MISSIONS—ASSUMING AN AVERAGE OF 7 SORTIES
PER MISSION (in numbers of missions)

Year	Military Region I	Military Region II	Military Region III	Military Region IV	Total South Vietnam
1967	527	284	269	10	1,090
1968	1,137	644	1,143	148	3,072
1969	319	440	1,777	98	2,634
1970	624	274	366	150	1,414
Total	2,607	1,642	3,555	406	8,210

5   **A B-52 Slows Noticeably When the Bomb Bays Open**
Richard R. Williams
June 3, 1972

There is a sudden, awesome roar that seems to shake the ground. Then the giant, eerie-looking, swept-wing engine of war begins to roll ever so slowly down the runway. It is one of the seventy-five or so B-52 heavy bombers stationed at Anderson Air Force Base here on the island of Guam that are now regularly employed in the demolition of South Vietnam and, when the President gives the word, North Vietnam. The plane's huge wings, filled with jet fuel and draped with 500-pound bombs, flap ponderously at first and then more rapidly as the 220-ton bomber gathers speed.

The eight jet engines blast deafeningly as the aircraft passes the 4,000-foot marker on the runway. Then the 6,000-foot marker is crossed. Will this monster, with its huge, black tail standing as tall as a five-story building, ever get itself into the air? The B-52 thunders past the 8,000-foot marker, still hugging the earth. Finally, at the 10,000-foot mark, its wings flapping wildly, the enormous airplane sails almost gracefully into the air. It is headed for a target in South Vietnam with a pay load of forty-two 750-pound bombs in its belly and twenty-four 500-pound bombs clinging to its wings.

At the controls is a thirty-year-old Texan named Robert E. Gill. A lean six-footer, Captain Gill has crew-cut hair and intense eyes that dart nervously as he speaks. He has been a bomber pilot for only a year but is already an old hand at this business. He settles down in his seat, from which he will not stir for more than twelve hours.

Gill appears relieved; the initial pressure is off. "I'm not surprised we got off the ground, but sometimes I wonder if we're going to make it," he remarks. "This airplane is about seventeen or eighteen years old, and there're all sorts of crazy squeaks, groans, grunts, and vibrations that express her age."

Gill is not exaggerating. The outside skin of his airplane is rippled almost like a washboard. "If *you* had the loads stuck in your belly and hanging from your arms that this old bird has, you would be marked with wrinkles, too," the pilot explains with a wry chuckle.

The feeling of relief among Gill and his four fellow crewmen is short-lived. It is time for the mid-air fueling operation. Fueling while in the air is necessary because these big bombers cannot take off efficiently with both a full load of bombs and a full load of fuel. Gill maneuvers his ship toward the swinging boom of an airborne KC-135 tanker.

As soon as the bomber separates from the tanker, Gill brings his plane into formation with two other B-52s, making up what is known as a "cell." Cells of various sizes, usually consisting of three or six B-52s, are composed and assigned to missions depending on the size of the target that has been selected for destruction.

This cell of bombers will not be over its target for another six hours. "I can't sleep on an airplane," Gill says. "There are just too damned many things to watch for and listen for." Throughout the flight Gill must keep a sharp eye on the turn-and-bank indicator, the air-speed gauge, and the altimeter as well as listen to and analyze weather reports from the navigator and other reports about the target and possible enemy activity from the radar operator.

Then, finally, after hours of tinkering with the controls of the aircraft, Gill hears the navigator sing out, "We are approaching assigned target area." Shortly, the navigator launches into a series of detailed instructions to guide the bomber directly over its target.

"Turn right ten degrees. Hold your present altitude and decrease air speed five knots."

"Roger."

"Radar navigator to pilot, hold her steady, Skipper."

"Okay."

Then the radar navigator presses a button to open the bomb-bay doors, and at that moment a computer takes charge of the mission. The crew feels a pronounced decrease in air speed when the bomb-bay doors open automatically but otherwise have no sensation of what is taking place. "There are no vibrations, no jumps or bounces of the airplane when the bombs leave," Gill explains. "It's not like in *12 O'Clock High,* when the old B-29s would jump up and down as the bombs left the plane. We can't even see into the bomb bays."

The B-52 carries its load of 750-pound bombs in a compartment sealed off from the cockpit. If the bomb bay *did* open into the cockpit, the crew would be sucked out of the plane as soon as the bomb-bay doors were opened, because the cabin is pressurized and the plane unloads its bombs from an altitude of 50,000 feet.

"Sometimes we see something below, and sometimes we don't," says Gill. "The only way we know the bombs are dropping is that the radar-nav tells us so. And he is told by an instrument. Sometimes, if I have the inclination to look, I might see some dropping off the left wing."

The cell of B-52s is flying in a tight formation as the bombs are released. The object, of course, is to shed them in a dense pattern. In a typical six-plane mission, for example, 150 tons of explosives are distributed over a one-and-a-half-square-mile rectangle. When the bombs explode, the blasts create a pressure exceeding three pounds per square inch throughout this entire area. And that is lethal. For comparison, the atomic bomb dropped on Hiroshima saturated six square miles—only four times the area covered by a B-52 bombing sortie—with three pounds per square inch of pressure.

The robotlike computer flying the aircraft during its bomb run signals with a light to the radar navigator that the pay load has been dropped, and the bay doors are automatically closed. Again suddenly, the crew feels the air speed pick up because the plane has become streamlined once more—and forty tons lighter.

"It's always a relief to know the mission is completed, and we're on our way back home," says Gill laconically. "But as far as emotions are concerned, frankly, I never have time to think. We never know what damage we have caused until maybe three or four days later. And even then we don't know if it's our crew that caused the damage. There are two other planes in the cell, and the report covers the entire mission, not any single airplane.

"Of course, we *hope* we hit something. After all, that's our job. We have put in more than twelve hours in the air, plus some tense moments on take-off and in refueling, and a couple of hours in briefings before the take-off. So, with that much time and effort put into something, you hope you did some good.

"But I don't get emotional or excited about it one way or the other," he continues dryly. "It's a job, one I have chosen for myself—and I work hard at it. I don't think of anything else. I don't think about the possibility of death. I don't think about the SAM missiles. I don't think about being captured. In fact, I don't even consider the possibility of being shot down.

"Five years ago I was a fighter pilot, flying against targets in North Vietnam. I was closer to the war then and, sure, I used to think. I used to think quite a bit. But my thoughts were about survival, staying alive, about doing my job.

"Do I miss my family? Hell, yes. I miss them more than I can describe to you. My son was born January fifth, and I left home on February twenty-first.

"Am I ever apprehensive? Sometimes, yes. But the only time I'm scared is on take-off. As I said before, it's an old bird we're flying. Sometimes I get the feeling that I can look back through the fuselage and see twenty thousand slaves pulling at the oars.

"Oh, she'll take off okay if you have enough runway. As long as the engines are roaring, she'll eventually climb into the air. But it's the 'enough runway' that worries me sometimes.

"And the night take-offs. Man, that's something else. It's like telling a ghost story. There are all kinds of sounds that are magnified. And ghostly colored lights inside and outside the airplane. A night take-off is like putting a black-painted fish bowl over your head.

"There's no real way of describing the take-off—my feelings, my thoughts, my emotions. We know that at the end of the 12,000-foot runway there are 650-foot cliffs that drop straight down into the Pacific.

"We know that either we're going to get off or we're not. It's that simple. There are only two things that can happen once we gain the ground speed where we can't stop this monster that's loaded with enough explosives to—well, enough, that's all, just enough. We either make it or we don't."

Two bombers have been lost at Anderson Air Force Base in the past three years when they failed to lift off the ground. There were no survivors from either crash. Five years ago two B-52s were lost when they collided in mid-air shortly after a refueling operation. There were no survivors that time either.

"On the return flight we are naturally a bit more relaxed," Gill goes on to say.

"But there are still systems to monitor continuously. I'm not much of an eater on an airplane, but the crew has a chance to pop in the oven a TV dinner or a frozen blueberry pie that someone picked up at the base commissary.

"Even though the landing is always a critical stage of any flight, I have a great deal more confidence at that point than I have on take-off. For one thing, there are no deadly weapons hanging from my wings or nestled in my belly."

And what about after the mission is over? "We don't sit around the BOQ or the officers' club and rehash the missions or talk about the merits of the conflict," he says. "We don't talk shop. We usually don't have time, and we're usually too damned tired to talk about war."

Document 6

North Vietnam's 1972 Easter Offensive came as a surprise to South Vietnam after a relatively quiet military season in 1971. Although the big ARVN invasion of Laos had failed early in that year, American and South Vietnamese military analysts saw lessened enemy pressure and gains in pacification of the countryside. The Easter Offensive showed, however, that North Vietnam had by no means abandoned its objective.

President Nixon's answer to the Easter Offensive was announced in a nationwide radio and television speech on May 8, 1972. The president reviewed his peace offers to the North Vietnamese government and expressed his great disappointment with their responses. Nixon announced that he was going to mine Haiphong harbor and escalate bombing of North Vietnam.

The president was careful to emphasize that he desired peace but that he would fight to prevent the success of the Easter Offensive. Nixon also tried to reassure the Soviet Union that the use of American might in Vietnam was intended to safeguard American lives and that the growing understanding between the two superpowers should be maintained and nurtured.

6   Address on Vietnam
Richard M. Nixon
May 8, 1972

Good evening. Five weeks ago, on Easter weekend, the Communist armies of North Vietnam launched a massive invasion of South Vietnam, an invasion that was made possible by tanks, artillery, and other advanced offensive weapons supplied to Hanoi by the Soviet Union and other Communist nations.

The South Vietnamese have fought bravely to repel this brutal assault. Casualties on both sides have been very high. Most tragically, there have been over 20,000 civilian casualties, including women and children, in the cities which the North Vietnamese have shelled in wanton disregard of human life.

As I announced in my report to the Nation 12 days ago, the role of the United States in resisting this invasion has been limited to air and naval strikes on military targets in North and South Vietnam. As I also pointed out in that report, we have responded to North Vietnam's massive military offensive by undertaking wide-ranging new peace efforts aimed at ending the war through negotiation.

. . .

Here is what over three years of public and private negotiations with Hanoi has come down to: The United States, with the full concurrence of our South Vietnamese allies, has offered the maximum of what any President of the United States could offer.

We have offered a de-escalation of the fighting. We have offered a cease-fire with a deadline for withdrawal of all American forces. We have offered new elections which would be internationally supervised with the communists participating both in the supervisory body and in the elections themselves.

President Thieu has offered to resign one month before the elections. We have offered an exchange of prisoners of war in a ratio of 10 North Vietnamese prisoners for every one American prisoner that they release. And North Vietnam has met each of these offers with insolence and insult. They have flatly and arrogantly refused to negotiate an end to the war and bring peace. Their answer to every peace offer we have made has been to escalate the war.

In the two weeks alone since I offered to resume negotiations Hanoi has launched three new military offensives in South Vietnam. In those two weeks the risk that a communist government may be imposed on the 17 million people of South Vietnam has increased and the communist offensive has now reached the point that it gravely threatens the lives of 60,000 American troops who are still in Vietnam.

There are only two issues left for us in this war. First, in the face of a massive invasion do we stand by, jeopardize the lives of 60,000 Americans, and leave the South Vietnamese to a long night of terror? This will not happen. We shall do whatever is required to safeguard American lives and American honor.

Second, in the face of complete intransigence at the conference table do we join with our enemy to install a communist government in South Vietnam? This, too, will not happen. We will not cross the line from generosity to treachery.

We now have a clear, hard choice among three courses of action: Immediate withdrawal of all American forces, continued attempts at negotiation, or decisive military action to end the war.

I know that many Americans favor the first course of action, immediate withdrawal. They believe that the way to end the war is for the United States to get out and to remove the threat to our remaining forces by simply withdrawing them.

From a political standpoint, this would be a very easy choice for me to accept. After all, I did not send over one-half a million Americans to Vietnam. I have brought 500,000 men home from Vietnam since I took office. But, abandoning our commitment in Vietnam here and now would mean turning 17 million South Vietnamese over to communist tyranny and terror. It would mean leaving hundreds of American prisoners in communist hands with no bargaining leverage to get them released.

An American defeat in Vietnam would encourage this kind of aggression all over the world, aggression in which smaller nations armed by their major allies, could be tempted to attack neighboring nations at will in the Mid-East, in Europe, and other areas. World peace would be in grave jeopardy.

The second course of action is to keep on trying to negotiate a settlement. Now this is the course we have preferred from the beginning and we shall continue to pursue it. We want to negotiate, but we have made every reasonable offer and tried every possible path for ending this war at the conference table.

The problem is, as you all know, it takes two to negotiate and now, as throughout the past four years, the North Vietnamese arrogantly refuse to negotiate anything but an imposition, an ultimatum that the United States impose a Communist regime on 17 million people in South Vietnam who do not want a Communist Government.

It is plain then that what appears to be a choice among three courses of action for the United States is really no choice at all. The killing in this tragic war must stop. By simply getting out, we would only worsen the bloodshed. By relying solely on negotiations, we would give an intransigent enemy the time he needs to press his aggression on the battlefield.

There is only one way to stop the killing. That is to keep the weapons of war out of the hands of the international outlaws of North Vietnam.

Throughout the war in Vietnam, the United States has exercised a degree of restraint unprecedented in the annals of war. That was our responsibility as a great nation, a nation which is interested—and we can be proud of this as Americans—as America has always been, in peace not conquest.

However, when the enemy abandons all restraint, throws its whole army into battle in the territory of its neighbor, refuses to negotiate, we simply face a new situation.

In these circumstances, with 60,000 Americans threatened, any President who failed to act decisively would have betrayed the trust of his country and betrayed the cause of world peace.

I therefore concluded that Hanoi must be denied the weapons and supplies it needs to continue the aggression. In full coordination with the Republic of Vietnam I have ordered the following measures which are being implemented as I am speaking to you.

All entrances to North Vietnamese ports will be mined to prevent access to these ports and North Vietnamese naval operations from these ports. United States forces have been directed to take appropriate measures within the internal and claimed territorial waters of North Vietnam to interdict the delivery of any supplies. Rail and all other communications will be cut off to the maximum extent possible. Air and naval strikes against military targets in North Vietnam will continue.

These actions are not directed against any other nation. Countries with ships presently in North Vietnamese ports have already been notified that their ships will have three daylight periods to leave in safety. After that time, the mines will become active and any ships attempting to leave or enter these ports will do so at their own risk.

These actions I have ordered will cease when the following conditions are met: First, all American prisoners of war must be returned.

Second, there must be an internationally supervised cease-fire throughout Indochina.

Once prisoners of war are released, once the internationally supervised cease-fire has begun, we will stop all acts of force throughout Indochina, and at that time we will proceed with a complete withdrawal of all American forces from Vietnam within four months.

Now, these terms are generous terms. They are terms which would not require surrender and humiliation on the part of anybody. They would permit the United States to withdraw with honor. They would end the killing. They would bring our POWs home. They would allow negotiations on a political settlement between the Vietnamese themselves. They would permit all the nations which have suffered in this long war—Cambodia, Laos, North Vietnam, South Vietnam—to turn at last to the urgent works of healing and peace. They deserve immediate acceptance by North Vietnam.

It is appropriate to conclude my remarks tonight with some comments directed individually to each of the major parties involved in the continuing tragedy of the Vietnam War. First, to the leaders of Hanoi, your people have already suffered too much in your pursuit of conquest. Do not compound their agony with continued arrogance; choose instead the path of a peace that redeems your sacrifices, guarantees true independence for your country and ushers in an era of reconciliation.

To the people of South Vietnam, you shall continue to have our firm support in your resistance against aggression. It is your spirit that will determine the outcome of the battle. It is your will that will shape the future of your country.

To other nations, especially those which are allied with North Vietnam, the actions I have announced tonight are not directed against you. Their sole purpose is to protect the lives of 60,000 Americans who would be gravely endangered in the event that the Communist offensive continues to roll forward and to prevent the imposition of a Communist government by brutal aggression upon 17 million people.

I particularly direct my comments tonight to the Soviet Union. We respect the Soviet Union as a great power. We recognize the right of the Soviet Union to defend its interests when they are threatened. The Soviet Union in turn must recognize our right to defend our interests.

No Soviet soldiers are threatened in Vietnam. Sixty thousand Americans are threatened. We expect you to help your allies, and you cannot expect us to do other than to continue to help our allies, but let us, and let all great powers help our allies only for the purpose of their defense, not for the purpose of launching invasions against their neighbors.

Otherwise the cause of peace, the cause in which we both have so great a stake, will be seriously jeopardized.

Our two nations have made significant progress in our negotiations in recent months. We are near major agreements on nuclear arms limitation, on trade, on a host of other issues.

Let us not slide back toward the dark shadows of a previous age. We do not ask you to sacrifice your principles, or your friends, but neither should you permit Hanoi's intransigence to blot out the prospects we together have so patiently prepared.

We, the United States, and the Soviet Union, are on the threshold of a new relationship that can serve not only the interests of our two countries, but the cause of world peace. We are prepared to continue to build this relationship. The responsibility is yours if we fail to do so.

And finally, may I say to the American people, I ask you for the same strong support you have always given your President in difficult moments. It is you most of all that the world will be watching.

I know how much you want to end this war. I know how much you want to bring our men home and I think you know from all that I have said and done these past three and one-half years how much I, too, want to end the war to bring our men home.

You want peace. I want peace. But, you also want honor and not defeat. You want a genuine peace, not a peace that is merely a prelude to another war.

At this moment, we must stand together in purpose and resolve. As so often in the past, we Americans did not choose to resort to war. It has been forced upon us by an enemy that has shown utter contempt toward every overture we have made for peace. And that is why, my fellow Americans, tonight I ask for your support of this decision, a decision which has only one purpose, not to expand the war, not to escalate the war, but to end this war and to win the kind of peace that will last.

With God's help, with your support, we will accomplish that great goal.

Thank you and good night.

Document 7

Since the withdrawal of American troops was well advanced by the spring of 1972, North Vietnam's Easter Offensive was an important test of the success of Vietnamization. Document 7, a publication of the U.S. Army Center of Military History, appeared in 1980. It gives a former ARVN general's retrospective view of how and why South Vietnam survived in the spring of 1972.

7   Summary and Conclusion, *Easter Offensive of 1972*
Lt. General Ngo Quang Truong
U.S. Army Center of Military History

Prior to the invasion of 1972, Hanoi had launched several large-scale offensive campaigns in South Vietnam, such as the 1968 "General Offensive—General Uprising" which included the siege on Khe Sanh Base, all with the commitment of multi-division forces. But none of these initiatives equaled the 1972 Easter Offensive—or the Nguyen Hue Campaign as the enemy called it—in scale and in importance. Undoubtedly, Hanoi had intended it to be a decisive military effort.

The importance and decisiveness of this effort were readily apparent by the forces Hanoi had committed—at least ten infantry divisions and hundreds of tanks and artillery pieces. The Hanoi leadership always timed its major efforts to exert maximum impact on American domestic politics. The 1972 Easter Offensive was in line with this policy. And true to their doctrinal precepts, the Communist leaders of North Vietnam evidenced little concern for personnel and equipment losses, provided that the ultimate objectives set forth by their Politbureau could be attained.

From its very beginning, this offensive was an ultimate challenge for South Vietnam. At various times in some geographical areas, victory appeared to be within reach of the enemy. Indeed, the initial stage of Hanoi's offensive had been successful beyond the capability of its forces to exploit. In northern Military Region 1, NVA units had in rapid succession taken one firebase after another in the DMZ area—14 in all—with little resistance from ARVN forces. In Military Region 3, three of Hanoi's divisions rapidly overwhelmed ARVN forces and seized Loc Ninh. In this area alone, they annihilated two ARVN regiments and laid siege to An Loc. In the Central Highlands, two other NVA divisions overran Dakto-Tan Canh and a series of firebases on Rocket Ridge overlooking Kontum City. The initial momentum of the NVA offensive was awesome.

After these unexpectedly easy victories, NVA forces concentrated their attacks during late April on Quang Tri City, captured this provincial capital and advanced toward Hue. This ancient city of great political importance was in grave danger. By mid-May, NVA forces in Military Region 2 were in position to slash across the width of South Vietnam from Kontum to Binh Dinh. Additionally, by the middle of May in Military Region 3, the enemy had seized a portion of An Loc just one hundred kilometers north of Saigon. NVA forces were also in control of several large, though remote areas which local governments had evacuated. However, the RVNAF consolidated its defense and stalled the momentum of the enemy invasion.

Even though United States strength in South Vietnam had been greatly reduced, both logistic and combat support was responsive and effective. Immediately following the initial attacks by the enemy, the United States initiated an emergency program to provide support to battered RVNAF units on all battlefields to assist them in regaining their strength and initiative. Combat support was provided by massed air and naval firepower against NVA units, their supply lines and bases.

Injected with new vigor, ARVN units resisted with determination. The enemy's desperate attempt to overwhelm our units again with his local numerical superiority was countered with B-52 and tactical air strikes. As he increased his assaults with massed infantry, the heavier his losses became. Finally, this attrition caused his offensive to run out of steam.

. . .

Many observers believed that Hanoi should have acted more cautiously after NVA forces lost the initial momentum and suffered subsequent defeats. But the Hanoi leadership was stubborn and intransigent, bent as always on the most belligerent course of action. The showdown was inevitable, and Hanoi apparently believed it could win. Hanoi's easy victories during April and May seemed to confirm this belief. Gearing up for the showdown, Hanoi probably continued to think that the RVNAF would collapse and only a final blow would be necessary to hasten the process.

Another possibility that might explain Hanoi's desire for a quick victory was its concern about the political discussions which were taking place between the United States and Russia and Red China. Was it possible that Russia and China, who supplied Hanoi with nearly all its war supplies, could be persuaded by the U.S. to reduce their support in the near future? . . .

But North Vietnam no longer had the forces needed to win. On the contrary, the odds were working against the enemy. As the fighting continued, Hanoi's chances of losing were increasing, not only militarily but also politically. Weakened and finally exhausted, the NVA forces were no match for the bolder South Vietnamese units. Contrary to the assessment of several observers, I believe that the last NVA effort in Quang Tri and Thua Thien failed to provide the enemy with any significant political advantages. Falling back in the wake of their defeat, NVA forces dispersed and switched to a less sanguine course of action: a well-orchestrated land and population grab campaign in preparation for a standstill ceasefire. And thus ended the 1972 NVA offensive.

In retrospect, Hanoi's conventional invasion of the South did not help it attain the major objectives desired. Although always the defender with an extremely disadvantageous strategic posture, South Vietnam emerged stronger than ever. Hanoi's effort had been thwarted by U.S.-RVN determination. The American response during the enemy offensive was timely, forceful and decisive. This staunch resolve of the U.S. to stand behind its ally stunned the enemy. Additionally, it brought about a strong feeling of self-assurance among the armed forces and population of South Vietnam.

Another major factor that contributed to Hanoi's military failures during 1972 was the reliability of RVNAF units. When Hanoi initiated its offensive, some had thought that it would be an ultimate test of Vietnamization and were not confident that the RVN could meet the challenge. But instead of defeat, the RVNAF had achieved quite the contrary.

Throughout the long months of the enemy offensive, the RVNAF performed like the mature, professional, dedicated fighting force it had become. Although this excellent performance was attributable to several factors, a definite tribute must be given to the U.S. advisers, especially the U.S. regional assistance commands. Even during this period of emergency, the U.S. advisory effort continued to help the RVNAF support machinery run smoothly, whether it was recruiting, equipping, training or replacing losses . . .

The final credit for our victory should go to the individual South Vietnamese soldier, regardless of branch or service. His gallantry, courage and determination were of the highest standard. No less admirable were the sacrifices and hardships endured by the common South Vietnamese people during this long ordeal. While modern weapons might help turn the tide of a battle, they could never replace the individual soldier on the battlefield. No matter how sound a battle plan or how good a commander, our success could never have been achieved without courageous soldiers. The average South Vietnamese soldier, who grew up in war, was not only audacious and devoted to the cause for which he had been fighting but he always took pride in his career and his heart was filled with love for his family, his comrade-in-arms and his people. He was indeed a heroic warrior who represented the noblest traditions of the Vietnamese people, a most ardent patriot, and an outstanding soldier. His success during 1972 had helped forge a new national spirit of solidarity and survival that was to prevail in the post–cease-fire years.

Document 8

In an October 1972 press conference Henry A. Kissinger, Assistant to the President for National Security Affairs, had announced to the American public that peace would soon be a reality. His "peace is at hand" statement, however, came back to haunt him when the agreement which had seemed so near unraveled in November and December 1972. The South Vietnamese government had refused to go along with the terms of the treaty.

In the text of his December 16, 1972, news conference (reprinted here as Document 8), Kissinger gave his explanation of what had happened to the peace settlement and what the future might hold.

8   Transcript of Henry A. Kissinger's December 16, 1972 Press Conference
    . . . We are now in this curious position: Great progress has been made, even in the talks. The only thing that is lacking is one decision in Hanoi, to settle the remaining issues in terms that two weeks previously they had already agreed to. So we are not talking of an issue of principle that is totally unacceptable. Secondly, to complete the work that is required to bring the international machinery into being in the spirit that both sides have an interest of not ending the war in such a way that it is just the beginning of another round of conflict. So we are in a position where peace can be near but peace requires a decision. This is why we wanted to restate once more what our basic attitude is.

With respect to Saigon, we have sympathy and compassion for the anguish of their people and for the concerns of their government. But if we can get an agreement that the President considers just, we will proceed with it.

With respect to Hanoi, our basic objective was stated in the press conference of

October 26. We want an end to the war that is something more than an armistice. We want to move from hostility to normalization and from normalization to cooperation. But we will not make a settlement which is a disguised form of continued warfare and which brings about by indirection what we have always said we would not tolerate.

We have always stated that a fair solution cannot possibly give either side everything that it wants. We are not continuing a war in order to give total victory to our allies. We want to give them a reasonable opportunity to participate in a political structure, but we also will not make a settlement which is a disguised form of victory for the other side.

Therefore we are at a point where we are again perhaps closer to an agreement than we were at the end of October, if the other side is willing to deal with us in good faith and with good will. But it cannot do that every day an issue is settled a new one is raised, that when an issue is settled in an agreement, it is raised again as an understanding, and if it is settled in an understanding, it is raised again as a protocol. We will not be blackmailed into an agreement, we will not be stampeded into an agreement, and if I may say so, we will not be charmed into an agreement, until its conditions are right.

For the President and for all of us who have been engaged in these negotiations, nothing that we have done has meant more than attempting to bring an end to the war in Viet-Nam. Nothing that I have done since I have been in this position has made me feel more the trustee of so many hopes as the negotiations in which I have recently participated. It was painful at times to think of the hopes of millions and, indeed, of the hopes of many of you ladies and gentlemen who were standing outside these various meetingplaces expecting momentous events to be occurring, while inside one frivolous issue after another was surfaced in the last three days.

So, what we are saying to Hanoi is: We are prepared to continue in the spirit of the negotiations that were started in October. We are prepared to maintain an agreement that provides for the unconditional release of all American and allied prisoners, that imposes no political solution on either side, that brings about an internationally supervised cease-fire and the withdrawal of all American forces within 60 days. It is a settlement that is just to both sides and that requires only a decision to maintain provisions that had already been accepted and an end to procedures that can only mock the hopes of humanity.

On that basis, we can have a peace that justifies the hopes of mankind and the sense of justice of all participants.

Now I will be glad to answer some of your questions.

Q. Dr. Kissinger, *could you explain what in your mind you think Hanoi's motivation was in playing what you called a charade?*

Dr. Kissinger: I don't want to speculate on Hanoi's motives. I have no doubt that before too long we will hear a version of events that does not exactly coincide with ours. I have attempted to give you as honest an account as I am capable of. I believe—and this is pure speculation—that for a people that have fought for so long it is, paradoxically, perhaps easier to face the risks of war than the uncertainties of peace.

It may be that they are waiting for a further accentuation of the divisions between us and Saigon, for more public pressures on us, or perhaps they simply cannot make up their mind. But I really have no clue to what the policy decisions were.

Q. Dr. Kissinger, *from your account one would conclude that the talks are now ended in terms of the series you completed. Is that true? Secondly, if it is not true, on what basis will they be resumed?*

Dr. Kissinger: We do not consider the talks completed. We believe that it would be a relatively simple matter to conclude the agreement, because many of the issues that I mentioned in the press conference of October 26 have either been settled or substantial progress toward settling them has been made.

Therefore, if there were a determination to reach an agreement, it could be reached relatively quickly. On the other hand, the possibilities of raising technical objections are endless.

So, as Le Duc Tho said yesterday, we would remain in contact through messages. We can then decide whether or when to meet again. I expect that we will meet again, but we have to meet in an atmosphere that is worthy of the seriousness of the endeavor. On that basis, as far as we are concerned, the settlement will be very rapid.

Q. Dr. Kissinger, you have not discussed at all the proposals that the United States made on behalf of Saigon which required changes in the existing agreement that was negotiated. Can you discuss what those were and what effect they had on stimulating Hanoi, if they did, to make counterproprosals of its own?

Dr. Kissinger: As I pointed out, there were two categories of objections on the part of Saigon, objections which we agreed with and objections which we did not agree with. The objections that we agreed with are essentially contained in the list that I presented at the beginning and those were the ones we maintained. All of those, we believe, did not represent changes in the agreement, but either clarifications, removal of ambiguities, or spelling out the implementation of agreed positions.

In the first sequence of meetings between November 20 and November 26, most of those were, or many of those were, taken care of. So that we have literally, as I have pointed out before, been in the position where every day we thought it could and indeed almost had to be the last day.

The counterproposals that Hanoi has made were again in two categories. One set of changes that would have totally destroyed the balance of the agreement and which, in effect, withdrew the most significant concessions they had made. I did not mention those in my statement, because in the process of negotiation they tended to disappear. They tended to disappear from the agreement to reappear in understandings and then to disappear from understandings to reappear in protocols. But I suspect that they will, in time, after the nervous exhaustion of our technical experts, disappear from the protocols as well. So there were major counterproposals which we believe can be handled.

But then there were a whole series of technical counterproposals which were absolutely unending and which hinged on such profound questions as whether if you state an obligation in the future tense, you were therefore leaving open the question of when it could come into operation, and matters that reached the metaphysical at moments and which, as soon as one of them was settled, another one appeared, which made one believe that one was not engaged in an effort to settle fundamental issues but in delaying action for whatever reason.

Now, those issues can be settled any day that somebody decides to be serious. Now, it is clear that the interplay between Saigon and Hanoi is one of the complicating features of this negotiation, but the basic point that we want to make here is this:

We have had our difficulties in Saigon, but the obstacle to an agreement at this moment is not Saigon, because we do not have, as yet, an agreement that we can present to them. When that point is reached, the President has made clear that he will act on the basis of what he considers just; but he has also made clear that he does not want to end such a long war by bringing about a very short peace.

Q. Can a useful agreement be made operative without Saigon's signature?

Dr. Kissinger: Well, this is a question that has not yet had to be faced and which we hope will not have to be faced. . . .

Q. Are we back to square one now, Dr. Kissinger, would you say?

Dr. Kissinger: No. We have an agreement that is 99 percent completed as far as the text of the agreement is concerned. We also have an agreement whose associated implementations are very simple to conclude if one takes the basic provisions of international supervision that are in the text of the agreement, provisions that happened to be spelled out in greater detail in the agreement than any other aspect, and therefore we are one decision away from a settlement.

Hanoi can settle this any day by an exchange of messages, after which there would be required a certain amount of work on the agreement, which is not very much, and some work in bringing the implementing instruments into being. . . .

Q. Dr. Kissinger, you already mentioned a fundamental disagreement in which you say it is the U.S. insistence that the two parts of Viet-Nam should live in peace with each other. Is that not the fundamental disagreement here?

Dr. Kissinger: As I said, I will not go into the details. I cannot consider it an extremely onerous demand to say that the parties of a peace settlement should live in peace with one another, and we cannot make a settlement which brings peace to North Viet-Nam and maintains the war in South Viet-Nam. . . .

Q. Dr. Kissinger, I am not quite clear on a technical point. You talked about agreements, understandings, and protocols. Are there in fact three different sets of documents under negotiation? What are these understandings?

Dr. Kissinger: There are agreements, understandings, and protocols. It always happens in a negotiation that there is some discussion which is not part of the agreement which attempts to explain what specific provisions mean and how they are going to be interpreted. This is what I meant by understanding. The protocols are the instruments that bring into being the international machinery and prisoner release. Their function is usually, in fact always, a purely technical implementation of provisions of an agreement.

These protocols do not, as a general rule, raise new issues, but rather they say, for example, with respect to prisoners, if the prisoners are to be released in 60 days, they would spell out the staging, the points at which they are released, who can receive them, and so forth.

Similarly with respect to international machinery, they would say where are the teams located, what are their functions, and so forth. Our concern is that the protocols, as we now have them, raise both political issues, which are inappropriate to implementing protocols, and technical issues, which are inconsistent with international supervision.

We have other protocols that deal with prisoners and withdrawals and mining that also present problems, but which I don't mention here because those are normal technical discussions that you would expect in the course of an agreement.

The press: Thank you.

Documents 9 and 10

When the November and December negotiating sessions between Kissinger and Le Duc Tho failed, President Nixon took a drastic step to bring the North Vietnamese back to the bargaining table: a twelve-day bombing campaign against the North. Although neither Nixon nor Kissinger defended the action in public, the American press reported a lot of controversy.

Anthony Lewis of the *New York Times* was the most outspoken national columnist against the war, and his opinions are reflected in Document 9. In Document 10, Art Buchwald, whose work was also syndicated throughout the country, used a very different literary device to comment on the president's policy.

9   Of Sodom and Washington
Anthony Lewis
January 4, 1973

London, England—When the Lord told Abraham that He was going to destroy Sodom for its sins, as it is said in Genesis, Chapter 18, Abraham asked, "Wilt thou also destroy the righteous with the wicked?" The Lord agreed that if there were 10 righteous men in Sodom, "then I will spare all the place for their sakes." But there were not 10.

In that episode the Bible gave early expression to an idea fundamental to Western civilization: the worth of the individual. The story teaches also that the individual has an inescapable moral responsibility to his society, for on him may depend the salvation of all.

One of the terrible aspects of the massive recent American bombing campaign against North Vietnam has been the inertness of the response in many quarters. Worst of all has been the failure of a single person in the United States government to break with a policy that many must know history will judge a crime against humanity.

Just One Purpose in Bombing: Terror

To send B-52s against populous areas such as Haiphong or Hanoi could have only one purpose: terror. It was the response of a man so overwhelmed by his sense of inadequacy and frustration that he had to strike out, punish, destroy.

An English newspaper that has taken a moderate line on the war, the Guardian, asked this week: "Does Mr. Nixon want to go down in history as one of the most murderous and bloodthirsty of American presidents?" But it no longer matters what he wants. The facts assure that he will be so recorded.

The American imagination has evidently ceased to be stirred by the facts of bombing. When people have not lived under bombs, as few Americans have, they perhaps cannot imagine the continuous fear.

They may not understand that bombs dropped in cities and villages kill human beings indiscriminately, the innocent with the wicked. They do not see themselves caught even hundreds of yards from the center of a B-52 raid, the concussion crushing their lungs or spewing out their insides.

The bombing that most notably evoked the sympathy of Americans was the

Nazi Blitz on Britain in World War II. How we admired the pluck of the British under those terrible raids.

In the nearly six years of World War II, less than 80,000 tons of bombs fell on the British Isles. In November alone, when American bombing was restricted because of the peace talks, US planes dropped 100,000 tons on Indochina. The total through the Johnson and Nixon administrations is now more than 7 million tons.

Whatever the cause, whatever the rights or wrongs of the parties in Vietnam, the means used by the United States in this war have long since passed the point when they could be justified by the end. Our war has failed the old and essential principle of proportionality, the moral doctrine that, in fighting, we must not do worse than the evil we oppose.

The Phenomenon Is Nothing New

But what is the cause? It is no longer even arguably to "contain China," or roll back communism, or make the peasants of Vietnam free. It is only, Henry Kissinger says, to make sure the American departure is "honorable." For that we have caused, are causing and presumably will continue to cause the most terrible destruction in the history of man.

Human indifference in the face of cruelty to others is hardly a new phenomenon. Supposedly civilized men and women said nothing while Hitler humiliated, tortured and eventually murdered millions of Jews. Freud made us see that there is an in-eradicable violence in us all.

Still, it does seem remarkable that no one in the United States government has now made himself a witness against what his country is doing. No members of the White House staff, no one in the Pentagon, no Air Force pilot. Not ten, not five, not one.

Public men always tell themselves that they do more good trying to moderate an evil policy from the inside, but at some point that self-deception has to stop.

They say also that one man cannot make a difference. That may be true, but it may not; and in any case it does not relieve anyone from the responsibility of trying. That is what we learn from the story of Abraham and Sodom.

10 Could Peace Prize Go to Bomber?
Art Buchwald
January 3, 1973

Washington—"The Nobel Peace Prize Committee will come to order. We will now start examining the list of candidates. Who is first, Mr. Secretary?"

"Richard M. Nixon. His name has been submitted by U. S. Sen. Hugh Scott."

"We can't have Nixon, not after the bombing attacks he ordered on North Vietnam last week."

"Au contraire, Mr. President. I think Richard Nixon is a very suitable candidate for the peace prize. He is eliminating the B-52 from the United States' arsenal of weapons."

"How is he doing that?"

"He is having them shot down by the enemy. The United States had only 100 B-52s. So far 12 have been shot down. At the rate they are going, they will all disappear in three months. What better gesture can one make toward peace?"

"It's out of the question, gentlemen. Nixon has bombed hospitals and schools and killed thousands of innocent civilians. We cannot give him the peace prize for this."

"But wait a minute. Does he not get credit for restraint? After all, he hasn't used atomic weapons against the North Vietnamese. A man who has the hydrogen bomb and doesn't use it against an enemy should certainly get the prize or at least an honorable mention."

"I do not dispute that but the Nobel Peace Prize has certain stipulations to it, and one is you do not award it to a man who has dropped more bombs on North Vietnam than have been dropped in all of World War II."

"Yes, Mr. President, but we must remember the "only" reason Nixon is bombing the North Vietnamese is to achieve a generation of peace for all mankind. If this bombing were punitive then I would say scratch him off the list. But Nixon is trying to find peace through war and he should be honored for it."

"I object. Nixon has been trying to achieve peace through war for four years. It hasn't worked and it will not work. If we award the prize to a man who believes the only solution to peace is destroying the other side, we will be the laughingstock of the world."

"What does the world know? Nixon has said he will stop the bombing any time the North Vietnamese come to the negotiating table and agree to a fair and just settlement of the war. I say a man who talks that way has gone the extra mile."

"But what is a fair and just settlement of the war?"

"That is not for this committee to decide, Mr. President. For years now, we have given the peace prize to people who have done a great deal of talking about peace, but have had no effect on anybody. This time we have a candidate who has done something about peace."

"What has he done?"

"He has shown everyone that he is dead serious about peace, even if he has to commit his entire Air Force and Navy to bring it about."

"That's true, Olav. But at the same time, wouldn't it be better to wait until the bombing stops before we give Nixon the peace prize?"

"By then it could be too late, particularly if he hasn't achieved peace in time. Don't you see what a fine gesture it would be if we gave the prize to a man who was working for peace but hadn't quite made it."

"We could be at this all day, gentlemen. Let's go on to the next candidate for the peace prize. Mr. Secretary, what is the second name on the list?"

"Henry Kissinger."

"Oh, boy."

Document 11

The Vietnam Agreement and Protocols went into effect on January 27, 1973. The document which was finally signed did not differ in any substantial way from the draft treaty which had been agreed upon by North Vietnam and the United States the preceding October, and South Vietnam, the main obstacle to the treaty back in October, was still not satisfied with many of its provisions.

The Thieu government however was confronted with a stick—the threat

that American aid would be withdrawn if Thieu did not sign—and a carrot—
Nixon's secret promise to come to Saigon's aid militarily if the regime was endangered—and so Thieu signed.

11   The Vietnam Agreement and Protocols, Signed January 27, 1973
Agreement on Ending the War and Restoring Peace in Vietnam

The Parties participating in the Paris Conference on Vietnam,

With a view to ending the war and restoring peace in Vietnam on the basis of
respect for the Vietnamese people's fundamental national rights and the South Vietnamese people's right to self-determination, and to contributing to the consolidation
of peace in Asia and the world,

Have agreed on the following provisions and undertake to respect and to implement them:

Chapter I
The Vietnamese People's Fundamental National Rights

Article 1

The United States and all other countries respect the independence, sovereignty,
unity, and territorial integrity of Vietnam as recognized by the 1954 Geneva Agreements on Vietnam.

Chapter II
Cessation of Hostilities—Withdrawal of Troops

Article 2

A cease-fire shall be observed throughout South Vietnam as of 2400 hours
G.M.T., on January 27, 1973.

At the same hour, the United States will stop all its military activities against the
territory of the Democratic Republic of Vietnam by ground, air and naval forces,
wherever they may be based, and end the mining of the territorial waters, ports,
harbors, and waterways of the Democratic Republic of Vietnam. The United States
will remove, permanently deactivate or destroy all the mines in the territorial waters,
ports, harbors, and waterways of North Vietnam as soon as this Agreement goes
into effect.

The complete cessation of hostilities mentioned in this Article shall be durable
and without limit of time.

Article 3

The parties undertake to maintain the cease-fire and to ensure a lasting and stable
peace.

As soon as the cease-fire goes into effect:

(a) The United States forces and those of the other foreign countries allied with
the United States and the Republic of Vietnam shall remain in-place pending the implementation of the plan of troop withdrawal. The Four-Party Joint Military Commission described in Article 16 shall determine the modalities.

(b) The armed forces of the two South Vietnamese parties shall remain in-place.
The Two-Party Joint Military Commission described in Article 17 shall determine
the areas controlled by each party and the modalities of stationing.

(c) The regular forces of all services and arms and the irregular forces of the parties in South Vietnam shall stop all offensive activities against each other and shall strictly abide by the following stipulations:

All acts of force on the ground, in the air, and on the sea shall be prohibited;

All hostile acts, terrorism, and reprisals by both sides will be banned.

Article 4

The United States will not continue its military involvement or intervene in the internal affairs of South Vietnam.

Article 5

Within sixty days of the signing of this Agreement, there will be a total withdrawal from South Vietnam of troops, military advisers, and military personnel, including technical military personnel and military personnel associated with the pacification program, armaments, munitions, and war material of the United States and those of the other foreign countries mentioned in Article 3 (a). Advisers from the above-mentioned countries to all paramilitary organizations and the police force will also be withdrawn within the same period of time.

Article 6

The dismantlement of all military bases in South Vietnam of the United States and of the other foreign countries mentioned in Article 3 (a) shall be completed within sixty days of the signing of this Agreement.

Article 7

From the enforcement of the cease-fire to the formation of the government provided for in Articles 9 (b) and 14 of this Agreement, the two South Vietnamese parties shall not accept the introduction of troops, military advisers, and military personnel including technical military personnel, armaments, munitions, and war material into South Vietnam.

The two South Vietnamese parties shall be permitted to make periodic replacement of armaments, munitions and war material which have been destroyed, damaged, worn out or used up after the cease-fire, on the basis of piece-for-piece of the same characteristics and properties, under the supervision of the Joint Military Commission of the two South Vietnamese parties and of the International Commission of Control and Supervision.

Chapter III
The Return of Captured Military Personnel and Foreign Civilians, and Captured and Detained Vietnamese Civilian Personnel

Article 8

(a) The return of captured military personnel and foreign civilians of the parties shall be carried out simultaneously with and completed not later than the same day as the troop withdrawal mentioned in Article 5. The parties shall exchange complete lists of the above-mentioned captured military personnel and foreign civilians on the day of the signing of this Agreement.

(b) The parties shall help each other to get information about those military personnel and foreign civilians of the parties missing in action, to determine the location and take care of the graves of the dead so as to facilitate the exhumation and repatriation of the remains, and to take any such other measures as may be required to get information about those still considered missing in action.

(c) The question of the return of Vietnamese civilian personnel captured and detained in South Vietnam will be resolved by the two South Vietnamese parties on the basis of the principles of Article 21 (b) of the Agreement of the Cessation of Hostilities in Vietnam of July 20, 1954. The two South Vietnamese parties will do so in a spirit of national reconciliation and concord, with a view to ending hatred and enmity, in order to ease suffering and to reunite families. The two South Vietnamese parties will do their utmost to resolve this question within ninety days after the cease-fire comes into effect.

Chapter IV
The Exercise of the South Vietnamese People's Right to Self-Determination

Article 9

The Government of the United States of America and the Government of the Democratic Republic of Vietnam undertake to respect the following principles for the exercise of the South Vietnamese people's right to self-determination:

(a) The South Vietnamese people's right to self-determination is sacred, inalienable, and shall be respected by all countries.

(b) The South Vietnamese people shall decide themselves the political future of South Vietnam through genuinely free and democratic general elections under international supervision.

(c) Foreign countries shall not impose any political tendency or personality on the South Vietnamese people.

Article 10

The two South Vietnamese parties undertake to respect the cease-fire and maintain peace in South Vietnam, settle all matters of contention through negotiations, and avoid all armed conflict.

Article 11

Immediately after the cease-fire, the two South Vietnamese parties will:

Achieve national reconciliation and concord, end hatred and enmity, prohibit all acts of reprisal and discrimination against individuals or organizations that have collaborated with one side or the other;

Ensure the democratic liberties of the people: personal freedom, freedom of speech, freedom of the press, freedom of meeting, freedom of organization, freedom of political activities, freedom of belief, freedom of movement, freedom of residence, freedom of work, right to property ownership, and right to free enterprise.

Article 12

(a) Immediately after the cease-fire, the two South Vietnamese parties shall hold consultations in a spirit of national reconciliation and concord, mutual respect, and mutual non-elimination to set up a National Council of National Reconciliation and Concord of three equal segments. The Council shall operate on the principle of unanimity. After the National Council of National Reconciliation and Concord has assumed its functions, the two South Vietnamese parties will consult about the formation of councils at lower levels. The two South Vietnamese parties shall sign an agreement on the internal matters of South Vietnam as soon as possible and do their utmost to accomplish this within ninety days after the cease-fire comes into effect, in keeping with the South Vietnamese people's aspirations for peace, independence and democracy.

(b) The National Council of National Reconciliation and Concord shall have the task of promoting the two South Vietnamese parties' implementation of this Agreement, achievement of national reconciliation and concord and ensurance of democratic liberties. The National Council of National Reconciliation and Concord will organize the free and democratic general elections provided for in Article 9 (b) and decide the procedures and modalities of these general elections. The institutions for which the general elections are to be held will be agreed upon through consultations between the two South Vietnamese parties. The National Council of National Reconciliation and Concord will also decide the procedures and modalities of such local elections as the two South Vietnamese parties agree upon.

Article 13

The question of Vietnamese armed forces in South Vietnam shall be settled by the two South Vietnamese parties in a spirit of national reconciliation and concord, equality and mutual respect, without foreign interference, in accordance with the postwar situation. Among the questions to be discussed by the two South Vietnamese parties are steps to reduce their military effectives and to demobilize the troops being reduced. The two South Vietnamese parties will accomplish this as soon as possible.

Article 14

South Vietnam will pursue a foreign policy of peace and independence. It will be prepared to establish relations with all countries irrespective of their political and social systems on the basis of mutual respect for independence and sovereignty and accept economic and technical aid from any country with no political conditions attached. The acceptance of military aid by South Vietnam in the future shall come under the authority of the government set up after the general elections in South Vietnam provided for in Article 9 (b).

Chapter V
The Reunification of Vietnam and the Relationship Between North and South Vietnam

Article 15

The reunification of Vietnam shall be carried out step by step through peaceful means on the basis of discussions and agreements between North and South Vietnam, without coercion or annexation by either party, and without foreign interference. The time for reunification will be agreed upon by North and South Vietnam.

Pending reunification:

(a) The military demarcation line between the two zones at the 17th parallel is only provisional and not a political or territorial boundary, as provided for in paragraph 6 of the Final Declaration of the 1954 Geneva Conference.

(b) North and South Vietnam shall respect the Demilitarized Zone on either side of the Provisional Military Demarcation Line.

(c) North and South Vietnam shall promptly start negotiations with a view to reestablishing normal relations in various fields. Among the questions to be negotiated are the modalities of civilian movement across the Provisional Military Demarcation Line.

(d) North and South Vietnam shall not join any military alliance or military bloc and shall not allow foreign powers to maintain military bases, troops, military advisers, and military personnel on their respective territories, as stipulated in the 1954 Geneva Agreements on Vietnam.

Document 12

Henry Kissinger was the key international political figure during the Nixon presidency. His brand of personal diplomacy took him all over the world, and his willingness to speak and spar with the press off the record made him a celebrity. Until after the peace settlements, however, Kissinger usually stayed behind the scenes.

This document is part of a transcript of a CBS News Special Report which was telecast shortly after the Vietnam Agreement was signed. In the course of the interview with Marvin Kalb, Kissinger discussed a wide range of issues on the international political scene. The following excerpts bear directly on the peace negotiations in Paris.

12 A Conversation with Henry Kissinger
CBS News Special Report
February 1, 1973

KALB: Dr. Kissinger, let's move the clock back about one month, at a time when the United States was engaged in a very extensive bombing program in the Hanoi-Haiphong area. We've never heard any explanation about why that was really necessary. Could you give us your own feeling on that?

KISSINGER: The decision to resume bombing in the middle of December was perhaps the most painful, the most difficult and certainly the most lonely that the President has had to make since he is in—has been in office. It was very painful to do this at that particular season, when the expectation for peace had been so high, and only six weeks before his inauguration. It was very difficult to do it under circumstances when the outcome was not demonstrable. There were really three parts to it. One: should we resume bombing? Two: if we resume bombing, with what weapons? That involved the whole issue of the B-52. And three: should we talk to the American people?—which was really implied in your question: there's never been an explanation.

With respect to the first part—why did the President decide to resume bombing—we had come to the conclusion that the negotiations as they were then being conducted were not serious; that for whatever reason, the North Vietnamese at that point had come to the conclusion that protracting the negotiations was more in their interest than concluding them. It was not a case that we made certain demands that they rejected. It was a case that no sooner was one issue settled that three others emerged, and as soon as one approached a solution, yet others came to the forefront. At the same time, the more difficult Hanoi was, the more rigid Saigon grew, and we could see a prospect, therefore, where we would be caught between the two contending Vietnamese parties with no element introduced that would change their opinion, with a gradual degeneration of the private talks between Le Duc Tho and me into the same sort of propaganda that the public talks in the Hotel Majestic had reached. And therefore it was decided to try to bring home, really to both Vietnamese parties, that the continuation of the war had its price. And it was not generally recognized that when we started the bombing again of North Vietnam, we also sent General Haig to Saigon to make very clear what—that this did not mean that we would fail to settle on the terms that we had defined as reasonable. So we really moved in both directions simultaneously.

Once the decision was made to resume bombing, we faced the fact that it was in the rainy season and that really the only plane that could act consistently was the B-52, which was an all-weather plane. The—You mentioned the Hanoi-Haiphong area. But major efforts were made to avoid residential areas, and the casualty figures which were released by the North Vietnamese of something like a thousand tend to support that many—that this was the case, because many of these casualties must have occurred in the target areas and not in civilian residential areas.

KALB: Yet a lot of the civilian areas were hit, apparently. There were pictures of that and—

KISSINGER: Well, you can never tell when a picture is made how vast the surrounding area of destruction is, but of course some civilian areas must have been hit. And I'm—I don't want to say that it was not a very painful thing to have to do.

Now, why did the President decide not to speak to the American people? The President can speak most effectively when he announces a new departure in policy and indicates what can be done to bring that particular departure to a conclusion. He could have done only two things in such a speech—which was considered. One is to explain why the negotiations had stalemated, and two, to explain under what circumstances he would end the bombing. The first would have broken the confidentiality of the negotiations, even more than was the case anyway through the exchanges that were going on publicly. And the second would have made the resumption of talks an issue of prestige and might have delayed it. And therefore the President decided that if this action succeeded, then the results would speak for themselves in terms of a settlement, and if a settlement was not reached, then he would have to give an accounting to American people—to the American people of all the actions that led to the continuing stalemate. Now, whatever the reason, once the Viet—once the talks were resumed a settlement was reached fairly rapidly. And I have—we have never made an assertion as to what produced it, but you asked why was the decision made to resume bombing, and this was the reasoning that led to it.

KALB: Dr. Kissinger, isn't the assumption that you're leaving with us that without that kind of heavy bombing the North Vietnamese would not have become serious—your term—and that therefore one could conclude that it was the bombing that brought the North Vietnamese into a serious frame of mind? I ask the question only because they've been bombed so repeatedly and for so many years and still stuck to their guns and their position. What was so unique about this?

KISSINGER: Well, that it came at the end of a long process—

KALB: Mm-hmm.

KISSINGER: —in which they too had suffered a great deal. But I don't think—at this moment, when I am preparing to go to Hanoi—it would serve any useful purpose for me to make any—to speculate about what caused them to make this decision. Obviously they made a big decision in October when they decided to separate the political and the military issues. And at this moment, I think, it is important to understand that the decision was not made lightly, that it was made in the interest of speeding the end of the war, and that now that the war has ended, I think, it is best to put the acrimony behind us.

KALB: Dr. Kissinger, let's talk for a moment about the man with whom you negotiated—how long was it with Le Duc Tho? Three and a half years, something like that?

KISSINGER: Three and a half years.

KALB: What kind of a person is he?

KISSINGER: When one talks about negotiations and looks at the pictures of my opposite number in a garden with me, joking and jovial, a great deal of emphasis tends to be put on the personal relationship. And, over three and a half years of extensive negotiations, of course we established a certain personal relationship, sometimes humorous. But one has to remember also what sort of a man he is, what his background is. Le Duc Tho is an impressive man who joined the Communist Party as a very young man. A man, therefore, driven, in the context of this time, by a certain missionary zeal. He spent seven years at extreme hard labor in a French prison, organized guerrilla movements, and finally, after long struggle, wound up in the Politburo of a country that itself—that then found itself at war almost immediately. He is a man who has never known tranquillity. And where we fight in order to end a war, he fights in order to achieve certain objectives he's held all his life. He holds values quite contrary to ours. And I never had any illusions about that. I didn't convert him to our point of view. He said when he left Paris that we were negotiators having different points of view who were always correct and courteous. I agree with this. And we achieved a conclusion when both of us had realized the limits of the strength that we had to achieve our objectives. And whenever he—when he realized that in the two phases, in October and then again in January—He could be maddening when he didn't want to settle and he was most effective when he did want to settle. He's a man of great theoretical interests and we used to joke with each other that after the peace we'd have exchanged professorships—he at Harvard and I in Hanoi. . . .

Critical Issues for Discussion

1. As a candidate for the presidency who believed in the reasons for American intervention in Vietnam, Richard Nixon had to establish a coherent position on that divisive issue. Document 1 indicates his stance.

What did Nixon consider to be America's mistakes in Vietnam? What did he think the United States should be doing there? How would these steps bring about an "honorable peace" in Vietnam? Nixon's campaign slogan in 1968 was: "This Time Vote Like Your Whole World Depended On It." What did he mean by that?

Nixon's argument that new leadership was needed to end the American role in Vietnam made sense to many. Why? Look at Document 2. What was Halberstam's message to Nixon? What was his warning? How did Halberstam account for the failure of the United States in Vietnam?

2. Richard Nixon believed in peace in Vietnam, but he did not want the United States to lose the military struggle there. He argued that "our defeat and humiliation in South Vietnam without question would promote recklessness in the councils of those great powers who have not yet abandoned their goals of world conquest."

Who were "those great powers"? What were their goals? How would an honorable peace in Vietnam avoid or avert those difficulties? What exactly is an "honorable peace"? What did Nixon assume about international politics?

3. Adlai Stevenson, the Democratic candidate for president in 1952 and 1956, was a liberal. Richard Nixon had once referred to him as "Adlai the appeaser . . . who got a Ph.D. from Dean Acheson's College of Cowardly Communist Containment." What did this phrase mean? In 1972, Nixon was the president who opened relations with China and worked for detente with the Soviet Union. What had happened? Had Nixon changed? How? Why? What were his underlying beliefs about the way the world works?

4. One of the major controversies of the war grew up around the strategy of bombing North Vietnam. The debate touched on many issues. With this in mind, consider Documents 3, 4, and 5.

What were the justifications for the bombing in 1972? What constructive purposes would it serve? What would happen to American soldiers without that policy? On what grounds did opponents of the bombing condemn it? Did these two sides in the dispute speak with each other, or were they talking different languages? Explain. Was morality an issue? How did the American pilot react to the discussion going on around him about his role in the war?

5. In Document 6, President Nixon explained why the United States had decided to take drastic steps against North Vietnam in the spring of 1972. What were those steps? How did the President make his case to the American people? What was the tone of his address? Was his account convincing? On what basis would his opponents have argued with his policy?

6. The North Vietnamese Easter Offensive which occurred during the spring of 1972 was seen as a referendum on Vietnamization. Document 7 presents the official U.S. Army history of this action.

How did the South Vietnamese do? How did the author account for their victory? Was the American role an important one? What were the factors which led to this assault? What were the results of the success of the South Vietnamese?

7. The failure of the negotiations between Henry Kissinger and Le Duc Tho in the fall of 1972 has been analyzed many times. Documents 8 and 12 present Kissinger's analysis. How did he view the breakdown of the talks? What did he think was necessary to make peace? What did he think about his North Vietnamese counterpart? What did he think about Saigon's attitude? How did he read Hanoi? Did he think that peace would ever come?

8. The Christmas Bombing provoked noisy protests at home. Documents 9 and 10 present the views of two popular newspaper columnists.

On what basis were these criticisms launched? How would President Nixon have responded? Were these articles convincing? Was either style more effective? Why?

9. Document 11 contains excerpts from the cease fire agreement of January 27, 1973. Was it an "honorable peace"? Did it solve the problems which had been debated and fought over for so many years? Which problems were shelved rather than solved? How would those problems be resolved? Did either side get a better deal? Why? What did the future appear to hold for all of the signatories of the agreement in January 1973?

10. Vietnamization was a military strategy. Did it have a diplomatic counterpart? Were the South Vietnamese involved in the negotiations over their future? What did the South Vietnamese government want from a peace treaty? Did the United States agree with those aims? Where did these allies agree? What were their differences? What did the "Americanization" of the negotiations mean to the peace process?

Follow Up One of the most important issues for any individual is the question of means and ends. The end which President Nixon desired was an honorable peace in Vietnam. Many have consistently questioned the means which he used to try to bring about that result.

Henry Kissinger commented that he questioned Nixon's decision to bomb Hanoi in December 1972 but that the President was proved right. What did Kissinger mean? Do you agree? How do you evaluate that gamble and Nixon's earlier ones: the Cambodian incursion of 1970, the Laos invasion of 1971, the mining of Haiphong harbor and bombing the north in May 1972? Did his ends justify his means?

Suggestions for Further Reading

Nixon and the Peace Negotiations

Aiken, George. *Senate Diary*. Brattleboro, Vt.: Stephen Greene Press, 1976.
Aiken, who supported Nixon until the Christmas bombing of 1972, provides valuable insights into congressional reactions to the Nixon presidency.

Goodman, Allen E. *The Lost Peace: America's Search for a Negotiated Settlement of the Vietnam War*. Stanford: Hoover Institute Press, 1978.
Goodman interviewed U.S. diplomats for this scholarly appraisal of the peace negotiations, which he sees as a defeat for the United States.

Kraslov, David, and Stuart Loory. *The Secret Search for Peace in Vietnam*. New York: Random House, 1968.
This short, readable account of early attempts at a negotiated settlement is still worth seeking out.

Porter, Gareth. *A Peace Denied: The U.S., Vietnam and the Paris Agreement.*
   Bloomington: Indiana Univ. Press, 1975.
   Using interviews with participants on all sides, Porter analyzes the failure of
   diplomacy to bring peace. He compares the Paris agreement to the 1954 Geneva agreements, with the United States again secretly planning to continue
   the war.
Szulc, Tad. *The Illusion of Peace: Foreign Policy in the Nixon Years.* New York:
   Viking, 1978.
   Because Szulc's massive book is organized chronologically, one must use the
   index to locate relevant sections on Vietnam. Szulc is highly critical of the
   high price in human lives which Nixon and Kissinger paid for the "unen-
   forceable platitudes" of the agreement.

Prisoners of War

Daly, James, and Lee Bergman. *A Hero's Welcome: The Conscience of Sergeant
   James Daly vs. the United States Army.* Indianapolis: Bobbs Merrill, 1975.
   Daly, a Black Jehovah's Witness, spent five years as a prisoner in Hanoi,
   where he joined a small group of antiwar prisoners called The Peace Com-
   mittee. His story raises important questions of patriotism and conscience.
Debris, Jean-Pierre, and Andre Menras. *We Accuse.* Washington: Indochina Mo-
   bile Education Project, 1973; distributed by American Friends Service Com-
   mittee, Philadelphia.
   Two Frenchmen who were jailed for two and a half years for raising the
   NLF flag in Saigon describe the conditions under which thousands of South
   Vietnamese political prisoners were held.
Rowan, Stephen A. *They Wouldn't Let Us Die: The Prisoners of War Tell Their
   Story.* Middle Village, N.Y.: Jonathan David, 1973.
   Rowan interviewed prisoners from all backgrounds about what they had en-
   dured and how they felt about it. Although the analysis is naive in places,
   the stories are interesting.
Rowe, James N. *Five Years to Freedom.* Boston: Little, Brown, 1970.
   A Green Beret major, captured in 1963 and held in South Vietnam by the
   Vietcong, Rowe succeeded in escaping on his fourth attempt, in 1968. For
   most of his five years in captivity, he was interrogated by the same V.C.
   officer, who never succeeded in winning Rowe over.
Risner, Robinson. *The Passing of the Night: My Seven Years as a Prisoner of the
   North Vietnamese.* New York: Random House, 1973.
   The highest-ranking American P.O.W. tells of his ordeal and of the convic-
   tions that kept him going.
Smith, George E. *P.O.W.: Two Years with the Vietcong.* Berkeley: Ramparts,
   1971.
   A member of the Special Forces, Smith was captured by the National Lib-
   eration Front in 1963 and spent his captivity in jungle camps in the south.
   He gives a detailed picture of life with the "Vietcong," whom he came to
   admire.

Hey, Hey, L.B.J. . . .
Peace demonstration at the Pentagon in the fall of 1967. President Johnson was pictured as a war criminal on one placard and was the subject of numerous chants and catcalls from the crowd. *U.P.I.*

Chapter 11
Homefront USA
Background

Historical Summary

Americans abandoned their traditional insularity during World War II, when the country assumed a major role in the struggle against German and Japanese aggression. Their leaders in the 1950s and 1960s maintained a posture of global activism, now aimed at the "containment" of Communism, which was seen as a massive international threat. Exemplifying this attitude, President Kennedy said in his inaugural address in January 1961 that America would "pay any price" and "bear any burden" to defend freedom everywhere.

World War II also set in motion enormous domestic changes. The need for industrial labor and the poor rural economy of the South encouraged the migration of blacks to northern cities and the West, and their demands for economic and social equality spawned a vigorous civil rights movement. Kennedy's assassination in late 1963 brought Lyndon Johnson into office; a long-time supporter of economic opportunity for the poor, Johnson was determined to promote progressive legislation to achieve the Great Society.

But there was the war in Vietnam. Seen initially as a minor test of America's worldwide obligation to stop the spread of communism, the war intensified until it consumed Johnson's political life. For, in his view, any sign of weakness in waging the war would unleash his right-wing political opponents and allow them to sabotage his liberal domestic program. So Johnson tried to limit the conflict, hoping that he could expend enough money and troops to win the Vietnam war without sacrificing his domestic "war" on poverty and ignorance. The strategy created a dilemma.

On the one hand, a small but vocal and growing minority protested against the war on moral grounds. They included students, teachers, clergymen, and others, soon to be joined by prominent black spokesmen like Martin Luther King, Jr., who believed in non-violence and felt that blacks were fighting for freedom in a far-off land when it had not yet been won at home. On the other hand, a substantial proportion of the American population, while favorable to the crusade against Communism, objected to Johnson's conduct of the war on the grounds that he was not acting decisively and forcefully enough.

Most Americans, though, were uncertain, confused and frustrated. They were troubled by the mounting casualty figures, the rising costs, and above all, the prospect of endless escalation of the war. Opinion surveys showed them alternating between support for negotiations and support for stronger action. Very few advocated unilateral withdrawal. Or, as one housewife told Samuel Lubell, the pollster: "I want to get out, but I don't want to give up."

The Congress mirrored this mood. Senator J. William Fulbright and a handful of associates seemed to personify antiwar sentiment. At the other extreme, hard-liners, like Senator John Stennis and Representative Mendel Rivers, who were close to the defense establishment, urged the president to unleash the military. But whatever their reservations about the war, the majority of the legislators went along with the president—partly because of his powerful influence and partly because they were susceptible to charges of not furnishing adequate backing for "our boys" in the field.

A dramatic turning point in support for the Johnson administration came with the Tet Offensive of 1968. The surprise Communist attacks affected U.S. public opinion only slightly; but Johnson's own advisers, in particular the new secretary of defense, Clark Clifford, began to have serious doubts.

Meanwhile, Johnson himself was being confronted by challengers within the Democratic party. Senator Eugene McCarthy of Minnesota registered an unexpectedly high vote in the New Hampshire presidential primary by espousing an antiwar platform. Then Senator Robert Kennedy, who had grown increasingly critical of the war, declared his candidacy. On March 31, 1968, Johnson announced that he would not seek or accept the Democratic nomination, saying that he did not want "the presidency to become involved in the partisan divisions that are developing in this political year." He may well have decided against running long before, but he appeared to the American public and to the world as a casualty of the war.

During the following months the United States seemed to explode. Martin Luther King, Jr., and Robert Kennedy were assassinated. Black neighborhoods in Washington and many other cities rioted. Campus demonstrations proliferated. And the unrest reached a climax in Chicago during the Democratic party convention as the police cracked down on protestors outside McCormick Hall.

Vice President Hubert Humphrey, the Democratic party nominee, was still loyal to President Johnson and therefore associated with his policies. Humphrey did not begin to express misgivings about the war until late September, by which time he lacked credibility. Reports circulated during the presidential campaign that Richard Nixon had a "secret plan" to end the war, and they may have contributed to his narrow victory over Humphrey.

Once in office, Nixon proceeded to withdraw American forces from Vietnam as part of his effort to achieve "peace with honor," winning considerable public approval from the "silent majority" of Americans. Yet anti-war protests multiplied, hitting a peak after the U.S. incursion into Cambodia in April 1970. Dissent, which had been expressed by a marginal few in 1964, had become a significant political factor—and would remain so until Americans stopped dying in Vietnam.

Points to Emphasize

- the assumptions which formed the general consensus in American politics as the 1960s began
- the ways in which the antiwar movement grew
- the reactions of different groups to the war in Vietnam
- the factors which led to the increasing polarization of American politics by the late 1960s
- the issues which arose during the election campaign of 1968
- the effects of the draft on American life
- the influence of the My Lai massacre on the American homefront
- the long-range effects of the heated debate on the Vietnam War

Glossary of Names and Terms

Spiro Theodore Agnew executive in Baltimore County, Maryland, 1962–1966. Governor of Maryland, 1967–1969. Vice President of the United States, 1969–1973. Resigned in financial scandal, 1973.

Daniel Berrigan Roman Catholic priest, poet, teacher, lecturer, and antiwar activist. Founder of the Catholic Peace Fellowship. Convicted of conspiracy and destruction of draft records in Catonsville, Maryland, in 1968. His brother Philip also involved in anti-war activities which led to arrests.

Samuel W. Brown National Volunteer Coordinator, Eugene McCarthy's Presidential campaign, 1968. Coordinator, Vietnam Moratorium, 1969. Treasurer of Colorado, 1974–1977.

William Sloane Coffin, Jr. worked in the C.I.A., 1950–1953. Ordained Presbyterian minister, 1956. Chaplain at Williams College, 1957–1958. Chaplain at Yale University, 1958–1975. Senior Minister, Riverside Church, New York City, 1977–present.

Daniel Ellsberg worked for Rand Corporation, 1959–1964, 1967–1970. Special Assisant to Assistant Secretary of Defense for international security affairs, 1964–1965. Senior liaison officer, American embassy, South Vietnam, 1965–1966. Assistant to Deputy U.S. Ambassador to South Vietnam, 1967. Member of the McNamara committee which produced the Pentagon Papers. Later leaked those documents to the Senate Foreign Relations Committee and, in 1971, to the press.

Lewis Hershey Deputy Director of Selective Service system, 1940–1941. Director, Selective Service System, 1941–1946. Director, Office of Selective Service Records, 1946–1947. Director of Selective Service, 1948–1970.

Hubert Horatio Humphrey Mayor of Minneapolis, 1945–1948. Democratic Senator from Minnesota, 1948–1964, 1971–1978. Senate Majority Whip, 1961. Vice President of the United States, 1965–1969. Defeated candidate for the presidency in the election of 1968.

John Kerry Yale graduate. Navy veteran who served in Vietnam and became a spokesman for the Vietnam Veterans Against The War in 1971. Elected Lieutenant Governor of Massachusetts in November 1982.

Martin Luther King, Jr. Baptist minister. Led Montgomery Bus Boycott, 1956. President and organizer of the Southern Christian Leadership Conference, 1957. A leader of the civil rights movement and nonviolent civil disobedience in the United States throughout the 1960s. Winner of the Nobel Peace Prize, 1964. Assassinated 1968.

Richard Milhouse Nixon Republican representative from California, 1947–1950. U.S. Senator from California, 1950–1953. Vice President of the United States, 1953–1961. Defeated candidate for the presidency, 1960. Defeated in gubernatorial election in California, 1962. President of the United States, 1969–1974. Resigned because of Watergate, 1974.

Dewey Canyon III five days of demonstrations in April 1971 organized by the Vietnam Veterans Against the War, whose chief spokesman was John Kerry. (Dewey Canyon I and II were U.S. military operations conducted in Vietnam.)

Kent State university in Ohio where students protesting at the time of the Cambodian incursion were fired upon by National Guardsmen on May 4, 1970. Four students were killed, sparking nationwide demonstrations.

My Lai a Vietnamese hamlet attacked by U.S. troops under Lieutenant William Calley on March 16, 1968. According to Seymour Hersh, the correspondent who later reported the story, 347 civilians were killed there.

silent majority President Nixon's term, used in a November 3, 1969 speech, for American citizens who supported his program for "peace with honor" in Vietnam.

Students for a Democratic Society (SDS) a radical student group with branches on many American campuses. Its national prominence began in 1962 with the Port Huron Statement, written largely by University of Michigan student Tom Hayden.

teach-ins begun at the University of Michigan in the spring of 1965 where professors organized all-night meetings of lectures and readings on the issue of the war in Vietnam.

Vietnam Moratorium Committee group which sponsored massive antiwar demonstrations in the fall of 1969.

Yippies members of the Youth International Party. Organized or, at least, named by Abbie Hoffman and Jerry Rubin. A protest group whose statements and actions shocked mainstream Americans.

Documents

Document 1

Senator J. William Fulbright of Arkansas served as Chairman of the Senate Committee on Foreign Relations. In that capacity, he had played a major role in easing the Gulf of Tonkin Resolution through the Senate in August 1964. By 1966, however, Fulbright had become a most persistent critic of U.S. policy in Vietnam. In his speeches, published in *The Arrogance of Power*, Fulbright's remarks about Vietnam expanded into a more general critique of American foreign policy throughout the world.

1 On America's Vietnam Policy
J. William Fulbright

The United States is now involved in a sizable and "open-ended" war against communism in the only country in the world which won freedom from colonial rule under communist leadership. In South Vietnam as in North Vietnam, the communists remain today the only solidly organized political force. That fact is both the measure of our failure and the key to its possible redemption. . . .

The major reason for the success of the Viet Cong in South Vietnam has not been aid from the North but the absence of a cohesive alternative nationalist movement in the South. Both the success of the communists in South Vietnam and their failure in India, Burma, Malaya, Indonesia, and the Philippines strongly suggest that "wars of national liberation" depend for their success more on the weakness of the regime under attack than on the strength of support from outside.

Our search for a solution to the Vietnamese war must begin with the general fact that nationalism is the strongest single political force in the world today and the specific fact, arising from the history to which I have referred, that in Vietnam the most effective nationalist movement is communist-controlled. We are compelled, therefore, once again to choose between opposition to communism and support of nationalism. I strongly recommend that for once we give priority to the latter. The dilemma is a cruel one, and one which we must hope to avoid in the future by timely and unstinting support of non-communist nationalist movements, but it is too late for that in Vietnam. I strongly recommend, therefore, that we seek to come to terms with both Hanoi and the Viet Cong, not, to be sure, by "turning tail and running," as the saying goes, but by conceding the Viet Cong a part in the government of South Vietnam. . . .

Present realities require a revision of priorities in American policy. The basis of my criticisms of American policy in Southeast Asia and Latin America is a belief that American interests are better served by supporting nationalism than by opposing communism, and that when the two are encountered in the same political movement it is in our interest to accept a communist role in the government of the country concerned rather than to undertake the cruel and all but impossible task of suppressing a genuinely nationalist revolution. In Vietnam we have allowed our fear of communism to make us once again the enemy of a nationalist revolution, and in that role we have wrought havoc.

. . .

Power has a way of undermining judgment, of planting delusions of grandeur in the minds of otherwise sensible people and otherwise sensible nations. As I have said earlier, the idea of being responsible for the whole world seems to have dazzled us, giving rise to what I call the arrogance of power, or what the French, perhaps more aptly, call "le vertige de puissance," by which they mean a kind of dizziness or giddiness inspired by the possession of great power. If then, as I suspect, there is a relationship between the self-absorption of some of our allies and the American military involvement in Vietnam, it may have more to do with American vanity than with our friends' complacency. Thus, by taking on foreign responsibilities for which it is ill-equipped, America not only strains her resources but encourages other nations to neglect their responsibilities, which neglect of course can only lead to added burdens for the United States. With this thought in mind, I turn now to what may be the most fateful of all of the fallout effects of the Vietnamese war: its effects on the American people and nation.

The Fallout at Home

The war in Southeast Asia has affected the internal life of the United States in two important ways: it has diverted our energies from the Great Society program which began so promisingly, and it has generated the beginnings of a war fever in the minds of the American people and their leaders.

Despite brave talk about having both "guns and butter," the Vietnamese war has already had a destructive effect on the Great Society. The 89th Congress, which enacted so much important domestic legislation in 1965, enacted much less in 1966, partly, it is true, because of the unusual productivity of its first session but more because the Congress as a whole lost interest in the Great Society and became, politically and psychologically, a "war Congress."

There is a kind of Gresham's Law of public policy: fear drives out hope, security precedes welfare, and it is only to the extent that a country is successful in the prevention of bad things that it is set free to concentrate on those pursuits which renew the nation's strength and bring happiness into the lives of its people. For twenty years beginning in 1940 America was greatly preoccupied with external dangers and accordingly neglectful of those aspects of domestic life which require organized public programs and sizable public expenditures. The reason for this, of course, was the exacting demands of two world wars and an intractable cold war, which required the massive diversion of resources from community life to national security. We felt ourselves compelled to turn away from our hopes in order to concentrate on our fears and the public happiness became a luxury to be postponed to some distant day when the dangers besetting us would have disappeared.

In the early 1960s a trend and an event coincided which seemed to create the opportunity for a revision of priorities on our national agenda. The trend—after if not before the Cuban missile crisis of 1962—was one toward relative stability in international relations, based on a fragile, tacit agreement between the great powers to live together in peaceful, or competitive, coexistence. The event was the coming to office in the United States of a creative new Administration, eager to arrange a détente with the Russians and eager as well to use a respite from international crisis to devise imaginative new programs for the betterment of American life. During the three years of his Administration, President Kennedy put forward imaginative and well-conceived plans for the improvement of health and education, for the conquest of poverty, pollution, and blight, and for the spiritual enrichment of American life.

President Johnson embraced and expanded upon these innovations. Elected in 1964 by a great popular majority and supported by a great Congressional majority, President Johnson used his extraordinary talent for leadership to make the first session of the 89th Congress the most productive in a generation. With a degree of partisan harmony that would have seemed inconceivable a few years before, the Congress in 1965 adopted sweeping legislation to expand education, to provide health care to the aged, to combat urban and rural poverty, to renew our cities and purify our streams, and to meet many other long-neglected problems. It seemed that the United States might be about to undergo something of a social revolution.

Then came Vietnam. The war had been going on for many years but before 1965 it had been a small and distant war and, as our leaders repeatedly assured us, a war which would be won or lost by the Vietnamese themselves. Then, in the first months of 1965 if not earlier, it became clear that the Saigon government was about to lose the war and we intervened with a large army, changing our role from adviser to principal belligerent. As a result of this radical change in American policy in Southeast Asia, we have had, after so brief an interlude, to turn back once again from our hopes to our fears, from the renewal of national resources to the avoidance of international disaster.

Vigorously executed and adequately funded, the legislation adopted by the 89th Congress can open the way to an era of abundance and opportunity for all Americans, but for the present at least the inspiration and commitment of the Great Society have disappeared. They have disappeared in the face of our deepening involvement in Vietnam, and although it may be contended that the United States has the material resources to rebuild its society at home while waging war abroad, it is already being demonstrated that we do not have the mental and spiritual resources for such a double effort. Politicians, like other people, have only one brain apiece, and it stands to reason that if they spend all their time thinking about one thing they are not going to be thinking about something else. The President simply cannot think about implementing the Great Society at home while he is supervising bombing missions over North Vietnam; nor is the Congress particularly inclined to debate, much less finance, expanded domestic programs when it is involved in debating, and paying for, an expanding war; nor can the American people be expected to think very hard or do very much about improving their schools and communities when they are worried about casualty lists and the danger of a wider war.

My own view is that there is a kind of madness in the facile assumption that we can raise the many billions of dollars necessary to rebuild our schools and cities and public transport and eliminate the pollution of air and water while also spending tens of billions to finance an "open-ended" war in Asia. But even if the material resources can somehow be drawn from an expanding economy, I do not think that the spiritual resources will long be forthcoming from an angry and disappointed people.

Document 2

Folk music thrived in the early 1960s. It became associated with the civil rights movement and soon carried over into the antiwar movement as well. Pete Seeger was a veteran troubadour whose left-wing political beliefs had kept him off network television since the political blacklists of the 1950's.

As opposition to the war escalated and the ranks of the protest singers swelled, Seeger remained in the forefront of the movement, and his song, "Waist Deep in the Big Muddy," left little doubt about his stance. His performance of the song on the Smothers Brothers television program, over the objections of some CBS Television executives, caused a sensation.

2   Waist Deep in the Big Muddy
Pete Seeger

It was back in nineteen forty two,
I was part of a good platoon.
We were on maneuvers in Loosiana,
One night by the light of the moon.
  The captain told us to ford a river,
  And that's how it all begun.
  We were knee deep in the Big Muddy,
  But the big fool said to push on.

The sergeant said, "Sir, are you sure,
This is the best way back to the base?"
"Sergeant, go on; I once forded this
  river
Just a mile above this place.
  It'll be a little soggy but just keep
  slogging.
  We'll soon be on dry ground."
  We were waist deep in the Big Muddy
  And the big fool said to push on.

The sergeant said, "Sir, with all this
  equipment,
No man will be able to swim."
"Sergeant, don't be a nervous nellie,"
The Captain said to him.
  "All we need is a little determination;
  Men, follow me, I'll lead on."
  We were neck deep in the Big Muddy
  And the big fool said to push on.

All of a sudden, the moon clouded
  over,

We heard a gurgling cry.
A few seconds later, the captain's
  helmet
Was all that floated by.
  The sergeant said, "Turn around men,
  I'm in charge from now on."
  And we just made it out of the
  Big Muddy
  With the captain dead and gone.

We stripped and dived and found his
  body
Stuck in the old quicksand.
I guess he didn't know that the water
  was deeper
Than the place he'd once before been.
  Another stream had joined the Big
  Muddy
  Just a half mile from where we'd
  gone.
  We'd been lucky to escape from the
  Big Muddy
  When the big fool said to push on.

Well, maybe you'd rather not draw
  any moral;
I'll leave that to yourself.
Maybe you're still walking and you're
  still talking
And you'd like to keep your health.
  But every time I read the papers

Words and music by Pete Seeger TRO © 1967 Melody Trails, Inc. New York, N.Y. Used by permission

That old feeling comes on:
We're waist deep in the Big Muddy and
The Big Fool says to push on.

Waist deep in the Big Muddy
And the Big Fool says to push on!
Waist deep in the Big Muddy

And the Big Fool says to push on!
Waist deep! Neck deep!
Soon even a tall man'll be
    over his head!
Waist deep in the BIG MUDDY!
AND THE BIG FOOL SAYS TO
PUSH ON!!

Document 3

The Reverend Martin Luther King, Jr., was the symbol of the civil rights movement. His leadership in the Birmingham Bus Boycott in 1955–1956 was followed by nationwide recognition of his ability as an orator and, more significantly, as a voice for moral change in America. His "I Have A Dream" speech which concluded the March to Washington in the summer of 1963 was a magnificent, eloquent, and influential address.

King opposed the war as early as 1965, but he did not voice his opposition publicly until 1967. In this speech, one of five lectures delivered by the Nobel Prize winner over the Canadian Broadcast Corporation in the fall of 1967, King explained why he felt that he, as a civil rights leader, had a moral obligation to speak out on the issue of the Vietnam War.

3   Conscience and the Vietnam War
Martin Luther King, Jr.

It is many months now since I found myself obliged by conscience to end my silence and to take a public stand against my country's war in Vietnam. The considerations which led me to that painful decision have not disappeared; indeed, they have been magnified by the course of events since then. The war itself is intensified; the impact on my country is even more destructive.

I cannot speak about the great themes of violence and nonviolence, of social change and of hope for the future, without reflecting on the tremendous violence of Vietnam.

Since the spring of 1967, when I first made public my opposition to my government's policy, many persons have questioned me about the wisdom of my decision. "Why *you?*" they have said. "Peace and civil rights don't mix. Aren't you hurting the cause of your people?" And when I hear such questions, I have been greatly saddened, for they mean that the inquirers have never really known me, my commitment, or my calling. Indeed, that question suggests that they do not know the world in which they live.

In explaining my position, I have tried to make it clear that I remain perplexed—as I think everyone must be perplexed—by the complexities and ambiguities of Vietnam. I would not wish to underrate the need for a collective solution to this tragic war. I would wish neither to present North Vietnam or the National Liberation Front as paragons of virtue, nor to overlook the role they can play in the successful resolution of the problem. While they both may have justifiable reasons to be suspicious of the good faith of the United States, life and history give eloquent testimony to the fact that conflicts are never resolved without trustful give-and-take on both sides.

Since I am a preacher by calling, I suppose it is not surprising that I had several reasons for bringing Vietnam into the field of my moral vision. There is at the outset a very obvious and almost facile connection between the war in Vietnam and the struggle I and others have been waging in America. A few years ago there was a shining moment in that struggle. It seemed as if there was a real promise of hope for the poor, both black and white, through the poverty program. There were experiments, hopes, new beginnings. Then came the build-up in Vietnam, and I watched the program broken and eviscerated as if it were some idle political plaything of a society gone mad on war, and I knew that America would never invest the necessary funds or energies in rehabilitation of its poor so long as adventures like Vietnam continued to draw men and skills and money like some demonical destructive suction tube. And so I was increasingly compelled to see the war not only as a moral outrage but also as an enemy of the poor, and to attack it as such.

Perhaps a more tragic recognition of reality took place when it became clear to me that the war was doing far more than devastating the hopes of the poor at home. It was sending their sons and their brothers and their husbands to fight and to die and in extraordinarily higher proportions relative to the rest of the population. We were taking the black young men who had been crippled by our society and sending them eight thousand miles away to guarantee liberties in Southeast Asia which they had not found in southwest Georgia and East Harlem. And so we have been repeatedly faced with the cruel irony of watching Negro and white boys on TV screens as they kill and die together for a nation that has been unable to seat them together in the same schools. We watch them in brutal solidarity burning the huts of a poor village, but we realize that they would never live on the same block in Detroit. I could not be silent in the face of such cruel manipulation of the poor.

My third reason moves to an even deeper level of awareness, but it grows out of my experience in the ghettos of the North over the last three years—especially the last three summers. As I have walked among the desperate, rejected, angry young men, I have told them that Molotov cocktails and rifles would not solve their problems. I have tried to offer them my deepest compassion, while maintaining my conviction that social change comes most meaningfully through nonviolent action. But, they asked, and rightly so, what about Vietnam? They asked if our own nation wasn't using massive doses of violence to solve its problems, to bring about the changes it wanted. Their questions hit home, and I knew that I could never again raise my voice against the violence of the oppressed in the ghettos without having first spoken clearly to the greatest purveyor of violence in the world today: my own government. For the sake of those boys, for the sake of this government, for the sake of the hundreds of thousands trembling under our violence, I cannot be silent.

For those who ask the question "Aren't you a civil rights leader?"—and thereby mean to exclude me from the movement for peace—I answer by saying that I have worked too long and hard now against segregated public accommodations to end up segregating my moral concern. Justice is indivisible. It must also be said that it would be rather absurd to work passionately and unrelentingly for integrated schools and not be concerned about the survival of a world in which to be integrated. I must say further that something in the very nature of our organizational structure in the Southern Christian Leadership Conference led me to this decision.

In 1957, when a group of us formed that organization, we chose as our motto: "To save the soul of America." Now it should be incandescently clear that no one who has any concern for the integrity and life of America today can ignore the present war.

As if the weight of such a commitment were not enough, another burden of responsibility was placed upon me in 1964: I cannot forget that the Nobel Prize for Peace was also a commission—a commission to work harder than I had ever worked before for "the brotherhood of man." This is a calling which takes me beyond national allegiances, but even if it were not present, I would yet have to live with the meaning of my commitment to the ministry of Jesus Christ. To me the relationship of this ministry to the making of peace is so obvious that I sometimes marvel at those who ask me why I am speaking against the war. We are called to speak for the weak, for the voiceless, for the victims of our nation, and for those it calls enemy, for no document from human hands can make these humans any less our brothers.

And as I ponder the madness of Vietnam and search within myself for ways to understand and respond in compassion, my mind goes constantly to the people of that peninsula. I speak now not of the soldiers of each side, not of the junta in Saigon, but simply of the people who have been living under the curse of war for almost three continuous decades now. I think of them, too, because it is clear to me that there will be no meaningful solution until some attempt is made to know them and to hear their broken cries.

. . .

Somehow this madness must cease. We must stop now. I speak as a child of God and brother to the suffering poor of Vietnam. I speak for those whose land is being laid waste, whose homes are being destroyed, whose culture is being subverted. I speak for the poor of America who are paying the double price of smashed hopes at home and death and corruption in Vietnam. I speak as a citizen of the world, for the world as it stands aghast at the path we have taken. I speak as an American to the leaders of my own nation. The great initiative in this war is ours. The initiative to stop it must be ours.

In the spring of 1967, I made public the steps I consider necessary for this to happen. I should add now only that while many Americans have supported the proposals, the government has so far not recognized one of them. These are the times for real choices and not false ones. We are at the moment when our lives must be placed on the line if our nation is to survive its own folly. Every man of humane convictions must decide on the protest that best suits his convictions, but we must all protest.

There is something seductively tempting about stopping there and going off on what in some circles has become a popular crusade against the war in Vietnam. I say we must enter that struggle, but I wish to go on now to say something even more disturbing. The war in Vietnam is but a symptom of a far deeper malady within the American spirit.

In 1957 a sensitive American official overseas said that it seemed to him that our nation was on the wrong side of a world revolution. I am convinced that if we are to get on the right side of the world revolution we as a nation must undergo a radical revolution of values. A true revolution of values will soon cause us to question the fairness and justice of many of our past and present policies. A true revolution of values will soon look uneasily on the glaring contrast between poverty and wealth. With righteous indignation, it will look across the seas and see individual capitalists of the West investing huge sums of money in Asia, Africa, and South America only to take the profits out with no concern for the social betterment of the countries, and say: "This is not just." It will look at our alliance with the landed gentry of Latin America and say: "This is not just." The Western arrogance of feeling that it has everything to teach others and nothing to learn from them is not just. A true revolution of values will lay hands on the world order and say of war: "This way of settling differences is not just." This business of burning human beings with napalm, of filling our nation's homes with orphans and widows, of injecting poisonous drugs of hate into the veins of peoples normally humane, of sending men home from dark and bloody battlefields physically handicapped and psychologically deranged, cannot be reconciled with wisdom, justice, and love. A nation that continues year after year to spend more money on military defense than on programs of social uplift is approaching spiritual doom.

This kind of positive revolution of values is our best defense against Communism. War is not the answer. Communism will never be defeated by the use of atomic bombs or nuclear weapons.

These are revolutionary times; all over the globe men are revolting against old systems of exploitation and oppression. The shirtless and barefoot people of the land are rising up as never before. "The people that walked in darkness have seen a great light." We in the West must support these revolutions. It is a sad fact that because of comfort, complacency, a morbid fear of Communism, and our proneness to adjust to injustice, the Western nations that initiated so much of the revolutionary spirit of the modern world have now become the arch-antirevolutionaries. This has driven many to feel that only Marxism has the revolutionary spirit. Therefore, Communism is a judgment against our failure to make democracy real and follow through on the revolutions that we initiated. We must move past indecision to action. We must find new ways to speak for peace in Vietnam and for justice throughout the developing world, a world that borders on our doors. If we do not act, we shall surely be dragged down the long, dark, and shameful corridors of time reserved for those who possess power without compassion, might without morality, and strength without sight.

Document 4

Civil disobedience became one of the strongest weapons in the arsenal of those who followed Martin Luther King, Jr. With a heritage traced to Gandhi, Tolstoy, and Thoreau, King's refusal to follow the established law in favor of conforming to a higher moral authority presented the government with a dilemma. When civil disobedience became a strategy of some members of the peace movement as well as of the civil rights movement, the state was in an even greater quandary.

An important focus of civil disobedience for the antiwar movement was the draft. Document 5, distributed in August 1967, was a call to young men to resist conscription, and based on it Dr. Benjamin Spock and the Reverend William Sloane Coffin, two major figures in the ranks of the dissenters, were indicted for counseling draft resistance.

4 Overt Act #1: A Call to Resist Illegitimate Authority

To the young men of America,
to the whole of the American people,
and to all men of good will everywhere:

1. An ever growing number of young American men are finding that the American war in Vietnam so outrages their deepest moral and religious sense that they cannot contribute to it in any way. We share their moral outrage.

2. We further believe that the war is unconstitutional and illegal. Congress has not declared a war as required by the Constitution. Moreover, under the Constitution, treaties signed by the President and ratified by the Senate have the same force as the Constitution itself. The Charter of the United Nations is such a treaty. The Charter specifically obligates the United States to refrain from force or the threat of force in international relations. It requires member states to exhaust every peaceful means of settling disputes and to submit disputes which cannot be settled peacefully to the Security Council. The United States has systematically violated all of these Charter provisions for thirteen years.

3. Moreover, this war violates international agreements, treaties and principles of law which the United States Government has solemnly endorsed. The combat role of the United States troops in Vietnam violates the Geneva Accords of 1954 which our government pledged to support but has since subverted. The destruction of rice, crops and livestock; the burning and bulldozing of entire villages consisting exclusively of civilian structures; the interning of civilian non-combatants in concentration camps; the summary executions of civilians in captured villages who could not produce satisfactory evidence of their loyalties or did not wish to be removed to concentration camps; the slaughter of peasants who dared to stand up in their fields and shake their fists at American helicopters—these are all actions of the kind which the United States and the other victorious powers of World War II declared to be crimes against humanity for which individuals were to be held personally responsible even when acting under the orders of their governments and for which Germans were sentenced at Nuremberg to long prison terms and death. The prohibition of such acts as war crimes was incorporated in treaty law by the Geneva Conventions of 1949, ratified by the United States. These are commitments to other countries and to Mankind, and they would claim our allegiance even if Congress should declare war.

4. We also believe it is an unconstitutional denial of religious liberty and equal protection of the laws to withhold draft exemption from men whose religious or profound philosophical beliefs are opposed to what in the Western religious tradition have been long known as unjust wars.

5. Therefore, we believe on all these grounds that every free man has a legal right and a moral duty to exert every effort to end this war, to avoid collusion with it, and to encourage others to do the same. Young men in the armed forces or threatened with the draft face the most excruciating choices. For them various forms of resistance risk separation from their families and their country, destruction of their careers, loss of their freedom and loss of their lives. Each must choose the course of resistance dictated by his conscience and circumstances. Among those already in the armed forces some are refusing to obey specific illegal and immoral orders, some are attempting to educate their fellow servicemen on the murderous and barbarous na-

ture of the war, some are absenting themselves without official leave. Among those not in the armed forces some are applying for status as conscientious objectors to American aggression in Vietnam, some are refusing to be inducted. Among both groups some are resisting openly and paying a heavy penalty, some are organizing more resistance within the United States and some have sought sanctuary in other countries.

6. We believe that each of these forms of resistance against illegitimate authority is courageous and justified. Many of us believe that open resistance to the war and the draft is the course of action most likely to strengthen the moral resolve with which all of us can oppose the war and most likely to bring an end to the war.

7. We will continue to lend our support to those who undertake resistance to this war. We will raise funds to organize draft resistance unions, to supply legal defense and bail, to support families and otherwise aid resistance to the war in whatever ways may seem appropriate.

8. We firmly believe that our statement is the sort of speech that under the First Amendment must be free, and that the actions we will undertake are as legal as is the war resistance of the young men themselves. In any case, we feel that we cannot shrink from fulfilling our responsibilities to the youth whom many of us teach, to the country whose freedom we cherish, and to the ancient traditions of religion and philosophy which we strive to preserve in this generation.

9. We call upon all men of good will to join us in this confrontation with immoral authority. Especially we call upon the universities to fulfill their mission of enlightenment and religious organizations to honor their heritage of brotherhood. Now is the time to resist.

Documents 5 and 6

By the end of the 1960s the Vietnam War had spawned extremism on both sides. Discussion was rare; debates most often degenerated into shouting matches; and nobody listened. In such a climate, only the most outrageous statements were recognized. The polarization between the diverse viewpoints allowed the wildest charges to be seen as representative of the mass.

During 1968, the Youth International Party, also known as the Yippies, planned to nominate their own candidate for president. Pigasus, their choice, was a pig. Document 6 was a leaflet distributed when the Democratic Convention was meeting in Chicago in August 1968.

The activities of groups like the Yippies shocked and annoyed many. One example is Tom Anderson's "Dear Brats" letter, which appeared in *American Opinion,* a conservative journal in June 1969.

5   REVOLUTION TOWARDS A FREE SOCIETY: YIPPIE!
A. Yippie
August 1968

1. An immediate end to the War in Vietnam. . . .
2. Immediate freedom for Huey Newton of the Black Panthers and all other black people. Adoption of the community control concept in our ghetto areas. . . .
3. The legalization of marihuana and all other psychedelic drugs. . . .

4. A prison system based on the concept of rehabilitation rather than punishment.

5. . . . abolition of all laws related to crimes without victims. That is, retention only of laws relating to crimes in which there is an unwilling injured party, i.e. murder, rape, assault.

6. The total disarmament of all the people beginning with the police. This includes not only guns, but such brutal devices as tear gas, MACE, electric prods, blackjacks, billy clubs, and the like.

7. The Abolition of Money. The abolition of pay housing, pay media, pay transportation, pay food, pay education, pay clothing, pay medical help, and pay toilets.

8. A society which works toward and actively promotes the concept of "full unemployment." A society in which people are free from the drudgery of work. Adoption of the concept "Let the Machines do it."

9. . . . elimination of pollution from our air and water.

10. . . . incentives for the decentralization of our crowded cities . . . encourage rural living.

11. . . . free birth control information . . . abortions when desired.

12. A restructured educational system which provides the student power to determine his course of study and allows for student participation in over-all policy planning. . . .

13. Open and free use of media . . . cable television as a method of increasing the selection of channels available to the viewer.

14. An end to all censorship. We are sick of a society which has no hesitation about showing people committing violence and refuses to show a couple fucking.

15. We believe that people should fuck all the time, anytime, whomever they wish. This is not a program to demand but a simple recognition of the reality around us.

16. . . . a national referendum system conducted via television or a telephone voting system . . . a decentralization of power and authority with many varied tribal groups. Groups in which people exist in a state of basic trust and are free to choose their tribe.

17. A program that encourages and promotes the arts. However, we feel that if the Free Society we envision were to be fought for and achieved, all of us would actualize the creativity within us. In a very real sense we would have a society in which every man would be an artist.

. . . Political Pigs, your days are numbered. We are the Second American Revolution. We shall win. Yippie!

6 "Dear Brats,"
Tom Anderson
June 1969

It is my annual custom at this time of year to write an inspiring message to America's militant youth. Since I always strive to make these messages sincere and "from the heart," I shall do my thing this year with that uppermost in mind:

Dear spoiled, deluded, and brainwashed brats:

I am sick of you. I am more sick of your professors, your administrators, your clergymen (if any), your parents, and others who have come very close to ruining an entire generation of young Americans.

The agnostic pragmatists who call themselves "Liberals" have taught you: (1) that there are no clear distinctions between right and wrong; (2) that there are no eternal verities, no absolute truths; (3) that environment determines truth and, since environment constantly changes, everything is relative; (4) that "life adjustment," not inculcation of principles and disciplines, is the aim of education; (5) that patriotism is absurd and out of date; and (6) that the government owes you a drink of some magic elixir called equality and a "decent" standard of living. The frauds further proclaim that you are not responsible for what you have become; that "Man is the product of his hereditary environment and you cannot expect him to rise above it." I doubt that many of you will.

You young militants, apparently brought up on the permissive nonreality of Dr. Spock, insist on running away from reality. You bemoan the world you "never made." What you fail to understand is that you must live in the world as it is and as it can be. My prayer for you is this: "Lord, give them the courage to change the things they can change, to accept those they cannot change, and—above all—the wisdom to know the difference."

Some things we can and should change, and some we can't and shouldn't. You can raise a pig in your parlor all right. But, it won't change the pig—only your parlor. So be *for* change as long as it's change for the better, recognizing that ruts are just graves with the ends removed.

Yet why change just to be changing? Why *destroy* the American system which has produced the highest standard of living in human history, just because that system is not perfect? Our Republic, with its capitalist economy, is indeed imperfect—but it is the least reprehensible system of government and economics which exists. There will never be a perfect system until there are perfect people; there will never be perfect people this side of Heaven. No society is better than the *individuals* in it. No nation advances except as the citizens who comprise it grow as individuals.

The collectivists, so-called "Liberals," seem to have convinced you that a socialist government can legislate unsuccessful people into prosperity by legislating successful people out of it. If that is true, why should a man work to succeed? The fact is that there is no such thing as equality. We cannot be free *and* equal. Free men are not equal and equal men are not free. While all men are created equal in the eyes of God and the law, they don't long stay equal even there. God penalizes unrepentant sinners, and the law penalizes repeating criminals.

So you want to replace "dog eat dog" with "dog love dog"? Both are animalism, and can only return civilization to the jungle.

Oh, I know you are constantly hearing that we must have equality not only here but with the rest of the world if we are to live in a peaceful socialist One World with our brothers. . . . The fact is that all mature men and women, all mature nations, are *inherently* unequal. That's why materialist America, with only six percent of the world's people and seven percent of the world's land, produces half of the world's goods. The sinister, selfish, and square American System of Free Enterprise (our profit and loss system) has enabled Americans to own seventy-one percent of the world's cars, fifty-six percent of its telephones, eighty-three percent of its TV sets, and (forgive me, hippies) ninety percent of its bathtubs.

The inventiveness of the American system has long been the envy of the world. The only new thing the Yippie Set has produced is a new drug mixing LSD and The Pill, so they can take a trip without the kids.

Meanwhile the voice from the Campus cries "hypocrisy!" at the community elders and the "Establishment." Students decry the "rat race," the "crushing materialism," our "money-mad society"—and then wire home, collect, for $200 to finance a spring bash of booze and sex at Fort Lauderdale, or a trip to New York for a parade to honor the Vietcong.

If you students want to rebel against "hypocrisy," why don't you rebel against an educational system whose "Liberal" teachers give you low marks unless you repeat their Leftist fairy tales at examination time?

If "hypocrisy" really offends you, why don't you rebel against the "Christian" heads of your Divinity Schools who are so quick to proclaim that they don't even believe in the divinity and resurrection of Christ?

If you want to rebel against the War in Vietnam, why don't you ask why our military is not being allowed to defeat a little country smaller than the state of Missouri?

If you want to rebel against the faceless, impersonal, giant corporations, why don't you demand to know why so many of them are trading with the arsenal of an enemy killing our soldiers in the field?

If you are opposed to materialism, if your heart bleeds for the disadvantaged, you guilt-ridden phonies should know that, just to help you defeat hypocrisy, you may turn over to me your new car, TV, stereo, tape-recorder, electric blanket, hair drier, camera, or fancy "mod" wardrobe, and I will personally see that they are distributed among the poor. Why don't you "idealists" practice what you preach?

Why don't you rebel against a rigged communications system which is brainwashing the American people? Not so? How long since you've seen an anti-Communist TV program or movie? Ever? Communism is the scourge of the world, yet you either ignore it or embrace it. It is the cause of most of the world's problems today, but you are almost never told the truth about it—not by your professors, movies, television, magazines, or newspapers. Why not, kids? Think about it a minute.

I don't blame you for being upset by the Establishment. You've been *had* by the Establishment. But the Establishment is *not* capitalism and the system of individual enterprise. Nor even what was formerly known as "Americanism." It is a combination of industrial cartelists, education and foundation bureaucrats, Leftist churchmen, and lightweight communicators who are deliberately trying to convert this nation into a Marxist-Fascist welfare state for their own aggrandizement and convenience. Most of these people are neither Marxists nor Fascists, but they are manipulated by Communists and are playing the Communist game. What is more, they are using *you* as pawns in that game.

Still, you never seem to learn.

One evening recently I spoke to a small crowd at Vanderbilt University. During the question and answer period, one sweet young thing with his hair on his shoulders stood and declared: "We're not Communists. We're anarchists. We don't want total government. We want no government. We believe in atheism, free love, and homosexuality between consenting adults."

How does a square like me "have dialogue" with that? I merely asked the shaven audience why they would sit there, inert, and let such slobs destroy their university, their country, and their freedom. No answer.

No, you never seem to learn.

If you "moderates," you uncommitted students, think that it is wrong and inexcusable to invite a self-proclaimed Marxist homosexual like Allen Ginsberg, a self-proclaimed criminal and anarchist like Eldridge Cleaver, or a head of the Young Communist League like Mike Zagarell, to speak on your campus, then why don't you do something about it?

People keep telling me that the campus anarchists, pacifists, Marxists, pot addicts, and "fairies" are a very small minority. Very well, maybe so. But tell me why an overwhelming majority of decent young people will sit by supinely while its universities are being hijacked and burned. More appalling than the outrages perpetrated by the collegiate punks, pinks, and perverts is the spineless acquiescence of the student majority.

We are constantly told that only two percent of you students are disrupting the campuses. But that is not true. The cowardly, apathetic, and silent ninety-eight percent of you who are *uncommitted* are guilty of letting it happen.

Most college students, according to a recent national survey, believe that the chief benefit of a college education is to increase one's earning power. Are these the same "idealists" who are bemoaning the cold commercial world they never made? Often they are. The point is that while money is not the main reason to go to college, neither is making over the world to suit the Marxist fairy tale.

Thousands of small businesses, such as the one I operate, couldn't care less whether employees went to college. The main reason to seek a higher education is to lift your horizon; to enable you to appreciate the finer things of life; to help you to make a good life, not a good living. When you graduate from college you are not educated. But you should have learned what it means to be educated; you should have the desire and the knowhow to *get* an education. The first thing an educated person learns to do is walk alone. Why don't you try it sometime? Get out of the mob, kids. Learn to be your own man. That's what integrity is all about.

Oh, I know that this sounds like tough talk. We so-called Conservatives are prone to such intolerance. But, one of the greatest problems of this country is that tolerance has become so excessive as to amount to cowardly permissiveness. In my book, one is not capable of genuine tolerance unless he is capable of honest conviction—which means a commitment to intolerance for lies and sham and fraud and perversion. A person unable to arrive at convictions is a person morally immature.

When things are morally and legally wrong, you are right to rebel. But your rebellion must be moral, legal, and constructive, else *you* are wrong. Students don't have a moral or legal right to "take over" a building. They are violating property rights and the rights of other students, and they should be routed out with tear gas, arrested, and given jail sentences. That's the way it is in the real world!

The first requirement and obligation of the institution of learning is to build character. "Free speech" and "search for truth" do not include the right to promote subversion, insurrection, anarchy, arson, murder, and treason. Nor does "academic freedom" include the right publicly to push drugs, free sex, and Communism. Communism and other such perversions are like rape—they are not moot questions. Communism is not just another ideology or a political Party, but a criminal conspiracy to enslave the world. Communists should no more be given a collegiate platform than murderers, dope pushers, or smut peddlers.

Discipline, order and character are the foundation of learning, not permissiveness, anarchy, and perversion. The main purpose of a school, in my opinion, should be to build and discipline character. Chancellors, administrators, and teachers devoid of character cannot, of course, build character. This is where our educational system has failed. This is the explanation for revolutionary anarchy on the campus. As historians Will and Ariel Durant have written:

> Violent revolutions do not so much redistribute wealth as destroy it. There may be a redivision of the land, but the natural inequality of men soon recreates an inequality of positions and privileges. The only real revolution is in the enlightenment of the mind and the improvement of character. The only real emancipation is individual, and the only real revolutionists are philosophers and saints.

Freedom without the discipline of character is an absurdity. "Freedom now!" sounds great, I suppose, to those of you who are wet behind the ears. But, the phrase you should be hearing is "Discipline now!" In a civilized society, freedom without discipline is impossible. Those who cannot discipline themselves cannot long be allowed to run free. People who cannot muster the discipline to govern themselves are destined to be disciplined by dictators. If the prevailing government is too decadent to do the job, then some other government, from outside or within, will replace it, by force if necessary. Thus individual violence is replaced by government violence. And freedom is replaced by slavery, as in Cuba, Mainland China, Czecho-Slovakia, Poland, Romania, Russia and elsewhere.

The campus revolution, if continued on its present course, will lead to an escalating revolution in the streets followed by dictatorship. And it will be a Communist dictatorship. The leadership of the "take-over generation" has been taken over by the Communists.

Your campus anarchists want a showdown—and they are going to get it. Millions of the taxpayers they consider milch cows are sick of paying for the destruction of their schools and their country. Millions of us are tired of the excess of tolerance become license, of trying to reason with unreason, of cant and Bolshevik clichés that were dated when your grandfather was in knickers. The academic leaders may be afraid of the militant young fascists and anarchists who are trying to turn our free Republic into a police state, but we the *people* are not.

Document 7

On October 15, 1969, a nationwide moratorium was held to oppose the policies of the Nixon administration in Vietnam. Hundreds of thousands of people marched, paraded, and demonstrated their disagreement. On October 19, 1969, in a speech in New Orleans, Louisiana, Vice President Spiro T. Agnew criticized the moratorium and its participants.

Agnew's attack was fierce, and his colorful rhetoric soon made him the leading lightning rod in American politics. Complaining about intellectuals, liberals, and radicals, Agnew stood as the clear enemy of all who considered themselves progressive. He argued that he was the representative of what the president would soon call "the silent majority."

The Vice President did agree with the dissenters that the draft needed reform. In the speech that follows, Agnew indicated the Administration's desire to alter the system of conscription and the broad support which underlay that proposal.

7   **Speech at a Citizens' Testimonial Dinner**
    Spiro T. Agnew
    October 19, 1969

Sometimes it appears that we are reaching a period when our senses and our minds will no longer respond to moderate stimulation. We seem to be approaching an age of the gross. Persuasion through speeches and books is too often discarded for disruptive demonstrations aimed at bludgeoning the unconvinced into action.

The young, and by this I don't mean by any stretch of the imagination all the young, but I'm talking about those who claim to speak for the young, at the zenith of physical power and sensitivity, overwhelm themselves with drugs and artificial stimulants. Subtlety is lost, and fine distinctions based on acute reasoning are carelessly ignored in a headlong jump to a predetermined conclusion. Life is visceral rather than intellectual, and the most visceral practitioners of life are those who characterize themselves as intellectuals.

Truth to them is "revealed" rather than logically proved, and the principal infatuations of today revolve around the social sciences, those subjects which can accommodate any opinion and about which the most reckless conjecture cannot be discredited.

Education is being redefined at the demand of the uneducated to suit the ideas of the uneducated. The student now goes to college to proclaim rather than to learn. The lessons of the past are ignored and obliterated in a contemporary antagonism known as the generation gap. A spirit of national masochism prevails, encouraged by an effete corps of impudent snobs who characterize themselves as intellectuals.

It is in this setting of dangerous oversimplification that the war in Vietnam achieves its greatest distortion.

The recent Vietnam Moratorium is a reflection of the confusion that exists in America today. Thousands of well-motivated young people, conditioned since childhood to respond to great emotional appeals, saw fit to demonstrate for peace. Most did not stop to consider that the leaders of the Moratorium had billed it as a massive public outpouring of sentiment against the foreign policy of the President of the United States. Most did not care to be reminded that the leaders of the Moratorium refused to disassociate themselves from the objective enunciated by the enemy in Hanoi.

If the Moratorium had any use whatever, it served as an emotional purgative for those who felt the need to cleanse themselves of their lack of ability to offer a constructive solution to the problem.

Unfortunately, we have not seen the end. The hard-core dissidents and the professional anarchists within the so-called "peace movement" will continue to exacerbate the situation. November 15 is already planned—wilder, more violent, and equally barren of constructive result.

. . .

Let us turn for a moment to a legitimate complaint of our young people—the draft.

The draft, at best, is a necessary evil—one that President Nixon wants to do away with as soon as possible. But while the draft is still necessary, our government has a moral obligation to make it as fair and as reasonable as possible. Our failure to do so mocks the ideals we profess so often.

What is it that makes our draft system so *unfair* and so *unreasonable*?

Essentially, there are two problems: first—the present system creates for our young men a long period of draft vulnerability, one which begins at age nineteen and stretches for seven long years—unless the young man is drafted sooner. During this time, his educational plans, his career, even his decisions concerning marriage and family are distorted by his inability to predict the impact of the draft. All of this constitutes a terrible pressure, a dark shadow which falls across the lives of young Americans at the very time when they should be greeting the opportunities of adulthood with the greatest sense of excitement and adventure.

Prolonged uncertainty is one problem with the draft. Unfair selection is the second. Though all are technically vulnerable to the draft, those who are able to go on to college and then into certain graduate programs or occupations are often able to escape induction. In short, the current draft system creates frustration and mocks justice; it is both unfair and unreasonable.

This is not my opinion alone. It is widely shared—by members of all age groups in all parts of the country. Two panels composed of distinguished citizens—one headed by General Mark Clark and one headed by Mr. Burke Marshall—have reached the same conclusion in recent years. So have the many leaders of both parties in the House and Senate.

Months ago President Nixon took the lead in the battle to reform the draft. On May 13, 1969, he sent a message to the Congress in which he asked that body to reduce the period of prime vulnerability from seven years to one year and to institute a fair, random-selection system. Under this arrangement, everyone would be eligible for the draft at age nineteen and would be randomly assigned a place in the order of call at that time. He would remain in a condition of prime eligibility for twelve months. If he were not drafted in twelve months, he would move into less vulnerable categories. Those who chose to take a deferment at age nineteen, to go on to college, for example, would do so knowing where they fell in that order of call and could plan their lives accordingly. They would then spend their year in the prime vulnerability group at the time they left school.

Few of the President's statements have brought more favorable reaction than his suggestions for reforming the draft. Despite the widespread dissatisfaction with the draft and despite the widespread praise which greeted the President's message—the Congress waited until this week to act. The House Armed Services Committee this week unanimously reported the bill favorably, and early House action is expected. Senate action will depend on prompt attention by Senator Stennis' Committee.

As Secretary Laird recently explained, all that is necessary is that one sentence be changed in the current draft law, a sentence introduced as a last-minute afterthought back in 1967. This single sentence now prevents the President from switching to the random-selection process. Now if they just take care of this one problem, if Congress takes care of that, the President can avoid doing it by administrative order which would eliminate the systematic inequity by scrambling the 365 days of the year and rearranging them so that birthdays fell randomly and the oldest in that year would not have to be taken. This is clearly the fairest system.

Certainly this is the time for the people to join the President in making their desires felt in this matter of draft reform. For if reform is frustrated, it will be a defeat not only for the President, but for the Democratic process. Above all it will be a retreat from the principles of reason and justice which we value so highly in this country, principles which we preach with great ardor to our young people, but which we have not yet achieved in our selective service legislation.

. . .

Great patriots of past generations would find it difficult to believe that Americans would ever doubt the validity of America's resolve to protect free men from totalitarian attack. Yet today we see those among us who prefer to side with an enemy aggressor rather than stand by this free nation. We see others who are shortsighted enough to believe that we need not protect ourselves from attack by governments that depend upon force to control their people—governments which came into being through force alone and continue to exist by force alone.

I do not want to see this nation spend one dollar more on defense than is absolutely necessary, but I would hate to see this nation spend one dollar less on defense than is absolutely necessary. Until the principle of open representative government exists among all nations, the United States must not abandon its moral obligation to protect by any means necessary the freedoms so hard won by past generations. The freedoms so hard won by the 400,000 Americans who made the ultimate sacrifice in dedicated belief that some things are more precious than life itself.

Document 8

People from all walks of life joined the antiwar movement, and by the early 1970s some Vietnam veterans had founded their own group. John Kerry, a representative of Vietnam Veterans Against the War, appeared before the Senate Committee on Foreign Relations in April 1971 and testified about what he had observed and learned in Vietnam.

Kerry's speech, which appears here as part of Document 8, received nationwide coverage in the media. The remainder of Document 8 shows that viewers of different news programs might have gotten different information and impressions of the same event. For example, at the end of the ABC version there was standing applause, but they edited out Kerry's criticisms of the nation's leaders. The CBS version deleted the applause and followed Kerry with a representative of the Veterans of Foreign Wars saying that the veterans protesting in Washington as part of Dewey Canyon III were not representative of American fighting men. On NBC there was no applause but a slow fade to black and silence before the next story.

---

8 Vietnam Veterans Against the War Statement by John Kerry April 23, 1971

Mr. Kerry: Thank you very much, Senator Fulbright, Senator Javits, Senator Symington, Senator Pell. I would like to say for the record, and also for the men behind me who are also wearing the uniform and their medals, that my sitting here is really symbolic. I am not here as John Kerry. I am here as one member of the group of 1,000, which is a small representation of a very much larger group of veterans in this country, and were it possible for all of them to sit at this table they would be here and have the same kind of testimony.

I would simply like to speak in very general terms. I apologize if my statement is general because I received notification yesterday you would hear me and I am afraid that because of the court injunction I was up most of the night and haven't had a great deal of time to prepare for this hearing.

I would like to talk on behalf of all those veterans and say that several months ago in

Detroit we had an investigation at which over 150 honorably discharged, and many very highly decorated, veterans testified to war crimes committed in Southeast Asia. These were not isolated incidents but crimes committed on a day to day basis with the full awareness of officers at all levels of command.

It is impossible to describe to you exactly what did happen in Detroit—the emotions in the room and the feelings of the men who were reliving their experiences in Vietnam. They relived the absolute horror of what this country, in a sense, made them do.

They told stories that at times they had personally raped, cut off ears, cut off heads, taped wires from portable telephones to human genitals and turned up the power, cut off limbs, blown up bodies, randomly shot at civilians, razed villages in fashion reminiscent of Genghis Khan, shot cattle and dogs for fun, poisoned food stocks, and generally ravaged the countryside of South Vietnam in addition to the normal ravage of war and the normal and very particular ravaging which is done by the applied bombing power of this country.

We call this investigation the Winter Soldier Investigation. The term Winter Soldier is a play on words of Thomas Paine's in 1776 when he spoke of the Sunshine Patriots and summer time soldiers who deserted at Valley Forge because the going was rough.

We who have come here to Washington have come here because we feel we have to be winter soldiers now. We could come back to this country, we could be quiet, we could hold our silence, we could not tell what went on in Vietnam, but we feel because of what threatens this country, not the reds, but the crimes which we are commiting that threaten it, that we have to speak out.

I would like to talk to you a little bit about what the result is of the feelings these men carry with them after coming back from Vietnam. The country doesn't know it yet but it has created a monster, a monster in the form of millions of men who have been taught to deal and to trade in violence and who are given the chance to die for the biggest nothing in history; men who have returned with a sense of anger and a sense of betrayal which no one has yet grasped.

As a veteran and one who feels this anger I would like to talk about it. We are angry because we feel we have been used in the worst fashion by the administration of this country.

In 1970 at West Point Vice President Agnew said "some glamorize the criminal misfits of society while our best men die in Asian rice paddies to preserve the freedom which most of those misfits abuse," and this was used as a rallying point for our effort in Vietnam.

But for us, as boys in Asia whom the country was supposed to support, his statement is a terrible distortion from which we can only draw a very deep sense of revulsion, and hence the anger of some of the men who are here in Washington today. It is a distortion because we in no way consider ourselves the best men of this country; because those he calls misfits were standing up for us in a way that nobody else in this country dared to; because so many who have died would have returned to this country to join the misfits in their efforts to ask for an immediate withdrawal from South Vietnam; because so many of those best men have returned as quadruplegics and amputees—and they lie forgotten in Veterans Administration Hospitals in this country which fly the flag which so many have chosen as their own personal symbol—and we cannot consider ourselves America's best men when we are ashamed of and hated for what we were called on to do in Southeast Asia.

In our opinion, and from our experience, there is nothing in South Vietnam which could happen that realistically threatens the United States of America. And to attempt to justify the loss of one American life in Vietnam, Cambodia or Laos by linking such loss to the preservation of freedom, which those misfits supposedly abuse, is to us the height of criminal hypocrisy, and it is that kind of hypocrisy which we feel has torn this country apart.

We are probably much more angry than that, but I don't want to go into the foreign policy aspects because I am outclassed here. I know that all of you talk about every possible alternative for getting out of Vietnam. We understand that. We know you have considered the seriousness of the aspects to the utmost level and I am not going to try to dwell on that. But I want to relate to you the feeling that many of the men who have returned to this country express because we are probably angriest about all that we were told about Vietnam and about the mystical war against communism.

We found that not only was it a civil war, an effort by a people who had for years been seeking their liberation from any colonial influence whatsoever, but also we found that the Vietnamese whom we had enthusiastically molded after our own image were hard put to take up the fight against the threat we were supposedly saving them from.

We found most people didn't even know the difference between communism and democracy. They only wanted to work in rice paddies without helicopters strafing them and bombs with napalm burning their villages and tearing their country apart. They wanted everything to do with the war, particularly with this foreign presence of the United States of America, to leave them alone in peace, and they practiced the art of survival by siding with whichever military force was present at a particular time, be it Viet Cong, North Vietnamese or American.

We found also that all too often American men were dying in those rice paddies for want of support from their allies. We saw first hand how monies from American taxes were used for a corrupt dictatorial regime. We saw that many people in this country had a one-sided idea of who was kept free by our flag, and blacks provided the highest percentage of casualties. We saw Vietnam ravaged equally by American bombs and search and destroy missions, as well as by Viet Cong terrorism, and yet we listened while this country tried to blame all of the havoc on the Viet Cong.

We rationalized destroying villages in order to save them. We saw America lose her sense of morality as she accepted very coolly a My Lai and refused to give up the image of American soldiers who hand out chocolate bars and chewing gum.

We learned the meaning of free fire zones, shooting anything that moves, and we watched while America placed a cheapness on the lives of orientals.

We watched the United States falsification of body counts, in fact the glorification of body counts. We listened while month after month we were told the back of the enemy was about to break. We fought using weapons against "oriental human beings." We fought using weapons against those people which I do not believe this country would dream of using were we fighting in the European theater. We watched while men charged up hills because a general said that hill has to be taken, and after losing one platoon or two platoons they marched away to leave the hill for reoccupation by the North Vietnamese. We watched pride allow the most unimportant battles to be blown into extravaganzas, because we couldn't lose, and we couldn't retreat, and because it didn't matter how many American bodies were lost to prove that point, and so there were Hamburger Hills and Khe Sanhs and Hill 81s and Fire Base 6s, and so many others.

Now we are told that the men who fought there must watch quietly while American lives are lost so that we can exercise the incredible arrogance of Vietnamizing the Vietnamese.

Each day to facilitate the process by which the United States washes her hands of Vietnam someone has to give up his life so that the United States doesn't have to admit something that the entire world already knows, so that we can't say that we have made a mistake. Someone has to die so that President Nixon won't be, and these are his words, "the first President to lose a war." — ★

We are asking Americans to think about that because how do you ask a man to be the last man to die in Vietnam? How do you ask a man to be the last man to die for a mistake? But we are trying to do that, and we are doing it with thousands of rationalizations, and if you read carefully the President's last speech to the people of this country, you can see that he says, and says clearly, "but the issue, gentlemen, the issue, is communism, and the question is whether or not we will leave that country to the communists or whether or not we will try to give it hope to be a free people." But the point is they are not a free people now under us. They are not a free people, and we cannot fight communism all over the world. I think we should have learned that lesson by now.

But the problem of veterans goes beyond this personal problem, because you think about a poster in this country with a picture of Uncle Sam and the picture says "I want you." And a young man comes out of high school and says, "that is fine, I am going to serve my country," and he goes to Vietnam and he shoots and he kills and he does his job. Or maybe he doesn't kill. Maybe he just goes and he comes back, and when he gets back to this country he finds that he isn't really wanted, because the largest corps of unemployed in the country—it varies depending on who you get it from, the Veterans Administration says 15 percent and various other sources 22 percent—but the largest corps of unemployed in this country are veterans of this war, and of those veterans 33 percent of the unemployed are black. That means one out of every ten of the nation's unemployed is a veteran of Vietnam.

The hospitals across the country won't, or can't meet their demands. It is not a question of not trying; they haven't got the appropriations. A man recently died after he had a tracheotomy in California, not because of the operation but because there weren't enough personnel to clean the mucus out of his tube and he suffocated to death.

Another young man just died in a New York VA Hospital the other day. A friend of mine was lying in a bed two beds away and tried to help him but he couldn't. He rang a bell and there was nobody there to service that man and so he died of convulsions.

I understand 57 percent of all those entering the VA hospitals talk about suicide. Some 27 percent have tried, and they try because they come back to this country and they have to face what they did in Vietnam, and then they come back and find the indifference of a country that doesn't really care.

Suddenly we are faced with a very sickening situation in this country, because there is no moral indignation and, if there is, it comes from people who are almost exhausted by their past indignations, and I know that many of them are sitting in front of me. The country seems to have lain down and shrugged off something as serious as Laos, just as we calmly shrugged off the loss of 700,000 lives in Pakistan, the so-called greatest disaster of all times.

But we are here as veterans to say we think we are in the midst of the greatest disaster of all times now because they are still dying over there—not just Americans, but Vietnamese—and we are rationalizing leaving that country so that those people can go on killing each other for years to come.

Americans seem to have accepted the idea that the war is winding down, at least for Americans, and they have also allowed the bodies which were once used by a President for statistics to prove that we were winning that war, to be used as evidence against a man who followed orders and who interpreted those orders no differently than hundreds of other men in Vietnam.

We veterans can only look with amazement on the fact that this country has been unable to see there is absolutely no difference between ground troops and a helicopter crew, and yet people have accepted a differentiation fed them by the administration.

No ground troops are in Laos so it is all right to kill Laotians by remote control. But believe me the helicopter crews fill the same body bags and they wreak the same kind of damage on the Vietnamese and Laotian countryside as anybody else, and the President is talking about allowing that to go on for many years to come. One can only ask if we will really be satisfied only when the troops march into Hanoi.

We are asking here in Washington for some action; action from the Congress of the United States of America which has the power to raise and maintain armies, and which by the Constitution also has the power to declare war.

We have come here, not to the President, because we believe that this body can be responsive to the will of the people, and we believe that the will of the people says that we should be out of Vietnam now.

We are here in Washington also to say that the problem of this war is not just a question of war and diplomacy. It is part and parcel of everything that we are trying as human beings to communicate to people in this country—the question of racism which is rampant in the military, and so many other questions such as the use of weapons; the hypocrisy in our taking umbrage at the Geneva Conventions and using that as justification for a continuation of this war when we are more guilty than any other body of violations of those Geneva Conventions; in the use of free fire zones, harassment interdiction fire, search and destroy missions, the bombings, the torture of prisoners, the killing of prisoners, all accepted policy by many units in South Vietnam. That is what we are trying to say. It is part and parcel of everything.

Kerry Statement *(continued)*

An American Indian friend of mine who lives in the Indian Nation of Alcatraz put it to me very succinctly. He told me how as a boy on an Indian reservation he had watched television and he used to cheer the cowboys when they came in and shot the Indians, and then suddenly one day he stopped in Vietnam and he said "my God, I am doing to these people the very same thing that was done to my people," and he stopped. And that is what we are trying to say, that we think this thing has to end.

We are also here to ask, and we are here to ask vehemently, where are the leaders of our country? Where is the leadership? We are here to ask where are McNamara, Rostow, Bundy, Gilpatrick and so many others? Where are they now that we, the men whom they sent off to war, have returned? These are commanders who have deserted their troops, and there is no more serious crime in the laws of war. The Army says they never leave their wounded. The Marines say they never leave even their dead. These men have left all the casualties and retreated behind a pious shield of public rectitude. They have left the real stuff of their reputations bleaching behind them in the sun in this country.

Coverage of the Kerry Statement by *ABC Evening News*

ABC Bob Clark

Clark: The witness invited by Senator Fulbright was a Vietnam veteran with a Silver Star and three Purple Hearts. Testifying for the anti-war protestors 27-year-old John Kerry delivered perhaps the most eloquent indictment of the war ever heard by the Senators.

Kerry: Each day to facilitate the process by★ which the United States washes its hands of Vietnam someone has to give up his life so that the United States doesn't have to admit something the entire world already knows. So that we can't say that we've made a mistake. Someone has to die so that President Nixon won't be—and these are his words—"the first President to lose a war." We are asking Americans to think about that. Because how do you ask a man to be the last man to die in Vietnam. How do you ask a man to be the last man to die for a mistake.

★See page 368.

by *CBS Evening News*

CBS Bruce Morton

Morton: . . . vets got a formal hearing when one of the organizers, John Kerry, testified before the Senate Foreign Relations Committee.

by *NBC Nightly News*

NBC Catherine Mackin

Mackin: A short time after the arrests one of their leaders, John Kerry, a former Navy gunboat commander, wounded three times in Vietnam, talked to the Senate Foreign Relations Committee.

Kerry: Each day to facilitate the process by★ which the United States washes its hands of Vietnam someone has to give up his life so that the United States doesn't have to admit something the entire world already knows. So that we can't say that we've made a mistake. Someone has to die so that President Nixon won't be—and these are his words—"the first President to lose a war." We are asking Americans to think about that. Because how do you ask a man to be the last man to die in Vietnam. How do you ask a man to be the last man to die for a mistake.

Kerry: We are here to ask, and we are here to ask vehemently, where are the leaders of our country. Where is the leadership? We're here to ask where are McNamara, Rostow, Bundy, Gilpatrick, and so many others. Where are they now that we, the men they sent off to war, have returned. These are commanders who have deserted their troops. And there is no more serious crime in the laws of war. The Army says they never leave their wounded. The marines say they never leave even their dead. These men have left all the casualties and retreated behind a pious shield of public rectitude. They've left the real stuff of their reputations bleaching behind them in the sun in this country.

We are here to ask, and we are here to ask vehemently, where are the leaders of our country. Where is the leadership? We're here to ask where are McNamara, Rostow, Bundy, Gilpatrick, and so many others. Where are they now that we, the men they sent off to war, have returned. These are commanders who have deserted their troops. And there is no more serious crime in the laws of war. The Army says they never leave their wounded. The marines say they never leave even their dead. These men have left all the casualties and retreated behind a pious shield of public rectitude. They've left the real stuff of their reputations bleaching behind them in the sun in this country.

★See page 368.

Kerry Statement *(continued)*

Finally, this administration has done us the ultimate dishonor. They have attempted to disown us and the sacrifices we made for this country. In their blindness and fear they have tried to deny that we are veterans or that we served in Nam. We do not need their testimony. Our own scars and stumps of limbs are witness enough for others and for ourselves.

We wish that a merciful God could wipe away our own memories of that service as easily as this administration has wiped away their memories of us. But all that they have done and all that they can do by this denial is to make more clear than ever our own determination to undertake one last mission—to search out and destroy the last vestige of this barbaric war, to pacify our own hearts, to conquer the hate and the fear that have driven this country these last ten years and more. And more. And so when 30 years from now our brothers go down the street without a leg, without an arm, or a face, and small boys ask why, we will be able to say "Vietnam" and not mean a desert, not a filthy obscene memory, but mean instead the place where America finally turned and where soldiers like us helped it in the turning.

Thank you.

by *ABC Evening News*

But all that they have done and all that they can do by this denial is to make more clear than ever our own determination to undertake one last mission. To search out and destroy the last vestiges of this barbaric war. To pacify our own hearts. To conquer the hate and fear that have driven this country these last 10 years and more. And more. And so when 30 years from now our brothers go down the street without a leg, without an arm, or a face, and small boys ask why, we will be able to say "Vietnam" and not mean a desert, not a filthy, obscene memory, but mean instead a place where America finally turned and where soldiers like us helped it in turning. Thank you.

(APPLAUSE, STANDING OVATION)

by *CBS Evening News*

Finally this administration has done us the ultimate dishonor. They have attempted to disown us and the sacrifices we made for this country.

We wish that a merciful God would wipe away our own memories of that service, as easily as this administration has wiped their memories of us. But all that they have done and all that they can do by this denial is to make more clear than ever our own determination to undertake one last mission. To search out and destroy the last vestiges of this barbaric war.

(More on VFW ways these vets are not representative.)

by *NBC Nightly News*

Finally this administration has done us the ultimate dishonor. They have attempted to disown us and the sacrifices we made for this country. In their blindness and fear they have tried to deny that we are veterans or that we served in Nam. We do not need their testimony. Our own scars and stumps of limbs are witness for others, and ourselves.

We wish that a merciful God would wipe away our own memories of that service, as easily as this administration has wiped their memories of us. But all that they have done and all that they can do by this denial is to make more clear than ever our own determination to undertake one last mission. To search out and destroy the last vestiges of this barbaric war. To pacify our own hearts. To conquer the hate and fear that have driven this country these last 10 years and more. And more. And so when 30 years from now our brothers go down the street without a leg, without an arm, or a face, and small boys ask why, we will be able to say "Vietnam" and not mean a desert, not a filthy, obscene memory, but mean instead the place where America finally turned and where soldiers like us helped it in turning. Thank you.

(FADE TO BLACK, SILENCE)

Documents 9, 10, and 11

To many in the antiwar movement, My Lai became a shorthand term for what was wrong with the whole war. To many soldiers, My Lai became a media circus in which outsiders took a terrible event and blew it out of proportion. To other observers, My Lai was just war; war was hell, and bad things happened.

The following three documents discuss this massacre of Vietnamese civilians. Document 9 is a letter from Ron Ridenhour, an American soldier who had served in Vietnam, to the Pentagon, the White House and 24 Congressmen. It revealed the conduct of American troops at My Lai in March 1968 and demanded a thorough investigation. The event became public in 1969, and a full investigation took place in 1971. By that time, Lt. William Calley had been held responsible for the actions of the troops under his charge. Document 10, the result of a Gallup Poll printed in *Newsweek* in April 1971, indicated popular reaction to the conviction and sentencing of Calley. Document 11 contains the thoughts of Bill Moyers in the wake of the controversy over the Calley verdict.

9   **Letter About My Lai**
    Ron Ridenhour
    March 29, 1969
    Gentlemen:
        It was late in April, 1968 that I first heard of "Pinkville" and what allegedly happened there. I received that first report with some skepticism, but in the following months I was to hear similar stories from such a wide variety of people that it became impossible for me to disbelieve that something rather dark and bloody did indeed occur sometime in March, 1968 in a village called "Pinkville" in the Republic of Viet Nam. . . .
        In late April, 1968 I was awaiting orders for a transfer from HHC, 11th Brigade to Company "E," 51st Inf. (LRP), when I happened to run into Pfc "Butch" Gruver, whom I had known in Hawaii. Gruver told me he had been assigned to "C" Company 1st of the 20th until April 1st when he transferred to the unit that I was headed for. During the course of our conversation he told me the first of many reports I was to hear of "Pinkville."
        "Charlie" Company 1/20 had been assigned to Task Force Barker in late February, 1968 to help conduct "search and destroy" operations on the Batangan Peninsula, Barker's area of operation. The task force was operating out of L. F. Dottie, located five or six miles north of Quang Nhai city on Viet Namese National Highway 1. Gruver said that Charlie Company had sustained casualties, primarily from mines and booby traps, almost every day from the first day they arrived on the peninsula. One village area was particularly troublesome and seemed to be infested with booby traps and enemy soldiers. It was located about six miles northeast of Quang Nhai city at approximate coordinates B. S. 728795. It was a notorious area and the men of Task Force Barker had a special name for it: they called it "Pinkville." One morning in the latter part of March, Task Force Barker moved out from its firebase headed for "Pinkville." Its mission: destroy the trouble spot and all of its inhabitants.

When "Butch" told me this I didn't quite believe that what he was telling me was true, but he assured me that it was and went on to describe what had happened. The other two companies that made up the task force cordoned off the village so that "Charlie" Company could move through to destroy the structures and kill the inhabitants. Any villagers who ran from Charlie Company were stopped by the encircling companies. I asked "Butch" several times if all the people were killed. He said that he thought they were, men and women and children. He recalled seeing a small boy, about three or four years old, standing by the trail with a gunshot wound in one arm. The boy was clutching his wounded arm with his other hand, while blood trickled between his fingers. He was staring around himself in shock and disbelief at what he saw. "He just stood there with big eyes staring around like he didn't understand; he didn't believe what was happening. Then the captain's RTO (radio operator) put a burst of 16 (M-16 rifle) fire into him." It was so bad, Gruver said, that one of the men in his squad shot himself in the foot in order to be medivaced out of the area so that he would not have to participate in the slaughter. Although he had not seen it, Gruver had been told by people he considered trustworthy that one of the company's officers, 2nd Lieutenant Kally (this spelling may be incorrect) had rounded up several groups of villagers (each group consisting of a minimum of 20 persons of both sexes and all ages). According to the story, Kally then machine-gunned each group. Gruver estimated that the population of the village had been 300 to 400 people and that very few, if any, escaped.

After hearing this account I couldn't quite accept it. Somehow I just couldn't believe that not only had so many young American men participated in such an act of barbarism, but that their officers had ordered it. There were other men in the unit I was soon to be assigned to, "E" Company, 51st Infantry (LRP), who had been in Charlie Company at the time that Gruver alleged the incident at "Pinkville" had occurred. I became determined to ask them about "Pinkville" so that I might compare their accounts with Pfc Gruver's.

When I arrived at "Echo" Company, 51st Infantry (LRP) the first men I looked for were Pfcs Michael Terry, and William Doherty. Both were veterans of "Charlie" Company, 1/20 and "Pinkville." Instead of contradicting "Butch" Gruver's story they corroborated it, adding some tasty tidbits of information of their own. Terry and Doherty had been in the same squad and their platoon was the third platoon of "C" Company to pass through the village. Most of the people they came to were already dead. Those that weren't were sought out and shot. The platoon left nothing alive, neither livestock nor people. Around noon the two soldiers' squad stopped to eat. "Billy and I started to get our chow," Terry said, "but close to us was a bunch of Vietnamese in a heap, and some of them were moaning. Kally (2nd Lt. Kally) had been through before us and all of them had been shot, but many weren't dead. It was obvious that they weren't going to get any medical attention so Billy and I got up and went over to where they were. I guess we sort of finished them off." Terry went on to say that he and Doherty then returned to where their packs were and ate lunch. He estimated the size of the village to be 200 to 300 people. Doherty thought that the population of "Pinkville" had been 400 people.

If Terry, Doherty and Gruver could be believed, then not only had "Charlie" Company received orders to slaughter all the inhabitants of the village, but those orders had come from the commanding officer of Task Force Barker, or possibly even higher in the chain of command. Pfc Terry stated that when Captain Medina (Charlie Company's commanding officer Captain Ernest Medina) issued the order for the destruction of "Pinkville" he had been hesitant, as if it were something he didn't want to do but had to. Others I spoke to concurred with Terry on this.

It was June before I spoke to anyone who had something of significance to add to what I had already been told of the "Pinkville" incident. It was the end of June, 1968 when I ran into Sargent [sic] Larry La Croix at the USO in Chu Lai. La Croix had been in 2nd Lt. Kally's platoon on the day Task Force Barker swept through "Pinkville." What he told me verified the stories of the others, but he also had something new to add. He had been a witness to Kally's gunning down of at least three separate groups of villagers. "It was terrible. They were slaughtering the villagers like so many sheep." Kally's men were dragging people out of bunkers and hootches and putting them together in a group. The people in the group were men, women and children of all ages. As soon as he felt that the group was big enough, Kally ordered an M-60 (machine-gun) set up and the people killed. La Croix said that he bore witness to this procedure at least three times. The three groups were of different sizes, one of about twenty people, one of about thirty people, and one of about forty people. When the first group was put together Kally ordered Pfc Torres to man the machine-gun and open fire on the villagers that had been grouped together. This Torres did, but before everyone in the group was down he ceased fire and refused to fire again. After ordering Torres to recommence firing several times, Lieutenant Kally took over the M-60 and finished shooting the remaining villagers in that first group himself. Sargent La Croix told me that Kally didn't bother to order anyone to take the machine-gun when the other two groups of villagers were formed. He simply manned it himself and shot down all villagers in both groups.

This account of Sargent La Croix's confirmed the rumors that Gruver, Terry and Doherty had previously told me about Lieutenant Kally. It also convinced me that there was a very substantial amount of truth to the stories that all of these men had told. If I needed more convincing, I was to receive it.

It was in the middle of November, 1968 just a few weeks before I was to return to the United States for separation from the army that I talked to Pfc Michael Bernhardt. Bernhardt had served his entire year in Viet Nam in "Charlie" Company 1/20 and he too was about to go home. "Bernie" substantiated the tales told by the other men I had talked to in vivid, bloody detail and added this. "Bernie" had absolutely refused to take part in the massacre of the villagers of "Pinkville" that morning and he thought it was rather strange that the officers of the company had not made an issue of it. But that evening "Medina (Captain Ernest Medina) came up to me ("Bernie") and told me not to do anything stupid like write my congressman" about what had happened that day. Bernhardt assured Captain Medina that he had no such thing in mind. He had nine months left in Viet Nam and felt that it was dangerous enough just fighting the acknowledged enemy.

Exactly what did, in fact, occur in the village of "Pinkville" in March, 1968 I do not know for *certain,* but I am convinced that it was something very black indeed. I remain irrevocably persuaded that if you and I do truly believe in the principles of justice and the equality of every man, however humble, before the law, that form the very backbone that this country is founded on, then we must press forward a widespread and public investigation of this matter with all our combined efforts. I think that it was Winston Churchhill who once said "A country without a conscience is a country without a soul, and a country without a soul is a country that cannot survive." I feel that I must take some positive action on this matter. I hope that you will launch an investigation immediately and keep me informed of your progress. If you cannot, then I don't know what other courses of action to take.

I have considered sending this to newspapers, magazines, and broadcasting companies, but I somehow feel that investigation and action by the Congress of the United States is the appropriate procedure, and as a conscientious citizen I have no desire to further besmirch the image of the American serviceman in the eyes of the world. I feel that this action, while probably it would promote attention, would not bring about the constructive actions that the direct actions of the Congress of the United States would.

Sincerely,
/s/ Ron Ridenhour

10 A *Newsweek* Poll On Calley's Fate
April 12, 1971

Newsweek commissioned The Gallup Organization to poll the U.S. public reactions to the Calley verdict. Telephone interviews surveyed a representative cross section of 522 Americans. The full questionaire and its results:

Do you approve or disapprove of the court-martial finding that Lieutenant Calley is guilty of premeditated murder?

Approve	9%
Disapprove	79%
No opinion	12%

(If you disapprove) do you disapprove of the verdict because you think what happened at My Lai was not a crime, or because you think many others besides Lieutenant Calley share the responsibility for what happened?

Not a crime	20%
Others responsible	71%
Both	1%
Other	7%
No response	1%

Do you think Lieutenant Calley is being made the scapegoat for the actions of others above him, or not?

Yes	69%
No	12%
No opinion	19%

Do you think the Calley sentence of life imprisonment is fair, or too harsh, or too lenient?

Fair	11%
Too harsh	81%
Too lenient	1%
No opinion	7%

Do you think the incident for which Lieutenant Calley was tried was an isolated incident or a common one?

Isolated	24%
Common	50%
No opinion	26%

Some people have suggested that the U.S. is guilty of war crimes in Vietnam for which high Government and military officials should be tried. Do you agree or disagree?

Agree	32%
Disagree	47%
No opinion	21%

11 Vietnam: What Is Left of Conscience?
Bill Moyers
February 13, 1971

We do not yet know the full extent to which the war in Vietnam has affected our moral sensibilities, but we do know enough to be troubled. News of continuing death and destruction appears fleetingly in the press and is quickly forgotten. In a recent national poll, people said they are more concerned with the economy than with the war. When during a television interview reporters finally asked President Nixon a question about the war, he wondered aloud, with a smile, why they had taken so long to bring it up. A consensus has been reached that the war is winding down, at least our active combat role in it; last month when 300 bombers roared over the countryside of Indochina dropping tons of bombs, barely a peep was heard in the land. There was relatively little outrage over the Cambodian invasion until four students were killed by the National Guard at Kent State. Campuses are quiet, I suspect, because the threat of the draft is disappearing. Americans do not seem able to sustain indignation over a situation that does not cost them personally. We do not mind war as long as we do not have to look at its victims.

A committee of the American Association for the Advancement of Science recently reported that chemical herbicides used by the United States have poisoned some five million acres of South Vietnam—one-eighth of that country; that we have used six pounds of herbicides per Vietnamese, including children; and that the defoliation program, intended to deny food to the Vietcong, often destroyed the crops of the Montagnards, who are supposed to be on our side. Pictures of once fertile mangrove forests look like pictures of the moon. The report was like a rock dropped into a bottomless well. After the first burst of news coverage, hardly anyone paid any attention to it.

When Col. Robert A. Koob was selected foreman of the court-martial panel for the trial of Sgt. Charles E. Hutto, one of the soldiers at Mylai, he was asked by the chief government prosecutor if an enlisted man should be prosecuted if he shot an unresisting prisoner of war at the order of an officer. Colonel Koob was quoted by *The New York Times* as replying: "Since the time I entered the service, I was taught that a soldier was trained to shoot and kill. Haven't we trained soldiers to be responsive to orders?" Koob was also quoted as saying that "this is not a conventional war. We have to forget propriety."

The problem with the colonel's statement is that nations always "forget propriety" in the waging of war, whether they are sending V-2 rockets into London or dropping an atomic bomb on Hiroshima. In all wars, men have observed Seneca's proposition: "Deeds that would be punished by loss of life if committed in secret are praised by us when uniformed generals carried them out."

However, there are exceptions: Lieutenant Calley and others *are* on trial for what allegedly happened at Mylai. But even here something seems amiss. What do we learn about ourselves when we realize that for all the outcry over events at Mylai and Kent State the public remains quiet over the bombs that continue to fall indiscriminately—they might as well be labeled "Occupant"—on Indochina? Are we indifferent to the destruction our newspapers are unable to describe? Why is it that men like Calley should bear the brunt of punishment for what has been an official policy of mass and impersonal devastation waged in our name in Vietnam? Are they more guilty than the men who fly the bombers? Than the men who give the orders from Saigon or CINCPAC in Hawaii? Than the men who make the policy in Washington? Than all of us?

I do not know how to deal with the dilemma of such questions. Collective guilt, like a trillion-dollar economy, is of such scope as to stagger my mind. I grew up believing in personal responsibility and individual guilt. Much of the country did, too, which perhaps explains why so many seem so little troubled by the anonymous and abstract manner in which we have destroyed so much of Vietnam in order to save it; in the diffusion of responsibility there is comfort. Perhaps it also explains our willingness to permit the Calleys to be scapegoats through whose sacrifice the rest of us arrive at some atonement. Seeing Calley on television as he is entering or leaving the place of trial, I sometimes find myself wishing the worst for him; the acts of which he stands accused seem so heinous a departure from propriety. But in the next moment, realizing that I have never been in war, have never been asked to kill for society, I am engulfed by sympathy for him, not willing that he alone of all of us should be judged. Perhaps it is these moral doubts to which Colonel Koob unwittingly referred when he said Vietnam is "not a conventional war." Americans have fought brutally in other wars. This is just the first time we have been forced to concede the brutality so frankly and publicly, the first time we have fought with a nagging conscience openly displayed on television, the first time we have acknowledged in such a wholesale way the discrepancy in justice for the individual soldier who kills in our behalf and the anonymous men who from 30,000 feet carry out official policies of mass destruction, also in our name. We have abandoned propriety before; we have never before doubted the reason for doing so, as we doubt it now.

No wonder our armed forces are being shaken. "The Troubled Army in Vietnam" was the title of a recent cover story in *Newsweek*. But we should not be surprised. War is so total a departure from the traditions of civility men have labored for centuries to achieve, so consuming in its requirement that ordinary men inflict upon one another such extraordinary terror that an army can never again be the same once its troops are denied general confidence that their cause is just. A totalitarian government can march men to war under threat of death; better to take one's chance with an uncertain fate on the battlefield than to die certainly at home by the hand of your own master. But if tyranny can force men to become killers, a democratic government must persuade its citizens that killing in behalf of their government is, in the nature of things, justifiable. Conscription in our kind of society can only work well when sufficient numbers of men believe they would not be asked to kill unless their leaders knew what they were doing. When enlisted men lose confidence in the rationale of the policy and begin to wonder if the killing is worth it, discipline and morale inevitably suffer.

Vietnam has demonstrated that Nietzsche was wrong; a good war does not "hallow every cause." War can defile a cause as it can degrade the men who fight it. Old war movies to the contrary, men who look down the barrel of a gun at another human being, intending his death, want to believe that the irrevocable act they are about to commit has grounds more defensible than the exhortation of politicians. When by intuition, observation, or experience they begin to suspect that the brutality being exacted of them is not only not heroic but futile as well—it will not accomplish what their leaders said it would accomplish, it cannot stay the forces of history—no Congressional resolution or Presidential order can make right to such men what their consciences suggest is wrong. War is the means by which a government can sanction our worse nature, enabling us to do collectively what singly we would abhor. But men have consciences if governments do not, and when the sanction of the state runs out, men remember what they did and what they became under its protection. This is why governments should not expect men lightly to go to war; governments never feel the need for forgiveness, but men do. If Samuel Johnson was correct when he observed that "every man thinks meanly of himself for not having been a soldier," governments ought not to require a man to act in such a way that he will think meanly of himself for having been a soldier. "In becoming soldiers," Cromwell's troops petitioned Parliament, "we have not ceased to be citizens."

When men are asked to forget propriety on a scale that challenges the fragile moral values by which they maintain some sanity and some dignity, many things can happen. Some will become more soldier than citizen—as may have happened at Mylai. Some will resist the right of the government to ask of them such an offense to what the Levelers called their "self-propriety" and will seek refuge in Canada or elsewhere. Some are never bothered because in handling the impersonal instruments of war—bombs and herbicides—they are never confronted with the particular consequences of their acts, the charred bodies of the victims or the Montagnard family without food. "I could take it," a young veteran told me last summer, "only because I was in the artillery. I never had to worry about who we hit. It might have been Charlie, it might have been somebody else. We never knew who we hit, so pretty soon we just stopped wondering. That was the best way for everybody."

Still others respond by becoming less soldier, less citizen. A Department of Defense task force reported last week that drug abuse among American military personnel in Vietnam has become a "military problem" for which no effective solution has been found, partly because many enlisted men want so much to get out of the service that they are prepared to risk less than honorable discharge to do so. According to *Newsweek,* since last June "the United States Army . . . has seen the time-honored medal-award system badly tarnished, witnessed large numbers of its troops take to drugs that are prohibited back home, and experienced a measurable decline in discipline and morale."

For a conscripted army, the only thing worse than defeat is the doubt that it should be fighting at all. There is a limit to how much savagery ordinary men in uniform can either absorb or inflict. Sooner or later they will stop wondering, stop caring, or go mad.

At home, we have also experienced "a measurable decline in discipline and morale." We have turned upon each other in spiteful and accusing fashion, which has

resulted in violence, division, charges of intimidation and conspiracy, increased sur-
veillance by the state of its citizens, and increased suspicion of the state by the citizen. Most disturbing of all is the ease with which so many tend to suppress their
indignation when they are not personally affected by injustice and suffering. Such is
what happens when in the name of its ideals a nation has to "forget propriety." Nations cannot abandon civility abroad and remain civilized at home.

Document 12

The draft was one issue which personalized the war and forced millions of people to come to a decision about it. James Fallows, a student at Harvard in 1969
who later worked in the Carter Administration, reflected on his attitude toward
conscription in an article written in 1975. Fallows' memories of the feelings of
Harvard students like himself toward the draft and the actions which they took
when they went to take their physicals were representative of those of many
young men in the same situation during that decade. Fallows' conclusions about
their behavior, however, have not been universally accepted.

12 What Did You Do In the Class War, Daddy?
James Fallows

Many people think that the worst scars of the war years have healed. I don't.
Vietnam has left us with a heritage rich in possibilities for class warfare, and I would
like to start telling about it with this story:

In the fall of 1969, I was beginning my final year in college. As the months went
by, the rock on which I had unthinkingly anchored my hopes—the certainty that the
war in Vietnam would be over before I could possibly fight—began to crumble. It
shattered altogether on Thanksgiving weekend when, while riding back to Boston
from a visit with my relatives, I heard that the draft lottery had been held and my
birthdate had come up number 45. I recognized for the first time that, inflexibly, I
must either be drafted or consciously find a way to prevent it.

In the atmosphere of that time, each possible choice came equipped with barbs.
To answer the call was unthinkable, not only because, in my heart, I was desperately
afraid of being killed, but also because, among my friends, it was axiomatic that one
should not be "complicit" in the immoral war effort. Draft resistance, the course
chosen by a few noble heroes of the movement, meant going to prison or leaving
the country. With much the same intensity with which I wanted to stay alive, I did
not want those things either. What I wanted was to go to graduate school, to get
married, and to enjoy those bright prospects I had been taught that life owed me.

I learned quickly enough that there was only one way to get what I wanted. A
physical deferment would restore things to the happy state I had known during four
undergraduate years. The barbed alternatives would be put off. By the impartial dic-
tates of public policy I would be free to pursue the better side of life.

Like many of my friends whose numbers had come up wrong in the lottery, I
set about securing my salvation. When I was not participating in anti-war rallies, I
was poring over the Army's code of physical regulations. During the winter and
early spring, seminars were held in the college common rooms. There, sympathetic

medical students helped us search for disqualifying conditions that we, in our many years of good health, might have overlooked. Although, on the doctors' advice, I made a half-hearted try at fainting spells, my only real possibility was beating the height and weight regulations. My normal weight was close to the cut-off point for an "underweight" disqualification and, with a diligence born of panic, I made sure I would have a margin. I was six-feet-one-inch tall at the time. On the morning of the draft physical I weighed 120 pounds.

Before sunrise that morning I rode the subway to the Cambridge city hall, where we had been told to gather for shipment to the examination at the Boston Navy Yard. The examinations were administered on a rotating basis, one or two days each month for each of the draft boards in the area. Virtually everyone who showed up on Cambridge day at the Navy Yard was a student from Harvard or MIT.

There was no mistaking the political temperament of our group. Many of my friends wore red arm bands and stop-the-war buttons. Most chanted the familiar words, "Ho, Ho, Ho Chi Minh/NLF is Gonna Win." One of the things we had learned from the draft counselors was that disruptive behavior at the examination was a worthwhile political goal, not only because it obstructed the smooth operation of the criminal war machine, but also because it might impress the examiners with our undesirable character traits. As we climbed into the buses and as they rolled toward the Navy Yard, about half of the young men brought the chants to a crescendo. The rest of us sat rigid and silent, clutching x-rays and letters from our doctors at home.

Inside the Navy Yard, we were first confronted by a young sergeant from Long Beach, a former surfer boy no older than the rest of us and seemingly unaware that he had an unusual situation on his hands. He started reading out instructions for the intelligence tests when he was hooted down. He went out to collect his lieutenant, who clearly had been through a Cambridge day before. "We've got all the time in the world," he said, and let the chanting go on for two or three minutes. "When we're finished with you, you can go, and not a minute before."

From that point on the disruption became more purposeful and individual, largely confined to those whose deferment strategies were based on anti-authoritarian psychiatric traits. Twice I saw students walk up to young orderlies—whose hands were extended to receive the required cup of urine—and throw the vial in the orderlies' faces. The orderlies looked up, initially more astonished than angry, and went back to towel themselves off. Most of the rest of us trod quietly through the paces, waiting for the moment of confrontation when the final examiner would give his verdict. I had stepped on the scales at the very beginning of the examination. Desperate at seeing the orderly write down 122 pounds, I hopped back on and made sure that he lowered it to 120. I walked in a trance through the rest of the examination, until the final meeting with the fatherly physician who ruled on marginal cases such as mine. I stood there in socks and underwear, arms wrapped around me in the chilly building. I knew as I looked at the doctor's face that he understood exactly what I was doing.

"Have you ever contemplated suicide?" he asked after he finished looking over my chart. My eyes darted up to his. "Oh, suicide—yes, I've been feeling very unstable and unreliable recently." He looked at me, staring until I returned my eyes to the ground. He wrote "unqualified" on my folder, turned on his heel, and left. I was overcome by a wave of relief, which for the first time revealed to me how great my terror had been, and by the beginning of the sense of shame which remains with me to this day.

It was, initially, a generalized shame at having gotten away with my deception, but it came into sharper focus later in the day. Even as the last of the Cambridge contingent was throwing its urine and deliberately failing its color-blindness tests, buses from the next board began to arrive. These bore the boys from Chelsea, thick, dark-haired young men, the white proles of Boston. Most of them were younger than us, since they had just left high school, and it had clearly never occurred to them that there might be a way around the draft. They walked through the examination lines like so many cattle off to slaughter. I tried to avoid noticing, but the results were inescapable. While perhaps four out of five of my friends from Harvard were being deferred, just the opposite was happening to the Chelsea boys.

We returned to Cambridge that afternoon, not in government buses but as free individuals, liberated and victorious. The talk was high-spirited, but there was something close to the surface that none of us wanted to mention. We knew now who would be killed.

As other memories of the war years have faded, it is that day in the Navy Yard that will not leave my mind. The answers to the other grand questions about the war have become familiar as any catechism. Q. What were America's sins? A. The Arrogance of Power, the Isolation of the Presidency, the Burden of Colonialism, and the Failure of Technological Warfare. In the abstract, at least, we have learned those lessons. For better or worse, it will be years before we again cheer a president who talks about paying any price and bearing any burden to prop up some spurious overseas version of democracy.

We have not, however, learned the lesson of the day at the Navy Yard, or the thousands of similar scenes all across the country through all the years of the war. Five years later, two questions have yet to be faced, let alone answered. The first is why, when so many of the bright young college men opposed the war, so few were willing to resist the draft, rather than simply evade it. The second is why all the well-educated presumably humane young men, whether they opposed the war or were thinking fondly of A-bombs on Hanoi, so willingly took advantage of this most brutal form of class discrimination—what it signifies that we let the boys from Chelsea be sent off to die.

The "we" that I refer to are the mainly-white, mainly-well-educated children of mainly-comfortable parents, who are now mainly embarked on promising careers in law, medicine, business, academics. What makes them a class is that they all avoided the draft by taking one of the thinking-man's routes to escape. These included the physical deferment, by far the smartest and least painful of all; the long technical appeals through the legal jungles of the Selective Service System; the more disingenuous resorts to conscientious objector status; and, one degree further down the scale of personal inconvenience, joining the Reserves or the National Guard. I am not talking about those who, on the one hand, submitted to the draft and took their chances in the trenches, nor, on the other hand, those who paid the price of formal draft resistance or exile.

That there is such a class, identifiable as "we," was brought home to me by comparing the very different fates of the different sorts of people I had known in high school and college. Hundreds from my high school were drafted, and nearly two dozen killed. When I look at the memorial roll of names I find that I recognize very few, for they were mainly the anonymous Mexican-American (as they were called at the time) and poor whites I barely knew in high school and forgot altogether when I left. Several people from my high school left the country; one that I know of went to jail. By comparison, of two or three hundred acquaintances from college and afterwards, I can think of only three who actually fought in Vietnam. Another dozen or so served in safer precincts of the military, and perhaps five went through the ordeal of formal resistance. The rest of us escaped, in one way or another.

The fifth anniversary report of my class at Harvard gives a more precise idea of who did what. There were about 1,200 people in the class, and slightly fewer than half wrote in to report on what had happened to them since 1970. Of that number, 12 said that they had been in the Army, two specifying that they had served in Vietnam. One had been in the Marine reserves. Another 32 people, most of whom had held ROTC scholarships in college, had put in time with the Navy. Two were in the Coast Guard, two in the National Guard, and seven more in unspecified branches of the military. That was the bite the military took from half my class at Harvard during a bloody year of the war—56 people, most of them far from the fighting. Besides them, seven of my classmates performed alternate service as conscientious objectors; and, though no one reported going to prison, one wrote from England that he was a "draft resister; beat the rap on a legal technicality," and another that he had "several years of legal entanglement with the draft and the Justice Department.

. . .

Moreover, a whole theoretical framework was developed to justify draft evasion. During many of the same meetings where I heard about the techniques of weight reduction, I also learned that we should think of ourselves as sand in the gears of the great war machine. During one of those counseling sessions I sat through a speech by Michael Ferber, then something of a celebrity as a codefendant in the trial of Dr. Spock. He excited us by revealing how close we were to victory. Did we realize that the draft machine was tottering towards it ultimate breakdown? That it was hardly in better condition than old General Hershey himself? That each body we withheld from its ravenous appetite brought it that much nearer the end? Our duty, therefore, was clear: as committed opponents of the war, we had a responsibility to save ourselves from the war machine.

This argument was most reassuring, for it meant that the course of action which kept us alive and out of jail was also the politically correct decision. The boys of Chelsea were not often mentioned during these sessions; when they were, regret was expressed that they had not yet understood the correct approach to the draft. We resolved to launch political-education programs, some under the auspices of the Worker-Student Alliance, to help straighten them out. In the meantime, there was the physical to prepare for.

It does not require enormous powers of analysis to see the basic fraudulence of this argument. General Hershey was never in danger of running out of bodies, and the only thing we were denying him was the chance to put *us* in uniform. With the same x-ray vision that enabled us to see, in every Pentagon sub-clerk, in every Honeywell accountant, an embryonic war criminal, we could certainly have seen that by keeping ourselves away from both frying pan and fire we were prolonging the war and consigning the Chelsea boys to danger and death. But somehow the x-rays were deflected.

There was, I believe, one genuine concern which provided the x-ray shield and made theories like Ferber's go down more easily. It was a monstrous war, not only in its horror but in the sense that it was beyond control, and to try to fight it as individuals was folly. Even as we knew that a thousand, or ten thousand, college boys going to prison might make a difference, we knew with equal certainty that the imprisonment and ruination of any one of us would mean nothing at all. The irrational war machine would grind on as if we had never existed, and our own lives would be pointlessly spoiled. From a certain perspective, it could even seem like grandstanding, an exercise in excessive piety, to go to the trouble of resisting the draft. The one moral issue that was within our control was whether we would actually participate . . . and we could solve that issue as easily by getting a deferment as by passing the time in jail.

Critical Issues For Discussion

1. Senator Fulbright's criticism of American foreign policy helped to shatter the consensus on the war. What distinction did the senator draw between communism and nationalism in Document 1? How did he urge the United States to react to those ideologies? What practical steps did he suggest to alter the situation in South Vietnam? What had the Vietnam War done to Americans who had stayed at home?

2. Pete Seeger was a leading figure in American folk music for decades. Why did this song, which appears as Document 2, create such a stir? What was the "Big Muddy"? What political message did the song deliver to you? Should Seeger have been allowed to sing this song while Americans were fighting and dying in Vietnam? Was the song in poor taste? Was it treasonous? Was it responsible criticism?

3. In a speech in Akron, Ohio, in October 1964, President Johnson had said: "Sometimes our folks get a little impatient. Sometimes they rattle their rockets some, and they bluff about their bombs. But we are not about to send American boys nine or ten thousand miles away from home to do what Asian boys ought to be doing for themselves."

This statement later came back to haunt the president. How could antigovernment spokespeople have used this statement? Could Johnson have answered them? How did each side explain the American presence in Vietnam?

4. Linking the civil rights and peace movements was a controversial step which always had its detractors. Read Document 3. Why did King feel that a connection between the two movements was logical? Why did he think it was proper? How would you evaluate his criticisms of American foreign policy? What did he mean by calling for a "radical revolution of values"? Which ones? Why did he consider a "radical revolution" so urgent?

5. Document 4 was one method of protesting the Vietnam War. On what bases were American policy decisions opposed? How were American decisions described? What kind of language did the authors of this document use? What did they mean by "moral"? What does that mean to you?

6. Francis Cardinal Spellman commented just after Christmas in 1966 that "this war in Vietnam, I believe, is a war for civilization. . . . American troops are there for the defense, protection and salvation not only of our country, but I believe of civilization itself." How would critics of the war have answered Spellman? What do you think he meant by civilization? What did he imply would happen if the United States did not send troops to Vietnam?

7. The Yippies were as interested in shocking Americans as they were in making political statements. Look at Document 5. What was the tone of this leaflet? How do you react to it? What kind of America were they seeking? What effect would this leaflet have on the average American citizen? Do you think that the authors of this leaflet would have gotten along with the authors of Document 4? Why or why not?

The author of Document 6 knew all about the Yippies. What political stance was he taking? Whom did he blame for the "bratty" nature of the younger generation? Why were those people to blame? What should be done about them? How might the "silent majority" have reacted to this piece? What did he think should be done to get the United States back on track?

8. During the presidency of Richard Nixon, his vice president served to comment on the use and abuse of dissent. Read Document 7. How did Agnew characterize intellectuals? Why was he so angry at the spokespeople for the youth of America? How did he view American education? How did his criticisms of the draft compare to those in Document 4? How did he define "moral obligation"? How did his definition of morality compare with that described in Document 4? What did Agnew consider to be the stakes involved in fighting in Vietnam?

9. John Kerry's speech, which appears here as Document 8, was a clear antiwar comment by a man who had served in Vietnam. What did he mean by a war crime? What are the rules of war? Had the United States acted immorally in Vietnam? What had the Vietnam War meant for Kerry?

All three television networks covered Kerry's speech as Document 8 indicates. Were there substantial differences in what was reported? How would you evaluate the accuracy of each network's report?

10. The My Lai massacre forced Americans to face themselves and the actions which their countrymen had taken. See Documents 9–11. What did Ron Ridenhour report? What led him to make these revelations? Why didn't he ignore the rumors which he had heard? Why did he not immediately release his letter to the media?

How did the public react to the conviction and sentencing of Lt. Calley? How do you account for that attitude? Why were war crimes an issue? What were the Nuremberg Trials? What was established there? Was Calley a scapegoat for his commanding officers? For the army? For the country?

An old saying argues that "all's fair in love and war." Do you agree? Why or why not? Did Bill Moyers express an opinion on this point in Document 11? Do you agree with Colonel Koob's contention that an unconventional war is a reason to "forget propriety"?

Moyers tried to connect events in South Vietnam to some at home. Was he convincing? Were the two "battles" related? Moyers argued that "nations cannot abandon civility abroad and remain civilized at home." Was that an accurate perception of what was happening in the United States while war raged in Vietnam? Explain.

11. One American soldier commented that "if everybody is left to decide when to fight for their country, we won't have a country." What was he saying? One issue which arose during the war was the question of "selective objection." Should an individual be able to claim that he was opposed to a particular war? How do you react to that concept? Are some wars just and others unjust? Who is capable of deciding that? Should a citizen accept his country's decision to go to war whether or not he felt his nation was wrong? Should one have to support everything one's country does or leave it?

12. The draft was the issue which divided millions of young men. James Fallows' recollections, in Document 12, were written half a decade after the event which he was describing. How had he avoided the draft? How does he portray the actions he and his fellow students took? What accounts for his attitude today? How might another individual regard the actions which Fallows and his friends took in 1969? Why was Fallows ashamed of what he had done?

Follow-Up The following exchange took place between Senator Wayne Morse and General Maxwell Taylor during testimony in the Senate Foreign Relations Committee on February 17, 1966:

Morse: You know we are engaged in historic debate in this country. There are honest differences of opinion. I happen to hold to the point of view that it isn't going to be too long before the American people repudiate our war in Southeast Asia.

Taylor: That, of course, is good news to Hanoi, Senator.

Morse: I know that that is the smear artist—that you militarists give to those of us who have honest differences of opinion with you. But I don't intend to get down in the gutter with you and engage in that kind of debate, General. I am simply saying that in my judgment the President of the United States is already losing the people of this country by the millions in connection with this war in Southeast Asia. All I am asking is if the people decide that this war should be stopped in Southeast Asia, are you going to take the position that it is weakness on the homefront in a democracy?

Taylor: I would feel that our people were badly misguided and did not understand the consequences of such a disaster.

Morse: Well, we agree on one thing, that they can be badly misguided. You and the President in my judgment have been misguiding them for a long time in this war.

The preceding discussion is an example of an important type of debate which went on during the war. What was responsible criticism? What was irresponsible? Where was the line between them? Was Morse giving aid and comfort to the enemy? Was Taylor trying to stifle democracy? Should freedom of speech and dissent be limited during wartime? Should politics stop at the water's edge and let all foreign policy be national rather than an issue of partisan disputation?

Suggestions for Further Reading

Domestic Impact of the War

Baskir, Lawrence M., and William A. Strauss. *Chance and Circumstance: The Draft, the War and the Vietnam Generation*. New York: Random House, 1978.
Effectively combining statistics and personal stories, two members of President's Ford's Clemency Board expose the inequities of the draft.

Chester, Lewis, Godfrey Hodgson, and Bruce Page. *An American Melodrama: The Presidential Campaign of 1968*. New York: Viking, 1969.
Three British reporters covered the dramatic events before the 1968 elections, including the intricacies of the Vietnam negotiations and their effect on the candidates.

Davis, Peter, and the Board of Church and Society of the United Methodist Church. *The Truth About Kent State: A Challenge to the American Conscience*. New York: Noonday, 1973.
This study tells the story with photographs of the events of May 4, 1970, and indicts the Nixon administration for failing to come to grips with the unanswered questions surrounding the deaths of four students shot by Ohio National Guardsmen.

Kendrick, Alexander. *The Wound Within: America in the Vietnam Years, 1945–1974*. Boston: Little, Brown, 1974.
This readable general history stresses the domestic impact of the war from its very beginnings.

Stevens, Robert Warren. *Vain Hopes, Grim Realities: The Economic Consequences of the Vietnam War*. New York: New Viewpoints, 1976.
Stevens analyzes in detail how blunders in economic policy-making made Vietnam the major negative factor affecting the domestic economy during the sixties and early seventies.

Ungar, Stanford J. *The Papers and THE PAPERS*. New York: Dutton, 1972.
Ungar, who covered the story for *The Washington Post,* gives a behind-the-scene narrative of the clash between the press and the government over the release of the Pentagon Papers.

The Antiwar Movement

Bryan, C. D. B. *Friendly Fire*. New York: Putnam, 1976.
Out of grief for their son Michael, Peg and Gene Mullen fought to find out how he was killed in Vietnam.

Chomsky, Noam et al. *Trials of the Resistance*. New York: New York Review, 1970.
This collection of essays describes the major trials of war resisters who committed civil disobedience in the late sixties and analyzes what they mean for the future of American political life.

Cooney, Robert, and Helen Michalowski. *The Power of the People: Active Nonviolence in the United States*. Culver City, Calif.: Peace, 1977.
This excellent visual history places resistance to the Indochina Wars in the

tradition of the struggles for labor unions, women's suffrage, disarmament and civil rights, as well as the efforts of those who resisted World Wars I and II.

Gaylin, Willard. *In the Service of Their Country: Draft Resisters in Prison*. New York: Grosset and Dunlap, 1970.
Six case studies based on interviews with the men in prison help to understand the type of men who resisted the war in this way and the motives that guided their actions.

Gray, Francine du Plessix. *Divine Disobedience: Profiles in Catholic Radicalism*. New York: Knopf, 1970.
Gray's essays on Philip and Daniel Berrigan illuminate the role of the radical Catholic left in the antiwar movement.

Heath, G. Louis, ed. *Mutiny Does Not Happen Lightly: The Literature of the American Resistance to the Vietnam War*. Metuchen, N.J.: Scarecrow, 1976.
Flyers, leaflets, reports, and other documents from groups that opposed the war from 1964 to 1974, with a chronology of antiwar actions during this period.

Lynd, Alice. *We Won't Go: Personal Accounts of War Objectors*. Boston: Beacon, 1968.
Sympathetic personal accounts of 24 men who decided to avoid or resist military service, including what influenced their choices and what happened to them as a result.

Williams, Roger Neville. *The New Exiles: American War Resisters in Canada*. New York: Liveright, 1971.
Himself an American exile in Canada, Williams gives both the collective history of the exodus and thirteen individual stories of deserters and draft resisters who left the United States.

Zinn, Howard. *A People's History of the United States*. New York: Harper and Row, 1980.
Zinn's chapter on Vietnam, "The Impossible Victory," focuses on the widespread sentiment against the war and credits it with bringing the war to an end.

Hanging on for Dear Life
In April 1975, as the South Vietnamese army fled toward Saigon, hundreds of
thousands of South Vietnamese citizens followed suit. Scenes like this one in Xuan Loc
were repeated as people attempted to board American helicopters which had brought
supplies to the army. Few could be accommodated in this hopeless scramble for a lift
to safety. *U.P.I.*

Chapter 12
The End of the Tunnel:
1973–1975

Background

Historical Summary

A semblance of peace came to Southeast Asia on January 27, 1973, when the parties involved in the Vietnam War signed a cease-fire agreement. South Vietnamese President Nguyen Van Thieu had resisted the settlement, but President Nixon obtained his cooperation—with both a stern warning and a secret pledge of U.S. intervention should the Communists violate the accord.

The last Americans to serve in Vietnam returned home as the U.S. prisoners of war held by Hanoi were released. By April, Vietnam had faded from newspaper headlines and television screens in America. But the war was not finished.

American aircraft were still bombing Cambodia, where the Communist Khmer Rouge were gaining ground. In South Vietnam, meanwhile, the Saigon government and the Vietcong—now legally recognized as the Provisional Revolutionary Government—were nibbling away at each other's territory.

For Americans, the focus of events had shifted to Washington, where President Nixon was under fire for the Watergate break-in. As it probed Nixon's purported misdeeds, Congress began to pull back the independent authority of the presidency in a number of areas, including Vietnam.

In August 1973, finally rejecting further American involvement in the region, Congress voted to halt all U.S. bombing of Southeast Asia.

Thieu, however, continued to believe that Nixon would honor his promise of U.S. intervention in the event of Communist attacks. Thieu stubbornly rejected any idea of a compromise with the Communists, and he was supported in his intransigence by Graham Martin, the new American ambassador in Saigon. Martin, a seasoned diplomat, urged the Nixon administration to continue aiding Thieu, optimistically maintaining that South Vietnam could survive with U.S. help.

But having voted the bombing cut off, Congress went on to pass the War Powers Act, which reduced the president's authority to commit American forces abroad.

The prospects for Thieu looked even bleaker after Nixon resigned rather than face impeachment. The new president, Gerald Ford, sought to reassure

Thieu, but the Communists were already planning an offensive in the South. They did not expect the offensive to succeed quickly, and they gambled that the United States, in the aftermath of Nixon's resignation, would not return to Vietnam.

North Vietnam's push started in March 1975 with an assault against Ban Me Thuot, a town in the central highlands of South Vietnam. Thieu's forces yielded and prepared to fight at Pleiku, another town in the highland region. But then Thieu, deciding to consolidate his forces for a defense of the populated areas to the south, abruptly ordered a retreat from Pleiku, and the situation quickly disintegrated.

Thieu had not made the reasons for his decision public, and rumors flew in all directions, demoralizing his troops. Confused, they fled toward the coast, their path clogged by thousands of civilians also fleeing in panic. Frenzied soldiers and refugees converged on the port of Danang, which became a chaotic scene as people, fearing either the Communist advance or being caught in battle, fought to escape by ship or air. Danang fell to the Communists at the end of March, by which time the South Vietnamese forces in central Vietnam had been routed.

President Ford appealed to Congress without success to rush renewed aid to Saigon. However, American officials attempted to organize an orderly withdrawal—though Ambassador Martin, still hopeful that the Thieu government could hold the line, refused to put an evacuation plan into action. The Communists pressed southward.

Americans and South Vietnamese, exploring the possibility of a compromise, felt by the middle of April that the Communists might agree to a settlement if Thieu quit. He resigned on April 21, but his successor, the elderly politician Tran Van Huong, could do no better. The Communists believed themselves to be nearing victory.

Huong resigned on April 28 and was replaced by General Duong Van "Big" Minh, a popular officer considered to be more acceptable to the Communists. But Minh lacked the military strength to bargain as the Communists swept to the outskirts of Saigon.

By now, Martin had become aware that his optimism was hollow. He finally ordered a last-minute evacuation of Americans and Vietnamese who had been closely associated with the United States and who might be vulnerable to Communist retribution. Thousands battled to enter the U.S. embassy compound in Saigon, to be flown to safety aboard American aircraft carriers deployed in the South China Sea. Thousands were left behind.

Martin himself departed on April 30, carrying the American flag, as North Vietnamese troops entered the presidential palace in Saigon to accept Minh's surrender. The offensive had succeeded far beyond the expectations of the Communists. They raised flags of victory over Saigon—soon to be renamed Ho Chi Minh City.

Chronology

	1973 Jan	Feb	Mar	Apr	May	Jun	Jul	Aug	Sep
Vietnam	Peace Agreement signed in Paris	Return of POWs begins	Last U.S. troops leave South Vietnam			Kissinger and Le Duc Tho meet again in Paris		U.S. bombing in Southeast Asia ends	
United States	Lyndon Johnson dies			Watergate investigation implicates president					Kissinger becomes Secretary of State
World Wide									Allende is overthrown in Chile

	1973 Oct	Nov	Dec	1974 Jan	Feb	Mar	Apr	May	Jun
Vietnam				Thieu declares war has begun again					
United States	Agnew resigns as vice president		Gerald Ford becomes vice president						Nixon visits Soviet Union again
World Wide	Yom Kippur War in Middle East	Energy crisis begins							

Chronology (cont.)

	1974 Jul	Aug	Sep	Oct	Nov	Dec	1975 Jan	Feb	Mar
Vietnam		Communists make military gains		Politburo of North Vietnam plans military strategy					North Vietnamese take Ban Me Thuot ARVN retreats from Pleiku North Vietnamese take Danang
United States		Nixon resigns. Ford takes over	Ford pardons Nixon		Democrats make big election gains				
World Wide									

	1975 Apr	Oct	Nov	Dec
Vietnam	Thieu resigns Saigon surrenders			
United States				President Ford visits China
World Wide	Khmer Rouge wins in Cambodia			King of Laos abdicates. People's Democratic Republic set up

Points to Emphasize

- the relationship between the United States and South Vietnam after the signing of the Peace Agreement
- the effect of domestic affairs on American foreign policy
- the debate over the continuation of the American bombing program in Southeast Asia
- the repercussions from the resignation of President Nixon
- the problems of Thieu's government in dealing with the South Vietnamese people
- the North Vietnamese decisions leading to the offensive in the spring of 1975
- the reasons for the chaos in South Vietnam as a result of North Vietnam's Spring Offensive in 1975
- the strong disagreements in the United States over whether or not to aid the Thieu government
- the factors leading to Saigon's fall

Glossary of Names and Terms

Sam J. Ervin Democratic Representative from North Carolina, 1946–1947. Senator from North Carolina, 1954–1974. Chairman, Separation of Powers subcommittee, Government Operations Committee; Presidential Campaign Activities Select Committee.

Le Minh Dao Brigadier General, ARVN. Commander of the 18th Division. Led troops at Xuan Loc.

Graham Martin Administrative Counselor to U.S. Embassy, Paris, 1947–1955. Ambassador to Thailand, 1963–1967. Ambassador to Italy, 1969–1972. Ambassador to South Vietnam, 1973–1975.

Paul McCloskey Republican Congressman from California, 1967–present. Ran unsuccessfully for the Republican nomination for President in 1972 as an opponent of Nixon's foreign policy.

Kenneth Moorefield battalion advisor in the southern delta in Vietnam, wounded in combat. Served in the presidential honor battalion in Washington. Appointed Ambassadorial Assistant by Graham Martin in 1973.

Peter Rodino Democratic Congressman from New Jersey, 1948–present. Chairman, House Committee on the Judiciary. Chairman, Impeachment Investigation of President Richard Nixon, 1973–1974.

Frank Snepp operative and analyst of European security affairs and North Vietnamese political affairs for the CIA, 1968–1976. Two tours, U.S. Embassy, Saigon, 1969–1971 and 1972–1975.

Tran Van Huong Vice President of South Vietnam under Nguyen Van Thieu. Replaced Thieu as president on April 21, 1975 and served for one week until Duong Van (Big) Minh replaced him.

Van Tien Dung Major General in Vietminh Army. Army Chief of Staff at the

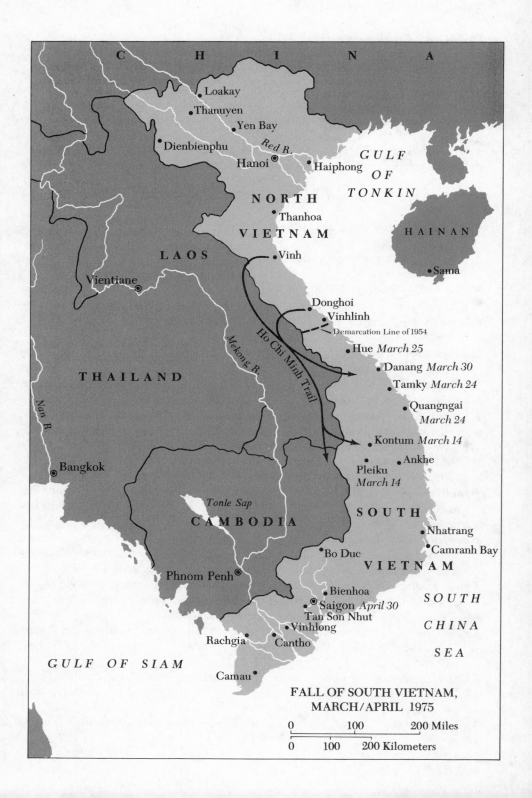

FALL OF SOUTH VIETNAM,
MARCH/APRIL 1975

0   100   200 Miles

0   100   200 Kilometers

time of Dienbienphu. Member of the North Vietnamese delegation to the First International Control Commission. Appointed to the North Vietnamese Politburo, 1972. Planned the 1975 Spring Offensive.

Frederick Weyand last Commander of Military Assistance Command, Vietnam, 1972–1973. Then Vice Army Chief of Staff and Chief of Staff. Sent to Saigon in the spring of 1975 by President Ford to assess the situation.

Ban Me Thuot town in South Vietnam. Scene of the first victory of the North Vietnamese Spring Offensive in 1975.

Convoy of Tears the frenzied evacuation of Pleiku by South Vietnamese civilians in March 1975; it symbolized the problems of the Thieu government during the final North Vietnamese Offensive.

Defense Attaché Office (DAO) office which replaced MACV as the official headquarters of the American military in South Vietnam after the Peace Agreement was signed.

Watergate a hotel-office complex in Washington, D.C., where an attempted burglary at the offices of the Democratic National Committee took place in June 1972. Impeachment proceedings against Richard Nixon stemmed from the subsequent investigation of the break-in.

Documents

Document 1

For the American public, the signing of the Vietnam peace agreement meant that American prisoners of war were coming home, that the last American combat troops were withdrawn, and America's longest and possibly most divisive war was over.

Few, if any, Vietnamese had that view. In this excerpt from a television interview, broadcast the same week the peace agreement was signed, President Thieu of South Vietnam was clearly not convinced that peace was at hand, nor did he seem to believe that America's military role in Vietnam had ended.

1   Mr. Thieu and the Fragile Truce
CBS News Special Report
February 1, 1973

. . . THIEU: Since the cease-fire, there [sic] have many violations. But I think that they have paid very expensive, very high cost of casualties and weapons. Up to now there [sic] have more than 1,300 killed, and so on. I think even if they would like to continue, they will be very limited on the capability, the real capability to do that—unless they would like to continue the war like before the cease-fire.

KALB: Well, I'm not—

THIEU: But if they would like to exploit only the first day following the cease-fire, they have to think over that because—whether or not it will be very advantageous for them to continue. And I hope that the—after that the control commission will be in place and will do their job correctly.

KALB: On the specific question, Mr. President, as to whether the other side will continue to make war in various scattered areas of the country or they will continue on a heavy way of continuing the war, which is your opinion?

THIEU: I think that they will continue the guerrilla on this remote area and they continue the infiltration. And they would like to capture as many as possible the hamlets and the people.

KALB: You do not see them, then, making a serious effort to respect the cease-fire?

THIEU: I think we have not to be confident on their goodwill. We have to be confident on the efficiency of the control mission.

KALB: Mr. President, you've talked about the new International Control Commission. In a speech the other night you called it inefficient and incompetent and you predicted that it would be, if I may use a loose translation of a word you used, useless.

THIEU: I think that with the experience we have in the past in Vietnam, in Cambodia, Laos, permit me to have such a kind of doubt. But it depends on how this new one, this new commission, will work.

KALB: There was a report here, Mr. President, that the South Vietnamese side—If I may interrupt, we hear the sound of some explosions in the distance from Saigon: that hardly sounds like a cease-fire.

THIEU: I think that the Communists have—are attacking at this hour some hamlets and we have to reply, because they fired the rocket in the civilian population many nights before.

KALB: Mr. President, is it accurate to say that—We know that the Geneva Agreement of 1954 divided Vietnam into two parts. Is it accurate to say that the latest agreement that has been signed in Paris has now divided South Vietnam into two parts: the Saigon part under the control of your forces and the parts of South Vietnam held by the Communist troops? Are there now three Vietnams, sir?

THIEU: We consider that South Vietnam belong to the South Vietnamese people and to this government. Now, to solve the problem with—between the South Vietnamese affection and particularly between this legal government and the NLF, certainly they have the armed unit. But the problem for us to do with them from now to six months is to have election and to solve the problem of South Vietnam once for all so we will have only one government, one territory of South Vietnam and one army. If the Communists win us in the election, certainly South Vietnam will be Communist. But when we win, the Communists in the election, they have to abide by the results and they may become a political party. And they have to abide by what the South Vietnamese people decide.

KALB: If the cease-fire were completely respected and serious talks were under way between the two sides and some kind of election date was set, would you go through, Mr. President, with the various proposals you have made before to resign in advance of the election?

THIEU: I think that we have to work on the new basis. I cannot predict what kind of election will be held in South Vietnam, but any kind of election will be agreed upon by the two sides.

KALB: Do you have any intention of asking the United States to return with some form of military power if the Communist side continues to violate the cease-fire, as you see it?

THIEU: You know, even if today we have no cease-fire agreement, the Vietnamese people now may continue the war without the full participation of the United States. And the Vietnamization have to be continued and we will fight alone with the military aid from the United States. And the Vietnamization plan will continue. Now, it depends on how the degree of the war the Communists will inflict again in the future.

KALB: If you went to a big degree, Mr. President—

THIEU: I think that first, we need the military aid from the United States. Secondly, I think the United States have to fulfill the responsibility, because, like President Nixon says, the "peace with honor." I understand peace with honor: that when the peace is respect and the political solution will be agreed and to consolidate the peace. Now, if the peace is violated by the Communists, I think that President Nixon will not consider it as a peace. So I think the responsibility United States will not be accomplished and I think that we do not call that peace with honor.

KALB: I wonder if I could be specific here, Mr. President. Are you saying that if there are what you would regard as massive violations by the Communist side of the cease-fire, that you would expect the United States to return to Vietnam with troops?

THIEU: No, not with troops—

KALB: With what, sir?

THIEU: Without troops. But the United States—

KALB: With air power?

THIEU: —have to react vigorously.

KALB: Well, sir, that's the point. "React vigorously" translates into what? U.S. air power returning?

THIEU: I think so. We never ask U.S. troops to come back here.

KALB: Air power, yes?

THIEU: Yes.

KALB: Now, Mr. President, there seems to be a distinction between the emphasis you are placing on the agreement and the emphasis another President—Mr. Nixon—is placing on the agreement. He has been talking about a peace with honor. You, President Thieu, have said this is a cease-fire, no more, no less: it is not peace. Now—

THIEU: Not peace yet.

KALB: Not peace yet. Now, someone listening can see a very different emphasis between two Presidents who are allies.

THIEU: No—

KALB: How do you explain this?

THIEU: —not the difference. Because even President Nixon agreed with the agreement. He said that this is a peace agreement. I agree with it: this is a peace agreement. But now, in the state of the things of today, I say that first the peace has to be begun from a standstill cease-fire. Now, to provide good condition for peace, it depends how the Communists will cooperate with us to elaborate—to establish peace in South Vietnam. If they continue to violate the treaty, we cannot call the treaty as a peace treaty. . . .

Document 2

There were no parades for conquering heroes when American troops came home from Vietnam. Many soldiers faced the hostility of an American public that had come to regard the war as an embarrassment at best. But the prisoners of war did receive a heroes' welcome.

In *Newsweek,* Shana Alexander took issue with the answer POWs were being given to the question "Who won?" ("South Vietnam didn't lose, and North Vietnam didn't win.") She suggested that the response was symptomatic of the effort being made to ignore uncomfortable questions about the meaning of the war and the suffering of the POWs. Her article voiced concern that both the military and the American people were now using the POWs to create a new set of justifications for our many years in Vietnam. As evidence, Shana Alexander pointed to the assignment of 80 military public-relations men—one for every two prisoners—to shield them from the press, and to the brief, almost uniform statements of loyalty and patriotism given by POWs during interviews.

In response, Colonel Robinson Risner, a POW for seven and a half years, wrote to *Newsweek* to explain how he felt about heroism, the war, his role in it, and his release (Document 2).

2 A POW Replies
Robinson Risner
June 16, 1973

In her March 5 column, Shana Alexander suggested that the returning American prisoners of war were actually "prisoners of peace with honor"—men who were coached by Pentagon public-relations brass on what to say on repatriation. Air Force Col. Robinson Risner, 48, a leader of the POW's own prison-camp command, gives his side of the story:

Dear Ms. Alexander:

Isn't it great to live in "the land of the free" where people with dissimilar beliefs can express themselves in the same publication? I must confess I had long taken this and other freedoms for granted. But after having been denied them for seven and a half years, I can sincerely say that I am acutely aware of even the simple privileges we as Americans possess.

You began your March 5 column with mention of heroes of past wars and referred to the returned POW's as Vietnam's *only* heroes. You were only partially right. There *were* heroes in the prison camps—men who were tortured and some who died at the hands of the enemy rather than compromise their principles; but there were *other* heroes of this war—men who fought with great valor and many who died on the battlefield fighting so that others might have some of the freedoms we enjoy.

Please don't misunderstand me, Ms. Alexander. I know that the Vietnam war was not perfect, either in its concept or in its conduct, but then few things are. At any rate, South Vietnam still remains free of Communist rule as does most of the rest of Southeast Asia. In addition, the U.S.A. is still a bulwark of freedom all over the world. And, although some would like us to believe otherwise, you can bet that our friends and allies continue to rely upon us.

I was speaking of heroes. Let me talk to you a moment about some of the unsung heroes, or rather heroines—our wives. These are the gals that took it on the chin and hung in there through thick and thin—our "velvet and steel" as some have called them. It would be impossible for me to relate here what these women have had to cope with through the years; just let it suffice to say that if anyone deserves recognition for "service above and beyond the call of duty," they do. So, Ms. Alexander, if perhaps the ladies seemed a little *too* radiant to you, all I can offer in their behalf is the thought that if you had been with these girls through these most trying years, perhaps you too would agree that not only did they deserve to put aside their cares and dry their eyes for this once-in-a-lifetime occasion, but also that their radiance was nothing less than genuine.

I must say that I am rather dismayed to find that you believed the grins, salutes, statements of gratitude, etc., were rehearsed. Just for the record, let me say that we received no briefing en route from Hanoi about our conduct or statements upon arrival at Clark Air Base. Do you believe that men who endured so much extra hardship and even death rather than allow themselves to be used as propaganda tools would permit themselves to be orchestrated? Don't you believe it!

During the time we were imprisoned and when it was possible for us to do so, we would discuss our basic beliefs and talk about what we considered to be major issues. Over the months and years we seemed to come to a meeting of the minds on some of these issues. Consequently, if our statements sounded similar, all I can say is that our beliefs—the beliefs that sustained us through these years—*were* similar.

'Basic Metals'

Let me try and explain it this way. If one were to take ore of varying grades and subject it to sufficient heat and pressure over a period of time, the basic metals would emerge. Men, too, are like that. What I'm trying to say, Ms. Alexander, is that we were not and are not unique. We are typical guys from Anytown, U.S.A., and although we were trained as fighting men, we cannot claim uniqueness even among the military. The qualities or "basic metals" that emerged in us are, I believe, inherent in most Americans and no matter what other differences we might sustain, these qualities are our common denominators.

Regarding the "protective shield" that was provided us upon our return, I can safely say that those of us who returned from Communist prisons, as well as our wives, were deeply grateful for the meticulous planning that went into the preparations for our release and return to normal life. They had every right to expect mental and physical deterioration as well as deep psychological problems. Believe me, I'm glad they planned for the worse and were pleasantly surprised.

"Who won?" When I am asked that question, I think, as I stated earlier, of South Vietnam and most of the rest of Southeast Asia which is still free of Communism, and the credibility of America's word with other nations. Yes, it was a very long war. It was not only long, it was the dirtiest kind of war. It was one in which deeds of valor became routine and taken for granted while a few deeds of which we were not proud were given the widest publicity. It was a war in which there were no clean-cut victories because there were no clean-cut front lines, no industrial complexes, no large cities to take. In short, it was a war to which Americans could not relate because it was unique in the history of American wars. It was a war in which

the word of a vociferous few, at times, drowned out the less vocal voices of the majority. I'm glad, though, that the majority was sustained and that a peace consistent with the commitments of three Presidents was concluded.

You said that "a nation cannot long sustain a war its own people don't believe in." I agree, and I would like to point out that despite the inherent American impatience, we fought in Indochina longer than in any other war.

Back to Freedom

Ms. Alexander, we came out of North Vietnam—back to freedom—grinning because for the first time in years we had a lot of things to grin about. The wives were radiant because they were happy to have their husbands back where they could touch them, love them and be angry at them if they wanted. The freed POW's made similar statements of gratitude to our Commander in Chief out of sincere admiration. While we were in the Communist prison, the North Vietnamese kept insisting that the Administration's Vietnam policy represented only a small minority and that the American people opposed it. The '72 election was an overwhelming rebuttal to that. Most of us felt that the President was personally responsible for getting us out "with honor." Maybe "with honor" isn't too meaningful to some but we would have stayed a lot longer rather than come home without it.

Document 3

Richard Nixon took particular pride in being the president to bring the American POWs home from North Vietnam. In May 1973, he hosted a dinner for POWs at the White House, and excerpts from his speech on that occasion are reprinted here as Document 4.

When the president had praised his guests for their courage, their endurance, and their sacrifices for their country, he went on to recount how he had ended the war and to detail his administration's foreign policy accomplishments—particularly the understandings he had reached with Russia and China. Part of Nixon's message dealt with the necessity for secrecy in the diplomatic process. He argued that secrecy and national security often went hand in hand and that those who denied that connection were not responsible critics of the government.

**3 Remarks of the President at a Reception for Returned Prisoners of War
Richard M. Nixon
May 24, 1974**

Gentlemen, as you can imagine during my term as President of the United States and also before that as Vice President, and in other offices, I have spoken to many distinguished audiences. I can say to you today that this is the most distinguished group I have ever addressed and I have never been prouder than I am at this moment to address this group.

I say that not simply because you are here and because the whole nation shares those views, as you know, some of you, I am sure, who have traveled around the nation since you have returned home, but I say it because I feel very deeply at this moment, when we have a culmination of the program which finally has all of you returned to the United States, that this is one of those critical moments in history that can change the world, and we need your help. . . .

Your sacrifice of all of your colleagues and comrades who died in Vietnam, and the sacrifice of all who have served in Vietnam, will have been worth it only if we build a world of peace now. That is what it was all about.

We didn't go to Vietnam for the purpose of conquering North Vietnam. We didn't begin this war, we haven't begun any war in this century, as you know. That is the greatness of U.S. foreign policy. We make our mistakes, but we always have as our motives defending peace, not breaking it, defending freedom, not destroying it.

But when we think in terms of whether your sacrifice then was worth it, we have to think then about the broader aspects of peace, whether or not the world you come back to, the America you come back to, is a better world or is it, shall we say, a world that is not as safe as when you went to Hanoi or whatever area you were kept in captivity.

I cannot put it in the context of 6½ or seven years, which some of you, of course, have been away. But I can put it in the context of the years I have been in this office. And perhaps we can see in perspective where we have been and where we are. But more important, where we are going to go.

First, when I came into this office 4½ years ago, 300 a week were being killed in action in Vietnam. There was no plan to end the war, no hope that it was going to be ended. Many of you were already prisoners of war. You had no hope.

Looking at the world scene, the United States had no communication whatever, in any meaningful sense, with the leaders of one-fourth of all the people in the world, those who govern the People's Republic of China. We were in constant confrontation with the Soviet Union, the other super power on the earth, with no thought or even hope that there was a chance for arms control, or trade, or a lessening of tension between these two great super powers.

There were other troubled areas in the world. Some of them are still troubled. But looking at those three areas and seeing what has happened since, and then looking at the United States, we see some progress has been made.

Some 4½ years ago, this nation was torn by riots. Hundreds of campuses were in flames. The American people seemed to have lost their way. There was a desire to move away from responsibilities in the world. There was a lack of national pride, a lack of patriotism. I don't mean among all the people, not even among a majority, but it was there. There was a crisis in terms of whether America, the greatest hope for peace in the world today, would dash that hope or whether it would be worthy of that hope. That was the situation 4½ years ago.

Now in describing that situation, I do not speak critically of those who preceded me in this office. President Eisenhower, John Kennedy, Lyndon Johnson loved this country. They worked for peace as I have tried to work for peace. They felt for you as I feel for you.

What I am simply saying is that in January of 1969 we did have a critical situation, and we started to move on it. And how I wish we could have moved faster. I remember that first Christmas in '69. I met with a group of the representatives of the League of Families down in the library and I talked to these wonderful remarkable women, and I saw their faith and their courage and their love of country, and I heard them tell me that their husbands had not gone to Vietnam simply for the purpose of getting back. In other words, they rejected totally the idea of "Get out, if you will give us our prisoners."

They said, in effect, and they didn't put it this way, but one of you put it very well, "Bring our men home, but bring them home on their feet and not on their knees." And that is what we have done.

And so that was our goal over those four years. That is why we couldn't achieve it perhaps quite as fast as we would have liked.

But the year 1972 saw remarkable progress, as you know. The year 1972, moving into 1973, in January, saw the return of all Americans from Vietnam, all of our combat forces, the return of all of our prisoners of war, the end of the American involvement in Vietnam, a peace agreement, which, if adhered to, will mean peace for Vietnam and Southeast Asia.

That was one accomplishment. That is the one that most people talk about. They say, "Thank God that war is over. Thank God we have got peace."

But in a broader sense, other events took place that will have even more meaning to the world and to peace than your return and the end of the war in Vietnam.

China, for example. That initiative, which was undertaken in early 1972, began in '71, the negotiations, has finally started communication between the leaders of the People's Republic of China and the leaders of the United States of America. Oh, it doesn't mean they aren't still Communists and that we are not still people who love freedom, but it does mean that instead of having hanging over us, looking down the road 10, 15, 20 years from now, a possible confrontation with a nation of the most able people in the world, armed with nuclear weapons equal to our own, instead of having that, there is a chance, a very good chance now, that we will have negotiations with them rather than confrontation, and that is the key to peace in the Pacific.

And then the second development was the meetings with the Soviet leaders. This did not happen just over a period of 1972. We worked for the whole four years. But it culminated in the summit in Moscow. You perhaps heard something about it since your return. But looking at that summit agreement, a great deal of emphasis can be placed on the aspects of trade, and our cooperation in space and other areas which are important, but the most significant development, undoubtedly, was the first step, and a very important step, in limiting the arms race in the nuclear field.

We have, therefore, an agreement with the Soviet Union on defensive nuclear weapons, where we are both limited, and we are moving now toward getting a limitation in the offensive field. . . .

One other subject that is somewhat sensitive that I will touch upon only briefly, that I would like to ask for your support on, is with regard to the security of the kind of negotiations that we have.

I want to be quite blunt. Had we not had secrecy, had we not had secret negotiations with the North Vietnamese, had we not had secret negotiations prior to the Soviet Summit, had we not had secret negotiations over a period of time with the Chinese leaders, let me say quite bluntly, there would have been no China initiative, there would have been no limitation of arms for the Soviet Union and no summit, and had we not had that kind of security, and that kind of secrecy that allowed for the kind of exchange that is essential, you men would still be in Hanoi rather than Washington today.

And let me say, I think it is time in this country to quit making national heroes out of those who steal secrets and publish them in the newspapers.

Because, gentlemen, you see, in order to continue these great initiatives for peace, we must have confidentiality, we must have secret communications. It isn't that we are trying to keep anything from the American people that the American people should know. It isn't that we are trying to keep something from the press that the press should print. But it is that what we are trying to do is to accomplish our goal, make a deal. And when we are dealing with potential adversaries, those negotiations must have the highest degree of confidentiality. . . .

I now want to talk about why the United States, after all that it has done for the world in World War II, after the billions that it has poured out since World War II, its sacrifices in Korea, its sacrifices in Vietnam, why we, the American people, have to continue to carry this load.

As I said earlier, believe me, as President, what a relief it would be to say, "Now that we have peace in Vietnam, we have a new relationship with China and Russia, we can simply turn away from the problems of the world and turn to the problems at home."

I can assure you gentlemen that if we were to follow that course, we would find very soon that we would be living in a terribly dangerous world. The world is safer today than it was four and one-half years ago. It can be more safe in the years ahead. But that will only happen provided we follow the course that I have tried to lay out to you here today.

As I look to that future, therefore, it is vitally important that the United States continue to play the world role.

Let's look at just this century. We don't need to go back any further than that. I can imagine some of you in those long hours of captivity were thinking back over several centuries. In any event, looking back just over this century, World War I, the United States could stand aside. After all, there was Britain, there was France, two great powers who thought as we did about the world, and they could carry the load. And then we came in toward the end in World War II. The United States, for a time, could stand aside because Great Britain was still strong and France at the beginning had some strength, but eventually we had to come in.

But today, look at the world. Among the free nations of the world there is no one else, not the Japanese, as you well know, even though they have the economic strength, they do not have the military strength, and cannot be allowed to acquire it under their constitution; and not one nation in Europe, by itself, or Europe collectively, has the strength to be the peacemaker in the world.

So it is all right here. It is in America. It is in that Oval Office, whoever is there, and it is there for the foreseeable future. In other words, the United States must maintain its strength in order to play a role between the great powers of the world and among the great powers of the world of reducing the danger of war, because our ideals and our goals—subject as they can be to much criticism as far as tactics are concerned in the world scene—our ideals and our goals are for a world of peace. Our ideals and our goals are for a world in which we reduce the burden of arms, and therefore, it is vitally important that this nation that has that kind of ideals and that kind of goals maintains its strength so that we can play that role.

But maintaining the strength alone is not enough. It must be respected. And that means that we must continue to have a policy which commands respect throughout the world. We must continue to insist on adherence to agreements that are made. We must continue to let the world know that while we have no aggressive intentions any place in the world, we will stand by our treaty commitments wherever they are in the world.

That, you see, is the language of peace rather than the language of bugging out of the world and turning to what people wistfully might think to be a fortress America. But let me tell you, fortress America might have been before World War

II a concept that was viable. Today it is ridiculous. We cannot be apart from the world, not when weapons that can destroy us are 30 minutes away.

And so we must play this role, and rather than playing it in terms of whining about it and complaining about it, let us do it proudly, because what greater mission could a people have than to say that in these years—the 70's—of 1971-2-3-4-5 and 6, when we reach our 200th birthday, the United States of America played a great role in the world and made the world safer not only for ourselves but for everybody in the world. That is the stake, that is the challenge we must meet.

Today then, I ask for your support, obviously, for a strong national defense. That is like the preacher talking to the choir. But I know as far as you are concerned, you will be for that, and I hope so many of you will stay in our armed forces. We need you.

But also, beyond that, I ask for your support in helping to develop the national spirit, the faith that we need in order to meet our responsibilities in the world. You have already contributed enormously to that by your statements on your return, by what you have said, what you have done, and I am sure you can contribute more to it in the future.

But the young people of America need to hear the truth. They will believe you. They will believe you because you have suffered so much for this country and have proved that you will do anything that you can to do what is best for America, not just for yourselves.

Because, at this particular point, America is the richest country in the world; militarily, it is the strongest, and will always have that potential because of its wealth. The only question is whether we face up to our world responsibilities, whether we have the faith, the patriotism, the willingness to lead in this critical period.

Gentlemen, by what you did and what you said on your return, you have helped turn this country around. You have helped reinstill faith where there was doubt before. And for what you have done by your faith, you have built up America's faith. This nation and the world will always be in your debt.

Those first four years in office were not easy ones for me on the international front, fighting for an adequate defense budget, fighting for a responsible foreign policy, but looking toward the balance of the second four years, let me say I feel better, because out in this room, I think I have some allies, and I will appreciate your help.

Thank you.

Documents 4 and 5

Vietnam reappeared in the headlines of American newspapers early in 1975, after having been largely ignored for two years by the American public. The North Vietnamese were advancing toward Saigon, and President Thieu's government had become desperate. Urgent messages came from Ambassador Martin in Saigon and the Ford administration pressed Congress for action, and Congress debated whether or not to send aid to President Thieu. The following articles from the *New York Times* reflect that debate.

Charles W. Wiley, the executive director of the National Committee for Responsible Patriotism, was a wholehearted supporter of America's presence in Vietnam. In Document 4 he asserted his belief that the North Vietnamese were testing the will of the United States to resist Communist aggression, and he expected this country to meet the test.

And a *New York Times* editorial (Document 5) explained why that paper did not favor a massive increase in aid to South Vietnam.

4 The United States Stake in Southeast Asia
Charles W. Wiley
February 19, 1975

Our country is at a crossroads of history. The United States has promised small nations that it would stand by them. And, based on our repeated pledges, millions of people have committed their lives—and those of their children—to the struggle. To turn away from them now would not be worthy of our great nation.

During nearly two decades of American commitment to stopping aggression in Southeast Asia—the policy of five Presidents and their parties—we have spent billions of dollars and lost thousands of lives. How can we dishonor the nearly 50,000 young Americans who gave their precious lives to the cause of freedom?

The old arguments of the critics are gone. Americans no longer need to fight in Southeast Asia. The South Vietnamese and Cambodians obviously have the will to fight their own battles.

Given the time to develop their nation and military strength, the South Vietnamese, despite awesome economic and strategic problems and years of suffering, are doing almost as well alone as when we were there with over a half million troops.

It is clear that many critics will not be satisfied until our South Vietnamese allies have been enslaved and the United States is judged a loser in the eyes of the world and our own people.

There is no way to cover up surrender to terrorists and aggression. Those who try to justify appeasement as a means of "avoiding fueling the conflict" only add lies to compound their shame. Aleksander Solzhenitsyn has described the "sickness of the will" in the free world. As he said in his Nobel Prize acceptance speech:

"The spirit of Munich prevails in the twentieth century. The timid civilized world has found nothing with which to oppose the onslaught of a sudden revival of barefaced barbarity, other than concessions and smiles. . . . And tomorrow, you'll see, it will be all right. But it will never be all right! The price of cowardice will only be evil; we shall reap courage and victory only when we dare to make sacrifices."

Not only is our honor at stake, but so is the survival of much of the world—its people and natural resources—and, ultimately, our very own existence.

The struggle in Southeast Asia has been a test of our will, and our response is being carefully studied by friend and foe alike. Some will decide their policies after asking themselves, Would a nation that turns its back on its own honored dead stand firm anywhere? And if they conclude, as they likely would, that the United States is a cowardly paper tiger without will, we can look forward to endless aggression across the globe. The Middle East and Asia are the likely next targets, but the danger is everywhere.

It is almost unbelievable that there can be serious opposition concerning continued material (not manpower) help to Southeast Asia. The amount of additional dollar aid being asked for both Vietnam and Cambodia is but a tiny fraction of our total commitment—far less than one per cent.

In Southeast Asia today we are like a poker player in a showdown hand. The table is piled high with chips—blue for treasure and red for the blood of our fallen sons—and we are hesitating to toss in a few white chips!

Will this not signal the world that we have washed our hands of honor and the will to survive?

Ours is a young nation of vibrant, courageous people. Our heritage is rich and our achievements great. But we still must learn from history. One lesson, perhaps the most important today, is that "staying power" is crucial. Those who would destroy freedom and our way of life have proved that they have it. Do we?

5   Commitment?
New York Times **Editorial**
April 6, 1975

What, if anything, do the people and Government of the United States now owe to the people and Government of South Vietnam? This question does not admit of any easy answer, entangled as it is in considerations of ethical responsibility, political commitment, and strategic self-interest, as well as the ambiguities of a shared history between a very powerful nation and a very weak one.

Beyond the clear call of human fellow feeling, there resides the hard and complex political question of the relationship between the United States and South Vietnam. The South Vietnamese Ambassador to Washington stated bitterly that the world could draw "only one possible conclusion: . . . that is, it is safer to be an ally of the Communists, and it looks like it is fatal to be an ally of the United States."

At his news conference last week, President Ford implicitly criticized the Democratic-controlled Congress for its failure to appropriate all the funds he had requested for Vietnamese military aid. Secretary of Defense Schlesinger meanwhile has repeatedly stated his view that this country has a moral—though not a legal—commitment to continue aid indefinitely to South Vietnam, a commitment allegedly given before Saigon agreed to sign the Paris peace protocols in 1973.

"I think that it was strongly stated to the South Vietnamese Government that the United States Government intended to see to it that the Paris accords were indeed enforced," Secretary Schlesinger said a few days ago.

It is clear that any such commitment, if it was ever made, has no legal basis. The Paris accords permit one-for-one replacement of military equipment but do not obligate the United States to provide such help. If Secretary of State Kissinger, the chief negotiator of those accords, offered private assurances of aid or, more ambitiously, intimated that the United States would respond to North Vietnamese violations with renewed bombing or the reintroduction of ground troops, he has never acknowledged doing so. At his news conference explaining the Paris agreements on Jan. 24, 1973, Mr. Kissinger said categorically: "There are no secret understandings."

If such understandings ever existed the Government of South Vietnam has been on notice for more than a year and a half that they would not be fulfilled. Effective Aug. 15, 1973, the Nixon Administration accepted a ban imposed by Congress against further bombing anywhere in Vietnam or Cambodia.

That leaves open the question of military aid, which has continued but on a declining basis. It has been the position of this newspaper, particularly in view of the intensified North Vietnamese attacks of recent months in open violation of the Paris agreements, that the United States should continue to provide military aid to South Vietnam for a definitely limited period, but possibly as much as the next three years. Legal commitments and diplomatic hints aside, there is always an implicit responsibility not to abandon a military ally if it has any prospect of making a go of it.

The sudden collapse of much of South Vietnam's army, however, makes the military aid question moot. Poor generalship and a breakdown in morale—not an immediate shortage of equipment and ammunition—caused the rout of recent days. Unless the Saigon Government can soon achieve a remarkable reversal of the military situation, the fate of the country will have been settled before further American equipment could make any difference.

It is never easy to come to terms with failure and disappointment, even if it is the failure of an effort that was mistaken in its basic premises, as America's involvement in Vietnam was. The United States made a fundamental miscalculation of its own national interests in intervening on a large-scale in 1965 and fighting there for three years. It then spent the next five years trying to extricate itself while at the same time hoping that "Vietnamization" of the war would gradually enable South Vietnam to fight successfully on its own. That gamble appears now to have failed.

If challenged, a nation's sense of its own honor can never much exceed its perception of its own vital interests. Southeast Asia has never been an area of vital American interest. Only the gratuitous American intervention made it appear to be such an area. The lives, money and energy expended were out of all proportion to any discernible American interest. When means and ends are so disproportionate, a shift in policy sooner or later becomes inevitable. For seven years since President Johnson withdrew as a candidate for re-election and initiated the Paris peace talks, the United States has been trying to withdraw from that over-commitment and yet create conditions in which South Vietnam could continue on its own. The events of recent weeks have sadly proved that South Vietnam could not prevail militarily unless helped by American bombing and probably also by American ground troops. Regardless of their lingering sense of obligation, the American people long ago rightly determined that those are heavy costs that they would not pay again in Southeast Asia.

Document 6

By the beginning of April 1975, the outlook for the government of President Thieu was bleak. Hundreds of thousands of refugees fled south before the advancing North Vietnamese army, and the fall of South Vietnam appeared imminent. At a news conference on April 3, 1975, President Gerald Ford put forth his views on the situation in Southeast Asia.

The President offered to help some South Vietnamese children escape from the ever-worsening situation by airlifting two thousand orphans to the United States. He reiterated his pledge to try to convince Congress to continue to aid the Thieu government. Finally, he vowed that the United States would remain a nation which stood by its allies.

6   Press Conference of the President of the United States
Gerald R. Ford
April 3, 1975
   . . . We are seeing a great human tragedy as untold numbers of Vietnamese flee the North Vietnamese onslaught. The United States has been doing—and will continue to do—its utmost to assist these people.

I have directed that all available Naval ships to [sic] stand off Indochina, to do whatever is necessary to assist. We have appealed to the United Nations to use its moral influence to permit these innocent people to leave, and we call on North Vietnam to permit the movement of refugees to the area of their choice.

While I have been in California, I have been spending many hours on the refugee problem and our humanitarian efforts. I have directed that money from a $2 million special foreign aid children's fund be made available to fly 2000 South Vietnamese orphans to the United States as soon as possible.

I have also directed American officials in Saigon to act immediately to cut red tape and other bureaucratic obstacles preventing these children from coming to the United States.

I have directed that C–5A aircraft and other aircraft especially equipped to care for these orphans during the flight be sent to Saigon. I expect these flights to begin within the next 36 to 48 hours. These orphans will be flown to Travis Air Force Base in California, and other bases on the West Coast, and cared for in those locations.

These 2000 Vietnamese orphans are all in the process of being adopted by American families. This is the least we can do, and we will do much, much more.

The first question is from Mr. George Dissinger of the San Diego Tribune.

QUESTION: Mr. President, are you ready to accept Communist takeover of South Vietnam and Cambodia?

THE PRESIDENT: I would hope that that would not take place in either case. My whole Congressional life in recent years was aimed at avoiding it. My complete efforts as President of the United States were aimed at avoiding that.

I am an optimist, despite the sad and tragic events that we see unfolding. I will do my utmost in the future—as I have in the past—to avoid that result.

QUESTION: Mr. President, I understand you are soon going to ask Congress for new authority to extend humanitarian aid in Southeast Asia. I wondered if you stand by your request, though, for more military aid for South Vietnam?

THE PRESIDENT: We do intend to ask for more humanitarian aid. I should point out that the Administration's request for $135 million for humanitarian aid in South Vietnam was unfortunately reduced to $55 million by Congressional action. Obviously, we will ask for more; the precise amount we have not yet determined.

We will continue to push for the $300 million that we have asked for and Congress had authorized for military assistance to South Vietnam, and the possibility exists that we may ask for more.

QUESTION: Mr. President, how and why did the U.S. miscalculate the intentions or the will of the South Vietnamese to resist?

THE PRESIDENT: I don't believe that we miscalculated the will of the South Vietnamese to carry on their fight for their own freedom.

There were several situations that developed that I think got beyond the control of the Vietnamese people. The unilateral military decision to withdraw created a chaotic situation in Vietnam that appears to have brought about tremendous disorganization.

I believe that the will of the South Vietnamese people to fight for their freedom is best evidenced by the fact that they are fleeing from the North Vietnamese, and that clearly is an indication they don't want to live under the kind of government that exists in North Vietnam.

The will of the South Vietnamese people, I think, still exists. They want freedom under a different kind of government than has existed in North Vietnam. The problem is how to organize that will under the traumatic experiences of the present.

QUESTION: Unilateral decision by whom?

THE PRESIDENT: It was a unilateral decision by President Thieu to order a withdrawal from the broad, exposed areas that were under the control of the South Vietnamese military.

QUESTION: Mr. President, what is your response to the South Vietnamese Ambassador to Washington's statement that we had not lived up to the Paris peace accords and that the Communists are safer allies?

THE PRESIDENT: I won't comment on his statement. I will say this: That the North Vietnamese repeatedly and in massive efforts violated the Paris peace accords. They sent North Vietnamese regular forces into South Vietnam in massive numbers—I think around 150,000 to 175,000—well-trained North Vietnamese regular forces, in violation of the Paris peace accords, moved into South Vietnam.

We have objected to that violation. I still believe that the United States, in this case and in other cases, is a reliable ally and although I am saddened by the events that we have read about and seen, it is a tragedy unbelievable in its ramifications.

I must say that I am frustrated by the action of the Congress in not responding to some of the requests for both economic, humanitarian and military assistance in South Vietnam. And I am frustrated by the limitations that were placed on the Chief Executive over the last two years.

But let me add very strongly, I am convinced that this country is going to continue its leadership. We will stand by our allies and I specifically warn any adversaries they should not, under any circumstances, feel that the tragedy of Vietnam is an indication that the American people have lost their will or their desire to stand up for freedom any place in the world.

QUESTION: Mr. President, can you explain why President Thieu, with our close military ties as allies, did not tell you what he was going to do in terms of the retreat?

THE PRESIDENT: I think the only answer to that can come from President Thieu.

QUESTION: Mr. Ford, recently you said the fall of Cambodia could threaten the national security of this country. Considering the probable fall of South Vietnam to Communist forces, do you feel that will threaten our national security, and if so, how?

THE PRESIDENT: At the moment, I do not anticipate the fall of South Vietnam, and I greatly respect and admire the tremendous fight that the government and the people of Cambodia are putting up against the insurgents who are trying to take over Cambodia.

I believe that in any case where the United States does not live up to its moral or treaty obligations, it can't help but have an adverse impact on other allies we have around the world. We read in European papers to the effect that Western Europe ought to have some questions.

Let me say to our Western European allies, we are going to stand behind our commitments to NATO, and we are going to stand behind our commitments to other allies around the world.

But, there has to be in the minds of some people, a feeling that maybe the tragedy of Indochina might affect our relations with their country. I repeat, the United States is going to continue its leadership and stand by its allies.

QUESTION: Are you, in fact, a believer of the domino theory of, if Southeast Asia falls, then perhaps some of the other countries in the Pacific are next?

THE PRESIDENT: I believe there is a great deal of credibility to the domino theory. I hope it does not happen. I hope that other countries in Southeast Asia, Thailand, the Philippines, don't misread the will of the American people and the leadership of this country to believing that we are going to abandon our position in Southeast Asia.

We are not, but I do know from the things I read and the messages that I hear, that some of them do get uneasy. I hope and trust they believe me when I say we are going to stand by our allies.

QUESTION: Mr. President, as you are well aware, there are about 7000 Americans still in Saigon. They are in danger not only from Communist attack, but from South Vietnamese reprisals. There are reports that the South Vietnamese are in a bad temper toward Americans.

Do you feel that under the War Powers Act and also under the limitations voted by Congress in 1973 on combat by Americans in Indochina, that you could send troops in to protect those Americans, and would you, if it came to that?

THE PRESIDENT: I can assure you that I will abide totally with the War Powers Act that was enacted by the Congress several years ago. At the same time, I likewise assure you that we have contingency plans to meet all problems involving evacuation, if that should become necessary. At this point, I do not believe that I should answer specifically how those contingency plans might be carried out.

QUESTION: Sir, you don't want to talk specifically. Can you tell us, however, if you do believe that you do have the authority to send in troops? You are not saying, I understand, whether you would, but do you have the authority?

THE PRESIDENT: It is my interpretation of that legislation that a President has certain limited authority to protect American lives. And to that extent, I will use that law.

QUESTION: Mr. President, despite your statement here this morning about war orphans, there apparently is a lot of red tape in Washington. A San Diego man who is trying to get four Vietnamese children out of that country has received hundreds of calls from people all over the Western United States wanting to help, even adopt children, but despite this outpouring of compassion by the American people, all he gets in Washington is, "No way."

There is nothing that can be done. Why is he running into this problem, if we are trying to help?

THE PRESIDENT: Having had some experience in the past with the Federal bureaucracy, when we had a similar problem involving Korean orphans, I understand the frustration and the problem.

But, I am assured that all bureaucratic red tape is being eliminated to the maximum degree and that we will make a total effort, as I indicated in my opening statement, to see to it that South Vietnamese war orphans are brought to the United States. . . .

Document 7

The resignation of President Thieu on April 21, 1975, did not come as a surprise. Throughout the North Vietnamese Spring Offensive, Thieu had been unable to launch an effective counteroffensive, and his decisions during that period were bitterly condemned by his critics. Thieu's resignation speech, part of which appears here as Document 7, reviewed at great length the circumstances leading to South Vietnam's increasing weakness and severely criticized the part the United States had played in his country's fate.

7 Resignation Speech
Nguyen Van Thieu
April 21, 1975

. . . The communist strategy is as follows: when they are strong militarily, they fight vigorously while holding talks perfunctorily. And when they are weak militarily, they fight that way but come on strong in the talks. They agreed to resume the peace talks. But after the talks between the South Vietnam-US side and the communist side resumed at the Paris conference table, we realized they were stalling.

At the time, there was collusion between the communists and the United States with a view to reaching the agreement of 26th October 1972. This agreement, which I spent much time explaining to our compatriots—I am sure that my compatriots still remember it—was an agreement by which the United States sold South Vietnam to the communists. I had enough courage to tell Secretary of State Kissinger at that time the following: if you accept this agreement, this means you accept to sell South Vietnam to the North Vietnamese communists. As for me, if I accept this agreement, I will be a traitor and seller of the South Vietnamese people and territory to the communists. If you accept it, this is for US interests or for some private reason which I do not know about. It is a sharing of interests among you powers that I do not know about. You make some concessions or exchanges among you. You want to sell the interests and lives of the South Vietnamese. As for me, a Vietnamese, I cannot do so.

I refused to accept this agreement. I opposed this agreement for three months.

. . .

I have therefore told them (the Americans): you have asked us to do something that you failed to do with half a million powerful troops and skilled commanders and with nearly 300 billion dollars in expenditures over six long years. If I do not say that you were defeated by the communists in Vietnam, I must modestly say that you did not win either. But you found an honourable way out. And at present, when our army lacks weapons, ammunition, helicopters, aircraft and B-52's, you ask us to do an impossible thing like filling up the ocean with stones. This is like the case in which you give me only three dollars and urge me to go by plane, first class; to rent a room in the hotel for 30 dollars per day; to eat four or five slices of beefsteak and to drink seven or eight glasses of wine per day. This is an impossible, absurd thing.

Likewise, you have let our combatants die under the hail of shells. This is an inhumane act by an inhumane ally. Refusing to aid an ally and abandoning it is an inhumane act. This is the reason why, on the day a US congressional delegation came here, I told the congressmen that it was not the problem of 300 million dollars in aid, but it was the question of complying with the US pledge to assist the Vietnamese people in the struggle to protect their independence and freedom and the ideal of freedom for which the Americans fought together with our people here and for which some 50,000 US citizens were sacrificed.

The United States is proud of being an invincible defender of the just cause and the ideal of freedom in this world and will celebrate its 200th anniversary next year.

I asked them: are US statements trustworthy? Are US commitments still valid? Some 300 million dollars is not a big sum to you. Compared with the amount of money you spent here in 10 years, this sum is sufficient for only 10 days of fighting. And with this sum, you ask me to score a victory or to check the communist aggression—a task which you failed to fulfil in six years with all US forces and with such an amount of money. This is absurd!

Gentlemen, compatriots and brothers and sisters: All this has led to the current situation in our country. I accept the criticism of the world people and our ally as well as the correct criticism of our Vietnamese people. I admit that some, but not all, of our military leaders were cowardly and imbued with a defeatist spirit and lacked the bravery of combatants in recent battles. In some areas, our combatants fought valiantly and I don't think that our allied troops could have fought as valiantly as they did.

We must be just. Therefore, I have said that wrongdoers must be punished and those scoring military achievements must be properly awarded. We do not try to conceal the shortcomings of those wrongdoers. We are proud to say that, in some of the recent battles, we scored achievements that our US allied troops probably could not have scored if they had been here.

. . .

I could stay on as President, to lead the resistance of all our armed forces and people. However, I am not in a position to supply adequate means for the army to fight. Moreover, I might also be misunderstood by the people as an impediment to peace and as continuing to cause mourning, destruction, misery, death and ruin. World public opinion continues to say that I am the cause of the fact that the South does not have peace at present. Let us wait and see whether the US Congress will prove that I am the cause or used me as a pretext for cutting military aid.

The second solution is to resign. This is one of the things I spoke of earlier. I think that my resignation is a very small sacrifice if all our people and armed forces will get abundant aid with which to fight and preserve the remaining territory, and if, without my presence, future negotiations with the communists can help protect a free and democratic South and achieve the right to self-determination of the South Vietnamese people in the spirit of the Paris Agreement. I call on all people, organizations, religions and politicians who have so far referred to me as an impediment to peace and considered me impotent in bringing about peace and protecting the South and unable to defeat the communists and restore peace, and thus only causing mourning and misery, for the sake of patriotism and love for the people, to assist President Tran Van Huong in bringing about peace, honour, freedom, prosperity and democracy; in ensuring strict implementation of the Paris Agreement with the communists forced to respect it; and in achieving the realization of the southern people's national right to self-determination as specified in the Paris Agreement. In short, I do not want anybody to use me—President Nguyen Van Thieu—personally as an excuse to maltreat this nation. Those persons, from this moment onward, can no longer use that excuse and must now show their sincerity and honesty.

Ladies and gentlemen, compatriots, brothers and sisters; I have served the compatriots, brothers and sisters for the past 10 years. As I have said, I do not lack courage. It is not that any demonstration or slander can discourage and demoralize me and prompt me to step down in a nonsensical and irresponsible manner. It is not due to the pressure of our ally or the difficult and hard struggle against the communists that I have to avoid responsibility and leave my office. The presidents of some big countries are proud of the fact that they have undergone six, seven or 10 crises. They have written books in which they proudly offer themselves as heroes and outstanding politicians. As for me, over the past 10 years, all years, months, days and all hours in my life have been bad, as my horoscope forecast. As regards my fate, I can enjoy no happiness; I have enjoyed no happiness, yet I have not sought ways to enjoy life. A ruler of a country can enjoy either honour or disgrace. He must accept this so he can lead the people. If I have some good points, the compatriots will praise me even if I do not want it. But if I have some bad points and errors, I am ready to accept judgements and accusations from the compatriots. Today, as I leave my office, I ask the compatriots, combatants and cadres, together with all popular organizations and religions, to forgive those errors I have committed against the nation during my presidential term.

I would like to thank the national assembly, all constitutionally established organs, all organizations, religions, individuals, compatriots of all walks of life and the brother and sister combatants and cadres for the co-operation and assistance they have given me through all the ups and downs of the country until the present. Our nation will remember forever the merits of these compatriots and friends. And personally, I will also keep them in my memory.

I am resigning but not deserting. From this moment, I place myself at the service of the President, the people and the army. As I step down, Mr Tran Van Huong will become President and our nation will not lose anything. Perhaps our country will gain another combatant on the battlefront. I will stand shoulder to shoulder with the compatriots and combatants to defend the country.

Now, I thank the compatriots, gentlemen and the brother and sister combatants and cadres throughout the country; and I say goodbye to them. I would like to repeat my request that the bicameral National Assembly and the Supreme Court allow, in the presence of you ladies and gentlemen, Vice-President Tran Van Huong to be sworn in as President in accordance with Article 55 of the Constitution. Thank you.

Documents 8 and 9

When Saigon fell to the Communists at the end of April 1975, the Office of the Secretary of Defense hired the Rand Corporation to study the loss of South Vietnam. The authors of the Rand report, part of which appears as Document 8, interviewed twenty-seven former high-ranking South Vietnamese military officers and civilians to discover their perceptions and explanations of the defeat.

Many South Vietnamese seemed to be placing the blame on the United States, and that proposed answer caused a commentator in the May 5, 1975 *New Yorker* to wonder anew about the reasons for American intervention in Vietnam (Document 9).

8   The Collapse in Retrospect

After all that has been said, there still remains a final set of questions about the fall of South Vietnam: Could the outcome have been different? Did our South Vietnamese respondents see the collapse as inevitable, and if not, what might have been done to avert the disaster?

As to the latter question, there is consensus among the respondents on one point: Had the Americans not "abandoned" Vietnam, the course of events would have been quite different. Most respondents agreed that an effective defense could have been sustained for some time had U.S. aid not been cut back after the Paris Agreements. Most also believed that the reintervention of U.S. airpower, especially B-52s, would have prevented defeat in 1975. None would contend that continued aid or renewed intervention would have ended the war or brought victory—significantly, the word "victory" does not appear in the interviews.

But beyond this fundamental conviction that U.S. support was crucial, the views of the respondents on "what might have been done" become more diffuse and complex, and must in part be distilled through inference. While some respondents offered explicit suggestions about what they believed to have been more promising options for the conduct of the war, the views of most must be drawn from the catalog of reasons they cited for the collapse. These range over a wide field: South Vietnam's armed forces were poorly led, stretched too thin, lacked an efficient general staff, and were improperly organized to cope with the threat at hand. It was difficult to mobilize national resources and impose the discipline necessary to fight a long war within the democratic norms the South was obliged to follow. Corruption was rampant. North Vietnam, by contrast, was a totalitarian society, geared for war, fully supported by its allies, and after 1973, free from direct attack, even in its southern sanctuaries.

The major points made included the following: Thieu should have been removed, along with, by implication, the corrupt and incompetent people he appointed. South Vietnam's territory should have been consolidated to make it more defensible. A more austere style of fighting should have been adopted. Manpower policies should have been changed. More divisions should have been activated. A coherent strategy for conducting the war should have been developed, along with more viable contingency plans in the event of a full-scale offensive. South Vietnam should have attacked the North, or at least harassed the enemy's lines of communication in the South. South Vietnam should have tried to hold out longer.

Although few said so directly, the respondents implied that had at least some of these and other things been done, the outcome of the war would have been different, which suggests that they felt defeat was not inevitable. But they did none of these things. One reason given for this is that such actions would have required America's acquiescence, if not its active support—after all, it was America that had insisted on the maintenance of democratic norms, organized the ARVN in the image of the U.S. Army, and refused to equip additional divisions. Moreover, South Vietnam's leaders seemed convinced that such painful reforms were in fact unnecessary, because the Americans could be counted on to bail out the South in an emergency.

But there was also one other fundamental factor that discouraged reform: None of South Vietnam's weaknesses seemed solvable in isolation; rather, each was part of an intricate web. According to this view, the causes of the collapse were so "inextricably interwoven" that no single change in the conduct of the war on their part alone would have affected the outcome and, in any case, they considered most reforms to be difficult, if not impossible to realize. (In contrast, American officials generally tended to consider South Vietnam's weaknesses to be discrete and individually remediable problems.) Change in South Vietnam often faced a vicious circle. It seemed impossible, for example, to get competent military commanders because of the corruption in the promotion system. Yet it was impossible to clean up corruption without concerted action on the part of President Thieu, who was himself in on or at least a "captive" of the system. But it was risky to get rid of Thieu because only he had the support of the Americans, and without American support the South Vietnamese could not carry on the war.

Thus, the principal causes of the disaster were seen as all interacting upon one another at any given time and encompassing a wide spectrum of military, social, political, and international factors. They embodied a composite of past errors, weaknesses, and misperceptions that left South Vietnam inherently vulnerable to an enemy superior in will and power.

Although it would be wrong to conclude that the South Vietnamese saw themselves as entirely helpless, they tended to see themselves as being "moved" rather than being "movers." This theme comes through quite strongly in the interviews. It appears first in their perceptions of how America was able to impose its will on Vietnam: In their view, the Americans, while they may not have been the architects of defeat, greatly contributed to it by simultaneously pushing for a vast range of different and irreconcilable objectives, more or less from the beginning of the war. The push for greater South Vietnamese military strength was incompatible with the push to encourage greater democracy and freedom. The Americans wanted the South Vietnamese government to create a broader political base and reduce corruption, but they continued to back Thieu. The Americans gave the South Vietnamese a military machine that was inherently costly to maintain and operate, and then wanted them to reduce military costs and operate with far less aid. The Americans wanted South Vietnam to demobilize men to transfer them to the civilian economy, while the enemy was increasing its military strength. This attempt to build a political and economic showcase in the midst of a hard war was regarded as unrealistic, and some South Vietnamese officials apparently felt squeezed—or in some cases suspended—between high-flown American plans and harsh military, economic, and political realities.

But the perception of being "moved" was reflected more fundamentally by those who saw South Vietnam to be but one piece of a larger contest. They viewed the war not simply as a conflict between themselves and the North Vietnamese but as part of a global struggle between the Soviet Union and China on the one side and the free world, led by the United States, on the other. In such a struggle, the will and the actions of the South Vietnamese could have but limited impact; the Americans held the real power. The course of the war and its outcome would depend on events and decisions made in a higher arena, and it was there they were to be ultimately failed. Détente with the Soviet Union and the rapprochement with China, together with the American President's Watergate troubles and America's inherent "impatience" (a condition they contrasted with their enemies' unlimited willingness to endure), combined to erode the desire and capacity of the United States to further resist Communist expansion.

Thus, the destiny of South Vietnam, in the final analysis, was regarded to have rested in the hands of others—and in this sense was a matter of fate, which, after all, is a concept deeply embedded in Vietnamese culture. And, as one respondent concluded, "Fate was not on our side."

9   Notes and Comments
The New Yorker
May 5, 1975

Last week, the war in Vietnam seemed to be moving towards its end, but something stranger than the victory of one side over the other was going on. Not only was the side supported by the United States collapsing; the world view that had given the war its importance in the eyes of American officialdom was collapsing, too. The system of friendships and enmities that had provided the policy with what Secretary of State Henry Kissinger calls its "coherence" was in disarray. The confusion was visible in microcosm in the positions taken on the issue of the Americans who remained in Saigon. The threats to these Americans came from some unexpected quarters. The principal threat, it seemed, came not from the North Vietnamese but from the South Vietnamese, America's ally. Drew Middleton, the military-affairs analyst for the *Times,* wrote of the mood of the South Vietnamese soldiers who had retreated from Danang to Saigon, "Ironically, these forces, who fought better than any other Government troops in the five-week campaign, are now regarded as the most serious danger to Americans in Saigon, as well as to politicians seeking an accommodation with the Communists infiltrating into the city." There was even fear that the South Vietnamese might hold the Americans hostage. Stranger still were reports that Mr. Graham Martin, the American Ambassador to South Vietnam, was slowing the evacuation—that *he* was holding the Americans hostage, in the hope of getting more aid for the South from Congress. Meanwhile, the "enemy"—the North Vietnamese—were promising a safe withdrawal for the Americans. The North Vietnamese, of course, have been trying to get Westerners out of Vietnam for some thirty years now.

The enmity of the South Vietnamese against the Americans was fast becoming the predominant emotion in Saigon. President Thieu, in his speech of resignation, put the blame for his government's plight not on the North Vietnamese but on the United States. The North Vietnamese may have had a supporting role, he seemed to be suggesting, but it was the United States that had "led the South Vietnamese people to death." He sounded as though the United States had been at war with South Vietnam, not North Vietnam, these last fifteen years. Thieu's opinion was apparently shared by the Ford Administration. In Washington, not long before, Mr. Kissinger—whom Thieu bitterly attacked in his resignation speech—had said that the United States must give Thieu more aid if it did not want to "destroy an ally." But while Thieu was blaming Kissinger for the collapse of the Saigon regime, Kissinger was blaming Congress. He contended that it was Congress that had not lived up to the American "commitment" to South Vietnam (Congress, meanwhile, was learning of the "commitment" for the first time, and was surprised at being accused of not having upheld a promise it did not know that the United States had made.) Moreover, as Kissinger was blaming Congress for its failures in the past, another member of the Administration, Vice-President Rockefeller, was looking to the future failures of Congress. Speculating that some thousands of Americans might be killed or captured in Saigon, he said that such an eventuality would make a campaign issue in the Presidential race of 1976; he also said that if Congress did not vote funds "and the Communists take over and there are a million people liquidated, we know where the responsibility will lie." Then, shortly afterward, President Ford said that Vietnam should not be a campaign issue in 1976.

Oddly, amid all this recrimination and talk of prospective massacres and campaign issues, there was very little mention of Russia, China, and North Vietnam—

the nations whose influence the United States had supposedly been opposing in South Vietnam. Indeed, President Ford, in his recent State of the World address, said that America's wounds were "self-inflicted." The foe had apparently been read out of the picture. We had been battling ourselves, it seemed, and had lost. What mention there was of the Communist powers tended to be cordial and understanding. Secretary of Defense James Schlesinger set the tone when he said, a few weeks back, during a discussion of the American presence in Asia, that the Chinese and the Russians sometimes found their Asian allies prone to "exuberance" and welcomed having the United States step in as a restraining influence. President Ford struck the same note in some remarks not long afterward. Speaking of the collapse of the Saigon forces in the northern part of South Vietnam, he said, "I don't think we can blame the Soviet Union and the People's Republic of China in this case. If we had done with our allies what we promised, I think this whole tragedy could have been eliminated." Instead, we could blame the members of our own Congress, who had voted down the extra military aid.

The remarks of the President and the Secretary of Defense seemed to evoke nothing less than a vision of a new world order. At one time, the government had told the public that the United States was fighting against Moscow and Peking in Vietnam, but now it seemed to be saying that these countries were our partners in the war. In the new world order, the great powers had apparently agreed that each would support its own allies in whatever wars were going on. Thus, a balance had been struck in which the Americans and the Russians and the Chinese were to live in peace while the Vietnamese would go on killing each other forever. The name of this order was "détente." But if the United States was in Asia to protect Chinese and Russian interests, as Mr. Schlesinger had said, Mr. Kissinger had not been told, for the day after the President had said we could not blame Russia and China for what was happening in Vietnam, Kissinger did blame them. "We shall not forget who supplied the arms which North Vietnam used to make a mockery of its signature on the Paris accords," he said.

The regime in Saigon was falling, but official Washington seemed at a loss to explain why. Some people were pointing the finger of blame at Russia and China, but others were saying that those countries were innocent. Some were saying that the fault was President Thieu's (while he was saying that the fault was ours). Some were saying that Congress was to blame, but then they were saying that there was enough blame for all Americans to share. The longest war in our history was at last coming to an end, and we did not know who the enemy had been.

Critical Issues for Discussion

1. An American reporter in Saigon made up a slogan for the American support of the last South Vietnamese government: "see it through with Nguyen Van Thieu."

What did this slogan mean? What was the attitude of the American government toward President Thieu? What was America's goal in supporting Thieu? What kind of government was the United States hoping for in South Vietnam?

2. The cease fire in Vietnam did not mean the same thing to the United States and South Vietnam. Document 1 represents President Thieu's opinion. What was his attitude towards the North Vietnamese? Was he optimistic

about the chances for peace? What was his vision of the political future of South Vietnam? What relationship did he foresee between the United States and his government? Who would be responsible for the success or failure of the cease fire? Why?

3. The U.S. prisoners of war came home as heroes, and their opinions about the war in which they had suffered so greatly were widely sought. Document 2 gives the views of POW Col. Robinson Risner.

How did Colonel Risner evaluate the time that he spent in captivity? How did he assess the American role in Vietnam? Was he proud of the part he had played? Was he defensive? What did he think about the president's desire for peace with honor? Did he think that this had been accomplished? How? What exactly did "peace with honor" mean?

4. In Document 3, President Nixon explained why he found secrecy to be one of the most important tools of diplomacy. What did Nixon feel were the results of his use of secret negotiations? Why couldn't these things have happened in other ways? Were there any negative results of the secret diplomacy?

5. Some people have argued that the Paris Agreement of January 1973 was a cynical maneuver on the part of the American government to allow the United States to leave Vietnam and to provide a "decent interval" before the Communists took over the South. What arguments could you make in defense of this theory? What criticisms would you offer? Did the cease fire agreement ever have a chance of keeping the peace in Southeast Asia? What were its strengths and weaknesses?

6. In 1975, Congress had to face the issue of Vietnam once again. Documents 4 and 5 reflect the debate on whether the United States should send additional aid to keep South Vietnam alive.

Which of these articles do you find more convincing? Why? What is its basic argument? What were the author's underlying assumptions?

Which article seemed more objective? Did it, nevertheless, have a point of view?

How would you have voted? Did the United States "stab an ally in the back" as some have suggested? Do you agree with the congressional decision? Why or why not?

7. President Ford explained his attitude toward the North Vietnamese Spring Offensive in his April 3, 1975 news conference. Look at his comments in Document 6.

What were his plans? What did he think those steps would accomplish? How did he assess the actions of the Thieu government? Why did he announce Operation Babylift? Did he think that South Vietnam could still be saved?

8. Document 7 presents portions of Thieu's resignation speech, and in Document 8 former South Vietnamese officials' assess the reasons for the collapse of their country. Why did Thieu resign? What had brought him to such a position?

How did he assess his term in office? What did he think about the American role in Vietnam? What actions or events would have been necessary for Thieu to have survived politically?

What did the former South Vietnamese officials have to say? Whom did they blame for their nation's collapse? How did they view Thieu? Would they have agreed with his speech? Which part? Did they see South Vietnam's fall as inevitable?

9. Colonel Risner commented that, despite the opposition to the Vietnam War in the United States, this country had stuck it out and had accomplished its purpose there. Vietnam was, as he noted, America's longest war. The commentator in the *New Yorker* article (Document 9) concluded that despite the length of the war, the United States never really knew whom it was fighting or why.

Why had the war lasted so long? Was that ability to endure a sign of American strength or weakness? Explain. Whose analysis was more in line with yours—Risner's or that of the author of Document 9? Why?

Follow Up The fall of South Vietnam set off a wave of questions and bitter comments in the United States. Who was responsible for South Vietnam's defeat? Was it a South Vietnamese failure? An American failure? A free world failure? All of these?

Who won the victory in Saigon? The National Liberation front? The North Vietnamese? All of the Vietnamese? The Russians? The Chinese? The Communists? All of these?

Suggestions for Further Reading

Hosmer, Stephen T., Konrad Kellen, and Brian M. Jenkins, eds. *The Fall of South Vietnam: Statements by Vietnamese Military and Civilian Leaders*. Santa Monica: Rand Corporation, 1978.
    Leaders of the Saigon forces give their analyses of why they were defeated.
Martin, Earl. *Reaching the Other Side*. New York: Crown, 1978.
    Martin is an American Mennonite who had been working with farmers in Quang Ngai. His journey to Saigon is full of stories of soldiers and civilians on both sides.
Nguyen Khac Vien, gen. ed. *Vietnamese Studies #47, Collapse of the Neo-Colonialist Regimes in Indochina*. Hanoi, 1977.
    This collection of essays analyzes the moral, political, military and economic weaknesses of the U.S.-sponsored regimes in Vietnam, Laos, and Cambodia as evidenced in their final collapse.
Snepp, Frank. *Decent Interval: An Insider's Account of Saigon's Indecent End*. New York: Random House, 1977.
    These memoirs of a former CIA staffer are a detailed indictment of the United States' failure to anticipate and prepare for the fall of Saigon.

Terzani, Tiziano. *Giai Phong! The Fall and Liberation of Saigon*. New York: St. Martin's, 1976.

Terzani, an Italian journalist and photographer, remained in Saigon during the Communist takeover. His story covers the Americans' leaving, the reunion of Vietnamese from all sides of the conflict, and their efforts to rebuild.

Van Tien Dung. *Our Great Spring Victory*. New York: Monthly Review Press, 1977.

The planning and execution of the final campaign by General Dung, chief of staff in the Hanoi military hierarchy.

Darrell Acree, *Vietnam Veterans Memorial Fund.*

How Will They Be Remembered?
Two architects' conceptions of what a memorial to Vietnam War veterans should look like.

Chapter 13
Legacies

The Vietnam war has many legacies, but they can be divided in two parts: those left to Vietnam and its neighbors—Cambodia and Laos—and those left to the United States. In Vietnam the end of hostilities did not bring the predicted bloodbath; in Cambodia, it did. Vietnam is not at peace: its armies are at swords' points with two former allies, the Chinese and the Cambodian Communists (the Khmer Rouge). Vietnam today is poorer than when it was at war; it is politically unified but rent with internal tensions; hundreds of thousands have fled its poverty and oppression. Vietnam's many wounds from thirty years of war will take many more years to heal.

Two and a half million Americans were directly involved in the Vietnam war, and 58,000 died there. The veterans' experiences, their memories are part of America's legacy, as are the experiences and memories of those who actively opposed the war, and of the majority of Americans who simply endured it. The presence of vast numbers of Southeast Asian refugees constitutes another part of America's legacy.

Probably the most significant legacy for most Americans is the continuing confusion about the Vietnam war—why it happened, why it lasted so long, why it ended as it did. Because of the controversy, many have tried to stop thinking about the war, stopped trying to understand it. But the controversy continues: over veterans' issues, over the treatment of refugees, even over the design of the national memorial to Vietnam veterans. And our judgments on the Vietnam war still color our responses to present-day concerns about foreign policy, the defense budget, arms control, human rights, and what the international role of the United States ought to be.

One writer noted in a work on the meaning of the Vietnam war that "again and again there is someone to say we have always been people who dropped the past and then could not remember where it had been put." Watching "Vietnam: A Television History" has, doubtless, led different people to different conclusions, but the process of thinking about significant and controversial issues will have one very important common result. It will help all of us to recognize the impact of the past on our present. A national memory of what happened in Vietnam—to the Vietnamese and to us—and an ability to explain the importance of that war to the next generations of Americans would be the most fitting monument to those whose lives changed because of it.

Note on the Documents in Chapter 13

The documents in this chapter are divided into two sections. The first group describes some of the "legacies" of the war—how it has affected the people and nations who were involved in it. The second group of documents outlines some of the "lessons" which Vietnam seems to offer to Americans—the "useful or salutary pieces of practical wisdom imparted or learned."

Both sections are a small sample of the vast literature on the war and its meaning, significance, and aftermath.

Legacies

Document 1

Although soldiers returning from any war have to undergo a period of adjustment to civilian life, Vietnam veterans sometimes found the adjustment extremely difficult, and even blamed themselves for their problems, thus intensifying them. It took considerable time for psychiatrists and clinical psychologists to conclude that conditions encountered in Vietnam, and upon homecoming, had created a special trauma for some veterans. In 1980 the Disabled American Veterans published a book on these problems, from which the following is excerpted.

1   **How the Vietnam Experience Differed from Previous Wars and Subsequently Predisposed the Combatant to the Post-Traumatic Stress Disorder: Delayed and/or Chronic Type**
    Jim Goodwin
        When direct American troop involvement in Vietnam became a reality, military planners looked to previous war experiences to help alleviate the problem of psychological disorder in combat. By then it was an understood fact that those combatants with the most combat exposure suffered the highest incidence of breakdown. In Korea this knowledge resulted in use, to some extent, of a "point system." After accumulating so many points, an individual was rotated home, regardless of the progress of the war. This was further refined in Vietnam. The outcome being the DEROS (date of expected return from overseas) system. Every individual serving in Vietnam, except general officers, knew before leaving the United States when he or she was scheduled to return. The tour lasted 12 months for everyone except the Marines who, known for their one-upmanship, did a 13-month tour. DEROS promised the combatant a way out of the war other than as a physical or psychological casualty (Kormos, 1978).
        The advantages were clear: there would not be an endless period of protracted combat with the prospect of becoming a psychological casualty as the only hope for

return to the United States without wounds. Rather, if a combatant could just hold together for the 12 or 13 months, he would be rotated to the United States; and, once home, he would leave the war far behind.

The disadvantages to DEROS were not as clear, and some time elapsed before they were noticed. DEROS was a very personal thing; each individual was rotated on his own with his own specific date. This meant that tours in Vietnam were solitary, individual episodes. It was rare, after the first few years of the war, that whole units were sent to the war zone simultaneously. Bourne said it best: "The war becomes a highly individualized and encapsulated event for each man. His war begins the day he arrives in the country, and ends the day he leaves" (p. 12, 1970). Bourne further states, "He feels no continuity with those who precede or follow him: He even feels apart from those who are with him but rotating on a different schedule" (p. 42, 1970).

Because of this very individual aspect of the war, unit morale, unit cohesion and unit identification suffered tremendously (Kormos, 1978). Many studies from past wars (Grinker and Spiegel, 1945) point to the concept of how unit integrity acts as a buffer for the individual against the overwhelming stresses of combat. Many of the veterans of World War II spent weeks or months with their units returning on ships from all over the world. During the long trip home, these men had the closeness and emotional support of one another to rework the especially traumatic episodes that they had experienced together. The epitaph for the Vietnam veteran, however, was a solitary plane ride home with complete strangers and a head full of grief, conflict, confusion and joy.

For every Vietnam combatant, the DEROS date became a fantasy that on a specific day all problems would cease as he flew swiftly back to the United States. The combatants believed that neither they as individuals nor the United States as a society had changed in their absence. Hundreds of thousands of men lived this fantasy from day to day. The universal popularity of short-timer calendars is evidence of this. A short-timer was a GI who was finishing his tour overseas. The calendars intricately marked off the days remaining of his overseas tour in all manner of designs with 365 spaces to fill in to complete the final design and mark that final day. The GIs overtly displayed these calendars to one another. Those with the shortest time left in the country were praised by others and would lead their peers on a fantasy excursion of how wonderful and carefree life would be as soon as they returned home. For many, this became an almost daily ritual. For those who may have been struggling with a psychological breakdown due to the stresses of combat, the DEROS fantasy served as a major prophylactic to actual overt symptoms of acute combat reaction. For these veterans, it was a hard-fought struggle to hold on until their time came due.

The vast majority of veterans did hold on as evidenced by the low neuropsychiatric casualty rates during the war (The President's Commission on Mental Health, 1978). Rates of acute combat reaction or acute post-traumatic stress disorder were significantly lowered relative to the two previous wars. As a result, many combatants, who in previous wars might have become psychological statistics, held on somewhat tenuously until the end of their tours in Vietnam.

The struggle for most was an uphill battle. Those motivators that kept the combatant fighting—unit *esprit de corps,* small group solidarity and an ideological belief that this was the good fight (Moskos, 1975)—were not present in Vietnam. Unit *esprit* was effectively slashed by the DEROS system. Complete strangers, often GIs who were strangers even to a specific unit's specialty, were transferred into units whenever individual rotations were completed. Veterans who had finally reached a level of proficiency had also reached their DEROS date and were rotated. Green troops or "fucking new guys" with almost no skills were thrown into their places. These "new guys" were essentially avoided by the unit, at least until after a few months of experience; "short timers" did not want to get themselves killed by relying on inexperienced replacements. Needless to say, the unit culture or *esprit* was often lost in the lack of communication with the endless leavings and arrivals.

There were other unique aspects of group dynamics in Vietnam. Seasoned troops would stick together, often forming very close small groups for short periods, a normal combat experience noted in previous wars (Grinker and Spiegel, 1945). However, as soon as a seasoned veteran got down to his last two months in Vietnam, he was struck by a strange malady known as the "short timer's syndrome." He would be withdrawn from the field and, if logistically possible, would be settled into a comparatively safe setting for the rest of his tour. His buddies would be left behind in the field without his skills, and he would be left with mixed feelings of joy and guilt. Interestingly, it was rare that a veteran ever wrote to his buddies still in Vietnam once he returned home (Howard, 1975). It has been an even rarer experience for two or more to get together following the war. This is a strong contrast to the endless reunions of World War II veterans. Feelings of guilt about leaving one's buddies to whatever unknown fate in Vietnam apparently proved so strong that many veterans were often too frightened to attempt to find out what happened to those left behind.

Another factor unique to the Vietnam War was that the ideological basis for the war was very difficult to grasp. In World War II, the United States was very clearly threatened by a uniformed and easily recognizable foe. In Vietnam, it was quite the opposite. It appeared that the whole country was hostile to American forces. The enemy was rarely uniformed, and American troops were often forced to kill women and children combatants. There were no real lines of demarcation, and just about any area was subject to attack. Most American forces had been trained to fight in conventional warfare, in which other human beings are confronted and a block of land is either acquired or lost in the fray. However, in Vietnam surprise firing devices such as booby traps accounted for a large number of casualties with the human foe rarely sighted. A block of land might be secured but not held. A unit would pull out to another conflict in the vicinity, and, if it wished to return to the same block of land, it would once again have to fight to take that land. It was an endless war with rarely seen foes and no ground gains, just a constant flow of troops in and out of the country. The only observable outcome was an interminable production of maimed, crippled bodies and countless corpses. Some were so disfigured it was hard to tell if they were Vietnamese or American, but they were all dead. The rage that such conditions generated was widespread among American troops. It manifested itself in violence and mistrust toward the Vietnamese (DeFazio, 1978), toward the authorities, and toward the society that sent these men to Vietnam and then would not support them. Rather than a war with a just ideological basis, Vietnam became a private war of survival for every American individual involved.

What was especially problematic was that this was America's first teenage war (Williams, 1979). The age of the average combatant was close to 20 (Wilson, 1979). According to Wilson (1978), this period for most adolescents involves a psychosocial moratorium (Erickson, 1968), during which the individual takes some time to establish a more stable and enduring personality structure and sense of self. This is an important step—identity versus role confusion—in Erickson's (1968) stages of psychosocial development. Unfortunately for the adolescents who fought the war, the role of combatant versus survivor, as well as the many ambiguous and conflicting values associated with these roles, led to a clear disruption of this moratorium and to the many subsequent problems that followed for the young veterans.

At this point, the reader is probably again wondering why there wasn't more incidence of immediate psychological breakdown among the troops in Vietnam. Again it is important to stress the prophylactic aspects of the DEROS system. In addition, as it is for many contemporary people, when one is confronted with overwhelming stress, one reaches for the quickest cure: medication.

The administration of tranquilizing drugs and the phenothiazines on the combat front first occurred in Vietnam (Jones & Johnson, 1975). This allowed some men, who might have been evacuated in an earlier war, to continue their duties until their normal rotation date.

By now, the use of illicit drugs in Vietnam has become legend. In order to aid the survival of her family, many a "mamasan" (GI slang for a Vietnamese women with a child) with whom GIs made contact had her own supply of cannabis, opium and heroin for sale. Bourne (1970), in fact, observed during his visit to Vietnam that there was widespread use of cannabis but that it had created almost no psychiatric problems. Quite to the contrary, it served its own medicinal purpose as a buffer against the stresses of the Vietnam experience (Horowitz & Solomon, 1975), submerging and delaying symptoms.

Many veterans who consumed the more powerful opiates or copious amounts of alcohol came to be recognized by their superiors because of side effects and aberrant behavior. The original reasons for their use of these buffers became secondary to the fact that they had become behavioral and medical problems for the services. Many men, who had either used drugs to deal with the overwhelming stresses of combat or developed other behavioral symptoms of similar stress-related etiology, were not recognized as struggling with acute combat reaction or post-traumatic stress disorder, acute subtype. Rather, their immediate behavior had proven to be problematic to the military, and they were offered an immediate resolution in the form of administrative discharges with diagnoses of character disorders (Kormos, 1978).

The administrative discharge proved to be another method to temporarily repress any further overt symptoms. It provided yet another means of ending the stress without becoming an actual physical or psychological casualty. It, therefore, served to lower the actual incidence of psychological breakdown, as did the DEROS. Eventually, this widely used practice came to be questioned, and it was recognized that it had been used as a convenient way to eliminate many individuals who had major psychological problems dating from their combat service (Kormos, 1978).

When the veteran finally returned home, his fantasy about his DEROS date was replaced by a rather harsh reality. As previously stated, World War II vets took weeks, sometimes months, to return home with their buddies. Vietnam vets returned home alone. Many made the transition from rice paddy to Southern California in less than 36 hours. Most made it in under a week. The civilian population of the World War II era had been treated to movies about the struggles of readjustment for veterans (i.e., The Man In The Gray Flannel Suit, The Best Years of Our Lives, Pride of The Marines) to prepare them to help the veteran (DeFazio, 1978). The civilian population of the Vietnam era was treated to the horrors of the war on the six o'clock news. They were tired and numb to the whole experience. Some were even fighting mad, and many veterans were witness to this fact. World War II veterans came home to victory parades. Vietnam veterans returned in defeat and witnessed antiwar marches and protests. For World War II veterans, resort hotels were taken over and made into redistribution stations to which veterans could bring their wives and devote two weeks to the initial homecoming (Boros, 1973). For Vietnam veterans, there were screaming antiwar crowds and locked military bases where they were processed back into civilian life in two or three days.

Those veterans who were struggling to make it back home finally did. However, they had drastically changed, and their world would never seem the same. Their fantasies were just that: fantasy. What they had experienced in Vietnam and on their return to their homes in the United States would leave an indelible mark that many may never erase.

The Catalysts of Post-Traumatic Stress Disorders for Vietnam Combat Veterans

More than 8.5 million individuals served in the U.S. Armed Forces during the Vietnam era, 1964–1973. Approximately 2.8 million served in Southeast Asia. Of the latter number, almost one million saw active combat or were exposed to hostile, life threatening situations (President's Commission on Mental Health, 1978). It is this writer's opinion that the vast majority of Vietnam era veterans have had a much more problematic readjustment to civilian life than did their World War II and Korean War counterparts. This was due to the issues already discussed in this chapter, as well as to the state of the economy and the inadequacy of the GI Bill in the early 1970s. In addition, the combat veterans of Vietnam, many of whom immediately tried to become assimilated back into the peacetime culture, discovered that their outlook and feelings about their relationships and future life experiences had changed immensely. According to the fantasy, all was to be well again when they returned from Vietnam. The reality for many was quite different.

A number of studies point out that those veterans subjected to more extensive combat show more problematic symptoms during the period of readjustment (Wilson, 1978; Strayer & Ellenhorn, 1975; Kormos, 1978; Shatan, 1978; Figley, 1978b). The usual pattern has been that of a combat veteran in Vietnam who held on until his DEROS date. He was largely asymptomatic at the point of his rotation back to the U.S. for the reasons previously discussed; on his return home, the joy of surviving continued to suppress any problematic symptoms. However, after a year or more, the veteran would begin to notice some changes in his outlook (Shatan, 1978). But, because there was a time limit of one year after which the Veterans Administration would not recognize neuropsychiatric problems as service-connected, the veteran was unable to get service-connected disability compensation. Treatment from the VA was very difficult to obtain. The veteran began to feel depressed, mistrustful, cynical and restless. He experienced problems with sleep and with his temper. Strangely, he became somewhat obsessed with his combat experiences in Vietnam. He would also begin to question why he survived when others did not.

For approximately 500,000 veterans (Wilson, 1978) of the combat in Southeast Asia, this problematic outlook has become a chronic lifestyle affecting not only the veterans but countless millions of persons who are in contact with these veterans. The symptoms described below are experienced by all Vietnam combat veterans to varying degrees. However, for some with the most extensive combat histories and other variables which have yet to be enumerated, Vietnam-related problems have persisted in disrupting all areas of life experience. According to Wilson (1978), the number of veterans experiencing these symptoms will climb until 1985, based on his belief in Erickson's psychosocial developmental stages and how far along in these stages most combat veterans will be by 1985. Furthermore, without any intervention, what was once a reaction to a traumatic episode may for many become an almost unchangeable personality characteristic.

Document 2

The literature on Vietnam continues to multiply, including poetry written and often published by Vietnam veterans. The poetry expresses many emotions, including pride in service, mourning for the loss of comrades, and sometimes strong disillusionment. Much of it, too, is questioning in tone, as in the following poem by W. D. Ehrhart, who saw combat in Vietnam in 1967 and 1968 as a sergeant in Intelligence.

2   **To Those Who Have Gone Home Tired**
     W. D. Ehrhart
     After the streets fall silent
     After the bruises and the tear-gassed eyes are healed
     After the consensus has returned
     After the memories of Kent and My Lai and Hiroshima
     Lose their power
     And their connections with each other
     And the sweaters labeled Made in Taiwan
     After the last American dies in Canada
     And the last Korean in prison
     And the last Indian at Pine Ridge
     After the last whale is emptied from the sea
     And the last leopard emptied from its skin
     And the last drop of blood refined by Exxon
     After the last iron door clangs shut
     Behind the last conscience
     And the last loaf of bread is hammered into bullets
     And the bullets
     Scattered among the hungry

     What answers will you find
     What armor will protect you
     When your children ask you

     Why?

Document 3

The ambivalence and controversy that surround so many aspects of the Vietnam war continue to manifest themselves. An architectural competition for a

Vietnam memorial resulted in an award to a design that was unlike any monument designed to commemorate any previous conflict, and the award proved highly controversial.

3   Vietnam Memorial: Questions of Architecture
Paul Goldberger
October 7, 1982

When a plan by Maya Yang Lin, a 21-year-old Yale architecture student, was selected last year as the winner of a nationwide competition to find a design for the Vietnam Veterans Memorial on the Mall near the Lincoln Memorial in Washington, it was hailed by the architectural press with words such as "stunning," "dignified" and "eminently right."

An Appraisal

The reaction was less enthusiastic from Vietnam veterans themselves, some of whom found the proposed memorial rather more cool and abstract than they would have liked. Nonetheless, Miss Lin's scheme, which is neither a building nor a sculpture but, rather, a pair of 200-foot-long black granite walls that join to form a V and embrace a gently sloping plot of ground between them, was approved rapidly by the Department of the Interior, the Fine Arts Commission and other public agencies that have jurisdiction over what is built in official Washington.

Construction began last March. Next week, however, the Fine Arts Commission will hold a public hearing to consider a revised design for the memorial, despite the fact that by now the granite walls—on which are carved the names of all 57,692 Americans who were killed in Vietnam from 1963 to 1973—are nearly complete. Opposition to the scheme from Vietnam veterans, which was muted when Miss Lin's design was first announced, later grew so intense as to lead to the unusual step of a proposed design change in mid-construction.

Threat to Integrity Seen

The hearing is scheduled for Oct. 13, and the battle lines have already been drawn fairly sharply. On one side, defending the changes, will be the Vietnam Veterans Memorial Fund, the organization that sponsored the architectural competition and had committed itself to building the winning scheme, as well as an advisory committee of Vietnam veterans who were among the more outspoken critics of the original design.

On the other side is not only Miss Lin, the designer, but the American Institute of Architects, which has taken a strong public position in defense of the original design and which sees the move to change the memorial as a threat to the integrity of the system of architectural competitions in general. Robert M. Lawrence, the institute's president, wrote this summer to J. Carter Brown, chairman of the Fine Arts Commission: "What we have here is nothing less than a breach of faith. The effort to compromise the design breaks faith with the designer who won the competition and all those who participated in this competition."

What has provoked the heated emotions, however, is less the integrity of architectural competition than the specifics of Miss Lin's design. To many of the Vietnam veterans, her scheme was too abstract to reflect the emotion that the Vietnam War symbolized to them, and too lacking in the symbols of heroism that more conventional monuments contain. They saw in the simple granite walls on which the names of the dead are inscribed not merely a means of honoring the dead, but a way of declaring that the Vietnam War was in some way different from past wars—from wars such as World War II, whose heroism could be symbolized in such a vibrant and active memorial as the Iwo Jima Monument just across the Potomac River, which contains a statue of marines struggling to raise the American flag.

A Statue Is Proposed

The changes in the Vietnam Memorial, therefore, have all been in the direction of making it less of an abstraction, and more realistic. When the Vietnam Veterans Memorial Fund decided some months ago to give in to criticism of the design from Vietnam veterans, it named an advisory committee consisting entirely of Vietnam veterans, in contrast to the jury of internationally known architects and design professionals who had selected Miss Lin's design. That committee selected Frederick Hart, a 38-year-old sculptor who had been a partner in a losing entry in the original competition, and commissioned him to create a realistic sculpture to act as the memorial's new centerpiece.

What Mr. Hart has created is an 8-foot-tall statue of three armed soldiers, one black and two white, which would be placed within the triangular piece of land between Miss Lin's granite walls. The revision of the design also includes a 50-foot-tall flagpole outside the granite walls, and thus it will change the view of the observer who is looking at the memorial in any direction.

Mr. Hart claims that his statue will "preserve and enhance" Miss Lin's design, and will "interact with the wall to form a unified totality." Miss Lin, however, disagrees and in a letter to the Memorial Fund on Sept. 20 she called the changes an "intrusion" that "destroys the meaning of the design."

Ironically, it is the very strength of the original design—its ability to be interpreted in a variety of ways—that is making for the current controversy. Miss Lin's original scheme is, in a sense, a tabula rasa, a blank slate—not a room, not a building, not a plaza, not a park, not a conventional memorial at all. It is a place of reflection, where the gradually sloping land, the thousands of carved names on somber granite and the view of the buildings of official Washington in the distance should combine to create an understated, yet powerful, presence.

It is a subtle design, like every great memorial capable of being given different meanings by each of us. The anguish of the Vietnam War is present here, but not in a way that does any dishonor to veterans. To call this memorial a "black gash of shame," as Tom Carhart, a Vietnam veteran who was another losing entrant in the competition, has said, is to miss its point entirely, and to fail to see that this design gives every indication of being a place of extreme dignity that honors the veterans who served in Vietnam with more poignancy, surely, than any ordinary monument ever could.

The Lin design is discreet and quiet, and perhaps this is what bothers its opponents the most. It is certainly what bothers Mr. Carhart, whose own design was described as "a statue of an officer offering a dead soldier heavenward." By commissioning the Hart sculpture and the flagpole, the Vietnam Veteran Memorial Fund seems intent on converting a superb design into something that speaks of heroism and of absolute moral certainty. But there can be no such literalism and no such certainty where Vietnam is concerned; to try to represent a period of anguish and complexity in our history with a simple statue of armed soldiers is to misunderstand all that has happened, and to suggest that no lessons have been learned at all from the experience of Vietnam.

Presence of the Names Speaks

The Vietnam Veterans Memorial, as it now nears completion, could be one of the most important works of contemporary architecture in official Washington—and perhaps the only one that will provide a contemplative space the equal of any in the past. The insertion of statues and a flagpole not only destroys the abstract beauty of that mystical, inside-outside kind of space that Maya Yang Lin has created; it also tries to shift this memorial away from its focus on the dead, and toward a kind of literal interpretation of heroism and patriotism that ultimately treats the war dead in only the most simplistic of terms.

For in the original design, the dead are remembered as individuals through the moving list of their names carved against the granite. It is the presence of the names, one after the other, that speaks. But if the statues are added, they will overpower the space and change the mood altogether. A symbol of loss, which Miss Lin's design is, will become instead a symbol of war. The names of the dead and the hushed granite wall will become merely a background for something else, and the chance for a very special kind of honor—and for a very special kind of architecture—will be lost.

Documents 4 and 5

Although we know less about the legacies of the war in Vietnam, refugees from that country and visitors to it bring their experiences with them. In Document 4, Nguyen Cong Hoan, who had been in the Buddhist antiwar opposition to President Thieu and later in the postwar National Assembly of Vietnam, explains why he risked his life to leave his country. He is one of the hundreds of thousands of "boat people" who found Vietnam unbearable after the war.

Document 5 is an article by Stanley Karnow, a long-time observer of the situation in Southeast Asia, who revisited Vietnam in 1981. This and an earlier piece published in the *Atlantic Monthly* are a succinct and perceptive look at life in Ho Chi Minh City, better known to most Americans by its old name—Saigon.

4   Why I Escaped From Vietnam
Nguyen Cong Hoan
October 31, 1977

The government of Vietnam has accepted triumphantly its full United Nations membership, to the cheers of what Hanoi calls "progressive mankind"—the Communist countries, much of the Third World and those in the West who opposed American Government policies during the war.

To a Vietnamese like myself, who detested the corrupt and repressive Thieu regime and considered the Communist victory a liberation, such an event should bring joy. But after living for nearly two years in Communist Vietnam, I feel precisely the opposite emotion.

I escaped from Vietnam to tell the world the truth about what is happening in my country. Within days after Hanoi's troops came to my town, such widely proclaimed policies of the Viet Cong's National Liberation Front as religious freedom, democratic liberties, peace and neutralism went out the window. Even the southern Communists were cast aside by northerners acting as conquerors, seizing all levers of power, inventorying and requisitioning everything.

For those bold enough to question, a vast network of prisons called "re-education camps" was established almost overnight—prisons where inmates were worked to death or starved. The prisoners included not only former Saigon military and civilian officials, but also many who opposed them—advocates of democratic liberties and a compromise peace. Apolitical professional, intellectual and religious leaders were also detained.

Prisoners

In my province, Phu Yen, alone, out of a total population of about 300,000, there were more than 6,000 prisoners in seven camps when I left Vietnam last spring. During the war, the population of South Vietnam was estimated at about 17 million, and was censused by Hanoi recently at about 24 million. If the Phu Yen prison population is characteristic of all of former South Vietnam, as is likely, from 340,000 to 480,000 could now be detained.

Outside the camps, many are unemployed and those with jobs can barely earn enough to feed one person, let alone a family. Thousands are press-ganged into non-paying, ostensibly "voluntary" labor brigades working on roads, canals and irrigation ditches. Large numbers are forced to resettle in remote, disease-ridden "new economic zones," a population dispersal aimed more at political control than at economic development.

The economy is in shambles. What agricultural wealth there is in southern Vietnam is siphoned to the north or exported for foreign exchange. Southern people have had their diet deteriorate from rice to yam and manioc.

The new authorities rule by force and terror. What little freedom existed under Thieu is gone. The An Ninh secret police are dreaded—worse than any previous Vietnamese regime. There is no freedom of movement or association; no freedom of the press, or of religion, or of economic enterprise, or even of private personal opinion. Rights of habeas corpus, or of property, are either unknown or flouted even as the government redefines these rights. Fear is everywhere. An indiscreet remark can make one liable to instant arrest and an indefinite prison term.

America is partly responsible for the tragedy befalling the Vietnamese. While the U.S. cannot, and should not, reintervene militarily, it can influence Hanoi to ameliorate the human-rights situation, just as it has obliged Hanoi to make some kind of accounting for MIA's. For example, virtually the entire An Quang Buddhist leadership has been arrested. As a Buddhist, I urge respectfully that Americans—certainly American religious leaders—express their concern publicly.

Many legislators active with me in opposing Thieu—and who were beaten and jailed by the Saigon government—are in prison again. These include democrats like Tran Van Tuyen, chairman of my opposition bloc in Saigon's lower house, whose case was recently taken up, I understand, by Amnesty International. As a political leader myself, I appeal to American political figures to express their concern to Hanoi and call for the release of Tuyen and many others I could help them list. The three men I escaped with, incidentally, want to come from Japan to America to provide their own eyewitness accounts of the suffering in Vietnam, but they need assistance.

An Appeal

I appeal also for help for the thousands of Vietnamese boat people who perish on the seas in river boats never meant for the severity of ocean passage. At least half who make it to international waters reportedly drown there as these flimsy boats go under. Who will rescue them if the United States does not participate? President Carter has agreed to accept at least 15,000 more Indochinese refugees, for which we are grateful. But a rescue project to pick people off those boats on the high seas is also needed.

Let me also mention energetically people whom I once opposed during the war: those who worked directly or indirectly for the United States. The U.S. has responsibilities regarding the fate of these people, comparable to the principle that American marines are said to have of not deserting their wounded.

To tell Americans what I have just said, I left my wife and children and risked my life on the seas. I appeal to Americans on behalf of the human rights of my people: please do not mute your voices on this subject. Before I escaped, there was great interest in my country in the human-rights stand of President Carter and other Western leaders. Vietnamese listen attentively to the Voice of America and the BBC. The cause of human rights comes up very often in conversations. Where hope is a rare commodity, the news that the world is watching, and cares, provides moral sustenance.

5   Saigon: "Liberated" but Still Capitalist
Stanley Karnow
November 1981

During the American war in Vietnam, when I served as a correspondent there, Saigon smelled of decay. Its bars were drug centers, its hotels brothels. Soldiers from Ohio and Georgia and Texas, black and white, their pockets crammed with cash, walked streets crowded with beggars, cripples, and other victims of devastation. South Vietnamese generals, enriched by silent Chinese partners, owned lavish villas near slums sheltering impoverished refugees from bombed villages. It was, in short, a city for sale.

A few months ago, I returned for the first time since the city's "liberation" by the Communists six years ago. As we sipped green tea under Ho Chi Minh's portrait in a salon of the ornate Hotel de Ville, the vice president of the People's Committee, the municipal administration, assured me that the "socialist transformation" is proceeding on schedule. His lecture was a formality. We both knew that while the Communists have swallowed Saigon, they cannot digest it. Therefore, they are doing very little to stifle its capitalistic vitality.

Communist rhetoric may fill the press and radio, but the present economic mood of Saigon is strikingly similar to what it was in the past—with one crucial difference. During the war, Saigon's inhabitants were competing for a piece of American aid, which ran to some $2 billion a year. Now they are struggling for a share of South Vietnam's scarce resources.

Campaigns against corruption are staged regularly, yet party cadres in severe tunics can be seen in "free" restaurants, where dinner costs more than their monthly wage. Periodic efforts are launched to purge speculators, yet the half-million

Chinese residents of Cholon continue to fix gold and black-market-money rates, and reportedly even arrange transactions for the state. The Chinese, who have unexpected ways of acquiring things, also furnish the government with spare parts for its automobiles and trucks.

A local official proudly told me one afternoon that prostitution, as well as other plagues of imperialism, has been "fundamentally" eradicated. But, that evening, three prostitutes accosted me with a ferocity I had never experienced during the American era, when clients were plentiful. My official, when I related the incident the next morning, remarked with a sense of humor: "Did I say 'fundamentally'? I meant 'theoretically.' "

Despite directives warning against the evils of "consumerism," avenues and alleys are jammed with peddlers hawking everything from English cigarettes and French wine to Australian butter and Japanese radios. The spectacle recalls old times, when goods filched from the American PX supplied illicit vendors, and it was even possible to buy guns and uniforms stolen from military warehouses. The major sources of merchandise at present, however, are the parcels sent by Vietnamese in the United States, France, Canada, Australia, and elsewhere to their relatives in Saigon, who make ends meet by selling the products. A weekly Air France Boeing 747 discharges freight as well as passengers, and a Cathay Pacific freight plane arrives irregularly from Hong Kong. In principle, the legal imports are meant to be consumed only by their recipients. Instead they augment the black market, which is tolerated and widespread. Without it, the Saigon economy would collapse.

The airlines bring in an average of 220 tons of cargo a month, its original value more than $10 million. By normal commercial measure, that amount is tiny. But it is significant to Vietnam, whose exports are so marginal that its foreign-currency reserves probably total less than $100 million. Moreover, the imported goods escalate astronomically in value, in terms of the purchasing power they can provide their owners.

Consider, for example, that the average Vietnamese worker earns roughly seventy dongs per month. A pack of American cigarettes sells at a street stall for forty dongs. Thus, if he is lucky enough to have an uncle in Cannes or Toronto who remembers him, that Vietnamese worker can make the equivalent of six months' salary with a carton of Salems.

Officials, including stalwart Communist Party members, rarely hide their involvement in the pervasive traffic. One of them, whose monthly wage of 160 dongs is relatively high, told me that his aunt in Paris sends him toothpaste, vitamins, and other such items, which he promptly sells on the "parallel" market. "I could not survive otherwise," he said.

The authorities recently gave a further boost to this trade by setting up the Ho Chi Minh City Import-Export Company, or Imex, designed to streamline the flow of articles into the city from overseas. Firms in Montreal, Hong Kong, and elsewhere can now channel remittances from Vietnamese abroad to Imex, which delivers duty-free gift parcels containing rice, sugar, condensed milk, soap, and cigarettes to relatives in Saigon, who then sell the merchandise. Imex, which also imports beer, whiskey, and other luxuries for the hard-currency shops patronized by foreigners, is a major source of merchandise that somehow makes its way into the hands of street vendors.

In this intricate and strangely sensitive economy, merchandise is more valuable than money. The lawful but unreal exchange rate for currency is nine dongs per dollar. Depending on fluctuations, the black-market rate is several times the legal rate. A bottle of aspirin, bought for a dollar in New York, can be sold in Saigon for two or three times as much. Merchandise is also safer to receive than money. Customs officers steam open letters, hoping to find banknotes, which they undoubtedly keep for themselves; and the prospective recipients cannot protest, since sending cash through the mail is illegal.

As in other socialist countries, which function in a fog of ambiguities, it is almost impossible to gauge the percentage of Saigon's 3.4 million people who gain from this fluid market mechanism. Mysteriously, though, the profits seem to filter down through layers of intermediaries and even reach out into the countryside. Goods from Saigon also stream up to Hanoi, usually on trucks that are supposed to be transporting rice and other cargo.

Top officials share in the profit-taking. Bureaucrats, who process the masses of documents required to operate here, expedite matters in exchange for gifts. Artisans would rather be paid in goods than in cash. And bourgeois families, once wealthy, dispose of their heirlooms in order to buy imports. Accordingly, rare antiques are sold at bargain prices. So are stamp and coin collections, and out-of-print books.

As the result of recent liberal measures, this unorthodox supply network has been reinforced by thousands of small enterprises, manufacturing such products as plastic buckets and electrical fixtures. These businesses can make what they like, as long as they pay taxes. Also new are the hundreds of coffee shops, where unemployed young people sit listening to rock music. At one such place, a throbbing song contained the appropriate words *"I see a boat on the river, it's sailing away . . . where to, I can't say."*

The basic aim of all this is to generate money for food. Vietnam's food shortage at the moment is severe. The starch ration, composed of rice, wheat, tapioca, and yams, averages thirteen kilograms per month, which is inadequate for an adult. The alternative is the free market, where a kilo of rice equals a worker's wage for a month. Meat is rationed, but pork can be bought on the black market for the equivalent of a month's salary per kilo—in effect, bartered against the shampoo sent by that brother in Boston. A professor of medicine I met has his own solution: he is raising a pair of pigs in his garden.

The peasants benefit from the trade, particularly if they are close enough to the city to bring in their yields. Originally discouraged by collectivization, they are now permitted to cultivate their own crops as a stimulus to production, as long as they deliver a quota to the state. Predictably, their output of private livestock and poultry and vegetables has increased, though not enough to satisfy demand. Market food prices, consequently, are within the grasp only of urban dwellers receiving goods from Chicago, Hamburg, or elsewhere.

The constant buying and selling, the hustling, conniving, and bargaining, have contributed to a pervasive cynicism, in which Marxist tenets have no place. Saigon's maxim is still, as it has always been, *"Chacun pour soi"*—or, this being a Confucian society, *"pour sa famille."*

One Vietnamese friend predicts that the Communists will sooner or later crack down on the extensive flow of goods, since the liberal trend is bound to accelerate, thus threatening their hope of creating a socialist structure in Saigon. I wonder, however, whether the Communists will be able to curb the city's entrepreneurial momentum. For the present, at least, they are plainly steering away from the revolutionary route. Perhaps they cannot afford to antagonize a population already unsettled by political controls.

At the end of April, 1975, as President Nguyen Van Thieu's inept regime crumbled, North Vietnamese divisions swept into Saigon, and were astonished by their easy success. They were greeted by a dazed people who welcomed peace for the first time in a generation.

The Communists rapidly began to alter the look of the city, covering its walls with slogans and putting their labels on buildings and streets. The modern Caravelle Hotel became the Doc Lap (Independence); the Rue Catinat, changed in the 1960s to Tu Do (Freedom), is now Dong Khoi (Uprising), but is still called Catinat by everyone.

Repression matched these cosmetics. Compared with Stalin and Mao Tse-tung, who slaughtered vast numbers of adversaries, the Vietnamese Communists were lenient. But 400,000 former South Vietnamese officials, army officers, doctors, lawyers, journalists, teachers, and others were sent to "re-education" centers, some for months and some for years, and about 80,000 continue to languish in camps. The penal decisions are hard to comprehend. A businessman, recently released, had been detained simply because his firm constructed roads for the American forces. I gather, though, that the warden of the notorious Con Son "tiger cages," in which suspected Communists and harmless dissidents died, is alive in jail, where he is being "reformed."

What irritates many Vietnamese, among them Communists who fought against the Americans and the former Saigon government, is the takeover by northerners. The Tet offensive of 1968, an ambitious bid by the Communists to win in one bold stroke, cost the lives of thousands of southern cadres of the National Liberation Front, as the Vietcong called itself. Thousands more were killed the following year in the Phoenix program, an operation directed by the American Central Intelligence Agency, which the Communists themselves now concede was extremely effective. Northerners moved in to fill the vacuum. To a degree, they are resented as outsiders. And they, in turn, tend to resent the southerners as former "collaborators" tainted by imperialism.

The political tension can be felt especially among the residual bourgeoisie. A student would like to practice his English over a lemonade, but he dares not, since being seen with me in a café might cause him trouble with the police. I sought out a former South Vietnamese general, recently released from a camp, to give him news of his family in America. An official advised me that a meeting was "inconvenient," implying sympathetically that I could hurt the former officer's chances of obtaining an exit visa for the United States. I refrained from attempting to see other Vietnamese acquaintances of mine.

The regime's pervasive interest in the behavior of Saigon's residents extends even to the city's "Cinderellas," girls hired by the government to dance with foreigners at a weekly ball. Saturday Night Fever takes place in the former American officers' club atop the Rex Hotel, now the Ben Thanh. Colored lights beam around the luxurious room as the band plays disco music and a singer, sinuous in her clinging gown, belts out the lyrics. The girls, office employees and shop assistants, are paid twenty-five dongs for their presence, and they are dazzling creatures, in stretch jeans and tight blouses. They dance with French, Scandinavian, and Russian partners, mostly technicians on projects, and they go home alone at midnight. Anything else would be too risky.

I am inclined to favor this puritanism, for the saddest legacies of the French and, later, American intervention in Vietnam are leftover children—some with blond hair and blue eyes and others partly black, outcasts who wander the streets, peddling and begging. Those fathered by French troops, European or African, are known as Eurasians. Those born during the American war are called "Amerasians." The Vietnamese care for a few in showcase orphanages. Privately, they tell Western refugee experts that the children can leave at any time. The problem is finding them sponsors overseas.

The French government has agreed to accept some 10,000 Eurasians born between 1946 and 1955, and some have already emigrated to France. The Vietnamese have privately expressed a willingness to let the Amerasians leave, but their entrance to the United States is blocked by immigration law, and a bill to reform the regulations has gone nowhere. There may be as many as 50,000 Amerasians. Their mothers, socially stigmatized by their misfit children, bombard the Red Cross and the United Nations offices with appeals for help. But even if the American fathers were willing to take their children, locating them would be close to impossible. A Vietnamese woman, her letter, in pidgin English, obviously prepared for her, writes to a Western refugee official:

"I was married an American citizen whose name was Dick. We have with each other a daughter. My husband left Vietnam on 1975. From then on we have lost contact. I hope you will come to our assistance so that my child may see her father and I shall be able to live. . . ."

It was a cruel war, and its aftermath is cruel. It disrupted this city while it was being fought, and the trauma is not over.

Document 6

One of many continuing controversies about the Vietnam War concerns the role of the media covering it: did their uncensored reporting encourage the public to oppose or to support U.S. government policies?

The issue flared up again when Great Britain and Argentina fought over the Falkland Islands in the spring of 1982. British reporters complained that they were hampered by government restrictions and that they deserved the same kind of free hand which American correspondents had supposedly had in Vietnam. In Document 6, Michael Arlen takes off from the British complaint to give readers his recollections of American reporting from Vietnam.

6   The Falklands, Vietnam, and Our Collective Memory
Michael Arlen
August 16, 1982
Though Vietnam, that strange war, slipped off our viewing screens some ten years ago, it never seems to be completely out of mind. Now it's the British, fresh (probably not the right word for it) from their Falklands scuffle with the Argentines, who invoke its ghostly memory. British war correspondents, back home from their tossing aircraft carriers and soggy airstrips, have been criticizing their government's traditional penchant for wartime censorship, press controls, and other hallowed United Kingdom methods of keeping journalists in the kitchen, and comparing their lot unfavorably with the seemingly free-floating experience of buccaneer American TV-news crews in Vietnam. At the same time, doyens of the British Ministry of Defence have claimed a similarly keen interest in American journalism in Vietnam—particularly in the effects of the combat coverage broadcast by the networks on the nightly

news, whose introduction of the horrors of battle into the American living room is now widely perceived as the chief motivation for the American electorate's having turned against the war.

To tell the truth, one can't very well blame the British journalists, confined to weeks of seasick quasi house arrest aboard the Hermes or the Invincible or the Dogmatic, for looking with a certain envy back in time toward the greener journalistic grass of Vietnam, where Jack Laurence, Dean Brelis, Morley Safer, and how many other safari-suited buckoes roamed (according to legend) like free spirits through the Indo-Chinese veldt. There's little doubt that American journalists in Vietnam had a freer hand than their British colleagues with the South Atlantic task force, who for the most part were required to report their war by means of still photographs accompanied by awkward, crackly telephoned commentary, as if their reports were proceeding not merely from another hemisphere but from another century. Still, this much said, there are other truths to be told and comparisons to be made, and the most interesting of the comparisons, I think, are not so much between the Falklands and Vietnam as between Vietnam and what is apparently now our collective memory of it.

In terms of a press role in war, two initial differences between the Falklands and Vietnam stand out—in addition to the obviously different military approaches involved in the two operations, one being preponderantly naval, the other mainly ground-based. To begin with, I believe it's fair to say that the American press in Vietnam was given its relative freedom for a variety of reasons, most of which had little or nothing to do with any overweening regard on the part of the American military establishment for the First Amendment. One of the reasons that American journalists moved about as they did was that Vietnam was not only an undeclared war (even more undeclared than the Falklands) but also a war in which the United States was theoretically not one of the key participants; our troops and our correspondents both got shot at, but each remained a "guest presence" in the country, amenable to controls and regulations often issued from very far away. But a more important reason for the wide-ranging presence of the American press in Vietnam was not simply the "need to know" on the part of the American electorate or American news organizations (a "need to know" that was kept mightily muted during most of the war) but was one of the great truths learned by the American military establishment in the Second World War; namely, the value of media exposure to high-ranking officers in wartime. In the Second World War, the generals and admirals learned to love the press; their pictures on the covers of *Life* and *Time* and *Collier's* were stepping stones out of the postwar military into defense contracting or senior government service—even into the Presidency. Of course, by the time of Korea the press had grown cool toward generals and admirals (with the exception of the national swoon over General MacArthur), and by the later stages of the Vietnam War the love affair was definitely over; military commanders were learning to duck for cover whenever a journalist came by. For the most part, though, in the year-by-year unfolding of our Vietnam involvement press wariness came slowly to the military—as slowly, perhaps, as a critical perspective came to our major news organizations. Originally, the American commanders not only allowed the press in; they welcomed it—especially the TV correspondents—the way all of us welcome anyone that we somehow instinctively assume will do something for *us*. And originally, and for many years, the press repaid the good will of its military hosts. For example, if General Paul D. Harkins did not grace as many news-magazine covers as the doughty Patton or the valorous Halsey, there he was at least (and not infre-

quently) in *Life* and *Time* and *Newsweek,* and on the nightly news, discoursing on
the merits of his Pacification (or was it Vietnamization? or was it Strategic Hamlets?)
program. Thus, from the outset in Vietnam the relative freedom enjoyed by American newsmen was colored by a certain element of trade-off in their relationship with
the military; whether the newsmen on the scene accepted the trade-off or not (and
most did not), American military commanders who had been tutored in the traditions of Second World War press coverage assumed that the press was there to give
them a boost—and not merely in a patriotic sense but in a more contemporarily
American sense of being an aid to their careers. (I suspect that it's less a matter of
superior morals and more a result of a different class structure—or, at least, of a different national approach to career advancement—that has sustained the British military establishment in giving a fairly steadfast cold shoulder to the art of public
relations.)

There was also a much more explicit form of interdependence in Vietnam between the press and the military—especially between the military and the television
networks—which took the form sometimes of routine military-press coöperation
and sometimes of powerful constraints on the supposedly freewheeling journalists.
The fact of the matter is that the type of press coverage that the military most
wanted and was most in awe of—the network television news reports—was also,
by virtue of its technology and its impedimenta, the type of coverage that most
needed military support and transportation. Military commanders couldn't control
what TV correspondents might say about their operations, but they could sure as
hell control where the correspondents went, and especially where they didn't go. In
other words, though Ernie Pyle in the Second World War may have bummed
around the Salerno beachhead with a notebook and pencil, CBS's Dave Schou-
macher and his Australian cameraman and his Vietnamese sound man, with their
seventy pounds of equipment, composed a troika that was neither mobile or particularly self-effacing. If a network camera crew wanted to cover something in Vietnam—say, a battle that might or might not be going well for United States forces—
a military officer ordinarily had to make it possible for them to get where it was
going on. Thus, while the audience watching the evening news back home might
assume that the scenes of the war that it was seeing were the important stories that
had occurred that day (or the day before), the stories on the evening news—though
technically uncensored—were in fact usually stories to which elaborate and expensive
helicopter access had been knowingly made possible by the military command.
Clever or aggressive correspondents could sometimes talk their way past guard-dog
colonels and wheedle or push their cumbersome crews and equipment into a temporarily empty Medevac helicopter. But often they couldn't. Often no helicopters
were "available" to television crews trying to report an independent story; the same
helicopters, however, always seemed in plentiful supply when the Army public-
information office mounted press coverage of one of the Army's famous sweeps of
"suspected Vietcong positions."

In short, while I think that the British correspondents in the Falklands have good
reason to complain about the nursemaid attitude that the military establishment took
toward them (especially the retentive attitude of the high command toward TV
transmission), I don't think they should waste time envying their American colleagues in Vietnam; a paradise of journalistic independence it was not. But more to
the point, I believe, is the question of what it is that everyone (not only the British
Defence Ministry) now seems to remember about the actual war footage that came
out of Vietnam, and what the effects of this war footage were on our body politic,

our citizen audience. Time and again, when I read accounts or reminiscences of the TV coverage of this period I note the phrase "horrors of war" or its equivalent. People generally, it seems to me, and maybe young people especially (many of whom were probably too young to have watched the news in those days), appear to remember having had to face almost Goyaesque images in their living rooms as the Vietnam War ran its course. "I can still remember all that shooting and killing," a young friend said to me recently. "I guess we had to look at it, but it was awful stuff."

This seems strange to me and makes me wonder what it is that many of us are keeping in our memory banks on the subject of Vietnam. Beginning in the summer of 1966, I watched television news of Vietnam, if not every night of the year for the next six years, then pretty close to every night of the year for the next six years, and what I remember most clearly about most of that time is the nearly total absence on the nightly network news broadcasts of any explicit reality of war—certainly of any of the blood and gore, or even the pain of combat. In fact, it seems to me that what a television viewer of the Vietnam War saw—at least for the first two-thirds of its duration—was a nightly stylized, generally distanced overview of a disjointed conflict which was composed mainly of scenes of helicopters landing, tall grasses blowing in the helicopter wind, American soldiers fanning out across a hillside on foot, rifles at the ready, with now and then (on the soundtrack) a far-off ping or two, and now and then (as the visual grand finale) a column of dark, billowing smoke a half mile away, invariably described as a burning Vietcong ammo dump. In 1966, I remember, for lack of any other human sense of the war, I wrote a column about Morley Safer (then CBS correspondent in Saigon) and how he was actually willing to be shown on camera a little scared and out of breath, in the field with some Marines after a brief firefight. Three Marines had been killed in the encounter, he said, but we didn't see any of them; the only human point of reference to combat in the story was Safer's own lack of composure at the time—a refreshing and quite unusual situation. On the Vietnam news, one almost never saw the dead or the dying, or even the wounded. In fact, on another occasion, in the spring of 1967, I remember writing about a brief Vietnam film clip that appeared on NBC one night—a routine story of another distanced American patrol but a story in which one could actually hear (though not see) a young infantryman who had been shot in the leg and was calling for help. So rare was this stark note on the nightly news that it seemed to warrant special mention.

By the last years of the war—by the time a majority of the country had come to realize, if not war's ghastliness, then at least the inefficacy of our Vietnam involvement—network news had become freer in its depictions of the ravages and miseries of war, as if to underscore the new irony in the tone of its correspondents' voice-overs. But during most of the war little shooting, little killing, and little death appeared on the home television screen. To put it another way, the "body counts" were usually announced each evening on the news, like eerie stock-market quotations or macabre baseball scores, but the bodies were almost never shown. Had somebody said *not* to show the bodies? For that matter, did a network president ever direct his senior news executive to tell his correspondents not to file negative stories about the war? It's possible, since all things are possible, but also unimportant; there was enough nervous self-editing and cautious autocensorship afoot in the major TV news organizations so that no official fiats were needed.

Received opinion today seems to hold that America's TV coverage of Vietnam was filled with harsh, unpleasant truths, and that these turned the country against the war. For what it's worth, when I set about trying to retrieve my own memory of those times I come up with a different recollection. Television's role was neither as inconclusive as some then claimed it to be nor as kinetic (or certainly one-sidedly kinetic) as some now claim it to have been. In the main, I think, television's role in our Vietnam experience was true to its own nature—a paradoxical nature, and therefore a paradoxical role. Granted, television helped get us out of Vietnam, but it also helped march us in. On the one hand, it projected for many years a determinedly bullish and enthusiastic—even, at times, a militaristic—tone; on the other hand, it showed us (or at least suggested) the chaos and destruction we were causing. The scenes it gave us were sometimes boyish (those swooping silvery Phantoms and their napalm strikes) and sometimes sanctimonious and bombastic (General Whatsisname reviews the ARVN), but mostly, in the end, I think, the Vietnam news was a crowded, overtalked, overfilmed, almost banal jumble, which was hugely difficult for people to relate to in any coherent fashion. But relate to it they finally did, and in more ways than received opinion now takes into account. In any case, the British Defence Ministry shouldn't have been so afraid, in its Falklands episode, of duplicating such untidy, basically circumscribed, essentially cautious (though perhaps ultimately democratic) news transmissions as were broadcast in this country during the Vietnam period. It wasn't scenes of bloody combat that turned Americans against their war; it was the war itself. One hopes there will not soon be a next time when both our countries can learn to handle such press coverage better.

Lessons

Documents 7 and 8

The debates on Vietnam have spilled over into the issue of how the history of the war should be taught. In 1981, H. Bruce Franklin, a professor of English and American Literature at Rutgers University in Newark, published an article on the subject in the November *Chronicle of Higher Education*. Franklin described his course, his methodology, and what he felt he had accomplished (Document 7).

The following month, the *Chronicle* published letters which called Franklin's objectivity, conclusions, and course itself into question. Four of these criticisms appear as Document 8.

7 Teaching Vietnam Today: Who Won, and Why?
H. Bruce Franklin
November 4, 1981

Teaching the Vietnam War started out as a subversive, radical, unpatriotic activity—as well as an unseemly violation of professional academic standards. And for good reason. The teach-ins of the mid-1960's threatened the official vision of American history, in which we always saw ourselves as good guys fighting, like our favorite comic-book hero, for "truth, justice, and the American way." The teach-ins also began to ask questions about higher education rarely heard since Thorstein Veblen published *Higher Learning in America* in 1918, shortly after he was fired by Stanford University.

The anti-war movement on the campuses soon challenged the decorum of the classroom, the methodological assumptions of several academic disciplines, and the social function of the university, whose massive participation in the war seemed to contradict its most cherished self-definition as an island of disinterested learning.

Teaching the Vietnam War now may be even more subversive. Today's undergraduates are products of the post–Vietnam War period, and their study of it can suggest to them where they come from, who they are, what America has become, and even what they might do about it.

Last year, I offered a course called "Vietnam and America" at the Newark campus of Rutgers University, a commuter college attended primarily by working-class students who hold jobs while trying to get the education required for such vocations as accounting and nursing. The unexpected overenrollment made me scurry for a lecture hall, rooms for two sections, and funds for a coadjunct.

In the opening half hour, the students were asked to write answers to three questions:

- When did the Vietnam War begin?
- Who won?
- Why?

Predictably, they gave a wide range of dates for the beginning of the war, running from 1954 through 1974. Several students expressed the view that "there are no winners in a war—everybody loses," but most thought the war had been won by the Vietcong, North Vietnam, "the other side," or "the enemy." The most common answer to the third question was that "we didn't try hard enough—we didn't really fight to win." This last illusion had to be dispelled right away. Understanding what America did to Vietnam is a precondition for understanding what the Vietnam War did to America.

It was certainly not sufficient to state the bare fact that the U.S. attack on Vietnam constituted the heaviest and most concentrated devastation one nation had ever carried out upon another. A few details were necessary: Between 1964 and 1969 alone, the United States bombed Vietnam with more than nine times the tonnage of high explosives dropped in the entire Pacific theater in World War II (500 pounds for each Vietnamese man, woman, and child). By 1969, North Vietnam was being hit each month with the explosive force of two atomic bombs. The Christmas, 1972, bombing alone ravaged Hanoi and Haiphong with more tonnage than the Nazis dropped on Great Britain from 1940 through 1945.

None of these comparisons includes the equally massive bombardments from U.S. ground forces and ships. Nor do they include the napalm, anti-personnel bombs, and other modern terror weapons that killed and maimed at random in the vast "free-fire zones" and turned much of a once lush country into a wasteland. By 1967, U.S. herbicides had poisoned over 50 per cent of the arable land in South Vietnam—more than 4 million acres. By 1971, these poisons had wiped out over 35 per cent of the hardwood forests—more than 6 million acres. The least toxic of the three main herbicides used to drench the rice fields and forests of Vietnam was Agent Orange.

The class had already reached a critical point in the educational process. For now the students wanted to know—as indeed they ought—why they should believe what they were now hearing rather than what they had always heard. *They* were the ones raising questions about sources, conflicting evidence, and the authority of teachers. The quest for my sources led them directly to the most useful tool for this course, *Teaching the Vietnam War,* that invaluable book by William L. Griffen and John Marciano, which compares the versions of the war found in the 28 leading high-school history textbooks with the Pentagon Papers and responsible scholar-ship. Later they would have firsthand experience with sources, as they conducted interviews with Vietnam veterans, read personal narratives such as Ron Kovic's *Born on the Fourth of July*, and saw documentary films of saturation bombing, na-palm raids, and U.S. soldiers using poison gas, torturing prisoners, and burning villages.

Teaching the Vietnam War brought them back to that crucial and perplexing ques-tion: When *did* the Vietnam War begin? In 1965, when Lyndon Johnson sent a full-scale invasion force? In 1962, when the number of U.S. military "advisers" reached 16,000? In 1954, when the United States set up a puppet government in Saigon and U.S. commando teams attacked Hanoi? In 1946, when a French invasion force, equipped by the United States, arrived in Haiphong aboard U.S. ships?

Or did the Vietnam war for national independence begin in the tenth century as resistance against Chinese occupation, transform in 1887 into an anti-colonial strug-gle against the French that lasted through 1940, become an armed guerrilla move-ment against Japanese occupation during World War II, and maintain this form against the postwar French reinvasion and against the U.S. forces that replaced the French after their defeat?

Teaching the Vietnam War makes one realize how the shape of a narrative deter-mines, and is determined by, its content. One cannot date the "beginning" of the Vietnam War without deciding whether it was an anti-colonial war for national in-dependence—and hence also the last in a series of wars of imperialist expansion by France, Japan, and the United States—or whether it was an invasion by "North Vietnam" of "South Vietnam," which was then supported by its "ally" the United States.

Instead of being given a date, the students found themselves thrown back in time to June, 1954, publication date of the essay "What Every American Should Know About Indo-China" (available in *Vietnam: The Endless War,* by Leo Huberman and others). The essay begins, "The war in Indo-China really began nearly a hundred years ago," and ends by warning that our intervention in Vietnam is about to jeop-ardize "the future of our country." Then we went back one more year to Vietnam in 1953, the scene of Graham Greene's classic 1955 novel *The Quiet American,* in which the students could witness the decline of the French colonial forces and the emergence of a figure later to be met again in many forms: the archetypal innocent, idealistic, anti-communist American liberal, literally walking in the blood he is spill-ing with the very best intentions.

Just as education about the war developed as a subversive activity, the main ide-ological defense of the war consistently depended on ignorance. This has led to an ominous sequel.

Students from the class were often seen arguing for hours with one another and with friends about the war and related issues. (Such discussion, a rare phenomenon on our campus, contains interesting implications about the causes of the "apathy" of students in the late 1970's and early 80's.) The students noted that most of their friends argued that the war began when North Vietnam invaded South Vietnam, and that we lost because we didn't try hard enough. When the students presented dates, statistics, or other evidence, they were often accused of being "brainwashed," a charge based not so much on their opinions as on the mere fact that they knew such detailed information. Education—at least about the Vietnam War—has appar-ently now become synonymous with brainwashing, implying that the only unsus-picious knowledge is ignorance.

Who won the war? And why? Much of the course addressed these questions. The most difficult intellectual task for the students was to confront two equally authoritative-sounding books—Frances FitzGerald's *Fire in the Lake* and Le Duan's *The Vietnamese Revolution*—both of which accept as obvious that the Vietnamese people united to defeat foreign invaders and their corrupt puppet governments, but which explain this with entirely contradictory visions of Vietnamese social reality. And on the home front, the students had to look at an increasingly divided America, with cities literally burning from open rebellions, crime rates soaring, an economy devastated by a war so unpopular that the government had to finance it almost entirely with deficit spending, and a social and political structure cracking if not disintegrating.

The students were especially interested in the anti-war movement, which they had associated almost exclusively with students, draft-card burning, demonstrations, and the counterculture. Most were unaware of the broad community base of the anti-war movement, and knew nothing at all about GI "fraggings," sabotage, and mutinies. And contrary to some of the main anti-war activities through 1968, the students tended not to regard electoral politics as a realistic way to address important issues. They were surprised at our early ignorance about who rules America.

The last two books they read focused on some particular ways the war changed the nation. *The Politics of Heroin in Southeast Asia,* a model of research and scholarship, shocked them with its painfully detailed account of how the Central Intelligence Agency established the Golden Triangle as the main source of heroin first for the GI's and then for the urban centers of America. Robert Stone's *Dog Soldiers* dramatized the domestic sequel. Stone's aptly named John Converse appears like a final avatar of Greene's quiet American, once an idealistic liberal bringing American democracy to Vietnam, now a self-serving cynic smuggling Vietnamese heroin to America. As Converse says to his equally self-deceived buddy in Vietnam, trapped by his lone-hero illusions: "We didn't know who we were till we got here. We thought we were something else."

Stone ends with a vision of post–Vietnam War America as a swamp of inescapable decay and depravity. Most of the students found a different message—about both their country and themselves—in their study of the war. Many went to Washington last spring to join the demonstration against America's intervention in El Salvador.

8   Letters to the Editor

To the Editor:

H. Bruce Franklin's article ("Teaching Vietnam Today: Who Won, and Why?" Point of View, November 4) should have been subtitled "The Marxist-Leninist View." Historical objectivity is an ideal to which we all aspire, and it should be mandatory that historians identify their ideological allegiances openly. The politics of historiography—and of the historical profession—are as important to our students as the research we pursue.

Mr. Franklin's views of the war in Vietnam are no doubt colored by his own well-known histrionics during the period. Of course, since he has tenure now, he may not have brought his own historical role to the attention of his students. But I note that Mr. Franklin's belletristic persuasion—he is a professor of English and American literature—may be the reason for his sloppy historical approach.

May one ask if the North Vietnamese, Vietcong, and their allies in Vietnam as well as in the United States cannot be considered the enemies of the United States? Does Mr. Franklin teach his "working class" students that one of the reasons for the failure of the war effort in the United States was that the privileged could ensconce themselves in undergraduate and graduate programs and legally avoid the draft while the working-class youths became cannon fodder? Does Mr. Franklin teach his students of the activities, bordering on treason to the United States, that were tolerated, even applauded, in the colleges and universities of the United States? Does Mr. Franklin teach his students that North Vietnamese by the hundreds of thousands would have rather died than live under Ho Chi Minh at the time of partition in 1954? Or that Ho Chi Minh ordered the disembowelment of pregnant Vietnamese women who had cohabited with Frenchmen?

In listing atrocities, does Mr. Franklin mention to his classes the numerous tortures inflicted on the Vietnamese Christians by the Vietminh, and the crucifixions of Vietnamese Catholic priests by Vietminh operatives? This catalogue could continue for several more pages. Now that all of Indochina has become a Marxist-Leninist satrapy, can Mr. Franklin explain to his classes the mass starvation of Cambodians, the innumerable atrocities and persecutions that continue to the present day?

The truth of history is concealed by Mr. Franklin. His skillful apologia for the left-wing critique of Vietnam does contain a number of unassailable facts, but true to the Marxist-Leninist model, it is loaded with half-truths and desiccated by concealment of relevant, qualifying information.

Hundreds of thousands of dedicated American servicemen served the cause of the United States in Vietnam. What of their sacrifice? Should a course on Vietnam not also focus on their valor?

We must endeavor to learn all of the facts of the war. Partial interpretations, Marxist-Leninist overviews, and concealment of relevant facts are a betrayal of history. Mistakes were made. Atrocities were committed. Let the truth be told, but let it be the whole truth.

MICHAEL SUOZZI
San Diego

To the Editor:

I almost never write letters to editors. But that piece of poppycock . . . really rang my chimes.

We lost the Vietnam War because we chickened out—because we forgot that when you get into a war you have to do *whatever* it takes to win it.

We had the wherewithal to win. But we just didn't have the guts to use it.

My source of information: my only son, a combat Air Force veteran. He told me when he got home in 1970 that he and his buddies could have won the war all by themselves in less than a month *if*—and that's an "if" that made all the difference—they had been allowed to do what they all knew had to be done. The Army and the Navy could have gone home; they were superfluous. But the green light to go ahead never came.

Vietnam was no "swamp of depravity," Professor Franklin. It was instead one of the noblest wars we ever fought—intended to gain nothing for ourselves but rather to save a frantic, helpless little land from brutal aggressors who invaded it.

One last word: If Harry Truman had been president in the 60's, the war would not have been lost. Ditto for Ronald Reagan. And you'd better believe it. So much for your "massive" American efforts, Professor. All it would have taken was the iron will to win. And that we didn't have.

MAX RAFFERTY
Distinguished Professor of Education
Troy State University
Troy, Ala.

Mr. Rafferty is former superintendent of public instruction in California.

—THE EDITOR

To the Editor:

I was very glad to see H. Bruce Franklin's essay on the Vietnam War. I join him in strongly urging that American education finally turn its attention to this important subject, and I'm naturally pleased that someone is willing to share his unhappy national experience with this generation of Americans.

However, several portions of his essay indicate that his approach lacks one important ingredient: objectivity. His "fact" that there was an "attack on Vietnam" by this country reduces a very complicated situation to terms that are at best simplistic and at worst a reckless falsehood. It's rhetoric that takes me back to the 1960's, when both the pro-war and anti-war people took great liberty with the truth in order to win the people in the center over to their respective sides.

In addition, he praises the book by William L. Griffen and John Marciano, which examines 28 high-school history textbooks and finds them to be woefully short on the truth. Perhaps they are, but critics have already seen through the one-sided presentation of the book, a kind of whitewash in reverse. The fact that millions of Americans (perhaps mistakenly) backed American involvement in Vietnam for the highest ideals has apparently been forgotten by both the authors and Mr. Franklin.

Thirdly, he makes a strong point about "GI fraggings, sabotage, and mutinies." The fact is that fraggings were very uncommon (I knew of no such incidents during the time I served with an Army infantry division in Vietnam from 1968 to 1969), and sabotage and mutinies, which were also extremely rare, often occurred for reasons unrelated to what Mr. Franklin implies—a belief that the war was wrong and reprehensible, and had to be stopped. Fragging incidents and mutinies merely presented a diversion for the American press, which has already been highly discredited for its reporting of the war.

I also decry the bloodshed and violence of the war, the ravaging of the land, and the death of hundreds of thousands of innocent people. I'm also upset by the fact that the war, as Mr. Franklin indicates, was carried on behind a wall of ignorance and deceit, perpetuated by the U.S. government.

But isn't Mr. Franklin, with his one-sided essay and questionable conclusions, committing an equal sin?

DALE E. REICH
Director
News and Publications Services
University of Wisconsin
Whitewater, Wis.

Mr. Reich is author of "Good Soldiers Don't Go to Heaven," an autobiographical look at the Vietnam War.

—THE EDITOR

To the Editor:

H. Bruce Franklin's Point of View brought back my own undergraduate experiences, while the war was going on. There seemed to be a great number of professors eager to "teach" the war, and to back up their versions with all sorts of data. The fact that each seemed to have a different version and to use different data wouldn't have bothered me, except they were so *sure*. They each knew The Truth.

They knew it so well that I often received a dose of it in courses that should have had nothing to do with Vietnam. Students who presented counters to whatever version the professor espoused were dismissed as naïve or foolish, no matter how well thought out their arguments or how well founded their data. Some were even graded accordingly. We experienced something called a "teach-in" during which 14 anti-war faculty members separately presented indictments of the war but none presented any other side. A suggestion that the event should have been called a "propaganda-in" was dismissed as stupid. This in a teachers' college.

I hope we have risen above that low level. I hope we have come to realize that just about any answer to Professor Franklin's questions on when, who, and why could be defended as "truth." There are no more hard truths to that war than to any war, only those sure they have The Truth. And I hope we can now teach the war and leave indoctrination behind. But I doubt it.

HAROLD J. ETTELT
Assistant Dean for Learning Resources
Columbia-Greene Community College
Hudson, N.Y.

Documents 9 and 10

Television journalist Bill Moyers served as President Johnson's Press Secretary during the period of the military buildup in Vietnam, until 1966. In 1980 he took up the subject of Vietnam in his public television series, "Bill Moyers' Journal." Documents 9 and 10 are two portions of the transcript of this program, "Vietnam Remembered." In Document 9, Moyers interviews Josiah Bunting—educator, novelist, and Vietnam veteran—seeking Bunting's interpretation of the Vietnam war. In Document 10, Moyers talks with the Kolor family of Pearl River, New York, about the "lessons of Vietnam."

9 Bill Moyers' Journal: Vietnam Remembered
Bunting Interview
March 20, 1980

MOYERS [voice-over]: Josiah Bunting joined the Marines when he was 17, went to Oxford as a Rhodes Scholar, then fought with the 9th Infantry Division in Vietnam. He returned as a major, to become one of the most popular instructors at West Point. He wrote a disquieting and highly praised novel about Vietnam called 'The Lionheads', the story of an ambitious American general in the Vietnamese delta who achieved success by burying his mistakes. Josiah Bunting left the military in 1972, frustrated with its leadership system, and is now president of Hampden-Sydney College in Virginia, where among the battlefields of the Civil War, he continues to study military history and modern society. [Exterior, Hampden-Sydney College, Bill Moyers and Josiah Bunting walking] I went to talk to him about the legacy of Vietnam today, and the rumors of wars to come. Do you think that Vietnam left indelibly an impression on us that we'll carry with us on the psychology of the nation, for a long time?

JOSIAH BUNTING: I think it probably showed us that we could lose a military conflict. I think it showed us also that we probably should not engage in a military conflict that we don't enter with some kind of unity, or at least, maintain during the conflict. I mean that in a particular way. If the cause cannot be explained to the American citizens in this democracy, then it probably isn't a very good cause. I see this war, incidentally, not as the creation of malevolent people, but of stupid people. Therefore, forgivable.

MOYERS: Stupid?

BUNTING: Stupid.

MOYERS: In what sense?

BUNTING: In the sense that they were very smart in executing and carrying out the minor policy chores, but they failed to examine carefully what the ultimate goal of the policy was to be.

[Interior, Bunting's living room]

MOYERS: What story were you telling in 'The Lionheads'?

BUNTING: I was trying to tell the story that there is nothing more tragic or horrible than that people who least understand why war is fought, are the ones that get killed, and people who make a profession out of fighting wars, survive.

MOYERS: Are you saying that the people who took us to Vietnam, who prosecuted the war, had the least to lose?

BUNTING: Well, in the ultimate sense that they were the ones least likely to be shot by a Viet Cong sniper. In some larger sense, they probably had as much to lose as practically anyone else, except their lives. I think what I was saying pretty much—well, I stand by my statement. It's a story about what a horrible thing it is when a boy who has no notion what he is doing in a war, is killed, and when those who make a profession of conducting the fighting, are not killed. In literature, there is such a thing as an ideograph, which is a person or an object which represents an idea, and I think these characters are somewhat more than ideographic.

MOYERS: If you reduced Vietnam to a single ideograph, what would it be?

BUNTING: Well, it would be General Lemming in that book. An efficient, hard-working, military person who didn't think very hard about what he was doing.

MOYERS: But did it because—why?

BUNTING: Because he was in uniform. Because he was there. Just like Erich Maria Remarque says. It's not very metaphysical. 'Their shoulders held the sky suspended, they stood, and earth's foundations stay. They took their wages and are dead. Off you go!'

MOYERS: You said once, that you couldn't wait to get to Vietnam. Why was that?

BUNTING: I was just terribly curious and wanted to get to Vietnam, I think, to see what the war was like, what I would be like in it, those kinds of things.

MOYERS: What did you find?

BUNTING: I found that the reality of the war and the reality of my own participation in it were not particularly exciting, not particularly moving, not particularly—They did not particularly fulfill what I expected. And I think that experience is much more common among people that went to Vietnam, than people who read about Vietnam know. I think there is a sharp skew in the direction of memoirs, conversations, films, books, and so on, which depict the war as being a terribly wrenching, emotional experience for everyone who went, which of course it distinctly was not.

MOYERS: Caputo's book, then, is more the experience of the ordinary soldier down in the conflict. Your book, 'The Lionheads' struck me as more the view written by somebody slightly above and off to the side of what was happening.

BUNTING: I think that's an accurate appraisal of the book. The last position I had in Vietnam, and I did it for about five months, was as an assistant chief of staff to an infantry division, and I saw very closely several general officers, several colonels,

majors, officers of that grade, who would come in from the various infantry brigades and battalions for meetings, briefings, and that kind of stuff. I had a pretty
good notion of how the American military machine functions at the higher levels in
a wartime situation.

MOYERS: How would you characterize the way it functioned in Vietnam, as you
saw it?

BUNTING: It was an efficient operation, but we lost sight frequently of the
object. I think a significant difference, of course, between Vietnam and other wars,
was that the people who prosecuted the war in Vietnam did so in one-year incre-
ments of time. In fact, less than that, since you tended to be moved from assignment
to assignment in Vietnam.

MOYERS: What was the consequence of that?

BUNTING: I think the consequence was to go as hard as you possibly could for
one year, but without any sense that the quality or nature of your effort bore directly on when the war would be over. There was no sense of fighting for victory.
There was a sense of fighting to do what you were trained to do about as well as
you could, and then you would go home.

MOYERS: What did this extraordinary experience, what did Vietnam do to the
American army?

BUNTING: Well, it did a number of things, and we're beginning now to be able
to see it from a distance, which, of course, is necessary. It robbed the Army of its
self-confidence. It robbed the Army of its confidence in the affection and esteem
which it imagined the American public held it in. The relationship of the American
public to its army has always been ambivalent and strange. But at least, the Army
thought, most of the time, when it began a war, that the public was behind it. I
think, those two things. The other thing it did, and it did this in common with certain other things that took place during this period from 1965 to 1975—it knocked
reason from its pedestal. It made the American people extremely suspicious of
smartness, of reason, of rationality, of wisdom. And I think, if you are looking for
an unhappy legacy, that was perhaps the unhappiest of all.

MOYERS: You once wrote an article in which you said, 'So long as the notion
persists, that sovereign states must make themselves strong in order not to fight'—
forget all this technological firepower—'it is likely they will keep on fighting.' Do
you really believe that's true?

BUNTING: I don't see how having a strong military force in a world filled with
sovereign predators, which answer to no higher allegiance—the United Nations
doesn't have an army to enforce its decisions—I don't see how they can avoid bump-
ing up against each other. And when they bump up against each other, given that
there's no court of arbitrament which can resolve the disputes that would come
about as a result of this, I don't see how they can avoid going to war. I think the
effect now of the fact that we all have nuclear weapons, or that the Russians and
ourselves have nuclear weapons, probably will change the bleakness of my prediction a little bit, or my observation a little bit, but I don't think it will stop countries
going to war at conventional levels.

MOYERS: Let me see if I understand what you're saying. The more nations arm,
the more likely they are to go to war, in principle, by your own admission?

BUNTING: Yes.

MOYERS: Well, nations now are arming to the teeth.

BUNTING: Arming to the teeth. I'm just trying to make the point that, yes, the
more they arm, the more likely it is that they will go to war, and the more horrific

will be the results; but at the same time, I ask you not to ignore the fact that there is no way out of the dilemma. It is, it seems to me, an inescapable part of the human condition so long as we are organized in sovereign states in the world.

MOYERS: You make me feel pessimistic, fatalistic.

BUNTING: Well, you should, Bill. You should feel pessimistic.

MOYERS: In the short term, do you see war soon?

BUNTING: I see a very good possibility of war in the next five years, certainly. I don't think it will be nuclear. I pray that it won't be. But I can't see how we should have any optimism about war, given the energy situation.

MOYERS: War between United States and other powers?

BUNTING: Possibly the United States and its proxies and our proxies, [sic] and the proxies of the Soviet Union, possibly in the Middle East, that kind of thing.

MOYERS: But won't we think awfully hard after Vietnam before we get involved in another war?

BUNTING: I think that there is now a public perception, which the President reflects, that those things that we need to survive are at risk, and that an American president would be strongly tempted to commit the country to war to protect them.

MOYERS: Those things being oil? If there were to be war—

BUNTING: And there is, you know there is a kind of a strange bellicosity, there are, in the old-fashioned phrase, there are a lot of rumors of war around the United States now. People are writing articles about the draft. Students are being questioned about the draft. You know, I mean there's a feeling, I think, of 'My gosh, we've been pushed around too much, we've had it now, we see that we reached a kind of nadir of our self-esteem and the world's notion of our self-esteem, between 1973 and now—and I guess we'd better build ourselves up and get ready for the long haul. These Russians really don't behave very well and we've got to get ready for them.'

MOYERS: Could a conventional war be prevented from escalating into a nuclear war? Let's say you're right. I know you're not arguing for war. But let's say that the inexorable tendencies of our times lead us to some conventional confrontation—could it be contained?

BUNTING: I think we are confronted again with a predicament which I would describe as existential and unanswerable. There will be tremendous pressures on the United States, on the American military, to make a conventional war nuclear at a very early stage of the fighting. That's inescapable. We do not have the kind of conventional infantry and armor, not to mention seaborne lift capability, transports and so on, to put a force into the Middle East, for example, which could do what we needed for it to do against the Russians. Nor do we have the allies who appear to be willing to help take up that slack. Therefore, there will be a great deal of felt pressure on the part of the local commander to employ tactical nuclear weapons. Whether he will accede to that pressure, whether an American president will make that decision for him, whether it will be felt that we could use tactical nuclear weapons, small yield, low yield weapons without escalating the conflict, I just can't say.

MOYERS: George Bush got into trouble recently by saying to a reporter, he thought we could survive a nuclear war. He talked about survivability. Is there such a thing, in your judgment, as a former military man, as a historian of military history, as a student of military affairs, is there such a thing as survivability in a nuclear war?

BUNTING: There certainly is. And it's a horrible thing to have to admit. And it's an even more horrible thing to contemplate. But, as Bush said, and he was exactly right, and people like Herman Kahn say it, and it's rather unpopular—but if the structure of a country remains, if 5 or 10 million people remain alive, the other side has no one alive, then we have won. It's a horrible, ghastly thing. But refusing to study it, or refusing to admit it, it seems to me, is more reprehensible, than pronouncing jeremiads against how horrible it will be if we have one.

MOYERS: But 'won' and 'lost' seem such anachronistic terms in that kind of conflict.

BUNTING: Yes, they do.

MOYERS: You're president of a college down there with what—800 young men?

BUNTING: About.

MOYERS: I mean, is there a willingness to go to war—

BUNTING: I think about most college-age students, there is neither a willingness, nor an unwillingness to go to war. If they're called, they will go. The kinds of comments I hear from students—one of them is really remarkable, and I'm kind of anxious as to its provenance. The student said to me the other day, 'When the war comes the next time, I want to be an officer. I sure want to be an officer.' It's like a World War II novel, or something.

MOYERS: One of the things implicit in the youngster's comment to you is part of the theme in Philip Caputo's book and in the movie they're making about a 'A Rumor of War'. And it's the seduction of war. It's the romanticizing of war throughout American history, throughout human history, I guess.

BUNTING: Well, again, it's a little more complex than that. We do romanticize war. Somebody said we are a bellicose people which hate militarism. We romanticize those portions of war in which we think we see our best characteristics, our best qualities as a people, reflected—our individualism, individual strokes of bravery, that kind of thing. The romance of war inheres in our willingness to see only those elements which we think are exciting.

MOYERS: Until we get there.

BUNTING: That's right.

10 Bill Moyers' Journal: Vietnam Remembered
Kolor Interview
March 20, 1980

MOYERS: Amidst new rumors of war, all of us, because of Vietnam, think harder about the circumstances in which we would again send our young to fight. So when President Carter announced plans for the registration of everyone aged 18 through 20, people responded strongly. This letter was written to her local newspaper by Mrs. Agnes Kolor of Pearl River, New York. She is the mother of four children. We saw it by chance and were moved by Mrs. Kolor's belief that if there is a next time, the burden must be shared. "Where is it written" she asked, "that only the young can kill or be killed. As citizens of the greatest country in the world, we feel it's time everyone pays their dues for living here, not just the young. We propose mandatory registration of all able-bodied men and women up to the age of 59. As to our young, we parents have learned much from the Vietnam war . . . "

. . .

MOYERS: What was behind this sentence in your letter: 'Where is it written that only the young should kill or be killed?'

MRS. AGNES KOLOR: Because I felt quite honestly, Mr. Moyers, that it's so much easier to go into war if there's just a certain group of people that you can shuffle off to war, but if you had to put your own life on the line, that you would start and really consider exactly what this action is that you're taking. Now, if there's a legitimate reason for that action, we must support it, because this is our country. I mean, we must support the country, if it's a legitimate action. But it's so easy, if you're not involved, if you're not personally involved, to not be too concerned about the lives and the actions of others.

MR. KOLOR: If people are making a decision for something that they themselves feel they're involved in, they'll take more care in making that decision. They won't just make it off the shoulder.

MOYERS: But the traditional attitude is that the young are able-bodied and are able to fight.

KOLOR: Well, why are our lives more valuable than the young? I mean, we're the ones who create the situation that put these young people in it.

MOYERS: But don't older people keep the machinery of our society in place?

KOLOR: Are we so important that we can't interrupt our lives? I mean, this is our country we're talking about.

MOYERS: So you're saying that if you drafted everybody, all of us between 18 and 59, it would make us think seriously about what we're doing?

MR. KOLOR: Yes, because it would make people sit down and say, do we really want to get into a war hysteria? Do we want to fan the cold war? Do we want to go to a part of the world—I'm not so sure that we're not involved in this war hysteria right now because of re-election politics, maybe oil interests. I don't see it as a vital interest of the U.S. the way it's made out to be.

KOLOR: I really in my heart believe that the only way there'll be peace is if everybody's put on the line. Do you know what I'm saying? If everybody has to get involved. Because too many people take the attitude it's not their problem, and what do they care.

MOYERS: What do you think we learned from the war in Vietnam?

KOLOR: I supported the war in Vietnam when it was going on, for the simple reason that I'm very anti-communist. You know, any of those boys who went over, they could have been my son, because if my son was old enough, being an American citizen, I would have thought it was his duty to go. And when I saw them come back, I said to myself, how must any mother or father feel who let— This is why I feel I must make a value judgment now.

MR. KOLOR: I don't want to see another Vietnam start. I think we should have learned a very strong lesson from Vietnam. I don't want to see us trying to fight a war in a part of the world that we can't win.

MOYERS: But what if today the government said we have to draw the line against communism in the Persian Gulf?

KOLOR: But we're smarter now. We're smarter now. I mean, being very honest, Mr. Moyers, in other wars before the Vietnam war, the reality of war was not brought home to us as easily as it was done on television, and we realize that wars aren't—I mean, I thought John Wayne was a great actor, but we realize that wars aren't like you see in John Wayne movies and other things, that there's a real reality to war, that people really get hurt, innocent people.

MOYERS: Did you learn anything from the protesters?

KOLOR: Oh, yes. I learned—Now, people have to understand, because I question something, I have the right as an American citizen to question it. I am not—If your child questions you about something, do you think your child is disloyal because he questioned you?

MOYERS: No.

KOLOR: Well, I am a child of this country, and I have a right to question the fathers of this country as to why they are doing a particular thing, because they expect me maybe to make the supreme sacrifice of taking my flesh and blood. And I have a right to ask them about these decisions. It doesn't mean I'm not supporting them.

MOYERS: So the real purpose of your letter is to say to the President, to the country, to all of us, what?

KOLOR: To think carefully before we embark on an action that we may be very sorry for, and to really feel that we all have to become involved today in helping our country out.

[End, "Listening to America"]

[Interior, Moyers' office]

MOYERS: Vietnam remembered should not make it impossible for this nation to defend itself and our liberties. But unremembered, Vietnam would leave us where it found us, thinking of war as fascinating instead of vulgar, of soldiers as warriors instead of men, of sacrifice as a measure of devotion to be asked of the young alone. Of such illusions are tragedies born and repeated. I'm Bill Moyers.

Document 11

American foreign policy decisions in the last decade have been made by people determined to avoid "another Vietnam." Although different administrations have drawn different lessons from the Vietnam experience, all have agreed that the U.S. involvement did not accomplish its aims.

In the winter of 1982, El Salvador was very much in the news. The Central American government was fighting what appeared to be a growing leftist insurgency, concern in Washington was evident and rising, and President Reagan was described as considering, among other options, the use of American combat troops to support the existing regime. Inevitably, the Vietnam analogy was used, by both proponents and opponents of intervention.

Document 11, which appeared in *Time* in February 1982, comments on the similarities and differences between El Salvador and Vietnam.

11 El Salvador: It Is Not Viet Nam
Strobe Talbott

For the past few weeks, Americans have been asking themselves some urgent and difficult questions about the ugly civil war in El Salvador. Will the latest guerrilla offensive succeed in disrupting and discrediting the elections scheduled for next month? Will the beleaguered civilian President, José Napoleón Duarte, be able to stave off the leftist challenge? Can he also rein in the right-wing military leaders with whom he shares what remains of central power—and therefore with whom he shares responsibility for atrocities committed by the security forces? And what can the U.S. do? Can it simultaneously foster land reform and counterinsurgency, especially when both campaigns are going so badly?

The crisis has also posed questions that more directly affect the American people: Is El Salvador a new Viet Nam? Is the U.S. about to repeat the mistakes that led it into the greatest single setback to its military power, political prestige and national self-confidence in this century? The news media have repeatedly been asking that of late. So have Senators and Congressmen in their interrogation of Government witnesses. So have academics and student leaders at teach-ins.

The natural tendency to draw cautionary comparisons with Viet Nam has already asserted itself to an unnatural, and certainly unhealthy, extent in the political debate about El Salvador. It has fostered prejudices over judgments and dogmas over lessons, both among conservatives (neo and otherwise), who are well represented in the Administration, and among their opponents on the left.

The liberal exhortation "No more Viet Nams!" could be a prescription for appeasement, passivism and isolationism; the hard-liners' rejoinder—"No more 'No more Viet Nams!' "—could translate into a recipe for macho bullying: "Let's go beat the stuffing out of somebody somewhere just to show that we're tough again." The danger of the first response is paralysis; the danger of the second is reflexive, unthinking action. Neither impulse makes for sound policy.

When U.S. fighters downed a pair of Libyan jets last August, two choruses sounded in counterpoint: "Hooray! We've finally put Viet Nam behind us!" and, from the other side of the stage, "Beware! The Gulf of Sidra may be another Gulf of Tonkin!" (thus bringing onstage, with clanking chains, the ghost of the 1964 naval skirmish off the coast of Viet Nam, which Lyndon Johnson used as a pretext to escalate American involvement there).

The Viet Nam syndrome has even clouded views of our adversaries' foreign entanglements. Some commentators, as well as some American Government officials, continue to toy hopefully with the idea that Afghanistan may turn out to be the Soviet Union's Viet Nam—never mind that Afghanistan is right on the Soviet border and that whatever else the leaders in Moscow have to worry about, they need not fear student marches on the Kremlin or peacenik political challengers in the next elections to the Supreme Soviet.

Still, it is inevitable, indeed understandable, that the Viet Nam analogy should arise in the context of the civil war in El Salvador. Precisely because the American debacle in Indochina was such a protracted, painful and preoccupying episode, it is sure to come to mind whenever the U.S. faces circumstances that are even superficially similar. Television coverage of El Salvador has provided some gnawingly familiar images: Marxist-led peasants *vs.* patrols of boy soldiers in ill-fitting uniforms and G.I.-style helmets, ambushes and massacres in the jungles, a trickle of American advisers into the embattled country, and, back in Washington, a Secretary of State telling a skeptical Congress that this is where the U.S. must draw the line against Communist adventurism.

But the parallels to Viet Nam are far outnumbered by the divergences. Viet Nam is 9,000 miles from the U.S.; El Salvador is a near neighbor. The military-civilian government in San Salvador is its own worst enemy, in the sense that it has alienated its own people and embarrassed what few friends it has left in the world. Still, the junta bears little resemblance to the assorted cliques and strongmen that the U.S. supported in Saigon.

Another difference between now and then: the Viet Cong had spent decades building up their cadres, fighting skills, command structure and supply lines; they also had North Viet Nam, with its huge regular army, first backing them up, then leading them in their conquest. The Salvadoran insurgency, by contrast, is limited to about 6,000 active fighters, many of whom are recent converts to the cause. The closest analogue to a North Viet Nam in Central America is Nicaragua, which is not really very close at all. The Sandinista regime there is still young and insecure. True, it is gravitating into the Soviet-Cuban orbit and building a formidable military machine, at least by Central American standards; but that buildup is partly in reaction to the Reagan Administration's implacable hostility. Much as the Sandinistas would like to see their Salvadoran comrades triumph, Nicaragua does not have a common border with El Salvador, and the extent to which the Sandinistas are shipping arms to the guerrillas is debatable. There is no equivalent of the Ho Chi Minh Trail and, far more important, of Ho Chi Minh himself.

In short, the Viet Nam analogy is really the Viet Nam fallacy. It is fallacious not just in the objective difference between the two situations, but in the way that indulgence of a false analogy can skew judgment. In general, foreign policy is better served by a conscious attempt to analyze each situation afresh, rather than by the wisdom of hindsight (which, of course, is really not wisdom at all). Soldiers, it has often been said, have the bad habit of waging the last war. Americans, in their current fretting over El Salvador, are similarly afflicted. Across the political spectrum, there is no one who wants to re-experience in Central America the defeat of Indochina. From that, the left is tempted to conclude: Better not to fight at all, anywhere, ever again. The right concludes the opposite: Fight somewhere, soon, only this time, by God, win!

The Administration's current policy, to prop up Duarte long enough to get some rudimentary democratic institutions and economic reforms in place, is in plenty of trouble on the ground in El Salvador; and it is couched in some of the more bellicose, almost hysterical idioms of Haigspeak back in Washington. But as long as the Administration seeks to curb the abuses of the regime and discourage the political ambitions of the military, providing American assistance against the guerrillas is a reasonable and responsible course. The humanitarian as well as geopolitical goal of the U.S. is to stop the escalation of violence in Central America, and that means exerting force against the insurgents through arms aid, as well as putting political pressure on our less savory clients to moderate their ways.

Should that policy fail, the Administration will face some excruciatingly difficult choices. If Duarte should lose out to one of his rightist rivals, does the U.S. withdraw its support and leave the repressive new regime to its own brutal but dwindling devices? More difficult still, if the guerrillas seem on the brink of military victory, does the U.S. send in combat troops? Friendly countries in the region and American allies around the world would almost unanimously oppose deeper, more direct American involvement; the Administration would also have to contend with massive political and popular resistance in this country, based as much as anything on distaste for the type of regime the U.S. would be trying to rescue. Besides, the rationale for the Administration's ends and means in El Salvador rests on the reassurances, repeated by Haig's deputy Thomas Enders only last week, that the U.S. seeks a political, not a military, solution. Sending in troops would undercut the already precarious credibility of that policy.

Those and other relevant considerations would be, and should be, enough to give the Administration plenty of reason to look for alternatives to military intervention. But the hard fact is that the U.S. cannot pre-emptively and categorically rule out more direct use of force in El Salvador, which is what some of Haig's crossexaminers in the Senate seemed to want him to do. Any nation, but especially a superpower, must reserve the option of armed action in defense of its vital interests. To foreclose that option in a nasty little crisis close to home would raise new questions about American defense commitments all over the world. The other half of the dilemma is that if the U.S. does resort to force, it must do so—and be seen to do so—in order to defeat real enemies in the here and now, rather than to exorcise ghosts from half a decade ago and half a globe away.

To the extent that policymakers and spokesmen for both left and right can avoid historymongering, so much the better. There is a converse to philosopher George Santayana's famous warning, "Those who cannot remember the past are condemned to repeat it." It is equally true that those who dwell obsessively on the past are prone to poor analysis, divisive debate, unconstructive criticism and bad decisions as they face the future. In short, they are doomed to ask the wrong questions, which can only yield the wrong answers.

Documents 12–19

In the course of preparing the television history, interviewers frequently sought retrospective views from participants. The following eight documents are brief excerpts from statements made in 1981 and 1982 by George Ball, Henry Kissinger, Dean Rusk, the Reverend William Sloane Coffin, former President Gerald Ford, Daniel Ellsberg, Jim Fallows, and William Ehrhart.

12 George Ball Interview

I think Viet Nam was the probably the greatest single error that America has made in its national history. I, that sounds like an overstatement, but I don't think it is. It demoralized our society. It ah ah for a whole generation there will be a mark left because they went through a period where the country was being torn apart. . . .

Viet Nam had, not only disastrous effects on the social fabric and social cohesion of America, but it, I think it set us back a very long way so far as foreign policy was concerned rather than enhancing our reputation which seemed to be the, the concern of my colleagues. I think it was disastrous because it gave the impression that the United States was reckless. The brutal bombing of Viet Nam, particularly that occurred under the Nixon administration, gave the impression that we were arrogant and, and had a disdain for the life of the local people, the indigenous people in the areas particularly in the Third World where we would consent, and that America's reputation as being a wise, powerful nation was enormously hurt by all of this. This, of course, was followed by Watergate so we had twin disasters, but I think that Viet Nam was the, will go down in history as a really a disastrous point in American history. A disastrous set of events that really did more than anything up to that point to diminish the, the reputation of the United States for wisdom and compassion, for generosity and understanding and all the things that we had tried to stand for. And, it'll be a long time overcoming that. Now, in addition, it has created inhibitions on the use of American power which, again, because they tend to be exaggerated, have ah ah are creating current problems for us. It tended us, contributed again to the unwillingness of Americans to serve in the armed forces, which I think we're suffering from now, and in in the deplorable state of our so-called volunteer army. I can't think of any event that had a worst set of series and set of consequences than the Vietnamese war.

13 Henry Kissinger Interview

Vietnam is still with us. It has divided the consensus that carried American foreign policy through a generation. It created a . . . doubts about American judgment, about American credibility, and American power. Not only in our country but in many, in many parts of the world. It has poisoned our domestic debate in which almost every issue now turns more on motives than on substance. And so we paid an exorbitant price for the decisions that were made in the middle 1960's in good faith and for good purposes. And the lesson we should learn is that we need some view both as to our ultimate purposes in the world about the objectives that are within our power to reach, and about the means that are appropriate to these objectives. And the second lesson we have to learn is that you cannot run a society by civil-war kind of debates. That there has to be something that a residue of what unites people must be preserved and that, that political opponents should strive not only for victories over each other, but that they'll ultimately be judged by their reconciliations.

14 Dean Rusk Interview

I think the principal impact is the erosion of the idea of collective security. And that we'd better be talking seriously about how we really propose to organize a durable peace in the world and prevent World War III. Now, there are those who would beat the drums and say you do it by simply building up your armed forces. That standing alone will not do it. A lot of other things have to be thought about. In our relations with the Soviet Union, there have been two main threads that are there at all times. The attempt to find points of agreement and the necessity for occasional confrontations when they go beyond the boundaries of permissable conduct and move into areas that threaten the peace of the world. Both elements are always there even though public opinion and many of our friends in the media tend to swing like a pendulum between something called detente and Cold War. Both elements are always present. It takes a good deal of sophistication in thinking to keep those two things in mind because sometimes the element of confrontation gets in the way of the possible search for points of agreement. (clears throat) You can't abandon that search for, for possible agreement because we and the Russians share a major common interest. The prevention of World War III. If we can find points of agreement that would help to broaden that base of common interest and reduce the range of issues on which violence can occur, we have to make the effort, because whatever anybody thinks of the Russians at the end of the day we and they must still find a way to inhabit this little speck of dust in the universe at the same time. Otherwise, forget it.

Q: And, do you think Viet Nam has diluted this, diverted people's attention . . . ?

A: I think it's diverted our attention from this central purpose. Viet Nam, I think, has at least for a period diverted our attention from this central issue of how the world is to organize itself to prevent World War III. Now, we'll come back to it, but I would like ah to see more public discussion.

15 William Sloane Coffin Interview

Yes, well it made a difference. I personally feel it made an enormous difference. I think in our, in the understanding of America's role in the world there has been a great change since the war in Vietnam. I started out thinking that the war in Vietnam was basically a diversion from our primary course in the world. Now I understand that it was part of our primary course. The United States is fundamentally an imperialistic country, we're still engaged in interventionist policies, so is the Soviet Union, a plague on both their houses. But I think a lot more Americans understand that what we did in Vietnam we're not ready to do again in El Salvador, Nicaragua,

Cuba, Guatemala, unless we watch it. I don't think now we have to be in the middle of the jungle to come to our minds. I think we know before we get into the jungle that this is a very bad move to make. So I think from that point of view it was, there was a lot of consciousness raising that took place. I think it's also very clear now, as it was not then, that you cannot have guns and butter. It's either guns or butter. And right now in our time we're saying that we're not even getting margarine, for heaven sakes. And that the expenditures on military adventures and the arms race just mean that the poor are going to be kept in their poverty indefinitely. And I think we learned a lot from that. We still haven't learned how to live with communist countries. We still look for military solutions to essentially political and social problems. We still haven't learned what pluralism in the world is all about. Great Britain managed to lose its power rather gracefully. The British have always sort of learned how to cooperate gracefully with the inevitable. Maybe they gave up their power after World War II because they were so convinced that the British (speaking in a British accent) were so much superior to everybody else. You know. But the French didn't. They fought like dogs in China, they fought like dogs in Algeria, and now the question is being addressed to us, I think. "Will you Americans be willing to relinquish some of the power that you had really almost in monopoly form after World War II, or will you insist on being the Hertz of the world when it comes to military strength? And my hope is that we Americans have enough in our tradition, enough remembrance of things past to remind ourselves, for instance, that our nation's influence was at its greatest when as a military power we were the weakest. And we stand for much better things then military intervention. And the kind of freedom that we represent at our best, the kind of openness that Lincoln stood for when he said, " . . . with malice toward none and charity for all," which makes Abraham Lincoln the spiritual son of American history. I keep hoping that those things in our history will help us get over this period into a time when we can live with greater intelligence and sanity with a lot of other nations.

16 Gerald Ford Interview

Q: Finally, looking back, what were the lessons of Vietnam?

A: The lessons of Vietnam, I think, are the following: Number 1: The United States has to make a firm decision that it will act in its best interests, of course, predicating its decision on sound legal grounds and sound moral grounds; secondly, the United States, in the future, must make a thorough analysis of all of the options, including the worst option, so that we are not caught without seeing what the most unfortunate circumstances might be. We've got to look at any challenge from the best to the worst and be fully prepared to meet whatever the contingencies might be. And thirdly, in any future challenge we have to make sure that the American people are fully informed to the best capability that a President has. A President has to be candid; he has to be forthright; he cannot hide anything—the good and the bad—from the American people. In that way, I really believe that ah, the American people, if they know the facts, will be supportive in a decision to act in the best interests of the United States.

17 Daniel Ellsberg Interview

In the last couple of years when students have asked me what Viet Nam was like and why we were there so long, I've had a more immediate answer to give them. I've said look at Afghanistan on your television screens and watch that operation closely. It's about the same. It's not hard for us to use the words aggression or invasion or imperialism about the Soviets in Afghanistan and all those words are right and they're right about what we did in Viet Nam. That was very hard for me to see as a U.S. official at the time. That the U.S. could commit war crimes, that we could be imperialist, that we could commit aggression. To go into a country whose leaders are people that we have put there for the purpose of asking us in, if necessary, doesn't constitute anything other than an invasion, and that's what we did in 1965. I think if Americans come to see the possibility that we're acting in the world the way we can see very clearly the way the Russians act in their sphere of influence we'll stay out of a lot of such interventions. I don't think the Americans want an imperial role, the American public, and if they don't want it, if they don't want this kind of great power bullying, they will have to participate more as citizens democratically. They'll have to act to take more democratic control of our foreign policy than we've had since World War II. That's the lesson I would like them to draw.

18 Jim Fallows Interview

Because you can't set up the rules for a nation on the principle that people will do heroic things. You can't expect that. You can't expect them to rise above self-interest. What you have to do is ally their self-interest with the things you want to see accomplished. Which is why, I think, that if there had been no student deferment during the middle 1960's, there would've been no war in Viet Nam. Because everybody would have known from the beginning the political cost that would be paid. It is why I think we are making a tragic mistake to have a volunteer force now. Because it's the same thing I was seeing at the induction day at the Boston Navy Yard, but institutionalized and more extreme. Because now no one from the good colleges is, very few people in the good colleges are going into the service, and it's much more foreign to our nation economically and educationally than it was even during, during Viet Nam. So, I think, the lesson I have drawn about society is that we need to have a universal draft with no exemptions if we want to avoid that painful experience again.

19 William Ehrhart Interview

I consider myself an American, a patriot. I love my country very much. I'm still here after all these years. But, for me the greatest legacy of the war in Viet Nam is that I will never believe my government again. I see things in El Salvador. The kinds of reports about the government and stuff, and it's the same thing all over again. And, the present administration says we got to put Viet Nam behind us and and ya they'd like me to forget. They'd like guys like me to shut the hell up and go away. Ah. But, I think that would be the greatest abdication of my responsibilities as a citizen to do that, to shut my mouth and forget about Viet Nam. I learned things about Viet Nam, about my country, about myself, about our place in the world. Ah. And, I'm not about to forget those things and if I can help it, I'd like to make sure that nobody can forget them either.

Critical Issues for Discussion

1. Soldiers who served in the Vietnam War have been more in the news recently than they were when they first came home. Document 1 summarizes
why this is so.

Was the Vietnam experience any different than duty in any other war? Why
or why not? If so, how? Why weren't steps taken to change the conditions under which Americans served in Vietnam? What reforms would you suggest to
help future servicemen cope with war?

2. Some veterans expressed their attitudes toward the Vietnam War through
poetry. Read Document 2.

What was Ehrhart saying? What images did he create? What was his attitude
toward the war? How can you tell? What issue concerns him the most?

3. The controversy over the Vietnam War has continued, even to the point of
a quarrel over the proper way to commemorate the war dead. In Document
3, the question of artistic expression is discussed.

What was the difference between the two images which have been described? What do most war monuments look like? Have they reflected the artistic modes of their time? Should the Vietnam Memorial be any different? Why
or why not? What is the purpose of building a memorial in the first place? What
do you think it should express?

4. As Documents 4 and 5 demonstrate, the Vietnamese are still living with the
consequences of the war in direct ways. What is your vision of Vietnam today based on the film and these documents? What are its strengths? What are its
weaknesses? What are the government's goals? How do you evaluate its methods? What are the major problems affecting that nation?

5. Historians have long argued that what really happened in the past is not
nearly as important as what people think happened. What do they mean by
that? Do you agree or disagree? Why?

Have your views of the Vietnam War been changed by the television series?
How? Does your new viewpoint affect how you see the world around you? In
what ways? Is the study of history worth anything?

6. The role of the media in the Vietnam War has been the subject of numerous
analyses, attacks, and debates in the last decade.

In Document 6, how did Arlen evaluate the role of the press in the Vietnam
War? Does he agree with the popular view of the actions and influence of the
media at that time? Some have argued that the press was responsible for the
American defeat in Vietnam. How would Arlen respond to that charge? How
would you?

What role should the press play during a war? Is critical reporting sabotage?
Is it treason? Is it a luxury which cannot be afforded? Is it necessary? Should a
free press be allowed to function during a war? When does national security
take precedence? How does the press influence national morale?

7. As veterans of a course on Vietnam, how do you react to Professor Franklin's article which appears as Document 7? How does it compare with the course you took?

Read the letters reprinted as Document 8. Were the critics correct to question Franklin's objectivity? How did you react to each letter? Did you agree with any? Disagree? What role should a teacher play in the classroom when studying controversial events like these? Should these events be studied? Why or why not?

What responsibility falls on the students?

8. In the fall of 1981 and the winter of 1982, the civil war in El Salvador received a great deal of press coverage in the United States. Comparisons between that struggle and the one in which the United States had intervened in Vietnam were constantly drawn.

What points did the essayist make in Document 11? What was his viewpoint? Were Vietnam and El Salvador comparable? Should the Vietnam experience have guided American policy makers in this case?

9. Documents 9 and 10, and 12 through 19 tried to look back and make meaning out of the Vietnam War. The perspectives of the speakers vary greatly, and so do their conclusions.

What do you do with so many conflicting views? With whom did you agree? With whom did you disagree? Why?

Did these speakers make any of the same assumptions? Where did they differ from each other?

What are your conclusions?

10. As early as 1947, Professor John K. Fairbank, an expert on the Far East, had pointed out that "our fear of Communism, partly as an expression of our general fear of the future, will continue to inspire us to aggressive anti-Communist policies in Asia and elsewhere, and the American people will be led to think and many honestly believe that the support of anti-Communist governments in Asia will somehow defend the American way of life."

How do you evaluate Fairbank's analysis? Was the United States fearful of the future? Did the United States look at the world through glasses which caused it to divide the world into "Communist" or "Free" nations? Does Fairbank's comment help to explain America's involvement in Vietnam? Does it still hold true today? What should determine American foreign policy?

Follow-Up The philosopher George Santayana made the oft-quoted remark that "those who cannot remember the past are condemned to repeat it." If you were to apply this to the American experience in Vietnam, what lessons would you extract from that struggle? Are these general truths or ones which are specific to Vietnam? What should the American public "remember" about Vietnam?

Suggestions for Further Reading

Legacies

Barry, Jan, and W. D. Ehrhart, eds. *Demilitarized Zones: Veterans After Vietnam.* Perkasie, Pa.: East River Anthology, 1976.

Soldier-poets focus on the struggle to take up their lives while haunted by the memories of Vietnam.

Cortright, David. *Soldiers in Revolt: The American Military Today.* Garden City, N.Y.: Doubleday, 1975.

A former GI activist gives a well-documented history of GI resistance to the war and an analysis of postwar problems with recruitment, the volunteer army, and continuing conflicts over racism and civil rights.

Elliott, David W. P., ed. *The Third Indochina Conflict.* Boulder, Colo.: Westview, 1981.

Asian scholars examine the complex problems of postwar Indochina, including the boat people, Vietnam's conflicts with Kampuchea and China, and the intersection of regional conflicts with global politics.

Emerson, Gloria. *Winners and Losers: Battles, Retreats, Gains, Losses and Ruins From a Long War.* New York: Harcourt Brace Jovanovich, 1976.

Based on her own experiences as a correspondent in Vietnam and three years of interviewing in this country, Emerson pieced together this passionate scrapbook of people affected by the war: small-town Americans who lost their sons, veterans who lost their limbs or eyes, Vietnamese who lost everything.

Grant, Bruce. *The Boat People.* New York: Penguin, 1979.

Based on interviews with refugees who came to Australia, Grant's book gives a comprehensive view of their experience in Indochina, the refugee camps and resettlement.

Horne, A. D., ed. *The Wounded Generation: America After Vietnam.* Englewood Cliffs, N.J.: Prentice-Hall, 1981.

Included here are excerpts from *Chance and Circumstance* and from several soldiers' first-hand accounts of the war, as well as a symposium of young men who came of age during the war years.

Gough, Kathleen. *Ten Times More Beautiful: The Rebuilding of Vietnam.* Vancouver: New Star, 1978.

Gough, a social anthropologist and supporter of the antiwar movement, spent ten days in northern Vietnam in 1976 as a guest of the Woman's Union of Vietnam. Although she details the war damage and injuries she saw, she came away impressed by the achievements and potential of the Vietnamese.

Klein, Robert. *Wounded Men, Broken Promises: How the Veterans Administration Betrays Yesterday's Heroes.* New York: Macmillan, 1981.

This indictment of the Veterans Administration hospital system by an investigative reporter is filled with the personal ordeals of veterans. Chapter

6, "The Poison Orange," describes the so-far unsuccessful efforts to have
the effects of Agent Orange recognized and to compensate its victims.

Zasloff, Joseph J., and MacAlister Brown. *Communist Indochina and U.S. Foreign
Policy: Postwar Realities.* Boulder, Colo.: Westview, 1978.
Analyzing the political and economic developments in Vietnam, Laos, and
Cambodia since 1975 and the policy issues facing the United States, the au-
thors recommend normalizing relations with Vietnam and providing post-
war reconstruction aid.

Lessons

Kinnard, Douglas. *The War Managers.* Hanover, N.H.: Dartmouth Univ.
Press, 1977.
Kinnard, a retired general and military historian, interviewed senior U.S.
Army officers on the conduct of the war and received a wide range of
responses.

Klare, Michael T. *Beyond the "Vietnam Syndrome": U.S. Interventionism in the
1980s.* Washington: Institute for Policy Studies, 1981.
Klare sees official attitudes in Washington veering once more in the direction
of armed intervention in the Third World, despite the American public's
disinclination to seek military solutions to world problems.

Lake, Anthony, ed. *The Legacy of Vietnam: The War, American Society, and the
Future of American Foreign Policy.* New York: New York Univ. Press, 1976.
Authors representing a wide range of opinion on the war look backward and
forward at its effect on the United States.

Nguyen Ngoc Ngan. *The Will of Heaven.* New York: Dutton, 1981.
This is the story of one Vietnamese, a soldier with the Saigon forces, who
after three years in a re-education camp chose to leave Vietnam.

Southeast Asia Resource Center. *Vietnam Is Still with Us.* Vol. 85 of *Southeast
Asia Chronicle* (August 1982).
"Reinterpreting the Vietnam Experience," pp. 3–7, gives an antiwar view
of the debate over the lessons of Vietnam. Other articles discuss veterans'
issues and the experience of Laotian refugees.

Summers, Harry G. *On Strategy: A Critical Analysis of the Vietnam War.* Novato,
California: Presidio Press, 1982.
Written by a colonel at the Army War College, this critique of the inappro-
priateness of U.S. military strategy has received much attention in military
circles.

Thompson, W. Scott, and Donaldson D. Frizzell, eds. *The Lessons of Vietnam.*
New York: Crane, Russak, 1977.
Papers from a colloquium on "The Military Lessons of the Vietnamese
War" which included representatives from the Rand Corporation, the De-
partment of Defense, and the armed forces.